914-631-8000 — BUSINESS
X 2285
2286

914-234-7320 - HOME

MANAGEMENT
Decisions and Behavior

THE IRWIN SERIES IN MANAGEMENT

CONSULTING EDITOR   JOHN F. MEE   *Indiana University*

MANAGEMENT
Decisions and Behavior

MAX D. RICHARDS
*Assistant Dean for Graduate Programs
and Professor of Management*

PAUL S. GREENLAW
Professor of Management

Both of The Pennsylvania State University

Revised Edition • 1972

RICHARD D. IRWIN, INC. *Homewood, Illinois 60430*
IRWIN-DORSEY INTERNATIONAL *London, England WC2H 9NJ*
IRWIN-DORSEY LIMITED *Georgetown, Ontario L7G 4B3*

The first edition of this book was published under the title: *Management Decision Making.*

Revised Edition

First Printing, November 1972
Second Printing, June 1973

ISBN 0-256-00474-9

Library of Congress Catalog Card No. 77–190542

Printed in the United States of America

To Wimp and Shirley

Preface

THE ORIGINAL impetus to writing the first edition of this book was our perceived need for teaching materials in the basic management theory course which would integrate with "traditional" management concepts both (1) scientific knowledge from the behavioral sciences about organizational behavior, and (2) the newer quantitative approaches to decision making. Our perceptions as to this need were reinforced with the appearance of the Carnegie and Ford Foundation reports on business education.

The same basic directions have been followed in this revised edition. In bringing the text up to date, newer behavioral and quantitative models have been introduced, such as the Fiedler Contingency Model in the area of leadership, and the s, S system of inventory control in Chapter 18. In no case, however, have we added materials requiring additional mathematical sophistication on the part of the student. We have also given increasing attention in this edition to some of the more important socioeconomic problems of today—for instance, we have expanded our materials on the social responsibilities of the businessman with respect to such problems as pollution.

The integrative conceptual framework utilized in the first edition of this book was one which views the business organization as an information-decision system, in which decision making represents the focus of activity performed by managers. This view emphasizes that in dealing with problems in all areas of organizational endeavor—from those involving interpersonal relationships to those requiring an economic analysis of revenue, costs, and profits—the manager is faced with choice situations, in which numerous alternative courses of action are possible, and for which certain information is prerequisite for effective decision making. In this revised edition, we have utilized a similar conceptual framework, with two exceptions. First, we have placed more attention on systems and have included a section on systems *theory*. Second, the first edition emphasized in *certain sections* that there are no universal rules for making managerial decisions, but rather that one has to look at the variables involved in the *specific situation* with which the manager is faced in order to come up with a problem solution. We have given much more attention to this "situational" approach (or, as it is sometimes called, "conditional management") in this edition than in the first.

As in the first edition, in order to provide the reader with a theoretical basis for understanding managerial decision making in the context of an information-decision system, considerable attention is given to the growing body of concepts and research findings from the social sciences which has been developed to explain and predict organizational behavior. Although at our present state of understanding, many organizational problems are not amenable to quantitative treatment, some of the variables and relationships developed theoretically can be explicitly described by mathematical models. To the extent that such models can assist in understanding the decision-making process (without involving sophisticated mathematics), they are utilized in this text. Attention is also given to the "practical" application of these theoretical concepts and to an examination of specific approaches which have been developed to handle business problems. In the presentation of these approaches, an overly descriptive orientation is avoided. For example, no attention is given to the design of inventory record-keeping forms. Rather, emphasis is placed upon the analysis of problem-solving approaches as they relate to key decision variables. What effect may different styles of leadership have upon employee motivation under various conditions? How may linear programming be utilized in making allocation decisions? These are some of the kinds of problem areas calling for managerial decisions upon which this text centers.

This book is intended to be an introductory general management text; that is, its use requires no previous study of management on the part of the reader. While the text focuses on the kinds of decision problems faced by managers at all levels and functional areas in the business organization, one of its functions is to provide a basic foundation for the subsequent study of more specialized fields such as sales, production and personnel management, and organization theory.

Some prior study of college algebra, economics, and accounting will be of value to the reader of this text, while having taken basic courses in psychology, sociology, and statistics will also be helpful. However, the materials in the text have been utilized successfully with students who have not completed prior work in all of these areas. We have made use of most of the textual materials in an undergraduate management course required of all College of Business Administration students at The Pennsylvania State University. Ordinarily, this course is taken during the last half of the sophomore or the first half of the junior year. Additionally, many of our graduate students have found numerous chapters of the text useful as reference sources in their graduate management theory courses.

As in the first edition, it is possible to utilize this book at several different levels of sophistication, depending on the materials employed with it. If case studies and problems are used along with the textual materials, for example, students can both intensify their *understanding* of the subject matter, and at the same time develop a degree of *skill* in applying concepts and analytical tools to specific problems. To help provide for various degrees of sophistication in usage, we have included numerous questions, problems, and/or short cases at the end of each chapter. Some of the questions so included are simply designed to test the student's knowledge of specific points covered in the chapters. Others, which are case and problem oriented, are intended to provide a vehicle for skill development in the application of concepts and tools to specific problem situations. Still others are geared toward having the student explore unresolved theoretical questions, examine overgeneralizations derived from management "folklore" in light of current theory, and so on. For some questions of these latter types, there may be few final answers—the chapter materials may merely provide a general basis for discussion.

This book has been organized in the following manner. Chapters 1–4 are designed to summarize the major historical and current trends in management thinking, to introduce the reader to the key phases of the decision-making process, and to provide an introduction to various basic approaches to decision making.

Chapters 5–11 focus attention on individual and group behavior, leadership, and organizational design. In these chapters, considerable attention is given to concepts and research findings from the social sciences which help to explain human behavior in organizations.

Chapters 12–19 focus attention on organizational planning and control. In these chapters, considerable emphasis is placed on the use of economic models to describe and explain decision processes. Since these models are quantitatively the most highly developed of those utilized to deal with organizational problems, these chapters generally have a greater quantitative orientation than do the previous ones. It is not our purpose in these chapters, however, to help enable the reader to become a mathematician or "operations researcher"; rather, emphasis is placed upon helping the student without a sophisticated mathematical background to better understand how quantitative approaches can be useful to managers in their decision making.

Finally, Chapter 20 provides a tentative conditional theory of management, relating many of the variables discussed in earlier chapters to the notions of the importance of uncertainty and complexity in managerial decision making.

As in the first edition, our basic rationale for placing most of the quantitatively oriented materials in latter chapters of the text was that their values and limitations become more meaningful to the student if he first understands the "behavioral environment" of the firm in which such quantitative techniques will be utilized. On the other hand, some instructors may find the following chapter sequencing also to be an effective one: Chapters 1–4; Chapters 12–19; Chapters 5–11; and Chapter 20.

We have been aided greatly in our writing efforts by the willingness of our colleagues at Penn State to utilize the materials in this book in their classes and to critically review the manuscript. We would like to thank especially Professors Sumer Aggarwal and Gary Kochenberger, for such assistance.

Appreciation is also expressed to Professor Michael Hottenstein, our department head, who gave us continuing encouragement to develop these materials as a means of upgrading our basic management theory course. As further encouragement, both he and Dean Ossian R. Mac-Kenzie have been most helpful in providing secretarial assistance and other resources. Finally, without the determined conscientiousness of our secretaries, and the encouragement of our wives, it is doubtful that this work could have been completed. While we appreciate the inestimable aid of all who have helped bring this project to fruition, we recognize our own complete responsibility for it.

October 1972   MAX D. RICHARDS
                                                           PAUL S. GREENLAW

Contents

Teams, etc. Diversity and Uncertainty. Managerial Coordination: Information, Influence, and Span of Control: *Managerial Coordination: Information and Influence. Span of Control Defined. Implications of Differing Spans of Control. Variables Affecting Size of Span. A Model of Span of Control.*

and Profitability Analysis: Values and Limitations. Comparative Analysis: Ratios and Percentages as Analytical Tools: *Return on Investment as a Tool of Analysis. Ratios and Percentages: Other Applications.* Cost-Utility Analysis: *Cost-Utility Analysis: Some Basic Characteristics. Some Inadequate Cost-Utility Approaches. More Adequate Cost-Utility Analysis.*

Growth of Simulation. Types of Simulation. The Structure of Simulation Models: *Simulation Languages. Iteration Specification. Input-Output Specification. Subsystems. Variables and Relationships. Handling Stochastic Variables: The Monte Carlo Technique.* The Future of Simulation.

Chapter 1

Management:
Past and Present

THE PURPOSE of this chapter is to introduce the study of management by describing management thinking and practice as viewed in different time periods by diverse schools of academic thought and practitioners. In succeeding chapters of this book, we will attempt to interweave these different concepts describing management into an integrated framework which may be utilized by the reader to guide his thinking as a manager in the business world.

To provide this perspective to the study of management, the first part of this chapter is devoted to a review of the historical developments which have brought about a need for rigorous intellectual thought about management. In the second part, the several dimensions along which different approaches to management thinking can be evaluated are shown. The third part examines some of the specific approaches to management offered by theorists and practitioners over the years. The fourth section summarizes the recent trends that management thought is experiencing. Finally, we conclude by presenting the basic approach this book takes to the study of management: an eclectic view which integrates the diverse approaches into a framework that focuses attention upon managerial decision making with a system's framework.

HISTORICAL FOUNDATIONS OF MANAGEMENT

As an art, management has been practiced since the early beginning of time. As John F. Mee has pointed out in his award-winning book, however: "Management thought is a product of the Twentieth Century."[1] Although we can find traces of managerial concepts in the Bible, in

---

[1] John F. Mee, *Management Thought in a Dynamic Economy* (New York: New York University Press, 1963), p. xviii. This book was a winner of the Academy of Management's McKinsey Book Award in 1963.

the writings of the Greek and Roman philosophers,[2] and in the works of early political economists,[3] no systematic or comprehensive approach for the study of management was developed until relatively recently. The foundations of probability theory, now applied to analysis for decision making, were developed by Cardan (1501–1576) and Pascal (1623–1662), but were not systematically incorporated into business decisions at a practical managerial operating level until the middle of the Twentieth Century, even though Laplace (1749–1827) had developed applications of probability theory to other types of decision making. Or, to cite another illustration, Charles Babbage (1792–1871), a professor at Cambridge University, developed the concept of the automatic computer in the nineteenth century. At the time, however, only mechanical devices were available for constructing his computer and friction prevented the practical application of his ideas. Babbage also wrote an essay in 1832—*On the Economy of Machinery and Manufactures*—which contained a number of forward-looking recommendations to management. Although his essay received some attention, it did not foster fundamental or widespread changes in management practice.

Probably the most important stimulus to management thought was the so-called Industrial Revolution which started in England around the middle of the eighteenth century. Prior to this time, most business enterprises were small, characterized by hand craftsmanship rather than mechanization, and faced problems much simpler than those faced today by typical firms in a complex industrial society. In consequence, relatively little need was perceived for giving systematic attention to the problems of management.

During the Industrial Revolution, many new inventions and technological developments occurred which made it possible to transform manufacturing from in-the-home production into large-scale factory operations, as, for example, was the case with textiles. Furthermore, developments within one industry spurred invention within others. For instance, the development of the metalworking screw lathe in 1797 made practical the extensive use of metals and interchangeable parts. The resulting demand for metals encouraged the development of Bessemer and open-hearth steelmaking methods which rendered large-scale steel production possible.

Providing impetus to the Industrial Revolution was a legal, social, and technological environment which tended to generate industrial growth and encourage entrepreneurs to invest in new industries. This environment was characterized by the Protestant ethic, which held that what was best for the individual coincided with God's will as well as with the general social welfare. Such an ethical philosophy of individual-

---

[2] For example, Cicero's *De Officiis*, Book II, chaps. 3–5.

[3] For example, Adam Smith, *Wealth of Nations*, Book I, chap. 1, p. 5 in Cannan's edition.

ism gave encouragement to business promoters and owners while, at the same time, tended to silence business critics. In the United States those who may have been injured through business excesses during this period could exercise the alternatives of settling new lands in the West or of forming their own businesses. The relatively large number of choices in employment which were available freed the individual from dependency upon business firms or the government for a livelihood.

This ethical philosophy of individualism was mirrored in the political-economic philosophy of laissez faire, which postulated that the greatest social good is realized when the individual business firm attempts to maximize its profits. Restraints upon business activities by governmental or social institutions should, therefore, according to this doctrine, be minimized so that the individual entrepreneur can be quite free to do whatever he wants to maximize his profits. Given these social and economic philosophies, it was often highly profitable to expand industry and to form new businesses.[4]

By 1850, England had been transformed from an agricultural and trading society to one characteristic of an industrial country. The Industrial Revolution occurred later in the United States and continued into the twentieth century. In the later stages of the Industrial Revolution, the closing western frontier in the United States reduced the opportunities for individuals to seek alternate employment opportunities. As the American society became an industrial one, individuals tended to become more and more dependent upon each other. Individual initiative became less relevant as a practical philosophy. No longer did the Protestant ethic and its emphasis on freedom and individualism provide such a realistic guide to a person's behavior. If one had a factory job the alternatives in employment open to him often were few. Social progress tended to become dependent upon cooperative effort and organization as well as upon individual effort. Fewer and fewer individuals were able to rely solely upon their own abilities and resources to earn their livelihoods. Reflections of this greater dependency came in many forms. The clergy paid less praise to the great captains of industry and pointed with alarm at the industrial "robber barons." Trade unions emerged to help protect the often relatively powerless individual worker against many business excesses. Legislation, such as the antitrust laws, were enacted to curb still other forms of business individualism.

---

[4] It is interesting to speculate whether the Industrial Revolution would have taken place as quickly if the legal, social, and technological environment of the times had been different. If communism or the divine right of kings had been the prevailing political-economic philosophy during the eighteenth century, the benefits of industrialization and technological development would have accrued to the state rather than to individuals. Under either system, would individual entrepreneurs or inventors have been motivated to create as they did? Or, would the state have been willing to risk the capital resources necessary to build factories and to design and utilize new previously untried machinery? Cf. Mee, *Management Thought,* pp. 36ff.

At the same time that these changes in the socioeconomic environment were taking place, a basic change in the form of management in many business firms was occurring. When the corporate holdings of an individual became very large, he needed assistance to manage and operate his enterprises. This need generated a *separation of ownership of business from its management.* The hired manager could not depend upon his ownership rights to ensure his livelihood. He usually had little, if any, stock ownership. Rather, he needed to rely upon his own competence as a manager in order to maintain his job. The owners were interested in employing those managers who could maximize the stockholders' returns. Managerial tenure became dependent upon performance rather than ownership.

IMPORTANT DIMENSIONS FOR THE STUDY OF MANAGEMENT

The development of a complex, interdependent society in which large-scale business firms were operated by professional managers created a need for much greater attention to the problems of managing. During the decades since this need emerged, developments in management thought have proceeded along several different lines. It is the purpose of this section to discuss these several dimensions of management thought to better understand and to analyze limitations and contributions of present-day management thinking.

Parts versus the Whole

A manager may deal with problems of wide or narrow scope; at high levels of the organization or low; occurring in New Delhi or New York; in production, marketing or finance. The scope of activities for which managers are responsible is so wide that research covering management processes must often focus upon relatively limited aspects of the total picture. To illustrate: Igor Ansoff has been interested in the processes of establishing corporate goals and the major strategies for changes in products and markets.[5] George Albert Smith's units of analysis have been the firms which incorporate decentralized operating units. He has studied the problems of organization and control of these units.[6] Joan Woodward has explored the relation between the types of production technology and organization structures of firms.[7] George Strauss has shown how the function of first-line supervisors is being altered.[8] None

[5] Igor Ansoff, *Corporate Strategy* (New York: McGraw-Hill Book Co., 1965).

[6] George A. Smith, *Managing Geographically Decentralized Companies* (Boston, Mass.: Harvard University Graduate School of Business Administration, 1958).

[7] Joan Woodward, *Industrial Organization Theory and Practice* (London: Oxford University Press, 1965).

[8] George Strauss, "The Changing Role of the Working Supervisor," *Journal of Business,* July 1957, pp. 202–11.

of these studies has encompassed a total explanation of management, although each has contributed something to our overall understanding of it.

There is a tendency for some writers, theorists, researchers, and practitioners to give the impression that their partial analysis is the central focus of management study. Readers must resist such a provincial view if they are to understand in total the complex process of managing. Since all managers do not engage in production, for example, a fairly complete study of manufacturing management would provide too narrow a base for generalizing about the executive behavior that one observes in other business functions such as marketing, engineering, or finance. Partial studies of activities or structures common to all managers can, however, provide an initial focus from which a broad management perspective may be developed. Thus a study of organization structure may progressively be enlarged to encompass communication and decision processes, leadership behavior, goal setting, and so forth.

Perhaps the ideal study of management would describe all relevant behavior for any manager at any level in any function in any cultural climate. Unfortunately, this ideal so complex and comprehensive is illusive. As a substitute, those interested in management need be cognizant of how parts contribute to an understanding of the whole. In reviewing publications dealing with subjects germane to management then, a conscious effort is necessary to maintain perspective.

Descriptive versus Normative Theory

A second dimension describing management theory is the descriptive-normative one.[9] Descriptive theory has the purpose of explaining "what is." In contrast, normative theory describes what "should be" or "ought to be." Normative approaches look for the best way. In order to prescribe what ought to be, however, the normative prescriber needs to have in mind some goal, some end, or some objective to achieve. For example, the best way to operate an organization may depend upon whether one wants to maximize return on assets or the percentage return on stockholders' equity. The choice of one goal over the other will have an effect on what are the best decisions for management to make.

It should be noted that the traditional physical sciences and social

---

[9] See Joseph McGuire, *Theories of Business Behavior* (Englewood Cliffs, N.J.: Prentice-Hall, Inc., 1964), pp. 11–12. Fritz Roethlisberger shows how the simple descriptive-normative dichotomy may not be as clear as one would like: "One of the problems is that these propositions which are intended to be descriptive from the point of view of the speaker do not remain descriptive very long from the point of view of the listener." He goes on to show that words used descriptively may acquire normative (good or bad) overtones (e.g., bureaucracy, democratic, nonlogical, group, conformity, deviance, dysfunctional and rational). See his "Contributions of the Behavioral Sciences to a General Theory of Management," in H. Koontz (ed.), *Toward a Unified Theory of Management* (New York: McGraw-Hill Book Co., 1964), p. 60.

sciences have been concerned with *descriptive* theory; i.e., attempting to describe, explain, and predict phenomena. The normative approach has its counterparts in these sciences, however. For example, in the study of economics, the economist *explains* the relationship between disposable income and consumer savings, but the politician or the legislator utilizes this knowledge to establish public policy for controlling inflation, establishing interest rates, and so on.[10] Some descriptive theorists pride themselves on being explanatory, concerned with "pure" phenomena, and tend to view the normative practitioner as merely a problem solver rather than a scientist. It should be made clear, however, that one may develop normative propositions about how an organization should operate by utilizing the scientific method. The whole area of management science as a school of management thought, for example, tends to be normative in its approach to the solution of problems in the firm. Its orientation to these solutions, however, is meant to be a logical and scientific one.

Practicing managers as a group tend to identify with the normative approach since they are interested in solving the problems of organizations. A descriptive scientist on the other hand is not necessarily interested in solving problems. He is interested in discovering truth, relationships, and understanding. At its extreme, of course, the descriptive theorist may be interested in knowledge only for knowledge's sake. Because one group of scholars is interested in descriptive approaches and others are interested in normative developments, there is often a lack of understanding between the two and a confusion to the uninitiated. It would appear reasonable for students of management to differentiate in their own minds between the descriptive and normative aspects of all materials they study.

Management as an Art or Science

The terms "scientific management" and "management science," are part and parcel of many of the writings in management. Thus, the contrasts between the science and the art of management thinking provide an additional dimension along which the student of management can view management concepts.

The Concepts of Science. The term "science" is associated with at least three separate ideas.[11] First, science consists of a verified, accumulated, and organized body of *knowledge.* Second, science connotates a

---

[10] Normative economists sometimes are said to work upon "policy" rather than theory.

[11] These concepts of science and scientific method are available in such general descriptions of science as Norman Campbell, *What Is Science?* (New York: Dover Publications, 1952) and Gustav Bergmann, *Philosophy of Science* (Madison, Wisc.: University of Wisconsin Press, 1957).

scientific *attitude* of objectivity, an impartiality toward facts and their discovery. Third, scientific progress has been associated with the *scientific method,* a systematic procedure agreed upon as a reliable means for verifying knowledge. The scientific method consists of (1) observation of phenomena; (2) making generalizations about the phenomena (the process of induction); (3) predicting other unobserved phenomena in the form of tentative hypotheses, the process of deduction; and (4) testing the validity of these hypotheses by means of controlled experiments.[12] If experiments do not uphold reasonable hypotheses deduced from the generalizations, it is necessary to reconceptualize or discard the generalizations. An interrelated set of these *verified* generalizations is called theory or law. Thus the body of codified knowledge of a science consists of interrelated facts, theories, and laws about some phenomena. In management, for example, the Gilbreths found that opposite and symmetrical hand motions at a workbench are less demanding, physiologically, than parallel nonsymmetric tasks. The process of scientific development of such generalizations is shown in Figure 1–1.

Figure 1–1. Relations among Scientific Method and Theory-Building Processes

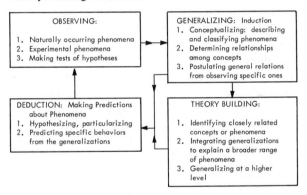

While it is important to understand what science is, it may be just as important to understand what it is not. Beliefs not based on facts but upon metaphysical concepts cannot be verified by experimentation but must be believed, if at all, as articles of faith. Although knowledge has advanced through the powerful insights of keen minds, these insight-

---

[12] The sequencing of these four steps suggested by this approach may not be completely realistic. For a highly personal description of the "scientific" discovery of the molecular structure of DNA, see the account by Nobel Prize winner, James D. Watson, *The Double Helix* (New York: Signet Books, 1968). He states ". . . science seldom proceeds in a straightforward logical manner imagined by outsiders. Instead, its steps forward (and sometimes backward) are often very human events in which personalities and cultural traditions play major roles." Further ". . . styles of scientific research vary almost as much as human personalities," p. ix.

ful concepts remained hypotheses in a scientist's view until controlled experiments could verify them. One of the attractions that Socrates has always had to scholars was his interesting perceptions about man and his mind. It remained for scientific psychology to verify some and reject others of his psychological ideas. Until this was done, the clever logic of his ideas remained hypotheses to be proven. Neither personal, nonsystematic observations, nor mere reporting constitutes scientific knowledge. Unless controlled repeatable experiments verify the generalizations reached, personal anecdotal experiences cannot be considered as verified scientific facts.

Theory and Research. As indicated previously, theory is considered basic to all sciences. Thus, some observations are also in order about the role of theory in applying the scientific method to management. A primary function of theory is to suggest to the researcher the phenomena most worthy of studying in order to further knowledge. Without theory, the collection of data for its own sake is questionable. Unless we had some theory to indicate that executives with red hair are more successful than other managers, for example, it would be highly speculative to look for any relationship between hair color and managerial success on the bare chance that some such relationship does exist. We can increase the probability of experimental success if data are collected to prove or disprove one of the yet unproved hypotheses derived from theory.

To illustrate, there is a growing body of knowledge about the behavior and characteristics of executives. Some of this knowledge supports the theory that executives are, on the whole, in better physical and mental health than are workers and that the higher his position the healthier the executive tends to be.[13] Using this theory, we might further hypothesize that executives enjoy better adjusted marriages than do workers. Then, to test this hypothesis, a measure of marriage adjustment or maladjustment might be developed (e.g., divorce and separation rates). If a representative sample of both executives and workers were taken and marital maladjustment measured and compared for the two groups, differences, if any, could be noted and the hypothesis accepted or rejected. In this way theory about executive behavior could be extended or modified based upon research results.

The purpose of the above example is to illustrate that hypothetical relationships developed on the basis of theory (mental health and executive level) are much more probable of being relevant and useful extensions of knowledge than are relationships based upon pure speculation

[13] This evidence contradicts the old wives' tale of the executive ulcer. See John R. P. French, Jr., "Status, Self-Esteem and Health," *Proceedings*, CIOS, XIII (New York: Council for International Progress in Management, 1963), pp. 735–38.

(e.g., red hair and executive success). Funds and time available for research are often extremely meager. We can ill afford research projects to test speculative whims of researchers or research supporters.

Theory and Practice.   In discussing the application of scientific methods to management, we should emphasize that the development of a body of knowledge does not assure its proper application. In spite of considerable knowledge about the adverse physiological effects of certain drugs upon the body, for example, drug addiction continues. In a similar way, managers may or may not utilize existing knowledge as they operate their businesses from day to day.

We would consider a doctor to be derelict or criminal if he ignores new scientific developments in treating patients. In management, however, some businessmen tend to discount the value of new scientific theories for they consider themselves extremely practical men. However, if it can predict the outcomes of various courses of action open to the manager, theory can be an extremely valuable tool. Managers can learn to *use* and *apply* management theory to their problems. The doctor and engineer have learned to apply the sciences underlying their practices. There is little reason to believe that managers cannot do the same.

Data, scientific or otherwise, can be detrimental, of course, if they are misapplied to business problems. One firm, for example, undertook a study to determine the product characteristics desired by the largest proportion of its customers, and then redesigned its product along these lines. However, the company ignored the additional fact that all of its competitors had similar designs. If the firm had selected a different, but exclusive, design, preferred by fewer consumers, the company might have had a market segment all to itself and been much more successful. This points up the fact that *applying* knowledge obtained through scientific investigation to the solution of management problems remains, to a considerable extent, an art, dependent upon the skill and expertise of the executive.

Concepts on Art and Management.   The concept of management as an art emphasizes the skills of the manager in solving problems. When managers act, they are not directly concerned with science, knowledge, and truth but with achieving some end, the attainment of which involves removing or preventing problems which inhibit attaining their goals. Similarly, as an artist places a piece of clay on the potter's wheel to produce a vase, he may be able to explain or predict in a scientific sense the adhesive properties of the clay, the possible elongations he can achieve, and the shapes he can produce if he exerts given forces at certain locations upon the clay. Yet these concepts, while true, are pushed into the background since the creation of aesthetic values is the main concern of the artist. Analogously, the manager's concern is achieving corporate goals by using whatever methods he has available, whether scientific or not. His ability to mold the elements into a smoothly operating whole is critical. Good managers often are said to possess a knack for getting things done, a "feel" for the situation facing them, and an "intuition" for the right decision.

Management: An Art or Science?   Now that we have discussed several facets of the meaning of the terms "art" and "science" and their implications for management, is management an art or a science?

There is one school of thought which contends that management can never become a science. This belief is partly based upon the complexity of the problems with which managers deal—there are so many variables which must be considered in making certain decisions and some of these are so ill-defined that the degree of precision and predictability usually attributed to a science do not appear capable of attainment. While conceding that a portion of managerial activity may be amenable to scientific analysis, some persons who conceive of management as an art contend that these portions comprise a relatively unimportant segment of the total managerial job. This is considered to be especially true at the highest and most important positions in an organization, where the problems which must be dealt with are most complex.

Taking a somewhat different view are those who believe that although knowledge about management can be classified and organizational behavior predicted and even prescribed, the science characterization is irrelevant. When managers decide or act, they do so not as scientists but as practitioners—as employers of science in the solution of their problems. They view the scientist's goal as truth and its discovery. Where knowledge exists, managers may use it. But even if knowledge does not exist, *the manager must still decide.* He must, in spite of knowledge or the lack of it, achieve results.

Those who view management as a science often admit that it is an emerging one. Generally acceptable techniques exist for the solution of some managerial problems, but there are still substantial gaps in the theory of management. In these areas, managerial decision making is based largely upon experience, judgment, and intuition. Yet scientific analysis of management problems progresses at a substantial pace. Projecting these developments over time, one might visualize a future in which comprehensive prescriptive laws for management behavior may be based upon sound verifiable theory.

The growing utilization of science in management may be exemplified by a study of short-term demand forecasting for power by a public utility. Over a long period of experience, repeated daily, one manager had developed a high degree of skill in anticipating what customer demand for power would be. By means of a scientific study of the variables influencing demand, two researchers with no experience in the utility industry were able to incorporate this and other knowledge into an efficient computer program which was substantially more accurate in its predictions than the experienced executive.

In some cases, however, the utilization of scientific methodology may not yield results better than those achieved by experience-based decision approaches. In a study of the scheduling methods used by foremen in one plant, for instance, an attempt was made to classify and simplify the decision rules currently being used. The researcher discovered that more than 30 different scheduling rules were being used by the foremen. These rules were being applied under different conditions of product demand, shop conditions, and worker availability. The study found that the varying conditions in the shop warranted the apparently large number of scheduling rules, and that the set of rules which had been established through experience were comprehensive enough to meet almost all contingencies which arose in the plant. Further, the results of the scientific analysis coincided with the same conclusions derived from long experience on the job. In this particular case, science was not able to improve to any major extent upon the art of management in the scheduling function.

In conclusion, it is clear that scientific analysis of managerial problems often improves managerial decision making. Conversely, management as a practicing art has provided many examples of success, some of which science has been unable to improve upon. Although management has not yet been reduced to a set of verifiable laws of behavior, continuous inroads are being made toward the development of a science of management.

Cultural Influences upon Management

In explaining or prescribing managerial behavior, it is necessary to consider the culture within which the analysis is framed. If, in a particular culture, promotions to higher ranks are given on the basis of seniority,[14] merit evaluations of an organization's personnel will not serve the same purposes as they do for some firms in the United States. In most developing countries, the education system ordinarily fails to provide the number or proportion of technicians needed to support the production and distribution technologies characteristically found in developed societies.[15]

Even within our own U.S. society, ethnic or religious groups tend to predominate in certain areas. A business located within such an area

---

[14] In Japan where employees in the past have ordinarily stayed with an employer for life, hiring and promotion practices used to vary quite a bit from those in other cultures (e.g., in the United States). See James Abegglen, *The Japanese Factory* (Cambridge, Mass.: Massachusetts Institute of Technology, 1959).

[15] See this reasoning expanded by Richard N. Farmer, "Organizational Transfer and Class Structure," *Academy of Management Journal*, 9 (September 1966), pp. 204–16.

finds that accommodations to the customs, mores, and norms indigenous to that cultural group are necessary. Manufacturing tents in the black ghetto of Watts in Los Angeles requires recognition of educational, skill, and motivational differences in the labor supply from those found in Wichita, Kansas. It may be that a particular management group inbred with the cultural impressions from one area will be unable to adapt its management style to a different cultural setting. It should be recognized, however that accommodations to critical cultural differences have allowed some firms to greatly expand the base of their operations not only nationally but on an international scale.

It may be contended that management and decision making are similar in all cultures: All that differs among cultures is the decision factors and their relative importance. According to this theory, setting up plants to process beef in Karachi or pork in Tel Aviv would merely constitute a failure to recognize religious taboos. Further, the same intelligence apparatus that supplies information such as shifts in consumer preferences, legislative attitudes, and economic forecasts would seem to possess rudimentary competence, at least, to recognize the varying importance of cultural differences upon corporate activities. At the very least, a firm's operations in new locales suggests the need to recognize new economic, political, social, and religious factors important to the design and operation of proposed activities. Whether these cultural differences impose substantive changes upon the processes of management is, perhaps, a philosophical question. Nevertheless, the student of management needs to recognize that these differences exist and that applications of the ideas from any one study may require modification to the cultural circumstances of the situation to which he gives attention.

Management as a Profession

In the writings about management, one often finds reference to professional managers and the need to make management a profession.[16] A profession is an occupation or calling possessing certain unique characteristics for admission to and for remaining in practice. The requirements for admission are often set by the States in conjunction with professional associations in the field. Minimum educational and/or experience requirements may be established as prerequisites for a license to practice the profession (e.g., medicine and law). In addition, an examination may be required (e.g., licensed professional engineers). Further, standards for being permitted to continue in practice may be established by law and by the professional associations (e.g., the prohibition against euthanasia by members of the medical profession). Members of a profession are also usually considered as having responsibilities

---

[16] See, for example, Mary Parker Follet, "When Business Management Becomes a Profession," *Advanced Management*, 20 (July 1955), pp. 22–26.

to their profession above and beyond their responsibilities to their employer. An accountant who is a CPA is expected to adhere to professional accounting standards in his work while at the same time helping meet the objectives of his employer.

In viewing management as a profession, it is true that managers perform similar activities, the sum total of which provides an occupational focus for a profession. In contrast to the more established professions, however, there are no common or widely accepted standards for admission to the practice of management. Although particular companies may establish and maintain a set of qualifications for managership in their firms, other enterprises may utilize quite different standards. Similarly, the standards for continuing in the practice of management show wide variability among different firms and even within the same firms. Furthermore, no government agency or professional association controls admission to or the practice of management. We may conclude, therefore, that although management is comprised of a set of occupational activities which form the basis for professional practice, the other accouterments normally associated with a "profession" are absent. As science evolves in management, it may be possible in the future to develop professional standards for management practice, but no agreement about what these standards are or might be exists at the present.[17]

Heterogeneity in Management Thought

We have examined a few of the more important dimensions along which thinking and writing in management can be examined. It is clear that each dimension may have many subdimensions (e.g., culture may be considered in terms of social, political, religious, and economic subdimensions). For purposes of exposition we have tended to simplify the classifications dichotomously along each dimension (e.g., normative or descriptive) rather than to consider each possible point along that dimensional continuum. If we were to explore each point on a large number of dimensional continua in all possible combinations, it would be possible to generate a very large number of approaches to management! Individuals writing in the field of management do not similarly restrict themselves (nor should they); and thus the field has a wide variety of writings. It has been the purpose of these sections to show the more important aspects of management thought so that these contributions from specific approaches to management can better be placed

---

[17] One argument opposing the establishment of a professional society to develop admission and practice standards for managers is as follows: There is a need for some people in our society to undertake risks and to perform entrepreneurial functions of business. If a professional society were to restrict individuals from initiating business enterprises on the basis that they had not met certain standards, this might have the effect of reducing competition. See, for example, Peter F. Drucker, *The Practice of Management* (New York: Harper & Bros., 1954), pp. 8–11, 47–48.

into a total perspective. One further word of caution is in order concerning these dimensions. Because any one approach to management lies at a particular point on a dimensional continuum does not necessarily condemn or commend it. Its contribution lies in the degree it enlightens, not in how it is classified.

"SCHOOLS" OF MANAGEMENT THOUGHT

Given that any conception of management may be examined along several dimensions, let us now turn our attention to considering how various management thinkers may be grouped together. These groupings are often referred to as "schools" of management thought with the idea that the individuals included within a "school" tend to posit similar ideas and philosophies about management. Each school represents a certain orientation to management. These classes are somewhat arbitrary, as is the inclusion of any particular writer within a school. Most exponents of logical and scholarly thought have had wide interests and have contributed in varying degrees to more than one facet of managerial thinking.

Scientific Management

One of the first and most significant persons to attempt to develop ways to meet this need for much greater attention to the problems of managing was Frederick Winslow Taylor, often referred to as the father of the "scientific management" school of thought.

Taylor was able to show, through both the logic of his writings and the application of his ideas as a manager, that the work of management can be analyzed scientifically so as to arrive at better decisions.[18] In 1878, Taylor started working at the Midvale Steel Works. As he progressed upward through the ranks of management, he was impressed by the lack of accurate knowledge at the disposal of managers. In attempting to set incentive pay rates for jobs, for example, no reliable estimates of the time required for performing the work were available. Taylor found that it would not be desirable to take the actual time of the best worker as a standard since the methods of some of the slower workers on certain parts of a particular job might be superior to those of the fastest worker. What was required was to determine the best possible method for each job segment by observing the performance of numerous workers, and from these data develop a best method for the job as a whole. Once the best method had been determined and taught to all workers, a time standard derived for it could

---

[18] Probably Taylor's most definitive and comprehensive work is his *Principles of Scientific Management* (New York: Harper & Bros., 1911).

be used for incentive purposes. This led to his development of a relatively accurate method of timing jobs called time study.

Taylor's success in setting time standards and incentives led him to apply the same methods of analysis to a wide variety of management problems including those involved in inventory control, production planning, metal cutting, cost accounting, and quality control. These analytical methods included: (1) *research* into the nature of the variables bearing upon problems; (2) *standardization* (applying the methods developed to *all* applicable jobs); (3) *selection* of workers best suited to performing the jobs analyzed and; (4) *training* them in the best method developed for performing the work. These research techniques implied that management could best determine the way that the work was to be performed, whereas previously trade skills had been passed down from master craftsman to apprentice. Thus, there was a separation of *planning* how the work was to be done from the actual performance of jobs by employees.

Managers and workers alike found it difficult to believe that an individual unskilled in a task could tell a master craftsman how to perform his job better. Consequently, Taylor's ideas were resisted by many whose positions were challenged by his work. When Taylor left the Bethlehem Steel Corporation after three years of work there, for example, many of his applications were discarded. His successes could not be ignored, however, and other analysts extended similar concepts into many industries. Frank and Lillian Gilbreth,[19] Harrington Emerson,[20] H. L. Gantt, and Henry Towne, among others, continued working along the lines followed by Taylor and were extremely active in formulating and applying scientific management approaches in business firms.

The advancement of these scientific management ideas—which have focused attention upon managerial problems faced at relatively low levels of administration in the firm, and upon the actual work performed by nonmanagerial employees—continues today in industrial engineering and production management departments at many universities. Depending upon the university involved, these departments are located organizationally either in colleges of engineering or of business administration.

The Functional or Process School

As indicated above, during the early part of the twentieth century, the management movement in the United States centered its attention upon managerial problems at the worker or shop level. Contemporary developments in European management thought, on the other hand,

---

[19] Frank B. Gilbreth, *Motion Study* (New York: D. Van Nostrand Co., Inc., 1911).

[20] Harrington Emerson, *The Twelve Principles of Efficiency*, 1913; H. L. Gantt, *Industrial Leadership*, 1916.

proceeded by concentrating attention at upper management levels. Henri Fayol, a French industrialist, conceived of the job of managing as consisting of several distinct *functions* or *processes:* planning, organizing, commanding, coordinating, and controlling.[21] Fayol's work was based less upon detailed research (illustrative of Taylor's work) than upon generalizing from his observations and his experience as a manager. Fayol's writings, however, were not translated into English until 1925 nor did they become widely available in the United States until 1949.

Fayol's work initiated what is referred to as the functional management school, or now frequently as the "classical" approach to management. Later contributions and elaborations of the functional approach came from Ralph C. Davis,[22] William Newman,[23] George Terry,[24] and Koontz and O'Donnell.[25]

The central focus of the classical school has been upon what the manager should do. The thinkers of this school have attempted to develop a set of principles to prescribe how the managerial functions should be performed. For example, one of the basic principles developed by the classical school is that the manager is limited in the number of subordinates which he can effectively manage. These principles have been derived largely from the experience and personal observation of managers and from studies by academic scholars.

The proponents of functional principles consider them applicable to management in all types of institutions (e.g., business, government, educational) and to all levels of management from the first line supervisor to the highest executive.

Bureaucracy

Max Weber, a Germany sociologist (1864–1920), formulated the basic concepts identified with bureaucratic organizations and administration.[26] Weber attempted to develop a normative rational management structure to deal with administering large organizations. He describes management thought as a rationalized complex administrative hierarchy characterized

---

[21] Henri Fayol, *Administration Industrielle et Generale,* 1916.

[22] R. C. Davis, *The Fundamentals of Top Management* (New York: Harper & Bros., 1951).

[23] William Newman, *Administrative Action* (Englewood Cliffs, N.J.: Prentice-Hall, Inc., 1950).

[24] George Terry, *Principles of Management* (5th ed.; Homewood, Ill.: Richard D. Irwin, Inc., 1968).

[25] Harold Koontz and Cyril O'Donnell, *Principles of Management* (4th ed.; New York: McGraw-Hill Book Co., 1968).

[26] See Max Weber, *The Theory of Social and Economic Organization,* trans. by A. M. Henderson and Talcott Parsons (London: Oxford University Press, 1947); and H. H. Gerth and C. Wright Mills, *From Max Weber: Essays in Sociology* (London: Oxford University Press, 1946).

by a high degree of specialization in the skills of workers and in the tasks to which they are assigned. Supposedly, through specialization each problem is thereby handled by an expert. To ensure that each specialist knew his job, each position in the organization is delegated a certain amount of authority to accomplish its task and a responsibility for accomplishing it. Further, the work for each job in the organization is prescribed by means of a description of the position. Relationships among positions are also defined by a system of rules and procedures. Action taken is to occur according to the stated procedures and rules.

The structure is designed as a prescribed hierarchy of specialized jobs and relationships rather than a social system of individuals. Therefore, a bureaucratic institution is, by nature, impersonal. One refers to the "office" rather than to the person. Problems are routed to the special *position* assigned to deal with that responsibility. Given that the individual in the position possesses the skills necessary to carry out the function, the solution of the problem is given the benefit of expert advice.

The system is designed to be *rational* since decisions are not made on the basis of personal desires or emotion, but rather upon the expertise of the office to which the problem is assigned. The bureaucratic system is designed to be *predictable* in that, given a certain problem, one can predict the manner in which it will be solved provided the rules, procedures, and organization of the bureaucracy is known. Thus, a bureaucratic organization tends to be *dependable*.

Large organizations need some way of ensuring themselves that day-to-day work will be performed. Without rules and procedures and assignments of jobs to specialists, managers could never be sure that any activity would be undertaken the same way twice. Too, job learning is facilitated with repetition of a particular activity so that determining the best rule or procedure of carrying out a function is a rational approach to the design of organizations. As a result, we still find many of the characteristics of bureaucratic structure in business organizations, educational institutions, and the government. Since certain aspects of bureaucratic organizations tend to be valuable concepts for the design of current structures, they will probably remain with us for a period of time.

The word "bureaucracy" also has some undesirable connotations. People talk about "fighting" the system and attempting to get through the maze of rules and procedures when something goes wrong. It is this difficulty in absorbing *unusual* problems that can make a bureaucratic structure inflexible. If all kinds of problems could be foreseen, the rules and procedures for dealing with each eventuality could be anticipated and programmed into the system.

A second kind of criticism to the prescriptive bureaucratic model stems from its cool impersonality, its calculated machinelike approach to individuals and the solution of problems by these individuals. The ideal bureaucratic structure tends to treat individuals as numbers, rather than as human beings. As a consequence, the full potential of individuals in jobs in such a bureaucratic structure are said to be rarely utilized. Rather, the special skills are developed to meet the needs of the job rather than the individual.

The study of bureaucracy has tended to be more popular in departments of sociology and public administration than in schools of business. This oversight on the part of the latter group may be unfortunate since many studies from scientists in bureaucracy are directly related to work going on in business management.[27] Perhaps the aversion to studying bureaucracy stems from a feeling that it constitutes poor administrative practice,[28] but current research in the two fields possesses so many parallels that cooperative endeavor seems most appropriate.

Human Relations

A school of management thought of significance today is the so-called human relations movement. This movement may be traced back to a number of experiments which were carried out at the Hawthorne Plant of the Western Electric Company in the 1920s. These experiments were initially directed toward determining, under controlled conditions, the effect of certain physical conditions upon worker output. For example, in one experiment, illumination levels were systematically varied at the workplace. In this experiment, it was found that worker output increased with increased illumination but when the illumination was then *decreased,* output *continued* to increase.

At first perplexed by their discovery, the researchers finally came to the conclusion that the productivity increases with lessened illumination were due to psychological factors—the performance of employees being studied was influenced to a considerable extent by the special attention that they were receiving as subjects of the experiment. This finding led the researchers to conclude that social and human factors in the place of work were often much more important than physical factors in influencing productivity.[29]

Whereas the scientific management school had focused primary attention upon the technology of the workplace, the human relations movement gave major consideration to individual and group relationships in organizations. Many disagreements between proponents of these two schools of management thought have been generated. The human rela-

---

[27] A sample of later writers in bureaucracy include Talcott Parsons, Robert K. Merton, Alvin Goulder, Peter Blau, R. Selznik, and Melville Dalton.

[28] See reasoning in footnote 9, supra.

[29] Reported in Elton Mayo, *The Human Problems of an Industrial Civilization* (New York: The Macmillan Co., 1933); and F. J. Roethlisberger and W. J. Dickson, *Management and the Worker* (Cambridge, Mass.: Harvard University Press, 1939).

tionists often have argued that irrespective of the technical efficiency of the physical layout, say for the mass production of an item on an assembly line, productivity would be impaired unless the psychological and sociological factors affecting worker output were considered. Certain persons in the scientific management school, on the other hand, have countered that placing too much emphasis on the feelings and needs of workers while ignoring costs and profitability is undesirable.

The work of human relations continues as an intellectual pursuit in the management departments of colleges of business administration as well as in departments of psychology, sociology, and in institutes dealing with human relations problems.

Behavioral Science

In the early writings about bureaucracy, scientific management and the functional school, their orientation as viewed now tends to give the impression that man and human groups acted primarily for their *economic* self-interest. The human relations school showed the importance of a multidisciplinary orientation to management thus making way for ideas from the other social sciences as theoretical background important to understanding management.

Some of the early work of the human relations school was undertaken with relatively little theoretical background to explain or to predict why a particular management technique worked or did not. In contrast, the later behavioral scientists put more emphasis on analyzing the functioning of a management system with reference to basic theory in the social sciences such as psychology, social psychology, and sociology. Rather than applying a technique on the basis that it has worked elsewhere in the past, the behavioral scientists have attempted with sufficient prior knowledge of the particular system under consideration, to predict the theoretical impact of the application of various types of solutions to problems.

Neither economics, psychology, sociology, nor anthropology explain the totality of behavior of individuals or groups. Together, with the behavioral sciences, the human relations school has provided better means for explaining and predicting organizational phenomena. Some research and writing in the behavioral sciences has occurred at the detailed microcosmic level, as exemplified by experimental studies of the change in one variable influenced by experimentally controlled variations in another.[30] Other behavioral science research has focused attention more at the macroscopic level. For example, Cyert and March have

---

[30] As examples, see Norman Miller and Donald C. Butler, "Social Power and Communication in Small Groups," *Behavioral Science*, 14 (January 1969), 11–18; or K. Roberts, R. Miles, and L. V. Blankenship, "Organizational Leadership, Satisfaction and Productivity: A Comparative Analysis," *Academy of Management Journal*, 11 (December 1968), pp. 401–14.

attempted to explain the levels of production, inventory, and employment in a firm through examination of a relatively few behavioral (and not just economic) variables.[31] The classical microeconomic model attempted to predict these same results with a limited number of purely economic variables. Thus, the Cyert and March model is seen as a substitute for the traditional microeconomic one.

Work in the behavioral sciences and human relations continues in many fields of academia including schools of business, public, educational, or institutional administration as well as in the more basic disciplines of psychology, sociology, economics, anthropology, and political science. The variety of sources and uses of knowledge in the behavioral sciences has also been part of the impetus given to the study of comparative administration.[32]

The Quantitative School of Management Thought

Another focus of managerial thought which has originated in the twentieth century is that of quantitative, mathematical analysis. During World War II, major applications of mathematical approaches to the solution of managerial decision problems were developed. Such problems as convoy makeup and submarine deployment were studied, analyzed, and solved mathematically. Then, after the war, many similar forms of quantitative analysis were developed by business firms. Many problems and subproblems that theretofore had been subjected only to intuitive experience-based analysis came under mathematical probing and scrutiny. The postwar development of automatic electronic computers greatly increased the ability of management analysts to perform complex quantitative studies of business problems since the large number of computations necessary in many types of these analyses cannot be handled easily without computers.

The rise of mathematical techniques has spawned new areas of business interest. One of these is often referred to as *operations research*. Operations research techniques are quantitatively based analytical methods useful in shedding insight into and in generating recommendations for action on a wide range of managerial problems. Also, a group of scholars, known as *management scientists* have developed additional and complementary quantitative techniques. Although it is often difficult

---

[31] Richard M. Cyert and James G. March, *A Behavioral Theory of the Firm* (Englewood Cliffs, N.J.: Prentice-Hall, Inc., 1963), see especially chap. 6.

[32] Comparative administration posits that a considerable portion of the management knowledge, skills, and techniques for business are applicable to the management of other kinds of organizations (e.g., governmental, educational, religious, and so forth). Comparative administration seeks to identify the similarities, differences, and causes of differences in the administration of different types of organizations, whether these are differences of kind or of degree. See Edwin Flippo (ed.), *Comparative Administration*, Proceedings, Academy of Management, 25th Annual Meeting, 1966, for differing views.

to distinguish the operations researcher from the management scientist, the management science movement is generally considered (by management scientists) to encompass a broader range of problems than does operations research, in that it also includes quantitative behavioral science approaches within its confines.[33]

The Systems Approach

One group of scholars describes its view of management as the systems approach. The meanings that various individuals attach to systems varies a great deal depending on the area to which the idea of systems is applied. Even within any particular area of management there may be disagreement among scholars as to the meaning and relevance of systems concepts. This diversity may be due to the fact that the ideas are of relatively recent origin, little attention to systems ideas for management being evident prior to 1950.[34]

A system is defined as an aggregate of component units each of which stands in a cause and effect relation to each other component. The behavior of any component or of the whole can be described by the same basic systems ideas: input, output, transformation, equilibrium, entropy, homeostasis, and others.[35] Not only do these concepts describe the state or the behavior of any component in a system, but also these system ideas can be used, rather universally, to describe any phenomenon or any organism, from man to computers, to airplanes. The universality of systems ideas and applications for explaining a wide range of phenomena is an important characteristic of the systems approach.

A second basic characteristic of systems is that each component affects every other. Take as an example an automobile engine. If an unconnected engine is running free on a test bed, it operates differently in terms of the inputs of gasoline and air that it needs than if it is attached to a transmission. Similarly, as more of the total automobile is added to the system, the engine operates still more differently. The mere change of automobile tires from regular two- or four-ply type to the radial

---

[33] It is interesting to note that many scholars are members of both the Operations Research Society of America (ORSA) and The Institute of Management Sciences (TIMS).

[34] Ludwig Von Bertalanffy, a biologist, is a proponent of the universality of systems theory explaining all phenomena. See his *Problems of Life* (New York: Harper & Bros., Torchbook edition, 1960). The role of information and the concepts of cybernetics are based upon original works by Norbert Wiener in *The Human Use of Human Beings* (Garden City, N.Y.: Doubleday & Company, Inc., Anchor Books edition, 1954). The application of systems to understanding organization is perhaps most completely covered in Stafford Beer's *Decision and Control* (New York: John Wiley & Sons, Inc., 1966).

[35] We will discuss the meaning of many of these concepts in Chapter 4 when we delve further into general systems theory.

type for the 1970 automobiles necessitated 250 minor changes in suspension parts. Thus a change in one component of the system has affected the operation of the others; if the output of the total system is to remain the same, the composition of the individual parts must change because they are so closely and sensitively related to the other components.

Environmental Elements as Components of a Larger System. As each component is sensitive to all others, the total system is similarly sensitive to its environment. For example, if an automobile engine were placed on the moon, it could not operate at all since no oxygen in the environment could be utilized as input. In managing a business, it is useful not only to explain and predict the behavior of the internal components of the organization but it is also useful and necessary to systematically analyze the effect of external factors on the operations of the firm. The external environment can include activities of the union, governmental controls over the industry in which the firm is a part, the actions of competitors in developing and pricing new products and the attitude of consumers toward the firm's products. Of course, if all of these environmental factors (i.e., the government, industry, competitors, and customers) were included into and composed as a larger system, the behavior of each of these could be considered as interacting with each other. Thus the analysis that one utilizes in the systems approach is dependent upon the *boundaries* of the system that the analyst draws. If components outside the firm are included as part of the total system, the analysis takes on a different flavor than if one merely considers the firm in relationship to its environment.

One can extend the building up of systems to include the firm, or a larger unit of analysis, the industry, then the economy, then the total world economy, then all the social systems in the world, and so on. For purposes of analysis, however, we can usually consider some component relatively independent of other components or we can assume that their relationships are fixed and stable. This isolation allows examining the particular component in detail, its functioning, and so forth. As we then change the inputs from the environment to the system, we can analyze how the component deals with these kinds of changes.

Role of Information. It should be noted, that in human organisms or human systems, the relationships among the parts are controlled and monitored by information flows. This explains the large amount of systems work going on in the areas of information processing and computers. In the human body, for example, the heart does not operate independently from the lungs. When increased muscular activity takes place, *messages* are sent to both the respiratory and the cardiovascular systems so that their operations may stand in coordinated relationship with each other and the rest of the body. In a similar way, when the sales activity of the firm changes, the producing operation needs to be notified so its actions may accommodate to the change.

We view a system as related components, each of which can be described as a system in itself. This idea of systems as boxes within boxes allows one to focus upon wholes rather than parts. While there is nothing new in trying to look at the forest rather than the trees, the systems approach provides a convenient way of doing this by showing that any system is a subsystem of something larger.

Systems ideas are relatively new and untried in comprehensive application to business operations and management but there are a number of management ideas which are illuminated by systems thinking. As a result, in this book we use these concepts in explaining and predicting various types of managerial behavior. Toward this goal, we undertake a more thorough examination of systems and their relationship to information in Chapter 4.

TRENDS IN MANAGEMENT THOUGHT

In the previous sections we have examined the major schools of management thought as they have developed since just prior to the turn of the twentieth century. The chronology of these developments is portrayed graphically in Figure 1–2. We will now consider these ideas

Figure 1–2. Chronology of Management Thought

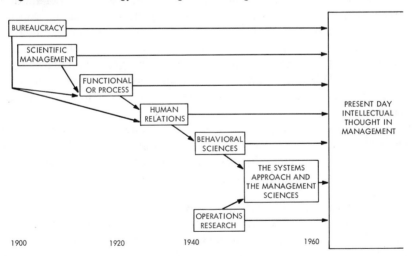

in light of the most significant current trends in the field of management.

In addition to the increasing examination of management in decision making and systems terms, four basic trends seem to be significant today in management thinking: (1) a broadening of the knowledge deemed to be relevant to management; (2) an increasing use of and dependence upon quantitative methods; (3) greater application of the underlying behavioral sciences to managerial understanding and decision making; and (4) the increasing application of computers to management.

Broadening of Management Knowledge

Prior to the twentieth century, management was often practiced in a way similar to the apprenticeship system with sons typically relieving fathers in administrative positions. Little conscious intellectual thought was given to improving or professionalizing practice until the emergence of the scientific management movement. This movement introduced the idea that scientific methods of analysis could be applied to managerial activity. Its applications were concerned primarily with factory-oriented relatively low-level managerial jobs, and with technological and cost considerations.

Weber's bureaucratic model and the classical school emphasized the notion that *all* levels of management in a wide variety of institutions warranted intellectual thought. They pointed up the importance of analyzing what managers should do as well as planning what workers should do.

Those scholars focusing attention on the human problems of organizations have brought us to the realization that knowledge of the social sciences (in addition to economics) could both aid the understanding of management and help improve managerial decision making. Neither the scientific management nor the classical schools of thought ignored human and social problems relevant to management, but the human relationists and behavioral scientists placed much greater emphasis upon these factors. Without doubt, these thinkers have broadened our ideas about the variables that management needs to consider in its day-to-day functioning.

The quantitative school of management thought has added mathematics and statistics as areas of knowledge important for effective decision making by managers. Finally, the systems thinkers have attempted to develop an integrating approach to many different kinds of phenomena.

Each of these schools of thought has broadened the scope of knowledge considered important to management. At the same time, their work has resulted in the management field becoming more complex and more difficult to conceptualize in any overall integrated sense. Further, sometimes these diverse approaches have arrived at quite opposing views as to how management problems ought to be analyzed and dealt with.

To cope with the dilemmas presented by this diverse and complex set of management ideologies, some scholars have restricted their attention to only those few management concepts most congruent with their own ideas. Such an approach runs the risk of ignoring important developments in other management areas. What management thought needs at this time is an integrating concept or focus through which knowledge from all subsets of management knowledge may be viewed. At the conclusion of this chapter, we will view the decision-information system concept as an integrating mechanism through which, in the remainder of this book, knowledge from these many diverse schools of management thought will be brought together.

The Increasing Use of Quantitative Methods

The second basic current trend of management thought is the increasing use of quantitative methods. Although, for example, statistical quality control dates from Shewhart's work in the mid-1920s, the application of mathematical approaches to management problems received its greatest impetus during World War II. Since that time, utilization of mathematical techniques by managers has extended considerably. The range of quantitative decision-making tools useful to management is becoming broader with the appearance of each issue of the scholarly journals. Present-day management makes use of linear, nonlinear and dynamic programming, statistical decision theory, inventory decision models, simulation and Monte Carlo methods, and many other quantitative decision tools. These have been applied to problems existing within the several functional areas of business such as production, marketing, and finance. In addition, these techniques have found application by managers of many other kinds of organizations such as hospitals, universities, both military and civilian governmental agencies, farms, and unions.

This increasing emphasis on quantitative approaches to management parallels earlier developments in the physical sciences. As problems, and the variables bearing on these problems, can be measured and stated in quantitative terms, a more precise prediction of behavior is possible. Progress in the physical sciences paralleled quantification and measurement in these fields. It is not coincidental, then, that many scholars and students of management thought consider progress in management theory closely related to the degree of quantification and measurement that can be associated with it. This also explains, to some extent, the emphasis which some managers and students place upon quantification and on the development of mathematical models for management.

Increasing Emphasis on the Behavioral Sciences

The third current trend in management thought is the growing emphasis on the behavioral sciences. Economics has long been recognized as the mother science of management. Much of the study of management has been focused upon the application of economic principles to administrative problems of organizations. For example, numerous inventory models have been utilized for a number of years as a means of minimizing the costs associated with the production or procurement of raw materials and parts. These models represent applications of cost-minimization principles from microeconomic theory. Since administrators are charged with the responsibility of achieving goals with limted resources, economics will continue to be one of the fundamental sciences underlying management.

As management thought has become more sophisticated both in theory and in practice, it has become evident that economics cannot explain or predict many types of organizational behavior of interest to managers. As an example, one of management's continuing problems is the training of its employees. Here, several concepts developed by learning theorists in the field of psychology have been helpful in designing more effective training programs. Similarly, personality theory has helped provide a basis for the design of the so-called sensitivity training approach, which is utilized to train executives in developing more effective interpersonal relationships with others.

In addition to economics and psychology, knowledge from other social sciences, such as sociology, cultural anthropology, and political science can be useful to the manager. Managers must deal with the behavior of work groups as well as that of individual employees in the organization; in the management of the firm's operations abroad, the cultural values of other nations and societies become important considerations, and many managerial problems must be dealt with in the light of existing governmental regulations and/or possible future legislation.

The relationship of management to the behavioral sciences is similar to that between engineering and the physical sciences or to that between the practice of medicine and the biological sciences. Medicine, management, and engineering are professional occupations whose activities are concentrated upon the solution of problems within their respective areas of endeavor. Doctors utilize the biological and physical sciences as a basis for analyzing health problems; engineers use the physical sciences in solving design problems in connection with chemical, electrical, and mechanical systems. Managers utilize the social sciences in an analogous manner since they are engaged in the solution of individual and group problems related to the achievement of organizational goals. The behavioral sciences furnish the underlying understanding of the behavior of individuals and groups necessary to arrive at knowledgeable solutions.

The Increasing Use of Computers

When computers became available for business use, they were employed initially upon the data processing functions such as accounting, inventory control, and other relatively routine data functions. When these simple applications had been computerized, the promises of reducing the cost of obtaining information for decision making led to a re-examination of the role, the need for, and the value of information in organizations. Prior to the computer, it often was too expensive to process some kinds of information. With modern processing capabilities, additional information could be made available to management although some processes still remain uneconomical. Thus, the computer became an important innovation which led to explicit recognition of the role of information in formal structures and decision processes within firms.

The quantitative developments in management could not have been brought to their present level of importance if the computer had not been available. Complicated quantitative techniques require a computer for their economical application since many problems would be almost impossible to calculate by hand within reasonable costs or time. Thus, the computer has made feasible the development and use of quantitative techniques for aiding management in decision making. In addition, research work in artificial intelligence has shown the analogy between human and computer thinking. As a result, the automation of decision making has received considerable emphasis as a computer research topic. From this research, it has been possible to develop certain computerized decision rules that can perform decision-making functions formerly undertaken by managers.

In addition to the above activities taking place within the business firm, the computer has permitted academic research activities to be carried out much more economically than had been previously possible. This research in management has benefited in that data reduction, statistical routines, and simulation has given greater insights into how organizations operate and how managers deal with these organizations.

The increasing use of computers as a trend in management is thus seen affecting not only routine data processes. Decision processes also are changing. The role of humans can be relieved from mundane and simple activities if computers and machines can undertake them.

THE APPROACH TO MANAGEMENT IN THIS BOOK

Decision Making

As we have shown in this chapter, there are many factors tending to make exposition of any treatise upon management, such as this one, a complex undertaking. There are several expository means that we employ to provide a comprehensive view of managers and their behavior. The first of these that we use is the initiating as well as the integrating focus of *decision making*. While managers actually undertake a number of activities such as reading, listening, speaking, writing, observing, and thinking, these activities are subsidiary means to achieving the goals of the business. The resources of any organization are limited so that goal achievement is constrained; goals cannot automatically be achieved without conscious choices of who, what, where, and when resources are to be committed to action. Thus, making these choices—i.e., the decision process—constitutes the prime responsibility of managers.

Systems

The second expository device employed in this text is the *systems approach.* The systems approach views each component of an organization as taking inputs (e.g., information and/or resources), transforming these inputs to create outputs, which, in turn, become inputs to some other component of the structure. Fortunately, these ideas about systems are useful in explaining decision and information processes as well as certain other nonmanagerial aspects of organization.

Basics: Environment, Decisions, and Systems

These fundamental ideas of decision making and systems are undertaken first as, in the next chapter, we describe the environment within which managers are called upon to make their decisions, and in light of this environment, the process of choosing what objectives the organization shall undertake. Although goals are established as semipermanent plans, their choice is fundamental to all other decisions. In Chapter 3, we examine basic decision approaches applicable to a wide range of managerial decisions. We complete the basic introductory materials by examining systems and information concepts in Chapter 4.

Types of Decisions

There are a number of types of decisions with which managers deal. In Chapters 5 through 10, we will treat those kinds of decisions relating to individuals and groups within formal organizations. To do this, we examine existing descriptive theory associated with these components of the system. To explain leadership, for example, it is convenient to rely upon theory relative to personality and leader-follower relations so that we better understand how leaders emerge and how followers react. Given these theoretical concepts as background, we can then discuss the effectiveness of leadership (the normative approach) under a variety of situations.

This same normative and descriptive presentation is followed in examining two other categories of decisions faced by managers: planning and control. Since both planning decisions and those related to evaluation and control are partially amenable to quantitative analysis, we explore the *quantitative decision* techniques primarily from the view of improving managerial decision making. Our purpose in the "quantitative" chapters is not to develop applied mathematicians but rather to reveal to the potential administrator the value and the role of quantitative approaches in the decision processes.

Dimensions of This Book

Given the above précis, how can the approach of this text be described in terms of the dimensions previously discussed in this chapter? In terms of parts versus the whole, we attempt to provide a comprehensive overview of the managerial process in business firms. While we make no pretense of presenting a study in comparative administration, many of the concepts brought forth are applicable to organizations other than business firms.

Since any chapter could provide the basis for one or several books, it is obvious that much detail is omitted. We do this by selecting those concepts substantiated where possible by scientific evidence. Since the number of studies relating to some areas is very large, we cite representative research rather than an exhaustive compendium. This is not to imply that all ideas herein are supported by scientific research. Where scholarly evidence is lacking, our purpose to provide a comprehensive view necessitates using the best available data, irrespective of its source, but our objective is to base the text on as scientific a base as is available.

By studying the concepts of management and decision making in this book, we aim to provide a base of knowledge from which successful development of managerial skills can emerge. Thus, we are interested in providing normative concepts to help shorten the reader's path to successful managerial performance. We are firmly committed, however, to the idea that the best techniques and rules for decision making are based upon sound descriptive theory. Effective management is seen to depend upon scientific descriptive theory of the behavior one is trying to manage.

No attempt has been made to provide a cross-cultural analysis of the applicability of these ideas. Implicitly, we assume the modern U.S. corporate setting as the cultural climate to which these ideas best apply.

We make no specific assumptions or reference to the idea of management as a profession. We believe that the development of such a position for management is relevant, perhaps, for the future, but not today.

In short, we are taking an eclectic view, integrating ideas from many "schools" and many thinkers; and our integrative framework is one which considers decision making (within a systems context) as central to the undertaking of managerial and organizational behavior.

In this exposition the reader will find that current management theory is *conditional* in the sense that under one set of conditions, one form of organization structure, one system for planning and control decisions, and one form of leadership are most appropriate while under different situations other forms of management are better. The conditions that influence the appropriate forms of management systems include the degree of uncertainty in the environment, the complexity and number of external factors bearing upon an organization and the rates of change of these factors. It is to these factors and the management systems that we now turn.

DISCUSSION AND STUDY QUESTIONS

1. Trace the historical events that provided impetus to the study of management.
2. The ideal study of management would describe all relevant behavior for any manager at any level in any function in any culture. Discuss.
3. The scientific method in management usually proceeds in a straightforward logical manner, consisting of several basic steps. Discuss.
4. The study of management does not need to focus explicit attention on cultural differences in other nations because the basic concepts of management will enable recognition of such differences. Discuss.
5. The schools of management thought represent historical happenings of little relevance to present-day management thought. Comment.
6. Compare and contrast the work of Frederick W. Taylor and Max Weber.
7. What is the difference between "operations research" and "management science"?
8. The systems approach to management allows one to look at the whole rather than the parts. Evaluate.
9. What is the basic difference between "descriptive" and "normative" theory? Which is of more interest to the manager?
10. Management decision making focuses attention upon the moment of actual decision choice from among alternatives. Comment.

SELECTED REFERENCES

BARNARD, CHESTER I. *The Functions of the Executive.* Cambridge, Mass.: Harvard University Press, 1938.

CHANDLER, ALFRED D., JR. "The Beginnings of 'Big Business' in American Industry," *The Business History Review*, 33 (Spring 1959).

COCHRAN, THOMAS C. *Basic History of American Business.* Princeton, N.J.: D. van Nostrand Co., Inc., 1959.

COPLEY, FRANK B. *Frederick W. Taylor: The Father of Scientific Management,* Vols. I and II, New York: Harper & Bros., 1923.

DAIUTE, JAMES R. *Scientific Management and Human Relations.* New York: Holt, Rinehart & Winston, Inc., 1964.

DAVIS, RALPH C. *The Fundamentals of Top Management.* New York: Harper & Bros., 1951.

DRUCKER, PETER F. *The Practice of Management.* New York: Harper & Bros., 1954.

FAYOL, HENRI. *General and Industrial Management.* London: Sir Isaac Pitman & Sons, Ltd., 1949.

FILIPETTI, GEORGE. *Industrial Management in Transition.* Rev. ed. Homewood, Ill.: Richard D. Irwin, Inc., 1953.

GEORGE, CLAUDE S., JR. *The History of Management Thought.* Englewood Cliffs, N.J.: Prentice-Hall, Inc., 1968.

GRAS, N., and LARSON, H. *Casebook in American Business History.* New York: F. S. Crofts & Co., 1939.

HARBISON, FREDERICK H., and MEYERS, CHARLES A. *Management in the Industrial World: An International Analysis.* New York: McGraw-Hill Book Co., 1959.

HURNI, MELVIN. "Characteristics of Management Science," *Management Technology,* December 1960, 37–46.

KOONTZ, HAROLD. "The Management Theory Jungle," *Journal of the Academy of Management,* 4 (December 1961), 174–88.

KOONTZ, HAROLD (ed.). *Toward a Unified Theory of Management.* New York: McGraw-Hill Book Co., 1964.

MAYO, ELTON. *The Human Problems of an Industrial Civilization.* Boston: Harvard Graduate School of Business Administration, 1946.

MAYO, ELTON. *The Social Problems of an Industrial Civilization.* Boston: Harvard Graduate School of Business Administration, 1945.

MEE, JOHN F. *Management Thought in a Dynamic Economy.* New York: New York University Press, 1963.

MERRILL, HOWARD F. (ed.). *Classics in Management.* New York: American Management Association, 1960.

MOONEY, JAMES. *The Principles of Organization.* Rev. ed. New York: Harper & Bros., 1954.

RICHARDS, M. D., and NIELANDER, W. A. (eds.). *Readings in Management.* 3d ed. Cincinnati, Ohio: South-Western Publishing Co., 1969.

ROETHLISBERGER, F. J. *Management and Morale.* Cambridge, Mass.: Harvard University Press, 1941.

SIMON, HERBERT. *Administrative Behavior.* 2d ed. New York: The Macmillan Co., 1957.

SIZELOVE, O., and ANDERSON, M. *Fifty Years of Progress in Management.* New York: American Society of Mechanical Engineers, 1960.

SMIDDY, HAROLD F., and NAUM, L. "Evolution of a 'Science of Managing' in America," *Management Science,* 1 (October 1954), 1–31.

SPRIEGEL, W. R., and MYERS, C. E. (eds.). *The Writings of the Gilbreths.* Homewood, Ill.: Richard D. Irwin, Inc., 1953.

STINCHCOMBE, ARTHUR L. "Bureaucratic and Craft Administration of Production: A Comparative Study," *Administrative Science Quarterly*, 4 (September 1959), 168–87.

SUMMER, CHARLES E., JR. *Factors in Effective Administration*. New York: Columbia University Graduate School of Business, 1956.

TAYLOR, FREDERICK W. *Scientific Management*. New York: Harper & Bros., 1947.

UDY, STANLEY H., JR. " 'Bureaucracy' and 'Rationality' in Weber's Organization Theory: An Empirical Study," *American Sociological Review*, 24 (December 1959).

URWICK, LYNDALL. *The Elements of Administration*. New York: Harper & Bros., 1944.

URWICK, LYNDALL. "Have We Lost Our Way in the Jungle of Management Theory?" *Personnel*, 42 (May–June 1965), 9–18.

WORTMAN, MAX S., JR. "Shifts in the Conceptual Approaches Which Underlie Principles of Management," *Academy of Management Journal*, 13 (1970), 439–48.

Chapter 2

Decision Making: Values, Objectives, and Social Responsibilities

INTRODUCTION

DECISION MAKING is gaining increased attention as a focal point for the study of business management. In fact, such a leading authority as Herbert Simon has considered decision making and management as synonymous terms.[1] With few exceptions, the work performed by managers involves or is related to the making of decisions in organizations. When, for example, a manager studies a report dealing with his competitors' pricing policies, the information which he obtains from it helps provide a basis for pricing decisions which he will subsequently make. When a manager communicates with his subordinates, this behavior results from some choice about what he believes they should know. Additionally, the information communicated by him provides a basis for the further making of decisions by his subordinates. When a manager decides to restructure his organization, he may have as an objective the improvement of interpersonal relationships and information flows so as to provide for more effective decision making in the future.

Although decision making does not encompass all dimensions of management, it does prove to be a highly useful focus for the analysis and study of management. Further, if one considers the entire decision-making process of gathering information and processing it, making choices from among alternatives, and effectively communicating decisions made to other members of the organization, there is little managerial activity which could not be considered within a decision-making framework.

---

[1] Herbert Simon, *The New Science of Management Decision* (New York: Harper & Bros., 1960), p. 1.

RATIONALITY IN DECISION MAKING

Sound and logical reasoning appears to be lacking to explain why certain decisions were made the way that they were. Some decisions appear to have been based upon personal reasons or emotional factors. Still others appear to have been ill-considered. When attempts are made to prescribe how decisions should be made, however, exhortations are given that managers ought to be "rational"—that they should put aside their personal feelings and emotions and base decisions on the facts of the situation. It is appropriate, then, to examine the concept of rationality in decision making and the extent to which managers are able to approach, in a rational way, the problems that arise within organizations.

Goal-Directed Behavior

The concept of "rational man" is not a perfectly clear one, but rationality cannot exist without the existence of a goal or goals, with behavior and decisions directed toward meeting the goal(s). Given the simplifying assumption that an individual has a single goal, any action on his part to detract from achieving that objective would be irrational. Conversely, decisions would be rational if they maximize achieving the goal. If only one of two possible decisions can be chosen, rational behavior would represent the selection of that alternative *most efficient* in achieving the desired goal. It would be irrational to select the less efficient method even if it does have some positive influence upon reaching the goal. With *multiple goals* and other factors involved in decision making, the concept of rationality becomes more complex.

Economic versus Noneconomic Factors

Some individuals hold that the rational man acts the same way as does the economic man of classical economic theory. This means that the manager would weigh the economic factors bearing upon organizational problems and decide solely with the objective of maximizing profits for the firm.

Noneconomic factors, however, have an important bearing on the outcome of many decisions in organizations. During the early days of the union movement, for example, many managers were baffled at the actions of their union members. These managers often made decisions based on the assumption that if the organization provided sufficient economic benefits to its workmen, this ought to suffice in satisfying their wants. Many workers, however, were interested in such so-called nonrational factors as their individual dignity and treatment as human beings. Since that time, psychological and sociological factors have gained increasing recognition as key ones in influencing the outcome of decisions, and the view that decision making involves only purely economic considerations has tended to disappear.

Not only may noneconomic factors have a bearing on whether a firm will meet its economic objectives, some enterprise objectives *themselves* may be noneconomic in nature. One firm, for example, has an objective of providing steady employment to its employees as a means of maintaining a satisfied work force. Decisions which may appear incongruent with achieving a company's economic (profit) goals may, in fact, be considered "rational" ones if these choices are directed toward such noneconomic objectives.

Perfect Information

Another complication involved in the concept of rationality comes from the fact that managers usually do not have complete information at their disposal for making decisions. Ignorance of this fact is still with us in some books and courses given in decision making. Frequently the decision maker is exhorted to get "all the facts" before he considers alternatives in making a decision. Compare this all-the-facts view of information needed with an example of the decision by a major television producer to integrate "backwards" to produce its own glass tube envelopes for color television, rather than purchasing them from an outside supplier as it had previously done. Although the corporation had, during the prior life cycle of color television, worked very closely with the glass suppliers of tube envelopes to establish specifications and tolerances, the TV manufacturer had no substantial experience in the construction of glass plants, in their operation, in the technical formulation of glass structures, or in glass forming. While the corporation had had varied experience in the use of glass, a substantial area of partial ignorance rather than "all the facts" characterized the decision to integrate so as to produce glass envelopes.

How close to an optimum solution to this problem was the organization able to come? Did the company have perfect knowledge or foresight? Did the persons making the decision have all the facts?

A great deal more time and money conceivably could have been spent by the company to search out the cost and revenue effects involved in glass production. Such variables as these can rarely be predicted precisely, especially if previous experience is lacking. Although the decision made may have been a good or satisfactory one, the particular series of actions undertaken could hardly have been optimum. There is a difference, however, between a satisfactory solution to a problem and an optimum solution. Rationality to achieve an optimum solution[2] is restricted by the search activity necessary for its attainment.

[2] M. Alexis and C. Wilson, *Organizational Decision Making* (Englewood Cliffs, N.J.: Prentice-Hall, Inc., 1967), p. 160.

Bounded Rationality

Humans cannot always make optimum decisions because their choices are bounded by the time and the costs involved in making such decisions. Rather than assay all possible alternatives, decision makers must be satisfied with the selection of the best decision from among a *limited* number of alternatives. Decisions may be optimum in the sense that the marginal cost of further search activity may exceed the marginal value of considering additional choices. That is, a better choice may have been uncovered through more search activity, but the extra cost of this search may have exceeded the added value of finding it. These limitations in decision making are sometimes referred to collectively as constituting "bounded rationality"[3]—the manager can rarely make decisions in the sense of having complete information and perfect foresight.

In summary, the managerial decision process can rarely achieve complete and objective rationality. Rather, many decisions typically are incomplete and subjective. Administrators can move toward rationality as they consistently attempt to achieve maximum attainment of organization goals given that this attempt considers the implications of the time and costs involved in obtaining information. Further, the goals toward which the organization strives may extend beyond economic ones. As will be shown in succeeding paragraphs, ethical, social, and religious factors may influence legitimate objectives for all organizations, including business firms.

Phases of Decision Making

It is convenient to think of decision making as involving several phases or steps.[4] First, the manager has to determine whether or not a decision needs to be made. This step may be viewed as an intelligence phase—i.e., finding the problems that require solution in an organization. To discover whether or not problems exist, it is often necessary to refer back to the organization's objectives. The second phase of decision making is that of developing or generating alternative strategies or courses of action to solve existing problems. Finally, the decision maker must select the most appropriate solution alternatives from those available. Although some writers treat the implementation of decisions as an additional phase

---

[3] Herbert Simon, *Administrative Behavior* (2d ed.; New York: The Macmillan Co., 1957), pp. 52 ff.

[4] Peter Drucker utilizes five phases of decision making in *The Practice of Management* (New York: Harper & Bros., 1954). Other writers consider anywhere from 1 to 20 steps or phases as comprising the decision process. Simon, *Science of Management Decision*, chap. 1, uses the three phases discussed below.

of decision making, we will consider implementation as still another problem requiring yet other decisions.

DETERMINING THE NEED FOR DECISIONS

Since the initial phase of decision making involves the determination that a decision is required on the part of the manager, why do problems occur and how may they be identified? If an organization were confronted with no problems, there would be no need to inject an explicit decision into the operation. This ideal situation rarely, if ever, exists in any organization, however, and the need for decisions arises because of the existence of problems. Organization problems may be created by either of the two following general conditions: (1) if the performance of the firm does not meet the goals which it has set, and/or (2) if the firm's objectives are inappropriate. A discussion of each of these conditions giving rise to problems—and thus the need for managerial decisions—follows.

Performance Inadequacies

Inadequate performance in meeting the objectives of an organization may result from several factors. First, the work of the organization may consist of activities which do not assist or aid in meeting the stated objectives. This is a case of misdirected effort on the part of the organization. Perhaps the organization could easily meet its objectives if its efforts were directed toward activities which would further these ends rather than being frittered away in meaningless (in terms of objectives) activities. If a businessman has the singular objective of obtaining a maximum profit but engages in many tangential activities which do not contribute toward meeting this objective, a problem may well exist.

Even though the activities of an organization are directed toward meeting its objectives, the performance may not be adequate and problems will result. That is, the level of effort is insufficient to meet the objective. Some businessmen, for example, may direct all of their efforts toward the profit objective and still be unable to meet it. Inefficiency in this effort or insufficient input of effort may cause the level of performance to fall short of meeting the objective.

Perhaps the most frequent cause of problems is the failure that accompanies some change in the performance of an organization or in its competitors. In a machine shop, a change in the supplier of castings may introduce a new and different hardness that causes difficulty in machining. On an assembly line, the absence of a key employee causes imbalance and a consequent slowdown in production. A salesman may fail to meet his quota because a competitor is obtaining a larger share of the market as a result of a price reduction. It is on account of such changing conditions that performance, formerly considered satisfactory, deteriorates. To detect these problems, information reporting systems are established to periodically monitor performance and report the status of the system to managers who, by comparing results to goals, are able to determine whether a problem exists, large enough to warrant corrective action.

Need to Change Objectives

Under relatively stable conditions, there may be little need to make decisions about the nature of the objectives in an organization. Under changing conditions, however, objectives tend to become obsolete. In such a case, the major decisions requiring attention in the firm will center around revision of objectives to accommodate the changed conditions. Decisions affecting the implementation of existing objectives tend to assume less importance because any such decisions are likely to be worthless if the objectives themselves are changed.

To illustrate how a change in environmental conditions may influence a company's objectives, consider the effect that the growing wave of corporate acquisitions and take-overs has had upon firms with relatively conservative financial structures. Some conservative firms recognize that generous cash balances and working capital positions provide safety from possible adverse conditions (e.g., a long strike). Furthermore, these balances also give flexibility to their operations by allowing rapid decisions to initiate new profitable products or promising research.

For a conglomerate seeking companies to acquire, however, the conservatively financed firm may be an attractive target since some of the costs of acquisition may be quickly recovered from the working capital balances of the acquired firm rather than from operating profits over a longer period of time.[5] If the management of a firm wished to avoid being taken over by another, it might well change its goals which give it financial safety and flexibility to ones which minimize the chances that it will be attractive to acquisitive firms. Thus, an external condition, such as the merger wave, may cause a firm to alter its goals and operating strategy.

A second reason that inappropriate goals may require decisions is that an organization's objectives may be unrealistic. If a firm finds that it is extremely easy or difficult to achieve its objectives, there is usually sufficient cause for their reconsideration. If General Motors, for example, set an objective of realizing a profit of $100 per year, the company would have a problem. Considering its investment in facilities and personnel this level of profit is ridiculously small. Similarly, an objective

---

[5] E. P. Foldessy, "Spryregen's Spring," *Wall Street Journal,* January 26, 1970, p. 32.

by NASA of "colonizing Venus" within the next 12 months would be out of the question under the present state of the art of space flight. Although these two examples are extreme ones, many problems in organizations come about because the performance that can reasonably be expected is widely at variance with the objectives which have been set.

Change and Problem Identification

We have noted that changes in the environment can result in dissatisfaction with the goals of an organization, thus creating a problem. Similarly, problems caused by performance inadequacies have been viewed as resulting from some change. Given that a business has been operating satisfactorily over a period of time, the sudden appearance of a particular problem can only result from a change of some sort. If change is indeed the basic cause of *all* problems, it ought to be possible to identify problem causes by close analysis of conditions before and after the appearance of the problem. Kepner and Tregoe use exactly this strategy in their systematic technique of isolating problem causes.[6] The significance of their approach lies in their method which depends upon a systematic reviewing of the changes that have occurred in all possible causes behind problems. If there has been a change in a possible cause, it is a much more likely reason for the problem than when no change has taken place. Since they agree that a new problem cannot evolve without change having occurred, this relationship allows the problem seeker to "zero in" on the reasons for a problem much more quickly, certainly, and systematically than he ordinarily does. They accomplish improved problem-seeking, logically enough, by searching for problem causes only in those areas which have experienced change rather than in all possible areas. "The search for the cause of a problem narrows down to the search for that change which could produce the precise effects observed."[7] If the decision seeker limits his search to those areas, he minimizes his time and costs of finding the basic cause of the problem.

The sources of organizational problems which we have discussed are summarized in Figure 2–1. It should be recognized that most managers spend a great deal more of their total time on decisions arising from "performance inadequacies" than from "the need to reset objectives." This does not mean that setting objectives is unimportant. Obviously if the company has established inappropriate objectives and if activity is directed toward meeting them, serious problems will occur in the

---

[6] Charles Kepner and Benjamin Tregoe, *The Rational Manager* (New York: McGraw-Hill Book Co., 1965), especially chaps. 3–8. While these authors focus upon change as causing inadequate performance, we also suggest it is change which results in the need to alter goals.

[7] Ibid., p. 89.

Figure 2–1. Sources of Problems

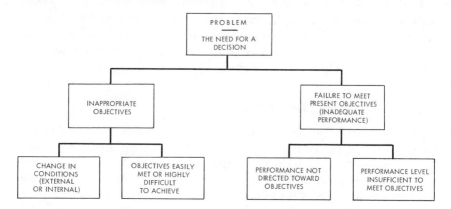

long run. When basic objectives are established, however, they tend to remain in effect over a relatively long period of time. There is a periodic, but not necessarily a continuous need for their review.

Since the problems and the decisions with which managers deal are related either directly or indirectly to the objectives of the organization, the remainder of our discussion of the "need for a decision" will center on this subject.

Intended Values and Business Objectives

Organizations, like individuals, are goal-seeking organisms. Their activities are performed so as to achieve some preset goal, some end, some objective. It is appropriate, therefore, to consider the sources of predetermined objectives developed for and by organizations.

From the viewpoint of society as a whole rather than that of the individual firm, classical economics holds that business exists to provide economic goods and services. The concept of profit can be considered as a measure of how well a firm is able to provide these goods and services to society. In strictly competitive markets, economic analysis shows that the maximization of profit by an individual business firm is consistent, in the long run, with the maximization of goods and services for society as a whole.

While most business firms attempt to achieve objectives other than purely economic ones, economic goals are fundamental in a capitalistic society. If profits are not achieved, the firm fails to survive. Yet, as will be shown, the profit goal can rarely be the only one with which managers want to or can deal.

Unintended Values: Dysfunctional Consequences. While the business firm may provide the locale for two potential lovers to meet and to socialize, the firm was not organized to provide such opportunities. In fact, business activity creates a large number of unintended effects which are incidental to its main purposes. While producing and selling a plastic resin, a chemical plant may be causing air pollution together with chemical and thermal pollution of a river. Although the chemical plant's manager has no intention or goal to achieve this pollution, an unintended result of seeking its intended goal may be the creation of other values held by some to be undesirable. Not only are certain consequences unintended, but it may often happen that as an organization becomes more successful in achieving its primary intended goals, it creates a greater degree of the undesired side effects. For example, as managers attempt to minimize capital investments, it may appear prudent for them to avoid purchase of dust collectors as a means of minimizing air pollution. Under similar circumstances, business management has often been criticized as indifferent or callous as it disregards social values in its fight for profits.

It is probably true in any and all kinds of organizations that excessive zeal toward achieving one set of values has an adverse effect upon the realization of others.[8] As a parent tries to exercise more rigid control over a child's behavior, this attempt risks being achieved at the expense of loss of love. As a city manager attempts to provide every and all services sought, he finds costs soaring beyond acceptable levels. Similarly, township trustees, congressmen, Peace Corps volunteers, hospital administrators, and all those who determine how energies or resources shall be used, find themselves constrained in their ability to maximize only intended values. Unintended consequences occur and they do so increasingly as singular attention is directed toward achieving a narrowly conceived objective.

But what is a narrowly conceived objective? Obviously, "narrowly conceived" is a relative term rather than an all-inclusive one which explicitly defines a goal's breadth. Interpretation of the narrowness or breadth of a goal depends upon the orientation of the individual making the judgment. To understand the establishment *and* interpretation of goals, it is necessary to consider the value orientations of the individuals setting goals, and those of others affected by the goals. In organizations, objectives are at least partially determined by the personal values of its executives. One may think of these values as ends which goal achievement serves. These relations can be diagrammed as below:

---

[8] J. Bruner and C. C. Goodman, "Value and Need as Organizing Factors in Perception," *Journal of Abnormal and Social Psychology*, 42 (January 1947), pp. 33–44.

Values and Value Differences. A value has been defined as an individual's conception of a desired state of affairs.[9] Obviously what is considered desirable is dependent upon one's background and experience. Individuals possessing similar education, and work experiences tend toward holding a similar set of values. Thus, lawyers tend toward similar sets of beliefs while scientists tend to hold a different set. The consideration of values is relevant because they are believed to influence goals, decisions, behavior, and conflict in a firm.

The values held by the top management of a firm are important in determining the intended values to be created through the organization's goals. If management possesses strong economic orientations, profit goals are likely to be emphasized. If, however, top management perceives economic values as not very important but rather upholds aesthetic values, profit objectives would tend to be subsumed to such goals as providing an attractive community and workplace or support for the arts.

Conflict. Individuals holding one set of values tend to establish goals and act in a manner different from individuals holding a different set of values. These differences in expectations can result in conflict and disagreement within an organization as Tagiuri has shown exists between scientists, research managers, and top management.[10] If accountants as a group tend to hold values in a manner inconsistent with professional personnel administrators, the likelihood of conflict between these groups is greater than if their value orientations are similar. Furthermore, this conflict may exceed that which one might ordinarily expect because one group tends to perceive another to hold sets of values *more extreme* than actually exist.[11] Businessmen may thus be *perceived* as desiring economic values even more strongly than they do. If this tendency to caricature or to view others' values in extreme terms persists, the probability that a manager will experience a lack of appreciation for his efforts in administering his business tends to increase. It would not be unusual if some individuals perceive business operations as overly concerned with economic considerations while overlooking social and ethical values. The literature abounds with examples of these differences and conflicting views.

Social Responsibilities

Just as value differences may cause conflicts within an organization, they may result in differences between management and groups outside

[9] Clyde Kluckhohn, "Values and Value Orientations in the Theory of Action," in T. Parsons and E. Shils (eds.), *Toward a General Theory of Action* (Cambridge, Mass.: Harvard University Press, 1951), p. 395.

[10] Renato Tagiuri, "Value Orientations and the Relationships of Managers and Scientists," *Administrative Science Quarterly*, 10 (June 1965), Table 3, p. 46.

[11] William Guth and Renato Tagiuri, "Personal Values and Corporate Objectives," *Harvard Business Review*, 43 (September–October 1965), pp. 123–32.

the firm. The pattern of values held desirable by individuals in the field of religion are different from those held by businessmen.[12] Similar differences compared to other groups exist. If a business manager attempts to maximize only those values he thinks important while either ignoring the creation of values desired and/or while creating values considered undesirable by others, he runs high risks that his position will be opposed. He is more likely to be considered as socially irresponsible, oblivious to needs broader than those of the business.

Some writers have summoned businessmen to forgo profit as their major objective and to give attention to sociologically derived values.[13] Others have placed emphasis on psychological values,[14] spiritual values, and human dignity.[15] These differences provide support to the fact that business responsibilities are broader than mere profit accumulation.

Another origin of social responsibilities stems from the authority that a business can exercise.[16] A business firm is powerful in many non-economic as well as economic ways. The ability of an industry or a firm to influence the general well-being and quality of life for broad segments of society through the effects that its acts have upon the level of employment, the quality of the environment, and the economic status of individuals and groups is substantial. These powers stemming from business acts not only have economic effects but social and psychological impacts as well. Because the activities of a firm influence various social, psychological, and spiritual areas of society, society expects business management to exercise its power in a manner benefiting others, not just the firm itself. Businessmen are expected to support the local social and health agencies. They are expected to buy locally, to support small businesses, to contribute to colleges and universities, to provide opportunities for blacks in management, to hire the handicapped, to man the hospital drive, to join the urban coalition, to train the disadvantaged, to participate in cultural affairs of the community, and so on. Business-

---

[12] Ibid.

[13] See, for example, Douglas McGregor, *The Human Side of Enterprise* (New York: McGraw-Hill Book Co., 1960), chap. 8.

[14] For example, Chris Argyris, *Personality and Organization* (New York: Harper & Bros., 1957).

[15] O. A. Ohmann, "Skyhooks with Special Implications for Monday through Friday," *Harvard Business Review*, May–June 1955, as reprinted in Max D. Richards and William A. Nielander (eds.), *Readings in Management* (Cincinnati, Ohio: South-Western Publishing Co., 1958), pp. 49 ff.

[16] The power of the business firm to influence others may evoke a countervailing rise of power from other segments of society. The powers of the business firms to influence the well-being of employees has had some bearing upon the introduction of labor unions so as to provide a countervailing influence. Similarly, business combinations, mergers, and trusts once became so powerful that opposing forces in government and the press successfully pressed for the passage of laws and regulation to offset this concentration of power. In general, as the power of any one segment of society becomes extremely strong, it tends to be offset by other segments so as to avoid undemocratic control and dominance by a small component of total society.

men can find much of their time and profit taken up by assuming duties related to social responsibilities.[17]

While external stimuli have frequently been cited as the sources from which concepts of social responsibility stem, the beliefs and ideals of businessmen themselves offer insight into the commitment of corporations to social problems. Although a businessman may place economic values at a relatively high level, this does not mean that he has no appreciation for social or ethical values. Businessmen express concern as do others about such social problems as urban decay, minority employment, environmental pollution, drug addiction, and crime rates. On one hand, these problems often adversely affect the ability of the firm to carry out its functions. At extreme levels, these problems offer threats to our ability to live and survive. Most all of the citizenry—businessmen and others—concern themselves to some extent with solving these social ills.

As managers have sought to analyze how social and business responsibilities might be integrated into operating realities of the business, the complexity of the relations between the firm and its environment became evident. To illustrate, in some instances, hiring hard-core unemployed can result in a more highly motivated hard-working work force, but this is not always the case. Similarly, in some processes, pollutants can be recovered and resold so that the costs of recovery can be offset entirely with income from recovered wastes. As larger and larger proportions of wastes are removed, however, the costs of removing them pro-

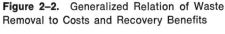

Figure 2–2. Generalized Relation of Waste Removal to Costs and Recovery Benefits

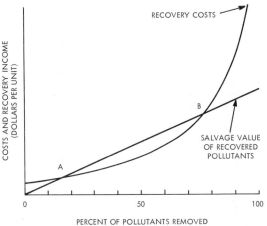

[17] Max D. Richards, "Management in the Social-Industrial Complex," in R. Millman and M. Hottenstein, *Promising Research Directions,* Proceedings, Academy of Management, Washington, D.C., 1967, p. 8.

gressively increase. Thus, while at one level of purity, less waste and higher profits are consistent, at other purity levels they are inconsistent. The general nature of this relation is illustrated in Figure 2–2.

Multiple Goals

One expression of the recognition of social responsibilities is that business firms in fact do not operate on the basis of a single economic goal. A multiplicity of objectives exists for all business firms. Typical are the objectives recommended by Peter Drucker: market standing; innovation; productivity; physical and financial resources; profitability; manager performance and development; worker performance and attitude; and public responsibility.[18] One reason for the existence of multiple objectives already shown, is that business firms attempt to provide multiple values and to meet social responsibilities. Another reason for multiple goals is that the overall objectives of the firm are *too general* to provide day-to-day guidance and must be supplemented with more narrowly circumscribed subobjectives. Consider the difficulty in decision making at the lower echelons of an organization if long-run profitability were the only objective toward which each manager were to direct his decisions. How could the production manager of a plant, for instance, realistically gear his efforts toward profit maximization unless he developed more specific subgoals such as the number of units to be produced, acceptable quality standards, and number of man-hours to be scheduled during each week? Nor is it probable that even such relatively specific subobjectives as these could be effectively implemented unless they, in turn, were further refined into even more narrowly defined subgoals. To attain an acceptable level of quality for its product, for example, the firm may find it necessary to increase the skills of its workers, to improve its materials, or to develop a greater degree of precision in its machining processes. Thus, most objectives of the firm may be viewed simultaneously as both ends toward which numerous subgoals are directed and as a means geared toward the achievement of higher level objectives. A somewhat similar pattern may be observed when we view the relationships between the long- and short-run objectives of the firm. A manufacturer of space systems, for example, may establish the development of a military missile as a short-run objective which in the longer run may provide the expertise for designing rockets for communications satellites. This latter objective, in turn, may provide a stepping-stone for someday sending a manned spacecraft to Mars.

Goals versus Constraints. Consider a student, perhaps typical of those who are candidates for an advanced degree. To graduate and obtain the most suitable employment, he is expected to attain a high level of academic achievement. Yet to maximize achieving highest grades,

---

[18] Drucker, *The Practice of Management*, chap. 7.

he must simultaneously trade off or give up some gratification of other pleasures (e.g., entertainment). Typically a student would be dissatisfied with no entertainment at one extreme or academic failure at the other. Some degree of achieving both goals is sought. The case can be viewed as one of multiple objectives.

An alternate formulation of this problem, however, is to consider achieving some satisfactory level of each goal as a necessary condition of a constraint in guiding behavior so that the individual will not fail in achieving other goals. One could establish that he will maximize grades given the constraint that he may devote two nights weekly to entertainment.

Achieving both the constraint and the goal require the use of his time resource. In fact, the constraint could be established so high that few resources remain to achieve the goal. If entertainment as a constraint were established at a level of five nights weekly, one might even question whether academic success still constitutes the goal. These observations merely illustrate that for voluntarily established constraints, there are resource trade-offs between them and the goals sought.[19]

Is it any different if one views societal-oriented goals as integral parts of goals that the firm establishes for itself or if social expectations are viewed as constraints to the strategy space within which managers operate to maximize the fundamental profitability objective? This resolution of how we formulate the social responsibility issue is a moot philosophical question. It does illustrate, however, the convenience of modeling the objectives of the firm in either a context of multiple goals or in a goal-constraint framework. Furthermore, the equivalencies in these formulations are useful in resolving the differing views concerning the role of business firms in undertaking social action, assuming social responsibilities, and facing fundamental economic realities.

Conflict between Objectives: Suboptimization

Conditions frequently exist in which the achievement of one organizational objective results in a less than optimum attainment of the others. This problem is often referred to as *suboptimization*.[20] From the point of view of the economist, an optimum overall condition for the firm exists when its marginal revenues are equal to marginal costs; and suboptimization occurs whenever the latter either exceed or fall below the former. In either case, greater profitability could be achieved by chang-

---

[19] H. Simon, "On the Concept of the Organization Goal," *Administrative Science Quarterly*, (March 1965), pp. 1–22.

[20] See Edward H. Bowman and Robert B. Fetter, *Analysis for Production Management* (rev. ed.; Homewood, Ill.: Richard D. Irwin, Inc., 1961), pp. 24 ff.; and Roland McKean, "Sub-optimization Criteria and Operations Research," Santa Monica, Calif.: The Rand Corporation, P-386, 22 (April 1953).

ing the firm's level of expenditures. In actuality, however, many types of expenditures cannot be directly related to revenue since they produce both economic and noneconomic values. Although theoretically it is possible to measure and weight all of the noneconomic objectives of a company—such as employee satisfaction—and thus relate them to its economic outputs so as to achieve overall optimization, in practice this would probably involve such a level of complexity as to be economically unfeasible.

From a less theoretical point of view, there are many cases in which (1) the attainment of two or more objectives is dependent upon a particular decision or set of decisions, and (2) no matter which course of action is chosen, some objectives will be realized only at the expense of the others. Two or more of the firm's overall objectives may conflict with one another; subobjectives may not be congruent with the overall objectives; or one subobjective may be in opposition to another. As an example of how these suboptimization conditions may arise, let us consider the production scheduling problems of a toy manufacturer whose demand reaches a high peak during the Christmas season. Should his production of toys be leveled over the year in which case inventories would build up during the slack season? Or, should production be geared directly to consumption with output greatly expanded and additional workers hired on a temporary basis each year to meet the period of peak demand? The production leveling alternative would be more congruent with the objectives of the personnel department, for the costs associated with the hiring, training, and laying off of the temporary employees would be eliminated. These savings, however, would be realized only at the expense of one of the prime objectives of the inventory manager—i.e., the reduction of inventory levels and their carrying costs. Further, from the point of view of the overall firm, neither of these two alternatives may represent an optimum course of action as far as profitability is concerned. Analysis of the problem may indicate, for example, that a partial leveling of production coupled with the hiring of just a few temporary workers during the peak season will result in the lowest total cost to the firm. Still this alternative might not be the optimum one if the company had established as one of its basic objectives the provision of steady year-round work for all of its employees.

There is still another important aspect of suboptimization. The attainment of short-run objectives may result in a lesser achievement of the long-run objectives of the organization. Our toy manufacturer may be able to improve his long-run profit considerably by increasing his expenditures for the development of new and different kinds of toys. Since such developments often do not pay off for some time, however, the achievement of this long-run objective may well be at the expense of profitability in the immediate future.

Measurement and the Weighting of Objectives

If the manager is to be able to evaluate effectively the success of his decision efforts, he must be able to measure the extent to which they contribute to the attainment of his objectives. In addition, when he seeks the achievement of a number of objectives which cannot all be directly translated into dollars of profit, it is important to develop means of weighting their relative importance. These two problems will be discussed briefly in the following sections.

Measurement. There are usually a number of different ways in which any given facet of organizational performance may be measured. For example, if the plant manager of a manufacturing firm has set as one of his objectives the prompt delivery of his product to his customers, several measures could be employed such as:

1. Number of orders shipped late.
2. Percentage of orders shipped late.
3. Total dollar value of the late orders.
4. Percentage of the company's total dollar volume shipped late.
5. Percentage distribution of orders shipped late by the number of days late.

Choice of any particular measures such as these should be conditioned not only by the value of the information so provided, but rather by the marginal value of the information as compared to its marginal cost. That is, the increased value of the decision payoff accruing from the marginal information should exceed the costs of obtaining the data.

In addition to measuring organizational performance, it is necessary for the decision maker to develop performance *standards* as a means of relating these measures to his objectives. For example, let us assume that the plant manager in our above illustration has decided that the best measure of the delivery objective is the "percentage of dollar volume shipped late." Suppose further that after having made this decision he observes that these percentages over the past four-week period have been 3.5, 4.2, 2.9, and 3.4. Is his objective being met? Does a problem exist? These questions cannot be answered until a specific percentage figure has been set to represent the successful attainment of the objective. If this standard has been set at 10 percent, for example, the delivery objective so defined would have been achieved in each of the four weeks indicated above. On the other hand, if the manager had decided that any number of delivery failures over 1 percent would represent failure on the part of the organization to meet its objective, a problem would have existed in each of these weeks.

Weighting of Objectives. If performance relative to the attainment of each of the subobjectives of a firm could be measured in dollars of profit, and the latter was the sole overall objective being sought, the manager would not be faced with the problem of determining the relative importance of each objective. In such a case, he would have a single criterion which could be applied to all organizational performance. Such an ideal measurement probably never exists, and, thus, the weighting of objectives is an important requisite for effective decision making. To illustrate, let us assume that a manager has decided that he wants to achieve three objectives, A, B, and C, and that he has developed an appropriate measure for each of these objectives. The basic question which he must then determine is: "How important is the attainment of objective A in relation to that of B and C?" If the manager believes that all three are equally important, for example, he might develop the following "model" to express the desired relationship between each and (O) his overall objective: $O = \frac{1}{3}A + \frac{1}{3}B + \frac{1}{3}C$. Although some authorities, such as Peter Drucker, believe that such attempts at weighting may prove fruitless at the overall level of company operations,[21] this process is essential for the development of certain types of operations research models.[22] An example of the establishment and weighting of objectives in such a specified decision-making situation is provided by the experience of the following company:

Company X manufactured a number of products, each of which required several different machining operations. Each time a different product was scheduled on any particular machine, change-over and set-up costs were incurred. The company attempted to develop an optimum set of decision rules to guide its dispatchers in scheduling the various products on the machines. Before this could be done, it was necessary to determine what objectives the firm was seeking to attain in its scheduling. Management decided that meeting its delivery promises to its customers and the minimization of operating costs were its two prime objectives, and an appropriate measure was developed for each. In deciding upon the relative importance of these two objectives, each was given equal weight. A mathematical model was then developed to represent the production operation and a series of past orders were "fed" into the model. Several different scheduling rules were tried out during these simulated production runs to determine which rule would provide for the greatest attainment of the two equally weighted objectives cost and delivery. In addition, the process was subsequently simulated with a different relationship between the two objectives incorporated into the model. This subsequent simulation indicated that different decision rules for the scheduling would be required whenever the weighting of the two objectives was modified.

This latter finding is what one would expect. If a firm's prime objective is to manufacture the highest quality product in the industry, its decisions would probably be quite different than if it were attempting to undersell all competition. Thus, the relative importance given to various

---

[21] Drucker, *The Practice of Management*, p. 62.

[22] C. West Churchman et al., *Introduction to Operations Research* (New York: John Wiley & Sons, Inc., 1957), p. 112. They present a discussion of the weighting of objectives.

objectives conditions the problems faced by, and consequently, the decisions required by an organization.[23]

SUMMARY

In the previous sections we have been concerned with organizational values, objectives, and problem identification. A summarizing flowchart

Figure 2–3.   Problem Identification in Organizations

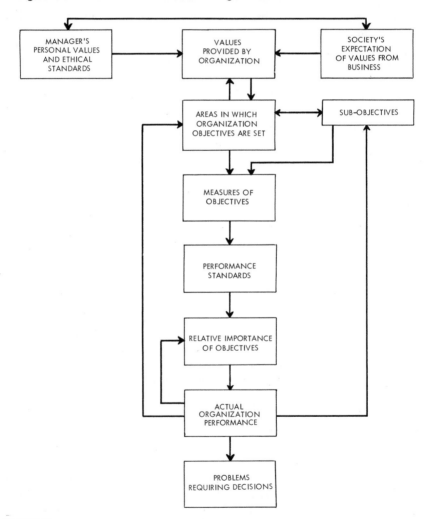

---

[23] In a discussion of goals, it is appropriate to examine the goal-setting process; how do managers go about establishing the firm's objectives? Such a discussion is delayed until the planning process is examined in Chapter 12. At that point a better understanding of organizations and the decision processes will allow a more rigorous treatment of the subject than is possible at this point.

of these aspects of the managerial process is presented in Figure 2–3. We have noted that problems exist when: (1) there is a difference between the current performance of an organization and its objectives, and/or (2) the objectives of the organization are inappropriate. Thus, the first requirement for decision making is the determination of objectives. The objectives are derived from the values which the company is attempting to provide to society—both economic and noneconomic. The manager's choice of values is conditioned both by what society expects of him and by his own philosophy and beliefs. A multiplicity of values and objectives exists for all business firms. In many cases, the full attainment of one objective results in a less than optimum achievement of others, and thus, suboptimization occurs. In relating the overall objectives of the firm to day-to-day decision making, it is necessary to develop additional detailed operational subobjectives, measures and standards of performance, and often, means for determining the importance to be attached to each objective. In addition, the decision maker will need to develop alternative courses of action to achieve his objectives. It is to this aspect of decision making that Chapter 3 will be devoted.

DISCUSSION AND STUDY QUESTIONS

1. What is the difference between "rationality" and "bounded rationality"?
2. Under what conditions do organizations need to make decisions?
3. What appears to be a "rational" way to systematically identify problems in organizations?
4. As an organization becomes more effective in achieving its primary goals, it creates dysfunctional side effects. Discuss.
5. What factor seems to increase the magnitude of value differences among different individuals and groups in organizations?
6. If managers are primarily concerned with societal expectations, their businesses are likely to suffer. Discuss.
7. The president of a small company was heard to comment: "With no pollution problems or the like to be concerned with, our firm has been successful with just one goal—profitability." Discuss.
8. What do we mean by suboptimization? What are some of the different types of suboptimization that may exist in a firm?
9. One production manager was heard to say, "My quality control is in excellent shape—rejects during the past month have been only 2.6 percent." Can you agree with this statement?
10. "I can be successful by carefully establishing the levels of my objectives at a point that operations can meet or exceed them." Comment.
11. A paper company produces one particular kind of product at each of several of its paper mills. One of these, its #3 mill, is located in a rela-

WRITTEN ASSIGNMENT
DUE 2/24/7(

tively small community in which the mill is the major employer. The mill is quite small and inefficient by modern standards.

The mill produces excessive air pollutants (such as sulfides) to which humans are particularly sensitive at very low levels of concentration in the air. Further, spent liquors and wash from production are expended to produce a degree of water pollution.

Although no known technology can eliminate all of these problems, control of pollution could probably be brought to acceptable levels if several million dollars worth of equipment were installed to monitor and control processes, preventing the creation of most of the undesired wastes. This investment might increase operating costs somewhat and would lower returns on an already depressed profit operation. Since the company has several plants that can produce the same products, and customer demand does not now require production at the No. 3 mill, management hesitates to install equipment into what is perceived as a marginal situation. Several studies have shown that for the same dollar investment a plant with three to four times the capacity of mill No. 3 could be equipped with pollution control equipment.

The company has received very few pollution complaints even though much of the time the local atmosphere literally reeks with offensive odors. Some managers reason that the townspeople believe that if complaints are made, they may result in a curtailment of plant operations and employment.

What should management do? Why?

SELECTED REFERENCES

Bowen, Howard. *Social Responsibilities of the Business Man.* New York: Harper & Bros., 1953.

Davis, Keith. "Can Business Afford to Ignore Social Responsibilities?" *California Management Review* (Spring 1960), 70–76.

Davis, Keith, and Bloomstrong, Robert L. *Business and Its Environment.* New York: McGraw-Hill Book Co., 1966.

Dent, James K. "Organizational Correlates of the Goals of Business Management," *Personnel Psychology,* 12 (Autumn 1959).

Drucker, Peter F. "Business Objectives and Survival Needs: Notes on a Discipline of Business Enterprise," *The Journal of Business,* 31 (April 1958), 81–90.

Eells, Richard, and Walton, Clarence. *Conceptual Foundations of Business.* Homewood, Ill., Richard D. Irwin, Inc., 1961.

England, George W. "Personal Value Systems of American Managers," *Academy of Management Journal,* 10 (March 1967), 53–68.

Greenwood, William T. *Issues in Business and Society.* Boston: Houghton Mifflin Co., 1964.

Guth, William D., and Renato, Tagiuri. "Personal Values and Corporate Strategy," *Harvard Business Review,* 43 (September–October 1965), 123–32.

McGuire, Joseph W. *Business and Society.* New York: McGraw-Hill Book Co., 1963.

Malik, Charles. "Reflections on the Great Society," *Saturday Review,* 49 (August 6, 1966), 13 ff.

Massarik, Fred. "Changing Social Values," *Academy of Management Proceedings, 1970,* San Diego, 1971, 63–76.

Peters, L. H., and Wotruba, T. R. "Goals and Directions—Two Aspects of Business Policy," *Northwest Business Management,* 4 (Spring 1967), 5–9.

Siri, Giuseppe Cardinal. "Management and the Spiritual Needs of Man," *Proceedings, CIOS XIII International Management Congress,* I (1963), 37–42.

Smith, George Albert, Jr. *Business, Society, and the Individual.* Homewood, Ill.: Richard D. Irwin, Inc., 1962.

Towle, Joseph W. (ed.). *Ethics and Standards in American Business.* Boston: Houghton Mifflin Co., 1964.

Chapter 3

Approaches to
Decision Making

THE PURPOSE of this chapter is to explain the decision activities that managers apply to the solution of their business problems. In the previous chapter, the methods of searching out and identifying problems were investigated. This chapter assumes that a known problem exists and that management wants to solve it, by first seeking alternative solutions and second, by applying methods of choice to those alternatives with the view of eliminating or reducing the intensity of the problem. (Eliminating a problem can be considered, alternatively, as meeting a goal more satisfactorily since a problem has already been defined as a difference between a system state existing and one desired.)

DEVELOPING ALTERNATIVE STRATEGIES

In Chapter 2, the three stages of decision making were discussed. The second of these involves the generation of alternative strategies or courses of action which the manager may take to solve his problems. While analysis is of central importance in discovering the problems of an organization, creativity tends to predominate in the generation of alternatives. In this section, consideration will be given to identifying the relevant factors involved in decision problems together with the creative means that the manager may use to generate alternative strategies.

Models of the Factors Influencing Achievement of Objectives

To improve the performance of an organization, any decision must modify the factors which have a bearing on the attainment of its objectives. If we know, for example, that the number of rejects of a particular product depends upon worker skill, degree of supervision, type of machine used and machine maintenance, any decision aimed at reducing the reject rate must result from a modification of one or more of these variables. To develop meaningful strategies for the solution of problems, then, it is important to understand both the objectives desired and the variables which influence the attainment of the objectives.

If the variables—including the objectives—can be identified and measured and the relationships between them explicitly stated, it is possible to construct a mathematical model of the behavior of the organization to the extent that it is influenced by these variables. Many readers of this book may be familiar with the representation of the value, A, of an investment, P, drawing interest, i, at the end of each year for n years as $A = P(1 + i)^n$. In this equation, the initial investment, the interest rate, and the number of years are *independent variables*, and the resultant value is the *dependent variable* in that it depends upon the values of the other variables. This model is a simple one in that the number of variables are few and the relationships between them not too complex. Many behavior patterns in organizations, however, cannot be represented by such elementary models, since a large number of variables are involved and the relationships between them can be extremely complicated.

A model of the variables influencing the attainment of objectives can be a useful device for generating alternative strategies. By substituting different values for the independent variables, it is possible to see what effect various changes in the firm's operations would have upon achieving the objective. For example, the manager may not need to actually increase his machine maintenance effort to observe how it would affect the reject rate. If he has developed a model of reject rate behavior, he can simulate modifications in this behavior by changing the values of the maintenance variable in the model and experimentally arrive at a satisfactory solution to the problem.

Although models may be useful for generating alternative strategies, their employment is limited if the manager is unable to identify all factors which have a bearing on the decision problem. Nor is it always possible to explicitly define the relationships between the decision variables, even when the manager is aware of their existence. In such cases, it may be necessary to develop novel strategies and approaches for the handling of problems. This development—as is also true with the formulation of new models—calls for creative thinking on the part of the manager.

Creativity in Decision Making

A new idea or a creative thought is the result of combining certain elements into new and different patterns. Consider as an example the electric bacon fryer. Although none of its separate parts were new, in and of themselves, their combination represented a new and radical departure in frying instruments. This case illustrates an instance in which old elements were brought together in a new combination. On the other hand, creativity sometimes results from a novel combination comprising previously unknown elements. The physicists have been discovering new and different parts of the atom for years, and the search for new sub-atomic particles continues. These discoveries, combined with knowledge already in existence, have provided a basis for creating new conceptions of the atom and of the universe itself.

Creativity in the form of generation of alternatives is a common need of managers for making decisions in their organizations.[1] Unique or unusual alternatives to meet organizational problems may defy development by any other means. Although an advertising manager may have a general idea of the effect of advertising on the sales of products for which he has responsibility, for example, each new advertisement requires creativity in the development of layout, copy, format, and, perhaps, media. The precise combination of factors for ensuring the success of the advertisement is not known for certain. It may not be possible to develop a formal model to ensure that a particular combination of elements will have the desired effect in attaining the objective. Furthermore, even if a model were developed to solve this problem, there is no assurance that the same combination of elements would bring about an equal degree of success over an extended period of time. That is, the model, if developed, may portray a dynamic and, perhaps, unstable condition. The existence of dynamic variables and relationships is not necessarily confined to advertising. Other decision problems exhibit similar characteristics.

The Creative Individual. Donald MacKinnon in reporting on a long-term research project at the University of California (Berkeley) by the Institute of Personality Assessment and Research concludes that those qualities most characteristic of the creative individual include

his high level of effective intelligence, his openness to experience, his freedom from crippling restraints and impoverishing inhibitions, his aesthetic sensitivity, his cognitive flexibility, his independence of thought and action, his high level of creative energy, his unquestioning commitment to creative endeavor,

---

[1] It is not clear that organizations develop an exhaustive list of alternative solutions to problems. Cyert and March conclude that the search for solutions is simple-minded and not very extensive, usually ending with the first *satisfactory* solution rather than continuing the search to find better or optimal ones. Richard Cyert and James March, *A Behavioral Theory of the Firm* (Englewood Cliffs, N.J.: Prentice-Hall, Inc., 1963), chap. 6. It must be noted, however, that the theory of Cyert and March involves describing and predicting behavior in a firm rather than seeking to improve performance. In the following sections dealing with creativity, we are dealing with normative prescriptions to generate solutions for problems. The heuristics section (following) deals with many of the issues Cyert and March posit.

and his unceasing striving for solutions to the ever more difficult problems
that he constantly sets for himself.[2]

While the sample of persons studied at Berkeley includes many creative persons outside the business field,[3] the results are relevant to decision making for organizations in several ways. They imply that training
can be effective for improving the creative output of an individual and
of organizations as the individuals in it are developed for creative thinking.[4] This implication is supported by the developmental programs of
various organizations which have implemented several types of training
programs to increase creative outputs. Brainstorming and several variations on its freewheeling theme for the creation of new ideas was first
presented by Alex Osborn.[5] The forced association technique, in which
attention is focused upon the several dimensions of a problem so that
alternatives can be adaptedly forced to comply with problem requirements, was developed by William J. J. Gordon. Other not as well-known
(although perhaps as successful) approaches have evolved in universities
and training departments of many corporations.

The second implication about the research upon creativity is that
some organizations will inhibit and perhaps even reject the creative
individual. To some extent it is logical and natural that bankers' interests
may be unlike those of highly creative individuals since conforming
to rules of the Federal Reserve Board, the Federal Deposit Insurance
Corporation, and other regulatory banking agencies does not allow a
maximum of "independence of thought and action" or freedom from
restraints or inhibitions. Order and fixed structure are characteristic of
large segments in the operation in banks. Conversely, however, banks
as organizations need ideas to survive and to flourish. Competition from
insurance companies and mutual funds, for example, provides an impetus
to develop imaginative bank trust investment approaches.

Encouraging Organizational Creativity. The potential conflict between business structure and creativity has been recognized by Frederick Randall,[6] who suggests that to promote creativity the executive

---

[2] Donald W. MacKinnon, "What Makes a Person Creative?" *Saturday Review,*
145 (February 1962), pp. 15–69. Copyright 1962, Saturday Review, Inc.

[3] In fact, highly creative individuals tend to have interests opposite those of
some groups in business: e.g., purchasing agents and bankers. Ibid.

[4] See I. Maltzman, "On the Training of Originality," *Psychological Review* 67
(1960), pp. 229–42; and Charles S. Whiting, "Operational Techniques of Creative
Thinking," *Advanced Management,* 20 (October 1955), pp. 24–30.

[5] Alex Osborn, *Applied Imagination* (New York: Charles Scribner's Sons, 1963).

[6] Frederick D. Randall, "Stimulate Your Executives to Think Creatively," *Harvard
Business Review,* 33 (July–August 1955), pp. 121–28. The following reasoning about
creativity in organizations follows Randall's thinking. See also T. North Whitehead,
"Permission to Think," *Harvard Business Review,* 34 (January–February 1956),
pp. 33–40.

needs to provide the atmosphere that will enhance idea production. Furnishing such a climate for subordinates involves several actions on the part of the executive. Since ideas consist of new combinations of concepts, people cannot be kept in the dark; they must be kept informed so as to have the raw materials for origination of ideas. Second, high pressure for accomplishing present tasks leaves little time for mulling over ideas. Overwork and conditions inducing anxiety thus tend to suppress ideation.

A third point made by Randall is that inhibitions to creation must be eliminated because creativity cannot be expected to bloom in an organization:

1. If there is rigid control over subordinates, jobs, and activities so that they have no influence on their content.
2. If there are extremely adverse consequences associated with individual failures rather than a willingness to allow people to make mistakes.
3. If a conditioned bias in thinking or a policy in the organization prevents junior executives from considering reasonable lines of exploration and giving comprehensive consideration to the problems they are attempting to solve.

While removing inhibitions will indeed "free up" the organization for the creation of ideas, not all organizations want new ideas. The captain of a sailing dinghy wants to be able to rely upon his crew to perform with fixed responses to his commands or to certain conditions. Rather than receiving new ideas, he wants to rely upon predictable acts. It may be that during the training phase or in planning for a race that new ideas would be welcome, but during execution, following a set routine is considered mandatory. Some people have no say in how they are trained or in planning. Such individuals may have little or no need for creativity in their jobs.

APPROACHES TO THE SELECTION OF ALTERNATIVES

If a number of reasonable and feasible solutions have been created to deal with a particular problem, the next stage in the decision process is to select the alternative or a combination of alternatives to be used in alleviating the problem. Methods for selecting alternatives possess several dimensions.

The rest of this chapter describes these several methods and criteria for considering their rational use to solve problems. There is a wide range in the degree of optimization possible with the different approaches to decision making. Some are relatively unsophisticated, while other techniques are based on rather complex analytical processes. We will discuss the less sophisticated approaches first, and follow by examining the more complex and "scientific" ones.

Personalistic Decision Making

Probably the most widely employed approach to selecting proper courses of action is to rely upon personal insight, intuition, judgment, and experience. In the history of many present-day organizations, the personal imprint of one or a few men has had a major impact upon the nature and success of the entity. Henry Ford, Harvey Firestone, Donaldson Brown of Du Pont, James Ling of LTV, and General Wood of Sears, set the patterns for their organizations with a combination of personalistic and systematic approaches. While the history of these corporate leaders dramatizes how the individualistic decision process can shape a giant corporation, these methods can be equally effective if employed by the foreman on the shop floor.[7]

If the manager can avoid overgeneralizing from past experience and accurately perceive how the key variables existing in new decision problems are similar to or different from those in previously encountered situations, experience-based decision making may prove quite effective. Further, personalistic methods may be necessary for dealing with the many problems which confront managers daily and for which there are no analytical or "scientifically based" solution methods available. Decision problems often have to be made quickly, and there may not be sufficient time to apply complex, time-consuming scientific analysis to their solution. Finally, the manager may sometimes deem it more profitable to purposely ignore scientific approaches even though he realizes that by doing so he may achieve less than optimum results. Achieving an optimum solution may not be sufficiently important to justify the considerable time and expense required to apply scientific approaches. The expense of developing an analytical solution may equal or exceed its contribution to improved decision making.

Such experience-based decision methods are, however, subject to certain limitations. Each manager's background is limited and his previous experience may not provide an adequate sample upon which to base current decisions. For this reason, decisions in new situations may fail because of false premises derived from past experience. Further, human memory, observation, and interpretation of data are fallible. Therefore, even if a manager's assumptions are correct, incomplete knowledge and faulty interpretation of data can undermine the effectiveness of experience-based decisions.

---

[7] For an attempt to systematically study the judgmental, "intuitive," and "insightful" aspects of managerial decision making, see Adrian J. Grossman, "An Approach for Formalizing Entrepreneurial Processes in Business," *Proceedings, CIOS XIII Management Congress* (New York: Council for International Progress in Management [USA], Inc., 1963), pp. 239–48.

Notwithstanding their continued wide usage, managers rarely place sole reliance upon experience-based judgmental decision approaches. Most blend scientific and experience-based methods. Further, the adoption of more scientific analytical tools is taking place at a more rapid rate than ever before. Wide availability of electronic computers has made possible the application of highly sophisticated tools for decision making, the use of which was not possible in the past because of prohibitive computational work. With rapid advances in decision theory, operations research, model building, and systems analysis, there is little doubt that the manager of tomorrow will rely on scientific methodology to a much greater extent than his counterpart of today.

Factor Identification and Weighting

It is difficult to assess the degree of rationality in personal judgments, hunch, and intuition. Managers may be unable to evaluate whether their decisions are consistent and comprehensive. The complexity of the decision tasks in managing most organizations of any size suggests that rational decision approaches be more systematic than simply personal judgment. Then, too, because experience and judgment are personal, they do not, necessarily, remain with the organization after the departure of the individual. While it would be both futile and unwise to try to abolish personalistic decision making, the organization also needs both systematic and more sophisticated approaches.

A simple start is merely to list the pros and cons of every alternative as a means of coming to a conclusion about which choice should be selected. For simple problems this technique is often valuable, but as the number of alternatives being considered and the number of variables bearing upon the problem increase, this approach becomes unwieldy. When using a listing of the favorable points of an alternative, for example, one soon finds that a point in favor of one alternative often turns out to be an unfavorable point for another. In selecting orange juice for a restaurant chain, the manager may be inclined to choose brand A because it is sweet, free of pulp, and easy to mix, but unfavorably inclined because of the manufacturer's business reliability and the price. Brand B is favored because of its easy availability, its price, and its national advertising but opposed because of its slightly sour taste and packaging. At least "price" and "degree of sweetness" are common factors for these two brands. If the decision maker can identify the factors or variables important in achieving the goal and reducing the problem, he can be more comprehensive by evaluating every alternative against all-important criteria.

Ranking, Rating. Figure 3–1 presents a hypothetical example of some of the factors which might be considered important in selecting an orange juice by a restaurant chain. Each brand is ranked relative to all

Figure 3–1. Factor Ranking of Juice Brands

	Alternative Brands					
	Brand Ranks by Factor				Rank Differences	
Factors	A	B	C	D	A	D
Color.................	1	3	4	2	1	
Sweetness.............	3	2	4	1		2
Price.................	3	2	4	1		2
Delivery time..........	1	3	4	2	1	
Availability...........	1	3	4	2	1	
Advertising............	3	2	4	1		2
Texture...............	1	3	4	2	1	
Ease in use............	3	2	4	1		2
Differences, Total......					4	8

others, factor by factor. Upon inspection of these data, brand C is inferior in all respects to all other brands and need not be considered further. It is said to be *dominated* by the other alternatives. Similarly brand B is dominated by brand D on all factors, leaving only A and D to be evaluated.

If all factors are considered equally important, there may be a predisposition on the part of the decision maker to select D over A since for those factors for which D is not superior, it is rated number two, while A is ranked number three in those instances where D is rated best. Or, if we sum the differences in ratings and attribute the differences to the superior alternative, (as is done in Figure 3–1 on the difference columns) D appears superior to A. However, this line of reasoning can be fallacious since we cannot by this means determine the relative worth of rankings across criteria. To illustrate this possiblity, consider the color factor. Brand A may be vastly superior to brand D for color, whereas for sweetness D may be only slightly superior to brand B or A. What obviously is needed is an estimate of the *degree* of superiority for each alternative rather than a *mere ranking*. Further, the relative importance of each factor to goal attainment is needed. Then a scoring scheme could be devised to provide a total score and a preferred choice.

To illustrate from the field of personnel administration, job evaluation is a technique of rating jobs for the purpose of determining their relative worth. Relative worth can then be translated into pay scales that reflect this worth. One evaluation technique starts by determining those variables (e.g., skill, effort, responsibility, job conditions) contributing to the worth of any job and assigning weights to those variables in the proportion that management believes the jobs ordinarily contribute their worth to the firms. A system might weight these variables as shown

Figure 3–2

Factor	Weight	Total Possible Points	Actual Weightings	
			Janitor	Machinist
Skill......................	10	250	85	200
Effort......................	3	75	65	35
Responsibility..............	4	100	40	75
Job conditions..............	3	75	65	30
TOTAL................		500	255	340

in Figure 3–2. To evaluate a job, it would be possible to compare each job by degree of difficulty relative to every other job on each of the many factors. Since hundreds of jobs typically are involved, this becomes cumbersome. Thus, more commonly, a rating scheme is devised to assign various numbers of "points" to a job up to a possible maximum (column 3) on a relatively small number of factors. After each job is rated (given so many degrees) on each factor, the points are totaled and represent the relative worth of those jobs (columns "Janitor" and "Machinist"). Detailed rating manuals are developed to attempt to ensure fairness and consistency in job ratings. In the example, the machinist job contributes more (340 to 255) than the janitorial job and would, supposedly, receive a higher pay.[8]

In evaluating various techniques of weighting and evaluating alternatives, Eckenrode found that simple ranking was equal to or superior to rating by several more complicated techniques (e.g., paired comparisons and successive comparisons).[9] Certainly, systematic procedures such as ranking methods can ensure that the decision maker considers factors explicitly and consistently. Decision complexity is reduced somewhat and apparent rationality is enhanced. The utility of systematic approaches is exemplified by the military services which employ variations of these techniques extensively in selecting weapons systems and their suppliers.

Principles of Management in Decision Making

Decision making goes on continuously in thousands of organizations all the time. To the extent that business acts are repetitive, it would

[8] For some of the problems involved in weighting factors and equitably determining the relative worth of jobs in wage and salary administration, see, for example, George Strauss and Leonard R. Sayles, *Personnel: The Human Problems of Management* (2d ed.; Englewood Cliffs, N.J.: Prentice-Hall, Inc., 1967), chap. 25.

[9] Robert T. Eckenrode, "Weighting Multiple Criteria," *Management Science*, (November 1965), pp. 180–92.

appear logical that if a rule of action governing specific decision conduct were available, managers could apply these principles appropriately to the problems they face. Under what conditions could a manager rely upon a principle for application to his problem? To answer this question it is useful to review methods of developing acceptable and reliable principles.

Development of Principles. Managerial principles may be derived in a number of ways. One source of principles is the experience of managers. If a manager finds one course of action successful in his practice, he tends to allow this to become a principle of action for him. If large numbers of managers in diverse situations find that the same course of action is successful in handling their problems, the principle may become generally accepted.

Experimentation and research may also be used in developing principles. The effectiveness of a course of action may be determined by observing its impact under controlled conditions, either in an actual organization or in a laboratory situation. If the observation reveals that a particular strategy is successful only under certain conditions, the principle prescribing its effectiveness must be modified to take into account these conditions. Control of as many variables as possible is attempted while the principle is being tested so that differences in results can be attributed to the effect of the principle rather than some other factor. Research by observational and experimental means is preferable to personal experience as a means of developing principles since extraneous or unobserved variables in experience may influence the effectiveness of the principle. Competent observation and experimentation isolate the effect of the principle from such variables.

In addition to the above methods, deduction may be used to develop principles. If a general theory of behavior exists, principles consistent with the theory may be logically deduced. For example, let us assume that one manager's theory about the behavior of individuals in organizations is as follows: "All people are inherently lazy and they abhor work." One principle which may be derived from this theory is that since people dislike work, "employee productivity can be increased only if forceful and threatening supervisory methods are employed." If the theory is valid, the principle should prove effective. We will examine the validity of this particular theory and its derived principles in a later chapter.

When first developed, no real life evidence of successful use of such logically deduced principles necessarily exists. The principles merely represent a logical extension of the general theory. When the principles are applied in practice they may or may not be verified. If not, either the original theory or the logic of the deduction is in error.

Values and Limitations of Management Principles. There is considerable disagreement as to whether many of the current so-called principles of management have the strength of truth implied by the definition of a principle. While some authorities title their books *Principles of Management*,[10] others writing about the same subject matter discuss instead the ". . . bases of effective thinking that condition the formulation of executive decisions"[11] or state that ". . . there are gaps in the information we possess, inconsistencies in other places, and frequently hypotheses not substantiated by demonstrated fact."[12] These authors do not make strong claims about the validity or reliability of their generalizations concerning managerial behavior. Still other scholars sharply criticize the validity of behavior prescribed by most principles of management[13] pointing out that one principle is often contradicted by another. When such contradictions exist, the decision maker has little basis for selecting the most appropriate principle.

Theoretically, it should be possible to learn from experience. Each time that a manager encounters a problem he should not have to consider it as entirely new and unique since countless managers before him have undoubtedly faced similar situations. If the causes of successful and unsuccessful results can be determined and understood, it should be possible to form generalizations about the appropriateness of prospective courses of action. This attractiveness of principles to guide decision making, however, has led some to leap to their formulation without sufficient factual data to support their applicability under varying conditions.

The major reason that current management principles fail to warrant more widespread scholarly support is the lack of comprehensive scientific evidence to indicate their truth or falsity. Rather than scientific evidence, the major support for management principles is from personal experience. Fayol, the progenitor of many management principles, distilled his principles from his personal managerial background. At their best, these "principles" are gems of insight and wisdom; at their worst, dangerous overgeneralizations.

At the same time, the so-called principles of management do have some value. In almost every case, there is some evidence to support their applicability, at least under certain conditions. If a manager's problem corresponds to the kind of situation under which the principle is applicable, it may provide him with a valuable guide for expediting and simplifying his decision making. In other situations, the principle

---

[10] See George Terry, *Principles of Management* (5th ed.; Homewood, Ill.: Richard D. Irwin, Inc., 1968), and Koontz and O'Donnell, *Principles of Management* (4th ed.; New York: McGraw-Hill Book Co., 1968).

[11] Ralph C. Davis, *The Fundamentals of Top Management* (New York: Harper & Bros., 1951), p. 29.

[12] William Newman, *Administrative Action* (Englewood Cliffs, N.J.: Prentice-Hall, Inc., 1951), p. 8.

[13] For example, Herbert A. Simon, *Administrative Behavior* (2d ed.; New York: The Macmillan Company, 1957), chap. 2.

may just be one factor or variable to be taken into consideration along with several others in making a decision.

To be able to apply a principle sensibly, then, the manager is well advised to inform himself as to the evidence providing support to the principle so that his use of it is rationally justified.

Heuristics and Behavioral Theories of Decisions

The process of balancing one's checkbook with a bank statement is a relatively routine procedure that can be described as checking the previous balance, deposits, and withdrawals on the bank statement with corresponding entries in the checkbook; then summing outstanding checks, and subtracting this sum from the previous checkbook balance to arrive at a balance that should be equivalent to that on the bank statement. If these two balances are unequal, one proceeds to one of several routines to identify the discrepancy. The rule of thumb procedures that are employed in such a process are called *heuristics*. They are important because they occur in many if not all types of personalistic decision making.

While many of the decision approaches to be explained in this book deal with how models or other decision approaches *should* be used in a prescriptive manner to achieve a firm's goals, research upon heuristics initially focused upon the descriptive question "How do people actually make decisions?" How does the mind work to deal with problems? What kind of decision behavior actually exists?

Human thought processes are typically considered as mysterious and unknown and one often is personally unable to reconstruct how he arrived at a particular conclusion. Some of the research on heuristic procedures, however, assumed that the essential thought process *could* be identified by the "protocol" method, by which the decision maker is asked to verbalize what he is thinking as he thinks through a problem. This verbalized reconstruction of thought processes is probably not descriptive of all of what goes on in the brain. By recording these verbalizations, flow diagramming the sequences of reasoning undertaken and the intermediate and final results of that thinking, however, it has been possible to construct a detailed written procedure that, if followed by another individual, can replicate the decision results of the original subject.

Probably many persons could sit down and write the heuristics used in balancing a checkbook with the bank statement—even to the extent of describing in detail the error-checking routines and their sequence of applications. If error free, another individual could use the procedure to arrive at the same result. This is a relatively simple routine, however, one that is subject to a known limited list of exceptions. Most basic heuristic research has focused upon complex problems in which the number of variables and their interrelationships have been large. The heuristics identified for complex problems have resulted in rather lengthy, detailed procedures more amenable to programming and calculation by computer rather than by man. Computer programs of such procedures are called heuristic programs.

Heuristic programs have been developed for the assembly line balancing problem,[14] the evaluation of potential job candidates by a consulting psychologist,[15] selecting a portfolio of investments by a trust investment office,[16] and playing games such as chess or checkers.[17] One objective of this type of research has been to automate the decision processes in organizations by replacing the decision maker with a computer, following routines (or improvements on them) formerly made by humans. This effort has been successful in such areas as assessing whether individuals are "normal" or "maladjusted" or a personality test, and in improving the PERT technique (which we will discuss in Chapter 16). A second more basic goal has been to illuminate the human thinking process and is closely related to the work in artificial intelligence which examines such technical and philosophical questions as whether computers can "think."[18]

Chess is a very complex game with literally thousands of considerations in the alternatives available for play. Neither the human mind nor the computer can process information fast enough to consider the optimum chess move (bounded rationality) and thus resorts instead to certain simplified heuristics, such as "dominate the center of the board," "protect the queen," and so forth, to evaluate possible plays of the game.

Simplifying the huge information requirements of a complex problem implies, however, that some variables and alternatives are not considered in a decision.[19] An analysis of the psychologist's thought process, for example, showed that in the sequence in which he examined information, he first sought that which allowed him to arrive at rapid conclusions. Some information would quickly disqualify a candidate for a particular

---

[14] Fred M. Tonge, *A Heuristic Program for Assembly Line Balancing* (Englewood Cliffs, N.J.: Prentice-Hall, Inc., 1961).

[15] Robert D. Smith and Paul S. Greenlaw, "Simulation of a Psychological Decision Process in Personnel Selection," *Management Science,* 13 (April 1967), B409–19.

[16] G. P. Clarkson, *Portfolio Selection: A Simulation of Trust Investment* (Englewood Cliffs, N.J.: Prentice-Hall, Inc., 1962).

[17] Newell, Shaw, and Simon, "Chess Playing Programs and the Problem of Complexity," *IBM Journal,* 2 (October 1958), pp. 320–35.

[18] H. L. Gelernter and N. Rochester, "Intelligent Behavior in Problem-Solving Machines," *IBM Journal,* 2 (October 1958), pp. 336–45.

[19] For a study of how variations in cognitive abilities affect the information processing and decision equality of individual decision makers, see Olof Lundberg, "An Experimental Investigation of Complex Decision Making as Influenced by Cognitive Style" (unpublished Ph.D. dissertation, University Park, Pa.: The Pennsylvania State University, 1971).

job, for example. These types of data tended to be examined first. The sequence of information search and evaluation varied depending upon what was concluded at each step of the heuristic. By sparsing the network of search, he proceeded to arrive at a final conclusion *without* examining all available information, only those data relevant *in light of* previously evaluated data.

Simplifying the information search procedure can also involve ignoring some relevant data. When the chess program applies the "dominate the center of the board" rule of thumb, it greatly cuts down the number of alternatively available moves to consider. By sequentially applying other heuristics, only a few alternatives from thousands need to be considered in detail.

In solving group or organizational problems, the search for solutions appears somewhat limited and simple-minded as well. Rather than seeking an optimum, patterns readily available and in the vicinity of those formerly used tend to predominate. Only when *satisfactory* solutions cannot be found does a widened search pattern evolve.[20] This implies that complex decision making is somewhat removed from rational and optimum approaches until problems become so serious that threats to individuals and the organization itself exist. This satisficing approach to decision making is partially a result of the huge information processing requirements involved in complex decisions and partially a function of the threat that managers perceive in the problems facing them.

Heuristic programs thus provide shortcut but not necessarily optimum solutions to problems. (Some programs may not be able to arrive at any solution for some cases.) As substitutes for human information processing and decision making, they can aid in automating organizational decision making. Furthermore, the computational costs of some mathematical optimizing approaches (e.g., linear programming) may be so great that research in these areas involves developing new heuristics to reduce computer costs even at the expense of always being able to reach an optimum solution. Finally, there are no feasible optimum methods for solving some kinds of problems (e.g., the locating of facilities within a plant). For these problems, the identification of human heuristics, improving them and developing complementary procedures allows consistent and computerized problem solving. As development in heuristics proceeds, narrowing the gap between satisfactory and optimizing approaches to decision making can be accelerated. Personalistic decision making can be relieved of routine and allowed to deal with more important, complex, and uncertain situations.

MODELS FOR DECISION MAKING

While intuition, heuristics, rules of thumb, tradition, principles, and even systematic methods exemplified by ranking techniques constitute

---

[20] Cyert and March, *A Behavioral Theory*, chap. 6.

very important managerial decision approaches, all of them suffer from an inability to arrive positively at the "best" answer for problems. Models can help to overcome this shortcoming and thus they are receiving increased attention as aids to decision making. The purpose of this section is to explain what models are, how they are constructed and how they may be used in handling decision problems. Models of business behavior represent one of the more sophisticated and scientific tools at the disposal of managers. They offer considerable promise for the manager of tomorrow. Although knowledge and skill in the use of mathematics and statistics are desirable for expertise with models, the following discussion and the application of the models presented throughout this book can be mastered with a minimum background in these subjects.

A model is a representation of some real situation or object. Lead soldiers and toy guns can be set up to represent a battle of war. Similarly, a model can represent the elements of a decision problem for a manager. It is not necessary for the model to duplicate in all the richness of life every detail of the real object or situation. It may serve its purposes by representing only the essential features. Few, if any, toy soldier battles represent the noise, emotion, and courage of combat. Yet the mock battle may serve a purpose by illustrating the effects of a military strategy. In a similar way, most decision models are abstractions from reality. In a model designed to aid in the selection of an individual for a job, for example, it may be unnecessary to show the color or existence of his hair or many other of his personal characteristics. Such abstraction from detail allows concentration on the essential or vital factors in decision problems.

Different models vary in their degree of abstraction (and conversely of reality). There are a number of factors which will condition the degree of abstraction desirable in a model. If a model is too abstract, the manager may lose confidence in it because it seems unrealistic to him. On the other hand, if the model is too concrete, he may feel that there are so many variables and relationships in it that he cannot move directly to the heart of the decision problem. For these reasons, a balance between abstraction and reality is desirable. In addition, there are cost factors related to the degree of abstraction appropriate for a model. Defining and quantifying each variable takes time on the part of the model builder, and thus, more highly abstract models may be cheaper to construct.

Model Types

Models may be classified in many different ways. The following classification is based upon the type of model construction. Three general types of construction can be distinguished: descriptive, analogue, and symbolic.

A *descriptive* model[21] attempts to represent a situation by picturing the way that it looks. A picture or a drawing of an automobile plant allows the viewer to imagine what the real plant looks like. A scale model, a blueprint, a pilot plant, a scale layout, a painting, all represent reality through imagery. These models possess a high degree of concreteness and relatively little abstraction. Descriptive models are relatively easy to construct but difficult to manipulate—e.g., it is cumbersome to change the variables in a picture. For this reason, the descriptive model is limited in application to the particular situation which it portrays and does not have general applicability to other situations. For the same reason, descriptive models usually do not lend themselves to portraying dynamic situations or causal relationships between variables although they may sometimes do so. Descriptive models, however, are valuable for obtaining a "feel" for a situation and for providing a stepping-stone for the development of other models with more abstract representations.

The second type of model is the *analogue* model. It represents the elements of a real situation by substituting for them other elements with different properties or forms. An airplaine is represented by a blip on a radar screen. Lakes are represented by blue colors on maps. Different materials for parts are represented by different types of cross-hatching on drawings. The flow of money and credit in the economy has been represented in a hydraulic analogue model by colored water, pipes, and valves. Analogue models are often more difficult and expensive to construct than descriptive models, but their value for decision making is also greater. Analogues can be constructed to portray more general conditions than is often possible with descriptive models and thus may be applicable to a greater variety of situations. They also may be more easily manipulated than most descriptive models, and causal and dynamic relationships may be more easily shown. In the money flow analogue, for example, the effects of a policy reducing the rates of interest paid by savings institutions could be traced throughout the system. Theoretically this policy would encourage additional consumption and discourage individuals from saving their incomes. These effects could be traced to other variables such as production and investment, by increasing or decreasing the water flows in the analogue model. The changes in water flow are analogous to the changes in the money and credit variables they represent.

The third type of model is the *symbolic* model in which symbols are employed to represent the variables existing in real life situations. Mathematical models or those based on symbolic logic are examples of this type of model. A major advantage of symbolic models is that

---

[21] C. West Churchman, Russell L. Ackoff, and E. Leonard Arnoff, *Introduction to Operations Research* (New York: John Wiley & Sons, Inc., 1957), refer to descriptive models as "iconic," p. 159.

the manipulation of variables as symbols is usually easier than the manipulation of analogues. Further symbolic representation often permits the use of powerful mathematical problem-solving techniques which are not applicable when situations are represented in descriptive or analogue terms. Symbolic models usually abstract from reality to a greater extent than do other models; however, the danger of misrepresentation is greater. Solutions to higher abstract models may have little applicability to real situations.

Model Choice.   The manager's choice of the type of model he wants to use will depend on the kind of problem with which he is dealing and the relative importance of the problem. As we indicated above, descriptive, analogue and symbolic models differ in the degree to which they possess several characteristics. These differences are summarized in Figure 3–3.

Figure 3–3.   Model Characteristics by Type of Construction

Model Characteristic	Type of Model Construction		
	Descriptive	Analogue	Symbolic
Degree of abstraction.............	3	2	1
Concreteness....................	1	2	3
Generality......................	3	2	1
Ease of construction.............	1	2	3
Ease of manipulation.............	3	2	1
Ability to Handle			
Dynamic changes................	3	2	1
Causal relationships.............	3	2	1

Note: The type of model possessing the greatest degree of a characteristic is denoted by a 1, the least by a 3.

If the manager is faced with a dynamic decision problem in which analysis of causal relationships is critical, a symbolic model would usually be most appropriate, provided it could be developed at a reasonable cost. On the other hand, if the manager wanted an easily constructed highly concrete representation of a relatively static operation, he might prefer a descriptive model. Whatever his choice may be, cost is an important consideration, as implied above. Model building may consume considerable time on the part of highly skilled personnel, and if a problem is relatively insignificant, the costs of developing a model may equal or exceed the benefits which may be derived from its usage. Consideration should also be given to the inclinations of the managers who will use the results generated from a model. If top management has a negative and suspicious attitude toward sophisticated mathematical analysis, the results obtained from a highly technical mathematical model may stand little chance of ever being used.

Objectives Served by Model Utilization

In the previous sections models have been shown to be highly useful aids to decision making. What specific functions do models serve? A fundamental advantage of model utilization is that it permits the manager to "try out various decision alternatives without interfering with the real system. The major advantage of this approach is that new policies and procedures can be tested without disrupting the operations of an organization, which would often be extremely costly and difficult, if not impossible to do."[22] For example, miniature machines in a scale-model plant can be moved around in order to determine their optimum layout much more easily than could real machines installed in the plant. Or, it might be more desirable for a firm to experiment with inventory reorder rules via a mathematical model than to try out the rules in "real life" where failure could be very costly. In short, the manager may experiment and make mistakes with models and then apply this knowledge to his actual operations.

Development of and experimentation with models may be carried out with either one or more of three specific objectives in mind: (1) to simply provide insight into an operation; (2) to predict organizational behavior; or (3) to prescribe managerial behavior. We will now examine each of these types of model utilization in detail.

Understanding and Insight. One purpose which models may serve is to provide the manager with a better understanding of certain phases of his operations. For example, the development of organization charts—in which each position in the company is represented by a box, and lines are drawn connecting these boxes to show the relationships between positions—may aid the manager in obtaining a better picture of his company's organizational relationships. Models such as this do not prescribe any specific courses of action for the manager to take, although they may enable him to predict, at least in a general way, how certain phases of his operations will function. Rather, their primary purpose is to help him gain insight which ultimately may provide the basis for improved decision making.

Prediction of Behavior. In certain other cases, models are designed primarily to aid in predicting the behavior of an organization or the conditions which it will experience, rather than simply providing understanding. For example, one company was interested in the impact that the successful introduction of a new product would have upon its operations. In analyzing the introduction of the product, the treasurer pre-

---

[22] Paul S. Greenlaw, Lowell W. Herron, and Richard H. Rawdon, *Business Simulation* (Englewood Cliffs, N.J.: Prentice-Hall, Inc., 1962), p. 9.

pared pro forma balance sheets and profit and loss statements of company operations during the proposed engineering, preproduction, testing, and production phases. These predictions in the form of financial models of the business operations showed that prior to any return of income through the sale of the product, a substantial outlay of cash would be required. If other cash needs of the company were to be met, additional outside capital would be needed. Having been shown by the model the extent and timing of the cash shortage, management was able to negotiate a flexible loan agreement with a banking group to alleviate the predicted cash need. It should be noted that although highly useful in guiding the decisions of the company's officers, this model did not show management what to do. It merely predicted a cash shortage. Given this prediction, management might have chosen other alternatives such as: (1) acquiring more funds through equity financing, and/or (2) slowing down the introduction of the product.

Prescribing Behavior. A third purpose of models is to prescribe managerial decisions. If the manager is able to develop a model closely representing the operations of his organization, analysis or experimentation with the model may allow development of a preferred course of action. In this way, decisions can be said to be prescribed through the use of models.

Assume for purposes of illustration that a simple symbolic model of profit for a company is as follows:

$$P = 78Q - \left(\frac{Q^2}{1,520} + 53Q + 70,000\right)$$

where P equals profit and Q equals the number of units produced and sold. The company may want to determine the level of output at which it will maximize its profit. In this case, by applying analytical techniques to the model, the manager can arrive directly at the optimum level of production, which is 19,000 units. For other models, however, no analytical methods are available. In still other cases, the computation by analytical methods is so cumbersome and time consuming that it is cheaper to experiment with the model—i.e., try out different values for the independent variables and evaluate their effect on the dependent variable. This process of experimentation is sometimes referred to as *simulation*, which we will discuss more fully in Chapter 19. Figure 3–4 illustrates experimentation with four values of Q for the company profit model indicated above. The profit level is calculated for four different levels of output: 10,000, 20,000, 30,000, and 40,000 units. It should be noted that the simulation alternative of 20,000 units approaches the optimum solution of 19,000 units. However, in this case the optimum may be directly arrived at by the use of the calculus, while reaching it by simulation may require substituting so many values for the inde-

Figure 3–4. Simulation and Analysis of a Profit-Quantity Model

Units Produced	Sales Revenue ($000) (78Q)	Total Costs ($000) $\left(\dfrac{Q^2}{1,520} + 53Q + 70,000\right)$	Profit ($000) (Revenue − Total Costs)
10,000.............	780	666.8	113.2
20,000.............	1,560	1,393.2	166.8
30,000.............	2,340	2,252.1	87.8
40,000.............	3,120	3,242.6	−122.6
*19,000.............	1,482	1,314.5	167.5

Model: $P = 78Q - \left[\dfrac{Q^2}{1520} + 53Q + 70,000\right]$, where P represents profit, and Q, the number of units produced and sold. $78Q$ represents sales revenue; and $\dfrac{Q^2}{1,520} + 53Q + 70,000$, represents total costs.

* Analytical solution obtained as follows: $\dfrac{dP}{dQ} = 25 - \dfrac{Q}{760}$; and $Q = 19,000$ when $\dfrac{dP}{dQ}$ is set equal to zero.

pendent variable, Q, as to be quite time consuming and expensive. For this reason, analytical means are preferred when they are available and when they do not require excessive computation.

Whether analytical or simulation techniques are used in manipulating models, they are intended to provide either optimum or highly satisfying solutions. Thus, the results obtained by their application prescribe courses of action for the manager to follow.

Model Construction

What are the steps involved and some of the methods employed in constructing decision-making models? The reader will note that these steps are similar to the phases of the decision-making process described earlier. It should also be noted that the construction approaches described are applicable primarily to symbolic models, and to a lesser extent, analogue models.

Objective Definition and Measurement. The initial step in model construction is to determine the objective to be optimized. In scientific terminology, an objective is referred to as a *dependent* variable. The same considerations in setting objectives that were discussed in Chapter 2 apply in determining dependent variables in model construction.

After the dependent variable has been defined, a measure of effectiveness or ineffectiveness of it is necessary. The measure of effectiveness of a sales organization might be total sales in dollars. Cost of production is a measure of ineffectiveness for a manufacturing plant. Effectiveness measures are intended to be maximized and ineffectiveness measures minimized.

In some models, it is desirable to optimize more than a single dependent variable, such as cost and quality—i.e., multiple objectives exist. When this is the case, it is most desirable to combine the measurement of all dependent variables in a single overall measure of effectiveness or ineffectiveness. If this is not done, manipulation of the model will result in no overall optimum solution, but merely a set of values for each dependent variable. For example, application of a simulation model in which product cost and quality are the dependent variables might indicate that a particular set of production decisions would (1) result in a reject rate of 3 percent and (2) a cost per piece of $0.50. For a different set of decisions however, the reject rate might be 2.7 percent and the cost per piece, $0.54. Which of these two conditions is preferable depends upon the relative value of the 0.3 percent reduction in rejects compared to the four cent increase in cost. Weighting the relative importance of objectives such as these may be accomplished after results are attained from the model, or the weighting decision may be built into the model itself. This latter alternative is usually preferable since it obviates the need for management to consider the question of weighting each time data are to be run through the model.

Determining Model Variables and Their Relationships. After the decision maker has determined the measures of effectiveness he wants to optimize in the model, the next step is to determine those factors which have some bearing upon the attainment of his objectives. These factors are referred to as *independent* variables. In developing a model, it is necessary to determine the type of relationship existing between each independent variable and the dependent variables. The following example will illustrate this process.

The management of a manufacturing operation wished to discover the relationship between the number of inspectors it employed and the number of poor pieces turned out by its employees. In a discussion of this problem, one manager held that when only a few inspectors were employed, some employees became careless, and more poor pieces were turned out than when the inspection force was adequate. Another manager agreed that, while such an inverse relationship between the number of inspectors and the number of poor pieces turned out did exist, the employment of additional inspectors led to fewer rejects only up to a point. He believed that when too many inspectors were utilized, some machine operators became antagonistic to their "snooping," and that this probably caused more rejects. From this discussion, management concluded that within a certain range, the number of rejects turned out was inversely and linearly related to the number of inspectors utilized, but that outside this range, the relationship had "tails" as illustrated in Figure 3–5.

In this example, we included only one independent variable. However, others can be treated in a similar manner. For example, management

Figure 3–5. Relationship between Poor Pieces Produced and Number of Inspectors

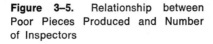
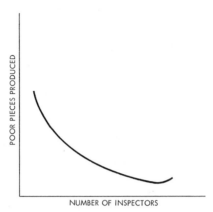

might also explore the relationship between employee scores on psychological tests and the number of rejects turned out. Such an analysis might indicate that there is an inverse relationship between an employee's performance on a manual dexterity test and the number of rejects he produces, up to a point, but that there is no significant relationship between intelligence test scores and the quality of production.

The method of determining relationships between variables described in the above example is essentially subjective in that it relies on the opinions of managers. Such opinions, however, may be checked against company records of past performance to discover if the managerial estimates are consistent with historical data. Another approach to model building is to start by analyzing company data rather than by obtaining executive opinions. Even when this is done, however, it may still be necessary for management to judge whether the periods covered by the data are representative of the company's operations. Thus, this approach also utilizes both data and opinion to serve as checks on each other.

If reliable data covering past operations exist, statistical techniques may be used to determine the importance and the effect of different variables upon the attainment of objectives. If, however, no reliable data are available and if opinion is considered unreliable, models may still be developed by experimentation. Experimentation may also be desirable when an operation has not been performed in the same way that it is planned for the future. For example, if we wanted to determine the factors which influence keypuncher productivity with direct data to tape machines when none had been used previously, an experiment using the new machines might generate sufficient data to develop a model. The model builder has, then, several options open to him in identifying and measuring the independent variables of the proposed model: opinion and discussion, statistical and mathematical analysis of company data, and experimentation.

Historically, managers in organizations have not always considered decision variables and their relationships in explicit, precise ways. Instead, a great deal of vagueness and many implicit assumptions about the behavior of organizations have existed in the minds of managers. When attempting to define and describe these variables from managerial descriptions then, the model builder may have considerable difficulty in arriving at satisfactory representations.

In addition, some important variables may be essentially qualitative in nature. A plant location decision model, for example, may require a consideration of community relations, but it may be quite difficult to derive a precise definition or measurement of this variable. The model may be constructed and tested, however, without this "soft variable." Then when the analysis is complete, explicit consideration of the community relations factor can be made. Thus this factor is not ignored, yet the difficulty of incorporating it into the model is avoided. Excessive use of this technique with several variables in one decision model, however, may lessen the value of the model as the decisions become primarily dependent upon nonquantifiable variables.

Refining the Model.   Examination often will show that some independent variables are relatively unimportant and that others have the same or a similar effect upon the dependent variable. Unimportant variables *may* be discarded from further consideration in order to ease the job of manipulating the model. If, for example, through analysis, worker age is found to be unrelated to productivity, it can be ignored in the construction of models in which productivity is *the* dependent variable. This approach creates a degree of abstraction, to be sure, but at the same time, it allows concentration on the most important elements comprising the decision problem. Further, independent variables affecting the dependent variables in the same way may sometimes be grouped together and considered as a single variable in constructing models. For example, "material costs" and "direct labor costs" often vary in exactly the same way and can be combined as "variable costs." Conversely, the manager may find that an independent variable affects an objective differently when tested with different sets of data or at different time periods. If so, the model builder should suspect that the definition and/or measurement of such a variable masks two or more separate subvariables operating in different ways. In this case, instead of combining variables, the independently acting subvariables should be separated for individual treatment in the model.

Symbolizing.   The final step in model building is to assign symbols to the dependent and independent variables. Basically, this amounts to developing abbreviations for the variables; such as P for profit, C

for costs, and so on. This process is applicable primarily in the development of symbolic models. However, in the hydraulic analogue models we could assign green tubes to the pipe representing consumption and red tubes to that pipe representing savings. The basic purpose in developing symbols is to facilitate manipulation of the model.

Following the above procedures results in an abstract representation of a real situation. The model-building process is useful in and of itself because it forces us to focus attention upon the key elements in decision problems and to disregard unimportant variables. Moreover, the existence of the model allows the use of powerful analytical and simulation techniques which would not be feasible unless this abstract mathematical representation existed. The cost of model building for business systems may be high, however, and these costs usually cannot be justified unless the model is subsequently manipulated to shed considerable light upon how a decision or a set of decisions should be made.

Use and Modification of Models. Upon completion, a model can be tested to determine its applicability to the decision problem for which it was designed. This testing can utilize data from past periods to show what decisions would have been best had the model been used during those times. A more rigorous test of the model with present and future data will disclose whether it can perform satisfactorily under less certain conditions.

If the tests of the model are successful, its use is justified under the conditions and within the limitations indicated in its design. It should be recognized, however, that the model was constructed under conditions of the past. If the variables are dynamic, modification of the model during its use may be necessary. At times it is possible to predict during the construction of the model that the variables and/or their interrelationships are subject to change. In such cases, it is sometimes possible to build self-modifying features into the model. In other instances, the variables may change without forewarning. If so, redesign of the model may be required. At a minimum, management should be aware of the assumptions underlying the models it uses for decision making. Additionally, a periodic, if not continuous, monitoring of the reality of the assumptions will allow management to modify decisions based on use of models as conditions change.

DECISION THEORY MODELS

One major branch of decision-making theory involves developing a normative approach to problems in which known alternatives are evaluated in the light of a number of possible conditions. Under the labels of "statistical decision theory," "normative decision theory," "expected value models," as well as others, the major components of these models involve evaluating payoffs under conditions of risk and uncertainty. This section discusses the basic role these approaches can play for management.

The attainment of objectives is dependent not only upon what the manager decides and does but also upon two other types of variables over which he has no direct influence or control. These are (1) *states of nature* and (2) *competitive strategies*. Both can have an effect upon the ability of the manager to meet his objective *regardless* of the strategies he chooses. For example, when a manager decides to spend $500,000 during a year to advertise his company's products, he expects the advertising to have a direct and positive effect on sales. The advertising may not be as effective as planned in meeting this objective, however, if a depression occurs or if competition spends larger sums on advertising than had been anticipated. In this instance, the depression is a state of nature, and the action of competitors in increasing the amount of advertising for their products is a competitive strategy. Although these variables are beyond the direct control of the decision maker, it may nonetheless be possible to force a competitor into particular competitive strategy by the actions which one takes.

Decision Making under Certainty

If a manager can determine what his competitors' strategies will be and what external conditions he will face, his decision simply involves (1) calculating the return or payoff that he can expect from each alternative strategy developed, and (2) then selecting that strategy which provides the highest return in terms of his objective. In such a case, his primary task is that of determining what these returns will be. Assuming that the objective is to maximize profit, the decision under certainty consists merely of selecting the strategy offering the greatest profitability.

In most cases, however, the manager will not be able to determine with certainty what his competitors will do or what states of nature will occur. In some cases, he will have no estimate at all of these two variables. This condition is known as "decision making under ignorance or uncertainty." In other cases, he will be able to estimate the probability that competition will choose certain strategies or that certain states of nature will occur. If so, we have a condition referred to as "decision making under risk." Since the manager is required to make decisions irrespective of his knowledge, it is appropriate to turn to decision making under these less certain conditions.

Expected Value, Conditional Value, and Decision Making under Risk

The concept of expected value is employed in decision making when the states of nature or competitive actions which will have a bearing on the effectiveness of the alternative decision strategies are not certain.

The *expected* value of any event (EV) is defined as: the value if it occurs (conditional value, $[CV]$) multiplied by its probability of occurrence, (p); or $EV = (CV) \cdot (p)$.[23] Suppose, for example, that a company has the alternatives of bidding on only one of two potential contracts and that: (1) the probability of receiving from customer A a $100,000 contract is 0.10; and (2) the probability of receiving a contract from customer B of $50,000 is 0.25. On which contract should the company bid? The expected value of the contract from customer A is $10,000 ($100,000 $\times$ .10); while the expected value of the contract from customer B is $12,500 ($50,000 $\times$ .25). Assuming that maximization of sales dollars is the objective, the company should bid for the contract of customer B, for the expected value of this contract is $2,500 more than that for customer A. It should be noted, however, that there is no assurance that the company's sales will be $2,500 greater *this particular time* if the company bids for the contract of customer B rather than that of customer A. The company may obtain sales of either $50,000 or $0 if the contract from customer B is bid upon. The reason for selecting customer B over customer A is based on the reasoning that if the company is faced with a great number of such decisions in which both the conditional values and probabilities remain the same, it will maximize its sales objective *over the long run* if it selects the strategy with the greatest expected value. That is, the *average* payoff for many such contracts would be $12,500 from customer B, as compared with $10,000 from customer A. This logic assumes, of course, the ability to estimate the conditional values of the events and the probabilities of their occurrence.

Figure 3–6. Conditional Payoffs for Warehousing Strategies (in dollars)

	States of Nature: Demand		
Strategies	*Low*	*Moderate*	*High*
Centralized.............	100,000	50,000	50,000
Decentralized...........	1,000	80,000	125,000

A convenient way of summarizing the expected values of the alternative decision strategies is by the use of a *payoff matrix,* an example of which is illustrated in Figure 3–6. The rows on the table represent the strategies open to the decision maker; the columns represent the different states of nature or competitive actions which may occur. In

[23] For a straightforward explanation of probability theory and its application to expected value problems, see Sheen Kassorf, *Normative Decision Making* (Englewood Cliffs, N.J.: Prentice-Hall, Inc., 1970), pp. 25–54.

the example presented in Figure 3–6, the decision involves a choice between centralized and decentralized warehousing strategies being considered by a company. These strategies are represented by the two rows designated centralized and decentralized. The three possible conditions of product demand which may occur during the time period under consideration are represented by columns "Low," "Moderate," and "High." The body of the table indicates the payoffs to the company under all possible combinations of demand and available strategies. These values represent the conditional values of the strategies. For example, if the decision maker selected the centralized strategy, and a moderate demand occurs, the payoff, or conditional value, would be $50,000. Once these conditional values have been determined, it is next necessary to calculate the expected values for all possible combinations of strategies and states of nature. These values are illustrated in Figure 3–7.

Figure 3–7. Expected Values for Warehousing Strategies (in $) (conditional values times probability of occurrence)

	States of Nature: Demand			
	Low	Moderate	High	
	Probability of Occurrence			Total Expected Value
Strategies	.10	.50	.40	
Centralized...............	10,000	25,000	20,000	55,000
Decentralized..............	100	40,000	50,000	90,100

The total expected value for each strategy is equal to the sum of its expected values under each possible state of nature; and represents the average payoff that would be obtained if the decision were made a great number of times. The total expected value for centralized strategy is $55,000, and for the decentralized one, $90,100. Thus, the latter represents the decision maker's best choice in order to achieve maximization of profits.

Determining Probabilities: Objective and Subjective Probability

An *objective* probability is one that can be determined on the basis of some past experience. We know, for example, that the probability of obtaining a head in the toss of a fair coin is .5 from experience in flipping a large number of such coins in the past. Similarly, previous company experience in the use of a particular psychological test to select managers may provide a basis for establishing the probability that a person obtaining a certain score on the test in the future will be successful. The process under analysis must continue as a stable one, however, if the experience of the past is to provide a valid basis for establishing the probabilities of events occurring in the future. If, for example, the managerial position referred to above now entails greater responsibilities than ever before, the probabilities associated with past use of the psychological test may not be valid for predicting the expected success rate for people now being hired.

In many cases the manager will not be able to determine from specific experience a suitable estimate of objective probability. Under such circumstances, however, he may be able to make a subjective estimate of the risks entailed in the decision making on the basis of his general knowledge of the problem under consideration. This involves what is referred to as *subjective* probability.[24] Although less precise, the use of subjective probabilities is better than completely ignoring the probabilities of occurrence of the different states of nature or competitor actions pertinent to the decision problem. Subjective probabilities are used in decision making the same way objective probabilites are used to arrive at the expected values for the various alternative strategies under consideration.

Utility. Thus far in the discussion of decision making under risk, it has been assumed that the managers attempted to maximize the attainment of objectives in terms of *dollars*. In many decision situations, this assumption is valid, providing that the decisions involve economic values. In other instances, however, the assumption of monetary maximization is inappropriate. Such a case—involving a small bakery—is examined

Figure 3–8. Payoff Matrix for a Small Baker

	Conditional Value		*Expected Value*		
	CS1	*CS2*	*CS1**	*CS2†*	*Total*
Strategy S1.......	−$60,000	$200,000	−$36,000	$80,000	$44,000
Strategy S2.......	10,000	12,000	6,000	4,800	$10,800

* Probability of Occurrence .60.
† Probability of Occurrence .40.

in Figure 3–8. Two strategies are available to the baker and either one of two competitive actions may occur. The probability of occurrence of each competitive strategy has been determined. S1 results in an expected value of $44,000 and S2, only $10,800.

---

[24] For a discussion of the concept and rationale of subjective probability, see Robert Schlaifer, *Probability and Statistics for Business Decisions* (New York: McGraw-Hill Book Co., 1959), chap. 1.

According to the expected value criterion, the baker should obviously select strategy S1. This choice will maximize this payoff in the long run. It should be noted, however, that if the baker selects this "optimum" strategy, and competitive strategy CS1 should occur, the bakery will suffer a loss of $60,000. Although the average value of strategy S1 *if made a large number of times* would be $33,200 greater than that for S2, the baker may never have an opportunity to make the decision more than once if the selection of S1 is coupled with competitive strategy CS1 because the $60,000 loss might well spell bankruptcy! Thus, the manager of the bakery might be unwilling to select any strategy, regardless of its average value, if it could result in the incurrence of such a large loss. Or, to put it another way, the value of the possible gain to the baker by choosing S1 ($200,000) is less than the disvalue of the possible loss of $60,000, even though in dollars the gain greatly exceeds the loss. The reader should not infer that this example indicates that probability theory is useless in decision making, however. Rather, it points up the fact that payoff measures in dollars are often not satisfactory guides when the amounts of money involved in the decision making are very large in relation to a firm's total assets. In terms of the economist, the *utility* of money to the manager is different when relatively large sums are an important consideration in decision problems. That dollars have a different utility to individuals under different conditions may be seen in the manner in which items are purchased just before and just after payday. Immediately prior to payday, many persons are quite cautious about how and upon what they spend their money. Immediately after receiving their paycheck, however, they usually exhibit much less inhibition. In general, as the amount of money possessed by an individual (or firm) increases, its utility decreases, and vice versa.[25] When money and expected values are employed as criteria for decision making, there is an assumption that the relationship between utility and money is approximately linear. For most business decisions, this assumption of linearity is probably valid, for the sums of money involved are not large in proportion to the total assets of the firm.

Decision Making under Uncertainty

In some decision problems, it is not possible to develop estimates of the probabilities that certain competitive strategies or states of nature will occur. In these cases, the manager cannot calculate the expected values of the alternative strategies which are available. There is no single optimum criterion for selecting any one strategy over another. There

---

[25] For alternative methods of measuring utility in its relation to money, see Schlaifer, *Probability and Statistics,* chap. 2; and William A. Spurr and Charles Bonini, *Statistical Analysis for Business Decisions* (Homewood, Ill.: Richard D. Irwin, Inc., 1967), pp. 211–17.

are, however, a number of criteria which have been suggested as rational ones to follow in evaluating the strategies. The initial step in decision making under uncertainty is to construct a payoff matrix by calculating the conditional values for each alternative strategy under each possible competitive strategy or state of nature. This step is identical to that employed in making decisions under conditions of risk. The next step involves the selection and application of a criterion for dealing with the conditional values that have been derived. To illustrate this process, we will first pose a hypothetical decision problem under conditions of uncertainty, and then indicate its solution by each of several different criteria.

As an example, assume that an aircraft manufacturer is considering the possibilities of designing a new high-performance jet fighter for the air force, and that three strategies are available: (1) the company can design a completely new plane from the ground up; (2) it can redesign an existing craft to meet the new military requirements; or (3) it can elect not to design a plane at all. Assume further that there are four possible states of nature which might occur that could affect the payoff of any one of the strategies: global war, limited war, cold war, and peace. After examining all evidence that might give some indication of the likelihood of which state of nature will occur, the company concludes that there is no basis for believing that any one is any more or less probable than the other. Given the conditional profit matrix indicated in Figure 3–9, what are some of the possible criteria that the company might employ in making this decision?

Figure 3–9. Conditional Values for Aircraft Producer (in $ millions)

	States of Nature			
Strategies	*N1* *Global War*	*N2* *Limited War*	*N3* *Cold War*	*N4* *Peace*
S1–New Craft..................	−5	6	4	4
S2–Redesign...................	2	2	2	1
S3–No Design................	0	0	0	1

The Laplace Criterion. If there is no good reason to believe that any one event is more likely to occur than any other, there is similarly no good reason for assuming that it will *not* occur with the same probability as the others. This concept, which is referred to as the *principle of insufficient reason,* provides the basis for one well-known criterion for decision making under conditions of uncertainty—the Laplace criterion.[26]

---

[26] This criterion is also referred to as the criterion of rationality and indifference, although it is no more rational than any other of the criteria discussed below.

This criterion simply applies equal probabilities to the occurrence of each state of nature or competitive strategy. In the aircraft problem, application of equal probabilities to the conditional values of each of the states of nature indicated in Figure 3–9 provides the expected values for each of the three strategies shown in Figure 3–10. Figure 3–10 was

Figure 3–10.   Expected Values for Aircraft Producer Applying Laplace Criterion (in $ millions)

	States of Nature				
Strategies	*N1 Global War*	*N2 Limited War*	*N3 Cold War*	*N4 Peace*	*Total Expected Value*
S1–New Craft........	−$1.25	1.5	1.0	1.0	$2.25
S2–Redesign..........	0.5	0.5	0.5	0.25	1.75
S3–No Design........	0	0	0	0.25	0.25

arrived at by assigning an equal probability to each of the four possible states of nature (i.e., $1.00/4 = .25$), and multiplying this figure by each conditional value in Figure 3–9. These values indicate that strategy S1, the design of a completely new jet fighter, should be chosen.

The Pessimism Criterion: The Maximin.[27]   The pessimism criterion assumes that the manager should always be pessimistic in assessing which competitive strategies or states of nature will occur. He should always act on the premise that the worst is going to happen, and then select the strategy which will maximize the payoff which he will receive under such adverse conditions. This guiding principle is often referred to as the *maximin,* because the manager attempts to maximize his gain under minimally favorable conditions—i.e., he tries to *maximize* the *minimum* possible gain. Inspection of Figure 3–9 indicates that if the aircraft producer were to apply the criterion of pessimism he would choose strategy S2—the redesign of his present jet fighter—for the following minimal conditions apply as shown in Figure 3–11. This strategy (S2) results in a maximum payoff of $1,000,000.

The Criterion of Optimism: Maximax.[28]   The maximin has been criticized on the grounds that to expect the most pessimistic conditions to occur all the time is not a rational approach to the selection of decision alternatives. One could just as well be completely *optimistic* about the

---

[27] This criterion was first suggested by Abraham Wald. For a discussion of it, see David W. Miller and Martin K. Starr, *Executive Decisions and Operations Research* (Englewood Cliffs, N.J.: Prentice-Hall, Inc., 1960), chap. 3; and Spurr and Bonini, *Statistical Analysis,* chap. 10.

[28] First suggested in the form discussed below by Leonid Hurwicz.

Figure 3–11

Strategy	Worst Condition	Payoff
S1.............	N1	−$5,000,000
S2.............	N4	1,000,000
S3.............	N1, N2, N3	0

occurrence of all future events. If the decision maker were to do the latter, he would select that strategy under which it is possible for the most favorable payoff of all to occur, on the optimistic assumption that *it will* occur. Our aircraft producer, for example, would select strategy S1 in Figure 3–9 since the most favorable payoff condition ($6,000,000) prevails when this strategy and state of nature N2 occur.

Neither complete optimism nor pessimism is probably very realistic. At any given time, the decision maker may be more or less optimistic, but not completely so. In such a case, it is possible for him to develop a scale—from 0 to 1.0—to indicate the extent to which he is optimistic or pessimistic. For example, assume that the aircraft manufacturer decides that he holds a .7 degree of optimism and a .3 degree of pessimism about the occurrence of the states of nature which bear on his design decision. If so, he would multiply the conditional value of the most optimistic state of nature for each strategy by his coefficient of optimism (.7). Then the conditional value of the most pessimistic state of nature for each strategy would be multiplied by his coefficient of pessimism (.3). Finally, these two values for each strategy would be

Figure 3–12. Application of Optimism Scale to Conditional Values for Aircraft Producer (.7 optimism and .3 pessimism) (in $ millions)

Strategy	Conditional Value* Best Condition		Conditional Value* Worst Condition		Weighted Value Best Condition	Weighted Value Worst Condition	Sum of Weighted Values
S1–New Craft.....	N2	$6	N1	−$5	$4.2	−$1.5	$2.7
S2–Redesign.......	N1, 2, 3	2	N4	1	1.4	.3	1.7
S3–No Design.....	N4	1	N1, 2, 3	0	.7	0	.7

* From Figure 3–9.

added together, and the strategy with the highest value as weighted by the optimism-pessimism scale selected. Figure 3–12 illustrates these calculations for the aircraft producer and indicates that S1 (new craft) would be the most preferable strategy.

The Criterion of Regret.[29]   A fourth criterion for decision making under conditions of uncertainty is the *criterion of regret*. It provides a method of selecting a strategy that *minimizes the maximum regret that could be realized*. The regret of a strategy is defined as *its payoff* under any given state of nature and/or competitive strategy *subtracted from* the *maximum payoff that is possible* with the occurrence of this event. For example, if state of nature N1 in our previous example occurs, the payoff for S1 is—$5 million; that for S2, $2 million; and that for S3, zero (see Figure 3–9). The regret for each strategy under the N1 state of nature is the difference between the maximum payoff ($2 million for S2) and its own payoff. Thus, the regret in this case for S1 is $7 million; for S2, zero; and for S3, $2 million. The amount of regret for all strategies and states of nature for the aircraft manufacturer is shown in Figure 3–13. This figure indicates that the maximum regret which the man-

Figure 3–13.   Regret for Aircraft-Producer in Selection of Alternative Strategies (in $ millions)

	States of Nature				
Strategy	*N1* *Global War*	*N2* *Limited War*	*N3* *Cold War*	*N4* *Peace*	*Maximum Regret*
S1–New Craft.........	7	0	0	0	7
S2–Modify............	0	4	2	3	4*
S3–Nothing..........	2	6	4	3	6

* This is a minimax solution—i.e., we try to *min*imize our *max*imum regret.
Source: Calculated from Fig. 3–9.

ufacturer may realize will be minimized if he selects strategy S2—$4 million. If he chooses S1, he might incur a regret of $7 million (if N1 occurs); and with strategy S3, a regret of $6 million is possible (with N2). If N1 does not occur, of course, the selection of S2 may not minimize the manufacturer's regret; however, he is assured that, no matter what state of nature prevails, his regret will never be more than $4 million.

Selection of an Uncertainty Criterion.   As we have indicated previously, there is no single best criterion for selecting decision strategies under conditions of uncertainty. In fact, to assess the effectiveness of any of these measures, it would probably be necessary to develop a set of criterion-evaluating criteria. One such set has been devised by

---

[29] L. J. Savage, "The Theory of Statistical Decision," *Journal of the American Statistical Association*, Vol. 46 (March 1951), pp. 55–67.

Figure 3–14. The Decision-Making Process in Organizations

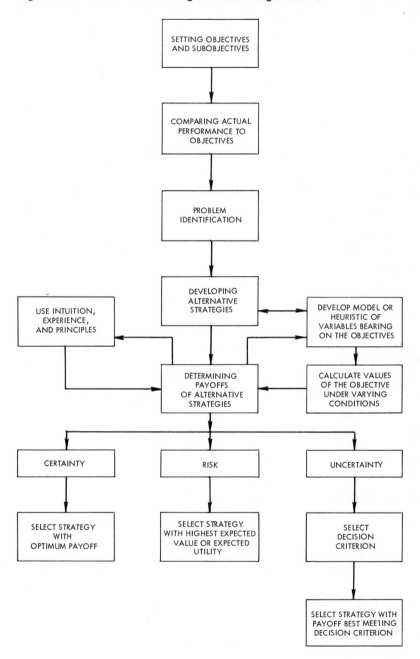

Milnor;[30] and the criterion of regret appears to satisfy a greater number of the Milnor criteria than any other presented in this chapter. In spite of the development of such criteria, however, the selection of an uncertainty criterion remains a matter of managerial judgment. There is no one best criterion, but only one which satisfies the decision maker.

SUMMARY

In this and the previous chapter the major phases involved in managerial decision making have been discussed. These phases are summarized by the flow diagram in Figure 3–14. After the firm has established its objectives and identified its problems, it is necessary to develop alternative decision strategies. One or more of these strategies is then chosen as representing the most appropriate course(s) of action. In the development and selection of strategies, it is sometimes possible to design mathematical models as decision tools. In other cases, the key decision variables and their interrelationships defy explicit quantification. Often, a considerable degree of creativity is required in the development of alternative strategies. In those rare instances in which the future events which will condition the effectiveness of various strategies are certain, the task of the manager simply involves the selection of that course of action which provides the greatest payoff to his firm. When some degree of risk is involved in the decision making, it is necessary to determine both the conditional and expected values of the alternative courses of action. If future events are completely uncertain, any one of a number of criteria may serve as guides to decision making. Although decision payoffs are frequently stated in terms of dollars of profit, many objectives of the firm involve noneconomic values. In addition, when the dollar value of different payoffs varies greatly, utility may be the most appropriate objective criterion.

DISCUSSION AND STUDY QUESTIONS

1. What can the business organization do both to encourage and to stifle its members' creativity? What does creativity have to do with decision making?

2. Under what conditions is "personalistic" decision making useful and valid?

3. A firm, considering handling one of four products, has ranked each on five factors as is shown below:
   a) Which products *dominate* any of the others?
   b) Which brand should management choose?
   c) What additional information would you like to have in making this decision?

---

[30] John Milnor, "Games against Nature," in R. M. Thrall, C. H. Coombs, and R. L. Davis, *Decision Processes* (New York: John Wiley & Sons, Inc., 1954), pp. 49–59. See especially the table on p. 52.

Factors	Alternative Products			
	A	B	C	D
1.............	1	2	3	4
2.............	2	1	4	3
3.............	2	1	3	4
4.............	3	4	2	1
5.............	4	3	1	2

4. What is a major criticism of management principles?

5. What is a heuristic program? What are some of the values of heuristic programs? What is the difference between a heuristic and a heuristic program? Between a heuristic and a personalistic decision approach?

6. a) What are the three model types discussed in this chapter?
   b) Which type would be used to the greatest extent with dynamic decision problems? Why?
   c) What are the basic objectives served by model utilization?

7. Management wants to develop a computerized model of its inventory system, and test the system with various ordering rules to see which one is best. Taking *one* item in the system, on a *daily* basis—considering raw materials of the part coming in each day, production, and items shipped on from this operation to the next one each day—indicate in general how you would go about designing a model of this one stage in the inventory system.

8. Farmer Jones, having heard of decision making under risk, has decided to utilize this approach in determining which one of four possible crops he should plant this spring. The conditional values in profits for these four crops, as well as the probability of occurrence of either of three weather conditions (which are important in determining the profit or loss, given any particular crop planted) are given below. Which crop should Farmer Jones plant?

States of Nature (weather)

Crops		Dry	Moderate	Wet
		Probabilities of Occurrence		
		.10	.50	.40
Crops	C1	−$4,000	$3,000	$4,000
	C2	$1,000	$6,000	−$2,000
	C3	−$3,000	$5,000	$3,000
	C4	$3,000	$3,000	−$2,000

9. As the weather actually turned out, Farmer Jones in the above question lost money by taking the strategy he did, and was heard to comment:

"This decision theory is all wet. Look at the money I've lost. Now I'm broke." Comment on Farmer Jones's statements.

10. *a*) The following year, Farmer Smith helped Farmer Jones financially and suggested exploring the planting of crops using an uncertainty criterion. Given the conditional values from Question 8 above, determine the best strategy applying:

    (1)   The Laplace Criterion 50-50

    (2)   The Criterion of Regret

    (3)   Using a .6 degree of optimism and a .4 degree of pessimism

   b)   Which of these uncertainty criteria worked out best in the problem?

11. If a decision is optimal, is it rational? If a decision is rational, is it optimal? Explain.

SELECTED REFERENCES

AIGNER, DENNIS J. *Principles of Statistical Decision Making.* New York: The Macmillan Company, 1968.

ANSCOMBE, F. J., and AUMANN, R. J. "A Definition of Subjective Probability," *The Annals of Mathematical Statistics,* 34 (1963), 199–205.

ARROW, KENNETH J. "Alternative Approaches to the Theory of Choice in Risk-Taking Situations," *Econometrica* 19 (October 1951), 404–37.

BRONOWSKI, JACOB. "Science as Foresight" in *What Is Science* (ed. JAMES R. NEWMAN). New York: Washington Square Press, Inc., 1961.

CHERNOFF, H., and MOSES, L. E. *Elementary Decision Theory.* New York: John Wiley & Sons, Inc., 1959.

CHURCHMAN, C. W. *Prediction and Optimal Decision.* Englewood Cliffs, N.J.: Prentice-Hall, Inc., 1961.

DIESING, PAUL. "Noneconomic Decision-Making," *Ethics,* 46 (October 1955), 18–35.

FISHBURN, PETER C. *Decision and Value Theory.* New York: John Wiley & Sons, Inc., 1964.

HADLEY, G. *Introduction to Probability and Statistical Decision Theory,* San Francisco: Holden-Day, Inc., 1967.

HALTER, ALBERT N., and DEAN, GERALD W. *Decisions under Uncertainty.* Cincinnati, Ohio: South-Western Publishing Co., 1971.

MAGEE, JOHN F. "Decision Trees for Decision-Making," *Harvard Business Review,* 42 (July–August 1964).

SIMON, HERBERT. *The New Science of Management Decision.* New York: Harper & Bros., 1960.

SIMON, HERBERT. "Theories of Decision-Making in Economics and Behavioral Science," *The American Economic Review,* 49 (June 1959), 253–83.

TERRY, HERBERT. "Comparative Evaluation of Performance Using Multiple Criteria," *Management Science,* 9 (April 1963).

TONGE, FRED M. "The Use of Heuristic Programming in Management Science," *Management Science,* 7 (April 1961).

WEIST, JEROME. "Heuristic Programs for Decision Making," *Harvard Business Review,* 44 (September–October 1966), 129–43.

Chapter 4

Systems and Information

In the first three chapters, attention was focused on managerial decision making and some of the approaches useful in making organizational decisions. As indicated in Chapter 1, a body of knowledge has been evolving contributing toward a theory of "systems." A basic objective of this chapter is to broaden the perspective of the decision process by examining it in the context of a systems framework. In this chapter, specific attention will be given to: "systems theory"; the organization as an information-decision system; and the role of computers and information in business systems.

SYSTEMS THEORY

Historical Background

The concept, "system," has been defined in a variety of ways. In somewhat oversimplified terms, a system may be conceived of "a complex of components in mutual interaction forming a unified whole." Further, various scholars have placed emphasis on different aspects, characteristics, and dimensions of systems. Although historically, many individuals have contributed to the development of systems theory, two may be singled out as having given special impetus to this field of endeavor— Ludwig von Bertalanffy and Norbert Wiener.

Von Bertalanffy, trained in biology, developed a *holistic, organismic* conception of biological systems, which he called "General System Theory." In doing so, he emphasized that such systems are comprised of a number of interrelated components in mutual interaction and that the behavior of these elements is influenced by and can be understood only in light of the state of the system as a whole.[1] To use Bertalanffy's words:

> . . . it is impossible to resolve the phenomena of life into elementary units; for each individual part and each individual event depends not only on conditions within itself, but also to a greater or lesser extent on conditions within the whole, or within superordinate units of which it is a part. Hence the behaviour of an isolated part is, in general, different from its behaviour within the context of the whole.[2]

Important to management thought is that Bertalanffy has extended his theories to fields other than biology. Noting that there were many basic similarities in ways that scientists in other disciplines viewed the phenomena with which they were dealing led Bertalanffy to the notions that: (1) There are certain general principles applicable to scientific inquiry in virtually all areas of endeavor; (2) A unification of scientific thought from all these areas can be developed; and (3) Underlying such a unification would be a "General System Theory."

A second "interdisciplinary" systems-oriented view conceived of as a unifying approach for science, was developed by the mathematician, Norbert Wiener, that of cybernetics. Taken from the Greek word, *kybernētēs*, meaning "steersman"—cybernetics may be defined as the science of communication and control. Wiener's thesis was that:

> . . . society can only be understood through a study of the messages and the communication facilities which belong to it; and that in the future development of these messages and communication facilities, messages between man and machines, between machines and man, and between machine and machine, are destined to play an everincreasing part.[3]

Having placed greater emphasis on communications and control than Bertalanffy, Wiener, for example, paralleled the functioning of electronic machine systems (e.g., computers) with that of man. He emphasized that both receive information to provide the basis for action; both possess memory mechanisms; both utilize the feedback of information from "outside" their own system as a means of comparing actual performance with intended performance; and both possess central decision organs which determine what is to be done on the basis of the informational feedback received. As Bertalanffy has viewed General System Theory

---

[1] Also central to this holistic view is the concept that the total system represents something more than and different from simply the sum of its parts, and exhibits characteristics absent from its isolated parts.

[2] Ludwig von Bertalanffy, *Problems of Life* (New York: Harper & Bros., Torchbook edition, 1960), p. 12. (Originally published by C. A. Watts and Co., Limited, London.) As as example, von Bertalanffy points out that: "The reflexes of an isolated part of the spinal cord are not the same as the performance of these parts in the intact nervous system."

[3] Norbert Wiener, *The Human Use of Human Beings* (Garden City, N.Y.: Doubleday & Company, Inc., Anchor Books edition, 1954), p. 16. Quoted with permission of the Houghton Mifflin Company, original publishers of the book.

as a unifying one in science, so also have Wiener and others held that "information theory, cybernetics, and other associated areas possess sufficient generality to warrant their extension into most every facet of the animate universe."[4]

It is useful and practical to explain many managerial phenomena in the language of systems theory. This is not to say, however, that systems concepts can *completely* explain organizations and how managers operate within them. (Even Bertalanffy has not reached that point in biology.) Still, a significant portion of the management literature utilizes systems terminology, and we find it convenient to undertake a fuller explanation of systems at this point so that we may utilize these ideas in our subsequent chapters.

Basic Types of Systems

Systems have been classified into two basic types: *closed* and *open*. At the expense of some oversimplification, closed systems may be defined as those which are isolated from any external environment, and do not exchange matter or information with any outside environment.[5] A basic characteristic of closed systems is that over time they become increasingly disorganized, deteriorate, and become more chaotic until eventually their elements become randomly distributed so that they reach an equilibrium where all processes come to a stop. A term, drawn from the physical sciences commonly used to describe (or measure) this tendency toward disorder is *entropy*.[6] A more concrete example of such a process in a closed system is provided by Scott:

Visualize a tank of water divided by a removable partition. On one side of the divider the water is colored with blue ink, the other side with red ink. If the partition separating the different colors of water is raised, the colors merge into an overall purple hue. The entropy of the system has in-

---

[4] William G. Scott, *Organizational Theory: A Behavioral Analysis for Management* (Homewood, Ill.: Richard D. Irwin, Inc., 1967), p. 175. Information theory, a field related to cybernetics, may be viewed as a mathematically oriented study of communications. See, for example, Claude E. Shannon and Warren Weaver, *The Mathematical Theory of Communication* (Urbana, Ill.: University of Illinois Press, 1949). Among other works of significant thinkers who have contributed to the development of cybernetics and/or information theory are: W. Ross Ashby, *An Introduction to Cybernetics* (New York: John Wiley & Sons, Inc., 1965); and Stafford Beer's *Cybernetics and Management* (New York: John Wiley & Sons, Inc., 1964), and *Decision and Control* (New York: John Wiley & Sons, Inc., 1966).

[5] It is beyond the scope of this book to explore: (1) the theoretical question of whether any system is completely closed, or (2) the problems in defining precisely degrees of openness in systems. We will indicate below, however, that the manager must sometimes treat open systems as partially closed (or isolated) for purposes of simplifying his analysis of them.

[6] The basic reason why closed systems tend toward entropy and have no purpose is probably that they do not exchange matter, energy, and information with their environments.

creased. Before the removal of the partition, a form of order existed with the red-ink molecules separated from the blue. But after the change, the molecules distributed themselves evenly throughout the tank, resulting in a single color.[7]

The second basic type of system—open—is of much greater concern to the manager. This is because the systems with which he must deal—individuals, groups, the business organization itself, and so forth—do interact with their environment. Further these open systems, influenced by both their own decisions and other variables may exhibit tendencies toward increasing order, rather than disorder. We will now explore several facets of open systems.

Basic Dimensions of Open Systems

Holism and Environmental Interaction.   As indicated above, open systems are composed of interrelated components comprising a unified whole. Instead of becoming randomly distributed as in closed systems, the components of open systems and their interrelationships tend to assume order.[8] This patterned ordering into a unified whole may be conceived of as the *structure* of open systems—one of their fundamental dimensions.[9]

A second basic characteristic of open systems is that, unlike closed systems, they interact with their environment—they both influence and are influenced by the external environment in which they function. Thus, there are two basic types of *system relations* common to open systems those: (1) among certain components *within* the system, and (2) *between* (some) of the system's components and external environmental variables.

Further, a mutual interrelationship or interaction often exists among systems components and/or between these components and external environmental variables. That is, changing one system component (or environmental variable) will influence one or more others, which in turn will, either directly or indirectly, influence the behavior of the original component (or variable) under consideration. The following is a highly simplified example, if we conceive of a business organization as an open system:[10] A firm may increase the price of one of its major products, which may result in a decrease in demand (from customers in the external environment), which may lead management to lower its prices,

---

[7] Scott, *Organizational Theory,* p. 178.

[8] At least in the short run. In the long run individuals will die, organizations may fall, civilizations may become extinct, and so forth.

[9] A common example is organization structure, which will be discussed in later chapters.

[10] The importance of viewing a system (and its boundaries) as something mentally conceived of will be discussed below.

which may in turn stimulate demand back to its original level, influencing production, purchasing, and so on.

Directionality of Relations. It is often useful to view such interrelationships, whether they exist solely among components within the system, or between the system and its environment in terms of directionality. In fact, in discussing the relationship between open systems and their environments Stafford Beer has pointed out that:

> In practice, the most noticeable feature of the interaction between the system itself and things outside it, is that the relationships are directional. Either the thing outside is affecting the system, or the system is affecting the thing outside—or both.[11]

In the above simplified example, the directional relationships between price and demand could be depicted schematically over time either (1) sequentially, or (2) as in "mutual interaction" as is shown in Figure 4–1.[12]

Figure 4–1. Price-Demand Directionality

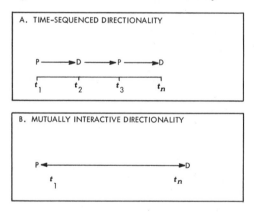

Flows. It may also be useful to conceive of the connectivity among certain system components (and between them and external variables) in terms of flows—using the word "flow" in a broad sense. These flows may assume the form of:

1. *Matter (or Materials) Flows.* E.g., the flow of raw materials into the firm, the subsequent flow of these materials through the firm's

---

[11] Beer, *Decision and Control*, p. 272.

[12] In some situations, dynamic action and reaction may occur so simultaneously that any schematic portrayal of the process such as $A \rightarrow B \rightarrow C \rightarrow \cdots N$ has little meaning. For both (1) a concrete (although quasi-closed system) example, and; (2) a philosophical discussion of viewing such situations, see Richard L. Schanck, *The Permanent Revolution in Science* (New York: Philosophical Library, 1954), pp. 34 ff.

production operations as they are converted into finished products, and the flow of these products to the consumer.

2. *Information Flows.* E.g., flows of information between a manager and his subordinates, of information into and out of a computer, and so forth; or

3. *Energy Flows.* E.g., the transmission of electrical power.

Such "flows" may assume either a constant or variable rate. As an example of how flows may create linkages among systems components, consider a simple production operation in which one raw material has to be fabricated into a finished product, inspected, and then shipped to customers. In such a case, the system variable (or component) raw materials inventory *level* at the end of each day will equal that at the beginning of the day plus the rate of flow of incoming raw materials during that day minus the rate of outflow of raw materials to the fabrication operation; the day-ending fabricated inventory level similarly will equal beginning fabrication inventories plus the inflow of raw materials minus the outflow of the fabricated product into inspection, and so on. It is also common to refer to information, matter, or energy coming into an open system (whether or not these be viewed in terms of flows) as *inputs* to the system; and conversely, when they go out of the system into its environment as *outputs*.

Boundaries. The above statement contains two phases "coming into" and "going out of" a system which pose a key question: "Exactly how can one define the *boundaries* of an open system which interacts with its environment?" Should we conceive of the total business organization as an open system with the economy as its external environment; the manufacturing department within an organization as a system within the rest of the organization of which it is a part as its external environment; and a group of individuals working in production as a system with the production department as its external environment?

Essentially, the answer to such questions centers around the notions that: (1) a "system" is simply a mental concept that we find useful in describing phenomena perceived to exist in the "world outside us," and consequently (2) that individuals will define "systems" and their boundaries differently depending upon their particular viewpoints and their specific *purposes* of analysis. As Stafford Beer has pointed out:

It may well be that systems detected in the world outside ourselves *are* models—mappings of our own brains on to the world. . . . We select, from an infinite number of relations between things, a set which, because of coherence and pattern and purpose, permits an interpretation of what might otherwise be a meaningless cavalcade of arbitrary events. It follows that the detection of system in the world outside ourselves is a subjective matter. Two people will not necessarily agree on the existence, or nature, or boundaries of any system so detected. Nor is it possible to *prove* that a system exists, or is thus and thus; it is possible to say only that the treatment of a certain collection of things as a system is helpful.[13]

The above discussion leads to three other points concerning open systems, their boundaries, and their environmental interaction. First, normatively, managers *should* define systems differently depending upon their analytical objectives—i.e., one system's "mapping" of real world phenomena often will prove more valid than another in any given situation. Second, it is often useful for analytical purposes to view smaller systems as existing within larger ones; and larger ones existing within still larger ones, and so forth. Systems conceived as being part of larger systems are commonly referred to an subsystems or sub-subsystems. For example, an individual manager may be considered as a subsystem functioning in a larger subsystem; a group of managers functioning in a still larger system; the organization can in turn be conceived of as a subsystem within the economy and so forth.

Finally, it should be pointed out that: (1) whether any phenomenon is viewed as a system *or* subsystem; and (2) whether information, matter, and energy crossing systems boundaries are inputs or outputs depends on one's vantage point. To illustrate, it may be most useful for the manager to view his organization as a system within the economy, and in this context the flow of finished goods from his firm to customers would be considered an *output*. From the point of view of a governmental analyst studying the whole economy, however, the manager's particular firm probably would be most conveniently viewed as a subsystem contained in the economic system; and an analyst would probably view the outflow of goods from this single firm as but one of many flows or *inputs* into the economic system.

Purposiveness of Open Systems and Steady State Behavior. Unlike closed systems which, as noted above, are isolated, open systems are purposive. Their basic purpose is viability—that is to survive, live, and grow.

Open systems, exchanging matter and information (and sometimes energy) with their environment with the purpose of viability, exhibit what is often referred to by systems theorists as *steady state* behavior. This term is *not* meant to imply complete stability, steadiness, or the existence of no change. Rather, steady state behavior may be defined more precisely as: (1) a probabilistic level of behavior, statistically distributed around some mean at *any given point in time*, with (2) changes in the steady state level possible and usually occurring over time. We will now illustrate both the maintenance and change aspects of the steady state with some concrete examples of both human and organizational behavior.

---

[13] Beer, *Decision and Control*, p. 243. Copyright © 1966 by John Wiley & Sons, Inc. The notion of purpose (central to open systems) contained in this quotation, will be discussed below.

Maintenance of Steady State Behavior.   In the human system, the mean steady state temperature of the healthy individual is 98.6° F. However, daily variations around this mean (e.g., 97.3°–99.1°) are also considered normal. The human system attempts to maintain the steady state temperature. When shock is introduced into the system (e.g., a viral infection), bodily mechanisms (possibly involving a fever) attempt to fight off this shock. When his system is able to successfully fight off an infection, accompanied by fever, his temperature will return to its steady state mean. (Should the individual's fever get too high, of course, his system may suffer permanent damage.)

Somewhat analogously, a firm's profits over a period of time may assume a mean of $5 million a month (with some variation, possibly due to seasonal factors). If the firm's sales and profits are suddenly seriously jeopardized by its competition's actions, management will (hopefully) take any one of a number of possible actions in an effort to restore its profit position to at least its previous steady state level. These examples illustrate the tendency of open systems to maintain steady state behavior against environmental shock harmful to them.

Improvement of the Steady State.   Open systems, with the basic purpose of viability, tend not only to protect themselves against shock (i.e., survive) but also to *improve* their steady state behavior—to grow, develop, and better themselves. The college student may study harder in order to learn more; the middle-aged executive may engage in daily jogging to improve his physical system. Analogously, to improve its profits and sales levels, a business firm may replace a number of its poorer managers with better ones, modify its research and development program, and so forth.

As a result of moving from one steady state level to a higher, improved one, open systems often experience some "shock," "discomfort," "disequilibrium," and so on. The man jogging may experience more fatigue than usual; the business firm replacing a number of managerial personnel may encounter training problems, negative attitudes among other current employees due to disruptions in interpersonnel relationships (that often occur with personnel changes), and so forth.

To draw on notions presented by Stafford Beer,[14] if open systems move too far from their current steady state in an effort to raise its level, they may damage themselves, and *not* be able to *maintain* the higher level steady state so desired. To put it another way, if an open system exceeds its capabilities in its steady state improvement attempts, it will suffer as a result of the overextension. For example, if the middle-aged jogger exercises too much, too quickly, he may strain certain muscles, which will set back his "steady state" improvement efforts. Or, consider a business firm expending excessive resources for research and development. If the firm reduces research too drastically, expenses may

---
[14] Ibid., pp. 289–90.

be cut to the extent that *short-term* profits will increase; but in the longer run such an action may put it in a position in which it is no longer able to compete effectively in its industry in the development of new products, and its profits will then decline.

Moderate movements (not exceeding current steady state capabilities), on the other hand, can enable the system not only to achieve but to *maintain* an improved steady state condition—e.g., moderate exercising, with the human, or some carefully analyzed reductions in unnecessary research expenditures by the firm.

There is, unfortunately, no clear-cut general answer as to how far any open system can move so as to maintain an improved steady state level. As Beer has pointed out with respect to the manager; the "intuitive recognition of the difference" between overextending and not overextending its capabilities in his effort to improve the steady state, is "in many circumstances, what makes a good businessman."[15]

Above, it was implied that open systems attempt to improve their steady state levels because they *want* to grow and develop. It should also be stressed that open systems may be *forced* to improve certain aspects of their current level of behavior if they are to *maintain* their overall current steady state condition because of environmental changes (or changes within the system). For example, an operations researcher may be compelled to master newly developed mathematical models if he is to be able to function effectively enough in a changing technology to *keep* his present job. Or, an automotive firm may be forced by governmental legislation to install more safety features in its new cars, if it is to continue in business. In short, environmental influences, as well as the open system's own characteristics, have an influence on its level of steady state behavior.

It can also be seen that some changes are continually taking place in open systems over time. This does not mean that all open systems' components constantly change to any significant extent (e.g., the relative constancy of the normal person's bodily temperature), but some of them do. Hence, a basic dimension of *all* open systems is that they are *dynamic* rather than static.

The Needs of Open Systems. In order to maintain and improve their steady state behavior, open systems need to possess certain abilities. First, since open systems function in a probabilistic environment, they must have *some* ability to forecast future events if they are to meet their objectives—e.g., even though a firm's sales may fluctuate in a manner not completely certain to him, its production manager needs to have some idea of the range of anticipated sales level if he is to develop effective production plans and schedules.

Second, open systems must also have some capacity for self-regulation (or control). A physicist in an organization's research department, for

---

[15] Ibid., p. 290.

instance, cannot be coerced into being creative solely by threats by his departmental manager—he, himself, must possess some degree of the self-discipline or self-control (internal motivation)[16] necessary to do such work.

A third essential for open systems is for them to receive feedback from their environment as to the appropriateness of their previous actions if they are to be able to correct past mistakes and improve future performance. Such feedback, (essentially one form of information) may assume different forms and may exist in both human and mechanical systems. For example:

1. Many firms have set up formalized performance appraisal systems, in which managers are periodically informed by their superiors of their performance—their strengths, weaknesses, and means of performance improvement.

2. Some computer systems[17] are designed so they will immediately stop any further calculations if any program fed into them contains a statement calling for the division of a number by zero. This procedure is based on the following premises. Because such division is, of course, not mathematically possible, something, thus, is wrong with the program. Running it further, rather than returning it to the individual who wrote it for correction, would result in wasted computer time and delayed feedback to the human programmer.

Fourth, open systems need to possess transformation components—i.e., such as mechanisms to effect changes in the system's structure and flows. The manager's decisions (to modify production schedules, discipline subordinates, change advertising programs, and so on) represent a basic type of transformation component in the organizational system—which we will discuss in greater detail later. As another example of transformation components, *decision rules* may be built into systems, as in the computer illustration given above.

Finally, open systems must possess a *memory* component for storing information gained from the past to serve as a guide to future behavior. In the business organization, memory components include both human (the memories of its members) and synthetic ones—e.g., data stored in files or on a computer.

The Complexity of Open Systems. Because of their large number of components in mutual interaction, the number of possible ways for open systems to behave is exceedingly large.[18] Further, open systems

---

[16] We will discuss motivation and leadership in greater detail in Chapters 5 and 6, respectively.

[17] Computers are not open systems in the sense that they are purposive (like humans); yet they do receive inputs, produce outputs, and so on.

[18] For example, the number of possible states which a simple system (called a "black box" in cybernetics terms) can assume with eight binary inputs and one binary output is 2^{256}. See Beer, *Decision and Control*, p. 296.

interacting in an uncertain environment are inherently probabilistic—it is not possible to predict precisely the behavior of any open system. For example, it is not possible to foresee in advance the exact profits, sales, inventory levels, employee safety performance, and so forth, of any organizational system. Because of their complexity, open systems are extremely difficult to conceptualize, analyze, and manage.

Faced with the problems of dealing with complex open systems, and with their "bounded rationality" as discussed in Chapter 2, managers must find various ways of simplifying their viewing and analyzing of such systems if they are to operate effectively. Otherwise, how could they deal on a day-to-day basis with a system so complex that it is difficult to understand or predict?

Simplification of the Complex

There are several ways in which managers simplify complex open systems problems for more effective analysis and handling.[19] In some cases, managers find it adequate to assume *certainty* in dealing with decision problems, even though they may be characterized by one or more probabilistic variables. First, for example, as we will discuss in Chapter 18, a relatively good approximation of minimal total costs in certain inventory problems may be obtained by assuming that demand is known (and constant), even though demand as a variable is probabilistic and cannot be predicted with certainty.

A second method used in simplification of the complex in open systems is to assume that *relationships* among variables are simpler than they are in reality. Many managerial decision models, for instance, assume *linear* relationships among variables, even though such relationships are not linear. Such is the case with linear programming models, which we will cover in Chapter 17.

Third, by means of heuristic programming, which was discussed in Chapter 3, complex decision problems are more easily coped with as they are broken down into a series of simpler subproblems, for which there is a greater likelihood that effective problem-solving techniques exist.

Fourth, is the technique of artificially *partially isolating* the firm (or one of its subsystems) from its environment. For one of the firm's subsystems (e.g., production) artificial isolation from the firm's marketing subsystem might be accomplished by the production manager's: (1) looking only at certain *key inputs* from marketing (e.g., demand schedules, customer complaints concerning production quality); while (2) ignoring others, such as the dollar sales volume of *particular* salesmen.

---

[19] For a more sophisticated treatment of simplification techniques, see ibid., chaps. 12 and 13, and Van Court Hare, Jr., *Systems Analysis: A Diagnostic Approach* (New York: Harcourt, Brace & World, Inc., 1967), chaps. 7 and 8.

Managers may also partially "close off" their own informational inputs from subordinates, by means of a technique commonly referred to as "exception" or "responsibility" reporting. Essentially, this involves reporting information to the manager concerning variables involved in his operations (e.g., production quality) only when they go (or are going) out of control (i.e., when a problem exists), thus relieving the manager of the task of examining information with respect to those portions of his operations which are "running smoothly."

Another simplification technique sometimes feasible occurs in situations when the manager *knows* that, among a total set of many decision alternatives available to him, the optimal alternative *has to be* one of only a smaller number (or subset) of these. For example, as we will show in detail in Chapter 17, in the graphic-algebraic method of linear programming, the optimal solution must always lie on one or more points of a polygon of feasible alternatives; and, hence all other alternatives may be excluded from consideration.

Still another simplification technique which will also be discussed later in this text is that of selective attention or control. In inventory control, for instance, much more emphasis is often placed on controlling the inventory levels of critical parts than those of less critical ones as will be indicated in Chapter 18.

Finally, statistical grouping of data is frequently useful as a simplification technique. One type of such method pointed out by Hare is that of arbitrarily converting *"a continuous variable to a discrete variable, which may assume several levels, or attributes."*[20] For instance, it may be useful for a firm analyzing a large number of customer orders ranging from $1 to $1,000, to convert the continuous variable, customer order size (in dollars) into several discrete categories—e.g., $1–$25; $26–$50, $51–$100, and so on.[21]

In utilizing any of the above simplification techniques, the manager faces a basic problem. This problem is that simplification may lead to *distortion of analysis,* and, hence, less effective solution. For example, assuming a known and constant demand in dealing with inventory problems in which actual demand is highly probabilistic (and widely fluctuating) would lead to a more costly solution than one in which demand variation is slight. Unfortunately there are no guidelines as to when simplification leads to distortion—essentially the problem is one of managerial intuition.

Systems Theory: Overview

As indicated previously, the concepts developed by systems theorists are being increasingly refined so as to render them more applicable

---

[20] Ibid., p. 175.

[21] This example was drawn from ibid.

to the analysis and handling of management decision-making problems. At the present time, the following generalizations may be made concerning the "state of the art" of systems theory:

1. Problems still exist in reducing many systems concepts to lower levels of abstraction so as to render them practically applicable to management systems, but increasing efforts by scholars and researchers directed toward overcoming this problem are taking place.
2. The notions derived from systems theory permit us to understand, explain, predict, and control *certain facets* of organizational behavior better than other forms of conceptualization.

In applying systems theory to management decision making, we find it especially useful to view the organization as an *information-decision* system. That is, to plan for and control organizations, managers need *information*, which they, then by their *decisions*, transform into courses of action in order to meet their objectives. Drawing on the concepts discussed above, we now turn attention to a conceptualization of management in information-decision systems terms.

INFORMATION-DECISION SYSTEMS

The systems concept may be applied in examining informational and decision processes of an organization in two different ways. First, we may view the decisions made by management and the information flows associated with these decisions as constituting an *information-decision* system. This view focuses attention on decisions as representing the transformation of information into courses of action. For example, when a gasoline station manager learns that a competitor has reduced prices by two cents a gallon, he may decide to follow suit. In systems terms, the manager's *decision* represents the *transformation* of the *information* that was obtained about his competitor into a specified course of action, or *output*.

Second, data processing operations in business firms may be viewed as *pure information* systems.[22] In pure information systems, as distinguished from information-decision systems, information is simply changed into different forms. No decisions are made, except those specifying what information is to be processed and how it is to be processed. In a job cost system, for example, data from manufacturing operations may be obtained, coded, sorted, and summarized. Although these data may ultimately be transformed into decisions by management, the data processing per se simply effects a change in form of the information.

---

[22] See, for example, Ned Chapin, *An Introduction to Automatic Computers* (Princeton, N.J.; D. Van Nostrand Company, Inc., 1957), chap. 4 and especially Figure 8, p. 51.

Whether we examine information-decision or pure information systems, their basic design is similar. Both types are comprised of the same kinds of *components* (the basic building blocks of a business system). These components can be grouped into three general classes: (1) information components, (2) transformation components, and (3) control components.

There are several different types of information components. First is the *input* component, which represents data *received* from outside the system. These data may come from other systems within the firm or from outside the organization. A special type of input is the *feedback* component, which refers to information reflecting results of the previous operations of the system which is fed back into the system to help guide future performance. Another type of information component is *output,* which centers around transmission of the results of a system to other systems. Finally, the *memory* component of a system stores and updates information in the system.

There are two basic types of *transformation* components. As indicated above, when considering an information-decision system, data from input, feedback, and memory are weighed and translated into a *decision;* whereas in a pure information system, data are simply changed into a different form.

The third basic type of component in these systems is the *control* component. This component, which is comprised of plans, policies, rules,

Figure 4–2. Schematic Representation of a System and Its Components

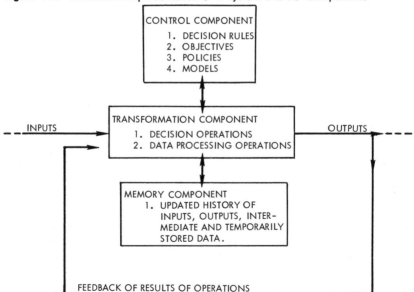

Note: Arrows indicate flow of information and its directions in the system. Examples of component contents are not necessarily all-inclusive.

and so forth, guides the way the total system of information and transformation components are to function.

The different types of systems components and their interrelationships are illustrated in Figures 4–2 and 4–3. Before examining each of these

Figure 4–3. Types of System Components

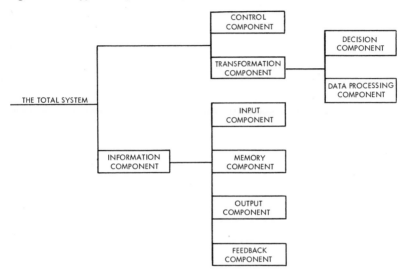

components in detail, we will illustrate their role in the business system with an example.

Consider that the manager is responsible for buying raw materials for a business firm. A certain portion of his time is devoted to the receipt of information. He needs to know the materials requirements of his organization. He also receives market information about materials from suppliers and salesmen. This portion of his activity spent in obtaining and receiving data represents an input component in the buying system.

After these data have been obtained, they may be processed into a standard form useful for reference. For example, a file of potential suppliers classified by type of material available from them is common. Similarly, a specification file is often maintained. These and similar parts of the information system constitute the memory component.

The decision to purchase a specified amount of material from a particular supplier represents activity in the transformation component in the system. Thus, information pertaining to the supplier and to needs of the firm is transformed into a specific purchasing decision.

The output component of the buying system consists of purchase orders and follow-up communications sent to suppliers. Further, information showing the status of outstanding purchase orders may be sent to the departments within the firm using the various materials for future planning. Most buying decisions of this type are not unique. Similar decisions have been made in the past. Company policies, objectives, and past decisions of buyers influence the transformation of data into decisions. The portion of the system which guides this transformation of data is the control component. In purchasing, one rule might be to restrict the total amount of any one order from a given supplier to a specified amount (e.g., $10,000). Other guides to making the decision might include the following: "Change suppliers for each material once each year." "Purchase from suppliers located within 100 miles." "Give preference to suppliers who buy from us." "Fifty percent of purchases shall be from small businesses." "Long-run lowest price is the primary criterion for selection of supplier." "For standard items, carload quantities are preferred if volume of usage allows." "Acceptance of gratuities from suppliers is cause for dismissal." These portions of the control component effect the supplier chosen as well as the data that is maintained.

Dividing a decision-information system into its components may appear artificial since a particular buyer may perform duties simultaneously to encompass all of the components. He may not make these distinctions between parts of his job. It is extremely useful to examine each system component separately, however, in order to focus attention on those parts creating difficulties and requiring revision. In large volume complex buying organizations, different parts of the system will be performed by separate individuals or machines. Under these conditions, consideration of each systems component becomes highly useful for analysis of decisions and information flows.

Inputs

The information inputs to a system are those data which are derived or developed to be helpful in making decisions. These data may come from other systems within the organization or from outside the company.

A common decision in plants operating assembly lines for the manufacture of their products is that of determining the number of hours per week that the plant should work. This decision may be made each week. One of the pieces of information valuable in arriving at this decision is the inventory of items in the possession of distributors and dealers. Trade association data or the company's own marketing operations may be the source of such data. Whatever its source, dealer inventories are useful in making the "hours per week" decision and would be considered as inputs.

The design of information inputs for a system is dependent upon the nature of the decisions and outputs desired from the system. If certain data are necessary to perform any of the functions required by a system, an input component must provide them. Thus, input component design is related to the design of other components of the system. Further, input design is influenced by the following factors:

1. The availability of data useful to the system. (Is it possible to obtain dealer inventory data?)
2. The cost of obtaining the desired inputs. (What is the relative cost of obtaining inventory data from the trade association as compared to a questionnaire financed by a company?)
3. The usefulness of available data to the system as a whole. (Can data more useful than dealer inventories be used?)
4. The timing need in the data receipt and use. (What if dealer inventory information were available monthly and the scheduling decision were made once per week?)

Memory

When a system relies on past actions, or when the arrival of the data inputs does not coincide with the time when they will be used, the memory component furnishes a means of storing these data for future use. In any office one observes file cabinets, safes, and desk drawers full of papers. These constitute the memory of past operations, decisions, and data stored for future use. For example:

In calculating social security deductions from employee earnings, a record of the total deductions for the year to date for each individual is necessary. The memory component of this system contains deductions identified by employee's name and social security number. The memory component is updated as further deductions are credited to each employee's account. If total deductions reach the maximum for an employee, no further deductions are made for him.

The form of the information in the memory component will vary considerably depending on the needs of the operation. However, certain generalizations may be made concerning memory design.

1. Its size is determined by the number of items to be sorted, their identification requirements, and the size of the items to be stored. For example, storing data for social security purposes requires a larger memory if (a) there is a larger number of employees; (b) an additional identification of each employee (such as age or sex) is desired; or (c) cumulative earnings as well as deductions are stored.

2. Its content is determined by the operation's or system's needs. Income tax rates would be superfluous in a system related only to social security deductions.

3. It is updated by input (or feedback) and the transformation component. As the employee works more hours (from input) the cumulative deductions in memory are updated. The addition of these to prior deductions is performed by the transformation component and the result is stored in memory.

4. The memory must be able to forget information on some planned basis. For the social security system, the memory is made to forget cumulative deductions at the end of each year or when an employee terminates employment.

Feedback

When the decision of a system is implemented, data about the *results* of the operation may be returned to the system so that the effect of past decisions can be evaluated and taken into consideration in making future decisions. This information flow in systems terms is referred to as "feedback."

The personnel department of one company selects and hires keypunch operators. During the selection process, considerable information concerning each applicant is obtained. These data are filed in the personnel jacket (a memory document) of each employee. Semiannually, supervisors rate the performance of the keypunch operators. These ratings are used for several purposes, and one copy of them becomes available to the person making the selection decisions. High and low production operators are grouped and compared with the criteria by which they were originally hired. One such analysis showed that there was no significant correlation between favorable personal recommendations given by former employers and the supervisors' ratings of the operators. By indicating that these recommendations were of little value in selection, the feedback of past results permitted decision refinement.

In the above example, the results of the decision were fed back into the system twice a year. Other systems may feed back data continuously and with little delay. One airplane landing system constantly monitors the position of each approaching aircraft in relation to a preselected guide path. As the position of the plane deviates from this path, the ground control operator feeds this information back to the pilot who makes flight corrections. One model of a landing system has a computer monitoring the radar data showing the position of each plane. As deviations from planned positions occur, the computer is designed to send radio messages to a control mechanism in the plane for realignment of its position relative to the guide path. Thus, the information flow and the reactions or decisions in this system are designed to be completely mechanized.

The feedback component of a system has several characteristics and requirements:

1. Some recording of the results of past decisions is required, as were supervisor evaluations in our example of the keypunch operators.

2. Processing of the recorded data into a useful form for subsequent decisions is usually necessary (as was interpretation of radar scope data by the ground control operator in our example).

3. Feedback information has time as well as content requirements (as may be noted by comparing the need for continuous and instantaneous data in the aircraft landing system with the delayed feedback in the selection of the keypunch operators).

4. Some systems require that certain information be designated as more urgent or important. It may have been that information relevant to the true state of the subsequently bankrupt Penn Central Railroad was masked by information suggesting satisfactory operations. Some members of the board of directors serving during the company's period of massive negative cash flows were said to believe they were not aware of the financial state at that time. If information had been presented to highlight deficiencies, precautionary decisions could, perhaps, have more readily been instituted. Similarly, when the ground control operator sees a plane leaving the guide path, he may raise the pitch and intensity of his voice to notify the pilot that this information is not ordinary.

5. Feedback of data is intended to stabilize the outputs of a system by focusing attention on deviations from planned output. If, however, the output of a system is oscillating between two points, it is possible for feedback to amplify deviations from planned performance rather than to dampen them. This will happen when the output operations are *out of phase* with the feedback—i.e., when information concerning the low phase of a cyclic operation is fed back at the time at which the system is performing at the high phase of the cycle. This feedback implies that the operations should be pushed higher in the cycle at a time that they are already too high, and vice versa.[23] The danger in delayed feedback can be seen by imagining that an incoming airplane is oscillating 20 feet above and below the guide path. If feedback is delayed to such an extent that the ground control operator indicates that the plane is 20 feet too high when it is 20 feet below the path, the consequences could be serious. Thus, the timing of feedback should be designed so that deviations from planned performance may be reduced. Operating oscillations are not uncommon. Feedback which amplifies variations can destroy the tendency toward equilibrium desirable in a system.

Output

The output of a system is information transformed into a useful form. An executive's decision is merely a mental concept until it has been translated into oral or written form. These forms of information represent the output of a system.

---

[23] If a system employs negative feedback, oscillations of output are reduced. Instability results when feedback is *positive*. Oscillations are then amplified and overcorrections occur. See, for example, Churchman, Ackoff, and Arnoff, *Introduction to Operations Research* (New York: John Wiley & Sons, Inc., 1957), p. 78.

The design of system outputs depends, first of all, upon the use to which they are to be put. If an output is to be used as an instruction to an employee, it may be merely a verbal statement. If it is a decision to introduce a new product to the company's line, on the other hand, the output may consist of a detailed plan of action which will in turn initiate additional studies, decisions, and actions throughout the company.

The prime criterion for designing systems outputs is the subsequent use to be made of them. However, the manager must also consider the cost of obtaining the output. Such costs are influenced by the availability of system inputs and the transformation of these into the desired output. For example, obtaining some kinds of market research data may be so expensive that any gains made possible through their use are not sufficient to justify their cost. Thus, the optimum specification for outputs is determined by their value to the system and by the costs of their production.

Transformation Components

Although the primary concern in this book is with managerial decision making, attention in the preceding sections has been focused on nondecision elements. This was done because of the critical importance of information transmission and processing in decision making. Most managers spend considerable portions of their time developing and managing information systems to obtain adequate data for their decisions. In fact, some managers are concerned solely with the selection of the most appropriate data collection, transmission, and processing methods.

The transformation component is at the heart of the decision-making process. As indicated earlier, there are two basic types of transformation components. Sometimes decisions are made to transform data into plans of action and orders. These are *substantive* transformations. For example, a substantive transformation is involved when a manager determines that he is going to reduce the number of hours his department will work the following week on the basis of feedback of his costs from last week's operation. Similarly, on the basis of inputs of market research data and cost projections, a company president may decide not to develop a new product. These decisions represent the transformation of information into a course of action to be taken.

Other transformations consist simply of data processing operations. These are referred to as *procedural* transformations.[24] When a clerk extends quantity and price per unit information on an invoice, he trans-

---

[24] Another term that conceivably could be used interchangeably for "transformation" in describing a decision-information system is "processor." Konvalinka and Trentin use that term, for example, in their article "Management Information Systems," *Management Science*, 12 (October 1965), pp. 27–39.

forms these two bits of data into a total price. When an employee files outstanding invoices by customer, he transforms data organized in a random manner to customer accounts receivable. The latter type of organized data can be used for decisions (e.g., credit for future orders from the customer), but the clerk does not perform decision transformations, merely data processing ones.

The design of a transformation component depends to a considerable extent upon the kind of outputs required from and the kind of inputs available to the system. Unless the form and content of the outputs are known, logical systems design is not possible. Consider a typical payroll operation in a plant manufacturing products to customer order. First, a timekeeper fills out a form indicating each job performed, the operator who performed it, the time taken, and the number of pieces produced. The payroll system then takes these pieces of data as inputs and transforms them into a paycheck for each employee. This involves adding each employee's time on all job slips during a given period, multiplying these times by the appropriate rate or rates, calculating deductions and net pay, and transforming these results into appropriate records and paychecks.

These same timekeeping data inputs could be used for determining departmental labor costs each week. This would require the transformation of the timekeeping slips into total labor costs for the plant and segregating these for each department. If the original timekeeping form identified the department in which the individual worked, this transformation could be performed by sorting the forms weekly by department, multiplying the hourly rate for each employee by the hours on each job, and adding the results. Although the inputs to the payroll and the labor cost system are the same, the *transformations* are different because the outputs required from the two systems are different.

It should be noted that if both of these outputs are required by the same organization, savings could be accomplished by integrating the two transformation operations. In both cases, hours worked are multiplied by the rate per hour, and duplication could be avoided by carrying out this operation only once. Once the multiplication has been accomplished, the data could be separated by employee's name for the payroll system and by department for the labor cost system. Further, the transformation of other data useful to the system such as the following could also be integrated with the multiplication operation:

1. Product costs. (The costs would need to be separated by job and the costs for all jobs on each product totaled.)
2. Time standards and estimates. (A time standard for an operation could be calculated by determining the total costs for each job and dividing by the number of pieces produced. This per unit cost could then be averaged with previous per unit costs for the same operation

to arrive at a historical time standard for the job. These standards might provide a basis for estimating future costs.)

The above example points up that there may be considerable common usage of certain system inputs. Thus, systems design, as a whole, should recognize the possibility of combining components of the different systems into one system with multiple transformations and multiple outputs. This concept of integration has wide applicability, and represents an important reason for considering decision making and information processing from a systems viewpoint.

Not only does the design of transformation components depend upon the nature of the inputs available and outputs desired, as has been indicated above, but it also must take into consideration two other factors. The first of these is the nature of the physical operations upon which the inputs may be based. For example, if an employee is paid the same rate per hour for each job he performs, the payroll system can total the hours he works in a period and make one multiplication to arrive at his gross pay. If, however, the employee receives a different rate of pay for each job, a separate multiplication must be made for each job and the results of these intermediate multiplications must be totaled to arrive at the employee's gross pay. Transformation component design also depends upon the availability of data in memory that may be transformed into an acceptable output. For instance, it may be difficult to generate departmental labor costs if the department in which the job was performed is not identified on the timekeeping form at the time the original record was made. The labor cost output could still be calculated, however, if the memory component contained a record of each employee's department. Since the timekeeping form contains the name of the employee, labor costs could be allocated to the various departments by reference to the intermediate memory record identifying the employee as a member of a particular department.

The Control Component

The "control" component in a system is that unit with the function of determining how the other components of the system are to operate. It is the brains of the system. It tells the transformation component what shall be done with the input and memory in order to produce the output required.

The control unit comprises objectives, policies, models, procedures, and programs as well as plans and controls. Any specific system might not include all of these types of controls, but it would include enough of them so that the people in charge of the system may meet their responsibilities to the organization (in terms of system outputs required) at a cost deemed reasonable. The choice of control methods will be conditioned by the effect that these different measures will have upon the efficiency of the system.

The control component can offer *general* guides as to how the system is to operate or it may provide highly *specific* operating rules. If only the objectives of the firm are given as a guide, the persons performing the transformation operation have considerable leeway as to how operations will be performed. In some cases the output of an organizational system is not even specified. For example, one man was hired by a machine tool manufacturing firm as "Chief Industrial Engineer." His duties were not specified. In general, he had a feeling that he was supposed to act "as industrial engineers act." Supposedly he could do this with respect to the office organization, the production group, or the sales staff. Here the industrial engineering system was able to determine its own outputs as well as the methods it would use to accomplish them.

Contrast this rather general specification control to the following situation: Through analysis of the flow of rejects of parts from a machining operation, one quality control organization determined that if the operating rejection rate exceeded a fixed percentage, the machines should be shut down for adjustment. This rule, made available to the foreman, provided a specific rule for operation decisions.

Overall Systems Design

As has been shown in the previous sections, each component of a system is dependent on each of the other components. The output is determined by the transformation, memory, and the input, and each of these is, in turn, related to each of the other components. At what point, then, should the design of a system begin? It is usually desirable to start at either the input or the output stage. Further, it is recommended that design begin with an analysis of the objectives that the manager wants accomplished by the system. Thus output design is primary. Then it is possible to determine whether the desired outputs can be produced economically or whether they must be modified in light of the costs of attaining them through the design of each of the other system components.

In considering the design of a system as a whole, it is not possible to stop after a consideration of a single output and the accompanying components necessary to provide that output. As was shown in the discussion of the payroll system, several different outputs useful in decision making in the organization can be developed from the same input data. Rather than design three or four different information systems to provide such needed data as these, it is more typical for organizations to combine input, memory, and transformation components so as to minimize systems costs. However, it should be recognized that excessive combination can result in compromises in the form and availability of the outputs. These compromises tend to reduce the effectiveness of the data as it is used in decision making. Consider a multiple payroll and departmental labor cost system. If labor costs are needed for decision making on a daily basis and payrolls are calculated semimonthly, the integration of these two systems tends to compromise the costs savings theoretically possible.

COMPUTERS AND INFORMATION

Computers: Basic Characteristics

The technology of information processing is integrally linked to the information structures available to managers, to the volume and timing of information, and to the flows of information in the firm. Basic to an understanding of that information technology is a knowledge of computer capability. Since the components of computers are directly analogous to the prior discussion of systems components, it is convenient to introduce a descriptive explanation of computers at this point for those with limited understanding of them.

Most modern digital computers are general-purpose internally stored-program machines that can operate upon data only if they are given (1) a program (which consists of a series of externally furnished instructions telling the computer how to start, read data, interpret it, store, calculate, print output, and stop),[25] (2) numerical values in the program designed to specify relationships, and so on, and then (3) data appropriate to and specified by the program. In the computer itself (referred to as hardware), the first component consists of an *input* unit which reads programs and/or data coded so that the unit can translate them into coded electronic pulses. A second component is the electronic memory unit into which the program is placed, data are stored and intermediate and final calculations kept until the program is completed. A third unit is the arithmetic unit or electronic calculator instructed by the program and to which data are brought to be operated on according to the program. A fourth unit is an output device which translates electronic pulses from the memory (or perhaps directly from the calculator) to the output forms required for subsequent computer use or for direct

---

[25] It is possible to build a programmed computer entirely of physical components with no externally inputed program if a fixed preconceived knowledge of the outputs desired, the inputs necessary, and the internal computations required are known. There are few computers like this since computer speeds are so high few applications can fully utilize their potential capacity. Further, changes in data needs, computational sequences, and available inputs would require a physical rebuilding of such a device. Realistically, therefore, computers consist, operationally, of both hardware (the physical components) and software (the programs).

human consumption. For example, a payroll program could print employee checks directly from a computer output unit.

A computer's internal language consists of a coded series of electronic pulses. In the early days of computers, programmers had to write in this machine code, memorizing the series of binary numbers that represented each computer instruction (e.g., add, divide, and so forth). Modern computer languages such as FORTRAN or COBOL more nearly representing sparsed English are used by programmers, but these "source" programs must be translated into a machine code before the computer can operate with them as a series of instructions. Fortunately, the computer can make these source to machine translations itself through standard intermediate programs called translators and compilers.

One of the features of digital computers making them so versatile is their ability to control, internally, the nature of the calculations that are to be performed. For example, a weekly program to update inventory levels by item, the amounts on hand, on order, and on reserve, together with net amounts available for use could have been outputed from the previous week's run. When these outputs are inputed for the current week together with the week's transactions (e.g., disbursements, orders, reserves, receipts), a new updated inventory status by item can be printed for scanning by inventory personnel to determine whether new orders should be placed. Consider a more versatile version of this inventory program in which the minimum desired level for each item is also maintained in the input data. If a series of instructions are used to find if the actual level is equal to or less than the minimum, a notation can be outputed that a reorder of that item is required. Such an output would not result for *all* items; only for those whose levels were low. The human inventory controller would only need an output list of items to reorder rather than a complete list of the status of all items. A separate output record for inputing the following week could maintain the detailed status of all items.

Internally, the computer would operate the reorder routine only if the actual inventory reached the minimum level. More complex versions could recalculate minimum levels of usage or delivery rate changes, recalculate the most economical order amount and even print purchase orders to replenish supplies. Note that a decision for reorder, formerly made by a human controller, has been automated. It is the ability of the computer to change its sequence and routines that give it the human-like ability to make decisions. The flexibility allows imaginative programmers to simulate human thought processes of a fairly complex nature. Through these procedures, some decisions formerly made by humans in organizations have been turned over to computers.

It is not always possible or convenient to specify all the detail of a program since it may have different uses with varying needs. It is possible to make a program flexible by leaving certain values of formulas or equations unspecified until a particular run of that program is made. For example, consider the exponential demand smoothing equation:

$$\bar{F}_t = \alpha D_t + (1 - \alpha)\bar{F}_{t-1};$$

where the value of α depends upon the particular use to which it is put.[26] It usually ranges from 0.01 to 0.3. If the value of α is set as a constant throughout the program (e.g., $\alpha = .10$), the program itself would have to be rewritten every time a different value for α was desired. If this variable is simply specified as the parameter, α, *in the program*, however, the same program could be used for different runs where different values of this variable are wanted, simply by punching the value of α on a *single input card* to be fed into the computer.

From this short description, it should be clear that a computer is a machine capable of tremendous processing throughout. It can lower

Figure 4–4. Major Digital Computer Components

Hardware Components	*Major Types Available*
Input Unit......................	—Punched card reader
	—Magnetic tape reader
	—Direct electronic signal from another computer or a terminal
Internal Storage.................	Magnetic core
	Semiconductor
	Disk
	Drum
	Tape
	Card
Calculation Unit.................	All calculate electronically, a variety of multiple calculators available
Output.........................	—Print on paper
	—Magnetic tape
	—Punched card

Software Components	*Major Types Available*
Source Languages	
Mathematically Oriented.........	FORTRAN
	ALGOL
Business Oriented..............	COBOL
General.......................	PL-1
	BASIC
	SIMSCRIPT
	GPSS
Compilers......................	One for each source language and machine*
Programs.......................	One for each application in machine and/or source language

* Not all computers can use every language. COBOL was designed as a most general-purpose source language for all machines.

---

[26] See Elwood S. Buffa, *Production-Inventory System: Planning and Control* (Homewood, Ill: Richard D. Irwin, Inc., 1968), pp. 35–40. In this equation, $\bar{F}_t$ represents the new forecasted average demand in the current period; D_t equals actual demand in the current period; $\bar{F}_{t-1}$, the last forecasted average demand; and α the smoothing constant or demand coefficient.

costs of information and make it economical to provide more of relevant information to managers. Further, its flexibility and capability for being instructed in logical processes—above mere calculations—aid the manager as an extension of and a substitution for part of his own logical and decision processes. The major components of digital computers are illustrated on page 116 in Figure 4–4. In the discussion following, factors affecting the economic feasibility of computer-based information systems serving these purposes are analyzed.

Data, Information, Intelligence, and Knowledge

Prior to discussing the design of information systems in organizations, it is useful to define just exactly what is meant by information. To improve the design of communications and information flows within an organization, the manager is interested in increasing his awareness of what the status and direction the organization is taking. Thus, data concerning the 1939 home run champion in the National League is irrelevant to most managerial jobs. Datum such as this consists of a message unorganized or unrelated to any conceptual scheme of the organization. In contrast, information as defined here is *ordered* and *assembled* to be useful in identifying and solving problems in a specific use. Information consists of an abstract representation of the physical, human, and other systems. If management were seeking to reduce accident rates, the number, location, timing, and severity of accidents could provide a starting point for identifying where to attack the problem. These data are organized as information for the accident problem for this company.

Intelligence represents a higher level or order of information. Intelligence not only provides data organized for solving problems but also *relates* one phenomenon to another. If accidents per 1,000,000 man-hours worked per department is used as a measure rather than mere number of accidents per time period, the effect of differing sizes of departments is automatically considered. Thus, to reduce accidents, the relation of accidents to number of hours worked may be a better relative indicator of potential problem departments than mere "number of accidents" alone. Indicating relationships then, adds another dimension (and intelligence) to information. The rate of return of profit on the firm's investment is more relevant for most managerial problems than is the sheer amount of profit. Share of market, production per man-hour, and similar *relational* concepts add relevance over their mere information components.

A further characteristic of information is that it possesses a surprise character. A utility company announcing a $9 dividend rate may provide little additional information to investors if over the last 20 years similar dividend announcements had always been made. If an event is almost certain, reports of its occurrence prossess little surprise or information.

In a stream of messages, an infrequent repetition of a message produces greater information content per occurrence than does a frequently repeated message. It should be noted that there is a mathematical theory of communication which examines the relationships among redundance versus certainty of message reception while introducing a number of other concepts. To date, however, mathematical communication theory has been much more useful in designing voice and data communication circuits for utilities than management information systems.

Perception. A related concept to the idea of surprise content in information is the "threshold" of the message receiver. If one is receiving a stream of messages such that the information content of the stream is low, the receiver tends not to perceive the message—i.e., he tunes it out. For any message in the stream to penetrate and attract the attention of the receiver, its impact must exceed a threshold level of attention. Surprise content is not enough; the data must also be perceived as important, exceeding the ordinary threshold. Thus, a computer center that distributes all the data it processes may, in fact, contribute to deadening the receptivity of a human receiver of the information. To increase perception, information considered important is highlighted. The concept of management by exception recognizes this principle in that it calls for only the exceptional, relevant, or problem information to be reported to the manager. Other data may be processed but not reported. The exception process (which provides one example of simplification of the complex) helps the manager to perceive that a problem exists.

Timing. Another factor bearing upon the relevance of information and intelligence is its timing. There is an optimal time that information should be reported to a manager. The costs of assembling information quickly may become quite expensive as the recording, transmission, processing, and reporting period is required to be shortened. Thus, it is uneconomical to have immediate access to all data. On the other hand, the value of the information for solving a problem often decays over time. Information indicating that a possibility of a negotiated purchase of common stock of a supplier at 25 percent discount below market prices can be useless if not acted upon before others learn of it. There are no general guides as to how "timing" may be optimized. We will, however, delve more deeply into the timing of feedback data in Chapter 13.

Value. When a purchasing agent receives a message that the supply of pencils is low and requires replacement and another input stating that starting next month the company's basic raw material costs are going to be increased 15 percent, he obtains information from both messages. In fact, the amount of information may be the same for both messages. The value of the second message, however, can greatly exceed the value of the first. What is the value of information? Its value stems from its use in *improving operations.* The utility of information is the utility derived with the information less the utility that would have existed without the information.[27]

What are the conditions under which information may possess value? Conversely, how can one estimate conditions in which additional processing of data will not change the decision to be made? When an information stream merely reinforces previously held conclusions, it provides no value since it changes no decision that could not previously have been made on the basis of prior information available. If the manager has developed a payoff matrix of his decision problem, additional information can have value if it changes the probabilities of the states of nature *and*, if consequently, an effective change in decision results. Consider the payoff matrix shown in Figure 4–5. If additional information

Figure 4–5. Payoff Matrix

	States		
	A	*B*	
Strategy	*p = 0.10*	*p = 0.90*	*Expected Value*
1.............	$100,000	$200,000	$190,000
2.............	170,000	160,000	161,000

were developed to show that the probabilities of states *A* and *B* actually occurring were really 0.05 and 0.95, respectively, is the new probability information of value? The expected value of strategy 1 is $195,000 with the new information and that of strategy 2, $165,000. Yet the optimal decision still remains strategy 1. There is no change in values that the organization will receive. There is merely a better estimate of those values as a consequence of the new information.

Consider another case in which the additional information changes the decision. If new information were developed for Figure 4–5 to show that the probability of *A* occurring is 0.5 and *B* is 0.5, the expected value of strategy 1 becomes $150,000 and strategy 2, $165,000. The optimal strategy now is changed to strategy 2 as a result of this new information. What is the value of the information that revises the manager's estimates of the state probabilities? Information value has been defined as the difference in utility arising from decisions made with the information. If these new probabilities were not available, strategy 1 with an expected value of $150,000 would have been selected. Given the new information, the second strategy with a $165,000 expected value is selected. The expected value of the information is the difference, $15,000.

---

[27] James C. Emery, *Organizational Planning and Control Systems* (Toronto: The Macmillan Company, 1969), pp. 67–69.

Significantly, the value of the information is not known until *after* the information has already been obtained. Consequently the manager will find it very difficult to decide whether or not to seek new information or new estimates. Information processing is costly and these expenses must be balanced against probable gains. Optimally, supposedly the manager should keep seeking additional information as long as its expected value exceeds its costs. Yet he does not know these values until he has already incurred the costs. Realistically, then, the manager must have some preconceived idea that his present information is inadequate before it is rational to seek more. This inadequacy of present information (1) could arise from the fact that the probable range of the estimates is so wide that more information could conceivably change the decision, or (2) because the differences in payoffs is so large that a small change in any estimate can alter the choice. These guidelines are fairly broad and imprecise, however,[28] and are, consequently, much more subjective and personalistic than we might otherwise desire.

Processing Functions Affecting Information Value and Cost

It is uneconomical for an organization to record data concerning every event that might affect it. While the promise of the computer has been to make more information available to management decision making, the information problem may not be a lack of quantity. Often analyses have shown that excessive data abound. What is needed is a balance between a lack and a surplus of information. This dilemma runs throughout the design of information systems. One way that is useful to consider how information systems can better meet the needs of management is to examine those data processing operations used to advance data to the states of information and intelligence.

Sampling. After having determined what measures of a process or an event in an organization need to be known for decision making, it may be possible to avoid a constant monitoring of that activity. Rather, it may be possible to record only a sample of data about it. Thus, in an activity such as quality control, data from a sample of products moving along a production line may provide sufficient information to take the corrective action if problems occur. Similarly, when it is desired to establish time standards for office positions, it is possible to take a random sample of activities as the basis for gathering data rather than to continuously record what is going on in the job. The use of sample information rather than complete data about a product or process

---

[28] A precise mathematically oriented model for the value of information exists, but the difficulty of estimating the levels of the variables in the model, similar to the difficulties for this example, reduce its usefulness. The model might thus be criticized as being impractical although managers of information centers will find its concepts useful for working toward improving information systems. See particularly, ibid., especially chap. 4.

is most permissible when the conditions are fairly repetitive and standardized—i.e., the system is stable. Unique events, of course, cannot be sampled. The use of sampling sometimes has been overlooked as the large processing capabilities of the computer have evolved. Rather than to develop a scientific base for the sampling process, some system designers have tended to record all events and processes. In cases of reports running to hundreds of computer printout pages, one could reasonably ask whether or not sampling of data might not provide as much information in a cheaper manner.

Compression. Although it may be necessary to record a great deal of detail about operations, the human processing capability for detail is so small that it is necessary to compress data into a more concise form if the manager is to be informed and to decide. *Filtering* is a common compression technique. The organization system itself tends to filter information by providing less and less detail information to the top of the organization. Hopefully, the information rises to the hierarchical level qualified to deal with the problems as intended by the sender of information. Furthermore, at any level, the systems designer needs to provide *aggregations* such as averages, summaries, measures of dispersion, and other statistical analyses that will allow the decision maker more insight into the meaning that can be gleaned from the data. A further factor affecting how data should be compressed is the time span over which the decision maker works. For a department store, *daily* sales figures would be quite relevant to the manager of the sports department while it may be possible for the store manager only to review *weekly* sales figures. For a chain of department stores, however, the top management of the chain may find little use for daily or even weekly sales figures since the decisions made at the top rarely affect operations during short-time intervals. Rather, top-level managers are concerned with decisions about whether or not to invest in new stores, the development of managers for the organization, and the design of new systems for planning and control. These contrasts in time periods suggest a differentiation in the filtering and aggregation of data for decision making. The above examples also provide another case of the simplifying of the complex.

Classifying and Indexing. Of course, it is possible to aggregate data so far that it has little meaning in making decisions. For example, if a firm is collecting information about absenteeism and turnover in a plant, the total plant turnover and absenteeism figures are probably less useful than some more detailed classification. In the case of turnover, for example, the company might reasonably expect that the rates would be different for men than for women and for people of different ages. By anticipating the possible problem causes, the systems designer can provide classification systems and indexing arrangements that allow the information to be extracted for a maximum impact on decision making.

Storage. Since decisions on most types of problems occur only periodically rather than continuously, data need to be stored so they can be available when the need for problem solving arises. There is a wide range for storage media available to the information systems designer. They range from magnetic core and transistorized main frame storage in an electronic computer to archival files of original documents recording past transactions that have taken place. Data that have a high expected value should be more readily available, while infrequently used and less valuable information should, ordinarily, be stored in less expensive storage media. Although the access time and cost of retrieval of infrequently used data may be high, the infrequency and low value in use suggest that the system minimize the costs associated with this storage.

As the costs of rapid storage media decline (such as has been the case of on-line disk storage, for example), it may become more economical to store detailed data rather than aggregations. Since ad hoc inquiries into a data base during some future period are very difficult to predict at the time the data is first stored, aggregating data can preclude the possibility of undertaking some types of analyses in the future. It would, obviously, be desirable to have the detailed data so that it could later be aggregated in any form thought to be desirable, but the cost of storing detailed data tends to mitigate against it.

Transmission. While data may be recorded in one location, it may not always be processed or used for decisions in that location. It may be more economical to transmit data from one plant to a main office to be processed and returned via electronic transmission lines to the branch plant for use. Historically, the cost per unit of calculation has declined as the size of the computer unit has increased. Thus it has been more economical to transmit data to a large computer rather than to use many small decentralized computers. The economics of centralized versus decentralized computer units change as technological developments continue to alter their relative advantages. At the present time, many small pre-processing computers feed information to distant computation centers and receive the completed computations back for printing as reports to management at that decentralized location. A related development in sharing computers among different companies has made it possible for some companies to provide large-scale computer services to small-scale users. Rather than owning a computer, the small user has a unit to input data to a transmission system linked to a large computer. The computer has a system for sorting out priorities of different users of the computer, such as calling for data bases and calling for the standard programs, as well as transmitting the processed information back to the appropriate user. Such arrangements make it possible for the small user to have enormous computation power while paying for only a small amount of time on the large computer. This can be cheaper than buying a small-scale computer since, as we have pointed out, the cost per unit of computation tends to decrease as the size of the computer increases.

Of course, electronic methods are not the only ones for transmitting data. As an extreme example, some firms whose data requirements are not immediate, airmail documents overseas to be keypunched onto cards, transferred to electronic tape, and flown back for analysis on the firm's computer. The reasoning behind this shipment of data overseas is the low cost of keypunching abroad compared to that in the United States.

Display. Not only must data be recorded, stored, aggregated, processed, transmitted, and so on, it must ultimately be made available to the manager. Thus, it needs to be displayed, hopefully, in some form in which the manager can spot problems and make decisions. Since a computer is a much more efficient large-scale processor of data than is man, computer printouts consisting of thousands of items appear an inefficient way of utilizing man's time. What is needed is a system of display that focuses on the unusual and exceptional, according to the problem areas under the domain of the individual receiving the display. For very important decisions (e.g., those of high levels), it is appropriate to spend extra time and money to prepare charts and graphs so that quick decisions can be made. The costs of developing these kinds of displays for further down the organization, such as at the foremen's level, are not justified to the same extent; the decisions made at that level ordinarily do not influence total cost or value to the organization to the same extent that they do at higher organization levels. One of the decision problems that the manager faces, of course, is finding whether or not problems exist in the organization. Therefore, it is convenient if some system can be devised in which the decision maker can explore the data base in such a way as to seek out problems. Some computer systems allow this search behavior by providing the manager a terminal with which he may call up any information which has been stored from a data bank, manipulate it in whatever way that the computer program permits, and print out that portion of the data he wishes to retain for later analysis. For example, the maintenance department of an airline schedules its equipment for repair on some sort of periodical basis. The interval between overhauls is conditioned by the amount of use the equipment received rather than a fixed time span. It would be useful to the maintenance manager in planning his work force over the next several months to have some estimates about usage on the equipment in the fleet. If he were able to search a data base and to find or calculate the projected time until overhaul on each item of equipment over which he has repair responsibility, he would be able to arrive at a more rational decision concerning his work force, equipment, and inventories. Since this particular example is a recurring need on the part of the manager, however, it might well be preferable to design a system which reports these data to him periodically rather than to have him interrogating the data base each time he feels compelled to make his own plans. It is for the more unique cases, decisions not anticipated and not regular, that a free-form type of investigation of the data base becomes most important.

SUMMARY

The concept of an open system interacting in an uncertain environment is descriptive of behavior in the business firm. Furthermore, associated with general systems concepts can be an information-decision system which describes organizational behavior in terms of linkages of information, feedback, and so forth, to the decision maker. This chapter has focused on analyzing the concepts that relate a system's behavior to an information system that can be used for decision making. Chapters 2 and 3 have provided a basic understanding of decision making; the following chapters turn to a description of individual, group, and organizational behavior.

DISCUSSION AND STUDY QUESTIONS

1. Compare and contrast the ideas of Ludwig von Bertalanffy and Norbert Weiner with respect to management thought.
2. What is entropy? How can the concept be applied in analyzing open systems such as business organizations?
3. How does one define the boundaries of an open system?
4. What are some of the techniques developed for "simplification of the complex"? What is the major benefit and danger in utilizing these techniques?
5. What is steady state behavior? What do most individuals and organizations attempt to do with respect to their "steady states"? What is the primary danger in these attempts?
6. Classify each of the following items as components of an information-decision system. In each case, give the reason for your answer.
   a) A performance appraisal interview between a superior and one of his subordinates.
   b) A company's policy of being an "equal opportunity" employer.
   c) A supervisor's selecting a man for a promotion.
   d) A deck of computer cards specifying certain variables and their relationships in the firm's marketing subsystem.
7. What are compilers or translators for computers and why are they important?
8. Would the score of the seventh game of the 1971 World Series be considered as information to the Pittsburgh Pirates' manager? Give reasons to support your answer.
9. What is the difference between information and intelligence?

10. One manager boasted that his firm's computer system "printed out all possible data in his organization, and, therefore, was one of the finest in the country." Comment on this statement.

11. Computers are merely extremely fast and complicated arithmetic machines. As such, they are no substitute for seasoned managers. Discuss.

12. If a system is extremely slow to react to environmental influences, an information system to monitor that environment can similarly be quite leisurely in the collection and feedback of environmental data. Comment.

13. Information can have no value if, on the basis of it, operations continue into the future as they have in the past. Discuss.

14. Mr. J. Fred Bimble is president of a small chain of 12 supermarkets operating in central Pennsylvania. Reporting to Mr. Bimble is the company's general manager, Joe Orsino, who directly supervises all the stores. The organization of each store is to have a head grocery clerk, head produce clerk, and head meat cutter reporting to the store manager. Mr. Orsino also does the buying for the chain.

   Mr. Bimble believes that his information-decision system could be improved if he rented computer time from a local firm. Does Mr. Bimble need a computer? Explain. If he does go to using a computer, what are some of the key inputs which would be required? What are some of the kinds of computer output data which would be needed by whom in the firm and at what time intervals?

SELECTED REFERENCES

ACKOFF, RUSSELL L. "Towards a Behavioral Theory of Communication," *Management Science*, 4 (1958), 218–34.

ACKOFF, RUSSELL L. "Management Misinformation System," *Management Science*, 14 (December 1967).

ANDRUS, ROMAN R. "Approaches to Information Evaluation," *MSU Business Topics*, 19 (Summer 1971), 40–46.

ARGYRIS, CHRIS. "Management Information Systems: The Challenge to Rationality and Emotionality," *Management Science*, 17 (February 1971), B275–92.

BOORE, WILLIAM F., and MURPHY, JERRY R. *The Computer Sampler*. New York: The McGraw-Hill Book Co., 1968.

Computers and Management, the 1967 Leatherbee Lectures. Boston, Mass.: Harvard University Graduate School of Business Administration, 1967.

DOLBY, J. L., and RESNIKOFF, H. L. "On the Multiplicative Structure of Information Storage and Access Systems," *Interfaces*, 1 (1970), 23–30.

FERRENCE, THOMAS P. "Organizational Communications Systems and the Decision Process," *Management Science*, 17 (October 1970), B83–96.

GLANS, THEODORE B. et al. *Management Systems*. New York: Holt, Rinehart & Winston, Inc., 1968.

GORRY, G. ANTHONY, and MORTON, M. S. "A Framework of Management Information Systems, *Sloan Management Review*, (Fall 1971), 55–70.

GREENWOOD, WILLIAM T. (ed.)   *Decision Theory and Information Systems.* Cincinnati, Ohio: South-Western Publishing Co., 1969.

HARE, VAN COURT, JR.   *Systems Analysis: A Diagnostic Approach.* New York: Harcourt, Brace & World, Inc., 1967.

HOMER, EUGENE D.   "A Generalized Model for Analyzing Management Information Systems," *Management Science*, 8 (July 1962).

JOYNER, ROBERT, and TUNSTALL, KENNETH.   "Computer Augmented Organizational Problem Solving," *Management Science*, 17 (December 1970), B212–25.

KANTER, JEROME.   *The Computer and the Executive.* Englewood Cliffs, N.J.: Prentice-Hall, Inc., 1967.

MARSHAK, JACOB.   "Producing, Storing, Transporting, and Using Knowledge," Western Management Science Institute Working Paper No. 165, 1970.

PARKHILL, DOUGLAS F.   *The Challenge of the Computer Utility.* Reading, Mass.: Addison-Wesley Publishing Co., Inc., 1966.

SCHODERBEK, PETER P.   *Management Systems.* New York: John Wiley & Sons, Inc., 1967.

STIGLER, GEORGE J.   "The Economics of Information," *The Journal of Political Economy*, 69 (June 1961), 213–25.

WEINWURM, GEORGE F.   "Computer Management Control Systems through the Looking Glass," *Management Science*, 7 (July 1961).

Chapter 5

Individual Behavior

INTRODUCTION

IT HAS BEEN STATED often that "management involves getting work done through people." Although this statement does not tell very much about the managerial process, it cannot be denied that human behavior is a key variable with which the manager must deal. In fact, all managerial decisions—from formalized policies and rules which guide the organization as a whole to a manager's interpersonal relationships with his subordinates—have an ultimate impact on the behavior of members of the organization. The installation of new machinery and equipment requires new work procedures to be followed by production employees. The decision to increase levels of production may necessitate overtime work or the hiring of additional employees; production cutbacks may effect layoffs or shorter working hours. The manner in which a supervisor decides to handle disciplinary problems in his department may have a marked effect on both the attitudes and behavior of his employees.

To perceive the ways in which decisions influence the behavior of the members of an organization, managers need to have some understanding of why people behave the way they do. Underlying the manager's decisions are certain assumptions (either explicit or implicit) about how other individuals will behave. Thus, if the manager's decisions are to be appropriate, it is necessary for these assumptions to be valid.

In addition to understanding human behavior, effective managerial decision making also requires *skills* in dealing with people in specific problem situations. A manager needs not only to have some understanding of why people are motivated to behave the way they do—he must also be able to make the kinds of decisions which will encourage his employees to direct their efforts toward the goals of the organization. Similarly, an understanding of how people learn and modify their behavior is insufficient if the manager is unable to apply this knowledge when the need arises for him to make decisions relative to the training of one of his workers.

Unfortunately, the development of skills in dealing with other people is usually a slow and difficult process, requiring both breaking well-established habits and considerable practice in trying out new ways of behavior. This is because our attitudes, perceptions, and ways of relating to other people are the product of lifelong learning processes—many of our behavioral patterns are deeply ingrained habits. Consequently, the development of skills in "human relations" is not something which can be accomplished simply by reading any textbook such as this. For this reason, our primary objective in this chapter is to help the reader develop a better understanding of human behavior, rather than to foster skill development. In doing so, we intend to provide (1) a basis for future skill development, and (2) a framework for our analysis in succeeding chapters of the influence of group membership, leadership, and organizational arrangements on the behavior of members of the business firm.

First, some observations will be made about individuals' "personality" and behavior. Second, behavior will be treated as being basically oriented toward the satisfaction of needs, three "motivational" models will be examined, and some of the more important types of human needs and the implications of the individual's success or failure in satisfying them will be discussed. Third, attention will be given to learning and some of the conditions under which learning new patterns of behavior seem to be most effective. Finally, certain aspects of the role that business firms play in providing individuals with opportunities for attaining job satisfaction in the organizational work situation will be dealt with.

The Concept of Personality

The term "personality" is one which has been defined in many different ways. Further, many different generalized personality characteristics have been defined and described by psychologists, such as mental ability, physical ability, feelings, attitudes, beliefs, interests, and emotional makeup. In turn, each of these has been broken down into a number of more specific characteristics. In the area of mental ability or intelligence, for example, measurements have been made of such abilities as verbal reasoning, mathematical reasoning, symbolic reasoning, and creative problem solving. As one might expect—considering the complexity of the human being and the difficulties involved in measuring such characteristics—considerable disagreement exists among psychologists in the ways they view personality.[1]

Most social scientists, however, do agree on considering personality

---

[1] To give some idea as to the diversity of common personality traits (or characteristics) which have been explored by social scientists, it is interesting to note that as far back as 1936, nearly 18,000 trait terms were found. G. W. Allport and H. S. Odbert, "Trait-Names: A Psycholexical Study," *Psychological Monographs,* 47, (1936). It should also be noted that attempting to identify common personality traits is only one among many approaches to the study of personality.

as representing the *totality* of a person's behavior and attitudes, and emphasize that each aspect of the individual's personality is interrelated with all of his others. That is, personality represents an *organization* of forces within the individual. Or, in terms of the discussion in Chapter 4, the individual's personality may be viewed as a dynamic, holistic, open system.

While most theories have viewed personality as an open system to some degree, they have varied in the emphasis given to the various dimensions of open systems. For example, as Gordon W. Allport has pointed out:[2]

1.   Most personality theorists have taken full account of the notions that: (*a*) there is material and energy exchange (or input and output) between the individual and his environment,[3] and (*b*) a vital need of the personality system is that of steady state maintenance—to satisfy needs, reduce tension, and maintain equilibrium.

2.   On the other hand, there has been less agreement among theorists in emphasizing (*a*) steady state improvement even at the expense of disequilibrium (e.g., psychological growth, self-actualization[4]); and (*b*) that in addition to matter and energy exchange, "there is extensive transactional commerce with the environment"[5] (e.g., social interaction).

Viewing the individual as an open system, the authors of this text agree with Allport's general conclusion that each of these dimensions should be given consideration in viewing human personality.

Determinants of Personality

The development of the human personality as an open system is influenced by the mutual interaction of two basic kinds of factors—*constitutional and environmental*. By constitutional factors is meant those inborn characteristics with which the individual is endowed through the processes of heredity. There are many different ways in which constitutional factors may condition a person's behavior, attitudes and ways of viewing life. As Kluckhohn and Murray have pointed out:

There are substantial reasons for believing that different genetic structures carry with them varying potentialities for learning, for reaction time, for energy level, for frustration tolerance. Different people appear to have different biological rhythms: of growth, of activity, of depression and exaltation. The various biologically inherited malfunctions certainly have implications for

---

[2] Gordon W. Allport, "The Open System in Personality Theory," *Journal of Abnormal and Social Psychology*, 61 (September 1960), pp. 301–10.

[3] For example, the individual's response (output) to some external stimulus (input), such as a bright light.

[4] We will give special attention to the concept of self-actualization later in this chapter.

[5] Allport, *The Open System in Personality Theory*, p. 303.

personality development, though there are wide variations among those who share the same physical handicap (deafness, for example).

Sex and age must be regarded as among the more striking constitutional determinants of personality. Personality is also shaped through such traits of physique as stature, pigmentation, strength, conformity of features to the culturally fashionable type, etc. Such characteristics influence a man's needs and expectations. The kind of world he finds about him is to a considerable extent determined by the way other people react to his appearance and physical capacities.[6]

The personality of the individual is also shaped by a number of environmental factors. One of the most important of these is the culture in which we live. The customs, traditions, standards, and values of our society, which are transmitted (and modified) from generation to generation, condition our behavior to a considerable extent.

The life history of the individual is first and foremost an accommodation to the patterns and standards traditionally handed down in his community. From the moment of his birth the customs into which he is born shape his experience and behavior. By the time he can talk, he is the little creature of his culture, and by the time he is grown and able to take part in its activities, its habits are his habits, its beliefs his beliefs, its impossibilities his impossibilities. Every child that is born into his group will share them with him, and no child born into one on the opposite side of the globe can ever achieve the thousandth part.[7]

As anthropologists have discovered, behavior considered appropriate in one society may be highly frowned on in another. As one would expect, many such differences reflect themselves in the behavior of individuals in their roles as members of business organizations. Until relatively recently, for example, in the Japanese business firm, attitudes and policies toward such factors as pay, promotions, and responsibility for decision making were quite different from our own.

Japanese workers are hired for life. They are practically never fired. Promotions go largely by seniority even at managerial levels. The incompetent executive moves up with advancing years to positions with titles appropriate to his age—even when this means devising types of duties that will keep him from interfering with the progress of the firm. The pay of workers bears no relation to their productivity. The pay envelope is the sum of a complex set of factors, in which length of service and number of dependents figure prominently. All management decisions are made on a group basis—at least

---

[6] Clyde Kluckhohn and Henry A. Murray, "Personality Formation: The Determinants," in Clyde Kluckhohn and Henry A. Murray, *Personality in Nature, Society, and Culture* (2d ed., rev.; New York: Alfred A. Knopf, Inc., 1956), p. 57. Copyright by Alfred A. Knopf, Inc.

[7] Ruth Benedict, *Patterns of Culture*, (New York: New American Library of Word Literature, Inc., 1934), p. 2; copyright by the original publisher, Houghton Mifflin Co.

normally. If an individual were credited with a certain decision that turned out to be unwise, then the individual would lose face. To spare management people from such humiliation, to all appearances the group as a whole shares responsibility in all decisions.[8]

It was reported by *The Wall Street Journal* in 1969, however, that several changes had been introduced by a number of Japanese firms into this traditional cultural pattern. For example, rapid promotions have been given to workers who have exerted extra effort; and productivity-based incentive plans have been installed by some companies; although employees generally, when joining a company, still stay with it until they reach 55, the usual retirement age in Japan.[9]

Within a particular culture many different kinds of personality patterns may be found. One reason for such variations is that the constitutional characteristics of individuals vary, as indicated above. In addition, different persons within any culture (such as in our own country) are exposed to dissimilar *subcultural* values, beliefs and standards—e.g., those found in the ghettos of many of our large cities, as contrasted with those in considerably more affluent upper income suburban areas.

Culture is transmitted to the individual by educational and religious institutions, by various groups with which he comes into contact during his life, and most important of all by the family. There is wide agreement among psychologists that a most critical factor in the development of personality is the child's relationships with his parents. The child's earliest and closest associations are with his family; he is rewarded or punished depending upon whether his behavior is approved or disapproved by his parents; and he learns their values, beliefs, and ways of behaving. The reader who is a parent has undoubtedly observed on many occasions how quick his offspring is to copy the behavior of father and mother (unfortunately, sometimes in public to the latter's considerable embarrassment). Whether the parents show love or hostility toward the child, whether they are overprotective and rarely let the child make any decisions of his own, or whether they are supportive of him and encourage his development—such relationships are likely to have a lasting influence on his behavior and ways of viewing life.

---

[8] William F. Whyte, *Men at Work* (Homewood, Ill.: Richard D. Irwin, Inc., 1961), p. 66. This quotation summarized certain aspects of a study published in 1958: James Abegglen, *The Japanese Factory* (Glencoe, Ill.: The Free Press, 1958). Similar findings 10 years later indicated that the Japanese firm was still regarded as a "family," in which there is virtually a lifetime commitment of both rank-and-file workers and managers to the firm which they first join: M. Y. Yoshino, *Japan's Managerial System: Tradition and Innovation* (Cambridge, Mass.: M.I.T. Press, 1968), esp. pp. 229 ff. These, as well as other aspects of Japanese business organizations are discussed in an intercultural context in: William F. Whyte, *Organizational Behavior: Theory and Application* (Homewood, Ill.: Richard D. Irwin, Inc., 1969), pp. 742–56.

[9] "Productivity Push: Japanese Firms Spur Employees with Plans Rewarding Hard Work," *The Wall Street Journal*, August 18, 1969, pp. 1, 11.

Finally, personality is molded by the experiences which befall the individual during his life, some of which may be quite accidental. Traumatic war experiences may lead to serious emotional disturbances; or a chance meeting of a high school student with his congressman may serve to inspire this student to pursue a career in politics. Similar experiences, of course, may be reacted to quite differently by different individuals, for their impact is a function of the personality structure as it has been molded previously by constitutional, family, and cultural influences.

In viewing *any* of the determinants of personality, it is important to recognize their interdependence and not consider them as isolated influencing factors. For example, if a child with a high degree of mental capacity is encouraged by his parents and teachers to develop this ability, and is given the opportunity for a college education, he may become a highly successful professional man. If, on the other hand, his brightness is ridiculed by his parents, and his cleverness supported by his peers only when it is directed toward antisocial ends, he may engage in juvenile delinquency and ultimately become one of a prison's most "intelligent" inmates. Thus, no single determinant may be viewed as being *the cause* of one's personality. Rather the development of the individual's personality system must be considered as having been conditioned by a number of interdependent factors in mutual interaction with one other, in an open systems sense.

Personality Development

Although each individual is unique, the personality development of most psychologically healthy people in *our culture* seems to proceed in certain similar directions. As Chris Argyris has pointed out, individuals:

1. Tend to develop from a state of passivity as infants to a state of increasing activity as adults. . . .

2. Tend to develop from a state of dependence upon others as infants to a state of relative independence as adults. . . .

3. Tend to develop from being capable of behaving only in a few ways as an infant to being capable of behaving in many different ways as an adult. . . .

4. Tend to develop from having erratic, casual, shallow, quickly-dropped interests as an infant to having deeper interests as an adult. . . .

5. Tend to develop from having a short time perspective (i.e., the present largely determines behavior) as infant to a much longer time perspective as an adult. . . .

6. Tend to develop from being in a subordinate position in the family and society as an infant to aspiring to occupy an equal and/or superordinate position relative to their peers.

7. Tend to develop from a lack of awareness of self as an infant to an awareness of and control over self as an adult.[10]

As we shall note in a later section, many observers such as Argyris believe that the demands of formal business organizations placed upon the individual are in many cases incongruent with the adult modes of behavior described here.

Two other observations should be noted concerning the development of personality depending upon both constitutional and environmental factors. First, there are considerable differences in the extent to which various individuals develop along the lines suggested above. The reader has undoubtedly met adults who are highly dependent upon others, whose interests are shallow and quickly dropped, or who show little awareness of their own behavior. With their development having somehow been stunted, such individuals may find it difficult to assume job responsibilities and may present problems to the manager. Second, regardless of the degree to which an individual has developed, his basic personality pattern tends to remain relatively constant once he reaches adulthood, and is extremely difficult although not impossible to change. For example, the degree to which an individual feels secure in life usually does not vary greatly even in the face of considerable environmental change.

No matter what the level of security may be, it is difficult either to raise or to lower it. . . . we find some tendency to hang on to the life style in the healthy as well as in the unhealthy person. The person who tends to believe that all people are essentially good will show the same resistance to change of this belief as will the person who believes all people are essentially bad. . . .

Personality syndromes can sometimes maintain a relative constancy under the most surprising conditions of external change. There are many examples of the maintenance of security feelings in emigrés who have undergone the most grueling and harrowing experiences. Studies of morale in bombed areas also give us proof of the surprising resistance that most healthy people have to external horrors.[11]

The reason for such constancy is that the ways of perceiving, thinking, and behaving have been repeated so many times by the time people become adults that they become deeply ingrained habits. Or, in more theoretical terms, these steady state patterns have been *overlearned* to such an extent that resistance to their modification is very strong.

The difficulty of changing many of the adult's basic ways of behaving has important implications for management decision making. In per-

---

[10] Chris Argyris, *Personality and Organization* (New York: Harper & Row, 1957), p. 50.

[11] A. H. Maslow, *Motivation and Personality* (2d ed.; New York: Harper & Row, 1970), p. 309.

sonnel selection, managers should be wary of hiring an individual lacking the personality characteristics desired for a job in the pious hope that "he's basically a nice guy and perhaps somehow he'll change once he's employed with us"—for such changes are usually not forthcoming. Those responsible for management training and development programs have also found that inducing change in basic behavioral and attitudinal patterns is often very difficult.[12] Although much money is being spent for such efforts every year by industry, research has shown that managers exposed to many such programs may show little positive change in their behavior after the training; and in some cases, negative change occurs.[13]

We should emphasize that the above observations are not meant to imply that people's behavior does not change; for the individual's personality system is a dynamic open one, and all normal individuals learn new ways of doing things much of the time. Rather, we are indicating that most people's *basic* patterns of behavior and *fundamental* attitudes remain relatively constant and are difficult to alter.

NEED SATISFACTION, MOTIVATION, AND BEHAVIOR

Why do people behave the way they do? Why does one manager closely watch the office clock prior to the close of each working day and leave the job promptly at quitting time, while his colleague at the next desk puts in two or three additional hours of work every evening after everyone else has gone home? Why does one person strongly prefer working alone with figures and cost data while another cannot tolerate "being chained to a desk all day" and enjoys only work which calls for him to make a large number of daily contacts with other people? Why are some individuals "yes men" and afraid to express any disagreement with their bosses, while others are not at all reluctant to criticize their superiors?

The answers to such questions as these, are based partly upon the unique personality of the individual. In spite of such *differences*, how-

---

[12] One training methodology which has become widely used (but also controversial) in attempting to help managers (and others) improve their human skills in relating to other people is sensitivity training. Although sensitivity training programs vary in content and duration, central to them are largely unstructured face-to-face group learning sessions, commonly referred to as "T-Groups." For an extensive review of the literature on sensitivity training, see, for example, John P. Campbell and Marvin D. Dunnette, "Effectiveness of T-Group Experiences in Managerial Training and Development," *Psychological Bulletin*, 70 (August 1968), pp. 73–104.

[13] There are probably a number of reasons for such negative training results. In some cases, the training itself may be ill conceived. Or, from a systems view, when managers are exposed to a training program outside their organizational system and then return to their jobs and attempt to try out new ideas and ways of behavior learned in the program, these efforts may be rejected by other members of the organizational system who have not been exposed to the training. For a discussion of this problem in systems terms, see Paul S. Greenlaw, "Management Development: A Systems View," *Personnel Journal*, 43 (April 1964), p. 209.

ever, there are certain needs, satisfactions, motivational forces, and so forth, which—although varying in strength and specific behavioral expression—tend to be *common* to all individuals.

There is general agreement among psychologists that, with a few exceptions, all behavior is *motivated;* people have reasons for doing the things that they do, and that behavior is oriented toward meeting certain perceived goals and objectives. Such goal-directed behavior centers around the desire for *need satisfaction*. All individuals have certain needs for which they are continuously seeking satisfaction. Among the human needs which have been distinguished by psychologists are: hunger, thirst, sex, companionship and belonging, love, recognition, security and safety, achievement, power, knowledge, and self-realization. One way of viewing the relationship between needs and behavior is that the existence of unsatisfied needs produces tension in the individual and that the motivation underlying behavior is to reduce these tensions. Although need satisfaction is generally accepted as constituting the prime determinant of behavior, disagreement exists among psychologists as to the number of human needs which exist and the relative importance of each. Before presenting some behavioral models for viewing human needs useful for the manager, a few comments are in order about these differences of opinion.

Human Needs: Some Differing Views

Most classical economists and early contributors to the scientific management movement placed primary emphasis on the individual's *rational* pursuit of *economic* objectives. These views hold that since man consciously and rationally strives to maximize his economic gain or utility, a prime means of motivating individuals is by providing them with monetary incentives. Although money is undoubtedly an important motivator for most people,[14] practically all psychologists emphasize that individuals seek to satisfy needs other than purely economic ones. Further, as Freud was the first to publicize widely as a central tenet of psychological thought, our behavior is often not rational and, in fact, is sometimes even self-destructive—many times our actions are conditioned by unconscious motives of which we are not aware.[15]

Although psychologists generally agree that man is motivated by the desire to satisfy a number of needs, some of which he is not consciously aware of, differences of opinion exist as to the nature and relative importance of these needs. There is also disagreement and a paucity of

---

[14] We will discuss more fully the role of money as a motivator later in this chapter.

[15] Not widely known is the fact that the concept of the unconscious mind was developed and explored long before Freud. See Lancelot Law White, *The Unconscious before Freud* (New York: Basic Books, 1960).

research as to the extent to which cultural variables affect need satisfaction.[16] Some psychologists have attempted to reduce all human needs to a few underlying types. Freud, for example, emphasized two basic classes of needs—the life instinct and the death instinct;[17] Adler focused primary attention on the drive for power or mastery; and Horney considered as a primary motive "the need for security and safety in a potentially dangerous world." Other thinkers, however, have taken a more pluralistic position, emphasizing that there are several types of needs,[18] the satisfaction of which is a prime determinant of behavior. This latter approach appears a more useful one for the manager in understanding and analyzing human behavior in organizations. We will now turn our attention to three such pluralistic models or theories. The first of these is that developed by the psychologist, A. H. Maslow, in his work, *Motivation and Personality*.[19]

Maslow's Hierarchy of Needs

Maslow's theory of motivation stresses that individuals are motivated to satisfy several different kinds of needs, some of which are more *prepotent* than others. Prepotency as it is used here means taking precedence over, and Maslow's theory states that if a number of a person's needs are unsatisfied at any given time, satisfaction of the most prepotent ones will be more pressing than that of the others. Maslow postulates the following five classes of needs in order of their prepotence: (1) physiological; (2) safety; (3) belongingness and love; (4) esteem; and (5) self-actualization.[20]

This conceptual framework, referred to as the *hierarchy of needs* because of the different levels of prepotency indicated, is diagrammatically illustrated in Figure 5–1.

---

[16] See, for example, John W. Slocum, Jr., "A Comparative Study of the Satisfaction of American and Mexican Operatives," *Academy of Management Journal*, 14 (March 1971), pp. 89–97, esp. p. 90.

[17] See, for example, Calvin S. Hall, *A Primer and Freudian Psychology* (New York: The New American Library of American Literature, Inc., 1955), pp. 55 ff. Copyright 1954 by The World Publishing Company.

[18] See David C. McClelland, *Personality* (New York: The Dryden Press, 1951), pp. 402–3.

[19] Maslow, *Motivation and Personality*. There have been, as indicated above, many different pluralistic need conceptualizations formulated. For example, in Marvin D. Dunnette and Wayne K. Kirchner, *Psychology Applied to Industry* (New York: Appleton-Century-Crofts, 1965), the four motives of security, affiliation, competence, and achievement are considered "among the most useful for helping us understand human behavior as it has been observed in industry" (p. 142). We prefer Maslow's conceptualization primarily because of its dynamic, holistic focus, as will be emphasized later.

[20] Maslow also considers cognitive and aesthetic needs as important, although he does not formally fit them into the hierarchy framework. Maslow, *Motivation and Personality*, 1st ed., pp. 93–98.

Figure 5–1. Hierarchy of Needs

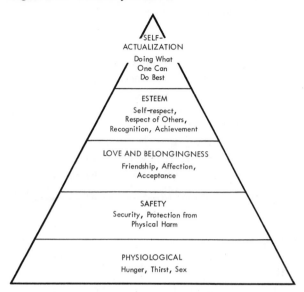

The prime prepotence of man's physiological needs is explained by Maslow as follows:

> Undoubtedly these physiological needs are the most prepotent of all needs. What this means specifically is that in the human being who is missing everything in life in an extreme fashion, it is most likely that the major motivation would be the physiological needs rather than any others. A person who is lacking food, safety, love, and esteem would probably hunger for food more strongly than for anything else.[21]

Once the individual's physiological needs are largely satisfied, the next level of needs in the hierarchy begins to emerge. These are the safety needs, among which are the avoidance of physical harm, illness, economic disaster, and so forth. In a similar manner, satisfaction of the safety needs gives rise to the emergence of belongingness and love needs, then the esteem needs, until the satisfaction of all of the above leads the individual to be primarily concerned with the highest level needs, those for self-actualization. Self-actualization is described by Maslow in the following terms:

> Even if all these needs . . . [the lower level needs] . . . are satisfied, we may still often (if not always) expect that a new discontent and restlessness will soon develop, unless the individual is doing what he is fitted for. A musician must make music, an artist must paint, a poet must write, if he is to be ultimately at peace with himself. What a man *can* be, he *must* be. This need we may call self-actualization.[22]

---

[21] Maslow, *Motivation and Personality*, 2d ed., p. 36.

[22] Maslow, *Motivation and Personality*, 2d ed., p. 46.

Several observations are necessary to clarify Maslow's needs hierarchy, which is central to, but only a part of, his overall conceptualization of personality. First, Maslow's multimotivational framework is *not* intended to be a static, rigid portrayal of the individual, in which each class of needs is unchanging and unrelated to the others. Rather, Maslow views human behavior in *dynamic* and *holistic* terms—i.e., the individual's personality may be conceived of as a dynamic system in which any given aspect of behavior can be understood only in light of his *whole* personality structure. Further, his emphasis on the emergence of higher level needs leading to self-actualization, places Maslow in the category of personality theorists who emphasize the dimension of steady state improvement (or growth) as discussed previously.

Second, in light of the dynamic, holistic nature of Maslow's needs hierarchy, it should *not* be inferred that only one class of needs exists for a person at any given time, and that once satisfied, it completely disappears giving way to the next higher level of needs. Rather, all levels of needs probably exist to some degree for the individual most of the time. Rarely, if ever, is any one need completely satisfied, at least for very long. Our hunger, as a simple example, may be fairly well satisfied after eating breakfast, only to emerge again before lunchtime (or perhaps to a lesser extent even sooner at the midmorning coffee break). It is also important to recognize that much behavior simultaneously satisfies several different needs, rather than just one. Participation at a luncheon with both his superior and peers, for example, may simultaneously satisfy a manager's hunger needs, his need to belong and be accepted by the group in which he works, or even as a possible means of letting his superior know about some important work in which he is engaged.

Third, it should be noted that, because of personality differences, there are certain exceptions to the relative degree of prepotency indicated by Maslow for each of the various levels of needs. That is, the physiological needs, although generally more prepotent than the safety needs, and so on up the hierarchy, are not always so. Among the more extreme of such exceptions is the behavior of those individuals who are martyrs, and are willing to sacrifice all other needs for the sake of an ideal or a religious, political, or social value.[23] The fasting of India's political and religious leader, Mahatma Gandhi, provides a good example of this type of behavior. Also, among more "normal" individuals, the relative importance of different classes of needs will vary depending on personality factors in mutual interaction with environmental variables. In the American economy, for example, the hunger and safety needs are generally fairly well satisfied and are not of the overriding concern as they are in some of the impoverished nations, in which getting enough

---

[23] For other exceptions see ibid., pp. 98–99.

to eat represents the primary focus of behavior for many. Or, in the American business firm, some individuals are strongly motivated by a need for recognition, while others are more interested in job security.

Fourth, viewing such individual differences in light of a central tenet of Maslow's theory of motvation—if a need is largely satisfied at any given point in time, it ceases to serve as an important motivator until reemerging again—is of considerable importance to managerial decision making. Organizations may be in a position to provide opportunities for the satisfaction of all five basic classes of employee needs, although the satisfaction of some is often difficult in work situations, as will be indicated in greater detail later. If management places emphasis on meeting needs which are not largely satisfied, rather than those already highly satisfied, its employees are likely to be more highly motivated to direct their efforts toward the goals of the organization. Thus, when management is interested in providing optimum motivational conditions for its employees, it is important that its decisions be based on the recognition that human behavior is primarily directed toward the fulfillment of *unsatisfied* needs.

Finally, some observations are in order concerning the validity and usefulness of Maslow's motivational framework. A number of research studies have explored various facets of Maslow's theory. Some have found that, in general, individuals tend to move toward placing greater emphasis on the satisfaction of higher level needs, as the lower level ones have become more fully satisfied—as the needs hierarchy predicts.[24] Conversely, a number of others have revealed findings not consistent with this tenet.[25] There are probably a number of reasons for such different findings. Among these, we consider especially important: (1) the inherent difficulties involved in the operational measurement of such a dynamic, holistic schema as Maslow's and, (2) the fact that various researchers have used different methodologies in their approaches to studying the needs-hierarchy framework.

There is also disagreement among scholars as to the practical usefulness of Maslow's conceptualization. Whyte, for example, considers such

---

[24] See, for example, M. Haire and J. Gottsdanker, "Factors Influencing Industrial Morale," *Personnel,* 27 (May 1951), pp. 445–54.

[25] See, for example, Douglas T. Hall and Knalil E. Nougaim, "An Examination of Maslow's Need Hierarchy in an Organizational Setting," *Organizational Behavior and Human Performance,* 3 (February 1968), pp. 12–35; James V. Clark, "Motivation in Work Groups: A Tentative View, *Human Organization,* 14 (Winter 1960–61), pp. 199–208; and R. A. Goodman, "On the Operationality of Maslow Need Hierarchy," *British Journal of Industrial Relations,* 6 (March 1968), pp. 511–58. Interestingly enough, these latter two findings, according to Chung, "seem to suggest that when an individual relatively satisfies a given need, he may move to satisfy higher level needs (not necessarily the next higher level need alone), and he may also move back down the scale to better satisfy lower level needs by upgrading the means of satisfying them." Kae H. Chung, "A Markov Chain Model of Human Needs: An Extension of Maslow's Need Theory," *Academy of Management Journal,* 12 (June 1969), p. 226.

schema as Maslow's as being "so broad and general that—except in extreme cases—they have little predictive value."[26] Sayles and Strauss, on the other hand, admit that there are both certain limitations to and operational difficulties involved in testing the needs-hierarchy hypothesis; but consider it useful in providing insights into human behavior, as long as other factors are considered.[27]

Notwithstanding such criticisms, Maslow's conceptualization continues not only to receive widespread attention in the management literature, but also to stimulate examination by newer research methodologies—e.g., through the application of one operations research technique, the Markov chain analysis.[28]

To summarize, we find the Maslow schema to be a useful conceptualization of motivation and behavior—all of which have both values and limitations, and still require further research to more fully explore their validity. We find the Maslow framework attractive because of its strong dynamic, holistic, systems orientation, which is highly congruent not only with our conception of personality, but also with the systems approach.

Herzberg's Duality Theory

The second motivational theory which we will examine is the so-called Herzberg "duality theory." Traditionally (and in the Maslow model) "satisfaction" and "dissatisfaction" were viewed as representing opposite extremes of a continuum; with a middle point in which the individual is neither satisfied nor dissatisfied, but neutral. For example, with respect to specific organizational variables, excellent opportunities for advancement, good pay, and high-quality supervision would represent factors contributing to satisfaction, whereas conversely, poor advancement, pay, and supervision would contribute to an individual's being dissatisfied.

In 1959, this conventional view was challenged by Frederick Herzberg and others,[29] and a new conception of satisfaction was postulated, often referred to as the dual-factor or duality theory. The basic assumptions of this theory are as follows. First, the factors contributing to job satisfaction are separate and distinct from those that lead to job dissatisfaction. That is: (1) the presence of certain job factors contribute to job satisfaction, while their absence is perceived as a "neutral" condition (*not* dissatisfaction); and conversely, (2) the presence of certain other job fac-

---

[26] Whyte, *Organizational Behavior*, p. 138.

[27] Leonard R. Sayles and George Strauss, *Human Behavior in Organizations* (Englewood Cliffs, N.J.: Prentice-Hall, Inc., 1966), p. 20.

[28] Chung, *A Markov Chain Model*, pp. 223–34.

[29] F. W. Herzberg, B. Mausner, and B. Snyderman, *The Motivation to Work* (2d ed.; New York: John Wiley & Sons, Inc., 1959).

tors leads to dissatisfaction; while their absence leads to a neutrally perceived condition, but *not* to satisfaction.

Among those variables considered as associated with satisfaction ("satisfiers") are primarily ones *intrinsic* to the individual's job—e.g., achievement, recognition, and opportunity for growth and self-actualization. Conversely, the "dissatisfiers" (sometimes called "hygienic" factors) are primarily ones extrinsic to a person's job, such as company policies, salary, and working conditions.

Second, the duality theory postulates that the satisfiers are effective in contributing toward the motivation of individuals toward better performance; but the hygienic variables are not. For example, greater opportunities for self-actualization would serve as an effective motivator; while improving poor working conditions (a hygienic variable) would not.

Since its initial postulation, the duality theory has led to both numerous research studies aimed at its confirmation, and to considerable debate and criticism.[30] Some of the research carried out has tended to substantiate the duality concept, while other studies have not. In surveying numerous of these studies, Behling et al. have concluded that those studies using Herzberg's research *methodology* have "almost without exception" given results supporting the duality theory; whereas, with "a similar degree of certainty," studies not utilizing this methodology have supported the single-continuum concept.[31]

The implications of the duality theory for management decision making are not certain at the time of this writing. As all theories of motivation and need satisfaction (including Maslow's), it has been criticized as being overly general. Further, as indicated above it has been considered as method-bound. This research does highlight the fact that the numerous, complex, interrelated determinants of human behavior are very difficult to measure; and the utilization of different measuring instruments will often lead to different conclusions. On the positive side, Herzberg's point that job factors contributing to the satisfaction of higher level needs (e.g., achievement and self-actualization) are important motivators is congruent with the thinking of other theorists (regardless of the validity of the duality theory *in toto*). On the whole, however,

---

[30] For a critical appraisal of the duality theory, see, for example, Robert J. House and Laurence A. Widgor, "Herzberg's Dual-Factor Theory of Job Satisfaction and Motivation: A Review of the Evidence and a Criticism," *Personnel Psychology,* 20 (Winter 1967), pp. 369–89; and Behling et al., "The Herzberg Controversy: A Critical Reappraisal," *Academy of Management Journal,* 11 (March 1968), pp. 99–108.

[31] Ibid., p. 106. Essentially Herzberg's methodology involved a semistructured interview approach, in which respondents were asked to recall any "critical incidents" which had been associated with either their satisfaction or dissatisfaction on the job. Conversely, the studies not supporting the duality theory generally have utilized more highly structured techniques of gathering information.

there seems to be an increasing degree of disenchantment with the duality theory.[32]

The Vroom Model

Victor Vroom has developed a motivational model which has been referred to as "preference expectation" or "instrumentality-valence" theory.[33] This model involves mathematical manipulations (unlike Maslow and Herzberg), and has been modified by others[34]—both of which aspects of the model are beyond the scope of this text. Basically, with respect to motivation, Vroom views the individual as a decision maker facing various courses of action from amongst which he must make a choice; and the model is designed to *predict* which choice the *individual* will make. Vroom has developed a set of terminology describing his model as follows:

1. *Expectancy* is the individual's *perceived* or subjective probability that an action (or activity) which he undertakes will lead to some (first-level) outcome or goal—e.g., the perceived probability of a production worker that his exerting a great deal of effort will result in his attaining a high level of production.

2. A *first-level outcome* is a goal which it is perceived will follow from successfully accomplishing the effort of activity undertaken—e.g., receiving more money for the high level of production in the above illustration.

3. *Instrumentality* is the *perceived* expectation that achieving the first-level outcome will lead to a *desired* second-level outcome (or goal)—i.e., the increased money received (first-level outcome) leading to more self-esteem, the ability to purchase a color television set, etc. Thus, first-level outcomes in the Vroom model serve as means for achieving second-level outcomes.

4. *Valence* refers to the strength of the desire (or need strength) the individual has for a particular outcome.[35] Obviously, individuals have valences for the second-level outcomes or goals. In Vroom's model, the valence of each first-level outcome to an individual is a continuously increasing function

---

[32] For example, John P. Campbell et al., *Managerial Behavior, Performance, and Effectiveness* (New York: McGraw-Hill Book Co., 1970), take the position "that the two factor-theory has now served its purpose [because it has stimulated considerable controversy and research] and should be altered or respectfully laid to rest" (p. 381).

[33] Victor H. Vroom, *Work and Motivation* (New York: John Wiley & Sons, Inc., 1964).

[34] For a modified Vroom model, see, for example, Campbell et al., *Managerial Behavior,* pp. 345–48.

[35] It should be noted that valences (or need strengths) may be either positive or negative (or zero). For example, the production worker in our illustration may not want to earn more money because such a goal would violate norms of the group in which he is working; or his level of performance may in no way effect any of his goals.

of the sum of the products of all second-level outcomes and his perceptions of its instrumentality for the attainment of the second-level outcomes.[36]

In short, the Vroom model assumes: (1) that an understanding of motivation must consider not only the goals "people hope to accomplish but the extent to which they believe that their own actions are instrumental in producing the outcomes they prefer";[37] and (2) that the individual will be motivated to choose taking actions which are perceived to be most desirable to him in terms of valence or meeting his need strength. The relationships among the above variables are illustrated in Figure 5–2.

Figure 5–2. The Vroom Model

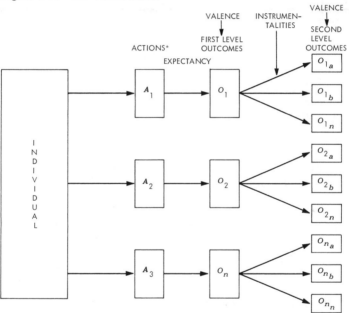

* Valences possible.

Several other observations are in order concerning the Vroom model. First, as may be noted from Figure 5–2, valences are possible not only for the first- and second-level outcomes, but also for the actions themselves. The reason for this is that there may be intrinsic job satisfaction (or somewhat similarly in Maslow's terms, self-actualization) attained simply as a result of the act of performing well itself. Second, how may the Vroom model be evaluated and compared with the Maslow

---

[36] Paraphrased from Vroom, *Work and Motivation*, p. 17.

[37] Alan C. Filley and Robert J. House, *Managerial Process and Organizational Behavior* (Glenview, Ill.: Scott, Foresman & Company, 1969), pp. 360–61.

and Herzberg theories? With respect to these questions, it should be pointed out that Vroom's model is not incongruent with these other theories. In both the actions the individual chooses to achieve outcomes, and the outcomes, themselves, can meet any of Maslow's needs or maybe one of Herzberg's "satisfiers." Unlike both the Maslow and Herzberg theories, however, Vroom's model attempts to *predict which decisions individuals will make* in a motivational context. Considering the emphasis on decision making in this text, it is this feature of the Vroom model that leads the authors to believe that it may ultimately be found to be the best of the three models under consideration. Although the model yet has not been extensively researched, a few studies have lent it empirical support. For example, in one study utilizing the model,[38] it was found that worker productivity was significantly related to supervisor support and money, and almost significantly to group acceptance; but not to fringe benefits and promotions. These findings appear logical in light of the Vroom model since there were relationships between the workers' performance-instrumentality-goal sequence and money, supervisory support, and to a lesser extent group acceptance; but *regardless* of worker productivity, the employees would still obtain the *same* fringe benefits and stand about the *same chance* of being promoted, since promotion was based primarily on seniority.

In spite of its promise, the Vroom model (and its variants) still poses certain problems. Two strong supporters of the model, for example, have pointed out that:

> We do not know all of the goals that have positive valence in a work situation. We do not know how much of a difference in force is necessary before one kind of outcome is chosen over another. Nor do we know what combination of measures yields the best prediction in a given situation. The answers to these and other questions await further research.[39]

Lack of Need Satisfaction: Frustration

As Maslow's model, in particular, emphasizes, unsatisfied needs produce tensions in the individual, and behavior is motivated to relieve these tensions. When an individual is unable to satisfy his needs, and thus reduce tension, he experiences *frustration*. The student who studies conscientiously every week only to flunk out of college at the end of his freshman year provides an example of a person who would be quite frustrated. His goal, that of receiving a college degree, the attainment

---

[38] Jay Galbraith and L. L. Cummings, "An Empirical Investigation of the Motivational Determinants of Task Performance: Interactive Effects between Instrumentality—Valence and Motivation—Ability," *Organizational Behavior and Human Performance*, 2 (1967), pp. 237–57.

[39] J. G. Hunt and J. W. Hill, "The New Look in Motivational Theory for Organizational Research," *Human Organization*, 28 (Summer 1969), p. 107. Reproduced by the permission of the Society for Applied Anthropology.

of which would have represented the satisfaction of many needs, such as status, prestige, greater earning power and pleasing his parents, has been blocked. Although most of us hopefully do not experience such serious frustrations most of the time, all of us are continuously frustrated to one degree or another, for our needs are never completely satisfied.

People react to frustration in different ways, just as the importance of different needs varies from person to person. Sometimes individuals react to frustration in a positive manner—that is, they search for realistic and constructive approaches to meet their unsatisfied needs. In other cases, however, when frustrated, people attempt to protect themselves from a threatening situation by evoking *defense mechanisms*. We will now examine each of these two kinds of reactions to frustration.

Constructive Behavior. Relatively little needs to be said about constructive problem-solving approaches since we are all familiar with this form of behavior. An employee frustrated because promotional opportunities in his company are not open to him because his education is limited may work for a college degree by taking evening courses at a local college. An individual who fails to achieve the recognition for his work which he desires may increase his effort on the job. In order to satisfy unmet belonging needs and gain acceptance from his fellow workers, an employee may conform to the values and standards of the work group of which he is a member.[40] These are but a few of the wide variety of constructive strategies which individuals may employ to satisfy needs and lessen frustration.

Defensive Behavior. When need satisfaction is blocked and frustration is experienced, a person may react by evoking one or more defense mechanisms instead of adopting constructive, realistic approaches to solving his problems. We will discuss this phenomena in somewhat greater detail than we did constructive behavior, not because it is more important or more common, but rather because it is not as generally well understood.

The concept of the defense mechanism appeared early in the writings of Freud.[41] The following summary of Freud's conception of the defense mechanism will serve to clarify its nature:

One of the major tasks imposed upon the ego is that of dealing with the threats and dangers that beset the person and arouse anxiety. The ego may try to master danger by adopting realistic problem-solving methods, or it

---

[40] Such behavior may be viewed as constructive from the viewpoint of the individual's meeting his needs; yet dysfunctional from the point of view of the organization—e.g., a worker's joining his work group to press management for higher wages may both help him meet his belongingness needs and lead to better pay, but at the same time be detrimental to management. We will discuss work group values and standards in greater detail in Chapter 7.

[41] For a discussion of the development of the defense mechanism concept, see Ruth L. Munroe, *Schools of Psychoanalytic Thought* (New York: The Dryden Press, 1955), pp. 90–93.

may attempt to alleviate anxiety by using methods that deny, falsify, or distort reality and that impede the development of personality. The latter methods are called *defense mechanisms* of the ego.[42]

All of us employ defense mechanisms to one degree or another. As Freud has hypothesized, they serve an important protective function in the development of the individual, especially when we are young and are not strong enough to face up to all of the demands that reality imposes upon us by rational means.[43] Or, in systems terms, the defense mechanisms essentially serve to maintain a particular steady state level of behavior. As the psychologically healthy individual matures, however, he becomes more and more able to cope realistically with the demands imposed on him, and his need for irrational defenses decreases. Those adults whose behavior continues to be dominated by defense mechanisms find it difficult to adapt to their work, responsibilities, and other people.

There are several different types of defense mechanisms which have been identified by psychologists. Among the more common of these are the following:

Rationalization. Rationalization refers to excusing one's behavior by presenting a reason for it which the individual sees as less ego destructive or more socially acceptable than the real reason. An employee's lack of proficiency on the job may be perceived as "poor working conditions," "low-quality materials," or "worn tools" rather than his own ineptitude which would be ego-deflating for him to admit to others.

Projection. Projection involves attributing one's own feelings or the reasons for one's own behavior to someone else. An employee may intensely dislike a colleague and attempt to make him look bad in the eyes of others whenever possible. At the same time, however, he may feel very guilty about this hostility, and attempt to justify it in terms of "my colleague is always out to get me." Projection of this type serves the purpose of changing an internal danger (one's own hostile impulse) which is difficult to cope with to an external danger (his dislike for me) which is much easier to handle.[44] Or, to put it another way, it

---

[42] Hall, *Primer of Freudian Psychology*, p. 85. Copyright 1954 by the World Publishing Company. Reprinted by arrangement with the World Publishing Company, Cleveland and New York. We should also note that the defense mechanisms must be evoked unconsciously if they are to be effective in reducing an individual's anxiety.

[43] Or, as Hall summarized Freud's thinking: "Why then do defenses exist if they are so harmful in so many ways? The reason for their existence is a developmental one. The infantile ego is too weak to integrate and synthesize all of the demands that are made upon it. Ego defenses are adopted as protective measures. If the ego cannot reduce anxiety by rational means, it has to utilize . . . [the defense mechanisms]." Ibid., p. 96. At the expense of considerable over-simplification the term "ego" here may be considered synonymous with the "self." Copyright 1954 by the World Publishing Co., and reprinted by arrangement with the World Publishing Company.

[44] Hall, ibid., pp. 89–90.

is less ego deflating to view someone else as trying to make life difficult for us than to think of ourselves as hostile individuals.

Reaction Formation. Reaction formation is a defense mechanism aimed at avoiding an unpleasant situation. "Here the person is so anxious to prevent the occurrence of the painful situation that he does the direct opposite of the thing he wishes to avoid."[45] In our previous illustration, for example, the employee may have felt so guilty about his hostility toward his colleague that instead of trying to make the colleague look bad, he expressed nothing but praise and admiration for him.[46] The purpose of such reactive behavior would have been to *conceal* the real feelings of hostility about which so much guilt existed.

Repression. Individuals sometimes *repress* unpleasant experiences or feelings from the conscious to the unconscious mind as a means of denying their existence. An occasion on which we were severely criticized by our parents (or boss), feelings of jealousy of which we are guilty, or fears experienced at one time or another may be "forgotten" because they are too painful to remember. Or, we sometimes find ourselves forgetting to take care of unpleasant tasks—they simply "slip our mind."

Regression. When frustrated, people sometimes revert back to earlier, more childish forms of behavior as a means of escaping from the unpleasantness of reality. This phenomenon is referred to as regression. One of the more common forms of regression of concern to the manager is horseplay on the job. Although a certain amount of regressive behavior may help to relieve tensions in stressful work situations, immoderate horseplay may not only interfere with productivity but also lead to accidents and injuries.

Aggression. A common reaction to frustration is aggression. In fact, some authorities believe that "the existence of frustration always leads to some form of aggression."[47] Essentially, aggression involves an attack (physical or nonphysical) with the intent of injuring the object of the attack. Sometimes aggression may be directed toward the person whom we perceive as the source of our frustration, e.g., a boss who is a perfectionist may engage in a bitter diatribe against a subordinate who has made a minor clerical error. In other cases, an individual's aggression may be *displaced* (or projected), i.e., directed toward a person or object other than the source of the frustration. The manager who comes to work after a heated argument with his wife at the breakfast table and finds fault with everything his subordinates do provides an example

---

[45] McClelland, *Personality*, p. 508.

[46] Expressed admiration such as this which is a product of reaction formation may be distinguished from real admiration in that it is exaggerated behavior. "Reactive love protests too much; it is overdone, extravagant, showy, and affected. It is counterfeit, and its falseness, like the overacting of the player-queen in Hamlet, is usually easily detected." Hall, *Primer of Freudian Psychology*, p. 92.

[47] John Dollard et al., *Frustration and Aggression* (paperbound ed.; New Haven, Conn.: Yale University Press, 1961), p. 1.

of displaced aggression. In addition, aggression is sometimes directed against oneself. In its milder form, the self-aggression may be simply denying ourself some pleasure because we have done something "wrong"; at its extreme, the self-punishment may manifest itself in suicide.

Avoidance (*Withdrawal*).   Sometimes people defend themselves against a painful reality by avoiding or withdrawing from those situations which are laden with frustration for them. Avoidance manifested in excessive absenteeism or tardiness, or a high turnover rate is not uncommon among workers holding jobs which provide little need satisfaction.

To summarize, many forms of defensive behavior such as aggressive acts or horseplay (regression) are basically nonproductive in orientation, and their occurrence on the job may interfere with the attainment of organizational objectives. All people rely on defense mechanisms to at least some extent. Thus, such behavior can never be completely eliminated in business organizations. Nor should attempts always be made to do, since, as indicated earlier, mild forms of regression, for example, may help to reduce work tensions. However, when defensive behavior is interfering with the attainment of organizational objectives, its occurrence may sometimes be prevented by managerial decisions which provide conditions under which employees will be able to satisfy more of their needs (and, thus, not experience considerable frustration) in the performance of their work. We will explore a number of decision approaches with this objective in mind in later sections of this book. Further, the manager may be able to deal with employees who do exhibit defensive behavior in such a way as to help overcome the frustrations of which the behavior is symptomatic. In many cases, counseling with an employee may enable the manager to pinpoint the source of the frustration, and provide insight as to possible actions which may be taken to help overcome the problem. For example, the manager's counseling with a subordinate who has become apathetic toward his job since being passed over for a promotion recently may lead to a training and development program for the man which will place him in a much stronger position to be considered for the next promotional opening.

Unmotivated Behavior

Although most behavior can be thought of as being motivated by the existence of unsatisfied needs, there are certain exceptions. Maslow, for example, has distinguished goal-oriented behavior from expressive or stylistic (style of life) behavior which is "simply a reflection of the personality."[48] In the latter category is included such behavior as the random movements of a child, the way in which a person walks, the

---

[48] Maslow, *Motivation and Personality*, p. 103.

pitch of an individual's voice, or one's preference for one type of music over another. Some expressive behavior, however, may be partially conditioned by a person's need structure. An executive may choose to play golf rather than tennis, for instance, to gain the acceptance of his superior who regularly shoots in the low 80s.

Behavior is also sometimes motivated by needs which *no longer exist.* This phenomenon has been referred to as *functional autonomy.*[49] To satisfy our needs at one time in our lives, we engage in certain types of behavior; we then continue these patterns of behavior even though they no longer serve to satisfy a currently existing need. The behavior which was once a *means* to an end now becomes an end in itself, largely through habit. Many examples of functional autonomy exist which may be of concern to the manager. An individual who was given high praise as a child by his parents for performing to perfection may, as an adult worker, be compelled to perfectionism even though his output and earnings suffer accordingly. A person who was mistreated by his father as a youngster may show hostility toward his present superior even though the latter does not mistreat him and such behavior is decidedly detrimental to his best interests. This example illustrates a point stressed earlier—our adult personalities are conditioned considerably by our experiences early in life, especially within the family.

Personality Differences and Motivation

In the above sections, primary emphasis was placed on certain common motivational dimensions of the human personality system, with only passing references to individual differences with respect to motivation (although as pointed out, the Vroom model provides for consideration of such differences). In this section, some additional observations will first be made concerning personality differences and motivation. Then, to illustrate more fully how specific needs may vary from individual to individual, we will examine some research findings delving into one of the needs explicitly included in Maslow's framework—the need to achieve, or the so-called achievement motive.

Personality Differences and Motivation: Some General Observations. As indicated previously, the relative strength and importance of differing needs do vary considerably from individual to individual depending upon one's personality structure, and only the Vroom model is geared to predicting individual choice behavior. Some people have a very strong need for security, which may reflect itself in an intense desire for a job which offers steady employment above all else. On the other hand, those individuals whose need for security is fairly well satisfied, but for whom esteem is highly important, may be primarily interested in work for which they can gain considerable recognition.

---

[49] This term was coined by Gordon W. Allport. See his *Personality* (New York: Henry Holt and Co., 1937), pp. 191 ff. for a fuller discussion of the concept.

Also, the strategies which an individual develops and employs for attempting to gain the satisfaction of a particular need is also a function of his personality. One person may strive to meet his esteem needs by gaining recognition on the job, while another may seek to meet the same needs by taking an active role in some community activity, such as the Boy Scouts. Or, in the choice of one's occupation, the boy who finds that he has an exceptional ability as an athlete may decide that he can gain the most recognition and earn the most money by becoming a professional baseball player, while the student highly proficient in mathematics may decide that he can meet these same needs best by entering the field of operations research.

Similarly, the manner in which a person reacts to and handles frustration is also a function of his personality. Individuals differ as to: (1) the kinds of situations in which they experience frustration, (2) the degree to which they evoke defense mechanisms when confronted with frustration, and (3) the kinds of defense mechanisms resorted to under different conditions. Some persons seem to have a relatively high *frustration tolerance,* while others do not. Some managers, for example, are able to function effectively without becoming emotionally upset in jobs in which considerable pressure exists, while others become easily upset and find emotional control difficult in such situations.

Finally, psychologists have emphasized that different individuals have different *levels of aspiration* depending upon the strength of their needs. One manager may never be very satisfied until he achieves the presidency of his firm, while another may aspire only to a middle-management position.

The Need to Achieve.   One need, the strength of which varies considerably among individuals depending on their personality structure (in mutual interaction with environmental factors), is the so-called achievement motive.

This achievement motive, which has been studied extensively by David C. McClelland and others,[50] basically represents one subset of Maslow's total class of esteem needs. Research exploring this motive has indicated that the high achievement-oriented individual tends to possess the following characteristics:

1.   The satisfaction he obtains from achieving is derived primarily from the *act of achieving itself;* rather than from any external rewards obtained from achieving, such as money.
2.   He wants to assume a considerable degree of personal responsibility for solving the problems with which he is faced.

---

[50] See, for example, David C. McClelland et al., *The Achievement Motive* (New York: Appleton-Century-Crofts, 1953); David C. McClelland, *The Achieving Society* (Princeton, N.J.: D. Van Nostrand Co., Inc., 1961); J. W. Atkinson and N. T. Feathers (eds.), *A Theory of Achievement Motivation* (New York: John Wiley & Sons, Inc., 1966).

3. He tends to set *moderate* achievement goals involving calculated risks, *avoiding*

   a) Work assignments (or other responsibilities) which are too easy to accomplish, because they do not present him with much of a challenge to achieve, and

   b) Responsibilities which are considered to be too difficult, because he perceives that his probabilities of successfully achieving their accomplishment are too low.

4. He has a strong need for *concrete feedback* as to how well he has done, so that he will know to what extent he has met (or is meeting) his achievement goals.

Given these characteristics, money does not serve as a motivator for the high achiever; rather it represents one form of the *concrete feedback* so strongly needed by him. Or, as McClelland has put it: "Money is not the incentive to effort but rather the *measure of its success* for the real entrepreneur."[51]

What are the implications of the research on achievement motivation for management decision making? There appears to be increasing agreement that higher achievement motivation may be stimulated for some individuals by managerial decisions which foster favorable environmental conditions in organizations. There are, however, two basic problems involved in doing so. These are determining:

1. Just how important achievement is for any particular organizational member, and

2. What kinds of goals are perceived by any given person to be important to him and at the same time reasonably attainable.[52]

In light of the personality characteristics associated with achievement motivation, some of the specific ways which have been suggested for stimulating achievement motivation in organizations are as follows:

1. Developing job and task structures in which individuals can work toward moderate risk goals—i.e., those which are perceived to be neither too easy nor difficult to achieve.

2. Making standards of performance expected by the organization explicit, and providing individuals with concrete fedback relative to their achievement of, and progress in achieving, organizational goals.

3. Developing an organizational environment in which the assumption of personal responsibility is encouraged.[53]

---

[51] David C. McClelland, "Achievement Motivation Can Be Developed," *Harvard Business Review*, 43 (November–December 1965), p. 7. The italics are ours.

[52] Drawn from Dunnette and Kirchner, *Psychology Applied to Industry*, p. 142.

[53] Drawn from Robert A. Stringer, Jr., "Achievement Motivation and Management Control," *Personnel Administration*, 29 (November–December 1966), pp. 3–5.

In short, research has pinpointed a cluster of personality characteristics associated with high-achievement motivation. Although there are still problems to be faced in applying these findings to industry, certain types of management decisions appear to have promise in helping stimulate higher achievement motivation for at least some organizational members.

LEARNING AND BEHAVIOR

In the preceding sections, numerous references were made to learning. We indicated that although certain capabilities and predispositions are inborn, much of our behavior is learned. It was also pointed out that although many of our basic personality patterns have been learned so thoroughly by the time we reach adulthood that their modification is difficult, we all continue to learn new ways of behaving throughout life.

An important task of management is to provide the conditions under which members of the organization will be able to learn the most effective and appropriate ways of behaving in order to meet the firm's objectives. The new employee in the organization must become familiar with company rules, regulations, and policies and must master the skills called for on his job. In our current era of rapid change, members of the organization are continually being compelled to respond to new technological developments, work processes, and competitive conditions. Crucial to the manager as he prepares himself for and assumes positions calling for greater responsibility in the organization are the development of greater knowledge and the learning of new skills and ways of behaving.

In this section, we will: (1) provide a brief discussion of the meaning of "learning"; (2) examine some of the more important conditions for effective learning; and (3) give attention to the use of "learning curves" for managerial decision making.

The Nature of Learning

In very simple terms, learning involves establishing for the individual (or organism) a connection (or association) between a stimulus and a response, where previously no such connection existed. That is, when an organism is exposed to a stimulus (or input) which evokes a response, representing some change in its behavior or attitudes, one may say that learning has taken place. For example, if a new employee on a production line is exposed to the fact (stimulus) that using the safety guard provided on his machine will negate the possibility that his hands will be injured, and uses the guard consistently (response), one may say that he has learned to be a "safer" worker.

Much complex learning, of course, involves more elements (or variables) than the simple stimulus-organism-response sequence indicated above. For instance, the role of understanding and insight as key variables in learning has been emphasized by many psychologists. Just how important such variables are is still open to disagreement among learning theorists. The field of learning theory is broad and complex; and different views have been taken as to exactly how different types of learning take place. To delve into these is beyond the scope if this text.[54] There are, however, a number of fairly widely accepted "principles of learning," that can be of value to the manager not only in the design of formal training programs, but also in his day-to-day assignment and development of subordinates. We will now turn our attention to some of the more important of these.

Basic Principles of Learning

Capacity of the Learner. Basic to deciding which individuals should learn what materials, skills, and so forth is a recognition of the capacity of the learner—one subset of his total personality system. Highly intelligent and educated people can master intellectual materials that those possessing a considerable lesser degree of these characteristics cannot; individuals with a high degree of manual dexterity can learn certain skills that those persons whose "fingers are all thumbs" could not. Recognition of this fact has obvious implications for personnel selection, promotion, and the assignment of work. Considerable attention has been given by many business firms to the measurement of the individual's learning capacity by means of psychological testing.

Repetition. Repeated practice is important for the effective learning of skills and certain types of factual information. The value of repetition has been recognized and its use incorporated into many training efforts in business organizations. For example, the Job Instruction Training (J.I.T.) method—which has been widely used in training employees in new job skills—prescribes that the trainer should demonstrate the job at least twice, and that the trainee should perform the job at least twice under the guidance of the trainer. How much repetition will be required in any specific training situation, depends on both environmental variables (e.g., task difficulty), and the individual's personality (e.g., his capacities and motivation).

Knowledge of Results. In learning, it is important for us to know how well or how poorly we are doing. Feedback of information as to the effectiveness of our learning enables us to correct our errors and

---

[54] A classic work delving into learning theory is Ernest R. Hilgard and Gordon Bower, *Theories of Learning* (3d ed.; New York: Appleton-Century-Crofts, 1966). For a simpler overview of some of the basic concepts and view of different schools of learning, see Ernest R. Hilgard, *Introduction to Psychology* (3d ed.; New York: Harcourt, Brace & World, Inc., 1962), chap. 9.

modify our behavior in the desired directions. The feedback will be most effective if it is immediate, for unless we correct our errors at once, we may continue learning the wrong things, and thus develop bad habits which may be difficult to unlearn. Knowledge of results and corrective feedback as a basis for modifying behavior are important not only in the learning of specific tasks, but are also central to organizational controls. In fact, the control process, which will be considered later in this book, may be thought of as a learning mechanism. Performance standards are established, information is fed back to the decision maker which enables him to compare actual with planned performance, and efforts then may be undertaken to correct for any variance which exists among the two.

Motivation. As the needs theory which was discussed earlier would indicate, learning for which there is a strong motivation is generally more effective than relatively unmotivated learning. However, motivation that is too strong or intense, may be accompanied by a high level of anxiety or fear that interferes with the learning process. Thus, moderate, rather than excessive, motivation is often more effective in many types of learning. Somewhat relatedly, learning which is motivated by the desire to obtain a reward seems more effective than that which is undertaken in order to avoid punishment. These observations raise serious questions as to the effectiveness of excessive supervisory pressures, under which emphasis is placed on the fear of losing one's job as a means of motivation.

Reinforcement. In the above paragraph, the notion of reward in learning was mentioned. Basic to learning and related to motivation is the need for the learning to be *reinforced.* That is, the individual must be rewarded in some way when he evokes the correct response(s) to stimuli in any learning situation. Such rewards may be either tangible or intangible—e.g., either praise and encouragement by his supervisor or an opportunity for promotion to a higher skilled job may serve as reinforcing mechanisms for a worker learning new skills correctly.

Participation and Involvement. It is generally more effective for an individual to participate in and become actively involved in the learning rather than simply assuming a passive role in the training. In learning a new job skill, for example, simply observing someone else's performance is of limited value by itself. If the trainee has an opportunity to perform the skill himself, more rapid learning will take place. Similarly, the neophyte manager will probably never learn to be an effective decision maker simply by watching his superior. He will learn faster if given the opportunity to participate actively in the decision making.

Realistic Goal Setting. In Chapter 2, we indicated the inappropriateness of organization objectives which are either too easy to accomplish or at the other extreme impossible to attain. Similarly, it is important in learning for realistic goals to be set by both the trainer and trainee. If goals are set too high, the learner will experience frustration and failure. On the other hand, goals which are too easily met will provide little learning challenge to the individual.

In the above paragraphs we have indicated some of the conditions under which individuals tend to learn new ways of behaving most effectively. As may be inferred from these comments, effective learning conditions in organizations may be influenced by a number of variables, such as supervisory behavior, organizational arrangements, and the types of rewards and/or punishments provided by the organization. We will explore these variables further with respect not only to learning but also to many other facets of human behavior in succeeding chapters.

Learning Curves

Over the years, many different learning curves have been developed. These show the relationship between: (1) improved performance; and (2) the duration of training, or the number of learning trials over time. Some of the work done on learning curves has been oriented primarily toward theoretical research objectives in psychology; other such efforts have focused their basic attention on logarithmic mathematical models for managerial decision making;[55] while still others have been based on empirical employee performance data. It is this latter type which will be discussed in this section.

Learning curves derived empirically from output records of employees have been used for many years in helping to make managerial decisions in industry—especially with jobs involving sensorimotor skills.[56] Frequently, in this type of learning curve application, output records of a number of employees as they are learning a new job are plotted over time, and these data are smoothed into a curve, which can later serve as a standard of "average" learning performance for the job.[57] One such hypothetical curve is shown in Figure 5–3.

[55] For more detailed information on the theoretical psychological learning curves, see, for example, W. K. Estes, "The Statistical Approach to Learning Theory," in S. Koch (ed.), *Psychology: A Study of a Science* (New York: McGraw-Hill Book Co., 1959), Vol. 2. Another basic work on statistical and mathematical learning theory in the field of psychology is Robert R. Bush and Frederick Mosteller, *Stochastic Models for Learning* (New York: John Wiley & Sons, Inc., 1955). For more information on the logarithmic mathematical models, see, for example, Rocco Carzo and John Y. Yanouzas, *Formal Organization: A Systems Approach* (Homewood, Ill.: Richard D. Irwin, Inc., 1967), chap. 10.

[56] A sensorimotor skill has been defined as one in which "muscular movement is prominent, but under sensory control"—e.g., a lathe operator following a blueprint and being required to stay within prescribed tolerances in his work. Hilgard, *Introduction to Psychology*, p. 268.

[57] In such cases, a single curve, showing average (or mean) learning performance for previous workers may be utilized. It is often more desirable, however, to develop additional curves from the sample or group of workers from whose performance the data were derived, showing some measure of dispersion of learning—e.g., ones depicting percentile ranges, or performance represented by one standard deviation from the mean. See, for example, Joseph Tiffin and Ernest J. McCormick, *Industrial Psychology* (5th ed.; Englewood Cliffs, N.J.: Prentice-Hall, Inc., 1965), p. 270.

Figure 5–3. A Representative Empirically Developed Type of Learning Curve

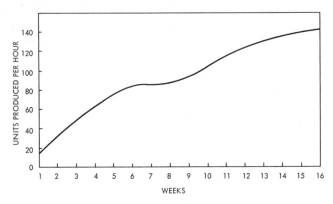

The shape of these curves will vary from task to task, depending upon its nature. However, generally:

1. Output tends to increase at a diminishing rate, and
2. Primarily for certain types of complex skills, there are periods in which no learning takes place—as, for example in weeks 5–7 in Figure 5–3. These periods are referred to as *plateaus*.[58]

Having available such learning curve data for various jobs can often be of considerable value in managerial decision making. For example, output data for an individual newly assigned to a job may be compared, during his training period, with the empirically derived "average" learning curve performance of previous workers. If the individual's rate of learning is considerably above average, it may indicate that he is "over-qualified" for the job. In such cases, depending on his motivation, management's needs, union constraints, and so forth, it may be desirable to consider him for reassignment to a more highly skilled job.

Conversely, if a new worker's output is increasing at a much slower rate than the average learning curve performance for his job, this comparative analysis might suggest: (1) that the worker does not have the skills to learn the job, and should be reassigned to a lower level task, or dismissed; or (2) additional training efforts will be required to improve his rate of learning.

ORGANIZATIONS, NEED SATISFACTION, AND MOTIVATION

In the preceding sections, a number of basic concepts and ideas useful to the understanding of human behavior have been presented. In this

---

[58] Several explanations have been suggested to explain the existence of plateaus. One is that there may often be a temporary decrease in motivation due to discouragement with the diminishing rate of learning common to learning curves.

section, we will turn our attention to certain facets of the role and success of organizations in meeting their members' needs and providing opportunities for satisfaction in the job.

Needs Which May Be Met by Organizations

Organizations are in a position to provide their members with a number of opportunities to help meet their needs on the job. Some of these are noneconomic in nature. Being accepted by one's superior and fellow employees is an important way in which the individual's needs for belonging are satisfied. Having our work recognized and performance praised by other members of the organization serves to satisfy our esteem needs. Further, certain types of work provide the individual with an opportunity for self-actualization. The manager who is given responsibility for making complex and difficult decisions or the engineer who develops new and creative production methods may be deriving considerable satisfaction from doing what they can do best. However, as will be discussed later, many jobs in business organizations provide very little opportunity for such self-actualization.

Business organizations also provide a number of economic rewards, which may contribute to individual need satisfaction. Our paycheck enables us to meet a number of our basic physiological and safety needs through the purchase of food, clothing, and shelter. Money may also contribute to the satisfaction of certain higher level needs. for example, that we are able to earn more than our neighbors, own the largest home in the community, afford a membership in the country club, or be a three-car family gives us status and prestige in the eyes of others. Or, in terms of the hierarchy of needs discussed earlier, money makes it possible for us to meet certain of our esteem needs.

The effectiveness of money as a motivator, however, has been open to considerable questioning. As Opsahl and Dunnette have pointed out: "Although it is generally agreed that money is the major mechanism for rewarding and modifying behavior in industry . . . very little is known about how it works."[59] For example, numerous surveys have shown that, following the introduction of wage incentive plans (in which bonuses were given for increased output), individual productivity has increased.[60] On the other hand, the achievement motivation research discussed previously, has indicated that for the high achievement-oriented individual, money serves, not as a motivator, but a feedback mechanism.

---

[59] Robert L. Opsahl and Marvin D. Dunnette, "The Role of Financial Compensation in Industrial Motivation," *Psychological Bulletin*, 66 (1966), p. 114.

[60] For a discussion of several of these surveys, as well as their limitations, see, for example, Alan C. Filley and Robert J. House, *Managerial Process and Organizational Behavior* (Glenview, Ill.: Scott, Foresman & Company, 1969), pp. 369–70.

In our opinion, the role of money as a motivator which seems most congruent with existing theories and research findings may be viewed as follows. Money by itself has no intrinsic meaning. Rather, money basically provides a symbolic function—it serves as a motivator only when an individual perceives that it has extrinsic value (or symbolizes it) as serving to meet certain needs or objectives considered important to him.[61] Or, in systems terms, money serves as a perceived input into the individual's open personality system. It will lead to different behavioral and attitudinal outputs, depending both upon how he has learned previously to symbolize the "value" of money, and his current life situation. For example, money might well serve primarily as a feedback mechanism for the 41 year old, high achievement-oriented, $25,000 a year manager (McClelland). On the other hand, for a financially overburdened father of eight in a low-income bracket, money may of necessity be primarily perceived as a means of maintaining his family's basic physiological and safety needs (Maslow).

Success and Failure of Organizations in Meeting Needs

Generally, American business organizations have been successful in providing their employees with an opportunity to meet many of their physiological and safety needs. Poverty, of course, still exists in segments of American society—e.g., in ghetto areas. However, most American workers are well fed, well clothed, and enjoy a relatively high standard of living. Although the nation is plagued with some unemployment problems, a fairly high level of economic security is enjoyed by most Americans. Among the forms of protection against economic insecurity which exist today are: unemployment compensation, workmen's compensation, seniority provisions in union-management contracts, health and medical insurance, retirement programs, and social security.

As Maslow's theory postulates, needs once largely satisfied cease to serve as important motivators. In light of this, one may question the effectiveness of management's continuing to focus its attention on providing its employees rewards geared to the lower level needs as a primary basis for the further motivation of its employees. As Zaleznik, Christensen and Roethlisberger have pointed out:

Because management has been so successful in satisfying its workers' subsistence needs, and because workers whose subsistence needs are satisfied are no longer motivated to satisfy these needs, management can no longer use its traditional rewards to motivate them. No amount of good wages, fringe benefits, and good working conditions in and by themselves will motivate workers to give more than minimum effort. Thus management seems to be

---

[61] This basic view of the role of money has also been postulated by Saul W. Gellerman, among others, in his *Motivation and Productivity* (New York: American Management Association, 1963).

left with obsolescent motivational tools on its hands that have not been "written off" for new ones.[62]

The points made in this quotation, it should be noted, are also congruent with Herzberg's thesis that extrinsic job factors such as wages and working conditions do not serve as motivators.

With employees' physiological and safety needs largely satisfied, it is important to appraise management's effectiveness in providing motivation through the opportunity for satisfaction of the higher level needs. Considerable evidence has been marshaled by contemporary observers to indicate that in many cases business firms have not been too successful in providing organizational conditions under which their employees are able to meet their belonging, esteem, and self-actualization needs. A salient characteristic of many firms, especially those geared toward mass production and assembly line operations, is a high degree of specialization of work. The work to be performed by production employees is broken down into simple repetitive tasks which often require little skill.[63] In many cases, assembly line work is machine paced, and even when it is not, the worker has relatively little control over the way in which he has to perform his job—he is expected to follow closely detailed step-by-step instructions for doing the work which have been developed by management. In addition, some assembly line jobs provide the worker with little chance for social interaction, either because of the need to give close continuous attention to his job, noise which renders conversation difficult, or because of physical isolation from other employees. Work of this type is often not conducive to the individual's satisfaction of his higher level needs. In those jobs where there is limited social interaction, the belongingness needs may easily be thwarted. When a person feels that his work is so simple that "a five-year old can come in and do it now,"[64] it may be difficult for him to develop a high level of self-respect or consider himself esteemed by others for the work that he does. Further, there is quite obviously little opportunity for self-actualization, unless, of course, one's abilities are extremely limited.[65] Nor are highly specialized, routine production jobs the only ones in organizations which may fail to substantially provide opportunities for

---

[62] A. Zaleznik, C. R. Christensen, and F. J. Roethlisberger, *The Motivation, Productivity, and Satisfaction of Workers, A Prediction Study* (Boston, Mass.: Harvard University, Division of Research, Graduate School of Business Administration, 1958), p. 402.

[63] For an interesting study of the automotive assembly line, which exhibits these characteristics, see Charles R. Walker and Robert H. Guest, *The Man on the Assembly Line* (Cambridge, Mass.: Harvard University Press, 1952).

[64] This is a statement by a worker on an automotive assembly line. Cited in ibid., p. 57.

[65] It is interesting to note that there have been cases in which mentally retarded individuals have proven to be highly satisfactory employees in routine production jobs. See, for example, Argyris, *Personality and Organization*, pp. 67–68.

the individual to satisfy his higher level needs. In many organizational positions, both managerial and nonmanagerial, the individual's behavior is closely directed and controlled; he has little opportunity to assume major responsibilities or make many important decisions himself, and is not able to fully utilize his abilities.

A number of management observers such as Chris Argyris and Douglas McGregor have expressed concern over the lack of higher level need satisfaction provided in many jobs in industry today. Argyris has taken the position that the requirements of formal organizations (especially with respect to lower level jobs) are basically incongruent with the needs of the mature individual in our culture. He has contended that:

> If the principles of formal organization are used as ideally defined, employees will tend to work in an environment where (1) they are provided minimal control over their workaday world, (2) they are expected to be passive, dependent, and subordinate, (3) they are expected to have a short time perspective, (4) they are induced to perfect and value the frequent use of a few skin-surface shallow abilities and, (5) they are expected to produce under conditions leading to psychological failure.[66]

To highlight this incongruency, the reader may wish to refer back to Argyris' description of the mature adult which we cited earlier.

McGregor also concluded that many of the individual's higher level needs are thwarted in organizations, although his position has been stated somewhat differently. He contended that traditionally management has tended to direct and control closely the behavior of its employees because it has adhered to a fallacious set of assumptions about human behavior. At the heart of this thinking (which McGregor referred to as Theory X) are the following beliefs:

> 1. The average human being has an inherent dislike of work and will avoid it if he can. . . .
> 2. Because of this human characteristic of dislike of work, most people must be coerced, controlled, directed, threatened with punishment to get them to put forth adequate effort toward the achievement of organizational objectives. . . .
> 3. The average human being prefers to be directed, wishes to avoid responsibility, has relatively little ambition, wants security above all.[67]

Disagreeing with these assumptions, McGregor postulated a converse set of assumptions (which he called Theory Y) that people do not inherently dislike work, and that they will assume responsibility and willingly direct their efforts toward the objectives of the organization *provided that* in doing so they are able to satisfy their higher level needs.

---

[66] Ibid., p. 66.

[67] Douglas McGregor, *The Human Side of Enterprise* (New York: McGraw-Hill Book Co., 1960), pp. 33–34. © Copyright and used by permission of the McGraw-Hill Book Company.

To what extent are criticisms such as those raised by Argyris and McGregor valid? To what extent are the demands of the organization incongruent with the needs of its members? To what extent do managements assume that people are inherently lazy and dislike work, and as a consequence closely control and direct the activities of their employees? As we indicated previously, when an individual's needs are not satisfied, he experiences frustration, and may react with negative and nonproductive behavior. Considerable evidence exists to indicate that when employee needs are thwarted on the job, workers may display hostility and aggression toward management, become apathetic and indifferent toward their work, or engage in some of the other forms of defensive behavior discussed previously. Tardiness, absences, strikes, slowdowns, and excessive numbers of grievances are among the more common forms of behavior which are often symptomatic of job frustrations. When confronted with such behavior, management may be tempted to conclude that employees are inherently lazy, dislike assuming responsibility, and must be coerced into directing their efforts toward the goals of the organization. Such a conclusion may lead management to exert more pressure on its employees and attempt to control their behavior more closely, which in turn often creates greater frustration and more nonproductive behavior. Thus, we may have what amounts to a vicious cycle. In jobs in which individuals are unable to fulfil many of their needs, frustration and behavior, not in accordance with management's objectives, occurs. This in turn convinces management to take actions which tend to magnify the kinds of problems underlying the behavior which it wishes to avoid.

Just how widespread management's "failure" to provide opportunities for members of the organization to meet their higher level needs is, however, open to considerable question. It should not be inferred that the individual's higher level needs are rarely if ever met in business organizations. Many managerial and some nonmanagerial positions afford the individual with considerable opportunity for creative endeavor, recognition, and self-actualization. Nor should we assume that all people want to engage in work in which they will be called on to assume considerable responsibility and make important decisions. Some persons are satisfied with routine work, like to be told exactly what to do and how to do it, and do not wish to asume any major responsibilities.[68] Thus, in appraising an organization's effectiveness in providing opportunities for on-the-job need fulfillment, one must guard against overgeneralization. It is necessary to look at each position within the organization separately and examine the demands of the job *in relationship to* the personality systems of the particular person who is filling it.

---

[68] In some cases this may be because the individual has continually been told exactly what to do and given few responsibilities since early childhood; in other cases a very limited mental capacity may be an important reason for one's desire for routine and uncomplicated work. See, for example, footnote 65 on page 159.

Organization Objectives and Member Needs: Integration

One further question needs to be explored before we conclude our discussion of the effectiveness of organizations in meeting member needs. To what extent *should* management attempt to provide conditions under which members of the organization can more fully meet their needs (especially the higher level needs)? We have indicated that the thwarting of employee need satisfaction often leads to behavior of a nonproductive type. As was pointed out earlier, however, it is possible that by devoting too much attention to member need satisfaction, organizations may be diverted from the attainment of their primary objectives, such as profitability. On the other hand, as McGregor has contended, it may be possible in many cases to create conditions under which individuals may satisfy their own needs *best* by directing their efforts toward the goals of the organization. This tenet, which is refered to as the principle of *integration* by McGregor, is based on the assumption that the individual does not need to be coerced to work toward the goals of the organization, but will willingly assume responsibility for meeting these goals under conditions which provide him with need satisfaction.

To what extent can such integration be achieved? Although there is no clear-cut answer to this question, it appears that a greater degree of integration of organization goals and member needs is possible than has existed in many traditionally managed firms in the past. A number of managerial approaches have been designed and utilized which have been aimed at more fully meeting individual need satisfaction while *at the same time* improving organizational effectiveness. We will discuss some of these in succeeding chapters. Realistically, however, most jobs will always contain certain aspects which are unpleasant, provide little need satisfaction, and are frustrating. Integration, thus, may be best thought of as an ideal objective, never to be fully realized, for some conflict will probably always exist between the objectives of the organization and the needs of its members.

SUMMARY

Most human behavior is motivated by the desire to satisfy certain needs. Although the behavior of all individuals is geared toward need satisfaction, the importance of different needs and the approaches taken to satisfy them vary considerably from individual to individual. The personality of each person is unique. An individual's personality is influenced in its development by certain inborn characteristics and environmental factors in mutual interaction. Although each personality is unique, the personality development of most normal individuals in our culture seems to proceed in similar directions. In other cultures, however, differing patterns of work important to management, have emerged.

Many "models" have been developed to deal with human motivation and need satisfaction in general. In this chapter, attention was focused on Maslow's hierarchy of needs schema, the Herzberg model, and the Vroom model—all of which examine general need satisfaction and motivation in a somewhat different way.

Important in personality development and motivation is learning. Some of the conditions under which learning seems to take place most effectively were discussed; and the usefulness of empirically developed individual learning curves dealt with.

Business organizations are in a position to provide their members with opportunities for satisfying many different types of needs. Although American business firms generally have been successful in enabling their members to meet most of their physiological and safety needs, many observers consider business organizations have failed to provide opportunities for the fulfilment of the higher level needs, especially among lower level jobs. The organization, however, has to be concerned not only with endeavoring to provide for the need satisfaction of its employees, but also with attaining its primary objectives, such as profitability. An ideal objective in managerial decision making would be the creation of conditions under which organization members could satisfy their own needs best by directing their efforts toward the objectives of the firm. However, it is likely that there will always be some degree of incongruency between organizational objectives and member needs.

DISCUSSION AND STUDY QUESTIONS

1. To what extent have personality theorists considered "personality" as an open system? Of the motivational models presented in Chapter 5, which is (are) the most "open systems" oriented?

2. The individual's personality pattern remains stable and constant once he reaches adulthood. What implications does this have for management?

3. Since environment influences personality, jobs ought to be designed to maximize the development of mature types of individuals. Comment.

4. Compare the "duality theory" with the Maslow model.

5. Compare and contrast the Vroom model and the Maslow model. To what extent are the models incongruent?

6. Assume in each of the following situations that you are sufficiently familiar with the individual concerned to conclude that he is employing a defense mechanism. What type of defense mechanism is being employed in each case, and why?

   a) The supervisor of a number of employees last week criticized strongly one of his employees; but since then the subordinate has expressed nothing but praise and admiration for his boss.

   b) In one research and development department, the department head gives very little supervision, rarely sets goals and gives his subordinates a minimum of direction. Often, the employees play mathematical puzzles two or three hours a day.

c) Your neighbor honestly forgot to bring home the loaf of bread he had promised his wife one evening.

d) You ask your neighbor how he likes his work and he says: "The work's OK, but I've got a terrible boss, the working conditions are poor, and there are too many company rules and regulations which I have to follow."

7. a) What are the basic characteristics of McClelland's high achiever?
   b) What is the relationship between McClelland's research and the Maslow and Herzberg models?
   c) What is the relevance of McClelland's research to management?

8. Show how motivations may affect learning on the job.

9. What objective does McGregor seek with his "principle of integration"? Discuss the extent to which you believe this objective can be attained within a business organization.

10. Mr. James Wilson, age 34, has a wife and two children and presently is assistant production manager at the Elco Electronics firm's Denver plant. He has been with the company for five years, having been promoted twice—from first-line foreman to general foreman to his present position two years ago. He enjoys his work, finds it basically challenging, gains a feeling of accomplishment from it and believes that there are further promotional possibilities ahead for him at Elco, unless corporate profits continue to sag as they have the past two years. Along with the sag in corporate profits, his salary increases (although not as much as many other managers at Elco) during this period have lagged. He is now making $15,000 whereas other comparable firms are now paying about $17,500 for positions with commensurate responsibility. He considers working conditions not especially good (e.g., an inadequate office in terms of space and convenience). He is somewhat frustrated by the technical incompetence of his superior (the plant production manager) and by a number of newly instituted rules and regulations which have added about 5 percent to the time he has to devote to "routine" paper work.

Mr. Wilson, in spite of the above advantages and disadvantages of his present position, has indicated privately that he plans to continue staying at Elco; and he continues to be a top-notch creative and productive manager. Explain his desire to remain at Elco and his continued high performance in light of:

a) Maslow's theory of motivation
b) Herzberg's theory of motivation
c) McClelland's achievement motive

SELECTED REFERENCES

ARGYRIS, CHRIS. *Personality and Organization.* New York: Harper & Bros., 1957.

ATKINSON, J. W., and FEATHERS, N. T. (eds.). *A Theory of Achievement Motivation.* New York: John Wiley & Sons, Inc., 1966.

BEHLING, ORLANDO, et al. "The Herzberg Controversy: A Critical Reappraisal," *Academy of Management Journal,* 11 (March 1968), 99–108.

CAMPBELL, JOHN P., et al. *Managerial Behavior, Performance, and Effectiveness.* New York: McGraw-Hill Book Co., 1970, chap. 15.

DOLLARD, J., and MILLER, N. E. *Personality and Psychotherapy.* New York: McGraw-Hill Book Co., 1950.

DUNNETTE, MARVIN D., and KIRSCHNER, WAYNE K. *Psychology Applied to Industry.* New York: Appleton-Century-Crofts, 1965.

GALBRAITH, JAY, and CUMMINGS, L. L. "An Empirical Investigation of the Motivational Determinants of Task Performance: Interactive Effects between Instrumentality—Valence and Motivation—Ability," *Organizational Behavior and Human Performance,* 2 (1967), 237–57.

HALL, CALVIN S. *A Primer of Freudian Psychology.* New York: The New American Library of World Literature, Inc., 1955.

HALL, CALVIN S., and LINDZEY, GARDNER. *Theories of Personality.* 2d. ed. New York: John Wiley & Sons, Inc., 1970.

HERZBERG, F. W., et al. *The Motivation to Work.* 2d ed. New York: John Wiley & Sons, Inc., 1959.

HILGARD, ERNEST R., and BOWER, GORDON. *Theories of Learning.* 3d ed. New York: Appleton-Century-Crofts, 1962.

HUNT, J. G., and HILL, J. W. "The New Look in Motivational Theory for Organizational Research," *Human Organization,* 28 (Summer 1969), 100–109.

KLUCKHOHN, CLYDE, and MURRAY, HENRY A. *Personality in Nature, Society, and Culture.* 2d ed. New York: Alfred A. Knopf, Inc., 1953.

McCLELLAND, DAVID. *The Achieving Society.* Princeton, N.J.: D. Van Nostrand Co., Inc., 1961.

McGREGOR, DOUGLAS. *The Human Side of Enterprise.* New York: McGraw-Hill Book Co., 1960.

MASLOW, A. H. *Motivation and Personality.* New York: Harper & Bros., 1954.

MUNROE, RUTH L. *Schools of Psychoanalytic Thought.* New York: Holt, Rinehart & Winston, Inc., 1955.

PORTER, LYMAN, and LAWLER, EDWARD, III. *Managerial Attitudes and Performance.* Homewood, Ill.: Richard D. Irwin, Inc., 1968.

SAYLES, LEONARD R. *Individualism and Big Business.* New York: McGraw-Hill Book Co., 1963.

VROOM, VICTOR H. *Work and Motivation.* New York: John Wiley & Sons, Inc., 1964.

WALKER, CHARLES R., and GUEST, ROBERT H. *The Man on the Assembly Line.* Cambridge, Mass.: Harvard University Press, 1952.

Chapter **6**

The Leadership Process

THE PREVIOUS CHAPTER focused attention on several aspects of *individual* behavior of importance to the manager. An understanding of the managerial process also requires an examination of *relationships among individuals,* for the functioning of the business firm viewed as a system centers around a complex network of interrelationships among many persons working together to meet organizational objectives.

There are two facets of human interaction which are of special concern to the manager. One of these is the impact of group membership upon individual behavior, which will be examined in the following chapter. The other is the phenomenon of leadership. In this chapter, leadership will be viewed as an influence process. We will examine this process in terms of both need satisfaction and social power. Finally, an examination will be made of various leadership styles available to the manager and some of the conditions under which each seems to be most effective.

In analyzing leadership, some of the same kinds of problems exist as in the study of individual behavior. The variables involved in the leadership process are complex and not well defined; and disagreement still exists among authorities as to their role and significance. However, a number of concepts have been developed which may provide the manager with a useful framework for understanding the phenomena of leadership and influence in business organizations. These concepts can be of value in analyzing his own role both as a leader and as a follower, and in selecting leadership strategies which will be effective for him in his interpersonal relationships with other members of his organization.

LEADERSHIP: A BASIC DEFINITIONAL FRAMEWORK

Leadership may be viewed as an *influence process.*[1] In this process, effective leadership may be defined as the *efforts* on the part of one

---

[1] It should be noted that a considerable amount of research has been carried

person (the leader) which *succeed* in influencing the behavior, attitudes, beliefs, or values of another person or persons (followers) toward the leader's goals *in any given situation.*[2]

Two observations are relevant to this conception of leadership. First, the leader's influence efforts may be directed either toward or against changing the behavior, attitudes, and so forth of others. For example, a manager may successfully influence one of his employees to do something—such as taking on some overtime work. Or, the leader may dissuade the employee from taking some action—such as refraining from scheduling his vacation at a time when the organization's work load is at its yearly peak. Second, this conception of leadership encompasses the leader's influencing the behavior of both (1) another individual, and (2) that of a number of individuals (or group of followers).

LEADERSHIP, FOLLOWERSHIP, AND NEED SATISFACTION

Although some individuals are obviously more influential than others, all people assume both leadership and followership roles to varying degrees. Our purpose in this section is to explore the nature of these roles and of the influence process by raising the following questions: (1) Why do individuals desire to seek influence over others and conversely; (2) Why are people attracted by situations in which they are in a position to be influenced by others? Since—as indicated in Chapter 5—most human behavior is motivated by the desire to satisfy needs, we will seek answers to these questions by analyzing the need satisfactions gained by both the influencer and the influencee.

out in an attempt to isolate personal characteristics differentiating leaders from other individuals. Although many authorities question whether there are any personality traits universally characteristic of leaders, certain traits do seem to be important factors in leadership. For example, it has been found that in general "leaders are more intelligent than their followers," but one of the most interesting results emerging from studies in this area is the discovery that they must not exceed the followers by too large a margin, for great discrepancies between the intelligence of leaders and followers militates against the emergence of the leadership relation, presumably because such wide discrepancies render improbable the unified purpose of the individuals concerned. Cecil A. Gibb, "Leadership," in *Handbook of Social Psychology*, Gardner Lindzey, (ed.) Vol. II (Reading, Mass.: Addison-Wesley Publishing Co., Inc., 1954), p. 886. For a discussion of the traitist approach to leadership, see also Alex Bavelas, "Leadership: Man and Function," *Administrative Science Quarterly*, 4 (March 1960), pp. 491–98.

[2] This definition framework is somewhat similar to that presented in Robert Tannenbaum, Irving R. Weschler, and Fred Massarik, *Leadership and Organization* (New York: McGraw-Hill Book Co., 1961), p. 24, but more systems and process oriented than some of the earlier so-called situational approaches. For an overview of the earlier situational approaches, and more recent attempts to view leadership as a dynamics systems oriented process, see, for example, Edwin P. Hollander and James W. Julian, "Contemporary Trends in the Analysis of Leadership Processes," *Psychological Bulletin*, 71 (May 1969), pp. 387–97. It should be noted that one person may influence the behavior of others merely by his presence, rather than by any overt efforts. A policeman, for example, may influence the driving behavior of passing motorists simply by standing at an intersection.

Need Satisfactions of the Leader

An individual may help satisfy many different needs by assuming the role of leader—in 'fact, probably all of Maslow's five basic classes of needs. The financial rewards given to those holding positions of considerable influence in our society are generally greater than those realized by persons exerting relatively little influence in their work. Such rewards, as indicated earlier, may enable the individual to help meet a number of his physiological, safety, and esteem needs. Further, some individuals seem to have a strong need to be in positions in which they have the power to control the behavior of others.[3] In some cases, their need for power may represent a manifestation of a need for security. That is, some insecure persons, who have relatively little confidence in their own abilities, may view other peoples' skills and abilities as a threat to themselves, that can be lessened if they have the power to control the activities of such other individuals. For example, the supervisor who fears that his subordinates may "take his job away from him" may feel more secure if he controls their behavior closely in such a manner as to stifle their creativity and prevent them from fully utilizing their abilities. As this example points out, leader behavior is not always constructively goal-oriented—it may also be *defensive* in nature (and have dysfunctional consequences to the organization).

Assumption of a position of leadership may also put the individual in a better position to satisfy both his belongingness and esteem needs. The reason for this is that individuals holding positions of influence in organizations and groups usually attain higher *status* than those who do not. By "status" we mean roughly the degree of prestige which an individual enjoys as a member of a group. As one observer has pointed out:

> The higher levels of status are believed to be, and usually are, the more pleasant to occupy. They involve more power and influence and they may bring higher financial returns. But the important factor in considering status as a motive in itself is that higher status gives entrée into attractive associations; it makes possible friendships and group memberships which, in turn, tend to maintain status and thus to satisfy important ego needs. This may indeed be one of the most important, and most general, satisfactions, to be had from occupancy of a leader role in any group.[4]

Further, as indicated in Chapter 5, the high achievement-oriented individual has a strong need to assume personal responsibility for the

---

[3] Research has been carried out exploring the need for power, or the power motive. See, for example, David C. McClelland, *The Achieving Society* (Princeton, N.J.: D. Van Nostrand Company, Inc., 1961).

[4] Cecil Gibb, "Leadership," in *Handbook of Social Psychology*, 2d ed., Gardner Lindzey and Elliott Aronson (eds.), Vol. IV (Reading, Mass.: The Addison-Wesley Publishing Co., 1969), p. 250.

projects which he undertakes; and positions of leadership in organizations may provide opportunities for the assumption of such responsibility.

Finally, assuming the role of leader may give the individual an opportunity to help meet his self-actualization needs. Many leadership positions in our society call on a person to direct and coordinate the efforts of others toward the solution of complex and difficult decision problems—e.g., the job of directing a large-scale research and development program (or some aspect thereof) in our nation's lunar space program. Some persons find that this type of endeavor is what they are best fitted for, and that they will experience "a new discontent and restlessness," to use Maslow's words, unless they are continually called on to deal with such challenging problems.

Need Satisfactions of the Follower

Many different types of needs may also be satisfied by assuming the role of follower. Acceding to the influence efforts of others may help provide satisfaction of some of the individual's physiological, safety, and belongingness needs. For instance, modifying one's behavior in the business organization in the directions indicated by his supervisor's influence efforts may lead to economic rewards in the form of a pay raise or promotion, greater assurances of job security, or a perception that he is more highly accepted by his superior. Moreover, an individual may help meet his esteem and self-actualization needs by taking the role of influencee in at least two different ways. First, there is strong evidence to suggest that some of a person's esteem needs may be satisfied as a follower, at least *vicariously* through the psychological process of *identification.* Identification, a concept attributed to Freud,

provides a means of incorporating the strength of another in ourselves. We can identify with strong individuals and with groups. The classic example of the vicarious strength obtained through identification is found in the small boy's assertion "My dad can whip your father." The individual feels strong if he has a close tie with another strong person. . . . Paradoxical as it may seem, followership may represent to the follower satisfactions of status needs very similar to those represented to the leader by his leadership.[5]

Second, satisfaction of the follower's esteem (including achievement) and self-actualization needs may be contributed to when the leader directs his efforts towards inducing the employee to behave in such manner that he will gain esteem and recognition and more fully utilize his abilities. For example, a manager may exert strong influence on an employee to take some courses at a local university which will enable him to develop certain skills and thus be in a position to perform better on the job and gain more recognition in the organization. Or, in terms

---

[5] Ibid., p. 253.

of achievement motivation, a leader may direct and influence his subordinates toward undertaking moderate-risk task goals, with opportunities involving the assumption of personal responsibility.

The Problems of Leadership and Followership

Although need satisfactions may be gained from assuming both leader and follower roles, either may present problems for the individual. The leader-follower relationship may be difficult for all concerned when the leader, in order to meet his needs and objectives, must exert influence aimed at inducing followers to behave in a manner incongruent with the satisfaction of certain of their needs. For example, in order to meet his responsibilities the manager may have to call on one of his employees to put aside some creative and highly interesting work and devote several weeks to a routine monotonous project which the employee dislikes intensely. In this case, the employee may gain the satisfaction of some needs by acceding to the influence of the manager (e.g., obtaining the approval of his superior, or conversely, avoiding being fired); but only at the expense of having certain other needs thwarted (e.g., esteem or self-actualization). Further, some managers may also find such a situation difficult and experience some feelings of guilt because of their exerting influence toward inducing the employee to behave in a manner which is unpleasant for him. Such conflict between leader and follower needs is not uncommon, and probably exists to some degree in most influence relationships. For this reason, a better understanding of leadership may be gained by an analysis of both the power of the influencer and of the follower's resistance to influence.

Before undertaking such an analysis, however, it will be useful to examine the problems involved in the leader-follower relationship from another point of view—in terms of the independence and dependence needs of the individual, and of the phenomenon of ambivalence toward leaders. As indicated in Chapter 5, as the psychologically healthy individual in our culture, he tends to move from a state of dependence on others to a state of relative independence. Whereas the child has to turn frequently to his parents (and other elders) for help with his problems, the adult generally neither needs nor has the desire to rely as heavily on others. Mature adults want to assume responsibilities, make their own decisions, and have some control over their own destinies. Such wants and desires are often referred to as *independence* needs.

There are limits, however, to the individual's desire for independence and freedom from direction and control by others. To rely primarily on ourselves rather than others, to stand alone in a complex, difficult, and uncertain world, to assume the responsibility not only for our own well-being but possibly also that of many others—can be very frightening for the individual. Consider as an extreme example of the heavy burdens of responsibility that the individual may be called on to bear, President

Truman's problem of whether or not to employ the atomic bomb against Japan in World War II. Although the President was able to seek counsel from his civilian and military advisers, it was he, and he alone, who had to bear the ultimate responsibility for his decision—a decision which meant the unleashing of a highly destructive force, but also one which might in the long run save many thousands of American lives.[6]

Most people do not have to face up to such difficult decisions. However, individuals are at times confronted with complex and uncertain situations in which it may be frightening to stand alone and depend on themselves rather than to seek direction from and rely on others. For this reason, persons sometimes attempt to "escape from freedom," as Erich Fromm has put it, by seeking out a strong leader upon whom they can depend.[7] For the child it is comforting to have a "strong powerful father" to whom he can go for help with his problems; similarly, for adults, it is sometimes comforting to have a strong leader or "father figure" to whom they can turn. Such yearnings for someone else to depend upon (especially at difficult times) are often referred to as *dependence* needs.[8]

However, as much as adults *sometimes* like to rely on others and seek strong leadership, most of them do not want to be completely dominated and controlled by someone else. As pointed out earlier, acceding to the influence of others may often mean that a person must sacrifice certain of his own needs, goals, and objectives. Consequently, most people have mixed feelings toward leadership—they want to be able to depend on a leader to an extent, but not completely so. Or, in psychological terms, individuals have *ambivalent* feelings toward leaders, "ambivalence" meaning an emotional attitude toward an individual involving the opposite feelings of love and hate. As one observer has pointed out:

Whatever the culture, followers have an ambivalent attitude toward the leader. Satisfactions of dependency needs are rarely without conflict for the

---

[6] Or, more recently, other American presidents, notwithstanding advice and counsel from both military and civilian advisors, have had to assume the ultimate responsibility for extremely difficult decisions—e.g., President Kennedy's handling of the Cuban missile crisis, and the many decisions of Presidents Johnson and Nixon with respect to Vietnam.

[7] Erich Fromm, *Escape from Freedom* (New York: Farrar and Rinehart, 1941). One of Fromm's interesting theses is that the rise of Hitler can be explained to a considerable extent by a strong need on the part of many Germans for a strong leader figure.

[8] The dependence and independence needs discussed in this section should not be considered as being distinct from and unrelated to those needs included in Maslow's hierarchy. Rather, they simply represent a different way of viewing some of the same kinds of motivational phenomena upon which Maslow's framework focuses attention. For example, the desire to have someone else to depend on reflects a basic need for security; while the need to assume responsibilities and make one's own decisions may represent the need for self-esteem, high achievement motivation, and/or self-actualization.

individual. Particularly is this true for the male adult, since in most cultures he is less free to express dependence and seems to sacrifice virility by doing so. . . . Almost any leader-follower relation one can think of involves this ambivalence because the follower needs the leader and his control but does not want to be exploited. . . . the father "may be an object of fear in one mood; in another an object of affection. The same is true of all the father surrogates, all the grandfathers and uncles, all the policemen and martial heroes, all the kings, presidents, and popes, who derive their first place in the child's experience as configural duplicates of his first experiences."[9]

A person may feel great affection for the leader when his support helps satisfy his own needs for dependence. On the other hand, he may become quite angry toward him when his influence efforts thwart his needs for independence and self-assertiveness. Further, such anger may also be felt when an individual perceives that the leader has failed to give him the support that his dependence needs require. An employee who needs to rely heavily on his supervisor for directions, for example, may feel "let down" and angry when the supervisor requires him to make more decisions on his own.

Certain other observations are relevant to dependence and independence needs in the context of management decision making. The relative strength of needs varies considerably from person to person, due to differences in individuals' personality systems. Further, although the basic personality system of any particular adult remains relatively constant: (1) the strength of his dependence and independence needs changes somewhat from time to time as different environmental circumstances prevail, and (2) in the longer run, basic steady state changes in his personality toward either more or less independence are possible.

In consequence, a basic problem that the leader is confronted with is to determine the relative strength of each of his follower's dependence needs both in terms of their current state and possible dynamic changes. Among the informational inputs which can be made available for making such a determination are:

1. Psychological tests, interviewing, and other relevant data obtained previously when the employee was hired.
2. Prior performance appraisal data, developed either by himself, or other managers in the organization for which the individual has worked.
3. His own day-to-day observations over time of the individual's performance.

Having such inputs, should the manager decide that the relative strength of any of his subordinates' dependence or independence needs are incongruent with his own objectives, optimally he should aim at

———
[9] Gibb, "Leadership," p. 254. The quotation used by Gibb is from G. Murphy, *Personality* (New York: Harper, 1947), pp. 845–46; and the Gibb quotation is from the 2d ed. of the *Handbook of Social Psychology*.

corrective action. For an overly dependent subordinate,[10] he might conclude that the individual's personality system is so rigidly fixed at this steady state level, that no personality change can be induced, and so, therefore, he can either (1) dismiss the individual; (2) accept him as he is; or (3) assign him to duties requiring the assumption of less individual personal responsibility.

On the other hand, if improvement toward a higher steady state level of independence is perceived by the manager, he may attempt to direct the individual toward such a level—i.e., gradually exerting leadership efforts to influence him to become more independent. The appropriate degree of such graduality, of course, will depend on the individual's personality system and the current environmental state. Of key importance in all cases is recognition of essentially the same point made in Chapter 4—i.e., if a subordinate (viewed as an open system) attempts to (or is influenced by his manager to) exceed his own capabilities in the movement toward a higher steady state level of independence, his improvement efforts may be set back with possible damage to his personality system. The manager's strategies with respect to overly dependent subordinates is illustrated from a systems point of view in Figure 6–1.

THE FORCES OF INFLUENCE AND OF RESISTANCE

Satisfaction of certain of the follower's needs may sometimes be thwarted if he permits himself to be influenced by the leader. Nevertheless, the individual often does allow himself to be influenced by others to behave in a manner distasteful to him—people are persuaded at times to do things which they strongly do not want to do. Such behavior may be better understood if it examined from two different points of view—(1) the consequence of the influencee's willingness to accept leader influence efforts, and (2) the nature of the forces which the influencer may bring to bear on the influencee.

Consequences of the Influencee's Willingness to Accept Influence Efforts

A person will decide to permit himself to be influenced by another if he perceives that he will probably gain greater net need satisfaction by doing so than by refusing to do so.[11] Such a decision is often a

---

[10] It should be noted that managers may also have problems with "overly independent" subordinates—e.g., the individual who has strong tendencies to go ahead and develop new projects without sufficient prior advice from his supervisor, resulting in mistakes being made which adversely affect organizational objectives.

[11] To the extent that the difference between the attractiveness of acceding to the influence efforts and that of not doing so is sufficiently great to be perceptible by the influencee. If not, there would be no basis for predicting the behavior of the influencee.

Figure 6–1. The Manager and the Overly Dependent Subordinate

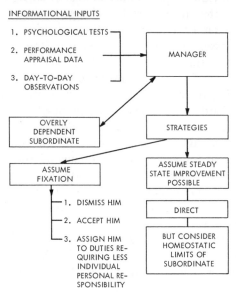

highly complex one, for the satisfaction of many different needs, each to varying degrees, may be involved. Further, the decision is not always "reasoned out" consciously, but rather is often influenced, at least in part, by unconscious forces of which the individual is not fully aware. To the extent that a person does "rationally" reason out the consequences of his willingness or refusal to accede to the influence efforts of others, however, he will probably consider both (1) the relative importance of those of his needs which may be affected by the influence acceptance decision, and (2) the probability of gains or losses in need satisfaction which will accrue from various alternative strategies open to him. The phrase "various alternative strategies" is important here because in addition to the complete acceptance or outright rejection of an influence attempt, a person may go along partially with the wishes of another, or do so in a mediocre way.

To illustrate these ideas, consider some of the questions which might be raised in the mind of an employee, with a high need to be creative, who is asked by his manager to devote several weeks to a routine and monotonous project:

1. If I refuse outright to do the work, what are my chances of being fired? Of losing a chance for a promotion? Of losing the approval of my supervisor? How important are each of these needs to me as compared with the frustration that I will experience if I consent to do the task?

2. If I cheerfully and gracefully undertake the distasteful work, will

my chances of getting ahead in the firm or of gaining my supervisor'
approval be materially enhanced?

3. If I chose another strategy—such as not openly refusing to do
the work but performing it in a mediocre manner, while at the
same time working on some other more creative projects that I want
to do—what will be the consequences?

Sources of Leader Power

The above example illustrates that the leader has certain *powers* to
provide, withhold, or take away need satisfactions which he may utilize
to induce influence acceptance—e.g., the manager's power to fire the
employee or to grant a promotion. To provide further insight into the
influence process we will now examine the bases of social power of
the leader.

One useful framework for understanding the bases, or sources of social
power that an individual may possess has been developed by French
and Raven.[12] The term "social power," as utilized in this framework
may be roughly defined as the *potential* ability of one person to influence
another. Or, to put it another way, social power represents the maximum
possible influence that one person may have on another as distinguished
from the influence which he actually exerts—i.e., people often choose
to exercise less than the full power at their command. A manager, for
example, may have the power to influence an employee to work overtime,
but not insist on the employee's doing so.

French and Raven have distinguished five different bases of social
power: (1) reward power, (2) coercive power, (3) referent power,
(4) expert power, and (5) legitimate power.

Reward Power. "Reward power is defined as power whose basis is
the ability to reward."[13] That is, an individual may be able to influence
others because he is in a position to reward them if they accede to his
influence efforts. Notice here that reward power is *not* the same as the
power to reward. Rather it is one's power to *influence based on* his power
to reward. In fact, a person may be in a position to dispense rewards,
and yet possess little or no reward power. For example, the parent may
have the power to reward his young son with a candy bar if he stops

---

[12] John R. P. French, Jr., and Bertram Raven, "The Bases of Social Power,"
in Dorwin Cartwright (ed.), *Studies in Social Power*, (Ann Arbor, Mich.: Institute
for Social Research, 1959), pp. 150–67. The discussion in this section draws heavily
on French and Raven's conceptual framework. It should be noted that other definitions of power have been put forth. For example, in Rocco Carzo, Jr. and John
N. Yanouzas, *Formal Organization: A Systems Approach* (Homewood, Ill.: Richard
D. Irwin, Inc. 1967), power is defined as an "ability to influence *through coercion*"
(p. 186); and congruently when "influence is successful *and it involves the presentation of force,* it is called power " (p. 183). The italics above are ours.

[13] French and Raven, "Bases of Social Power," p. 156.

hitting an older sister; but be unable to induce the desired behavior by promising such a reward.

The reward which the influencer has at his disposal may represent either (1) an increase in positive need satisfaction or (2) a reduction in need dissatisfaction. For example, the manager may influence one of his employees to do an exceptionally good job on a work project by promising him, if he does so, either an increase in pay or relief from certain unpleasant aspects of his job in the future.[14]

The term "promised rewards" is also important in the analysis of the dynamics of reward power. This is because the influencer may or may not actually provide the reward to the influencee once the prescribed influence efforts have been conformed to. Whether or not the influencer *does* live up to his promises of reward, however, is of considerable importance. If he does so: (1) his reward power will tend to be augmented because the influence is likely to attach a greater probability to the fulfillment of future reward promises, and (2) his attractiveness as a person to the influencee will tend to increase, thus enhancing his referent power, the nature of which will be discussed below. Conversely, the failure to fulfill reward promises will tend to reduce both the influencer's reward power and his attractiveness to the influencee. From these observations, two prescriptive statements may be made about leader behavior: the leader should refrain from promising rewards (1) that he cannot fulfill, and (2) for behavior which it is not possible for the influencee to attain (e.g., a pay raise for a level of production so high as to be impossible for the influencee to meet).

Coercive Power.   Coercive power refers to the potential ability of the individual to influence others because he is in a position to punish them if they do not follow his wishes. The parent may influence his child to stop jumping on the living room sofa by threat of a spanking; the professor may influence his students to attend class by virtue of his power to fail them if they do not do so; the manager may influence his employees to produce at high levels by threat of dismissal. Again—as with reward power—it is important to distinguish between the power to punish and the power to *influence* others by threat of punishment. The professor, for example, may be unable to induce certain students to come to class even though he has the power to give them a failing grade.[15]

---

[14] Whether or not the influencee will fully or partially accept influence efforts based on reward power will depend on his perceptions with respect to the gaining of greater net need satisfaction, as discussed in the previous section.

[15] As the reader may observe, coercive power is in some respects quite similar to reward power, and at times it may be difficult to distinguish between the two. Withholding a reward may be much the same as doling out a punishment; or conversely, withholding punishment may be equivalent to giving a reward, depending on the way that the influencee *perceives* the influence effort. French and Raven, however, contend that the dynamics of these two types of power are different. See French and Raven, "Bases of Social Power," p. 158.

Referent Power. A third basis of social power, already mentioned in passing, is referent power—one person accedes to the influence efforts of another because he is attracted to him, wishes to identify with him, and wants to be like him. The young son may be more than willing to help his father build a cupboard for his mother because he wants to be like his father and do the things his father does. Or the employee may be very enthused about carrying out a request of his superior because he admires him and wants to identify with him. As indicated previously, such identification provides a mean for the individual to incorporate, psychologically, the strength of another in himself.

A person may also identify with *groups* of people as well as with individuals. Such identification may provide a basis for his being influenced by the values, standards, and modes of conduct considered desirable by the group. In fact, groups also derive social power from their ability to provide punishments and rewards in much the same way as do individuals, as will be indicated in the following chapter.

Finally, in discussing referent power (and identification with "father figures") it should be noted that at various times in history, individuals have achieved very strong power positions primarily because of the force of the extraordinary nature of their personalities alone. Such individuals, frequently political leaders, have been termed "charismatic" leaders by the sociologist, Max Weber.[16] In more primitive societies, such leaders have often been perceived as revered "father figures," possessing magical qualities.[17]

The question of whether charismatic leaders simply possess an extremely high degree of referent power, based on identification with father figures, or whether this type of leadership involves different psychodynamics, is open to debate.[18] There are, however, certain aspects of the phenomenon of charisma which deserve attention. First, unless the charismatic leader makes himself a dictator:

he is usually doomed to a relatively short career in power. Nothing is so fatiguing as greatness—to the nongreat. People become numbed by excitement and sacrifice, grow weary of the grand view from the mountaintop, and long for a return to normalcy.[19]

---

[16] See, for example, H. H. Gerth and C. Wright Mills, *From Max Weber: Essays in Sociology* (New York: Oxford University Press, 1958), pp. 295–96.

[17] For example, "peasants in Turkey . . . believed that Dictator Kemal Atatürk was impervious to bullets." "Whatever Happened to Charisma?" *Time*, 94 (October 17, 1969), p. 41.

[18] Hollander and Julian, "Contemporary Trends," p. 394, have indicated that the study of identification has been largely ignored in leadership research, that the quality of "charisma" has had a "history of imprecise usage," and have suggested that more research concerning the "sources and consequences of identification with the leader" is an important need.

[19] "Whatever Happened to Charisma?" *Time*, 94 (October 17, 1969), p. 41. Reprinted by permission of Time, the Weekly News Magazine. Copyright Time, Inc., 1969.

A classical example of this phenomenon occurred when, after the crisis of World War II, the British people voted out their charismatic prime minister, Winston Churchill, in favor of a leader figure, Clement Atlee, possessing considerably less dramatic personality characteristics.

The above discussion also points out that, in spite of their power, charismatic leaders are strongly influenced by those whom they lead (in any democratic situation, at least), and hence will have difficulty in being "successful" if their views and actions differ too greatly from those desired by their followers.

Somewhat related, in taking the position that very few charismatic leaders existed in the United States in 1969, *Time* pointed out that (1) at that time, this country had no clearly defined national purpose, and (2) having such a purpose was an essential precondition for the ascendancy of a charismatic leader:

> Before there can be a crusade, there have to be, after all, crusaders. Before there can be a Moses, adds Political Scientist Sidney Hyman, "there must be a people of Israel who want to get out of Egypt." What ever happened to charisma? It is waiting—not for the man but the purpose.[20]

Expert Power. The fourth basis of social power distinguished by French and Raven is *expert* power. Expert powers refers to the potential ability of one person to influence others because of his superior knowledge or understanding of a particular situation. Many examples of the exercise of expert power could be cited—the patient's acceptance of his doctor's prescribed treatment, the student's acceptance of his professor's recommendation to read a particular book as preparation for a term paper, or the plant superintendent's acceptance of his personnel manager's interpretation of a psychological test.

Generally, the *range* of expert power is fairly narrow—i.e., individuals tend to be influenced by another person because he is an expert only within his area of expertise. For example, most people would probably not pay much attention to their doctor's advice regarding their legal matters. In fact, a person's expert power may be reduced if he attempts its exercise in an area in which he is not truly knowledgeable. We recall one labor relations assistant, for example, who proclaimed to be an expert on everything from high fidelity systems to the preparation of exotic oriented foods, and who was continually trying to get his colleagues to accept his "expert" advice on all sorts of different matters. Although this individual was highly competent in his own field of labor relations, even here his colleagues began to become suspicious of his expertise because they seriously questioned the validity of his claims to knowledge in other areas.

Legitimate Power. The fifth, and perhaps most complex, basis of social power is *legitimate* power. Legitimate power refers to the indi-

---

[20] Ibid.

vidual's permitting himself to be influenced by others because he believes that it is the right thing to do. That is, a person's conscience, or his own internalized value system, tells him that another person has the right to influence his behavior and that he has an obligation to accept this influence.

There are at least two different types of legitimate power. First, a person may feel an obligation to do as another requests because he has previously made a promise to do so and believes that it would be morally wrong to break that promise. Second, and of greater relevance to organizational behavior, is legitimate power based on one's belief that other individuals *holding certain positions* have the right to influence his behavior. If a person

> . . . accepts as right the social structure of his group, organization, or society . . . [he] . . . will accept the legitimate authority of . . . [a person] . . . who occupies a superior office in the hierarchy. Thus legitimate power in a formal organization is largely a relationship between offices rather than between persons.[21]

Legitimate power of this second type is quite similar to the idea of formal "authority," which has long been a central concept in management thinking.

The Organizational Bases of Social Power

Above we indicated that the holding of positions in an organization may provide one important base of social power—legitimate power. We will now explore certain other ways in which individuals may derive power from the organization and how organizational decisions may explicitly be made to modify the degree of a particular manager's sources of power.

First, let us consider a distinction frequently made in analyzing the leadership process—that between formal and *informal* leaders. A *formal* leader is defined as one, like the business manager, who derives considerable power by virtue of having been appointed to a position in an organization. An informal leader, on the other hand, is one whose position of influence is conferred on him solely by the membership of his group itself—e.g., a work group in a manufacturing plant may choose one of its members to be its spokesman, to present its grievances to management, etc.[22] Although many of the concepts which we are examin-

---

[21] French and Raven, "Bases of Social Power," p. 160.

[22] It should be mentioned that a person may assume the role of both formal and informal leader depending upon the specific influence situation in which he is involved. For instance, in his relationships with his subordinates, a first-line supervisor would be viewed as a formal leader; while the same individual may have emerged as an informal leader within a group of first-line supervisors of which he is a member.

ing in this chapter are applicable in the analysis of both formal and informal leadership, there are certain differences between these two types of influence relationships which we will point out in the next chapter.

With respect to formal leaders, the organization has at its disposal many means of enhancing (or diminishing)[23] a particular manager's power bases. This may be illustrated by examining a particular organizational power problem which has been of concern to many companies in recent years—the erosion of power of the first-line supervisor.

Fifty or sixty years ago, many first-line supervisors (or foremen) in production operations had considerable power—power to hire, fire, and promote their employees, and to make decisions regarding many phases of their operations. With the growth of unionism, however, both disciplinary and promotional procedures have come to be spelled out in many union-management contracts. For example, whereas the foreman once could fire a man for being absent a day without a justifiable reason, today under some union-management contracts he can only give the employee an oral warning for the first such offense.[24] In addition, some companies have taken the hiring decision from the foreman and transferred it to the personnel department. Thus, the *coercive, reward,* and *legitimate* bases of the foreman's social power have all been reduced in scope. Further, as business organizations have become technologically more complex, the foreman has come to be surrounded by a myriad of staff specialists in production control, quality control, industrial engineering, personnel, maintenance, and so forth, all of whom have some say as to the way in which his department should be run. This has often led to an erosion of the supervisor's *expert* power.

In recent years some companies have taken certain steps to help overcome the problem of the first-line supervisor's diminished power bases. A few have concluded that the foreman has become obsolete and have restructured their organizations so as to abolish this type of position altogether.[25] A number of others, on the other hand, have attempted to deal with the problem by attempting to strengthen the foreman's bases of social power. In order to help enhance his referent power, for example, some companies have given back to the foremen the right to hire new employees—on the assumption that the new employee may be more attracted to and identify more with a supervisor who has per-

---

[23] For example, some firms will transfer a long-tenured "loyal" manager nearing retirement, who has "slowed down" to the point where he no longer can handle his present position effectively, to one involving less important responsibilities, rather than dismiss him and thus cause him to lose his retirement benefits.

[24] For further offenses, more serious measures are usually in order—e.g., a one-day layoff for the second such offense, a one-week layoff for the third, and discharge for the fourth. This type of disciplinary approach is often referred to as *progressive discipline.*

[25] See, for example, " 'Upgrading' Foreman with an Ax," *Business Week* (February 11, 1961), pp. 110, 112.

sonally chosen him, than with one who has been forced to hire him by the personnel department.[26] Firms have also attempted to augment the foreman's referent power by training him in human relations skills. The reasoning here is that if a person is able to develop more effective interpersonal relationships with others, they will tend to be more attracted to him and identify with him to a greater extent.

Business firms have also considered the possibility of enhancing the foreman's expert power. Efforts have been made to increase the foreman's knowledge and understanding of many different phases of his company's operations—e.g., by providing him with training programs on the meaning of the provisions in the firm's union-management contract, on time study procedures employed in the plant, and so forth. In addition, some companies have attempted to augment the supervisor's expert power by (1) communicating to him more information about decisions being made by top management and/or (2) permitting him to sit in on higher level management committee meetings and participate actively in these discussions.

Reliance on the Bases of Social Power. In analyzing the influence process it is usually necessary to consider simultaneously more than one power base. This is because we rarely find only one base underlying any given influencer-influencee relationship at any particular time in the business organization. When a subordinate agrees to carry out a work assignment in the manner specified by his superior, for example, it may be because he not only feels a moral obligation to do so, but also has confidence in his superior's expertise and identifies with him.

It should also be emphasized that most managers probably derive some of their power from all of the five sources in the French and Raven conceptual framework to varying degrees. All managers, by the very fact that they occupy positions in the organization hierarchy (as formal leaders) possess certain legitimate rights to influence others, and, unless they are extremely ineffective, are able to derive *some* power from this source. Most managers also possess some power to reward and punish on the basis of which they are able to influence, and hopefully have attained some degree of expertise and have some qualities which will lead others to want to identify with them. There are, of course, wide differences among managers not only as to the degree to which they are able to draw on but also actually do utilize the various classes of power. For example, the manager of a research department doing work in cryogenics in an aerospace firm may be a recognized authority in his field and rely heavily on his expertise in influencing his colleagues. On the other hand, a newly appointed production supervisor with little technical knowledge of the operations of which he is in charge, but who is supportive of and had the ability to inspire others,

---

[26] Giving the foreman responsibility for hiring his own men also makes it more difficult for him to "pass the buck"—i.e., when things go wrong to blame the personnel department for the "poor" men which it compelled him to hire.

may draw largely upon his referent power. Further, the same manager may rely more heavily on one source of power in some situations at certain times and another source at other times. A supervisor may find, for instance, that at a particular time, one of his subordinates both recognizes his expertise and identifies with him, while another is somewhat hostile toward him and can only be induced to accept his influence efforts if he threatens punishment (coercive power) for his failure to do so. At a future time, however, the latter's hostile relationship with the manager may change for the better,[27] thus creating a basis for a shift away from emphasis on the part of the manager in his reliance on coercion as a primary power base. In short, the reliance on multiple power bases, which may change over time, points up that the French and Raven framework should be viewed in open systems terms, in which dynamic, mutual interaction takes place in the leadership process.

THE LEADERSHIP PROCESS: SUMMARY

We have indicated that the leadership process centers around the efforts of one person (the leader) to influence others (the followers) either to change their behavior, attitudes, and so on, or to refrain from doing so; and that this process must be viewed in dynamic, open systems terms. The leader possesses social power—reward, coercive, referent, legitimate, and expert—by virtue of his ability to provide, withhold, or take away certain need satisfactions of the follower. We have suggested that a person will choose to accept the influence of another when he perceives that he will gain greater net need satisfaction by doing so than by refraining from doing so. These concepts are summarized graphically in Figure 6–2.

LEADERSHIP EFFECTIVENESS

In the evaluation of leader effectiveness, there are no simple, clear-cut answers. Insight into this problem may be gained, however, by focusing attention first on leader objectives, and then upon leader approaches (or styles of behavior) employed to meet these objectives from a dynamic systems viewpoint.

Leader Objectives

In Chapter 2 we indicated that the activities of organizations are geared toward the attainment of goals and objectives. So also is one of the basic functions of a manager as a leader to help provide objectives for those subordinates whom he supervises. The objective or goal-setting

---

[27] For any one or more of a number of reasons—e.g., the manager's learning how to deal more effectively with such hostility; or an increasing degree of maturity on the part of the subordinate enabling him to manage more constructively his hostility toward "leader figures."

Figure 6–2. A Model of the Leadership Process*

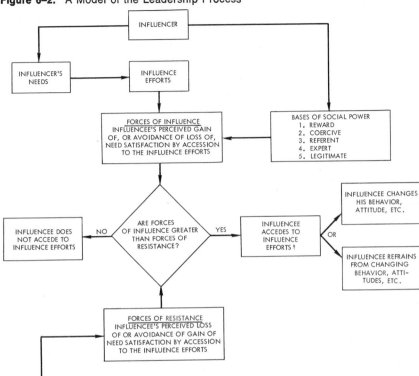

* It should be emphasized that this model is intended to portray a dynamic process—e.g., the influencer's needs, influencer's efforts, the follower's forces of resistance, will often change over time.

† Accession may be either complete or partial.

activity of leaders has generally been neglected in the study of the leadership process; although its "importance appears considerable."[28] For example, in one study of this aspect of the leadership processes involving discussion groups, it was found that the leader's failure to provide directions in setting goals resulted in tensions, antagonisms, and absenteeism among the members of his group.[29]

Two other observations are in order concerning the leader's role in goal setting. First, as implied above, managers will usually set multiple objectives. The criteria of effective leadership may be measures of such factors as "productivity and efficiency and measures of worker satisfaction, personal growth, or 'self-actualization.' "[30]

[28] Hollander and Julian, "Contemporary Trends," p. 390.

[29] P. J. Burke, "Authority Relations and Descriptive Behavior in Small Discussion Groups," *Sociometry*, 29 (September 1966), pp. 237–50.

[30] Gordon E. O'Brien, "Leadership in Organizational Settings," *The Journal of Applied Behavioral Science*, 5 (January–March 1969), p. 46.

Second, the objectives established by managers may not always be congruent with the goals of the organization as a whole. In some cases a manager may successfully influence his subordinates to direct their efforts toward his own personal goals, which are dysfunctional with respect to his firm's objectives. For instance, in order to "strengthen" his own position in the firm, a supervisor may induce his employees to develop an inaccurate report which will make one of his managerial rivals look bad in the eyes of top management. Such a report may have negative repercussions in terms of the firm's attainment of its objectives, yet possibly enhance the supervisor's own personal ambitions. In short, the "leader is not effective merely by being influential, without regard to the processes at work and the ends achieved."[31]

Leader Approaches or Styles

There is no single generally accepted theory which prescribes which "strategies," "approaches," or "styles" a particular leader should take to effectively influence his followers to meet his goals. A number of research studies dating back to the 1930s, however, have focused attention on two major "clusters" of leader behavior. These clusters (or styles) have been variously labeled "autocratic" as opposed to "democratic"; "task-oriented" versus "human relations-oriented"; concern for production versus concern for people; "authoritarian" versus "democratic" leadership, and so forth. Although these different cluster terms are not synonymous, they do have certain features in common.[32]

In discussing leadership styles, two approaches which appear especially useful will be presented, both of which may be viewed in dynamic situational systems terms: (1) the degree of leadership direction and control in an authoritarian—democratic—laissez-faire continuum framework, and (2) a more systematically formulated and researched approach to leadership—Fiedler's "contingency model."

The Authoritarian—Democratic—Laissez-Faire Continuum. Individuals holding positions of leadership in organizations and groups differ widely as to the degree to which they attempt to direct and control the behavior of those in subordinate positions. At one extreme of the directiveness continuum is a pattern of leader behavior which is often referred to as *authoritarian* leadership. The highly authoritarian leader:

1. Makes decisions and gives directions often without consulting with his subordinates. He supervises his people closely, checks on their behavior frequently, spells out in detail how they should perform

---

[31] Hollander and Julian, "Contemporary Trends," p. 393.

[32] Fred E. Fiedler, "A Contingency Model of Leadership," in Leonard Berkowitz (ed.), *Advances in Experimental Social Psychology*," Vol. I (New York: Academic Press, 1964), p. 150.

their work, and gives them little latitude in making decisions on their own.

2. Places emphasis on obedience and upon the status differences between himself and his subordinates. As the leader, he is the most important, the central person, the individual with the greatest status and prestige, and it is the duty of those working under him to defer to him.

As the reader may note, such a style represents a highly supervisor-centered type of leadership, in which the leader is the focal point of attention and wields considerable power.

At the other extreme of the directiveness continuum is a cluster of behavior which is sometimes called *laissez-faire* leadership. The laissez-faire leader rarely sets or helps set objectives for his work group, and gives his followers little or no direction. Rather, he allows them almost complete freedom to do what they wish to do. Or, as the term "laissez-faire" implies, he "lets his people alone" and attempts to exercise very little influence over them. As an example of laissez-faire leadership, we cite the following experience:

The manager of a research-oriented staff function in a large corporation often found it difficult to decide just what his department's objectives should be or what kind of work his employees should be engaged in. His employees would frequently complete a particular work project and submit it to the manager. (These were often filed away by the manager because he couldn't decide just what should be done with them.) The manager would then be asked: "Boss, what project do you think we should work on next?" The reply: "Well, I don't know. Do whatever you want to do." The employees would then raise some suggestions as to possible courses of action which might be appropriate. Again, however, the manager would find it difficult to commit himself, and the conversation would often end with no conclusions being reached as to what work should be undertaken.

The style of other managers falls somewhere in the middle range, rather than at either extreme of the directiveness and control continuum. This range is often referred to as *democratic* leadership or general supervision.[33] The democratic leader:

1. Unlike his laissez-faire counterpart, sets objectives, makes decisions, gives direction and does not give his subordinates extreme latitude in their behavior;

---

[33] As indicated previously, many researchers have utilized only two "clusters" or categories in examining leadership approaches or styles, rather than focusing explicit attention on a continuum of behavior. For example, D. Katz, N. Maccoby, and N. Morse, in their *Productivity, Supervision, and Morale in an Office Situation* (Ann Arbor, Mich.: Institute for Social Research, 1950), have utilized the two categories "close supervision" as contrasted with "general supervision." Their conception of general supervision, however, does not imply the complete or near complete lack of direction characterized by laissez-faire leadership but rather is similar to the democratic leadership pattern as above.

2. Unlike the authoritarian, however, does not attempt to control his subordinates closely or insist on spelling out in detail the ways that they should behave. Rather, he encourages his followers to help set objectives and make decisions, gives them considerable freedom to act on their own within certain prescribed limits, and encourages their creativity and development. Although he recognizes status differences, he does not emphasize them—rather he treats his followers more as equals than does the authoritarian leader. Nor does he stress obedience as does the authoritarian—he invites criticism of his own ideas and welcomes the suggestions of others when they are appropriate.

A number of research studies which have examined the influence process in groups and organizations *in our culture* have suggested that the democratic leadership pattern (or general supervision) is *generally* the most appropriate.[34] Supporters of democratic leadership have pointed out that when followers are permitted to participate in making decisions for their group or organization they will tend to: (1) gain a greater understanding of the work in which they are involved, and (2) give greater support for the programs developed and decisions made.[35]

Other observers, however, have seriously questioned the efficacy of the democratic pattern, at least in the modern business organization.[36]

---

[34] Much of this research has been conducted by the Institute for Social Research at the University of Michigan. See, for example, Katz, Maccoby, and Morse, *Productivity, Supervision, and Morale,* and D. Katz, N. Maccoby, G. Gurin, and L. G. Floor, *Productivity, Supervision, and Morale among Railroad Workers* (Ann Arbor, Mich: Institute for Social Research, 1951). Many of the ideas drawn from the research of the Institute may also be found in Rensis Likert, *New Patterns of Management* (New York: McGraw-Hill Book Co., 1961). It should also be noted that other research has indicated that a greater degree of leader direction may be more effective in certain other nations, where cultural values are different. As Cecil Gibb has noted: "Many studies, particularly of the German culture, have given support to the hypothesis that authoritarian leadership is more highly valued, and more efficient, in authoritarian cultures." "Leadership," 1st ed., p. 910.

[35] It should also be noted that the democratic pattern seems to provide a better answer to the problem of leader succession than does the authoritarian pattern. If, in the business organization, a manager allows none of his subordinates to make any important decisions or to assume any major responsibilities, it is not likely that any of them will be prepared to take over his duties when he leaves the company or is promoted to a higher position. On the other hand, if he has given his subordinates considerable responsibility, one or more of them may be ready to step into his job immediately should the need arise.

[36] Some small group research has also indicated that under certain conditions the democratic pattern may be less effective than the authoritarian. For example, in one such study, it was found that in making repetitive routine decisions with a computerized business simulation, groups comprised of both authoritarian leaders and followers (as measured by a psychological test) performed more effectively than groups comprised of either: (1) equalitarian (democratic) leaders and equalitarian followers or (2) equalitarian leaders and authoritarian followers. See M. William Frey, "An Experimental Study of the Influence of Disruptive Interactions Induced by Authoritarian-Equalitarian Leader-Follower Combinations upon the De-

Robert N. McMurry, for example, in suggesting as an ideal managerial leadership philosophy one which he refers to as "benevolent autocracy," takes the following position:

> I do not doubt . . . [that the humanistic or democratic-participative philosophy of management] . . . is superior to blind autocracy, especially when the latter leads to the development of a great inchoate and bumbling bureaucracy. Democratic leadership is obviously more productive. It stimulates and builds men; it invariably enhances morale. It has everything to recommend it except for the one fact that only in a relatively few small, socially well-integrated, and homogeneous groups—for example the New England town meeting, the British Foreign Office, or some types of family-run firms—can it really be made to work.[37]

To support these generalizations, McMurry argues that many individuals prefer regimentation, that most top-level managers in business organizations tend to be autocratic, and that most decision making in the firm must be centralized and structured. Following McMurry's reasoning further, if the probability of having *some* autocratic superiors is great, "democratically" made decisions at lower levels in the organization could arbitrarily be reversed, thus vitiating these democratic processes.

Unlike the democratic and authoritarian approaches, the extreme laissez-faire pattern of leadership has relatively few supporters today, and generally does not seem to be too effective, unless the system and organization cannot be structured due to a high degree of environmental and technological uncertainty. As indicated earlier: (1) the goal-setting activity of the leader is an extremely important one, and (2) most people have some need for dependence and at times want to rely on and receive direction from a leader figure. A complete, or almost complete lack of direction in helping to establish goals and objectives usually leads to a highly ambiguous and unstructured situation for the followers, tends to frustrate their dependence needs, and tends to result in chaos, confusion, and hostility toward the leader.

Regardless of the advantages and disadvantages of the leader approaches discussed above, the key question for managerial analysis and decision making is *not* which leadership style is *generally* most effective. Rather, of prime importance is understanding of what styles are effective under *what specific conditions*. Further, viewing the leadership process from a systems point of view, it is important to consider the interrelationships between leader styles and variables relevant to leader effectiveness.

One useful framework for examining leadership effectiveness under

---

cision-Making Effectiveness of Small Groups." Doctoral dissertation, The Pennsylvania State University, 1963.

[37] Robert N. McMurry, "The Case for Benevolent Autocracy," *Harvard Business Review*, 36 (January–February 1958), p. 85.

different conditions has been developed by Tannenbaum and Schmidt.[38] These observers have suggested that in analyzing managerial leadership one must examine certain forces: (1) in the subordinate, (2) in the organizational situation, and (3) in the manager. We will now examine each of these three classes of variables separately—recognizing, however, that they are dynamic and mutually interdependent.

The Follower Variable. In selecting influence strategies, it is important for the manager to consider the personality system of the follower. As indicated previously, some individuals have fairly strong dependence needs and function best when they are closely directed and controlled; while others prefer to assume more responsibility, to be given greater freedom, and to rely less heavily on the leader for direction. In addition, the knowledge and experience of the follower are important considerations in the manager's choice of a leadership style. A new and inexperienced employee may be unable to deal with the problems he faces on the job unless the method of handling them is spelled out in detail for him by his supervisor. The manager, of course, as indicated previously, may in some cases help such individuals attain an improved level of performance by gradually giving them more responsibilities.

On the other hand, a highly capable, seasoned employee may have the knowledge and experience to perform most of his duties with relatively little supervision. Further, as Tannenbaum and Schmidt have pointed out, less directiveness tends to be required by the manager when his subordinates are: (1) interested in problems; (2) perceive that such problems are important; and (3) have an understanding of and identify with the goals of the organization.[39]

The Situation Variable. The leader's degree of directiveness should be conditioned by the follower variable in relation to certain other forces existing in the particular organizational situation where his influence is exerted. The *time available* for making a decision is one variable which must be considered when a leader is deciding to what extent he should permit his subordinates to participate in making a particular decision. When decisions have to be made quickly, there may not be time for consultation, and he may be forced to act on his own. Leader decisions involving the amount of subordinate participation should take into consideration the nature and complexity of the problem involved. In some situations,

> the more complex a problem, the more anxious a manager will be to get some assistance in solving it. However, this is not always the case. There will be times when the very complexity of the problem calls for one person to work it out. For example, if the manager has most of the background

---

[38] Robert Tannenbaum and Warren H. Schmidt, "How to Choose a Leadership Pattern," *Harvard Business Review,* 36 (March–April 1958), pp. 95–101.

[39] Ibid., p. 99.

and factual data relevant to a given issue, it may be easier for him to think it through himself than to take the time to fill in his staff on all the pertinent background information.[40]

It is also important to know how serious the consequences may be if a problem is handled improperly. Failure on the part of a subordinate to deal correctly with a relatively minor problem may cost the company only a few dollars; and the loss may be offset by the learning gained from the experience. If, however, a poor decision may cost his company many thousands of dollars, the manager may be much more likely to make the decision himself, rather than delegating its handling to any of those who work for him.

The type of organization or group in which the leader functions will have a bearing on the varying degrees of directiveness which seem to be appropriate. The informal leader, for example, generally needs to consider the needs and objectives of his group to a greater extent than the formal leader. For this reason, he is more constrained than the formal leader with respect to the degree of both authoritarian directiveness and laissez-faire behavior which his group will accept.[41] Furthermore, in the formal organization the behavior, attitudes, and philosophy of top-level members often condition the directiveness pattern of its lower level managers to a great extent. For example, if the president of a corporation believes in and practices either close or general supervision, his pattern will often be transmitted to his subordinates, in turn to their subordinates, and so on, down through the organization.[42] The basic reason for this is that the manager may find it necessary to practice the type of leadership that his own supervisor believes in if he wants to gain his manager's approval and move ahead in the organization.

There are also many other organization variables which may have an influence on the leadership pattern of the manager. For example, if a manager is called on to supervise a large number of subordinates, he may not have time to direct each of them closely, and may be forced into a pattern of general supervision. Or, if a manager's subordinates work in locations quite distant from him geographically (e.g., a field sales force), he may be compelled to give them considerable freedom

[40] Ibid., p. 100.

[41] Gibb, "Leadership," 1st ed., p. 908.

[42] Katz, Maccoby, and Morse, *Productivity, Supervision, and Morale*, for example, in their study of productivity and morale among office workers, found that close supervisors more frequently worked under managers practicing close supervision and that general supervisors more often worked for supervisors who practiced general supervision. This same point of the transmittal of leadership styles has been emphasized in a more recent survey of the literature: O'Brien, "Leadership in Organizational Settings," p. 48. The effects of the congruence of leadership styles from one level of supervision to the next upon productivity are less clear. See, for example, Stanley M. Nealey and Fred E. Fiedler, "Leadership Functions of Middle Managers," *Psychological Bulletin*, 70 (November 1968), p. 325.

in making day-to-day decisions. We will discuss in greater detail organizational variables such as these in later chapters on organization.

The Leader Variable. Finally, it should be recognized that both the needs and values of the leader may have a considerable influence on the type of leadership style which he *will* choose. In this respect, the leader's choice of an influence strategy may often be *constrained* by the nature of his own personality system. That is, even though a specified degree of directiveness may be theoretically most effective with regard to the follower's needs and abilities in any given situation, the leader may find it uncomfortable and difficult or in some cases impossible to make such a choice. For example, the individual who has learned to function, say in an authoritarian manner, may be unable to tolerate psychologically the thought of giving his subordinates considerable latitude in making decisions on their own. Or, the manager's general level of confidence in himself and others may have a bearing on his choice of a leadership pattern. There appears to be a considerable difference among managers as to the degree of confidence they have in other individuals, including the employees they supervise. If a manager has relatively little trust in his subordinates, he may believe it necessary to supervise their work closely; whereas if he has considerable faith in their abilities, he is less likely to do so. Furthermore, confidence in his own ability to function in uncertain situations is likely to condition his choice of leadership strategies. This is because the manager becomes less certain as to how it will be handled when he turns the responsibility for dealing with a problem over to a subordinate. For this reason those individuals who have a strong need for predictable and unambiguous situations often find it very difficult to delegate major responsibilities to others.

Fiedler's Contingency Model

Professor Fred E. Fiedler, after several years of studying leadership, has developed a model of leader effectiveness, commonly referred to as the "contingency model." This model is dynamic and situationally oriented, emphasizing interaction among key systems variables like the authoritarian—democratic—laissez-faire approach described above. However, it is more systematically framed, lending itself more to organized research aimed at testing its validity. The contingency model and research, unlike the approach described in the previous section, also has been confined explicitly to an analysis of leader effectiveness in supervising *groups* of subordinates.[43] Although further research is needed

---

[43] Fiedler has distinguished three different types of groups: (1) interacting, in which the efforts of members are interrelated in meeting some common goal; (2) coacting, where members work independently on a common task (e.g., a bowling team); and (3) counteracting, where individuals work together in negotiating and/or reconciling conflicting objectives. See Fred E. Fiedler, A *Theory of Leadership*

to validate this model, it has gained considerable support, and from a behavioral science viewpoint appears to have considerable theoretical soundness.

In his research, Fiedler identifies two basic styles of leadership by use of what is called the Least Preferred Co-worker Scale (LPC):[44]

1. Those individuals who rated their least preferred co-worker (the person with whom they could work least well) highly tended to be permissive, considerate, and human relations oriented in supervising their groups of followers. This type of leader appears to gain "his major satisfaction from establishing close personal relations with his group members."[45]

2. Conversely, those individuals who rated their least preferred co-workers low, tended to be active, controlling, structuring, and task oriented in supervising the members of their groups. The low LPC leader obtains "his major satisfaction by successfully completing the task, even at the risk of poor interpersonal relations with his workers."[46]

Perhaps the most attractive aspect of Fiedler's model is that "it predicts which style of leadership will work more effectively as the ease of exerting influence varies,"[47] *depending* on the *interaction* of certain basic situational variables.

In the contingency model, three basic situational variables are postulated, the existence of which in *different combinations*, will indicate which of Fiedler's two leadership styles will be more effective. These are:

1. Of *primary* importance, *leader-member relations,* or the degree to which the members of a leader's group like him, trust him, have confidence in him, and so forth.

Effectiveness (New York: McGraw-Hill Book Co., 1967), pp. 18–20. It should be emphasized that the contingency model is based on an analysis of leader effectiveness in interacting groups only.

[44] Two notes are in order here. First, Fiedler also used a second scale in identifying these styles—Assumed Similarity of Opposites (ASO)—which correlates highly with the LPC scale. Second, Fiedler does not consider his two styles of leadership as completely dichotomous categories, but recognizes that they represent a continuum.

[45] Fred E. Fiedler, "Style or Circumstances: The Leadership Engima," *Psychology Today,* 2 (March 1969), p. 40.

[46] Ibid.

[47] Walter Hill, "The Validation and Extension of Fiedler's Theory of Leadership Effectiveness," *Academy of Management Journal,* 12 (March 1969), p. 35. Fiedler defines "leadership style" in terms of the *basic* needs of an individual, which remain relatively constant over time; as opposed to specific *acts* of leader behavior which appear to be more variable over time. See Fiedler, "Style or Circumstance: The Leadership Enigma," p. 40. This definition is basically congruent with the point made earlier in the discussion of the Authoritarian—Democratic—Laissez-Faire framework—i.e., the leader's choice of an influence style may often be constrained by his own personality system.

2. *Task structure,* with high-task structure situations—ones in which the work done by the leader's followers can be programmed or spelled out in detail; and conversely, low-task structure situations— ones in which the work is vague, nebulous, and undefined.
3. *Leader position power.* This variable does not refer to any power the leader may possess as a result of his personality alone. Rather, it is derived from characteristics of his position in the organization—e.g., the power to discipline, fire, promote, and grant salary increases to his workers.[48]

Fiedler has categorized combinations of these three situational variables in his model into eight distinct "cells"; with leadership (viewed as the case of any leader's ability to influence) becoming increasingly more difficult as one progresses from Cell 1 to Cell 8 (see Figure 6–3). As is shown in Figure 6–3, the permissive, human relations style of lead-

Figure 6–3. Fiedler's Contingency Model of Leadership

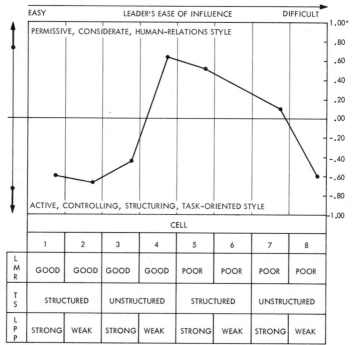

LMR = Leader-Member Relations
TS = Task Structure
LPP = Leader Position Power

* Median correlations between leaders' LPC scores and group effectiveness.

---

[48] Fiedler has postulated that there probably is some overlap between position power and leader-member relations; and that position power is the least important of his three situational variables.

ership in the contingency model is most effective in the middle cells; whereas, the active, controlling, task-oriented style is most effective in the extreme cells; i.e., those in which the combination of situational variables renders leader influence *both the easiest and the most difficult.*

That both highly favorable and unfavorable leadership conditions should logically call for directive active, task-oriented style may be illustrated by the following comments of Fiedler:

Where the situation is very favorable, . . . [e.g., Cell 1] . . . the group expects and wants the leader to give directions. We neither expect nor want the trusted air-line pilot to turn to his crew and ask, "What do you think we ought to check before takeoff?"[49]

Conversely, if in a Cell 8 situation, "the disliked chairmen of a volunteer committee asks his group what to do, . . . [rather than exercising a directive style] . . . he may be told that everybody ought to go home."[50]

Analysis of some of the middle cells in the contingency model is perhaps somewhat less obvious;[51] which the following examples should help clarify.

1. A well-liked project manager supervising a group of engineers working on the initial stages of a new space vehicle is faced with a highly nebulous and ill-defined work situation in which his position power may well be weak; i.e., a Cell 4 situation. Here, the human relations, permissive style in which he consults with his subordinates, asks them for their ideas, encourages their creativity, and so on, would be more appropriate than a directive, structuring style.

2. A recently hired college graduate who majored in business administration, is placed with little on-the-job training as a first-line supervisor over a number of "old timers" with lesser education but considerably more technical experience in a highly structured fabricating operation in a manufacturing firm. In such a situation, some jealousies and antagonisms may well exist toward him by the group on the grounds that management has superimposed upon them as a supervisor a "bright young college kid who doesn't really know what's going on around here." In such a Cell 5 or 6 situation (depending upon the strength of the new supervisor's position power), a human relations, rather than a highly directive controlling type of leadership in which the supervisor "orders the men what to do," would appear intuitively much more appropriate, as the contingency model would predict.

Finally, it should be emphasized that the contingency model is not only situationist-systems oriented, but also conceives of leader influence

---

[49] Fred E. Fiedler, "Engineer the Job to Fit the Manager," *Harvard Business Review,* 43 (September–October 1965), p. 119.

[50] Ibid.

[51] For a discussion of the theory underlying these middle cells, see Fiedler, *A Theory of Leadership Effectiveness,* p. 145. It should also be noted, that according to Hill, "Validation and Extension of Fiedler's Theory," p. 45, no actual studies have ever been conducted specifically examining Cell 6 in the contingency model.

operating in a *dynamic* context. As Fiedler himself stresses, the key situational variables affecting the ease of any manager's influence efforts, often change over time, so that different leader styles may be more effective in a managerial position at different points in time.[52] As may be noted, this view of Fiedler's is congruent with that which we took in viewing leadership in terms of the authoritarian—democratic—laissez-faire continuum.[53]

ORGANIZATIONAL DECISION MAKING AND LEADER EFFECTIVENESS

Previously, two basic points were made concerning human behavior in general: (1) the adult's *basic* personality patterns are relatively fixed, yet (2) viewing the individual's personality system as a dynamic open one, in which steady state improvement is possible, changes in people's behavior do take place. Relating these concepts to the fact that the variables affecting leader effectiveness are dynamic, we will now explore the question: "To what extent can organizational decisions contribute to increasing leader effectiveness under dynamic situational conditions?"

Basically, leader effectiveness may be enhanced by: (1) changing the manager's personality (and behavior) to adjust to the different leadership conditions with which he may have to deal; (2) modifying certain other systems elements to *fit* the manager's personality; or (3) some combination of the above two approaches.

Greenlaw has pointed out that it may often be easier to improve managerial performance by modifying certain systems elements than by attempting to "change" the manager by means of formalized management training and development programs.[54] Fiedler has also stressed the problems involved in changing managers' personalities as opposed to fitting jobs to managers in discussing his contingency model. He has taken the position that "executive jobs are surprisingly pliable," that fitting "the man to the leadership job by selection and training has

---

[52] For example, in the planning stages of a research project, the manager should probably be permissive, and let members of his group speak up freely and contribute their ideas. After the research plan has been developed, however, the situation will tend to become much more structured, calling for the manager to prescribe tasks in considerable detail. See Fiedler, "Engineer the Job to Fit the Manager," p. 116.

[53] It should be noted that the Fiedler model has been critiqued on both conceptual and methodological grounds in an article of which Fiedler himself was a co-author— Terence R. Mitchell et al., "The Contingency Model: Criticism and Suggestions," *Academy of Management Journal*, 13 (September 1970), pp. 253–67. Among the theoretical criticisms is that the LPC scale may be a measure of "cognitive complexity" rather than of the individual's basic style of leadership.

[54] Paul S. Greenlaw, "Management Development: A Systems View," *Personnel Journal*, 43 (April 1964), pp. 205–11.

not been spectacularly successful," and that it is "surely easier to change almost anything in the job situation than a man's personality and his leadership style."[55]

In discussing how it may be possible to "engineer" jobs to fit the manager's personality and leadership style in terms of the contingency model, Fiedler has made a number of suggestions, some of which are as follows:[56]

1. *Leader-member relations* may be improved by restructuring the manager's group of subordinates so that its members are more homogeneous—e.g., in terms of cultural, linguistic, technical, or educational backgrounds.
2. The leader's *task structure* may be modified in either direction by: (*a*) giving him and his group more explicit instructions or clarifying the task situation in greater detail; or conversely (*b*) providing a task situation with more general instructions framed in more vague and nebulous terms.
3. *Leader position power.* As indicated earlier, the organization has a number of ways by which it can enhance or diminish the manager's social power, as defined by French and Raven. Somewhat similarly, Fiedler has indicated that the leader's position power may be: (*a*) enhanced, for example, by providing him with higher rank in the organization; or (*b*) diminished by being given "subordinates who are equal or nearly equal to him in rank."[57]

Whether all suggestions such as the above are feasible in terms of the realities of organizational constraints is open to question. For example, to what extent can the organization change a manager's group of subordinates to make them more culturally homogeneous, in light of possible technological disruptions which might result from such a modification?[58] Nonetheless, some organizational change decisions suggested in this chapter appear to have merit; so that the possibilities of enhancing leader effectiveness by modification of organizational variables should be considered as decision-making strategies for organizational improvement.

---

[55] Fiedler, "Engineer the Job to Fit the Manager," p. 115. It should be noted, however, that Fiedler recognizes that training programs can be developed to help a manager learn in which situations he can perform most effectively. See Fiedler, "Style or Circumstance: The Leadership Enigma," p. 43.

[56] These points are discussed in both of the two references cited in the preceding footnote.

[57] Fiedler, "Style or Circumstance: The Leadership Enigma," p. 43.

[58] For example, regrouping employees by shifting some individuals with skills into a department calling for different skills may require considerable retraining. Further, the regrouping of workers who are union members may be prohibited by the firm's contract with the union.

TECHNOLOGY AND LEADERSHIP

Although we have referred to technological variables at various points in this chapter, it may well be that one of the most important organizational variables influencing the appropriateness of different leadership styles is *technology*. Specifically, key technological variables appear to be the degree of uncertainty and complexity involved in the work processes within which the leadership is being exercised. In the project manager illustration referred to earlier, for example, there were no well-defined set procedures or routine operative rules to prescribe behavior. Rather, the engineering technology was characterized by experimentation, trial and error, and uncertainty as to what behavior is appropriate. In this context, followers with high dependency needs and leaders depending upon authoritarian approaches will feel out of place—i.e., their needs are inappropriate to the complexity and uncertainty of the technological requirements. Followers with needs for autonomy and self-sufficiency and leaders leaning toward democratic and laissez-faire approaches may tend to be more successful. These ideas are more fully developed in organization structural terms in Chapters 8–11, but a further example may clarify them.

In a mass-production technology, there is extensive planning of the production processes, individual work procedures, the relations between jobs, the inputs, the outputs, and so on. This structuring of the work processes is designed to eliminate exceptions and uncertainty in the technological operations. In such organizational settings, there is little formal requirement for structuring and laissez-faire behavior and democratic leadership styles may labor under the handicap of preplanned decisions having eliminated the desirability for individual autonomy. The needs for conformity in such structures may lead to dysfunctional results by workers. Individual workers, for example, to create variety where little exists in the work routine, may resort to "fouling up" the routine by such actions as welding pop bottles in auto frames, and so on.

In fact, there may be a degree of self-selection of the individuals with various personality types (and thus propensities toward certain leader styles) in relation to types of organizations. Persons with a high dependence needs may tend to be attached to organizations designed for stability and simplicity. Individuals with high autonomy needs, conversely, would tend to be less comfortable in structured situations and would seek out organizations offering relatively more opportunity for individual expression. Further, while democratic and laissez-faire leadership opportunities do exist even in highly structured technological organizations, their greater applicability to organizational units possessing more uncertainties and greater complexities appears reasonable. Appropriate leadership style is thus seen as perhaps considerably affected by the organization's technology, especially as it influences the amount and extent of uncertainty and complexity.

The above analysis, as may be noted, raises questions as to just how much organizations can be changed to better provide for the meeting of leader and follower needs, as we suggested in the preceding section. Research has not yet provided us with an answer to this question. Perhaps the ultimate answer will be that the technological and environmental variables mentioned above do impose *basic* constraints on the organization's ability to modify its systems elements which otherwise would provide better conditions for effective leadership; but within these basic constraints there are still opportunities to "engineer the job to fit the manager."

SUMMARY

Leadership may be most appropriately thought of as a situational influence process. A number of needs may be satisfied by the assumption of either the leader or follower role, although neither is without its problems. Analysis of the individual's inclination to accept the influence efforts of others may be undertaken in terms of both his own need system and of the social power of the influencer. Many different degrees of directiveness may be chosen by the leader in his attempts to influence others, ranging from highly directive to highly permissive. The appropriateness of these strategies may be viewed as varying along an authoritarian—democratic—laissez-faire continuum, and as depending upon the leader, the follower, and the specific situation in which they are utilized. Or, leader styles under different situational conditions in interacting groups may be examined in light of the more formally structured Fiedler contingency model. Both of these approaches to leadership effectiveness are situationist ones, in which we ask not what kind of leadership is universally best, but rather, *under what conditions* do each of the various types of leader patterns seem most effective.

DISCUSSION AND STUDY QUESTIONS

1. *a)* What is charismatic leadership? Can it be related to French and Raven's bases of social power? Explain.
   b) Name someone whom you believe is an important charismatic leader today.
2. One manager was heard to say: "My superior is terrific; I get along beautifully with him, and we never have any disagreements." Comment on this statement on the basis of leadership theory.
3. Identify the primary basis of social power implied in each of the following statements by leaders to their subordinates:

a) "I'd think very highly of you if you could do an especially good job on this."

b) "If you are absent without notice again, I'll give you a week's layoff."

c) "If you can get the Blakeslee account, I'll try to get the 'big boss' to give you a 'fat raise'."

d) "I know you don't like the decision I've made, but I'm your boss, and it's your duty and responsibility to follow up on this decision the best you can."

e) "My marketing staff has come up with this computer model which is most imposing, and we should follow up on it immediately."

4. The objectives of managers as good leaders are congruent with those of their followers and the goals of the organization. Comment.

5. You have just, after finishing college, been appointed to be a first-line supervisor in a highly structured production line situation. Most of the workers are Spanish-American; you are not of Spanish descent, but you have majored in Spanish in college. Top management has given you support. What kind of a leader would you be (depending on your personality) and in which cell of the Fiedler model would your situation fall? Explain.

6. To what extent do you agree with Fiedler when the point is made to engineer the job to fit the manager, rather than to fit the manager to the job?

7. What are some of the situational variables that affect leader effectiveness in the authoritarian—democratic—laissez-faire continuum conceptual framework?

8. Which of French and Raven's bases of power is generally narrowest in scope? Why?

9. "Empathy" has been defined as the ability of one person to imagine himself in the position of another. How would this ability be useful in the leadership process?

10. What problem might arise if an employee with very strong independence needs were supervised by a manager whose leadership style was quite controlling and autocratic?

11. Describe the problems you might have as a manager if your superior were highly authoritarian, and your subordinates preferred a participative form of leadership. How might you resolve these problems?

12. Joe Shultz was a first-line supervisor of a group of assembly line workers at the Supreme Manufacturing Company. With a high school education, he had been with Supreme in this department as an assembly worker himself, and had been promoted to supervisor five years ago. His leadership style had been what might be called "active, controlling and task oriented"; he was of the same ethnic group as many of his subordinates (German); would often "kid" with them in Germanic slang; and would on a few occasions join them at the local Hofbrau after work on Fridays. He was well liked by his subordinates and their work performance was among the best in the company.

Joe was recognized as being highly intelligent and mechanically expert, and had been encouraged to take some night courses at the local university in engineering, which he did (and performed well in) for three years.

Recently, with a respectable (although not expert) engineering background, he was promoted to assistant supervisor in the company's drafting department. Here he had the technical skills necessary to supervise his employees, and the work he supervised was also highly programmed, as in the assembly department. The draftsmen whom he supervised were of diverse ethnic backgrounds, and many of them had been in the department for 8–10 years. There was a feeling on the part of some of his new subordinates that one of them, Fred Keen, should have been promoted to the position Joe was given. This feeling was not too strong, however, as Fred Keen was disliked by certain members of the group.

Joe continued his basic leadership style (as described above) in his new job; but somehow productivity in the drafting department fell. Numerous antagonisms developed under Joe's leadership and a couple of his better subordinates resigned within a period of three months.

a) Explain why Joe encountered these problems in his new job in terms of:

    1) French and Raven's framework.

    2) Fiedler's contingency model.

b) What, if anything, should his supervisor attempt to do to correct this situation?

SELECTED REFERENCES

BASS, BERNARD M. *Leadership, Psychology and Organizational Behavior.* New York: Harper & Bros., 1960.

FIEDLER, FRED E. *A Theory of Leadership Effectiveness.* New York: McGraw-Hill Book Co., 1967.

FRENCH, JOHN R. P., JR., and RAVEN, BERTRAM. "The Bases of Social Power," in DORWIN CARTWRIGHT (ed.). *Studies in Social Power.* Ann Arbor, Mich.: Institute for Social Research, 1959.

FROMM, ERICH. *Escape from Freedom.* New York: Farrar and Rinehart, 1941.

GOULDNER, ALVIN W. (ed.). *Studies in Leadership.* New York: Harper & Bros., 1950.

HOLLANDER, EDWIN P., and JULIAN, JAMES W. "Contemporary Trends in the Analysis of Leadership Processes," *Psychological Bulletin,* 71 (May 1969), 387–97.

JENNINGS, EUGENE E. *An Anatomy of Leadership: Princes, Heroes, and Supermen.* New York: Harper & Bros., 1960.

LIKERT, RENSIS. *New Patterns of Management.* New York: McGraw-Hill Book Co., 1961.

LINDZEY, GARDNER, and ARONSON, ELLIOTT (eds.). *Handbook of Social Psychology*, Vol. 4. 2d ed. Reading, Mass.: Addison-Wesley Publishing Co., Inc., 1969.

MCMURRY, ROBERT N. "The Case for Benevolent Autocracy," *Harvard Business Review*, 36 (January–February 1958), 82–90.

MITCHELL, TERENCE R., et al., "The Contingency Model: Criticisms and Suggestions," *Academy of Management Journal*, 13 (September 1970), 253–67.

NEALEY, M. STANLEY, and FIEDLER, FRED. "Leadership Functions of Middle Managers," *Psychological Bulletin*, 70 (November 1968), 313–29.

O'BRIEN, GORDON. "Leadership in Organizational Settings," *Journal of Applied Behavioral Science*, 5 (January–March 1969), 45–63.

STRAUSS, GEORGE, and SAYLES, LEONARD R. *Personnel: The Human Problems of Management*. 2d ed. Englewood Cliffs, N.J.: Prentice-Hall, Inc., 1967, chap. 4.

TANNENBAUM, ROBERT; WESCHLER, IRVING R.; and MASSARIK, FRED. *Leadership and Organization: A Behavioral Science Approach*. New York: McGraw-Hill Book Co., 1961.

Chapter 7

Group Behavior

THE BEHAVIOR of the member of the business firm is influenced by a number of variables in mutual interaction with one another. One of the most important of these is his membership in one or more groups within the organization. Beginning with the classic "Hawthorne" studies conducted at the Western Electric Company in the late 1920s,[1] research into organizational behavior has indicated that employees usually do not react to their work environment as isolated individuals. Rather, their behavior and attitudes toward their jobs and toward management are conditioned to a considerable extent by the values, standards, and expectations of the work groups to which they belong. For this reason, it is important for the manager to have some understanding of the dynamics of those groups in the organization with which he must deal so as to have a basis for predicting the impact of his decision strategies on their attitudes and behavior.

The purpose of this chapter is to provide a conceptual framework for understanding the behavior of organizational work groups. In doing so, attention will be focused on both (1) some of the kinds of group behavior in organizations of greatest concern to managerial decision making, and (2) certain major classes of variables which influence these patterns of behavior.

GROUP BEHAVIOR: SOME FUNDAMENTAL CONSIDERATIONS

People belong to many different groups. Some are comprised of many members; others are small in size. Some function for only short periods of time; others may endure for many years. Membership in some groups is extremely important for the individual, while his association with other groups may contribute only slightly to his need satisfaction.

The primary and most basic group to which the individual belongs is his family. Here, he is cared for as an infant and child; frequent

---

[1] For a report of this research, see F. J. Roethlisberger and W. J. Dickson, *Management and the Worker* (Cambridge, Mass.: Harvard University Press, 1939).

interaction with others takes place, and close and enduring relationships are developed. In addition, many people belong to a number of other groups—school groups, church groups, social clubs, civic groups, and, of most concern to us here, business organizations and groups *within* business organizations.

Definition of a "Group"

Although most individuals are familiar with many of these different kinds of groups, the meaning of the term "group" is subject to many different interpretations. Our preference is to view a group as *two or more persons, working together in pursuit of some common objective or objectives, the attainment of which through concerted effort will provide some need satisfaction for each.*[2] Thus, a number of teen-age boys who associate with each other as a "neighborhood gang" would be considered a social group. Or, in the business organization, a team of engineers working together toward the development of an intercontinental ballistic missile would constitute a group, as would a number of employees who band together to protest to their supervisor about a new work rule which they consider to be unfair.

One further observation needs to be made concerning our definition of the term "group." Above, work groups were referred to as existing *within* organizations. However, the organization *itself* may also be considered as a group. Business firms (except for small one-man operations) are comprised of two or more persons working together to meet certain organizational objectives; and the attainment of such objectives enables their individual members to gain some need satisfaction. As has been pointed out by two observers in the field of social psychology:

> Although we can distinguish between psychological groups and social organizations, these two have much in common. In the first place, the very same social group can, at certain times and under certain conditions, simultaneously qualify as either. . . . In the second place, and this is of the greatest significance . . . many of the most basic generalizations about psychological groups apply to social organizations. This is merely a reflection of the fact that both kinds of groups are special instances of social groups.[3]

---

[2] This definition is somewhat similar to that suggested by: Cecil A. Gibb, "Leadership," in *Handbook of Social Psychology*, ed. Gardner Lindzey, Vol. II (Reading, Mass.: Addison-Wesley Publishing Co., Inc., 1954), p. 879. It should also be noted that for purposes of conceptualization and analysis, groups have been classified by type in many different ways. For example, as noted in Chapter 6, Fiedler in his leadership research has classified groups as being coacting, interacting, or counteracting. Later in this chapter, a different typology will be utilized which we consider more appropriate for the analysis and understanding of organizational groups.

[3] David Krech and Richard S. Crutchfield, *Theory and Problems of Social Psychology* (New York: McGraw-Hill Book Co., 1948), p. 370. Copyright © 1948 by and used by permission of the McGraw-Hill Book Company.

In effect then, the business firm may be viewed as one large group system comprised of many smaller group subsystems. It will be upon these subsystems that we will focus primary attention in this chapter. Then, in Chapters 8–11, we will examine the organizational structure of the firm as a whole, and its relationship to the behavior of these smaller groups.

Group Membership and Need Satisfaction

People join groups and organizations for many different reasons. In some instances, an individual's membership in a particular group may be completely involuntary—e.g., the baby has no choice whatsoever as to the family group into which he is born. In other cases, a person has some choice as to his group memberships, although there may be strong pressures imposed upon him to join (or not to join) a particular group. For example, an employee in the business firm who has been transferred to a department in which he does not care to work, may be able to avoid membership in the new work group only by giving up his job and leaving the organization. In still other cases, one's group memberships may be on a highly voluntary basis. For instance, the individual may be under little or no pressure from others to join, or not to join, a bridge club, bowling team, or civic group.

As is true with most behavior, people are motivated to join groups and participate in their activities in order to help satisfy certain needs. More specifically, the following observations may be made concerning group membership and individual need satisfaction.

The satisfaction of any or all of the five basic classes of needs discussed in Chapter 5 may be contributed to by virtue of an individual's membership in a group. For example, satisfaction of many of the child's physiological, safety, and other needs obtains from his membership in the family group; the individual may gain considerable acceptance and recognition from his association with the other employees in his work group; or a person's endeavor in a civic group may contribute to the satisfaction of his self-actualization needs.

Groups are not equally responsive to the needs of their various members. As will be indicated more fully later, some group members usually enjoy greater prestige and status, and have more influence than others. In fact, groups are often dominated by a few individuals, while the remaining members assume a relatively passive role in making group decisions. In consequence, most groups serve to meet the current needs of their more influential members and "the function of any group can be better understood in terms of the major needs of its more dominant members than in undifferentiated terms for all of its members."[4]

---

[4] *Ibid.*, p. 382.

A certain amount of conflict will probably always exist between group objectives and the needs of its members. The reader will recall from the discussion in Chapter 5 that some observers have held that some of the requirements of formal organizations are incongruent with the needs of the mature individual. Although the small face-to-face group may often be more responsive to its member needs than the large organization, even in such groups we may expect to find some degree of incongruency. One reason for this is that, as indicated above, these groups are often dominated by a few members, with the remaining membership having relatively little say in making group decisions. In addition, the individual may find himself in a conflict situation by virtue of his membership in a number of groups of which two or more have opposing objectives. For example, an employee (1) whose family group places a high premium on hard work, and (2) who has considerable loyalty to the business organization for which he works, may find himself a member of a work group within the firm which imposes strong pressures on him to restrict production.

The above discussion raises the questions: (1) Under what conditions will an individual decide to join or leave any given group (assuming he has any choice in the matter); and (2) To what extent will he be inclined to accept the values and objectives of any group of which he is a member? In answering these questions, we suggest—as we did previously in Chapter 6 with respect to the individual's acceptance of leader influence efforts—that a person will join, withdraw from, or accept the values of a group when he perceives that he will probably gain greater net need satisfaction by doing so, than by not doing so. Or, as one observer has pointed out in summarizing propositions developed by certain group theorists:

> . . . When two (or more) people interact, each elects to express a behavior which will provide him with the greatest reward and the least cost . . . almost any behavior is both rewarding and costly, and the decision to express a given behavior is based on the balance of reward and cost for that behavior in comparison with the reward-cost balance of a potential alternative.[5]

For example, as will be pointed out more fully below, an organizational employee may restrict his production and hence his earnings in order to avoid being rejected by his work group because the psychological belongingness needs at stake provide more important rewards than the economic returns sacrificed.

---

[5] Clovis R. Shepherd, *Small Groups: Some Sociological Perspectives* (San Francisco: Chandler Publishing Company, 1964), p. 46. In this quotation, Shepherd was specifically referring to the group model developed by John W. Thibaut and Harold H. Kelley in *The Social Psychology of Groups* (New York: John Wiley & Sons, Inc., 1959); but also in the context that these propositions are similar to those developed by George C. Homans in his *Social Behavior: Its Elementary Forms* (New York: Harcourt, Brace & World, 1961).

WORK GROUP BEHAVIOR: A SYSTEMS ANALYSIS

Historical Background

Analysis of group behavior is complex because of the large number of interrelationships existing among the many variables involved. Further, there is no *one single* best theory or model yet developed by group theorists which adequately describes all aspects of the behavior of groups in organizations.

Two basic trends, however, appear to be gaining impetus in examining group behavior. The first of these is that of viewing groups as open systems. One of the classic systems-oriented group models is that developed by George C. Homans.[6] Although the work group systems model which we will develop below focuses attention on different variables than the basic ones in Homan's model, a brief description of the latter will provide further perspective to the understanding of groups as systems.

The Homans model categorized three basic forms of *interdependent* behavior which exists in all groups:

1. *Sentiments*, which refer to the feelings, beliefs, attitudes, and so on of members of groups,
2. *Activities*,[7] i.e., actions which individuals in a group take with respect to either nonhuman objects or other people; e.g., working on a milling machine or shaking hands with a co-worker, and
3. *Interactions among individuals*, such as working together or playing together.

Taking a systems view, Homans has contended that these three basic forms of behavior are dynamically interrelated, and that consequently, changes in any one are likely to induce changes in the others. For example, "if the scheme of activities is changed, the scheme of interaction will, in general, change also, and vice versa."[8] Further, Homans has also taken an open systems viewpoint, emphasizing that groups (and their basic types of behavior) are both affected by and affect their external environment.

---

[6] Homans postulated his basic model in *The Human Group* (New York: Harcourt, Brace & Company, 1950); and elaborated upon it in *Social Behavior: Its Elementary Forms*.

[7] It should be noted that Homans conceives of the term "activity" in a broader and somewhat different sense in his *Social Behavior: Its Elementary Forms* than he does in his *The Human Group*. For a discussion of this point see, for example, Shepherd, *Small Groups*, p. 44; and Rocco Carzo, Jr. and John Yanouzas, *Formal Organization: A Systems Approach* (Homewood, Ill.: Richard D. Irwin, Inc., 1967), p. 144, footnote 12.

[8] Homans, *The Human Group*, p. 102.

Second, both group and organization theorists and researchers have increasingly emphasized the interrelationships between *technology* and work group behavior, rather than focusing attention almost exclusively upon interpersonal relations within groups and between groups and other members of the organization.[9] These individuals have frequently used the term "sociotechnical system" to describe their work.[10] As one observer has pointed out, historically:

1. Many social scientists took the findings of the Hawthorne Experiments and other research "to mean that the environment was unimportant and the *social climate* between superior and subordinate was all that counted," while on the other hand;

2. "Industrial engineers tended to focus on people's *performances* at work"; and

3. It has only been fairly recently that there has been real progress in research which was primarily concerned in an integrated way "with the reciprocal relation between the technical and the human organizations."[11]

Two further observations are in order at this point. First, the term technology has been broadly defined, including such variables as machines, materials, the physical and mental requirements of specific jobs themselves, and the sequential flow of work from one employee to another (or lack of it), type of production systems (e.g., firms based primarily on a technology which calls for the production of units to meet customers' requirements as opposed to the continuous flow production of liquids and gases and crystalline substances,[12] and so forth.

Second, some research falling in the "sociotechnical" category has placed greater emphasis upon the relationships between technology and the organizational structure of the firm as a whole;[13] while other research has focused more attention on these interrelationships at the work group

---

[9] William F. Whyte has emphasized that the research findings which have focused sole attention on interpersonal relations have been rather meager and has postulated that: "recent work . . . has indicated that future theorizing on organizational behavior should be based on a foundation of knowledge of technology, work flow, and formal organization structure." William F. Whyte, *Organizational Behavior* (Homewood, Ill.: Richard D. Irwin, Inc., 1969), p. 715.

[10] Much of the pioneering work in examining "sociotechnical" systems has been done at the Tavistock Institute of Human Relations in London by E. L. Trist and others. Apparently the term itself "as used to refer to a specific set of phenomena in the real world first appeared" in these writings, according to Peter B. Vaill, "Industrial Engineering and Socio-Technical Systems," *The Journal of Industrial Engineering*, 18 (September 1967), pp. 530–38. Among these classic British publications are: E. L. Trist et al., *Organizational Choice* (London: Tavistock Publications, 1963); and A. K. Rice, *Productivity and Social Organization* (London: Tavistock Publications), 1958.

[11] Vaill, "Industrial Engineering," pp. 531, 532. The first italics in these quotations are ours.

[12] These are two of a number of different types of production systems categorized as influencing organizational behavior in Joan Woodward, *Industrial Organization: Theory and Practice* (London: Oxford University Press, 1965).

[13] For example, see ibid.

level within organizations.[14] We will make reference to sociotechnical relationships of both types in this and the following chapters which deal with organizational behavior.

Work Group Behavior: A Systems Model

There are many different ways in which one could: (1) view groups as open sociotechnical subsystems in organizations; and (2) define the inputs and outputs of such subsystems. Our preference is to conceptualize the behavior and attitudes of work groups as the outputs of such systems, which are generated by group member decisions.[15] For the purposes of conceptualization, these outputs are grouped into three general classes:

1. Group objectives and norms.
2. Patterns of differentiated member behavior—i.e., differences among individuals in the kinds of attitudes and behavior which they exhibit as members of any particular group.
3. Concerted action taken by group members.

The decision transformations made by the members of the group are in turn, influenced by many different kinds of *inputs* into the subsystem. In our model, these are grouped into two major classes:

1. Group membership—i.e., the outputs of any group are influenced considerably by the needs, values, and so on, of the *particular* personalities of which it is comprised.
2. The organizational environment in which the group functions—types of work performed and other technological variables, supervisory actions taken affecting the group—also influence its outputs.

A schematic model of this systems view is shown in Figure 7–1.

The nature of each of the two input classes in this model, as well as group decision transformations and outputs, are conditioned considerably by various types of managerial decisions, as we will indicate later.

The basic reason why this work group model is framed in terms of inputs and outputs rather than independent and dependent variables is that the variables involved are dynamically and reciprocally *interde-*

---

[14] See, for example, Leonard R. Sayles, *The Behavior of Industrial Work Groups* (New York: John Wiley & Sons, Inc., 1958). It should be noted that Sayles focused his attention on departmental units, which were sometimes small groups, but in some cases encompassed as many as 100 workers.

[15] For another organizational sociotechnical conceptualization, see, for example, John A. Seiler, *Systems Analysis in Organizational Behavior* (Homewood, Ill.: Richard D. Irwin, Inc., 1967), esp. Figure 1, p. 33. Seiler's inputs are classified as human, technological, social, and organizational. He views the actual behavior of groups as being comprised of Homans' three elementary forms of behavior indicated above (activities, interactions, and sentiments); and the outputs of the organizational system as productivity, satisfaction, and development.

Figure 7-1. Work Group Behavior: A Systems View

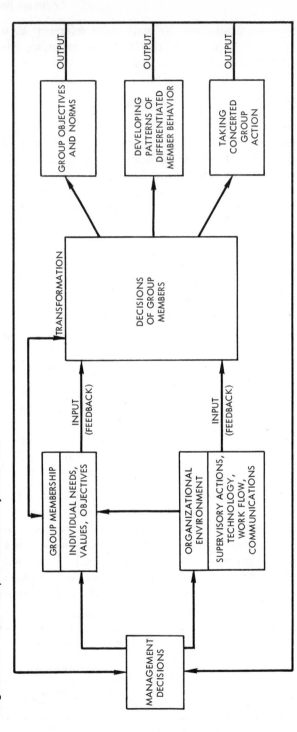

pendent, in an open systems sense as discussed in Chapter 4. For instance, not only may concerted action by a work group be influenced by management decisions, but it in turn may also influence actions taken by management. Such dynamic interdependence among these variables may be illustrated by the following example:

A number of employees in a manufacturing plant where the work performed was frequently quite dirty made it a habit of leaving their workplaces 15 or 20 minutes before quitting time to wash up. This was done even though no provision existed for clean-up time in the union contract. Their departmental supervisor decided to curb this practice and posted a notice to the effect that those who left early in the future would be disciplined. The members of his work group resented this action, and decided that they would ignore the supervisor's warning. The following day all but three members of the group left their workplaces 17 minutes early and were subsequently given an oral warning (the first step in the company's disciplinary procedure) by the supervisor. Angered by the action, the group decided that it would engage in a production slowdown and restrict its output to the minimum acceptable level. After the slowdown had been in effect for three days, the matter was brought to the attention of top management. Shortly thereafter, a compromise agreement was negotiated with the union whereby employees in the department were given 10 minutes of clean-up time at the end of each day.

As may be observed, the above example illustrates what might be termed a "behavioral chain reaction" in which a series of mutually interdependent actions were taken by management and a work group. From the point of view of the group as a subsystem, the supervisor's actions constituted information inputs on the basis of which group decisions (substantive transformations) were made to engage in protest behavior (output). On the other hand, if one were to view this situation from the viewpoint of management and the total organizational system, the group's behavior would represent information inputs from a subsystem, with the supervisor's decisions constituting transformations, and his actions, outputs. The behavior illustrated in the example is viewed from the vantage point of both the total organizational system and the group subsystem in Figure 7–2.

Group Membership and the Organizational Environment Inputs. Each of the two interdependent input classes in our group subsystem model are influenced by managerial decisions. Through employee selection and assignment, management determines where specific personalities are to be placed within the organization. Such placement decisions, coupled with those establishing the types of work environment in which each member of the firm is to function, influence considerably the formation and composition of particular work groups. *Once formed,* the behavioral and attitudinal outputs of any such group will in turn be a function of the specific personalities which comprise it and the organizational environment in which it exists. We will now turn our attention

Figure 7–2. The Work Group Subsystem and the Organizational System

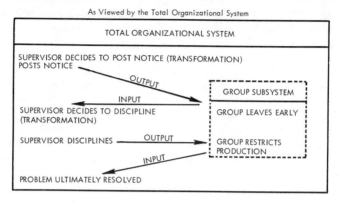

As Viewed by the Total Organizational System

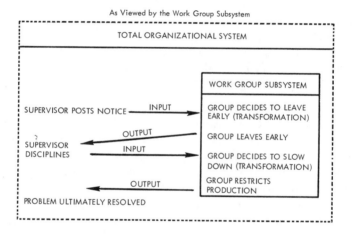

As Viewed by the Work Group Subsystem

to these two basic input categories: group membership and the organizational environment.

In examining work group behavior, it is important to recognize that the employee in the business organization frequently is *not* a member of a *single* group. Rather, he often enjoys membership in more than one such group. Among the different types of work groups to which the individuals may belong, the following categorization developed by Leonard R. Sayles is quite useful:[16]

1. The *command* group, which is comprised of all employees reporting to the same supervisor.

2. The *task* group, which is made up of those employees who collaborate in some way on a given job or task. Within a research and

---

[16] Leonard R. Sayles, "Work Group Behavior and the Larger Organization," in Conrad Arensburg et al., *Research in Industrial Human Relations,* Industrial Relations Research Association (New York: Harper, 1957), pp. 131–45.

development department, for example, four or five engineers may work closely together over a period of time on a particular subphase of a project.

3. The *interest* group, which includes those employees who have banded together in order to promote some common objective relating to the organization. Employees forming such groups may or may not work together on a common task, or be under the command of the same supervisor. A number of milling machine operators in a plant, for example, regardless of department, may unite to press management for looser production standards, or improved seniority rights.

4. The *friendship* clique, comprised of those members of the organization who associate together on the basis of ties of friendship. Such groups may converse with each other during working hours, take their coffee breaks together, or sometimes extend their on-the-job associations to such outside activities as a bowling team or monthly poker club.

The composition of any given command ar task group within the organization is basically determined by managerial *selection* and *assignment* decisions. Once employed by the organization, an individual may succeed in being transferred away from the command of a particular supervisor, or may have some say as to the tasks to which he will be assigned. However, it is management which ultimately decides which employees it will hire, to which department they will be assigned, and (to perhaps a lesser extent depending on technological variables) upon which tasks they will work.

Management, on the other hand, does not explicitly assign particular organizational members to any given interest group—groups of this type are voluntarily formed. However, the composition (membership inputs) of interest groups may be influenced considerably by any one of a different number of managerial decisions. For example, workers who are assigned to perform the same jobs, receive the same pay, and so forth, will tend to have more interests in common than those who do not; and consequently are more likely to band together to enhance their position.

Membership in the friendship clique is also basically voluntary. These groups represent

. . . the diverse interests of the worker placed there by the organization. The boundaries of these clusterings appear to reflect the employees' off-the-job interests and associations or previous work experience. Age, ethnic background, outside activities, sex, marital status, and so on, comprise the mortar that binds the clique together.[17]

Even though membership in the friendship clique is largely voluntary, its composition is influenced by the formal command and task structure and the specific technology of the firm. This is essentially because indi-

---

[17] Ibid., p. 133.

viduals who have greater opportunities to communicate with each other tend to develop closer friendship associations. Such communication opportunities are largely a function of spatial and temporal[18] constraints imposed on workers by their jobs in relation to technology. The physical proximity of workers is a key variable here because it is generally "easier for people to talk to each other when they are close to each other in space than when they are separated."[19] Noise, other perceptual barriers (such as walls),[20] and the degree to which workers can move from their work locations, rather than being stationed at one position all day, however, must also be considered as spatial constraints modifying physical proximity per se.

Researchers have found that the degree of communications possible among workers may vary considerably under different types of technologies. Meissner, for example, found that communicational opportunities among workers were generally greater in both technologically "underdeveloped" situations (e.g., heavy manual hauling) and at the most advanced levels of technology (automation) than in intermediate technologies such as assembly lines.[21] In his study, it should be noted that Meissner was refering *not only* to verbal messages among workers; *but also,* for example, in automated systems, the sending of messages through technical transmitters. That there may be less *direct* interpersonal in some computerized situations, however, has been suggested by Whisler. He has indicated, for example, that the introduction of electronic data processing in 15 insurance companies studied led to *less* direct interpersonal communications among insurance clerks and both their peers and superiors.[22]

The above discussion indicates that both of the two major input classes in our group subsystem model are influenced by managerial decisions, including those involving technology, to which increasing attention is being given. Through employee selection and assignment decisions, management determines at what locations specific personalities are to be placed within this organization. Such placement decisions *in mutual*

---

[18] By temporal constraint, we mean that people must be together (as qualified below) at the *same time* in order to communicate.

[19] Abraham Zaleznik and David Moment, *The Dynamics of Interpersonal Behavior* (New York: John Wiley & Sons, Inc., 1964), p. 299.

[20] Martin Meissner, in discussing spacial constraints with respect to communication possibilities has classified distance between work stations into four categories: talking distance, shouting distance, seeing distance, and beyond seeing distance. *Technology and the Worker* (San Francisco: Chandler Publishing Co., 1969), p. 21.

[21] Ibid., p. 239. It should also be noted that Meissner concluded that from the limited amount of information available in his study concerning automation, the individual's choice of workers with whom he could converse directly in this type of technology was restricted to a considerable extent. Ibid., p. 241.

[22] Thomas L. Whisler, *Information Technology and Organization Change* (Belmont, Calif.: Wadsworth Publishing Company, Inc., 1970), p. 77. Whisler also notes that the longer companies have used the computer the greater the decline in interpersonal communications among the insurance clerks (p. 78).

interaction with those establishing the nature of the work environment, influence directly the formation and composition of particular work groups. Mutual interaction is emphasized because different personalities will perceive and react to technological and other variables differently, and their attitudes and behavior as members of groups will be influenced by these perceptions. *Once formed,* the behavioral and attitudinal outputs of any such group will also be a function of the specific personalities which comprise it and the organizational environment in which it exists.

Group Objectives and Norms

Work Group Objectives. Work groups, as indicated previously, establish objectives; these objectives are conditioned considerably by member needs, and are also influenced by the organizational environment.

Although the objectives of different work groups will vary considerably, certain observations may be made about their goals. First, with respect to small groups in general, Shepherd has pointed out that successful groups tend to have clear-cut objectives, rather than vague ones; and also objectives which are the same as or compatible with the personal objectives of the members of the group:

If the group's objectives are vague the members will probably be working at cross purposes since they are unlikely to have the same or compatible personal objectives. Consequently, the more time a group spends in developing agreement on clear objectives the less time it need spend in achieving them and the more likely the members' contributions will converge toward a solution.[23]

Second, both the command and task groups are explicitly formed to meet organizational objectives—employees are assigned to specific departments and tasks in order to carry out the work to be undertaken by the firm. Task and command groups, however, may or may not fully accept the objectives laid down for them by management, and may develop goals of their own. For example, task groups often develop work methods that may depart from the organization's original conception of the job, or at least "fills in" the specific details of the operation not specified in the formal work plan. Thus, employees may exchange repetitive jobs, although such trading is illegal; one worker may do two jobs while a colleague rests; or, . . . they may change the sequence of the operations to reduce tensions and provide shortcuts.[24] Both interest groups and friendship cliques, on the other hand, are voluntarily formed to meet member objectives rather than those of the organization.

[23] Shepherd, *Small Groups*, p. 122. It should be noted that the objectives of any "successful" group may or may not be congruent with the organization's objectives.

[24] Sayles, "Work Group Behavior and the Larger Organization," p. 136. For a more thorough discussion of the extent to which workers may perform their work differently than originally conceived of by management in relation to technological constraints, see, for example, Meissner, *Technology and the Worker*, pp. 25 ff.

The objectives of the interest group, as indicated above, are geared toward enhancing or protecting some common interest of its membership such as improved work methods, and pay. A primary goal of the friendship clique, on the other hand, is to meet the belongingness needs of its members on the job. Somewhat relatedly, membership in the friendship clique also "provides a source of personal security in an impersonal environment." This is because:

> Loyalty, even attachment, to the total organization with its impersonality, extended hierarchy, and social distance becomes ambiguous. However, attachment to the immediate and easily perceived face-to-face group is the predominant reality of organization experience.[25]

Work Group Norms. As a means of gearing member actions toward their various objectives, work groups invariably develop certain attitudinal and behavioral standards to which it is expected that their members will conform. The attitudes and viewpoints which group members are expected to share and those patterns of behavior toward which conformity is expected are often referred to as *norms*. We have already observed the manifestation of a group norm in the illustration presented in a previous section—i.e., concerted action to restrict output in protest of the supervisor's efforts to curb the practice of leaving the job early to wash up.

Several basic observations concerning norms are in order at this point. First a norm always refers to something specific—a particular form of behavior or attitude (a tendency to behave). Second, the *number* of different norms which may exist in different groups may vary considerably.[26] So also will the amount, degree, or range of behavior (or attitude) that is considered appropriate with respect to any particular norm. In one work group, for example, it may be considered appropriate for members to turn out 120–150 pieces per hour; while in another group performing the same task, the norms may be established at 110–130 pieces per hour. Finally, a wide variation exists in regards to the *intensity* of a group's approval or disapproval of any of its member's behavior (or attitudes) with respect to a particular norm. "In certain areas of behavior, a transgression is punished severely; in others there seems to be little concern by members of a group regardless of how individuals behave."[27] For example, a work group may be relatively indifferent as

---

[25] Sayles, "Work Group Behavior," p. 133.

[26] In some cases it is possible for there to be a conflict between the behavior expected by one group norm and that of another. This may lead to a situation in which members find it difficult to obtain approval for their behavior, which creates a conflict situation for them. For a discussion of this point, as well as a more detailed examination of norms and their characteristics, see Jay M. Jackson, "Structural Characteristics of Norms," in Bruce J. Biddle and Edwin J. Thomas, *Role Theory: Concepts and Research* (New York: John Wiley & Sons, Inc., 1966), pp. 113–26.

[27] Ibid., p. 116.

to whether its members wear green or blue shirts, but very much concerned about their production levels.

Enforcement of Norms. Various degrees of conformity to different norms may be found among members of any particular work group. While some group attitudes and standards of behavior may be accepted by all members, others may conflict strongly with the needs and values of certain individuals within the group, and for this reason be rejected. For example, an employee in a work group in which the restriction of production is viewed as an important norm may refuse to limit his output because he feels a strong need to earn as much money as he can so as to be able to send his children to college.

Notwithstanding such differences, however, strong pressures are often exerted by the work group on its individual members which renders nonconformity to norms difficult if they are to remain within the group. This, of course, is especially true with high-intensity norms as discussed above. The nature and effectiveness of these pressures can perhaps be best understood by drawing on some of the concepts which we have examined previously—by viewing the group's ability to influence its member's behavior in terms of member needs and the bases of social power which the group possesses.

A basic reason why individuals are often inclined to be influenced by group norms, even though such conformity may conflict with certain other needs experienced and values held, is that they want to identify with, be a part of, and be accepted by the group. In much the same way as with identification with authority figures which we discussed in Chapter 6, identification with the group may enable the individual to incorporate psychologically the strength of others in himself. Further, groups often have considerable power to reward those members who conform to its values and standards, and to punish those who do not. In addition to bestowing acceptance—a most powerful reward—upon the "regular" member, the group may be in a position to provide assistance to its members and help "protect" them from management. For example, the older, and more experienced members of a group may inform those newer members who have become accepted of shortcuts in work methods unknown to the supervisor which will result in greater earnings with less effort, ways of avoiding being caught by supervision for breaking unpopular work rules, and so on. On the other hand, the group can be extremely punitive to those of its members who do not abide by the norms which exist. The nonconformist member may face ostracism—his fellow workers may refuse to talk with him, or permit him to engage in any of their social activities. Or, some cases have even been noted in which the machines of nonconformists have been sabotaged as a punitive measure by other members of a group. As suggested earlier, whether any *particular* individual will accede to the influence efforts exerted upon him by the group, will depend upon whether he perceives that he will probably gain greater net need satisfaction by conforming than by not doing so.

Directionality of Norms. Some observations are now in order regarding the *direction* toward which work group norms are geared in terms of management's objectives—i.e., to what extent are such attitudinal and behavioral standards directed toward meeting organizational objectives, or, conversely, toward thwarting the aims and goals of management?

Many research studies to date have focused attention on norms and standards *negatively* directed in terms of organizational objectives. One of the most significant areas of negatively directed work group behavior which has been observed in a number of firms, and especially among production employees in manufacturing enterprises, is that of output restriction. Even in cases where incentive systems are in effect, under which employees are rewarded by additional pay for each piece of work turned out above a standard established by the firm, many work groups have been known to develop and enforce output restrictions. For example, where company work standards are set at 100 pieces per hour for all members of a particular task group, and where a majority of the employees could turn out 140 pieces with relatively little extra effort, the group may, nevertheless, attempt to enforce the restriction of output by its members to not more than 110 pieces.

There seem to be at least three basic reasons for such behavior. First, work groups may attempt to restrict output because they fear that if they do not some of their members will be out of jobs. Such fears may be well justified, especially when the demand for a firm's products is relatively inelastic. When this is the case, the company may not be able to sell the increased production that would be turned out if all workers put forth their maximum efforts, and consequently, some employees might have to be laid off. Further, in some firms subject to highly fluctuating seasonal demand patterns, policies are followed by which numbers of employees are temporarily laid off each year during slack periods. Here also, work groups may feel that the magnitude of such layoffs will be reduced if output is restricted.

A second motive for output restrictions is to protect group members against the "tightening" of work standards by management. Sometimes incentive standards on a particular job may be set so that they can be exceeded by, say 60 or 70 percent, by most employees with maximum effort. Production at such high levels, however, might well convince management that the standards have been too loosely set, and that they need to be restudied and made more realistic. On the other hand, if the group makes sure that member output never exceeds the company established standards by perhaps 20 to 25 percent, such actions on the part of management are less likely to be forthcoming.

A third reason for the development and enforcement of output restriction norms is to protect the older members of the work group. In our culture a commonly held value is that older and more experienced employees should enjoy greater earnings than their younger and less-experienced colleagues. In the professions and in many skilled nonprofessional jobs, the individual's earnings normally do increase as he gains experience and becomes more competent in his work. However, in many production jobs in which (1) earnings are directly related to output and (2) considerable physical effort and vigor are called for, this cultural value may be violated in the absence of output restrictions. This is because individuals in such jobs often slow down physically as they grow older to the extent that they could be outproduced by their younger, more vigorous colleagues if the latter were to put forth maximum effort. If this were permitted to occur, many of the more experienced workers would be dealt a serious status blow, for their weekly earnings might be considerably less than those of even some of the newest men in their work group.

Although work group norms are sometimes geared in directions which conflict with organizational objectives, often they are not. In fact, some work groups develop and attempt to enforce upon their membership performance standards calling for both a high quality and quantity of work. Members of a firm's research and development department, for example, may adhere to high professional standards, and look down upon and reject any of their colleagues whose sloppy performance does not meet these standards. Or, in some university departments, one's prestige, status, and acceptance by his fellow professors are enhanced by a high level of output in research and writing.

Patterns of Differentiated Member Behavior

We will now turn our attention to the second major class of outputs in our subsystem model—the many differences found among members of the work group in their attitudes, behavior, and participation in group activities. In doing so, we will examine member differentiation from the point of view of: (1) role; (2) status; and (3) informal leadership.

Role Differentiation. One way of viewing differences among individuals as members of groups is to focus attention on the *roles* which they assume.[28] A role has been defined as:

. . . a patterned sequence of learned *actions* or deeds performed by a person in an interaction situation. The organizing of individual actions is a product of the perceptual and cognitive behavior of person *A* upon observing person *B*.

---

[28] For a more detailed but not overly technical discussion of the concept of "role," see William G. Scott, *Organization Theory* (Homewood, Ill.: Richard D. Irwin, Inc., 1967), chap. 8. It should also be noted that the concepts of role and status are inseparable, but we treat them as does Scott under different sections for analytical purposes.

B performs one or a number of discrete acts which *A* observes and organizes into a concept, a role. On the basis of this conceptualization of the actions of *B*, *A* expects certain further actions from *B*. . . . Once having located or named the position of . . . [*B*] . . . *A* performs certain acts which have been learned as belonging to the reciprocal position; these actions are conceptualized as *A's* role.[29]

There are a number of variables which determine the roles which individuals are expected to assume in their relationships with others such as age, sex, and other personality characteristics, job or position held, values of the particular culture in which they live. In the family, a different role is expected for the father than for the mother. At the university, the professor and the student assume different roles. Similarly, different roles are assumed by different members of organizational work groups. New members may be expected to show deference to those with greater seniority in the group; a member who is highly intelligent and adept at communicating ideas to others may be looked to as a spokesman for the group in presenting complaints to the foreman; an individual whose religious or ethnic background is different from that of the majority of group members may be looked down upon and expected to play a passive role as far as influencing group decisions is concerned.

Status Differences.   Implied in the above discussion is the fact that in the work group (as in other groups) some members enjoy a greater degree of status than others—i.e., they are viewed as being more important or prestigeful.[30] Within the business firm, an individual's status is a function of two major classes of variables: (1) certain of his personal characteristics and (2) his position in the "formal" organization. *In general,* men enjoy a higher status than women; individuals of the same ethnic and religious background as the majority of the members in their group enjoy a greater status than those with different backgrounds; and a person's status is enhanced by personality characteristics which appeal to others—e.g., intelligence, a "warm and friendly" disposition, and so forth. As far as one's position in the formal organization is concerned, those persons holding more important, more highly paid, and more skilled jobs will often enjoy a higher status than those who do not, all other factors being equal. In addition, a person's status may be enhanced if his job calls for him to be physically located in such a manner that he can interact frequently with other members of his group—as opposed to being physically isolated from his colleagues.

From the above discussion, the reader may observe that an individual may possess some attributes which would tend to give him a high status

---

[29] Theodore R. Sarbin, "Role Theory," in *Handbook of Social Psychology*, Vol. I, p. 225.

[30] For a more thorough discussion of the concept of status, see William G. Scott, *Organization Theory*, pp. 182–92.

position within his group, and others which would tend to lower his status. For example, a member of a race or religion different from that of some of his colleagues might be the most intelligent and most highly paid employee in a particular work group. When such is the case—i.e., when inconsistent or a person's status indicators are considerably "out of line" with his others—the individual is referred to as being characterized by a *low degree* of *status congruence.*

Some observations are in order concerning status congruence, which has become increasingly recognized as an important behavioral variable in groups. First, there are generally only a few status factors in any particular group which are regarded important by its members, and therefore which contribute substantially to the degree of status congruence possessed by any member. The importance of these factors varies considerably from group to group. Second, individuals with low-status congruence generally tend to have feelings of "stress, frustration and dissatisfaction."[31] Such individuals may attempt to cope with such frustrations by either constructive or defensive behavior as discussed in Chapter 5. For example, a low congruence individual may withdraw and fail to participate in the group (avoidance); or conversely, constructively attempt to modify one or more of his status factors in an attempt to make them more congruent with the others[32] (e.g., increase his education). Finally, with respect to interpersonal relationships within groups, when an individual's status factors are incongruent, others will usually find it difficult to know how to react to him since he is high on certain status dimensions and low on others. Such ambiguity

tends to result in stress and various other reactions. . . . For example, a college educated assembler might disturb other assemblers in a department who would then either ignore him or behave in an unfriendly way toward him and thus cause him to be uncomfortable.[33]

It should also be pointed out that the individual's *total status* as well as his status congruence seem to have considerable influence on his

---

[31] J. G. Hunt, "Status Congruence: An Important Organization Function," *Personnel Administration,* 32 (January–February 1969), p. 20.

[32] Two observations are in order here. First, some attempts to modify status factors in an effort to make them more congruent may result in conflict within the group (ibid.). Second, attempt to change status factors (other than by withdrawal) may not always represent constructive behavior. For example, an individual may "distort his perception, so that he perceives the dimensions on which he ranks high as more important, and those he ranks low as relatively unimportant." Gerald I. Susman, "The Concept of Status Congruent as a Basis to Predict Task Allocations in Autonomous Work Groups," *Administrative Science Quarterly,* 15 (June 1970), p. 165. For a more detailed discussion of some of the ways people attempt to reduce status incongruence, see both of ·the above references. For a review of the literature on status congruence, see also Edward E. Sampson, "Studies of Status Congruence," in L. Berkowitz (ed.), *Advances in Experimental Social Psychology, 4* (New York: Academic Press, 1969), pp. 225–70.

[33] Hunt, "Status Congruence," p. 22.

relationships with the work group. In a classic study conducted by Zaleznik, Christensen, and Roethlisberger, for example, it was found that both the individual's need satisfaction and his inclination to conform to group norms were conditioned by these two variables.[34] It was found that those individuals possessing both high total status and status congruence were more likely to be accepted by the group as "regular" members. Further, these regular members tended to be satisfied and to conform to the norms of the group, while the nonregulars (those not accepted by the group) tended to be less satisfied and not to conform to the norms. Or, in terms of needs and motivation, those individuals who were in a position to gain some satisfaction of their belongingness needs by virtue of their acceptance by the group were willing to abide by its norms, while those for whom such acceptance was not forthcoming were not inclined to do so.

The implications of lack of status congruence for management decision making are not yet clear. However, as Hunt has noted, incongruence can be considered by management as a possible problem "when there is evidence of interpersonal conflict or stress and/or performance is not up to par."[35] He also suggests, for example, that the status congruence variable may have an influence on such diverse aspects of management as union-management relations, worker compensation systems, acceptance of organizational change, and supervisory behavior.[36]

Informal Leadership.   In Chapter 6, we indicated that employee behavior in the business organization is influenced not only by formally appointed supervision, but also by members of work groups who evolve as "informal leaders." Many different patterns of member influence may be observed among organizational work groups. In some groups, little or no informal leadership may evolve. In others, efforts directed toward influencing the behavior and attitudes of the group membership may be centered largely in one individual. In still others, we may find more than one person assuming the role of informal leader.

Many of the observations which we made about leadership in Chapter 6 apply to the informal as well as the formal leader—e.g., those concerning the needs satisfied by assuming the leader role, the ambivalence of the followers toward the leader, and so forth. There is, however, one important difference between the formal and the informal leader— the latter lacks many of the powers which the former enjoys. Unlike the formally appointed manager, the informal leader within the work group lacks both the power to discipline (or fire) his colleagues if they

---

[34] A. Zaleznik, C. R. Christensen, and F. J. Roethlisberger, *The Motivation, Productivity, and Satisfaction of Workers: A Prediction Study* (Boston: Harvard University, Division of Research, Graduate School of Business Administration, 1958).

[35] Hunt, "Status Congruence," p. 23.

[36] Ibid. For example, Hunt suggests that there are good reasons to believe that more and different kinds of grievances will be filed by those individuals who are lower in status congruence.

do not accede to his influence efforts, and the power to reward them with promotions or pay increases based on meritorious performance. Neither may he have the power to make many other types of decisions which may have an important bearing on member need satisfaction, such as scheduling overtime work, assigning employees to jobs or work projects which they may especially like or dislike.

Why then, is the informal leader, although he lacks many of the powers of the formal leader, often in a position to induce other members of his group to accede to his influence efforts? Probably the most fundamental reason for the work group's acceptance of one or more of its member's assumption of the leader role is that it is necessary for this role to be fulfilled if many of the group's objectives are to be achieved. Plans of action must be initiated by one or more members of the group and then communicated to the rest of the membership. Someone must attempt to compromise differences of opinion which may exist among the group and to influence members to take a common stand on basic issues if concerted action is to be undertaken. Dealings with management can often be facilitated if one or more members are chosen as spokesmen to communicate the group's position to supervision. In short, the informal leadership serves to plan, organize, coordinate, and provide direction for the work group in its efforts to achieve its objectives.

One final question should be raised concerning informal leadership within work groups: What are the characteristics of those individuals who do emerge as informal leaders? First, as indicated previously, physical proximity among workers (a function of managerial decisions including technology) tends to facilitate friendship patterns; and in many cases the informal leader will be an individual who is in close proximity to a number of the members of his group with whom he has developed ties of friendship.[37] Second, as the situationist analysis presented in the previous chapter would indicate, there are few, if any specific personality characteristics universally possessed by those assuming such leader roles. Rather, the characteristics of informal leaders tend to vary considerably from group to group. However, the informal leader will usually be a member whose values, objectives, behavior, and so forth, will tend to be congruent with that considered desirable by the group. In a work group dominated by French-Canadian membership and values, he is likely to be of French-Canadian origin. Or in a work group in which

---

[37] Other technological variables may also have an influence upon the type of informal leadership, if any, which evolves in a group. For example, Leonard Sayles in his *Behavior of Industrial Work Groups* (New York: John Wiley & Sons, Inc., 1958), identified, on the basis of a number of technological variables, four basic types of work groups. In one type of group (called apathetic) Sayles generally found no well-defined leadership existing; while in another type (erratic) autocratic leadership was found to be common. It should be noted that Sayles's approach in developing this classification of four different types of groups has been subject to criticism—e.g., see Meissner, *Technology and the Worker*, p. 253.

output restrictions have been developed, he is likely to be a member whose productivity comes close to the standard set by the group. Thus, both the organizational environment in relation to the characteristics of the individual himself will influence just who becomes an informal leader.

Concerted Group Action

Now that we have discussed some of the basic differences among member behavior within the work group we will turn our attention to those conditions under which group members behave similarly—i.e., unite to take concerted action to meet their objectives. In our discussion we will examine the concept of "cohesion" and some of the more important relationships between the inputs into the group subsystem and the concerted action output.

Work Group Cohesion. One concept which has frequently been utilized by researchers in their study of organizational work groups is that of *cohesion* or *cohesiveness.* To date, two different major approaches have been followed in attempting to measure group cohesion. Some researchers having given attitude questionnaires to various groups, have judged as highly cohesive those groups where the members have shown positive sentiments toward the group, and negative ones toward the possibility of leaving the group, and have attempted to relate cohesion to productivity.[38] Other researchers, on the other hand, have focused attention on the concerted behavior of work groups toward management in order to achieve some goal.[39] As the reader may note, the latter approach focuses attention on one of the three general classes of output in our group subsystem model—concerted action. Considering this view more useful than the "positive sentiments" concept of cohesiveness, we will use the terms "cohesion" and "concerted action" synonymously in the following discussion.

Subsystem Inputs and the Concerted Action Output. Research has shown that different work groups in the business organization vary considerably in their cohesiveness. In this section, we will indicate some of the relationships between our two major classes of subsystem inputs— group membership and the organizational environment—and work group cohesion. In doing so, we will make some observations about the impact on cohesiveness of certain subvariables within each of these two classes,

---

[38] A major study utilizing this concept of cohesion is Stanley Seashore, *Group Cohesiveness in the Industrial Work Group* (Ann Arbor, Mich.: Survey Research Center, 1954). Basically Seashore found that (1) average cohesiveness of groups was not related to productivity; but (2) that in low-cohesive groups, member ranges of production varied much more widely than in high-cohesive groups.

[39] A classic study utilizing this approach to cohesion is Sayles, *The Behavior of Industrial Work Groups.*

assuming in each case that all other factors are held the same. The reader should recognize that for any given work group, some of these inputs may tend to predispose the group to a high degree of cohesion, while others may have an influence in the opposite direction. Thus, in attempting to predict the degree of concerted action to be exhibited by any particular work group, one would have to consider and weigh each of the inputs in relationship to each other.

Before discussing the impact of the subsystem inputs on cohesion, it should be reiterated that concerted work group actions may be directed toward the objectives of the organization or in opposition to them. For this reason, it may be either desirable or undesirable in the eyes of management for a particular work group to be highly cohesive, depending upon the nature of the objectives toward which its concerted actions are taken. Thus cohesiveness, per se, can be considered as neither "good" nor "bad" by the organization. Further, regardless of norms restricting production (mentioned previously) or concerted action taken *against* management (to be discussed below) the existence of work groups is *essential* to the firm's successfully meeting its objectives. In studying a number of British firms, for example, Joan Woodward concluded that:

> It was found . . . that organizational objectives were frequently achieved through the informal rather than formal organization. A dysfunctional formal organization could be compensated by contributive informal relationships. This was particularly noticeable in relation to technical change.[40]

Technical organizational change will be discussed later in Chapter 10.

The Group Membership Input.[41] In general, homogeneous work groups—i.e., those whose members possess similar personal and social characteristics—tend to be more cohesive than heterogeneous groups. Among such characteristics which seem to have an influence on homogeneity are ethnic affiliation, social class background, and educational background. In addition, at least one researcher has expressed the opinion that "a one-sex work group is likely to be more cohesive than one in which both sexes are represented.[42] There is also some evidence to suggest that the degree to which a group's members' psychological orientation is toward their peers rather than their superiors has some

---

[40] Woodward, *Industrial Organization*, p. 75. It should be noted that Woodward defines informal organization as "the pattern of [interpersonal] relationships which actually emerges from day-to-day operations" (p. 74). Thus, her definition of informal organization is broader than one just encompassing work groups—it would include individual supervisor-subordinate relationships, managerial-peer interrelationships, and so forth.

[41] Our discussion in this and the following section is influenced considerably by William F. Whyte, *Men at Work* (Homewood, Ill.: Richard D. Irwin, Inc., 1961); and William F. Whyte, *Organizational Behavior.*

[42] Whyte, *Men at Work*, p. 541.

influence on its cohesiveness. For example, William F. Whyte has observed on the basis of his research that:

Some people seem to look primarily to their organizational superiors for approval, whereas other people seem to look primarily to their peers. . . . These orientations represent two extremes; of course, many people seem to fall somewhere in between, being pulled in both directions. A work group consisting of members who are oriented toward their peers will naturally be more cohesive than those in which a substantial proportion of the members are oriented toward their organizational superiors.[43]

As Whyte suggests, such personality differences are probably conditioned to a considerable extent by the degree to which the individual grew up under firm parental control and has had previous peer group experiences.[44]

The Organizational Environment Input. There are a number of organizational factors including technological ones which also seem to have an important influence on the degree to which work groups will engage in concerted behavior. In general, homogeneous groups with respect to *jobs performed* are more likely to be cohesive than those groups in which members hold dissimilar jobs. A basic reason for this relationship is that individuals performing the same kind of work, earning the same pay, and subjected to the same working conditions are more likely to be affected *uniformly* by management decisions, and hence have a more common basis for uniting to take concerted action.

A second organizational input which seems to have an important bearing on cohesion is the degree to which interactional opportunities are available to members of the work group. In general, those groups whose members find it difficult to converse with each other, either because of a high noise level or physical separation will find it more difficult to effect concerted action than those groups in which greater communication among members is possible.[45]

---

[43] Ibid., p. 542.

[44] To quote Whyte: "The individual who grows up under the firm (and accepted) control of his parents and who has little peer group experience will tend to be vertically oriented; the individual who does not experience such parental control and who has led an active peer group life will tend to be horizontally oriented." Ibid., p. 543.

[45] However, if members of work groups who perform identical jobs work very closely together, and an extremely great degree of interaction is possible, emotional support for concerted action may develop rapidly and lead to uncontrolled outbursts. This seemed to be the case with a number of the "erratic groups" described by Sayles in *The Behavior of Industrial Work Groups.* A somewhat similar phenomena was found by William F. Whyte in a study of a French-Canadian plant comparing the operations of a chemical and a smelting division (comprised of vat lines and a caustic plant) where there was more group cohesion and militancy in the latter. See Whyte, *Organizational Behavior*, p. 481. It should be noted that Whyte's generalizations from this study were derived from examining fairly large organizational work units, rather than small groups.

The importance to management of the jobs performed by work groups is another organizational input affecting cohesion—especially when concerted action is taken to pressure management to improve the position of the work group. As William F. Whyte has pointed out:

If the group's work is exceedingly important to management, the group is likely to perceive this importance and assume that management is more likely to respond to this group's collective pressures than it would to the pressures of some work group whose operations seemed more peripheral to the enterprise.[46]

In a study conducted by Leonard Sayles,[47] for example, those work groups which engaged in concerted action to the greatest extent were frequently found where: (1) there was a flow of work among departments, and (2) a production slowdown or wildcat strike on their part would have halted total plant operations more readily than would have similar behavior on the part of many other work groups in the organization.

A final organizational input influencing cohesion which should be mentioned is the degree to which the work group has been previously successful in achieving its objectives through concerted action. There is evidence to suggest that if a particular work group finds that it can effectively pressure management into giving in to its demands by concerted behavior (such as a wildcat strike) it will be more predisposed to engage in such tactics on future occasions. Strong management resistance to the group's demands, on the other hand, tends to reduce the probability of the recurrence of such behavior. This relationship again points up the interdependence between the group subsystem inputs and outputs. Concerted action (output) will touch off a response on the part of management (input), the nature of which will influence the group's concerted action output in the future.

MANAGERIAL DECISIONS AND WORK GROUP OUTPUTS

As has been pointed out in previous sections, work group behavior is quite complex, and may be influenced by many different kinds of

---

[46] Whyte, *Men at Work*, p. 545.

[47] Sayles, *The Behavior of Industrial Work Groups*. Whyte, in his French-Canadian study noted above, also found less work group militancy in the chemical division than in the smelting division where the work was considered more important to management. See Whyte, *Organizational Behavior*, p. 483. Whyte additionally found certain other work variables related to cohesion and militancy against management in this study. For example, the more cohesive workers on the vat lines in the smelting division had poorer working conditions and less job security than the workers in the less militant chemical division. To what extent the job security and working condition variables would lead to cohesion in other situations is open to question in terms of motivation theory. For example, both of these two variables are "hygienic" ones and not motivators in the Herzberg model discussed in Chapter 5.

managerial decision. For this reason, prescriptive statements as to *specifically* how management should deal with *any particular* work group cannot be made validly without first analyzing its membership, objectives, norms, the organizational environment in which it functions, and so on.

It is possible, however, to make some observations about certain *general* approaches which may be useful to the manager in influencing work group behavior and attitudes.

Deference to Group Norms

Work group norms, as emphasized earlier, may sometimes conflict with organizational objectives. For example, a norm which holds that dirty or unpleasant tasks should not be performed by the high status members of a group may conflict with the optimal assignment of work in a department.

In cases such as this, the supervisor is often faced with a dilemma or, in decision-making terms, a suboptimization problem—if he takes actions which violate a norm, his objective of good relationships with his group may suffer, while, on the other hand, if he defers to the group, certain other organizational objectives may not be as fully achieved. To resolve such problems, the supervisor must assign some weight to each of the conflicting objectives and assess the strategies open to him accordingly. If the organizational objectives at stake are major ones, he may decide to disregard group norms, even though he recognizes that his actions may lead to strong protests and negative group behavior. On the other hand, if the objectives are minor in comparison with the negative group actions which he believes will follow if the norms are violated (e.g., a production slowdown), it may be more advisable for him to defer to them. For example, in a department examined in the Hawthorne studies, one supervisor permitted his men to falsify their output records (to effect a belief held by the group that output should be kept relatively constant) because, to have enforced the company's rules:

. . . would have required his standing over the men all day, and by so doing he would have sacrificed all hope of establishing good relations with them. . . . He would have lost even that minimum of influence that he needed if he was to do any kind of a job at all. Under these circumstances he chose to side with the group and wink at much that was going on. . . .[48]

In short, what we have been emphasizing in this section is that the supervisor must be sensitive to the attitudinal and behavioral norms

---

[48] George Homans, *The Human Group*, p. 63. This supervisory strategy apparently created no serious problems for the company. In fact, in spite of the falsification of records, output was generally considered good by management.

of the group, and that in some cases deference to them, even at the expense of certain organizational objectives, may enhance his overall influence with the group in the long run.

Working through the Informal Leader

Another influence strategy which the supervisor should be aware of is the possibility of working through his work group's informal leadership. As we indicated earlier, one or more individuals often emerge as informal leaders within the work group, and are in a position to exert considerable influence on the remaining membership. If the supervisor can (1) identify such individuals, and (2) build and maintain good relationships with them, he may be able to persuade them to influence the group to take action in accordance with his objectives. For example, obtaining a group's acceptance of a new work rule may be facilitated considerably if the informal leadership has been first convinced of its merits by the supervisor.

There is, however, one danger in working through informal group leadership which the supervisor should recognize. If the informal leader identifies too greatly with the supervisor or comes to be regarded as his "pawn," his influence within the group may diminish greatly. Moreover, the strategy of working with the informal leader is sometimes not possible because (1) little, if any informal leadership exists within a group, and/or (2) group attitudes are strongly antimanagement rendering any form of cooperation with the supervisor difficult.

Group Participation in the Decision Making

In some cases, the supervisor may gain a group's support for certain of his objectives by permitting its membership to participate in determining how the objectives are to be realized. For example:

One unpleasant task which had to be performed by members of a group of car hops in a drive-in restaurant after closing hours each night was that of picking pieces of broken soda pop bottles from a wire mesh bin—a job that often resulted in cut fingers. When particular car hops were assigned to the task by the supervisor, they frequently balked and offered excuses as to why they couldn't stay on to do it. Finally, the supervisor called the group together, pointed out that the job had to be done and asked the group to assign the responsibility for deciding which of its members were to perform the task each night. The group agreed, worked out a system of taking turns, and exerted strong pressures on any of its members who attempted to avoid their turn. From that point on, the supervisor was relieved from all haggling as to who was to perform the unpleasant job each night.

Several comments are in order concerning the group participation approach. First, the theory underlying the approach is that (1) individuals will tend to identify with, and hence give greater support to decisions which they have participated in making, and (2) groups tend to exert influence on their membership to conform to courses of action agreed upon—influence which may be more effective than that of the supervisor. In the illustration given above, for example, the car hop group would "needle" any member who offered what the group considered a "lame" excuse for avoiding his turn to pick up the broken bottles.

Second, the group participation approach has certain limitations. In some cases, groups may resist any such participative efforts on the part of the supervisor because they are apathetic or hostile toward management. Moreover, depending upon such factors as technology work groups may not possess the knowledge and skills which would permit them to contribute effectively to the making of some kinds of decisions affecting their work—e.g., whether or not the introduction of a new machine is economically justifiable. Finally, we should mention that group participation has sometimes been used as a means of helping to overcome resistance to changes within organizations. We will illustrate this application of the participative approach in Chapter 11.

SUMMARY

The behavior of the organizational employee is influenced considerably by his membership in one or more work groups. For this reason, it is important for the manager to have an understanding of the nature of work groups, and of the impact of his decisions on such behavior.

For conceptual purposes, the work group may be viewed as an organizational subsystem. Its behavior is influenced by two major classes of subsystem inputs—group membership and the organizational environment—both of which are influenced considerably by decisions (including technological ones) made by management. To achieve their objectives, groups develop both attitudinal and behavioral standards, and are often in a position to exert strong pressures on their membership to abide by such norms. Accession to these norms permits concerted group action, which may be directed either toward or in opposition to the objectives of the organization. Although groups often take concerted action to meet their objectives, many differences exist among their membership in roles played, status enjoyed, and influences exerted. These three classes of group attitudes and behavior—objectives, norms, and concerted action, and member differentiation—may be viewed as the outputs of the group subsystem. Important to recognize in analyzing organizational work groups is the interdependence which exists among the system's elements. Group inputs, such as managerial decisions, not only influence such outputs as concerted action, but the latter may in turn condition the nature of future organizational decision inputs.

DISCUSSION AND STUDY QUESTIONS

1. The sociotechnical approach to group theory is basically incongruent with the systems explanation of their behavior. Do you agree? Explain.

2. One manager was heard to say, "I want a good cohesive group working for me in which everyone likes each other because I'll get more productivity out of my workers." Comment.

3. What are some of the basic conditions (or variables) that lead work groups to be cohesive in the sense of the taking of concerted action toward management's decisions?

4. Which of the following would you define as a "group" in the light of the definition of a group given in the text:
    a) Two divers diving into the municipal swimming pool.
    b) Two passengers sitting next to each other on a bus.
    c) A policeman who is giving directions to a motorist, lost in a strange city.
    d) A group of people on the mailing list of a firm sending out unsolicited brochures.
    e) A teen-age boy and girl sitting next to each other on a park bench on a moonlight night.

5. Leaders of voluntary groups are respected and admired since they directly satisfy group members' needs. Discuss.

6. Indicate how the formation of friendship groups, where membership is voluntary, is influenced by managerial decisions.

7. Adherence to group norms by group members is dysfunctional in terms of management's goals. Discuss.

8. a) What is status incongruence?
    b) What tends to happen in groups where status incongruence exists?
    c) What are the implications of status incongruence for management?

9. What limitations are there to the use of group participation in management decision making?

10. There are three secretaries doing the clerical and secretarial work for an English department comprised of 10 professors in a large midwestern university. Two of the three, Alice and Betty, have been working in the department for over two years, while the third, Carol is a relative newcomer. All three girls report to the department head and do basically the same kind of work. However, Alice and Betty are both in the same higher classified position, and make slightly more money than Carol. There are no strong frictions among the three girls but Alice and Betty each lunch and socialize together more by themselves than with Carol. Alice and Betty will also often help each other when their work gets behind, but rarely help Carol when she has a work overload. (The work such as typing of letters, manuscripts, and exams is given to each secretary by the professors themselves, based on their preferences, rather than being routed through the department head to the secretaries.) When Alice and Betty do not have any work to do, which happens

occasionally, they sometimes play rummy together, rather than helping Carol, who may be overloaded with work at the time. When Carol is free, she will sometimes help the other girls, or sometimes read magazines. There have been no major criticisms of any of the girls' work by the professors. Generally the work done is of high quality, although in a few cases it is turned out behind schedule.

Is there any problem here? Explain. If so, what should the department head do?

SELECTED REFERENCES

ASCH, S. E. *Social Psychology.* Englewood Cliffs, N.J.: Prentice-Hall, Inc., 1952.

BERELSON, BERNARD, and STEINER, GARY A. *Human Behavior: An Inventory of Scientific Findings,* chaps. 8–16. New York: Harcourt, Brace & World, Inc., 1964.

CARTWRIGHT, DORWIN, and ZANDER, ALVIN. *Group Dynamics Research and Theory.* 3d ed. New York: Harper and Row, Publishers, 1968.

CARZO, ROCCO, JR., and YANOUZAS, JOHN. *Formal Organization: A Systems Approach,* chap. 6. Homewood, Ill.: Richard D. Irwin Inc., 1967.

DAVIS, KEITH, and SCOTT, WILLIAM G. *Human Relations and Organizational Behavior.* 3d ed. New York: McGraw-Hill Book Co., 1969.

DUBIN, ROBERT. *Human Relations in Administration,* 3d ed. Englewood Cliffs, N.J.: Prentice-Hall, Inc., 1968.

HECKMANN, I. L., JR., and HUNERYAGER, S. G. *Human Relations in Management.* 2d ed. Cincinnati, Ohio: South-Western Publishing Co., 1967.

HOMANS, GEORGE. *Social Behavior: Its Elementary Forms.* New York: Harcourt Brace & World, Inc., 1961.

INDUSTRIAL RELATIONS RESEARCH ASSOCIATION. *Research in Industrial Human Relations.* New York: Harper & Bros., 1957.

KELLY, JOE. *Organizational Behavior,* chap. 5. Homewood, Ill.: Richard D. Irwin Inc., 1969.

KRECH, DAVID, et al. *Individual in Society.* New York: McGraw-Hill Book Co., 1962.

LEVY, RONALD B. *Human Relations—A Conceptual Approach,* Scranton, Pa.: International Textbook Co., 1969.

LINDZEY, GARDNER, and ARONSON, ELLIOTT (eds.). *Handbook of Social Psychology,* Vol. 4. Reading, Mass.: Addison-Wesley Publishing Co., Inc., 1969.

LITTERER, JOSEPH, A. *Organizations: Structure and Behavior.* Chap. 6. 2d ed. New York: John Wiley & Sons, Inc., 1965.

MEISSNER, MARTIN. *Technology and the Worker.* San Francisco: Chandler Publishing Co., 1969.

PORTER, DONALD E., et al. *Studies in Organizational Behavior and Management.* 2d ed. Scranton, Pa.: International Textbook Co., 1970.

SCOTT, WILLIAM G. *Organization Theory.* Homewood, Ill.: Richard D. Irwin, Inc., 1967.

SHEPHERD, CLOVIS. *Small Groups: Some Sociological Perspectives.* San Francisco: Chandler Publishing Company, 1964.

TUCKER, W. T. *The Social Context of Economic Behavior.* New York: Holt, Rinehart & Winston, Inc., 1964.

WHYTE, WILLIAM F. *Men at Work.* Homewood, Ill.: Richard D. Irwin, Inc., 1961.

WHYTE, WILLIAM F. *Organizational Behavior: Theory and Application.* Homewood, Ill.: Richard D. Irwin, Inc., 1969.

ZALEZNIK, ABRAHAM, and MOMENT, DAVID. *The Dynamics of Interpersonal Behavior.* New York: John Wiley & Sons, Inc., 1964.

Chapter **8**

Organizational
Processes

INTRODUCTION: COMPLEXITY OF ORGANIZATIONS

THE PRECEDING THREE CHAPTERS have been devoted to a discussion of
the behavior of individuals and small groups in complex organizations.
It is the objective of this chapter and the next to extend this explanation
to large and complex forms of social organizations, especially those of
business firms. This chapter focuses upon the theoretical factors which
are important in determining the organization forms appropriate to the
tasks undertaken by companies. The next chapter describes different
forms of complex organizations resulting from the theoretical considerations presented in this chapter.

In productive social organizations typical in underdeveloped societies,
simple rather than complex organizational forms tend to predominate.
While early armies and the churches were required to develop some
complexity of organizational forms to deal with their tasks and the environment impinging upon them, it was not until the Industrial Revolution that businesses developed the technology suggesting the need for
complex organizations. When the technological knowledge and skills
of an industry were in the minds and hands of master craftsman, each
craftsman could perform all functions required to produce and distribute
the product without large-scale aid from a social organization. Chapter
1 related the key role that inventions of equipment played in developing
a need for larger financial investment for business firms and the resulting
technological need for large-scale complex organizations. Since it is these
complex organizations that are typical of enterprises in the United States
and other developed countries, the attention of this chapter is devoted
to their explanation.

Basically two contrasting, but simultaneous, processes occur in organizational formation. First, there is a need to separate the total tasks
of the organization into operable jobs and combinations of jobs. This
is the differentiation process. Second is the need to tie the separate

and differentiated parts so formed into a whole. This is the integration or coordination process. It is to these two processes, the factors influencing them, and approaches to their use that we now turn.

DIFFERENTIATION AT TASK LEVELS

In complex organizations, the work that is performed is divided so that specialized tasks are assigned to individuals. Rather than calling on each employee to perform all of the different kinds of work necessary to meet a firm's objectives, certain individuals may be assigned to the task of selling, others may be assigned to devote their full time to operating a particular machine, and so on.

A key decision problem involved in designing an organizational structure is that of determining just how much specialization should exist—i.e., of deciding how large or small the scope of work performed by each employee should be. For example, in a manufacturing operation comprised of three steps—setting up a machine, operating the machine, and inspecting the pieces turned out on the machine—should management:

1. Structure the work so that each employee performs all three of these tasks? or
2. Provide for even greater specialization by having some workers just do the setup work; others, just the machining; and still others do nothing but inspection?

In general, specialization of activity, *up to a point* enables the individual to be more productive than would be the case were he to try to perform a job calling for the application of a wide variety of different types of skills. Certain tasks in organizations, however—especially at the nonmanagerial level—have become so highly specialized as to lead to problems which may tend to reduce the productivity of the majority of employees performing them. In this section attention is focused upon some of the advantages of specialization and some of the problems of overspecialization and nonmanagerial levels in the business organization.[1] Then some of the approaches utilized by business firms to help overcome such problems are examined.

Advantages of Specialization

Most highly specialized nonmanagerial positions have short-*cycle times*—i.e., a task requiring only a short duration of time to complete

---

[1] The reader should recognize that specialization of work, with both its advantages and disadvantages, also occurs at *managerial* levels in most business organizations. In consequence, certain of the observations which we will make in this section have some degree of applicability to at least certain managerial positions. Specialization of work at the managerial level, however, is rarely, if ever, carried to the extreme that it often is at the worker level in many firms.

is repeated over and over again. As was indicated in Chapter 5 in our discussion of learning theory, learning generally is more effective when there is repetition of the activity being taught. Further, activities requiring only very short-cycle times often require only relatively low skill levels in their performance. Thus, highly specialized nonmanagerial jobs, such as those found on many production lines, often can be learned more quickly than those calling for a broader scope of activities to be performed. In one study of assembly line positions, for example, it was found that jobs with three-minute cycles required approximately three times as many repetitions as jobs with one-half minute cycles before standard levels of production were reached.[2]

Shorter learning times required for jobs are advantageous to the firm for several reasons. For one, the cost of training employees to perform on new jobs is reduced. Further, interruptions in production due to absences, vacations, or resignations can be minimized because new workers can be quickly trained as replacements. When such is the case, the organization becomes less dependent upon any one employee—his skill becomes relatively unimportant since it can be so easily replaced.

Not only may training time be less on short-cycle jobs; additionally, workers may often become more proficient on such jobs as compared with less highly specialized ones. As the short-cycle job is repeated over and over, the individual learns to eliminate wasted and ineffective motions. False starts and mistakes tend to be reduced. In one study, for example, it was found that the ultimate attainable level of proficiency for certain TV chassis assembly jobs with one-minute cycles was 16 percent above that of those with three-minute cycles.[3]

Disadvantages of Specialization

There are at least three potential disadvantages which may accrue to the organization when jobs become specialized. First, as indicated previously in Chapter 5, when employees are called on to perform simple repetitive tasks which require little skill, satisfaction of their esteem and self-actualization needs may be thwarted; and the resultant frustrations may lead to defensive behavior such as excessive absenteeism, and hostility toward supervision. Moreover, by greatly reducing the firm's dependence upon the skills of any single employee, specialization has sometimes tended to threaten the security needs of workers. When an employee performs a low-skill-level job which almost anyone can do, his superior may be more inclined to fire him for arbitrary or capricious reasons, than if he possessed skills not easily replaceable. One way of the employee's overcoming such problems has been through

---

[2] Maurice Kilbridge, "A Model for Industrial Learning Costs," *Management Science,* 8 (July 1962), p. 522.

[3] Ibid., p. 520.

unionization and the design of union-management contracts protecting workers from arbitrary discipline or dismissal by their supervisors. In fact, some observers of the labor scene attribute much of the organizing success which unions have enjoyed to the failure of management to provide job security to operating employees as their jobs have become highly specialized.

In addition to these psychological problems, the specialization of work beyond a certain point may effect inefficiencies due to technological considerations. For instance, shortening cycle times to an extreme degree may result in an increasing amount of handling time required in the performance of a task, as may be illustrated by the following hypothetical example.

A firm has an assembly line job in which the operator: (1) picks up a subassembly, (2) drills and reams four holes in it, (3) assembles inserts into the holes, and (4) replaces the subassembly on the line. We will assume that the standard times for each of these four elements of this task are those shown in Figure 8–1.

Figure 8–1. A Technological Limit to Specialization (illustrative example)

Present Job		*Proposed Additional Specialization*			
Job: Drill, Ream and Assemble		*Job 1: Drill and Ream*		*Job 2: Assemble*	
Operation	*Time in minutes*	*Operation*	*Time in minutes*	*Operation*	*Time in minutes*
Pick up	.04	Pick up	.04	Pick up	.04
Drill and Ream	.26	Drill and Ream	.22	Assemble	.16
Assemble insert	.19	Replace	.04	Replace	.04
Replace	.04	Subtotal	.30	Subtotal	.24
Total work and handling time	.53	.54 min.			
Total work time	.45	.38 min.			
Total handling time	.08	.16 min.			
Handling as percent of work	18%	42%			
Increased efficiency in work elements	—	20%			

The firm's industrial engineers estimate that if this job were further broken down with the machining tasks assigned to some workers, and the assembly of inserts to others, an overall increase in efficiency of 20 percent could be expected for these two work elements. If this further specialization of the job were effected, however, both the machining operator and the assembler would have to pick up the subassembly and replace it on the line, whereas these steps have to be performed only once for each subassembly under the present setup. Given the standard times shown in Figure 8–1, the total time required for the job would be lengthened by .01 minute by the further specialization, rather than decreased, because the additional handling time required more than offsets the increased efficiency which could be realized in the performance of the work elements.

When tasks are subdivided and assigned so as to be performed sequentially or serially as parts of the total task, there is a tendency for individuals assigned to these tasks to isolate themselves from the whole jobs, i.e., to assume responsibility for only their assigned subtask. This serial system of task arrangement and assignment tends to work well as long as there is a minimum of variation in the total task and in the sequence of application of the subtasks. If, however, the proportion or the sequence of application of subtasks vary, composite task assignments in which individuals perform a larger number of main tasks have resulted in productivity increases.[4] Serial task assignment, on the other hand, assumes, in effect, a known sequence and proportion of subtasks to the total.

In the repair of auto engines, for example, it might be possible to have repair experts for each major component such as valve, crankshaft, ignition, and carburetor. The repair needs of any engine varies from the next, however, so that a line, serial-type assignment of tasks would find some workers idle if several autos did not require their specialty in the repair. If an automobile mechanic possesses multiple skills, however, he can apply his skills as the repair task requires. Versatility in work force skills allows management to deal more effectively with task variability even if the versatility must be compensated for in higher hourly wages.

Techniques for Dealing with Specialization Problems

To help overcome the adverse effects of specialization, several techniques have been developed and utilized by business firms. We will now examine several of these.

Employee Selection. One way of offsetting some of the adverse psychological effects of specialization is to *select* workers who do not perceive the firm's highly specialized jobs to be monotonous. Although it may be difficult to predict how a potential employee will view a particular job, this approach theoretically offers a solution to the monotonous tendencies induced by specialization and sometimes has been effective,

---

[4] See F. E. Emery and E. L. Trist, "Socio-Technical Systems" in F. E. Emery (ed.) *Systems Thinking* (Middlesex, Eng.: Penguin Books, Ltd., 1969), pp. 281–296. We will discuss this point in further detail later when we consider "job enlargement."

as noted in Chapter 5. However, most people may consider a large majority of a company's highly specialized jobs as monotonous. If, for example, a firm were to build a new plant calling for 3,000 highly specialized jobs to be filled in an area with a labor supply of 5,000 individuals available for work, perhaps as many as 4,500 or 90 percent of them might view practically all of these jobs as monotonous. That such a 90 percent figure may not be unreasonable for mechanically paced, repetitive jobs is indicated by the following finding from a study of workers on an automobile assembly line:

> Roughly 10 percent of our sample of workers preferred or were indifferent to jobs with basic mass production characteristics such as mechanical pacing and repetitiveness. The great majority expressed in varying degrees a dislike of these features of their job situations at Plant X.[5]

Thus, although sometimes practicable, worker selection oftentimes may not provide a widely applicable means of overcoming the psychological problems associated with high degrees of specialization.

Participative Methods. Frustration in achieving higher level needs arising from specialized job design may be partially overcome by utilizing the participative management approach discussed in Chapter 7. If this approach is employed, it may be possible to provide decision opportunities which allow employees to achieve some degree of fulfillment of their self-actualization needs. However, in many cases participation may not be consistent with job specialization. If a job is highly routinized and its steps prescribed in engineering detail, to what degree can an employee's decisions affect his own work? Yet some latitude for employee participation in decision making may exist even in highly repetitive routine jobs. For example, in one toy manufacturing firm, a paint spraying operation, staffed by girls, was plagued by absenteeism and employee turnover. The girls doing this work were called in to talk with their supervisor to discuss the problems which they faced on their jobs. Among other complaints, the girls pointed out that they were frustrated by the constant speed of the conveyor belt which brought them the toys to paint. They suggested that they be permitted to "adjust the speed of the belt faster or slower depending on how we feel."[6] Then,

> With great misgivings, the foreman had a control with a dial marked "low, medium, fast" installed at the booth of the group leader; she could now

---

[5] Charles R. Walker and Robert H. Guest, *The Man on the Assembly Line* (Cambridge, Mass.: Harvard University Press, 1952), p. 141. It should be noted that some observers believe that a higher percentage of individuals than the figure cited here can find satisfaction in repetitive work; and that greater advantage may be gained from utilizing the selection approach for jobs of this type. See, for example, Theodore O. Prenting, "Better Selection for Repetitive Work," *Personnel*, 41 (September–October 1964), pp. 26–31.

[6] William F. Whyte, *Money and Motivation* (New York: Harper & Bros., 1955), as reprinted in Charles R. Walker, *Modern Technology and Civilization* (New York: McGraw-Hill Book Co., 1962), p. 117.

adjust the speed of the belt anywhere between the upper and lower limits that the engineers had set. The girls were delighted. . . . Production increased, and within three weeks . . . the girls were operating at 30 to 50 percent above the level that had been expected. . . .[7]

As the reader may note, not only was the approach utilized here participative in nature; it also resulted in the employees being freed to a considerable extent from machine-pacing, a mass-production characteristic objectionable to many workers.

Job Enlargement. Another approach sometimes utilized to help offset the adverse effects of specialization is *job enlargement.* As its name implies, job enlargement is the opposite of dividing up work into minute subtasks—it is a form of *de*specialization in which work is restructured so that each job contains *more,* rather than fewer, elements. Although enlarged jobs require longer training time, monotony tends to be reduced and job interest increased in comparison with that in extremely specialized jobs. In this way, job productivity (after training) may be increased.

An example of job enlargement is provided by the IBM Corporation.[8] The work of certain of its machine operators at one time consisted solely of placing a part into their machine, and removing it when the machine processing was completed. These jobs allowed little ingenuity or challenge. Job enlargement was effected by additionally assigning both the setup of the machines and the inspection of completed parts to the machine operators. This broadening of responsibility necessitated a higher level of operator skill because setup (formerly performed by a specialized setup man) is a more highly skilled function than is machine operation.

Increasing the operator's skill, of course, required commensurate upgrading of their rate of pay. Additionally, as a result of the job enlargement, certain increased costs had to be incurred due to the need for extra inspection equipment. The company believed, however, that these costs were worth their investment because three valuable benefits accrued from the enlargement:

1. A better product quality resulting from an increased sense of worker responsibility.
2. Less idle worker time, with a 95 percent reduction in setup and inspection costs because the workers no longer needed to wait for a setup man to come along before starting on a new batch of parts, or for an inspector to check their parts.
3. "Job enrichment" due to greater job interest, variety, and responsibility than was present before.

---

[7] Ibid.

[8] Information about the IBM experience described in this and the following paragraphs was drawn from C. R. Walker, "The Problem of the Repetitive Job," *Harvard Business Review,* 28 (May 1950), pp. 54–58.

In spite of numerous successful applications, however, there are limitations to the applicability of job enlargement. If jobs are too greatly expanded in scope, many of the advantages of specialization discussed earlier will be lost. Further, due to technological constraints, no job enlargement may be possible for certain classes of jobs. For example, at certain stages of some manufacturing operations, setups may be very infrequent, with no inspection being carried out until later stages in the production process. In such cases, there may be no additional tasks available for enlarging the scope of the work of those individuals tending the machines, unless the technological process were to be considerably revamped.

Job Rotation. A final approach designed to help overcome some of the problems arising from specialization which deserves mention is that of *job rotation.* With job rotation, neither the worker's task nor its cycle time is extended as with job enlargement. Rather, workers are trained in performing several jobs, rather than one. Then, periodically during the day (or at less frequent intervals), they are rotated from one job to another by switching jobs with one another. For example, an employee may be assigned to rotate among three jobs along with two other workers.

Job rotation is usually a simpler approach to inaugurate than job enlargement, since it does not call for the redesign of jobs. Further, it tends to provide more flexibility in relating the assignment of workers to their own skills and capabilities. Since skill levels, capabilities, and perceptions of monotony vary from worker to worker, the enlargement of all jobs in a particular operation may be highly beneficial for some workers while less so for others. Under job rotation, on the other hand, it may be relatively easy to schedule the work so that: (1) those individuals with limited capabilities, and who experience little or no boredom when assigned to routine tasks, be given just one job and not rotated, while at the same time (2) those individuals who want to switch jobs periodically be provided with an opportunity to do so. ᴵ

Task Specialization: Summary

The factors which must be considered in determining how specialized jobs at the worker level should be, consist of two opposing types: (1) those which tend to increase productivity with greater degrees of specialization (e.g., faster learning), and (2) those which may result in decreased productivity as specialization increases (e.g., boredom, monotony, and lack of job interest). The magnitude of these tendencies will vary considerably from one situation to another. A particular repetitive, machine-paced job may be quite satisfying to one individual, for example, while being equally unsatisfactory for another. Thus, both in the initial design of jobs of the types we have been discussing, and in considering organizational modifications by such approaches as job enlargement and job rotation, a situational approach is called for.

DIFFERENTIATION OF GROUPS AND DEPARTMENTS

The preceding section examined the factors associated with differentiation and specialization of tasks at the worker level. In this section, attention will be given as to how groupings of departments and hierarchy are determined. A series of recent research studies (especially those of Woodward,[9] Lawrence and Lorsch,[10] and Thompson[11]) suggest that *under certain conditions,* particular forms of organization appear to emerge while if other conditions exist, a different organization structure is called for. Thus, the type of theory of organizations that these studies suggest is a *conditional* one; there is no one best way to organize all organizations. Rather, the "best way" depends upon a series of interrelated factors which, if they can be determined, provide information as to both how typical structures emerge and how they should be designed. The theory is thus both descriptive and normative since it reveals actual and preferred designs. The theory is conditional in the same sense that Chapter 6 suggested a situational theory of leadership in which there is no one best leadership style most effective for all conditions.

Strategy and Structure

In Chapter 12, devoted to planning, the nature of corporate strategy in relation to other planning decisions will be undertaken in some detail. As will be shown there, a corporate strategy includes a set of decisions about what products or services the firm will provide and the markets in which each product will be sold. Given the capabilities of the firm together with the opportunities and constraints in the environment, a rational strategy attempts to provide a means for translating corporate activity most appropriately into the achievement of corporate goals. Of significance to this chapter is that different strategies call for different organization structures. It is obvious that a company whose strategy is to make and sell high fashion women's shoes in major metropolitan markets will have no need for a rolling mill department that an integrated steel mill would need. Their task technologies differ. Similarly, two companies selling competing products to the same consumer electronics industry (i.e., one producing solid state devices and the other

[9] Joan Woodward, *Industrial Organization: Theory and Practice* (London: Oxford University Press, 1965).

[10] Paul R. Lawrence and Jay W. Lorsch, *Organization and Environment* (Homewood, Ill.: Richard D. Irwin, Inc., 1969).

[11] James D. Thompson, *Organizations in Action* (New York: McGraw-Hill Book Co., 1967).

electronic tubes) would require different departmental arrangements for producing these differing products because of their different production technologies. On the other hand, the marketing departments of these two firms could be quite similar since their products are loosely substitutes for one another and could be sold in a similar manner to the same customers.

Not so obvious are the differences between a textbook publisher and a publisher of popular science fiction books. The production technologies would tend to be similar (except for some differences in editing, perhaps) and their production structures would thus tend to exhibit similarities (e.g., editing, typesetting, printing, binding). Since, however, the ultimate consumers of these products, the distribution channels, and the consumer decision processes differ, the two marketing organizations would tend to have less congruence with each other than would the productive system.

A textbook publisher does not deal directly with the ultimate consumer (the student) but at the college level with professors who typically specify books for courses they teach. At the secondary educational level, however, textbook decisions are made by teachers, school administrators, county superintendents, or state boards of education. The selling function to these two markets is so different that many texbook publishers have separate selling departments for college and secondary texts. Unlike textbooks, a science fiction publisher needs to get his books in front of the ultimate consumer to generate sales. His sales organizations are, therefore, geared to servicing retail book stores, wholesale news distributors, and so forth. In addition, advertising may assume an important role in drawing customers to ask for a particular book at the outlets. College or secondary school sales departments would be out of place here, but retail and wholesale sales departments would not be. Further, coordination between advertising and the sales departments would tend to assume greater importance than for a textbook publisher.

These preceding examples are intended to show that the particular product-market strategies selected by a firm have a direct effect upon the technology used and the tasks required to implement that strategy, and, as a result, directly influence the task departments that the firm employs.

Domain of Strategy

An additional factor having a bearing upon the specific technology that a firm selects is the *domain* of its strategy. The domain of a strategy or of a firm's operations refers to the intensive-extensiveness of its product line, its market coverage, and its market penetration. Some integrated oil companies produce a very wide line of petroleum products for sale to both industrial and consumer markets on a worldwide basis and possess relatively high market shares in at least some of these markets. Their throughput of crude oil per day is high and thus they can use the most highly developed exploration, production, refining, transportation, and marketing technologies. In contrast, a smaller U.S. oil firm whose domain is restricted to marketing only consumer products refined from crude oil purchased on the open market and selling within a limited geographical area would require only a subset of the technologies needed by the large integrated firm. Furthermore, its refining technology could not be as highly developed because its volume would not warrant the investment. The extensiveness of domain obviously affects the volume that exists and volume, in turn, influences the technology employed. The organization structure of the smaller firm would be simpler and less differentiated than the large producer.

In crude petroleum storage tanks, for example, some petroleum wax precipitates out of the crude as it awaits processing. Eventually the tanks need to be cleaned of this wax which can be refined and different fractions sold for a variety of needs. A small refiner would have a small volume of wax as a by-product. It would not be economical to establish a tank cleaning department, wax refining, and marketing organizations to dispose of it although a large refiner might find such a structure useful. Since the function of cleaning tanks to remove wax is necessary in either case, the small firm tends to contract this activity to firms specializing in wax refining and marketing.

Technology

While we have shown that organization structure is influenced by the technology employed and that this technology is further determined by product-market strategy and its domain, a question remains as to whether any general theoretical statements can be made about these relationships.

In her study of manufacturing companies, Joan Woodward identifies three major classes of technology: (1) *unit* production and small batch in which "one-of-a-kind" products or small numbers of units are produced; (2) *large-batch and mass-production* technology in which products are produced in volume quantities, some intermittently and some more or less continuously; and (3) *process* technology characterized by continuous flow at all production stages, sequentially arranged to balance, approximately, throughputs of one state to the input needs of the succeeding stage—e.g., a chemical plant or an oil refinery.[12] She

---

[12] Woodward, *Industrial Organization*, chap. 3. Thompson provides a technological classification encompassing more than manufacturing firms, the domain of Woodward's classes. He uses three classes: a *long-linked* technology involving serial relations among units; a *mediating* technology which links clients (e.g., banks); and an *intensive* technology in which diverse expertises bear upon an object. The series of application of expertises may vary among objects. Thompson, *Organizations in Action*, chap. 2.

further subdivides these three major technologies into 11 minor ones. Her research is important as it empirically relates technology to structure in an explicit and descriptive manner. Some of these relations between technology and structure are shown in Figure 8–2. It is clear by examination that differences in the organization factors depend upon the type of technology the company employs as Figure 8–2 shows.

Figure 8–2. Organization Parameters by Manufacturing Technology

Parameters	*Unit and Small Batch*	*Large Batch Mass Production*	*Process Production*
Typical span of control of first-line supervisors....................	21–30	41–50	11–20
Staff to production workers........	8	5.5	2
Direct to indirect workers.........	9	4	1
Average percent cost of wages......	15	32	40
Levels of management.............	3	4	6
Most critical function.............	Development	Production	Marketing
Tendency toward line-staff forms........................	Little	Marked	Little

Source: The data are adapted from Joan Woodward, *Industrial Organization Theory and Practice* (London: Oxford University Press, 1965). The precise definition of these parameters is given in Woodward's study. We will define these variables in general terms in this and the following chapter.

In relating the success of companies to structure, Woodward further shows that firms deviating from the median values of span of control of first-line supervisors for their technological class are less successful than those firms possessing median values.[13] Similarly, parameters such as the principles of limited span of control for the chief executive, unity of command, and clear separation of line from staff activities appear to be necessary for success in large-batch production, but detrimental to success in unit or process production. Her results suggest the dependency of rational organization structure to the technology employed and deviation from the organization norms in a technological class appears to bring about a reduction in achievement.[14]

Environmental Diversity

To some extent, it has already been shown that external conditions of market size and dispersion influence the technology that a firm employs and thus its tasks and organization structure. Two additional factors in the external environment influence the need for a differentiated internal organization structure. The first of these is the diversity of ex-

---

[13] Woodward, op. cit., chap. 5.

[14] In a later work, Woodward attempts to uncover the reasoning behind the Technology-Structure relations. See Joan Woodward (ed.), *Industrial Organization: Behavior and Control* (New York: Oxford University Press, 1970). In fact, technology may merely affect uncertainty and complexity as they influence differentiation.

ternal factors bearing upon the firm's operations. Consider a supermarket chain operating only in typical suburban neighborhoods. The class of clientele in terms of taste, income, product preferences, service, and so on, tend to be more homogeneous than for a similar firm operating supermarkets in a variety of ethnic neighborhoods. For the latter, separate merchandising skills, knowledge, and, perhaps, organizations will be required to meet this diversity of customer needs. Similarly an airframe manufacturer selling air transports to both military and commercial customers will require twin marketing, legal, service, repair, and, perhaps, production capabilities. While it is possible to combine the military and civilian activities of each of these functions, Lawrence and Lorsch have shown that the most successful firms of those facing diversity in external environmental conditions are those that provide a differentiated internal structure.[15] Conversely they show that firms enjoying a relatively monolithic stable environment with little change in price policies, technological development or product change are able to operate most effectively with a relatively simple nondifferentiated organization structure—i.e., with fewer separate departments. A key factor in determining to what extent a structure should be differentiated or combined is the need arising from diversity of environment and tasks rather than need based on "Parkinsonian tendencies."[16]

Environmental Uncertainty

The degree of uncertainty of the environmental conditions facing the firm is a further factor influencing the degree of differentiation required in organization components. Thompson contends that firms attempt to deal with uncertainty by first isolating their "core technologies" from environmental variations by creating input and output units of organization.[17] For a mass-production organization facing seasonal demands, for example, a final inventory is built up in slack sales periods to buffer the production line's efficiency from the ups and downs of demand. This may require an organizational unit to plan, store, and control final inventory variations. For firms which produce only when customer orders are on hand, however, there is no need to buffer output and no need for a differentiated department to deal with these types of problems. Such firms may set up a unit of their organization, however, to differentiate their input processes so as to stabilize the effect that external variations will have upon its internal operations—e.g., it may add a department that will only accept or solicit orders which provide it a degree

---

[15] Lawrence and Lorsch, *Organization and Environment,* chap. 11.

[16] Ibid., p. 213. Parkinsonianism refers to the hypothesized tendency of an organization to proliferate departments or personnel without regard to task.

[17] Thompson, *Organizations in Action,* pp. 19, 20.

of stability. (Alternatively it may price its products to achieve this buffering effect.) Thus, either structural or decision system changes are involved.

Technological Change

While organizational buffering provides some relief from environmental uncertainty, differentiation beyond merely adding input and output departments may be required for other types of uncertainty in the environment. For example, for some firms their products and the processes for producing them are undergoing rapid technological change while for other firms, product and process stability has been achieved. Consider a firm making AM radios, the fundamental design of which has been established for a number of years. True innovations in this field are few. A firm can compete in terms of design with relatively minor adaptations other than using major research or developmental expenditures. Consequently, there is no need for a basic research group or a product development activity separate from tool engineering or process engineering. The processes are so well known and similar in approach that any differentiation would make for distinctions without any real differences.

In contrast, consider firms which develop software programs for computers. These firms must first develop new programs that will help their customers meet their computational needs. Computer technology is new and changing rapidly so that a program design must be innovative and consider a number of different approaches if it is to be efficient and effective. For example, the design of a program to estimate costs for construction firms bidding upon multistory office and apartment buildings would involve research into the types of costs, types of subcontracts, excavation and erection rates, their relation to each other, and so forth, as well as the fixed and variable portions of each before a general computer program could be started.

After a program or a series of programs have been developed, it is necessary for a different function to be performed—that of selling. This process differs from selling relatively standard products such as AM radios for which standards have been developed. There is a need for *adapation* of the general programs to the customer's particular computer, testing the inputs available, and evaluating the results. Some software firms have been successful at developing the basic programs but have failed in their efforts to successfully adapt them to meet customer needs. These two activities—research and adaptation—differ in several important respects.[18] By comparing fundamental and applied research organizations (to which these two respective computer tasks can be

---

[18] Lawrence and Lorsch, *Organization and Environment*, p. 36.

compared), Lawrence and Lorsch found that the fundamental research group tended to have: (1) less formality of structure; (2) more of an orientation to task than to interpersonal relationships; and (3) a longer time orientation than the applied research group in the same company. Following these findings, a tendency toward organization and personal conflict as well as uncertainty of assignments would occur if these computer groups were combined into one department. The establishment of different organizational units appears to be warranted by the differences in the uncertainties associated with the technological conditions facing the two activities. Conversely, Lawrence and Lorsch found that a relatively simple undifferentiated structure was more appropriate for container manufacturing firms whose product and process technologies were relatively well known and not rapidly changing.[19] The can company's primary research and development activity, for example, occurred at the production floor to adapt machinery to accommodate customer variations. No department performed packaging research or new product development since environmental activity in these areas was relatively lacking.

Differentiation: Summary

The degree of organization differentiation of structure is seen to depend upon factors, both controllable by and independent of the decisions undertaken by the firm. Technological change, uncertainty of competitive acts, and diversity of customers use of its products are examples of factors usually considered exogeneous variables not under the direct influence and control of an organization's management. Yet, rational organizational differentiation is influenced by them. A firm could isolate itself from variation and uncertainty to a degree if it were to select a strategy such that these external variations are minimized. Often, however, a firm's prior investment and expertise does not allow a completely free choice of strategy but rather it must attempt to match its own competencies with environmental needs. Additionally, it is often in the diverse and uncertain market areas that the greatest profit opportunities exist.

Organization is thus seen as an open system, one whose boundaries interact with a set of competitive, technological, legal, and social environments. When these environments are benign, stable, and relatively simple, an organization can behave as a less-open system. Further, although not completely closed, such systems tend somewhat more toward entropy, a condition in which differentiation of the system parts is reduced, as pointed out in Chapter 4. For firms facing the more certain and less-complex environments, less differentiation in time perspective

---

[19] Ibid., pp. 52, 176.

and fewer specialized departments to deal with environmental uncertainty exist.

INTEGRATION OF GROUPS AND DEPARTMENTS

As tasks and departmental groupings become more differentiated for whatever reasons, there develops the need to coordinate or integrate the disparate suborganizations and activities toward the common goals of the total organization. There are several factors in addition to differentiation which influence the need for integration. These integration requirements will be discussed in connection with the approaches appropriate for achieving coordinative efforts.

Interdependence and Integration

Not all activities depend directly upon all others for proper performance of their function. Rather, a suborganization may be relatively independent of some counterpart groups while relying heavily on others. Thompson identifies three types of interdependence: pooled, serial, and reciprocal, respectively increasing in integration needs.[20] These types of interdependence stem at least partially from the technical requirements of the tasks. *Pooled* interdependence means that although departments do not contact or interact directly with others, the performance of each affects the whole and vice versa. A branch retail store in Chicago does not ordinarily contact or interact with another retail branch of the same company in Louisville. Yet each contributes to the overall company's well-being which in turn affects each branch to some extent. This type of interdependence requires a minimum of communication and decision making for effective operation. Thompson states that the most appropriate management systems for integrating pooled interdependence utilize *standardization*. By establishing normal stock levels, limits of discretion at the store level, standard policies for action, and standard reporting and control procedures, the contributions of each branch store may be controlled, and to some extent its performance better assured. Communication control and decision making (and thus integration) are carried out by these standard procedures rather than through day-to-day communications.

Serial independence arises from tasks in which the output of one unit is the input to another in a sequential fashion such that B depends on A, and C depends on B. Serial interdependence is more critical than pooled and requires more communication and decision making. Appro-

---

[20] Thompson, *Organizations in Action*, chap. 5. The following discussion of interdependence follows Thompson's analysis.

priate integration is affected by *planning* rather than through standardization since the actions of B can only partially be programmed from the actions of A.

In a general machine shop, for example, work in the foundry precedes the work to be performed in the machine shop which precedes assembly

work. A production planning operation to determine the sequencing or timing of orders through these departments is essential if delivery goals are to be met. Although the foundary ordinarily would have little knowledge of machine processing, operations or assembly times required, its timing and sequencing of castings produced could vitally affect the performance of subsequent operations. A planning unit superordinate to these producing departments can achieve the coordination required by the serial task interdependence.

The most complex form of interdependence is *reciprocal* in which the output of A is the input of B and the outputs of B are the inputs to A. Since they are mutually interactive, they must, under natural circumstances, work closely together. Communication and decisions are extensive and integration of their efforts is accomplished through *mutual adjustment.*

Consider a builder of earthmoving equipment who makes special order draglines and excavators on specifications requested by strip miners. In selling such a machine, the salesman must work closely with the customer and the engineering department in his own company to ensure that the specifications can be met or to obtain adjustments from the customer if alternate performance specifications seem advisable. Further, the engineering department might need to get aid from their tooling, production, and materials departments—even suppliers of special materials—to determine whether or not the proposed machine can be built to do the job outlined. A great deal of interdepartmental communication and mutual adjustment of requirements among the several departments, suppliers, and customer is required prior to final delivery.

One way of isolating the integration needs of reciprocal interdependence is to isolate components or tasks requiring it within a single department. In the excavator case, a project team with appropriate technical representatives from the customer, sales, engineering, tooling, production, and material departments could be formed and given the authority to make the decisions needed to accomplish the goal of design, production, and delivery of the excavating system. If such teams were established for each new project, reciprocal interdependence could greatly be reduced among the remaining departments. It should be noted that serial interdependence between project teams would still exist and that pooled interdependence would continue to exist among organizational units. The three types of interdependencies discussed above are shown in Figure 8–3.

Figure 8–3. Basic Types of Interdependence

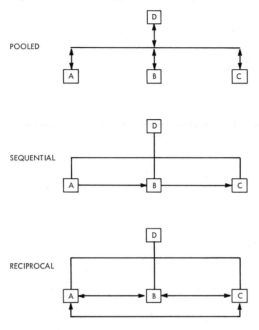

Interdependence and Structural Groupings

Since coordination through communications and decision making is expensive, it is rational to attempt to minimize the costs of integration. One way of doing this is to group together the tasks having reciprocal interdependence so as to isolate these effects from the rest of the organization (e.g., by project teams). If reciprocal interdependence can be isolated by grouping tasks requiring it, only serial and pooled interdependence are not coordinated. Thus, the remaining integration efforts can revert to less costly planning. For example, the project teams for designing excavators can through mutual adjustment accomplish their tasks, but top management still must consider which projects have priority and plan production and material schedules appropriately.

As coordinating reciprocal interdependence is more costly in terms of communications and decisions than in integration of serial interdependence, so too are its planning requirements more costly than coordination by standardization methods of a pooled interdependence. Thus, in grouping activities together or contiguously, operations that are serially dependent are to be combined or located adjacently after reciprocally coordinated tasks have been isolated. The general rule in grouping activities, then, is to attempt to first combine reciprocally interdependent tasks or departments and then to group serially interdependent units leaving only integration of units possessing pooled interdependence to be accomplished.

Coordination via Hierarchy, Project Teams, etc.

When groupings to isolate reciprocal interdependencies become very large in size, however, the resulting group coordination activities can become very great. As a consequence, smaller groupings encompassing the most critical interdependencies tend to be formed first and then coordination among such first-level groups is performed by the next higher level of organization. Although proper combining of interdependent tasks and hierarchy are able to account for many coordination needs, the remaining coordinative requirements may suggest the use of committees, task forces, liason assignments, and project teams, the use dependent upon the degree of remaining interdependency.

Diversity and Uncertainty

Above it was shown that increasing environmental uncertainty and diversity tended to generate a need for increased task and group differentiation. Lawrence and Lorsch have noted further that these conditions also tend to evoke a need for coordination at relatively low hierarchical levels of organization.[21] These conditions are ones which appear to engender reciprocal interdependence and the need for on-the-spot mutual adjustment of difficulties. Conversely, a relatively stable and simple environment provides little uncertainty to the organization and it can more easily be coordinated from the top hierarchical levels. It thus appears that the greater the diversity and uncertainty in the environment, *ceteris paribus,* the greater is the need for integrative efforts at the *lower* levels of an organization's hierarchy and vice versa.

MANAGERIAL COORDINATION: INFORMATION, INFLUENCE, AND SPAN OF CONTROL

In the previous section, the need for coordination of segregated tasks and groups has been shown as well as how some of these integration requirements can be met by task groupings and hierarchy. It is to the role of the manager in the hierarchy and in performing integrating functions that we now turn.

---

[21] Lawrence and Lorsch, *Organization and Environment,* p. 91.

Managerial Coordination: Information and Influence

Work performed by different individuals in the firm must obviously be *coordinated* if company objectives are to be met. If each organizational member were to define his own performance output without giving consideration to its relationship to work performed by other individuals in the firm, a high degree of organizational chaos could result.

A basic function of and need for managers in the business organization is to provide such coordination. The plant manager in a manufacturing firm, for example, must coordinate the work of engineering, production, and quality control so that the items produced meet specifications; the production and sales efforts of the firm must be coordinated so that there is sufficient number of salesmen to sell the units of product produced, or so that production can turn out a sufficient number of units to meet customer orders.

Essentially managerial coordination is effected by (1) *providing information* to subordinates and other organizational members, and (2) *influencing* these individuals to *accept* the content of their communicational messages. The foreman, for example, needs to inform his workers as to what work he wants them to accomplish; then he must influence them to direct their efforts toward meeting these work objectives.

These information-providing and influence needs of the coordinative process have two basic implications for organizational design. First, in structuring jobs, not only must the work content of the job be considered, but attention must also be given to its *informational* requirements. If the production worker is to be able to operate a particular machine, he must be given information as to how to do it; if the manager is to make effective decisions, his informational inputs must be adequate, and so on. Further, not only must information *content* be defined, informational *flows* and communications *channels* must be given explicit attention in organizational design. *From whom* is the production control manager to obtain information needed to establish the plant's production schedules for the following week? Once a scheduling decision has been made, then *to whom* must such information be communicated if the decision is to be effectively implemented?

Second, organizational design implies the structuring of *power* and influence relationships among individual holding various positions in the firm. By virtue of the fact that he has been appointed to a position of "boss," the first-line foreman is usually perceived by his subordinates as possessing a certain amount of legitimate power. By designing a managerial position so that its holder has the power to hire, fire, promote, demote, and give or withhold salary increases to subordinates, coercive and reward bases of power are established.

In summary, the design of an organizational hierarchy, in which managers at one or more levels are called on to coordinate and direct the efforts of their subordinates toward organizational goals, implies the structuring not only of work content, but also for informational flows and power and influence relationships among various members of the organization.

Span of Control Defined

In our previous discussion, we indicated that the job of organizing involves subdividing a total task into smaller and smaller subtasks until jobs are defined for individual workers. Then, we pointed out that in order to coordinate specialized tasks, appropriate structure and formal leadership in the firm are necessary. Reliance on both specialization and coordination implies that organizations be comprised of a set of groups, each consisting of a number of specialized workers and a formal leader or manager. In determining how large these groups should be, considerations that limit a manager's ability are now to be contemplated.

Quite obviously, any individual is limited in what he is able to accomplish. We are limited by time, and by our knowledge, skills, interests, and motivation. These limitations upon the scope of a manager's activities within any given period of time are considered explicitly in organization design by the notion of span of control.[22] The concept of span of control may be stated as follows: "There is a limited number of subordinates who may be *supervised effectively* by any single manager." We will now examine some of the organizational implications of different size spans of control, and some of the key variables which must be considered by management in determining what the span of control ought to be at various levels in the organization.

Implications of Differing Spans of Control

Management's choice as to the width of the span of control at each level in the organizational hierarchy can have numerous implications of significance for the firm. Several of these implications may be visualized by examining three possible alternative spans of control for a small (hypothetical) organization consisting of 16 operating employees: (1) a narrow span of 2, (2) an intermediate span of 4, and (3) a wide span of 16. These three possibilities are illustrated graphically in Figure 8–4, and some of the organizational implications of each summarized in Figure 8–5. For purposes of simplicity, we are assuming in this exam-

---

[22] "Span of control" is also sometimes referred to as "span of management" or "span of supervision."

Figure 8–4. Alternative Spans of Control

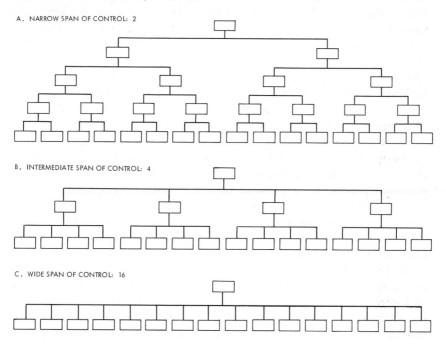

A. NARROW SPAN OF CONTROL: 2

B. INTERMEDIATE SPAN OF CONTROL: 4

C. WIDE SPAN OF CONTROL: 16

Figure 8–5.   Effects of Alternative Spans of Control

	Narrow	Intermediate	Wide	Organization Level
Span of control.....................	2	4	16	
Number of nonsupervisory employees........................	16	16	16	1st
1st level supervisors..............	8	4	1	2nd
2nd level supervisors.............	4	1	0	3rd
3rd level supervisors.............	2	0	0	4th
4th level supervisors.............	1	0	0	5th
Total management levels..............	4	2	1	
Total organization levels..............	5	3	2	
Number of managers.................	15	5	1	
Total employees.....................	31	21	17	
Managers as a percent of total employees........................	49%	23%	6%	

ple that the span of control is the same at each level in the organization, although, as we will indicate later, spans usually do (and should) vary at different organizational levels.

Generalizing from Figures 8–4 and 8–5, we may note that, all other factors being the same, the smaller the span of control in an organization, the larger will be the number of: managers, total employees, and both managerial and total organizational levels. In consequence, the larger the span of control in an organization tends to be, the smaller the administrative costs, since salaries do not have to be paid to as large a number of managers.[23] Further, *vertical* communications—i.e., such as the transmission of verbal messages, written reports, from top management down to lower levels in the organization, and, conversely, from lower level managers up to the top—tend to pose fewer problems with wider spans of control. This is because with a smaller number of levels in the organization, there are fewer managers through whom messages must pass in going from their source to their ultimate destination. For example, suppose that in the hypothetical organization of 16 operating employees discussed previously, a problem involving certain work procedures on a particular job arises that should be decided upon by top management, rather than at any lower level, because it has several important implications for the overall operations of the firm. With a span of control of four, as illustrated in Figure 8–4, pertinent information on the problem would have only to be transmitted from the manager of the department in which the problem arose to the president of the firm. With a span of control of two, on the other hand, the information would have to be additionally brought to the attention of two other managers (the first-line supervisor's boss, and, in turn, his boss) before it was received by the president. One disadvantage of such "longer" communications channels as opposed to shorter ones is that messages tend to become *distorted* as they pass from one individual to another, since different individuals' knowledge, levels of understanding, perceptions, needs, and so forth are different. Further, more time is usually required for a message to reach its destination when it must be transmitted to and then be retransmitted from numerous individuals in the organization. In consequence, delays in obtaining information needed quickly to provide the basis for decision making may pose a greater problem in multilevel firms where the vertical communications channels are quite "long" than in those organizations characterized by a relatively small number of hierarchical levels.

Now that some of the positive implications of a wide span of control have been considered, let us examine the disadvantages of this form of organizational structuring. As indicated earlier, the primary disadvantage accruing from a span of control which is "too wide" is that the job of supervising may become so great that the manager cannot perform

---

[23] Decreasing the number of managers in an organization by increasing span of control may not always result in lower administrative costs. For example, each manager whose span is increased may be paid more than he previously was due to the added responsibilities which he has been given; and such salary increases may more than offset any cut in costs resulting from the employment of fewer managers.

his work effectively. In explaining the increased supervisory burden facing managers as their span of control is increased, attention has often been given to the fact that:

As the number of individuals reporting to a manager increases, the number of supervisor-subordinate *relationships* which may exist in this department increases at a *much faster rate.*

To illustrate, if a supervisor, A, has only a single subordinate, B, only one relationship may exist within the department—that between A and B, which may be denoted A:B. With 2, 3, or 4 subordinates, however, the number of possible supervisor-subordinate relationships increases to 3, 7, and 15, respectively, as is illustrated in Figure 8–6.

Figure 8–6. Possible Supervisory-Subordinate Relationships with Two, Three, and Four Subordinates

Two Subordinates	*Three Subordinates*	*Four Subordinates*	
A:B	A:B	A:B	A:CD
A:C	A:C	A:C	A:CE
A:BC	A:D	A:D	A:DE
	A:BC	A:E	A:BCD
	A:BD	A:BC	A:BCE
	A:CD	A:BD	A:BDE
	A:BCD	A:BE	A:CDE
			A:BCDE
3	7	15	

TOTAL

Important to recognize is the fact that the supervisory-subordinate relationships which have been discussed are simply *possible* ones. In some instances some of them may rarely, if ever, exist or, even if they occur relatively frequently may involve only a very small amount of supervisory time. Referring back to Figure 8–6, for example, supervisor A may have to spend only 10 minutes a month instructing, helping to resolve problems among, or in other ways communicating with subordinates B, C, and E, as a group—the relationship A:BCE. On the other hand, he may find it necessary to spend several hours each week in his supervisory relationship with B and D (A:BD). Thus, although wider spans of control do mean the existence of increasingly larger numbers of possible supervisor-subordinate relationships, the *importance* of such relationships in terms of supervisory burden is often influenced considerably by other variables. Attention will now be turned to some of the key variables which do influence span of control.

Variables Affecting Size of Span

Considerable variations may be found in the number of subordinates considered most desirable for managers to supervise in different organizational situations. In some cases, firms have found a span of control of as small as 2 or 3 to be the largest which certain of their managers could handle effectively; while in others, effective supervision with spans of 30 or more have been reported. Our purpose in this section is to examine some of the variables of importance in determining what the manager's span of control should be under various conditions.

Interrelated Work among Subordinates. One important variable which will influence the amount of attention which a manager will have to give in helping to resolve problems *among* his subordinates (relationships of the type A:BC, A:BCD, and so on) is the degree to which the work performed by the subordinates is *interdependent.* In general, other factors being the same, a manager may effectively supervise a larger number of subordinates when the work performed by each is relatively *independent,* since fewer problems of *coordination* arise. This point may be illustrated by reference to two research studies which have been made on span of control.

In a study of Sears, Roebuck retail stores, James Worthy found that a large span of control (sometimes over 30) for store managers seemed to be more effective than a small span.[24] In contrast, a study made by James Healey of manufacturing firms in Ohio indicated that a relatively narrow span of control for plant managers was more often used and considered desirable.[25] These opposing research results may be reconciled if the differences in the relationships requiring management attention in each are examined. In Sears, Roebuck stores, the work of various departments is relatively *independent,* possessing essentially pooled interdependence. Work in the hardware department, for example, is only loosely related to work in the women's clothing, sports, or appliance departments. Thus, few interrelationships among the work of the department managers require attention by the store manager and a relatively large span of control is feasible.

In contrast, the plant managers studied by Healey supervised a number of departments performing interrelated work—such as engineering, tooling, production planning and control, manufacturing and inspection. In such manufacturing operations when the engineering department has completed a design and the drawings for a part or a product, the tooling department must then design and manufacture tools for its production.

---

[24] James Worthy, "Organizational Structure and Employee Morale," *American Sociological Review,* 15 (April 1950), pp. 169–79.

[25] James H. Healey, *Executive Coordination and Control* (Columbus, Ohio: Bureau of Business Research, The Ohio State University, 1956).

After obtaining estimates as to what volume of sales can be expected, production planning must determine when and on what machines parts are to be produced; manufacturing produces the product and quality control inspects it. Since actions in one department may seriously affect the operations in others, a much greater degree of coordinative supervision is required by plant managers in manufacturing than by store managers in retailing operations such as Sears. The interdependence exhibited in the manufacturing companies is of the serial type requiring considerably more communications and decision making than does pooled interdependence.

Figure 8–2, page 243, shows the impact of technology upon organization parameters. Woodward's results suggest different average spans for different technologies. In the unit technology, a custom operation, different tasks are brought to operate on a unit of product. Since product design is uncertain, mutual adjustment among the tasks is required and reciprocal interdependence appears to exist among tasks. Extensive coordinative efforts would be required and a small span of control called for as Woodward's data show. In mass production, serial interdependence would require less communication and permit larger spans; these expectations are also confirmed in Woodward's data. Finally, the process firms (e.g., automated chemical operations) exhibit small average spans indicating reciprocal interdependence. These relations stem from the need for close control over optimizing the operations of the processes rather than from uncertainties in the product as in the unit case. While the empirical evidence is small (but growing) thus far, task interdependencies apparently as influenced partially by the type of technology used help determine the span of control.

Complexity of Work Performed. Another variable influencing span of control is the complexity of the work performed by the manager's subordinates. If the work carried out by employees in a department is highly programmed, routine, and not subject to frequent change, less supervisory attention will usually be required than if the work is of a more dynamic and complex nature. It is for this reason that organizations typically exhibit wider spans of control at lower levels than at upper levels. First-line supervisors, who are able to rely upon precise job descriptions, operating instructions and work rules to aid them in defining and coordinating subordinate actions, often are able to effectively supervise 20, 30, or more employees. At upper levels in most organizations, on the other hand, managerial problems tend to be much broader in scope and more dynamic, with fewer precise *precedents* for decision making and action available. Under such nonroutine conditions in which many problems are ill-defined, executives must spend considerable time working out plans for action with their subordinates; and hence, the effective span of control tends to be fairly narrow. As we have seen, however, the need for flexibility and nonroutine tasks does not necessarily apply only to upper executive levels but rather these needs may also arise at lower levels due to technological and product uncertainties.

Leader and Follower Characteristics. The personality characteristics of both the manager and his subordinates may also have an important bearing on span of control. If a manager's subordinates are well trained, competent, and able (and willing) to plan their own work and make decisions for themselves, there will be less need for supervisory attention; and a larger span of control will be possible. Moreover, if the manager himself is highly skilled in planning, instructing subordinates, handling employee problems, and so on, it may be possible to give him a larger span than would be the case with a less adept supervisor.

Physical Contiguity. When a manager's subordinates are separated physically from one another, it may be necessary for his span of control to be narrower. This is because supervision is rendered more difficult by his inability to "oversee" all of his subordinates at any given time. Physical separation inhibits instruction, and other forms of communications. Organization analysts sometimes try to offset the span-narrowing impact of physical separation by utilizing approaches to make the manager's supervisory task less burdensome. For example, short written forms to ease superior-subordinate communications are often introduced (e.g., salesman report forms). Or, individuals selected for remotely located positions may be given special instruction and training, necessitating less supervisor attention and communication. All other factors remaining the same, however, physical separation does tend to reduce the manager's effective span of control.

Administrative Assistance. Another factor influencing span of control is the amount of assistance or aid available to the manager in coordinating the efforts of his subordinates. As Ernest Dale has suggested, it was possible for General Eisenhower to allow 50 corps commanders direct "access" to him because he had an intervening level of staff officers who relieved him from handling numerous day-to-day problems.[26] Or, in the Sears stores mentioned previously, an assistant manager, who was responsible for dealing with several managerial functions, can be considered as contributing to the effectiveness found with a wide span of control. Somewhat similarly, by assigning a training assistant and a paper-work clerk to certain of its first-line foremen, IBM was able to widen their span of control and as a result eliminate one level of management.

Just how much coordinative assistance should be provided the manager will, of course, depend on a number of variables. For example, consider providing a manager with one administrative assistant, which would have the effects shown in Figure 8–7. Whether the additional

---

[26] Ernest Dale, *Planning and Developing the Company Organization Structure,* Research Report No. 20 (New York: American Management Association, 1952), pp. 56–57.

Figure 8–7. Addition of an Administrative Assistant (hypothetical example)

	Without Assistant	*With Assistant*
Manager's salary	$10,000	$10,000
Assistant's salary	—	7,500
Span of control possible	10	15
Administrative cost/subordinate	$1,000	$1,167

$7,500 in salary paid to the assistant would be justified would depend on such factors as the following: How much more effectively can the manager run his department with the assistant? By increasing his span of control (and possibly that of other managers by providing them with assistants) would it be possible to reduce the number of managers and organizational levels in the firm? In short, providing administrative assistance will tend to increase the manager's effective span of control; but whether such assistance is desirable depends upon a number of factors.

A Model of Span of Control

In the previous sections we have illustrated how several different variables may influence the appropriateness of different sized spans of control. We have not, however, examined the *relative importance* which should be given to each of these variables in determining what span of control is most effective in any given organizational situation.

Unfortunately, little research evidence yet exists which will permit the development of any definitive quantitative model explicitly specifying the relationship between the variables involved in making span of control decisions. However, one firm—the Lockheed Missile and Space Company—has experimented with the design and utilization of a simple span of control "model," in which several variables believed to be of considerable influence on span of control have been weighted.[27]

What Lockheed did was to first weight six separate factors believed to affect span of control. These factors, and their maximum ratings (and hence, relative weights) were as follows:

1. (Dis)similarity of functions performed by subordinates—5
2. Geographic separation of employees—5

[27] The material in this and the following paragraphs was drawn from: Harold Stieglitz, "Optimizing Span of Control," *Management Record*, 24 (September 1962), pp. 25–29. A more mathematical approach using waiting line theory is used to model "optimal spans" in Lawrence S. Hill, "The Application of Queuing Theory to the Span of Control," *Academy of Management Journal*, 6 (March 1963), pp. 58–69.

3. Complexity of jobs performed by subordinates—10
4. Degree of subordinate direction and control required—15
5. Degree of coordination of subordinates required—10
6. The scope and complexity of and precedents available for the planning required in the supervisory position—10

Then, each managerial position was rated by these factors and the ratings were summed to give a supervisory "index." Next, by analyzing numerous supervisory positions, several different suggested spans of control were established based on the point value of the supervisory indices. For example, for middle-management positions, an index of 40–42 indicated a suggested span of four or five subordinates, and index of 31–33, of from five to eight subordinates, and so forth.[28]

Once designed, the Lockheed "model" was applied to a few units of the company, and the following results reported:

> One . . . [application] . . . extended the average span for 3.8 people to 4.2 and reduced supervisory levels from five to four; another broadened the average span of middle managers from 3.0 to 4.2 and cut levels from six to five; and in a third case, the average span went from 4.2 to 4.8 persons and levels dropped from seven to five. The reductions in managerial personnel and supervisory payroll were "substantial."[29]

Admitting to its successful application in a few cases, let us now consider the question: "How may the Lockheed approach in general be evaluated?" In our opinion, a primary advantage of this approach is that it focuses *explicit* and *systematic* attention on the problem of span of control in organization design. In doing so, it may warn against developing a small-span, many level organization which is expensive in supervisory salaries, and which tends to magnify problems in vertical communications; while at the same time, it may help assure narrow enough spans of control for effective supervision.

As the analysts who designed this approach have been quick to point out, however, the index cannot be applied "blindly" and without thought to supervisory positions; rather its successful application requires considerable reliance on managerial judgment.

> Judgment, for example, is called for in evaluating the extent to which the six factors are present in a particular job situation. And even greater judgment is needed in deciding whether the "suggested span" is truly appropriate in a given situation.[30]

Thus, the model should not be viewed as one in which the manager can routinely "plug in" values and obtain optimum results. Rather, it

---

[28] It should be noted that in utilizing the supervisory indices, consideration was also given to the amount of administrative assistance which various supervisors had.

[29] Stieglitz, "Optimizing Span of Control," p. 29.

[30] Ibid.

is intended as a general guide, which, when supplemented with managerial judgment, may aid in making more effective span of control decisions.

SUMMARY

Whether one is examining propositions concerning the natural form and evolution of an organization or its deliberate design by management, there are a number of interacting factors bearing upon the final result. These factors and some interrelations among them are shown in Figure 8–8 which is used as a basis for this summary discussion. The environ-

Figure 8–8. Model of Organizational Differentiation and Integration

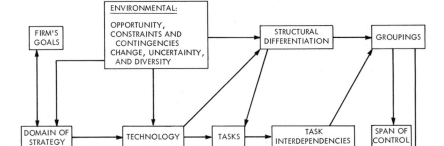

ment, especially in terms of markets, provides opportunities for a firm to meet its goals if it selects a strategy to link the firm's particular and unique capabilities to market opportunities. The selection of strategy in terms of the products provided and the markets served circumscribes a set of technologies available to perform the processes necessary to achieve product-market anticipations.

The existing set of resources and skills in an organization feed back upon the selection of a strategy in such a way as to achieve a unique and, hopefully, superior relative advantage for the organization in relation to competitors and market opportunities. Once the technology is determined, several alternate task assignments are possible, the choice being one of optimizing task assignments and the degree of specialization on the one hand with job uncertainties, technological constraints, and psychological factors on the other.

Choices from among alternate task assignments gives rise to task inter-dependencies which along with the structural differentiation appropriate to the technology and environmental diversity and uncertainty determine the types of tasks that are grouped together and/or adjacently. These groupings achieve a large measure of intertask integration, but some groups thus formed will be too large for effective supervision. In these cases, the factors which influence the proper span of control are taken into consideration to form hierarchies spanning the unintegrated group-ings. Integration or coordination is achieved through the supervisor of the groupings requiring it. If sufficient coordination is not achieved through the management hierarchy, other integrative devices such as committees, task forces, and project groups, may be employed.

These processes result in a differentiated and integrated organization exhibiting certain behaviors and capacities, both in the formal and in-formal social systems. If the capabilities of these systems are reconsid-ered in the light of existing strategy, a reevaluation of the firm's strategic orientation can take place to better match internal strengths and weak-nesses to the external opportunities.

Before progressing to new topics, the dynamic open-system nature of this model should be reemphasized. A number of external factors bear upon strategy, technology, differentiation, and the need for integra-tion. Thus, stability of organization structure will only be achieved if the environment is stable or the firm ignores changes. While not all environmental change will require internal organizational adaptation, perception of change and evaluating its implications to structure are an ever-present need.

Finally, it should be noted that this is a model in which every variable ultimately influences every other. This characteristic points again to the view that organization theory can only explain phenomena if at some point these systems are considered as open ones.

DISCUSSION AND STUDY QUESTIONS

1. Describe the differences between organization structures appropriate to a large retail appliance store and a national chain of appliance stores.

2. In considering the type of businesses it should enter as part of its strategy, why would a firm enter complex and uncertain areas especially in view of the increased differentiation and integration of organizational efforts such strategies might entail?

3. Compare job enlargement with job rotation as approaches to minimizing the dysfunctional, psychological consequences of increased job specialization.

4. As an organization increasingly differentiates tasks so that each worker has less of the total task to perform, what human effects might this evolution create?

5. What, in organization terms, is the relationship between the process of differentiation from that of integration?

6. The Wagner Corporation produces highly engineered pumps for jet fuel aboard aircraft in one division located in Denver and office furniture in a division whose plant is located in Pennsylvania. Both divisions have similar primary functional organizations: design, parts production, assembly, and sales. The design sections perform the necessary engineering and styling, the parts production groups produce parts on a job shop basis, parts are assembled, and the sales departments are responsible for the selling functions.

    a) Draw an organization chart of the Wagner firm.
    b) Describe the departments between or in which pooled, serial, and reciprocal interdependence are likely to exist.

7. In terms of organizational design, are learning and motivation theories consistent? Explain.

8. a) If a firm employs 64 workers who are not supervisors, what would be the span of control if the organization included two managing levels with the same span at both levels?
    b) If the span were divided in two, how many organization levels would exist?
    c) Draw a chart of the two organizations.

9. If the interdependence among tasks in a group increases, what impact would it have upon the desirable span of control? Explain.

10. A highly successful company engaged in electronic research and development has, as a matter of policy, set aside a portion of its earnings to work on projects in which it possessed competence and in which potential for economic success was believed to be high. The success of company-financed projects, in general, has been quite low. Most of the income to the firm has been provided by contracts to produce research and prototypes of electronic systems or subsystems for the government, to other prime contractors for the government, and for a limited number of commercial firms.

    As a result of one of its own internally financed projects and spin-offs of information from several government contracts, however, the company has developed a unique low-cost electronic calculator believed to have substantial market potential in office and home uses.

    The firm has been organized primarily on a task or project basis with contract bids as well as research and developmental work being carried out by the project team of experts possessing the particular skills necessary to accomplish the mission of the contract assigned to it. A typical team might originally consist of research engineers to assemble and create the basic knowledge to allow design to progress rationally, development engineers whose task it is to take the basic knowledge and to create a workable design concept, and production engineers whose function consists of creating a working prototype from the design. Since considerable uncertainty faced these teams, the initial designs and prototypes were frequently at variance with the contract specifications so that considerable redesign, adjustment of components, and even basic research might be acquired.

It was anticipated that the new electronic calculator could be mass-produced to perform most of the functions of existing calculators at a cost to allow a $125 selling price, considerably below the prices of existing mechanical or electronic calculators.

As a result of the design breakthrough, the company was considering the possibility of producing the calculator itself.

a) What changes in the environmental factors facing the firm could be anticipated if it decided to produce the calculator?

b) What effect might the components have upon the structure and functioning of the organization?

c) What alternative might the company consider to isolate its current primary functions from these environmental and organizational changes?

SELECTED REFERENCES

BARNARD, CHESTER I. *The Functions of the Executive*, chaps. 5–12. Cambridge, Mass.: Harvard University Press, 1938.

BARNES, L. B. *Organizational Systems and Engineering Groups*. Boston: Division of Research, Graduate School of Business Administration, Harvard University, 1960.

BLAU, P., and SCOTT, W. R. *Formal Organizations*. San Francisco: Chandler Publishing Co., 1962.

BURNS, T., and STALKER, G. M. *The Management of Innovation*. London: Tavistock Publications, 1961.

DALE, ERNEST. *Planning and Developing the Company Organization Structure*. Research Report No. 20. New York: American Management Association, 1952.

HAIRE, MASON (ed.). *Modern Organization Theory*. New York: John Wiley & Sons, Inc., 1959.

HARVEY, E. "Technology and the Structure of Organizations," *American Sociological Review*, 33 (1968), 247–59.

HICKSON, D. J.: PUGH, D. S.; and PHEYSEY, D. C. "Operations Technology and Organization structure," *Administrative Science Quarterly*, 14 (1969), 378–97.

HILL, LAWRENCE S. "The Application of Queuing Theory to the Span of Control," *Academy of Management Journal*, 6 (March 1963), 58–69.

HUNT, RAYMOND G. "Technology and Organization," *Academy of Management Journal*, 13 (September 1970), 235–52.

INDIK, BERNARD P. "The Relationship between Organization Size and Supervision Ratio," *Administrative Science Quarterly*, 9 (1964), 301–13.

MARCH, JAMES G. *Handbook of Organizations*, Chicago: Rand McNally & Co., 1965.

MARCH, JAMES G., and SIMON, H. A. *Organizations.* New York: John Wiley & Sons, Inc., 1958.

MILLER, E. J., and RICE, A. K. *Systems of Organization.* London: Tavistock Publications, 1967.

MILLMAN, R. WILLIAM. "Some Unsettled Questions in Organizational Theory," *Academy of Management Journal,* 7 (September 1964), 189–95.

PERROW, C. A. "A Framework for the Comparative Analysis of Organizations," *American Sociological Review,* 32 (1967), 195–208.

PUGH, D. S. et al. "A Conceptual Scheme for Organization Analysis," *Administrative Science Quarterly,* 8 (1963), 289–360.

SCOTT, WILLIAM G. "Organization Theory: An Overview and an Appraisal," *Journal of the Academy of Management,* 4 (April 1961), 7–26.

THOMPSON, J. D., and BATES, F. L. "Technology, Organization, and Administration, *Administrative Science Quarterly,* 2 (1957), 325–42.

THOMPSON, VICTOR A. "Hierarchy, Specialization, and Organization Conflict," *Administrative Science Quarterly,* 5 (1960), 485–521.

WALKER, CHARLES R. (ed.). *Modern Technology and Civilization.* New York: McGraw-Hill Book Co., 1962.

Chapter 9

Formal Organization: Departmentation

IN THE LAST CHAPTER, the process of *differentiation*, determining the manner in which total activities are to be subdivided—and of *integration*—providing the means to coordinate the parts so separated, were shown to be influenced to a considerable extent by the kinds of businesses the firm selected as its domain and the nature of the environmental factors bearing upon its operations. The purpose of this chapter is to show how differentiation and integration result in certain typical forms of structural arrangements. While the organization structures of all firms may not exactly fit the classes shown in this chapter, the types of departments that emerge and the relationships of one grouping to another tend to vary by the types of departmentation which will be discussed. Thus, understanding a structure and its operations is enhanced by this overview of types of departmentation.

A second major purpose of this chapter is to examine some of the additional variables important to determining and modifying structural groupings. If managers understand these and the processes of the last chapter, they have the basis for modifying ailing organizations or designing new ones.

ALTERNATE BASES FOR DEPARTMENTATION

There are several ways in which departmental areas of responsibility may be arranged.[1] Four basic types of grouping are examined in this section by: (1) function or process, (2) territory or geographical, (3) product or service, and (4) project. These approaches to formation of

---

[1] In addition to these four bases, work activities are sometimes grouped on the basis of customers served. For example, one sales department might sell certain products to one group of customers, while another sales department sells the same products to a different group of customers. This form of work grouping which is sometimes referred to as departmentalization by *clientele* is not nearly as widely utilized as the four bases which we will discuss in this section.

the primary or basic departmentation reflect the *first-level* differentiation and integrating processes that determine the types of groupings that occur at the *top level* of an organization. Second-level differentiation, third, and so on further down the hierarchical structure reflect differentiation of these four types as well as that of staff and service activities.

Functions Performed or Processes Employed

A common form of organizational structuring is that of departmentalization on the basis of functions or processes performed. In a manufacturing firm, for example, all activities involved in purchasing might be assigned to one department, and all engineering work to another department, with production, sales, and finance activities assigned to still other major departments. In retailing, a department store organized on the basis of functions performed might include the following major departments: (1) merchandising, to decide upon, purchase, and promote the lines of goods to be sold; (2) receiving, to inspect, store, and distribute goods to the selling floor; (3) sales, to which all the store's sales clerks are assigned; (4) credit, to grant credit, and handle collec-

Figure 9–1. Examples of Functional Departmentalization

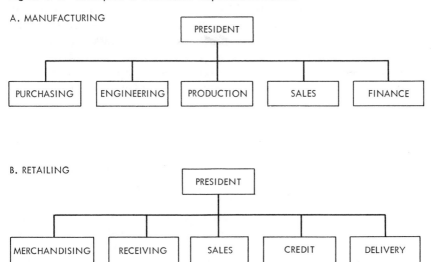

tions; and (5) delivery, responsible for distributing goods to the store's customers. These two examples of functional departmentalization are illustrated in Figure 9–1.

In process departmentalization, workers operating the same (or similar) types of machinery or equipment are grouped together and report to the same supervisor. In a machine shop, for example, one might find drill press, milling machine, lathe, screw machine, punch press, and stamping departments, as illustrated in Figure 9–2. Although process departmentalization is probably most common in manufacturing operations, this form of organizational structuring may be found elsewhere as well. For example, in an office situation, typists may be grouped together into a typing pool; or, in a large computer center, all keypunch operators may report to the same supervisor in a keypunch department.

It should be noted that process and/or functional departmentation may be of a "pure" form as shown in Figures 9–1 and 9–2, or it may

Figure 9–2. Example of Process Departmentalization

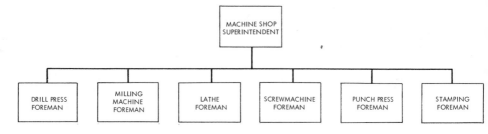

be combined with the other forms of departmentalization which will be explained below. (Alternative department forms are shown in Figure 9–4.) In fact, since process and functional departmentation represent separate work activities necessary to accomplish the tasks of the firm, some form of them occurs at some level in every organization. In their purest forms, they occur primarily in smaller and simpler organizations.

Product or Service Departmentalization

In many cases, all duties related to one or more products or services may be assigned to a particular department. In a large chemical firm, for example, the major operational departments might be plastics, oils, and chemicals, as is illustrated in Figure 9–3. Within each of these three major divisions, all activities involved in producing and selling the product classes assigned to the division would be carried out. As is also illustrated in Figure 9–3, the basis of departmentalization *within* a major product division may vary—the work performed within the chemical division in our example is broken down on the basis of product; while functional departmentalization exists within the oil division.

Conceptually similar to departmentalization based on products is that based on the grouping of similar services. Illustrative of a service departmentalized organization would be that of a large bank, in which departments were established to handle: (1) customer deposits and withdrawals, (2) mortgage and other loans, and (3) trusts.

Figure 9–3. Example of Product Departmentalization

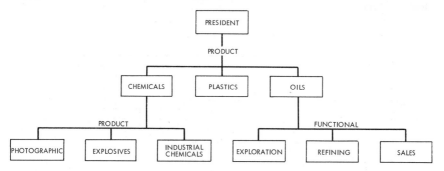

It should be noted that the differentiation in a bank's operations into these separate departments is partially a function of environmental constraints and diversity. The trust operations (in which the bank serves as a trustee of its client's money invested in securities of companies) can gain inside information about a company invested in if the bank also makes commercial loans to the firm in question. This example of potential conflict of interest from the point of view of the general investing public has even raised the question of whether departmental separation of banking activities is a sufficient protection to investors or whether legally separate organizations are more appropriate.[2]

Geographical Departmentalization

In many instances, firms will assign the activities involved in servicing a given geographical area to a particular department. In one large supermarket chain, for example, over 20 geographical divisions exist—a division encompassing all stores in the greater Cincinnati area, a Pittsburgh division, a Detroit division, and so forth. In addition, in this organization the activities carried out by these major geographical divisions are further broken down on the basis of territory serviced—the divisions are divided into a number of zones or districts, each comprised of several stores.

In addition to retailing operations such as the above in which a number of physically dispersed stores exist, many firms' sales and international operations are departmentalized geographically. It is fairly common for firms selling goods throughout this country to have a number of major territorial sales divisions (and offices)—e.g., Eastern, Midwestern, Southern, and Far Western—with, in many cases, further geographic subdepartmentalization within each region. For instance, a company's Eastern sales region might be divided into the following districts: (1)

---

[2] "The Battle over $300-Billion in Bank Trusts," *Business Week*, Number 2186 (July 24, 1971), pp. 64–65.

Figure 9–4.   Several Possible Basic Departmentalization Alternatives for a Hypothetical Firm

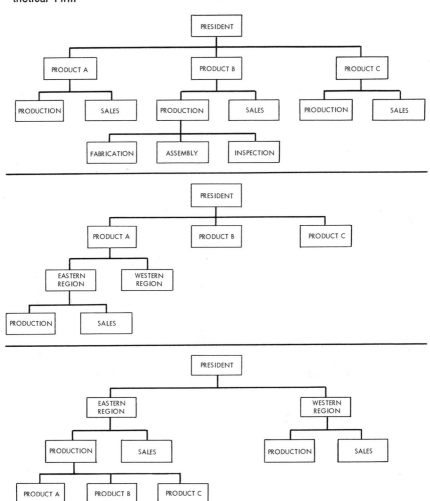

New England, (2) New York, (3) Pennsylvania, and (4) New Jersey, Maryland and Delaware. Because of the many special environmental conditions involved in doing business abroad, many companies have established separate divisions to encompass all of their international operations, and in many cases the activities of international operations departments are subdivided on a geographical basis. For example, in 1960 the Quaker Oats Company "owned twenty-one plants located in ten countries in Latin America, Canada, and Europe,"[3] and its interna-

---

[3] Thomas J. McNichols, *Policy Making and Executive Action,* (3d ed.; New York: McGraw-Hill Book Co., 1967), pp. 635–78.

Figure 9–4. *Continued*

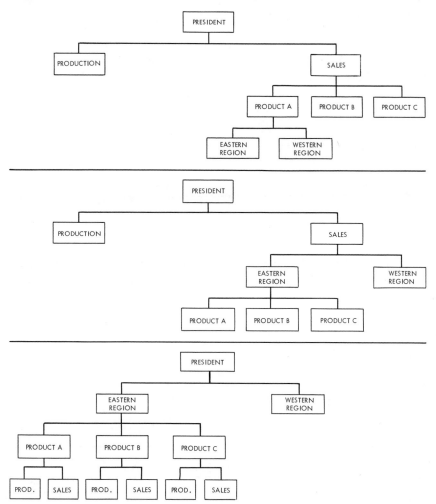

tional operations division was divided into three departments, one responsible for operations in each of these three geographical areas.

In some cases, the scope of responsibilities assigned to a geographic unit may be quite broad. Such is sometimes the case with department store chains which give each branch store considerable latitude to operate as a quasi-autonomous unit. In other instances, however, the scope of functions performed by territorial divisions or departments may be much narrower. Many regional sales divisions, for instance, are permitted only to contact customers and obtain orders, with advertising, pricing, marketing research, promotion and other activities encompassed by the marketing function assigned to a centralized marketing department.

Project-Matrix Departmentalization

In recent years, a special type of product departmentalization which deserves special attention has been developed in certain types of organizations. This structural form is referred to as *project* departmentalization in which departments are formed on a semipermanent basis to complete a program or project.

Figure 9–5. Alternative Project Departmentation

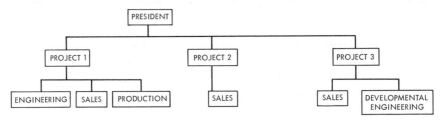

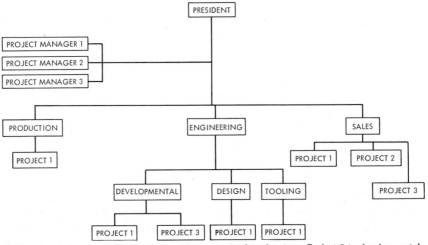

Note that in both cases Project 2 has evolved to only the sales stage, Project 3 to developmental engineering, while Project 1 is in production.

In "pure" project departments, the project manager has direct supervisory power over all personnel assigned to him from the various functional departments. Under such an arrangement, individual engineers, research personnel, and so on, typically report to project supervisors, who in turn report to the project manager.

In a somewhat different type of project organization—the matrix form—the basic departmentation is both functional and project with personnel assignments made from the functional group to the project as the needs of the latter dictate. A functional specialist could work on several projects in a week and be responsible to both the functional and project managers.

A third type of project organization is one in which the basic departmentation remains functional although project managers are also appointed with the power to "oversee" functional operations as they relate to his project (see Figure 9–5B). The power of the project manager in this kind of arrangement may be great or, conversely, quite limited if all he is authorized to do is to report the status of project cost, quality, and delivery. Under such circumstances he must work through and rely upon functional managers to achieve his project's goals. On the other hand, the functional manager by giving priority to the needs of one project manager may interfere with his own ability to satisfy obligations to meet the needs of other project managers. This type of project arrangement creates, thereby, the potential for conflict among project departments. If greater power over functional managers is given to project managers, moreover, some interproject coordination is essential to prevent project conflicts within functional operations.

In American firms, a major impetus to project departmentalization was the missile and space race touched off by the Soviet launching of Sputnik. After that time, crash programs aimed at ensuring the delivery of space systems were undertaken. Under such conditions of urgency, separate project departments were established so that special managerial attention could be given to high-priority programs. When a project is in progress, a project department is in many ways quite similar to a product-based department, especially if the departmental manager has control over the functions, activities, and resources necessary to achieve a specified output. The generation of output in a product department is expected to continue more or less indefinitely, but the work of a project department has a limited life-span. The work required for the completion of some projects may take only a few months or less. For others, however, several years of effort may be needed—e.g., work on a complex manned space vehicle system.

During the life cycle of many large projects, relative changes will occur in the types of work activities which need to be performed. In a five-year missile project, for example, the bulk of the engineering efforts required might be expended during the first two years, with the peak utilization of tooling facilities subsequently following. Then, at a later time, the number of production man hours required for the project would be at its maximum. Thus, a problem faced by many project managers is that of frequently having to build up certain functions while, at the same time, having to decelerate or disband others.

In general, project departments have been utilized, and tend to be justified to the greatest extent, when one or more of the following conditions exist:

1. The size of the project is *large* relative to the capacity of the organization, and the per unit dollar value is high.
2. Some aspect of the project (e.g., delivery or cost) is considered *critical* to the success of the organization, either in the short or long run.
3. When required by the customer. (To obtain a large space system contract, one contractor firm felt compelled to guarantee the contracting government agency that it would initiate a complete product organization to manage the design and production of the system.)

Even when the above conditions do exist, project departments have been criticized as resulting in overorganization and overmanning in a company. With this type of organizational arrangement, a firm not only has to employ functional managers but also a number of project managers and supervisors. Also, the question has been raised: "What is so different about the work of one-time contracts that the work required on them could not be assigned sequentially to each of a firm's functional departments, as would be work on a *special order*, say, of furniture for a new hotel? A furniture company can merely sequence work on such an order in its regular stream of work along with its other orders, even though it might require some special and unique operations. Many firms do produce specially ordered, unique items for which there is no recurring demand. Why couldn't contract work on a large defense project be handled in a similar manner?

On the other hand, project departmentalization—which is fairly common in some industries which do considerable contract work, such as in the aerospace industry—has been defended on the grounds that it does help assure the meeting of project goals. As the general manager of an aerospace division employing almost 10,000 people, doing contract work for several military organizations and foreign countries, and handling several hundred contracts at a time, has pointed out:

I have a project manager for every contract, no matter how small. Perhaps we don't need them for spare parts contracts since these are almost production runs, but project managers are vital for research and development contracts where numerous uncertainties exist with respect to performance, delivery, and cost. With project managers, I am assured that someone is seeing to it that we meet our commitments and that we make a profit on each contract if at all possible. If we just ran these projects through our functional departments without individual attention, many of them would get lost in the shuffle.

Some people refer to project managers as glorified expediters, but they are responsible for more than just getting the work out on time. They are responsible for working with the customer to ensure that our designs meet their needs. They are responsible for costs and profits. The expense of project management is justified in my mind since it relieves me from having to worry and getting involved in running down these problems. I couldn't keep on top of them all by myself. The manager of our largest contract has a staff of 11 people, but his contract comprises about 45 percent of our total business at present. In effect, he has about 4,500 people working for him. The expense incurred in operating his office is relatively small. In contrast, for some of our smaller contracts, one manager may supervise up to a dozen separate contracts.

Furthermore, functional departmentalization, as an alternative approach, also has its limitations. For example, under a functional type organization in the Department of Defense, each functional service in the Army often felt the need for a detailed review of proposals for new weapons systems, and a lengthy evaluation of the performance of contractors on such systems contracts. With many different groups responsible for different phases of development and procurement, it was believed that the lead time on Army weapons "was excessive, that in some cases costs were higher than necessary and that performance once in the field, was not always equal to the needs of combat."[4] As a result, separate project organizations were established for different major systems.

One further observation is in order concerning project departmentalization—particularly of the matrix type. If a firm has a large number of smaller contracts, each of a relatively short duration but still utilizes project managers, personnel tend to be shifted frequently from one project (and project manager) to another. In some such cases, individuals may be assigned to one project for one week or more, and then be shifted to another. In other cases, personnel from the functional departments may be called on to work part time on several projects during any given time period.

When an individual works for a project manager on a part-time or temporary basis, he will normally take orders from and report to the project manager. Yet, the basic responsibility for deciding upon any pay raises and promotions which he may obtain is in the hands of the manager of the functional department to which he is permanently assigned. In effect, then, he is working for two supervisors, which violates one of the so-called principles of management—unity of command—which prescribes that an individual should have only one "boss." While the functional manager and the project manager may work closely together in guiding and evaluating an individual's work performance, if

---

[4] Lt. General F. S. Besson, Jr., "Project Management within the Army Matériel Command," in Fremont E. Kast and James E. Rosenzweig (eds.), *Science, Technology and Management* (New York: McGraw-Hill Book Co., 1963), p. 92.

conflicts arise among the two managers, the subordinate would tend to follow the lead of his functional supervisor, upon whom his future in the organization depends to a greater extent. The existence of this problem again points up the fact that project departmentalization tends to be more suited to firms working on large projects of relatively long duration.

Some of the difficulties arising in project organizations result in human problems. In comparing functional to project employees, Reeser found that project personnel were less loyal to the organization and perceived greater ambiguity as to who their boss was, a higher frustration from the lack of formal procedures and role definitions, conflict among personnel as being more serious, and a greater lack of concern for their personal development. Further, as the project drew to a close, they expressed greater anxieties about loss of position, higher frustration with "make work," and greater concern that setbacks would occur in their careers.[5] While some of these problems would appear to occur in other kinds of departmentalization at times, this apparently greater frequency in project organizations suggests planning for this occurrence when project groupings are formed and administered.

STAFF DEPARTMENTATION

In describing alternative bases for departmentation in the last section, the emergence of the fundamental departments and their subdivisions were shown. In order to manage a large enterprise organized by any of the bases shown, the president, if he were to manage it alone, would need to have a wide variety of knowledge and skills: a top-flight legal talent, a scientific knowledge of the product and process technologies, a financial knowledge and skill, and many others as well as his basic administrative knowledge. Obviously, no individual has the time or the aptitude to learn all the knowledge or to acquire all the skills necessary to properly evaluate the problems arising in a complex organization as was pointed out in the discussion on span of control in Chapter 8. To provide these competencies, special tasks, assignments or departments are established as advisors to the chief executive. By appointing individuals to provide legal, scientific, financial, and other expertise, the chief executive can draw upon all the knowledges and skills that he does not personally possess. These individuals are distinguished from

---

[5] Clayton Reeser, "Some Potential Problems of the Project Form of Organization," *Academy of Management Journal*, Vol. 12, No. 4 (December 1969), pp. 459–67. In a preliminary study of management in project organizations (Apollo), David L. Wilemon and John P. Cicero also hypothesize a number of tendencies in project organizations, but reasoning shows that their propositions could apply as well to certain product departmentalized and other types of organizations. See their "The Project Manager-Anomalies and Ambiguities," *Academy of Management Journal*, 13 (September 1970), pp. 269–82.

other departmental personnel by designating them as "staff" personnel. While the managers in charge of the basic four types of departments discussed above typically report to the chief executive in a manner similar to the staff personnel, these former are typically designated as line executives to distinguish them from staff.

The need for staff expertise can arise at any level of managerial hierarchy in the organization, not just the top level. The second level marketing executive, for example, may be able to justify forecasting experts, marketing researchers, new product analysts, and other specialties in order to carry out effectively his selling responsibilities.

Such experts deal with some limited part of the total managerial job, and provide specialized knowledge or services to the rest of the organization. Among the more common staff departments found in business organizations today are personnel, accounting, marketing research, engineering, legal, public relations, and production control. To differentiate staff from those managers who supervise workers *directly engaged* in the firm's primary activities of producing or selling its goods or

Figure 9–6. Hypothetical Organization Chart Illustrating Line and Staff Managers (and Departments)

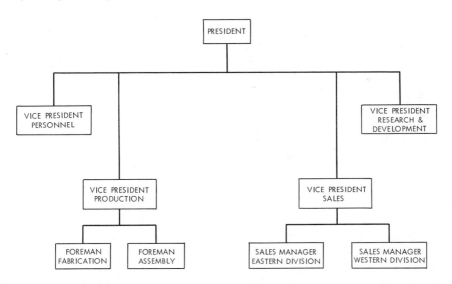

services (i.e., the line managers), distinctions or organization charts are made such as that illustrated in Figure 9–6:

1. The firm's president is its top line manager with the production and sales vice-presidents, the foremen in charge of fabrication and assembly, and the sales managers for each division all being line officials;

2. The vice-presidents for personnel and research and development are designated as staff managers.

Two other observations concerning the concepts of line and staff are in order at this point. First, not all managers designated as "staff" are experts in some particular specialized area as described above—there are certain exceptions. For example, in some firms staff assistants who are "generalists" are employed to relieve top managers of many of the burdensome details of their work. These staff assistants are frequently designated "assistant to"—e.g., "Assistant to the President."

Second, it should be emphasized that the distinction between "staff" and "line" is in many ways a blurred one; and considerable differences of opinion exist as to what precisely are the differences between the two.[6] Furthermore, some departments (and functions) are designated as "staff" in some firms, but as "line" in others. This is perhaps especially true for the engineering function in business organizations.

Types of Staff Work

To clarify the functions which staff personnel perform in organizations, we will now examine three types of specialized assistance which staff departments may provide to the business organization.

One of the most common functions performed by staff managers is that of studying and analyzing problems and developing problem solutions. The personnel department, for example, may design psychological tests for use in selecting job applicants, and through the utilization of such tests and other selection techniques, make recommendations as to whether specific job applicants should be hired. Or, the firm's operations research department may develop a mathematical model for inventory control; its marketing research department may analyze the market potential for a proposed new product, and so forth.

In addition to analyzing managerial problems, staff specialists may undertake the function of preparing and processing data which line managers need for making decisions. Top- and middle-level line managers, who usually do not have close daily contact with work being performed at lower levels in the organization, must rely heavily upon indirect methods, rather than direct observation, to determine what is going on at these levels. Information about operating performance may be provided by various staff departments such as cost data by accounting, and labor turnover and accident rate data by personnel. Since many managers in a firm may require similar types of information about oper-

---

[6] Compare, for example, the discussion of line and staff in John M. Pfiffner and Frank P. Sherwood, *Administrative Organization* (Englewood Cliffs, N.J.: Prentice-Hall, Inc., 1960), chap. 10, with that in Harold Koontz and Cyril O'Donnell, *Principles of Management,* (4th ed.; New York: McGraw-Hill Book Co., 1968), chap. 15.

ating performance, integrated systems for data collection and processing are often economical. For example, accounting departments frequently collect all types of cost and financial data from all parts of the organization for use by all managers in the firm. Since they often are experts in data *analysis* as well, such departments are frequently charged with preparing financial analyses, cost estimates on new projects, and so forth. Thus, many staff groups, such as accounting, perform the function of problem analysis as well as that of data collection and processing.

Service Departments

While legal staffs, accounting departments, and other groups are formed to meet the special needs for managerial expertise as staff, still other departmental groups arise from a differentiation of the tasks performed within the normal scope of the basic departments. Such groupings are often called service departments in that their activities provide a service (but not necessarily advice as do the normal staff groups)[7] to the basic departments. A maintenance department may be initiated, for example, to undertake and be responsible for maintaining equipment, the rationale for its formation being that experts are required for this function over and above that normally required of a semiskilled machine tender. If machine operators were required to possess skills necessary to maintain their machines, they would command wages commensurate with the higher level maintenance skill workers even during the majority of the time that they would merely be operating the machine.

Similar reasoning goes into the creation of specialized engineering groups with some individuals and departments assigned to basic research and product development, others to product design, and still others to process or production engineering for development equipment methods to manufacture products, and so on. Each engineering department provides a differentiated service to the organization as a whole. Yet these specialized groups are not staff in the usual sense of the word in that they are not formed to provide advisory expertise as staff groups do, although they *may* often do so. Nor do service groups work directly on the product as supposedly do line departments. Thus, service groups do not meet either of the definitions strictly applied to staff or line departments.

The distinction between service and line departments is blurred just as is the distinction between staff and line. Consider, for example, a company manufacturing custom products sold to machine tool manufacturers. Each order, because it is custom tailored to the customer's

---

[7] It should be noted that service groups sometimes do provide advice to both line and staff departments—e.g., a maintenance manager advising management that a particular machine is "too worn out for further repairs."

needs requires some product engineering so that blueprints and specifications can be provided. These engineering activities are required in the same sense that lathe operations are required to produce parts for the product. What is different about the required nature of the engineering activity from the production activity so that the latter is designated line and the former "service"? The requirement that a line department works directly on the product as do sales and production departments seems equally applicable to engineering in this case. The same could be said of purchasing, transportation or materials departments.

Neither can one say that a staff department is identifiable as one that provides advice to superiors since all departments are expected to contribute to advising their superiors. Thus, we see that attempting to classify departments into line, staff, or service departments may be quite futile at times. What the manager and organization designer need to determine, however, are the kinds of differentiation of managerial work and basic departments needed along with the particular powers, relationships, and reporting requirements expected from the specialized department. This confusion in classification should not stop management from creating needed differentiation; it should, instead, suggest the need for delineating the scope and powers of the service departments.

Staff and Service Powers

When staff and service positions and departments are created separate from the line organization, the question is posed: "What powers shall their personnel be given: to *study* problems only, to *provide the results* of those studies undertaken to line managers for their use, to *recommend* actions that line managers should undertake or, to *tell* or *dictate to* line management those courses of action which should be taken based upon staff study and analyses?" The range of powers given to staff and service groups may fall anywhere on this continuum—from simply studying problems to actually "calling the shots" as to what line management should do—and may be illustrated by the following story about the president of a small brewery:

The president of the brewery found himself so burdened with work that he hired an economist to help him keep his knowledge of the raw materials market up to date. Since the cost of grains constituted such a large percentage of the firm's total expenses, the president had personally purchased all these raw materials.

The president first explained to the economist the data he needed, their sources, and the kinds of analyses he had been utilizing. He trained the economist in the *collection* and *preparation* of these data.

After a few months had gone by, the president requested *recommendations* from the economist as to which grains should be purchased. In many cases, the recommendations were discussed at length by the two. The president, however, continued to make all final decisions on grain purchases. Before long, the president gained considerable confidence in the economist's work. He became dependent on the economist to prepare the *purchase orders,* and to submit these to him along with the economist's recommendations.

One day when he was exceptionally busy, the president signed the purchase orders without bothering to read the recommendations. Soon thereafter, he regularly omitted reading the orders and eventually prepared a rubber stamp with his signature for use by the economist. Some time later, the rubber stamp was lost, and from that time on, the economist signed all purchase orders himself.

The gradual expansion of staff power as illustrated in this example is not uncommon. In many cases, staff personnel may initially simply provide information sought by the line, then be called on to make recommendations, and ultimately, as line management gains more and more confidence in their abilities, be given the power to make decisions formerly made by line.

We should also note that staff personnel and service personnel probably to a lesser extent actually possess what might be termed "*implicit decision powers*" even when they are only called on to study problems and make recommendations. If staff or service has the power to recommend, it has, at the same time, the power *not to recommend.* The number of possible alternatives which staff or service personnel *might* consider in many cases may be very large. When a staff manager recommends only one or two such alternatives, he may, in effect, be conditioning to a considerable extent the ultimate decision which will be made. This is because line managers—lacking time to research problems further and having confidence in their staff advisors—often have a tendency to consider only those alternatives explicitly recommended by the staff.

The powers which staff and service groups possess may also be examined in terms of their *control over information.* As was emphasized in Chapter 4, decisions made by managers are strongly influenced by the informational inputs at their disposal. For this reason, staff managers, who generate the basic data on which line decisions will be largely based, may influence these decisions considerably by the way in which the information is developed and presented to line management. The methodology which a staff manager employs in developing information may be biased by his educational and/or professional background. Further, his own personal prejudices may lead to his "slanting" the information in one direction or another. For example, if a personnel researcher has a strong anti-union bias, this bias may well influence the data he prepares with respect to the firm's contract negotiations. Although such biases may not be conscious or intentional, they nonetheless, may have a considerable impact on decisions made by line management.

The distribution of powers to service organizations similarly represents a problem to which organization designers should give attention to.

Should the maintenance manager have the power to suspend operations in a production department in order to make a needed overhaul on a drill press or should this production stoppage be allowed only with the foreknowledge and approval of the foreman? Similarly, questions as to the freedom that a production foreman has to deviate from engineering tolerances are the kinds of questions that can be resolved by formal consideration in organization design. If formal power is not assigned, variation in practices can occur until a mutually satisfactory informal working arrangement evolves. Clearly assigning powers to staff, service, and line groups involves considering an immense complex of possible interrelations. Obviously all possibilities cannot and should not be anticipated and formally covered in an organization chart for the respective departments. However, some formal structuring of relationships is certainly useful in helping to overcome the frictions possible among departmental groups.

Line-Staff Frictions

A problem which appears common to most large organizations is that of numerous conflicts and frictions existing between line, staff, and service departments. There are many different reasons why such conflicts may arise. Some of the more important of these are examined in this section.

In many firms, staff departments have expanded their scope of activities considerably over the past several decades. In many cases, this expansion has led to an erosion of the power of certain line managers. As was pointed out in Chapter 6, many of the decision areas for which first-line foremen were once responsible in some companies have been assigned to various staff (and service) departments such as personnel, quality control, and industrial engineering. Although first-line foremen have undoubtedly welcomed the opportunity to have staff departments relieve them of certain responsibilities, in other instances they have grown resentful of staff personnel "usurping" more and more of their powers.

A second reason for the emergence of problems in line-staff relationships is that in some cases both line and staff may have certain responsibilities for dealing with a particular problem, but there may exist no clear definition as to what powers each possesses with respect to resolving the problem. To illustrate, in one manufacturing plant, the manager of training, who reported to the personnel manager (as is illustrated in Figure 9–7), was given the responsibility of developing a training program for a number of new production workers who had recently been assigned to the plant's fabrication department. The general foreman, who *also* had the responsibility of making sure that his new employees were trained adequately, resisted many of the training manager's

Figure 9–7. Partial Organizational Chart for Plant Situation Illustrating Line-Staff Conflict

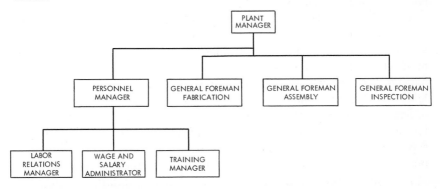

ideas for the program as being "new-fangled" and "too theoretical"; and he took the position that his people should be trained by certain methods which had been followed in the past, but which the training manager considered unsound in terms of learning theory. In this case, the training manager had no power to command the general foreman to follow his program, even though if his program was rejected and the training of the new employees, as a consequence, was to be ineffective, he would be held (at least partially) responsible for the failure. On the other hand, the general foreman realized that if he rejected the training manager's program, and the training then failed, he might be severely criticized by the plant manager for not bowing to the wishes of the staff specialist. Further complicating the relationship between the training manager and general foreman were numerous *status incongruences.* The training manager held a graduate degree while the general foreman had never finished high school; he was considered an expert in training methodology while the foreman was not. Yet, the general foreman held a higher level position in the firm's organizational hierarchy, earned several thousand dollars more per year than the training manager, and had been with the company about 20 years longer. Such incongruences, we should point out, are not uncommon in line-staff relationships. In general, staff groups tend to be better educated, more articulate and younger than many of their line counterparts, whereas many of the line managers with whom they must deal enjoy higher level and better salaried positions in the organizational hierarchy.

One additional observation is in order concerning the above illustration. Ultimately, the disagreements between the training manager and general foreman were brought to the attention of the plant manager. Among the decision alternatives available to him for resolving this problem were: (1) to support the staff specialist's position, (2) to support the general foreman, or (3) attempt to get the two to work out some sort of compromise solution themselves. In this case, the plant manager chose the latter alternative.

The bringing of this dispute to the plant manager's attention illustrates another common problem emanating from the existence of line and staff and service departments—the problem faced by top-line managers as to what to do when line-staff or line-service frictions do exist. If top management consistently supports the staff in such situations, the lower level line manager may come to perceive that he might as well take orders directly from the staff, since he will ultimately be directed by his superior to bow to the wishes of staff. On the other hand, consistent support of lower line by top management may lead staff to feel frustrated because of an inability to gain acceptance for their programs.

Two further sources of conflict between line and staff deserve mention. First, in some cases, staff managers are called on to develop and to present to top-line management data for control purposes on the operations of lower line managers, which makes the latter appear in an unfavorable light. For example, a personnel manager's monthly safety report may indicate that the accident rate among workers under the supervision of the plant's fabrication foreman is exceptionally high. Or, cost data developed by the accounting staff for the plant manager may indicate that costs are way out of line in the foreman's department. Since this type of work performed by staff may pinpoint weaknesses in the line departments, the line managers may come to perceive the staff as posing a threat to them. This threatening aspect of staff work may be minimized if the staff reports any performance inadequacies detected in the line manager's department directly to the line manager himself, rather than to his superior. For instance, the head accountant might inform the fabrication foreman that his costs are out of line, discuss with him ways for dealing with the problem, and the problem might readily be overcome by the foreman himself.

Second, conflicts may sometimes arise in organizations when several line departments are competing for services performed by staff (and especially service) groups. For instance, if all maintenance crews in a plant are already overloaded with work, and each of two production supervisors has a machine which "has just broken down and must be repaired at once if production schedules are to be met," the maintenance manager would be faced with the problem as to which of the two line supervisor's requests should be given priority. Such problems—which, of course, tend to occur more frequently when staff services are being fully utilized—may in some cases be resolved not so much on the basis of which priority choice is optimal for the firm as a whole as upon friendships among the staff and certain line supervisors and/or staff's perception of the status and power of the different line supervisors making the requests for services.

It should be noted that frictions do not necessarily arise because one department is staff or service while its counterpart is line. Frictions arise from differences in subgoals of the two units as well as differences in perceptions, time orientation, and so forth as discussed in Chapter 8. Those differences may be greater in comparing line to staff than between two line departments, but line-line frictions exist also and for the same reasons of subgoal and perception differences. For example, to minimize rejects, a foundry foreman (line manager) may design his molds oversize in some dimensions so that the flow of molten metal to form the castings is facilitated. Castings are machined to precise dimensions by other line departments and oversize castings result in more machining costs there to remove the excess metal. Attention to subgoals by the foundry creates the potential for friction with the machining foremen.

One final observation is in order concerning frictions. The reader should *not* infer that all conflict between managers is *inherently bad*. In some cases, managers may have differing perceptions as to how a certain problem should be handled, each of which has some merit. In the situation involving the training manager and general foreman discussed previously, for instance, the training manager's program as originally conceived was probably too theory-oriented, while the general foreman's thinking did not give sufficient emphasis to some valid theoretical concepts. In this situation, a compromise solution was ultimately worked out which incorporated the thinking of both the line and staff manager. In many respects, the compromise program was probably more effective than the training would have been had just the ideas of either of the two managers been followed. Because different managers will have different backgrounds, perceptions, and objectives, some degree of conflict will always exist in organizations, not only among line and staff, but among different line managers, and different staff managers as well. What is important to the firm is that the disruptive effects of conflict be minimized, and that a constructive resolution of conflicting viewpoints be effected.

Location of Staff and Service Activities

Another decision problem often faced by management is that of determining where staff departments are to be located in the organization. If the services of a staff or service department are utilized extensively throughout an organization, there may be a need to locate it relatively high up in the hierarchical structure. Many firms, for example, have centralized staff departments handling legal, public relations, and personnel problems relative to all divisions in the company and headed by a vice-president, who reports directly to the president. If all staff groups of this type should report to the president, however, his span of control may become so large that he cannot give adequate attention to them.

Some large organizations, with many staff groups, have attempted to overcome this problem by combining numerous staff functions into a smaller number of departments, each with a fairly broad scope of responsibility. General Electric, for example, has utilized a Vice-President of Relations, given responsibilities encompassing personnel and industrial, as well as public relations.

If a staff or service group is designed to provide services to a single function in contrast to many throughout the firm, on the other hand, it is only logical to subordinate the staff to that function. For example, draftsmen, who assist engineers, would normally be grouped within a firm's engineering department. Or, even though they may provide some services to many departments in an organization, purchasing and quality control groups may report to a firm's top manufacturing manager because the major portion of their assistance is provided to manufacturing.

One further observation needs to be made concerning the location of staff departments. In many large organizations with multiple product or territorial divisions, staff departments dealing with the same functional area will be created both: (1) centrally, and reporting to the president, and (2) within each product or geographical division, and reporting to the divisional manager. This phenomenon is often referred to as *staff parallelism.* In a large geographically dispersed supermarket chain, for example, parallel staff departments as illustrated in Figure 9–8 might well be found. In such a case, the centralized staff departments would normally be responsible for such activities as research, developing overall company policies, and providing technical assistance to the geographical

Figure 9–8. Staff Parallelism

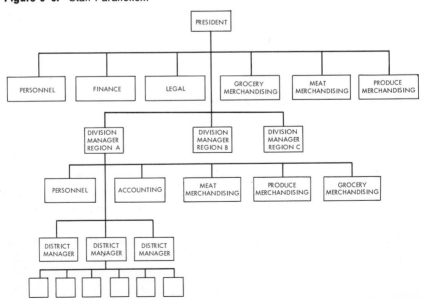

divisions; while the divisional staff groups would focus attention on implementing company policies and on the day-to-day operational problems of their divisions. For example, consider the area of personnel selection:

1. The centralized personnel staff might develop and validate psychological tests for use in all divisions, determine what scores on the tests should be attained by job applicants if they are to be considered for employment by the firm; develop brochures for use by the divisional personnel managers outlining the company's selection procedures, and possibly train the divisional staff in such facets of selection as interpretation of the psychological tests; while

2. Each divisional personnel department might be responsible for: placing ads announcing job openings in the supermarkets in local newspapers; interviewing, giving the psychological tests to job applicants, and interpreting the test results; arranging for physical examinations and credit checks on applicants; making recommendations to its divisional line management as to whether particular job applicants should be hired, and so forth.

When parallel staff or service departments exist, not only must the organization be concerned with line-staff relationships (and frictions), but staff-staff (or service-service) relations must also be given consideration. To illustrate, a divisional personnel manager in the above example reports to his divisional manager, yet at the same time he may be expected to follow the policies and procedures developed by the central personnel staff. Although the central staff has no direct command power over him, he may feel strong pressures to abide by their wishes. One reason for this is that he may be aiming for a future promotion to the central staff (or to a personnel position entailing greater responsibilities in another of the firm's divisions) rather than to a higher level position outside his speciality in his own division; and, thus, want to be looked upon favorably by the central staff group, who probably would have considerable influence on any such promotional decisions. Thus, divisional staff personnel may often have divided loyalties—loyalties to both their own division and to the central staff group in their function. This condition may lead to no special problems in many instances, for the divisional manager may be in full accord with the policies, procedures, and so on, which the central staff wants his own staff to follow. However, when the central staff's influence efforts are incongruent with the philosophy and wishes of the divisional manager, his staff may find themselves in a conflict situation.[8]

---

[8] There are, of course, many different strategies that the staff might employ in dealing with such problems, depending on their objectives and perception of the situation—e.g., following central staff's policies completely and ignoring their own boss's reactions; attempting to influence their superior that the central staff position should be adhered to; following their superior's position while trying to placate the central staff, and so forth.

VARIABLES INFLUENCING DEPARTMENTALIZATION DECISIONS

In the last chapter the differentiation and integration processes showed the need for departments and how some of the resulting groupings would be formed. Now that the different organization forms have been explained in terms of line, staff, and service departments, additional considerations need to be examined to give insights as to why these structures emerge. As was pointed out previously, departmentalization involves determining which activities should be grouped together at *each level* in the firm, and in large multilevel firms, the range of possible departmentalization alternatives which could be chosen may be quite large. Figure 9–4, shown previously, depicts only a few of the many different forms of basic departmentalization which might be conceived of for a company manufacturing three products for sale throughout the United States. Further, the variables which will influence the effectiveness of any particular work grouping choice are often both considerable in number and interdependent. In the following sections we will consider several of these variables which we consider to be of importance.

The Physical Location of Operations

When the technology or the environment forces a company to maintain some of its operations on a geographically dispersed basis, these locations tend to suggest certain kinds of basic departmentation. For example, a large paper company is unable to concentrate all its paper production in one location because of limitations to the availability of sufficient pulpwood. Consequently, it has a number of separate papermaking plants throughout the country. Rather than to allow each plant to produce all products, however, each plant is assigned different product lines so that specialized equipment, pulp trees, and skills can be used. Thus the necessary dispersion of production has allowed differentiation and specialization of departments by products produced.

Firms with widely dispersed operations frequently utilize some form of geographic departmentalization. Some of the reasons why physical dispersion of operations may render geographic departmentalization an effective choice may be noted by considering the operations of a supermarket chain with stores in many locations. In most firms of this type, each separate store will have its own manager, with a head meat cutter, and head clerks for produce, grocery, and sometimes dairy departments reporting to him. Rather than such geographical departmentalization at the overall store level, however, product departmentalization would theoretically be possible. For example, in a 12-store chain encompassing a geographical area with a 200-mile radius: *one* meat manager might supervise the head meat cutters in *all* 12 stores, one produce manager might supervise all 12 head produce clerks, and so on, with no one serving as manager of the overall operations of any one store. Among the reasons why most grocery chains do prefer to have one manager responsible for all operational areas of each store, rather than the alternative form of product departmentalization are as follows:

1. Some one person with full responsibility for the operations is physically proximate and available for handling emergencies or other problems affecting the store as a whole such as fire, theft, power failure, and customer injuries in the store.
2. Better coordination of efforts among the product departments may be obtained. For example, the store manager could instruct his head grocery clerk to temporarily assign one of his people to help handle a work overload in the produce department; whereas, if the head produce and grocery clerks reported to different product managers, neither of whom was physically proximate, such reassignments would often be much more difficult to effect.

Additionally, giving one person the responsibility for coordinating all efforts in one geographical location may help develop his coordinative skills, which may better qualify him for higher level managerial work. We will discuss this variable with respect to departmentalization more fully in the next section.

Decentralization, Coordination and Managerial Skills

A second important variable affecting departmentalization is the degree to which various alternative structural forms will permit the *decentralization* of decision making in the organization—i.e., the delegation of decision-making responsibilities by upper level managers to their counterparts at lower levels in the organization. The decentralization of decision making may be desirable not only because it may help relieve the work burden of upper level managers, but also because it may provide lower level managers with more challenging work, and hence, greater opportunities for meeting their higher level needs. Further, such assignments develop managerial skills.

Decentralization tends to be feasible when the delegated decision responsibilities do not have an impact on departmental subsystems in the organization other than those under the jurisdiction of the manager making the decisions. Decisions made in the firm will differ widely in the extent to which they have an interdepartmental impact. To illustrate, one manager, upon assuming a position in a firm, found that he was expected to approve all salaries in his division above $5,000 per year. He decentralized this decision-making responsibility by setting up constraints in terms of a salary budget and salary policies, and allowing his subordinate managers to make salary decisions within these defined limits. The establishment of the constraints minimized any possible negative interdepartmental impact of the decisions delegated—e.g., inconsistencies in salaries from one department to another resulting from different policies followed by each of his subordinate managers.

Decentralization of salary decisions, as discussed above, could be effected with any form of departmentalization—product, functional, process, or geographical. Some types of managerial decisions, however, can be delegated to a much greater extent with certain types of departmentalization than with others. For example, suppose that a manufacturing plant produces three products, each requiring three processing operations, fabrication, assembly, and inspection, in that order; and that the technology is such (e.g., ways in which the machinery and equipment could be located) that either a product or process type of departmentalization were possible—as is illustrated in Figure 9–9. In these operations, the decentralization of certain types of decisions would be possible under the product departmentalization alternative, whereas it would not be

Figure 9–9.   Example of Product v. Process Departmentalization

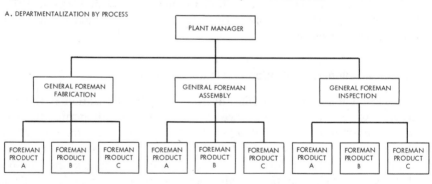

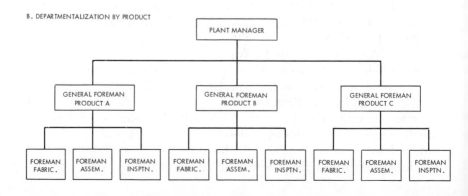

with the process structure. For example, important to such operations is the coordinated scheduling of each operation so that there is a smooth flow of work from one process to the next. If, for instance, only enough workers were scheduled to permit the fabrication of 500 units a day, while the assemblers assigned to work could turn out 2,000 units per day, the latter would not have a sufficient number of pieces to keep them busy (unless large inventories of fabricated, but yet unassembled units were available). With the product form of departmentalization illustrated in Figure 9–9, worker scheduling decisions could be delegated to the *general foreman* since each would have responsibility for all of the three *interdependent* phases of work flow required in turning out his product. With the process structure, however, these interdependent scheduling decisions would have to be made *centrally* by the *plant manager* (or one of his assistants), since coordination of work schedules among all three major process departments is necessary.

Several other observations are in order concerning the impact of departmentalization on decentralization, coordination, and managerial decision making. First, departmentalization by either process or function tends to result in serial and reciprocal *interdependent stages* of work flow being assigned to *different supervisors* (as illustrated in the above example) to a greater extent than does either product or geographical departmentalization. For this reason, the decentralization of many decision-making responsibilities tends to be more difficult with either a process or functional grouping of activities than with either a product or geographical one where only pooled interdependence may exist. This does not mean, of course, that all, or even most, decision responsibilities can easily be decentralized to lower level managers in a product or geographical-based organization structure. For example, if a supermarket chain with 20 stores in a large city were to permit each store manager to determine what meat specials (and prices) would be offered in his store each week:

1. The firm often would not be able to obtain as good prices on its meat purchases as it would if larger quantities of the same meat item were bought for sale in all stores; and,
2. Its problems of local newspaper and television advertising would be complicated, since no single ad could apply to all stores.

In consequence, most chains operating under such conditions generally do not delegate the responsibility for determining and pricing weekly specials to their store managers.

Second, observations are sometimes made that a firm employing product or geographical departmentalization is, *because of* its departmentalization choice, *necessarily* a "decentralized" organization. While we have shown that it is generally easier to decentralize certain decision-making responsibilities in product- or territorial-based departments, it may also be quite easy to *centralize* decision making in such departments. Consider, for example, a "Five-and-Ten" retail chain with several hundred stores. Since the operations of each store are basically similar, many of the decisions made for one store would be applicable to others in the chain. To the extent that such is the case, firms of this type often have found it more economical to have experts in store layout, merchandising, counter display, employee training, and so forth make these decisions for all of their stores. It is inappropriate, therefore, to refer to a firm as "centralized" or "decentralized" in its decision making simply on the basis of the type(s) of departmentalization it employs. Whether a company decentralizes many of its decision responsibilities depends more upon other factors. Again, however, the decentralization of many decisions can be more readily effected in product- or territorial-based departments than in functional or process based ones.

A third aspect of departmentalization of importance to managerial decision making is that the coordination of activities tends to be a more complex problem for managers of product- and geographical-based departments than for those managing process or functional departments. This is especially true when several *interdependent* work processes are placed under the jurisdiction of a product or territorial manager. In the previous example of the plant manufacturing three products, each calling for fabrication, assembly, and inspection, relatively little coordinative work scheduling could be carried on by the general foremen under the process form of departmentalization discussed; whereas, under the product structure, each general foreman could be permitted to schedule his fabrication, assembly, and inspection operations so as to provide for a smooth flow of work through these interdependent processes.

The additional coordination which may be required with a product or territorial grouping leads to two important implications for management. First, and somewhat related to the previous discussion of decentralization, is that one of the basic reasons why many large, multiproduct firms establish separate product divisions is to allow the delegation of many coordinative responsibilities from the presidential level to lower levels in the organization. For example, consider a large electrical firm manufacturing household appliances, light bulbs, and power generation equipment. In such a firm, coordinating the various functions and stages involved in producing and selling any particular product would involve many more complex problems than would interproduct coordination. For instance, for each product: production schedules have to be coordinated with sales forecasts (or orders sold); pricing policies may have to be made in light of production costs; customer complaints as to defective products received by the firm's salesmen may have to be worked out with quality control; and so forth. If such a firm's primary departmentalization were functional, the burden of resolving all coordinative problems among production and sales for all products would be placed upon the shoulders of its president, whereas with primary product divisions, such problems could be handled at one level lower in the organization, by the product vice-presidents. These effects of departmentalization are illustrated in Figure 9–10.

Figure 9–10.   Coordinative Problems—Functional v. Product Departmentalization

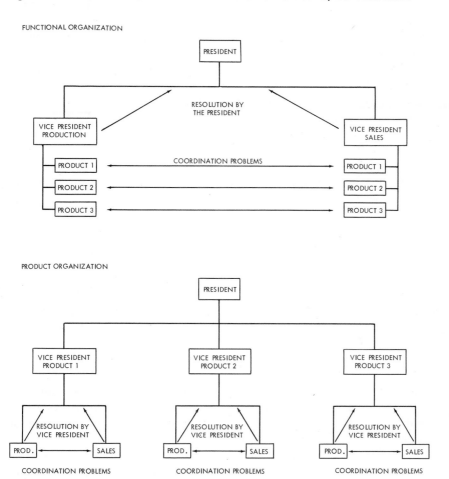

A second important implication is that the more frequently product and geographical managers are faced with coordinative problems, the more *experience* they will gain in dealing with these problems. At the top levels in a firm, the manager must perceive and deal with the operations of his organization as an integrated whole, and in doing so, manage the interrelationships among numerous organizational subsystems. Managerial experience at lower levels in the organization constitutes probably the most important experience that aspirants to top-level executive positions can have. As a training experience for top-level positions, the management of process and functionally based departments has limitations, since the problems which managers deal with in such departments tend to be relatively narrow in scope, focusing upon a work stage or a processing technology rather than upon the coordination of many interdependent activities. A manager's advancement within a functional department such as engineering may depend to a considerable extent upon his becoming a more and more skilled and knowledgeable specialist in engineering. If encouragement is given to learning more about such specialized areas as this, expertise in the function may be developed at the expense of perceiving and dealing with interrelationships among different functions—i.e., those executive qualities considered of prime importance at upper levels in the organization. The manager may gain experience in perceiving and dealing with interrelated work stages before he reaches top executive levels if he is given an opportunity to manage departments organized in such a way as to require interfunctional or interprocess coordination—i.e., departments established on a territorial or product basis comprising multiple interdependent functional and process responsibilities.

Duplication of Work

In most large organizations many of the same types of work are carried on at more than one location. For example, checking out customers at the cash register will take place in every one of a firm's 150 physically dispersed supermarkets; interviewing prospective applicants for employment may be done at each of a company's eight manufacturing plants, and so forth. In many cases, such simultaneous performance of identical (or very similar) activities at numerous locations in a firm is necessitated, not because of the way its organization is structured, but because a need exists to provide services on a dispersed basis. For example, customers would have to be checked out in each of the 150 supermarkets, mentioned above, regardless of whether the chain was organized on a product or geographical basis.

In some cases, however, business firms will be afforded a choice as to whether certain types of similar activities should: (1) be all grouped together in one process or functional department, or (2) be dispersed, with some of them being performed in each of a number of product- or territorial-based departments. One problem which sometimes may occur when the performance of similar tasks is so dispersed is that an uneconomical *duplication of effort* takes place. For example, in one firm in which several product divisions existed, each of two of its divisions was simultaneously developing a complex computer program for handling payrolls. Neither division was aware of the fact that the other was engaged in what was essentially the same project. If the firm had been organized such that the development of all such computer programs were carried on in one functionally based department, the duplication of effort probably would not have occurred. We should point out that problems such as this may be minimized when those managers responsible for the performance of similar functions in different product or geographical divisions are in communication with each other regarding the projects which they are working on and/or contemplating for the future. Nonetheless, the problem of unnecessary duplication of work tends to be a greater one with both product and territorial departmentalization than with either functional or process forms.

The Balancing of Work Loads

Another reason for establishing process- and functional-based departments which we have not yet discussed is to permit a balancing of work loads. To illustrate, in one manufacturing plant three different product lines are produced; the basic departmentalization is a product one, with a general foreman responsible for each product reporting to the plant manager. However, all time study work in the plant is assigned to one centralized industrial engineering department, rather than having three or four industrial engineers reporting to each general foreman. One reason for the functional grouping of all industrial engineering activities is to provide greater balance in the work loads of the engineers.[9] Frequently, during certain time periods considerable time study work is required in one of the product departments, with relatively little work called for in the others. With the functional departmentalization, any or all of the engineers can be assigned to any of the product departments as the need may arise, whereas if a few engineers were assigned to work only in one department, they would on occasion be overloaded with work, while those engineers assigned to the other product departments might have little to do. It is for a similar reason that in many office operations—in which clerical work relative to several different functions (or products) is carried on—typist pools are established. In such cases, typists are grouped together under one supervisor (process departmentalization), and handle work sent to the typing pool from executives, who may be responsible for such diverse areas as marketing, engineering, personnel, and finance.

---

[9] Such a functional grouping of all industrial engineers under the same department head may also help ensure that the engineers are consistent in establishing work standards—i.e., that some engineers do not set rates which are much "tighter" or "looser" than others. For a discussion of the problem of consistency in developing time standards, see George Strauss and Leonard R. Sayles, *Personnel: The Human Problems of Management* (2d ed.; Englewood Cliffs, N.J.: Prentice-Hall, Inc., 1967), pp. 646 ff.

Conflict of Interest

A final variable considered here for determining department differentiation arises if two tasks assigned to one manager involve a basic conflict of interest. Internal auditors are responsible for seeing to it that proper accounting controls are exercised to preserve and report on company assets. Many firms separate the internal audit function from the accounting department responsible for designing and operating the accounting system. This separation allows higher level management an independent check upon the workings of the accounting department. Even though auditors and accountants have similar training, perceptions, and interests, an internal auditor reporting to the chief accountant may not have the same opportunity to remain independent in his reports than if he reported to the general manager. Separation of other potential conflicts of interest (e.g., quality control from production) are made for the same reason.

SUMMARY

In the last chapter an organization was viewed as acting as an open system adapting to factors impinging upon it from the environment and to changes in those factors. In this chapter, the results of this adaptation was shown to result in typical line, staff, and service departments. While environmental factors cannot be ignored in organization design, management usually has some alternative organizational approaches for meeting both external and internal demands. Further, some of the variables affecting choice of structure tend to be offsetting ones. While reciprocal interdependence might suggest that two activities be grouped together, for example, conflict of interest between the two tasks may suggest they be separate. Thus, organization structure is seen to be a compromise that takes into simultaneous consideration a large complex of variables. Such a system is too complex to model optimally. Since, too, the value of important variables influencing organization structure are different from organization to organization, one could expect that no two organizations will be the same. Adaptation to individual skills, geographical location, and market conditions will almost certainly result in different structures if these factors are rationally considered.

The above discussion of organization has not considered organizations specifically in a dynamic setting. The analysis has been primarily a static one although the notions of environmental change and adaptation have been introduced. The next two chapters focus upon the need for and the factors involved in organization change.

DISCUSSION AND STUDY QUESTIONS

1. If staff members are assigned advisory powers, how is it that, as a group, staff members may dominate the affairs of an organization?

2. Explain the differences in decentralization possible if the firms' primary departmentation is:
   a) functional versus product
   b) geographical versus product

3. Explain why each of the following would be line or staff personnel:
   a) an assembly line worker
   b) a highly skilled operator of a numerically controlled machine tool
   c) an internal cost auditor
   d) a labor contract negotiator
   e) a newspaper editor

4. The Bobous Electrical Company produces small electrical motors for sale to various commercial and industrial customers. While a majority of these motors are standard items and can be ordered off the shelf from inventory, some are special orders requiring adaptation of wiring, grounding, and waterproofing. Does the special order variation require a differentiation in organization structure?

5. Would the duplication of functions (e.g., two sales departments) as an organization phenomena indicate excessive differentiation in structure?

6. When the coordination costs of a functional or process-based organization are seen to be excessive, what alternatives are available to the management in terms of alternate structural types to reduce these costs?

7. Different types of project organization are appropriate or refer to several distinct types of power structures, especially as they relate to the head of the project as he is impowered to, by reason of his delegated responsibilities, call upon resources of the organization. Explain the different types of powers that are related to the different kinds of project departments.

8. Staff groups are restricted to and are exclusive purveyors of expert advice in an organization. Comment.

9. Clarity of an organization's structure is important to individuals working in it. The design of a system using multiple bases for departmentation is confusing and thus should be eliminated or at least minimized. Comment.

10. A major automobile and truck manufacturer has received a large special order from a foreign government. The firm manufactures approximately 70 percent of its parts and purchases the rest. While one of the company's standard trucks forms the basic vehicle to be delivered, the order specifies a number of special characteristics not available currently in the options on any of the firm's models. The order was obtained under highly competitive price and delivery constraints with late delivery penalties. The

company has a potential interest in the possibility of follow-on orders and those from other countries. Since, moreover, there is disagreement concerning the potential profitability of such orders, the president has directed that a special study be made for this order so to provide evidence about the problem.

a) Does the firm face greater uncertainty and diversity because of this order? Explain.

b) If so, what kind of greater organizational or task differentiation appears appropriate, if any?

c) Would your answer be the same if the truck order could be assembled from currently available standard options? Explain.

11. How might a legal department be classified as both a service and a staff department? Would anyone in a large legal department have line relationships with others? Explain.

12. Failure to differentiate an operations research staff group in an organization is primary evidence that the quality of quantitative analysis in the organization suffers. Comment.

13. If the personnel department engages in developing personnel procedures, policy, and regulations, the nature of staff member requirements differs from a personnel department whose focus is upon research—e.g., examining the types of successful versus unsuccessful applicants, the causes of turnover, and so forth. Explain.

14. Distinguish between a product basis of departmentalization and a project basis when the project group's primary responsibility is creating and producing a product.

15. In a project organization, individuals should possess characteristics of dependency, obedience, and need for structure. Comment.

SELECTED REFERENCES

BAUM, BERNARD H. *Decentralization of Authority in a Bureaucracy.* Englewood Cliffs, N.J.: Prentice-Hall, Inc., 1961.

BELASCO, JAMES A. "Line and Staff Conflicts: Some Empirical Insights," *Academy of Management Journal,* 12 (1969), 469–77.

BENNIS, WARREN G. "Organizational Developments and the Fate of Bureaucracy," *Industrial Management Review,* 7 (Spring 1966), 41–55.

DALTON, MELVILLE. *Men Who Manage.* New York: John Wiley & Sons Inc., 1959.

FISCH, GERALD G. "Line-Staff Is Obsolete," *Harvard Business Review,* 39 (September-October 1961), 66–79.

HAIRE, MASON (ed.). *Modern Organization Theory.* New York: John Wiley & Sons, Inc., 1959.

HENSKEY, ROBERT L. "Organizational Planning," *Business Topics,* 10 (Winter 1962), 29–40.

MARCH, JAMES G., and SIMON, H. A. *Organizations.* New York: John Wiley & Sons, Inc., 1958.

MYERS, C. A., and TURNBULL, JOHN G. "Line and Staff in Industrial Relations," *Harvard Business Review*, 34 (1956), 113–24.

RUBENSTEIN, ALBERT H. "Organizational Factors Affecting Research and Development Decision-Making in Large Decentralized Companies," *Management Science*, 10 (July 1964), 618–33.

SCHOLLHAMMER, HANS. "Organization Structures of Multinational Corporations," *Academy of Management Journal*, 14 (September 1971), 345–65.

SMITH, G. A., JR. *Managing Geographically Decentralized Companies.* Boston: Division of Research, Graduate School of Business Administration, Harvard University, 1958.

STIEGLITZ, HAROLD. "Staff-Staff Relationships," *Management Record*, February 1962, 2–13.

URWICK, L. *Profitably Using the General Staff Position in Business.* General Management Series, No. 165. New York: American Management Association, Inc., 1953.

WICKESBERG, A. K., and CRONIN, T. C. "Management by Task Force," *Harvard Business Review*, 40 (November-December 1962), 111–18.

ZANNETOS, ZENON S. "On The Theory of Divisional Structures," *Management Science*, 12 (December 1965), B49–B68.

Chapter 10

Formal Organizational Change

A SALIENT CHARACTERISTIC of most business firms is that they face frequent changes. Modifications take place in tasks performed by individual workers, in the way jobs are grouped together, in the areas of responsibility for decision making held by various managers, in the patterning of communications, and so forth.

Some organizational modifications effected by business firms are of considerable magnitude—e.g., a major redepartmentalization may be made in which the areas of responsibility of the department heads reporting directly to the president of a company are changed from functional-based ones to product-based ones. Changes such as these, which are usually geared toward overcoming major organizational problems and which often lead to considerable upheaval in the firm, are generally effected at infrequent intervals. On the other hand, many more minor organizational changes take place almost continuously in most firms—e.g., a manager may modify the work assignments of one or more of his subordinates; his own span of control may be temporarily enlarged by the hiring of part-time help during a rush period of work, and so on. Unlike major restructurings of the organization, which represent "formal" planned changes by management, many of the minor day-to-day organizational modifications are effected "informally," and, in fact, sometimes even without the knowledge of management. For example, production employees in a manufacturing operation may modify their work procedures, or perhaps engage in job trading with one another without their foreman's being aware of such task modifications. In short, the changes which one may find taking place in the way organization structures are designed may vary considerably in magnitude and scope, frequency of occurrence, and degree of formality.

In the previous two chapters our view of the organization has been primarily a static one, although we have given some attention to such organizational redesign techniques as job enlargement and job rotation.

300

Our purpose in this and the succeeding chapter is to focus more explicit attention on several basic facets of change in organizations. In this chapter, our discussion will cover: some of the reasons for restructuring organizations, the identification of problems necessitating such changes; and certain approaches to organizational redesign utilized by business firms. Then, in Chapter 11, we will examine the behavior and reactions of individuals and groups within the firm with respect to organizational change.

PROBLEMS NECESSITATING ORGANIZATIONAL CHANGE

In some cases, firms find organizational change necessary because their task assignments, spans of control, and so forth, were inadequately structured in the first place. In defining the scope of work for production workers, for example, a company may have given insufficient attention to the psychological problems of specialization, only to find that absenteeism and turnover have become an acute problem with these individuals.

In many other cases, however, organizational restructuring may be necessitated by changed environmental conditions facing the firm rather than by ineffective initial organizational design. We will now examine the basic types of change which may give rise to the need for organizational redesign.

Environmental Change

As shown in Chapters 4, 8, and 9, an organization can be considered as an open system interacting with and adapting to its environment. Following the open-system conceptualization, one would naturally expect that changes in environmental conditions could induce change in the internal systems of affected organizations. Some of these adaptations could be major as was the impact of legislation designed to minimize air pollution by motor vehicles. As public realization of the extent of pollution by autos and trucks became known, some auto manufacturers first reacted to *dispute* pollution claims. When laws were passed, the auto organizations attempted to *liberalize* the amount of emissions allowed. In addition, added research and design activities were undertaken to perfect the antipollution services necessary to meet government standards.

This example illustrates the systems nature of organizations in that the initial disturbance in the environment engendered can affect the organization to attempt to reestablish its original equilibrium by ignoring or eliminating the disturbance (discounting the extent of auto pollution). When it becomes clear that eliminating the disturbance is not possible, the system attempts to modify the impact of the change upon it (attempting to liberalize the extent of emissions by autos). While both of these means of resistance to environmental change obviously influenced the tasks and level of activity of the public relations and legal staffs of the affected organizations, the discounting and liberalizations adaptations may have been achieved without substantial structural organization change.

The development of a pollution research and design activity, however, illustrates the adaptation to change by additional organizational differentiation to form, perhaps, a project organization.[1] The rise of the consumer movement in the United States has similarly triggered additional differentiation by leading organizations to add departments whose function is to accommodate consumer complaints and fears. These departments have been formed in both commercial and governmental organizations. Internal task and structural changes such as these illustrate a more severe form of adaptation of the system to external disturbances. Of course, there are continual changes in the markets, competition, technology, legislation, and so on which influence an organization. The discussion of these follows, such as output, input, and transformation changes.

Changes in Types of Output Desired

When the firm desires to modify its output specifications—e.g., changing its product line or providing for new services to meet changed competitive conditions—its work loads, assignment of tasks, skills required by its workers, and so forth, may also need to undergo modification, thus necessitating some degree of organizational redesign.

An illustration of organization changes accompanying shifts in product objectives is afforded by the airframe industry. Prior to the time that missiles began replacing airplaines as prime Air Force defensive and offensive weapons, the organizations of major airframe contractors were frequently characterized by a ratio of from .2/1 to .5/1 between (1) research and development, and engineering personnel and (2) production workers. As missile systems advanced to the state in which they were able to replace airplanes, it became evident for airframe concerns going into missiles that:

1. These systems would utilize rocket engines instead of jet, jet-prop, or reciprocating engines. In fact, the latter two had already become obsolete through the use of the pure jet engine for many other purposes.

---

[1] For a general discussion of the open-systems nature of adaptation, see D. Katz and R. L. Kahn, *The Social Psychology of Organizations* (New York: John Wiley & Sons, Inc., 1956), esp. chap. 2; and James Thompson, *Organizations in Action* (New York: McGraw-Hill Book Co., 1967).

2. Airframes—the manufacture of which was a complex and expensive operation requiring large amounts of labor—would be replaced with missile envelopes whose production component would be less relative to its technical and engineering component.

3. Automatic electronic systems for the control of missiles would become more important, complex, and expensive as compared to the human-electronic systems in airplanes.

4. The reliability needs would be greater in missile systems, with less dependence upon human correction or compensation.

For those firms entering the missile business, these changes in product, and therefore in output objectives, were reflected in major differences in the costs of components. Notable was the relative reduction in the labor to produce the carrier (missile fuselages as opposed to airframes). Concurrently an increased number of engineers was needed to design, test, and mate the complex electronic equipment. For example, after it had gone into missiles, at one time Martin's Denver facility is said to have required a ratio of seven engineering personnel to one laborer.

If the objectives of an airframe company were to encompass missile production, rather major organization changes were required. For example, North American Aviation Company set up separate divisions designed to produce: (1) subsystems for missiles, (2) electronic control and communication devices, (3) rocket engines, and so on, as well as (4) one to continue airplane manufacture. Some other companies decided not to enter the missile business, but rather to attempt to gain a larger share of the dwindling airplane business. Still others decided to enter the missile business but to subcontract from established electronic and engine firms those subsystems for which they did not have superior capabilities. In one such firm, even though sales were not reduced substantially, a major cut in employment took place as considerably fewer manufacturing employees were required. At the same time, however, there was a large increase in the employment of scientific, research, engineering, and test personnel. These major organizational changes were necessary because of modified product objectives and because of the particular methods that the company chose to meet these objectives.

In addition to changes in product objectives, changes in other objectives such as public or personnel relations may also require organizational restructuring. For example, recognition of a union by the management of a firm will require an output of relations not therefore needed, such as preparing for and conducting contract negotiations, and designing and following an agreed upon grievance procedure. In some companies, such tasks may simply be handled by enlarging the scope of responsibility of existing managers; while in others new staff specialists may be hired and staff departments either expanded or created to deal with labor relations.

Changes in Inputs Available

The Mesabi iron ore fields of Minnesota have long constituted an input of raw material to the blast furnaces of the iron and steel industry. Over time, the high-grade Mesabi deposits became so scarce that benefication (upgrading of iron content) plants were built to process low-grade ores to improve their iron content prior to shipping on the Great Lakes to the Chicago-Pittsburgh-Cleveland area steel producers. While raw high-grade ores had averaged 50–55 percent iron content, the low-grade ores were improved to 60 or 65 percent iron content. In addition, they were formed as pellets or sinter by the benefication process. To the blast furnaces, the switch from natural to beneficated inputs represented change, but the change was not sufficient to require new equipment, new organization, or new task assignments. However, new procedures in terms of rate of feed of air, pressure regulation, and temperature controls were affected. The change in input did not materially influence the structure or job assignment in the system. Only operational procedures were influenced.

Some changes in inputs may be accommodated without any substantial change, even in procedure as when a supplier changes the length of the discount period from 10 to 15 days. The flexibility of the system to accommodate such change is sufficiently wide. In contrast, the change from transistor to integrated circuits as inputs to construction and design of computers has resulted in a substantial change in the production operations by eliminating the need for many previously required wiring and assembly operations.

Transformation Changes

Technological change in the process of creating goods and services also has a variety of organizational influences for affected firms. As a minor disruptive influence, consider the replacement of a worn machine tool such as a milling machine. While new models of milling machines are constantly emerging and ease of operation and automaticity tend to be greater in newer models, the basic function (i.e., to remove material to produce a flat surface) remains basically the same. A new tool may require very little operator training or change in skills. The difference may be similar to the contrast between driving a 1960 and a 1970 automobile.

That transformation changes may have considerable impact on the firm's organization, however, may be illustrated by the experience of a company, which produced industrial equipment, motors, and pumps.

Although the company's management believed that it had a reasonable market share for the products which it manufactured, its volume on any one product was not sufficiently large to justify mass-production methods. Many of the parts for its various products were machined on the same general-purpose equipment in relatively small lots. Some of its products were designed in such a way that they had several different end uses. For example, certain motors were designed so that they could be used by several different customers. This alleviated but did not overcome completely the problem of short machine runs on parts. In analyzing their competition on each product, company executives noted that they and their five competitors had approximately equal market shares for one particular pump. Each firm's sales volume was relatively low; and none could produce the pump as cheaply as could be done with mass-production methods. The executives predicted that if they had 50 percent of the market, they could afford to invest in special-purpose equipment and tooling so as to mass-produce the pump. Since mass production would reduce costs considerably below that of its competitors, the company would be able to price the pump sufficiently low to obtain a greater market share. The decision was made to go ahead with the plan, and within several years, the company had captured a major share of the market.

In the above example, the firm's basic product was not changed. Both its market share objective and transformation methods, however, were modified. A new building was constructed, new special-purpose equipment was installed, and a new organizational division was created. With mass production of the pump, a greater degree of worker specialization was effected on many jobs, and lesser skill levels were required for these jobs. Thus, both departmental and task restructuring resulted from the change in transformational methods of producing the firm's product.

Organizational Growth and Decline

In the example given in the previous section, we saw how transformation changes coupled with organizational growth (i.e., the production and sale of more pumps) necessitated organizational redesign by a firm. Of importance also in understanding the business firm is the fact that organizational growth per se, even in the absence of changes in basic technological processes utilized, may render organizational change necessary or desirable. A number of researchers have found that as firms become larger, not only do their departments become larger, with simply more people doing the same kinds of jobs—but certain changes usually occur in their organizational *"shape."*

Several investigators have attempted to show that the shape an organization takes as it grows is a *natural* phenomenon. Mason Haire has suggested that the square-cube law might be utilized in explaining organization shape.[2] In living organisms, the square-cube law has been used to explain changes in the relationship between an organism's area and volume as it grows. In applying this "law" to companies, Haire has classified employees as being either "outside" or "inside." Outside employees include salesmen, purchasing agents, labor negotiators, and other individuals performing work dealing with entities outside the firm. The square-cube law, as applied by Haire to organizational growth, predicts that for any size of firm the square root of the number of external employees (area) varies as the cube root of the number of internal employees (volume); or, $\sqrt{\text{external employees}} = \sqrt[3]{\text{internal employees}}$. Haire's evidence shows that, when plotted, data from a number of actual companies over a period of time seem to indicate that the rate of growth in the number of internal employees is less than that predicted by the formula.

A somewhat different type of relationship has been postulated by Ralph C. Davis in examining organizational growth. In predicting the relative size of staff groups as opposed to line, Davis has stated:

> The complexity of functional relationships tends to increase in geometric progression as the volume of work that the organization must handle increases in arithmetic progression. Staff organizations tend to grow faster than the line organizations they serve. There is some evidence that the growth relation between them also involves geometric progression until we approach the optimum organization size.[3]

Haire's data indicates that this tendency for rapid staff expansion in relation to that of the line is descriptive of early stages of company growth; but that line and staff groups tend to grow at similar rates after reaching some "established" (and indefinite) size.[4] This conclusion has been supported by data by Despelder.[5]

Still another study, conducted by Alan Filley, however, disputes all of the above-mentioned conclusions:

> The fact that either line or staff executives may perform necessary supportive functions seems to have been generally overlooked in management literature and research. Research designs which purport to measure a natural-order result of growth are, in fact, measuring only the extent to which circumstances or policy has dictated the creation or restriction of staff units. Nor do such

---

[2] Mason Haire, "Biological Models and Empirical Histories of the Growth of Organizations," in his *Modern Organization Theory* (New York: John Wiley & Sons, 1959), pp. 272–306.

[3] Ralph C. Davis, *The Fundamentals of Top Management* (New York: Harper & Bros., 1951), p. 232.

[4] Haire, "Biological Models," Figures 13, 14, 15, and 16.

[5] Bruce Despelder, *Ratios of Staff to Line Personnel* (Columbus, Ohio: Bureau of Business Research, The Ohio State University, Research Monograph No. 106, 1962).

designs consider the conditions militating toward the retention of such functions by top management and against delegation to subordinates.[6]

Filley found the data from the various studies so different and conflicting
he concluded that there is no *natural* order to organizational growth
or to the shape of this growth. His contention is that the staff units
formed in organizations are dependent upon management *decisions.* In
one growing firm that he studied staff personnel remained at an approximately constant ratio of one to nine to line personnel. But Filley indicated that this firm could probably have economized by adding more
staff units to benefit from greater managerial staff specialization.[7]

It is obvious that a staff group cannot be initiated without managerial
decision and action. The fact that some managements do not choose
to differentiate their management functions by forming staff *departments*
as the firms become larger does not deny that there is some relationship
between the staff *work* to be performed and the size of the firm. On
the other hand, there are probably more basic reasons for staff growth
than any "natural order." A basic reason why it is "natural" for a personnel staff to form when a firm reaches a size of approximately 175 people,[8]
for example, is that by that time the number of personnel activities
and problems being handled by the line has usually become large enough
to justify the addition of a specially trained and competent professional
personnel manager. Whether or not a differentiated task, position, or
department exists in an organization to perform a specialized function,
there still may well be a need for that activity. A firm may not be
large enough to utilize fully the talents of a tax expert, for example.
As alternatives to employing a full-time expert, the company can use
a part-time consultant or an accountant with a general knowledge of
accounting rather than tax expertise. Obviously in the latter case the
level of skill used is less than that available. As a firm becomes large
enough to be able to utilize several tax experts full time, failure to
differentiate these more specialized functions at some point from the
other accounting operations may exemplify a lack of differentiation of
tasks to diversity in the environment (in this case the effect of tax
law and rulings on the firm). Whether or not a tax department ought
to be established should be determined by the relative economies in

---

[6] Allan C. Filley, "Decisions and Research in Staff Utilization," *Journal of the
Academy of Management* 6 (September 1963), pp. 220–31.

[7] Comments by Filley at the original presentation of his paper cited in footnote 6
at the Midwest Management Conference, April 26, 1963.

[8] Haire, "Biological Models," p. 293. It should be noted that in companies whose
employment is dependent to a considerable extent upon obtaining one or more
large contracts, the growth in some staff or auxiliary functions (e.g., purchasing,
engineering) tends to *lead* increases in worker employment whereas the work load
of other functions (e.g., handling accounts receivable) may lag peak worker
employment.

use of a consultant versus internal experts, the size of the tax staff, the interdependence of tax activities to others in the firm, and so forth.

While the above changes have been in terms of the *total* growth of the firm, differences in the *relative proportions* of organizational segments may have similar impact upon the need for change. When the railroad passenger business declined precipitously with the popularity of air travel, for example, large segments of departments within the passenger divisions were eliminated and collapsed into consolidated units even though total volume of sales increased. Some firms completely eliminated the function of advertising for passengers, for example.

Directly related to the relative line-staff growth patterns is the ratio of indirect to direct workers and the change in this ratio as the size of the firm varies. As a firm grows, the need for indirect workers often is not recognized as quickly as the growth occurs so that addition of indirect personnel tends to lag behind additions to direct workers (see Figure 10–1). When contraction of operations takes place, however, there

Figure 10–1. Hypothesized Growth Tendencies of Direct and Indirect Workers

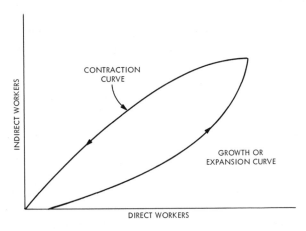

is a tendency for the reduction of indirect workers to lag behind other reductions, due to the inability to see quickly the need for reductions and to evaluate as precisely the contributions of indirect personnel to the operation. Translating these effects to overhead costs results in higher relative profits in expansion periods and lower profits at the same volume during contraction. These examples illustrate differentiation and its converse, consolidation, as growth and contraction of activities in the firm occurs. While only general tendencies are shown, managers ought to be aware of constrained operations that could be freed by further differentiation and, at the same time knowledgeable of slack that can be consolidated.

PINPOINTING ORGANIZATIONAL PROBLEMS

In the previous sections, we have shown several different types of conditions under which organizational restructuring may be needed by a firm. In order for management to undertake organizational redesign (or any other approach) for dealing with its problems, it is first necessary to identify and analyze the nature of these problems facing it. The purpose of this section is to explain some of the approaches used by management in pinpointing organizational problems.

Before discussing any of these, it is important to emphasize that an inappropriate organizational structure is only *one* possible cause of a firm's problems. Difficulties can and do arise from many other sources. A combination of many factors, including organizational design, often contribute to the problems of a firm. Since organization structure, job design, leadership, the personal capabilities of the firm's members, and so forth, are often all interdependent in influencing the output of an organization system, one manifestation of a firm's problem may simply be the result of another variable in the system. For example, the supposed weakness of a manager may be due more to faulty organization design which fails to provide the timely data necessary to make the decisions assigned to him, than to his own inadequacies.

Analysis of Day-to-Day Operations

Many times organizational redesign arises from problems identified by managers in their day-to-day operations of the firm. Management may find that its costs are increasing, that an increasing number of late deliveries on its products are taking place, and so forth, and, after subsequent analysis of such problems, decide that one or more kinds of inadequacies exist in its organization structure. An example of this type of problem identification and analysis is provided by a manufacturing firm which experienced a late delivery problem.

For over a year, the firm in question had been plagued by frequent late deliveries. To help overcome this problem, several expedients were attempted by the production department such as: overtime; splitting processing runs on parts into two or more lots; using expediters to push particular jobs through the shop; and utilizing rush and special rush orders which took precedence over ordinary jobs.

These actions resulted in high costs from duplicate machine setups and overtime work. The late deliveries, however, continued. Analysis showed that 20 percent of the lots *entered* the machine shops up to one month after machining on them had been originally scheduled to start. Eighty percent of the parts *left* the machining shops behind schedule partially because rush orders took priority in processing and delayed other orders which previously had been on schedule. The work flow of an order through the organization was as is shown in Figure 10–2.

Figure 10–2. Work Flow of Orders in an Illustrative Firm

Neither the firm's sales volume nor its organization structure had changed significantly for several years. The delivery problem, however, had appeared only during the last year. Further study showed that somewhat prior to this time, the distribution of order *sizes* entering the plant had changed from few orders of a relatively large lot size to many orders of a relatively small lot size. The basic products had not changed, but the *average size* of orders had been reduced.

Although the organization had been able to produce effectively the large lot size mix, it was not able to handle as successfully the production of many orders of small size. The smaller lots required relatively more engineering time, tooling, scheduling, and setups per dollar of sales. Failure to differentiate and to coordinate these changed requirements among the firm's departments other than production constituted a basic reason for the late delivery problem that arose. While organization changes had been made in production to correct the *resulting* problems, no attention had been given to eliminate their *causes* in those departments *preceding* production in the work flow.

Once the real problems had been identified, several organizational redesign steps were undertaken in an attempt to correct them. Data on product mix were developed (and projected) by the sales department so that engineering, tooling, and production could anticipate the size and nature of their work forces. By also having these data, production was able to organize separate crews for off-shift maintenance and for setups, which permitted the reduction of overtime work. Organization adjustments of similar types in the engineering and tooling departments also helped make it possible to process orders into the shop on time.

As the above example illustrates, inadequacies in the structure of organizational tasks and information flows may manifest themselves in a host of resultant problems. Further, the inadequacies underlying such problems are often not immediately apparent, but may be uncovered only after considerable analysis. If management focuses attention solely on the resultant problems, without attempting to identify the variables underlying them, it may develop a "patchwork" organizational redesign which only scratches the surface, and effects little fundamental improvement in its operations.

Intervening Performance Indicators

In the example given in the preceding section, an organizational problem was ultimately manifested in a measurable output deficiency—an increasing number of deliveries were late. Managers are also sometimes able to uncover problems by examining what may be referred to as "intervening" measures of performance. These measures are so-named because they "intervene" between the firm's operations and such ultimate measures of operating performance as costs and profits. Among those intervening measures commonly examined by management are employee attitudes, labor turnover, absenteeism, number of grievances, and accident rates. Measures for many of the more commonly utilized intervening performance indicators exist, so that it is possible for managers to note both the development of trends and to compare the performance of particular departments with that of other departments or their firm's performance with that of other companies.

When intervening performance indicators are "out of line," the firm may or may not experience any basic problems in meeting its output objectives. For example, even though the number of employee grievances in a particular department has increased, its cost, production quality, and delivery schedule objectives all may still be met. When such indicators do give "negative readings," however, it may be a warning of impending difficulties.

If, for example, employee turnover or absenteeism in one department of a firm is significantly higher than in other organizational units, there is some indication that its employees do not wish to associate or identify with the department or other individuals in it. Although the reasons for such possible nonidentification are not indicated by the intervening performance measures per se, the measures do give the manager a warning that certain problems may exist, or be in the making. These problems, of course, may not be due to inadequate organizational design alone; they might reflect poor supervisory practices or any one of a number of other conditions.

Periodic Surveys

In their day-to-day analysis of data concerning their operations, managers may often be able to pinpoint organizational problems, as was indicated previously. However, because of imperfect information, time pressures, and other limiting factors, many organizational problems or potential problems that might be uncovered in day-to-day operational analysis may go long undetected by the manager.

To help overcome this problem, managers sometimes obtain periodic reviews or surveys of certain facets of their operations by individuals or groups outside their department. Such reviews may be conducted by outside consulting firms or by staff groups within the organization. Such periodic surveys may focus attention on both direct measures of output, and upon intervening performance measures. Illustrations of such reviews of organizations are provided by the periodic inspections held by the Armed Services, the periodic evaluation of university departments by outside experts, and employee attitude surveys which are conducted from time to time by many business firms.

Attitude surveys have often been used as a means of determining the sentiments and viewpoints of employees in a company. Replies from such surveys are often segregated and summarized for the subordinates reporting to each manager. This permits managers to compare the attitudes of their subordinates with those of subordinates in other departments and with the attitudes of all employees as a whole in the plant or company. In some companies, attitude surveys are conducted on a planned periodic basis—e.g., every two years. If the same questions are asked in each such survey so that the results from one survey to the next are comparable, not only may absolute "levels" of employee attitudes be determined, but also *changes* in attitudes may be discerned. In some attitude surveys, questions are asked about conditions in the employees' own departments and about overall plant or company conditions—e.g., attitudes may be obtained about employee benefit programs, the company newsletter, or the plant cafeteria.

Two final observations are in order concerning the value of attitude surveys in pinpointing problems which may call for organizational redesign. First, some of the problems revealed by such surveys may not be ones of organizational inadequacy. For instance, negative attitudes toward the plant's cafeteria may be due to nothing more than overly hot conditions in the summertime which could be corrected simply by the purchase and installation of an air conditioner. Second, as is also true of many of the intervening performance indicators discussed in the previous section, survey results frequently indicate only that an organizational problem may exist, but do not give a complete picture of what the problem is or what its underlying causes are. For example, if most of the employees in a particular department express the opinion that they "are given little opportunity to express their ideas on the job," such sentiments might reflect the practicing of close supervision by their foreman. Or, on the other hand, the basic reason for these attitudes could be that work in the department has, through overspecialization, become so routine that little creative expression is possible.

Environmental Monitoring

Since diversity, uncertainty, and change in the environmental factors influencing a firm's operations have an impact on the degree of differentiation and the need for integration, the recognition and interpretation of these external factors in terms of their effect upon internal operations is needed but is frequently a function that is not well done. A reason for failure is the tendency of the firm to isolate itself from environmental effects as was shown in the last chapter. A second reason for a short circuit in information flow from the environment is a typical lack of responsibility for monitoring external events. For example, who has the responsibility for knowing about proposed legislation and interpreting this information as it might affect the firm? Often, the individual departments most affected are expected to develop systems to deal with these data, but uncertainties as to relevancy of external events suggests that a firm may not receive all pertinent data in a timely manner. Further, information influencing one department may never reach it even if knowledge of the event is known by some other department but not transmitted. Finally, some firms have a relatively stable and certain environment. Thus, there is little need to gather and evaluate data on external events even though these conditions leave the firm somewhat unprepared to deal with change if and when it ultimately occurs.

Through product and market research, firms are able to maintain viable perspectives on customers and competitive actions, to be sure. These activities constitute typical ongoing functions that allows the firm to continuously adapt to market and technological conditions. In contrast, it is the more uncertain and unique environmental events that are more probable of being ignored.

While the need for knowledge of external factors' bearing upon a firm's operations have been shown, the associated need for development of a rational information system for monitoring the totality of the environment has not, in our opinion, received adequate attention in either the literature or in the operations of firms.[9]

ADAPTATION TO CHANGE

The preceding sections have examined a number of problems which give rise to the need for change in the operations of organizations. The purpose of this section is to show how decisions to accommodate these problems result in an adaptation of the organization's functioning. While these managerial responses can take a great variety of forms, this discussion focuses upon three major categories of change: in managerial systems, information flow restructuring, and structural changes.

Change in Management Systems

As was shown in Chapter 8, different degrees of explicitness in the planning and control systems evolve as variations in the behavioral and

---

[9] For possible exceptions to the lack of information concerning external events, see James Emery, *Organizational Planning and Control Systems* (London: Collier-Macmillan, Ltd., 1969), chap. 3.

problem-solving tasks confronting those operating the system occur. These "exceptions" to the operating routines, their frequency, and importance can also change, resulting in a need to adapt systems, structure, and/or power assignments. For example, a manufacturer of standardized industrial and office lighting equipment decided to provide a specialized design and manufacturing service to architects desiring unique specially adapted lighting fixtures for new buildings and redesigned offices. Since this new service was different for each order, a job order system of planning the work and controlling its progress from purchasing to shipment had to be adopted over and above the previous system which had not required the internal operating system to differentiate one customer's order from another. The number of exceptions from routine processing was a direct function of the number of special orders received by the firm. Eventually a separate set of job-processing routines were established for special orders so that the diversification of products resulted in a separate planning and control system.

Note, too, that the variations inherent from special orders require flexibility in tasks, processes, and the sequence of their application by the work force. While standardization of products allows task specialization (and relative rigidity in assignment), product variation implies greater need for workers capable and adaptable to a number of different assignments. Both training and the personality types required to accommodate to these different management systems may be quite at variance with one another. For example, workers seeking certainty and safety might prefer the standardized routines[10] while those seeking variety and risk would seek the nonroutine.

Information Flow Restructuring

In some cases, organizational problems have arisen because of inadequacies existing in the manner in which informational outputs from one organizational subsystem have flowed as inputs to another subsystem in the firm.

An example of this type of problem is provided by William F. Whyte's analysis of communications and work flow in certain restaurants.[11] Whyte has shown that inadequate informational structuring in some restaurants has been a source of organization conflict. Waitresses give customer orders to cooks. During busy periods, customers pressure waitresses resulting in the waitresses pressuring cooks for their orders. The work

---

[10] Paul Lawrence and Jay Lorsch, *Organization and Environment* (Homewood, Ill.: Richard D. Irwin, Inc., 1969), pp. 243–45, hypothesize that workers with different personality types are attracted to organizations matching their personality needs.

[11] "Social Structure of the Whole Organization: The Restaurant," *American Journal of Sociology*, 54 (January 1949), pp. 302–8.

load of the cooks is most efficiently handled if it is bulked (i.e., if a dozen salads can be made at one time rather than individually). In contrast, the work load of the waitress is most efficiently handled if all orders for a table are batched together. Thus, the most efficient work flow in the waitress subsystem is different from that in the kitchen subsystem.

Another variable influencing the relationship between waitresses and cooks is status. The cook is a highly skilled, highly paid male. He enjoys a relatively high status in a restaurant's hierarchy of positions. On the other hand, waitresses are relatively low skilled, low paid, and females and hence of a lower status. In the work flow, the lower status waitresses give orders to the higher status cooks. This condition has been a source of many tensions and conflicts in restaurants.[12]

A third variable in the waitress-cook relation is the type of communication used between them. When oral communications are used, there is likely to be more disagreement and conflict when errors are made in orders than if the orders are written. Whether the waitress errs in obtaining the order from the customer or whether the cook errs in receiving the oral order from the waitress is often difficult, if not impossible to determine. Further, with oral communications, waitresses must often stand in line during peak periods waiting to call their orders in to the cook.

A restructuring of the work between cooks and waitresses has been accomplished in some restaurants through the use of a circular spindle upon which waitresses place their *written* orders and from which cooks establish their work sequence. This spindle turns so that the cook may scan all orders and batch together common items from all waitresses. This allows more efficient kitchen operation. Since the spindle intervenes between the cooks and the waitresses, the tensions and conflict occasioned by verbal orders being given from lower status to higher status employees are reduced. Direct face-to-face contact is eliminated as a necessary condition of communication. Further, the use of written orders tends to overcome errors arising from miscommunication by oral means; and when an error does occur, the person responsible for it can be determined by reference to written communications. As Porter has pointed out,

> The waitress prepares the order slip and the cook works directly from it. If the waitress records the order incorrectly, it is obvious to her upon examining the order slip. Similarly, if the cook misreads the slip, an examination of the order slip makes it obvious to him. . . . [A function] . . . of the spindle, then, is to provide "feedback" to both waitress and cook regarding

[12] For an explanation of the reasons for these tensions and conflicts in terms of both psychological, sociological and anthropological theory, see Elias H. Porter, "The Parable of the Spindle," *Harvard Business Review*, 40 (May-June 1962), pp. 58–66.

errors. The spindle markedly alters the emotional relationship and redirects the learning process.[13]

Additionally, the spindle serves as a queuing device in two ways:

It holds the order in a proper waiting line until the cook can get to them. When dependent on his memory only, the cook can get orders mixed up. It also does all the "standing in line" for the waitresses. They need never again stand in line to pass an order to the cook. This makes their jobs easier—especially during the rush hours.[14]

As the reader may note, the above analysis of the restaurant problem illustrates application of the systems concept which we discussed previously in Chapter 4. A central focus of attention was upon the flow of information from one organizational subsystem to another. This example also illustrates that organizational design decisions should take into consideration not only *what* information is transmitted to a particular subsystem but *how* it is transmitted. The introduction of the spindle did not significantly alter the *content* of messages transmitted from waitresses to the cooks. Rather, it helped overcome both psychological and work flow problems by modifying the form which the messages took (verbal to written), and the timing of the message transmission and receipt—i.e., the waitresses did not have to wait to transmit orders, while the cooks could *time their own receipt* of the informational inputs contained in the written orders, so as to plan their work more effectively.

Structural Changes

While the introduction of some changes will require only procedural adaptations, more severe changes call for changes in the organization structure itself. In the example of the lighting manufacturer cited above, the procedural changes in the planning and control of the special orders through the production system were emphasized although the actual production processes also had to be changed from the standard ones because different materials and processes were often required. Almost any kind of organizational change can result from the addition or elimination of task variation. This section focuses upon several recurring types of adaptations in structure: the introduction of project groups, permanent differentiation or consolidation, and (de)centralization.

Introduction of Project Groups. Since some exceptions to routine operations are perceived as being temporary, there is no need to establish a permanent change in structure or procedure to accommodate the variation. Such a case is illustrated by a manufacturer of commercial air

---

[13] From ibid., as reprinted in Max D. Richards and William A. Nielander, *Readings in Management,* (3rd ed.; Cincinnati, Ohio: South-Western Publishing Company, 1969), p. 101.

[14] Ibid., p. 100.

transports who received a special order from the government for three planes for the President, Vice-President, and so on. The prestige value of this order was high and the specifications for interior accommodations was different from those of the commercial airlines. As a consequence, a special project team was established to deal with the customer and to follow the progress of the planes through design and manufacturing even though they followed many standard routines. When delivery was made, the team was disbanded.

Even if a permanent service or product is being introduced, it may be useful initially to establish a project group to spearhead its introduction. If an auto manufacturer plans a new entry for the market (e.g., a Mustang or a Vega), the problems of researching the potential market, product design, procurement, tooling, and production may be different enough initially to suggest that these activities be separated from the relatively routine operations for already established products. A separate project group allows these latter standardized procedures to be undisturbed and permits efficiency in present operations. The project also provides a focus for top management to better assure itself that the new product is receiving adequate attention. Even with these differences, there will be commonalities between standard operations and the project group in such areas as suppliers, parts, use of plants, and dealers. Further, at some point in the introductory phase of the product, its operations will tend to become similar to the standard ones and management will consider integrating project operations into the established hierarchy. At that point, the project group starts disbanding.

Permanent Differentiation. While the uniqueness and variation of tasks facing an organization may be temporary and accommodated by a short-term project organization, sufficient differences may remain to justify a permanent new differentiated organizational group. When oil companies developed chemical affiliates to take advantage of the integration of refinery outputs to the potential profits in the sale of chemicals rather than oil products, the new production, research, and marketing expertise was so different that separate organizations, and even subsidiaries, persisted over time.

Much of the differentiation or conversely, consolidation of organizational groupings occurs because of the growth or decline in the size of operations. Line-staff shifts illustrate these changes. When organizations reach a size such that enough specialized work handled by line managers exists to justify the hiring of staff specialists, the work is often shifted from the line to a newly created staff group. In some cases, such staff groups are set up organizationally *within* existing line departments. Subsequently, however, the magnitude of work performed by the new staff group may become large enough to justify its being broken away from its "parent" department to form a separate organizational unit. For example, in some companies, executive manpower planning—i.e., projecting the firm's managerial needs in future years, the future movement of managers into higher level positions, and so forth—was handled first by line management, subsequently assigned to the personnel staff, and finally made the responsibility of a separate organizational planning unit. This type of line-staff shift as contradistinguished from consolidation is illustrated in Figure 10–3.

Figure 10–3. Two Types of Line-Staff Shifts

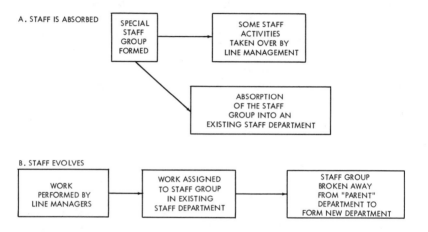

Centralization-Decentralization. Analysis of a firm's organizational problems may indicate that either greater centralization or decentralization of decision-making responsibilities is appropriate. That is, as we indicated in Chapter 9, decisions previously made at one organizational level may be shifted upward (centralization) or downward (decentralization) in the firm's managerial hierarchy.

There are many possible reasons for the desirability of shifting the level at which decisions are made. Enlarging the scope and importance of the decisions lower level managers are responsible for may better prepare them to assume higher level positions with greater responsibilities. Decentralization may be utilized as a means to allow quicker and more appropriate decisions. For example, in one large company, all grain purchases had to be approved by the president. On many occasions the firm's head purchasing agent had an opportunity, if he could act quickly, to make purchases at especially favorable prices; however, he could not contact the president for approval in time to take advantage of these opportunities. This problem was later overcome by giving full responsibility for purchases to the agent.

Two other observations are in order concerning modification of the organizational levels at which decisions are made. First, effective decentralization is possible only when lower level managers possess the skills and competence to handle those decisions formerly made at higher levels. If the purchasing manager mentioned above was prone to make poor decisions, continued approval of all grain purchases by the president might have been more appropriate, notwithstanding the problems of delay which the need for such approval sometimes created. Furthermore, shifting certain types of decision making downward may not be possible when the work performed by several functional departments is highly interdependent, and requires centralized coordination—e.g., manufacturing firms producing many small lots of different items, which flow from one department to another in their manufacture, have centralized production control departments in order to coordinate work scheduling among the various production departments.

Second, although many different types of technological change may give rise to a need for centralization or decentralization, one technological development—computerization—may have far-reaching consequences for organizational design, especially at managerial levels. With electronic computers, it is possible to generate more and better data for decision making much more quickly than has heretofore been possible. In consequence, top managements of many firms are now often able to make more detailed decisions, which were formerly the responsibility of lower level managers.[15] With the science of decision making and information processing developing at a rapid rate, the opportunities for top management to plan and control in detail the operations at lower levels are increasing. To the extent that these opportunities are taken advantage of, the decision latitude of middle-level managers is greatly reduced, and the need for middle management is lessened. Leavitt and Whisler have predicted that middle management will assume much less importance within the next 20 years because top management, aided by computers and a staff of experts, will be able to make or to program in detail many of the decisions now made by middle-level managers.[16] Whether these precise effects will occur is open to considerable debate, but their possibility has arisen from computer technology.

SUMMARY

Viable organizations are dynamic systems in which procedural and structural changes frequently take place. Modifications may be triggered by environmental change, changes in inputs utilized, outputs produced, and/or transformational methods employed. Further, growth or decline per se in operations may lead to organizational redesign. The information

---

[15] For one company's experience, see, for example, L. G. Wagner, "Computers, Decentralization, and Corporate Control," *California Management Review*, 9 (Winter 1966), pp. 25–32.

[16] Harold J. Leavitt and Thomas L. Whisler, "Management in the 1980's," *Harvard Business Review*, 36 (November-December 1958), pp. 41–48.

that may signal the possibility of organizational change can come from a manager's analysis of his day-to-day operations, periodic analyses, and from monitoring environmental factors having bearing upon a firm's operations. Both changes in the management system and in the organization structure can result from a decision that change is required.

While this chapter has shown that organizational adaptation is often rational, little attention has been given to the human elements which have bearing upon the extent and rapidity of change. It is to these human centered variables that the next chapter is directed.

DISCUSSION AND STUDY QUESTIONS

1. The Ivy College, organized along traditional disciplinary departments, is considering whether it should develop a new interdisciplinary major in environmental sciences. What organizational changes might evolve in such a study and the implementation of the new major? What parts of the system will require no organizational change but only task changes within the system? Can parts of the system accommodate such a change with no organizational or task changes?

2. One automobile firm is reported to be spending over $100 million per year and to be employing over 1,000 employees on pollution and safety research whereas only a few years ago this activity used only a small number of people (less than 100) and cost considerably less. In light of the increased cost of this activity (approaching or exceeding yearly model change costs), the company was considering a change in policy about its yearly models. Why was such a major change in expenditures of the firm made so suddenly? Why hadn't the change in model policy been anticipated so that it could be coordinated with its engineering and sales units?

3. Only a subset of the environment has impact upon a firm's operations. If the environmental factors impinging upon it are relatively stable and predictable, the firm can be operated much like a closed rather than an open system. Discuss.

4. Examine the statement "You either grow or you die. You just can't stand still. Organizations must grow to be successful." Comment.

5. While reviewing personnel statistics regularly compiled and reported to the top management of the company, an assistant personnel manager in charge of personnel data collection noticed an upward trend in absenteeism, lateness, and turnover in the shipping department. In reviewing the operations of that department he subsequently discovered that a new general manager had been appointed to the shipping organization. He was unsure what action he should undertake. Does the organization have a problem? If it does, has the assistant personnel manager uncovered the cause? Discuss.

6. The president of Ivy University had heard rumors of widespread faculty and student dissatisfaction in one of the major laboratories. The president

had been urged by his Dean of Graduate Studies to replace the head of the lab, but the head had been its director for a number of years and had an outstanding international reputation as a scientist and scholar. What might the president do?

7. We have grown from 100 to 1,000 employees without modifying the basically small administrative staff. We believe this is quite an achievement. Comment.

8. In an annual U.S. Sailboat Show, there was only one of over 300 boats whose hull was made of wood. Plastic hulls dominated entries in the show. One builder not in the show commented that he would never change to plastic since the beauty and finish of wood could not be duplicated in plastic. Further, his yard possessed no skills to lay off current employees who had been with him for years, and he did not "like" plastic. Can his position be defended? Is he operating his business as an open system?

9. If a small firm producing a fairly broad product line of standard machine tools in limited volume per item acquired an invention that when used in one of its models gave it a high exclusive advantage over its 20 competitors, what effect might use of the invention on the tool have on the systems of decision making in the firm?

10. In the past, relatively high-priced middle-level managers reviewed inventory levels, evaluated usage, and reordered items to replenish stocks. Today such a system of inventory management has been structured so that a computer can perform these functions using a formulae that provides greater accuracy than managers could. As similar structuring of management decisions are developed, the changes in management systems of planning and controlling operations tend to move the nature of systems from unstructured to structured. Evaluate these statements and the tendency toward structured systems.

11. If a threat to U.S. National Security were perceived by the Congress and the administration to necessitate a one-third increase in the defense budget, what impact might this have upon:
   a) a company which is designing a space system for a manned landing on Mars? or
   b) a firm manufacturing military rocket systems?
   c) a business selling pizza to college students?
   d) an electronics firm selling to commercial and industrial customers?

SELECTED REFERENCES

BLAKE, ROBERT R., and MOUTON, J. S. *The Managerial Grid.* Houston, Tex.: Gulf Publishing Co., 1964.

DALTON, GENE; BARNES, LOUIS, B., and ZALEZNIK, ABRAHAM. *The Distribution of Authority in Formal Organizations.* Boston: Division of Research, Harvard Business School, 1968.

GLUECK, WILLIAM. "Organization Change in Business and Government" *Academy of Management Journal,* 12 (1969), 439–49.

HAIRE, M. *Modern Organization Theory.* New York: John Wiley & Sons, Inc., 1959.

JACQUES, ELLIOT. *The Changing Culture of a Factory.* London: Tavistock Publications, Ltd., 1951.

LAWRENCE, PAUL R. *The Changing of Organizational Behavior Patterns.* Boston: Division of Research, Graduate School of Business Administration, Harvard University, 1958.

MORSE, NANCY, and REIMER, E. "The Experimental Change of a Major Organizational Variable," *Journal of Abnormal Social Psychology,* 52 (1956), 120–29.

RICE, A. K. *Productivity and Social Organization: The Ahmedabad Experiment.* London: Tavistock Publications, Ltd., 1958.

ROY, DONALD. "Quota Restriction and Gold-Bricking in a Machine Shop," *American Journal of Sociology,* 57 (March 1952), 430–37.

SAYLES, LEONARD. "The Change Process in Organizations," *Human Organization,* Summer 1962, 62–67.

SEASHORE, S. E., and BOWERS D. G. *Changing the Structure and Functioning of an Organization.* Ann Arbor, Mich.: Monograph 33, Survey Research Center, University of Michigan, 1963.

TRIST, E. L., and BAMFORTH, K. W. "Selections from Social and Psychological Consequences of the Longwell Method of Coal Getting," *Human Relations,* 4 (1951), 6–38.

VAN ZELST, RAYMOND H. "Sociometrically Selected Work Teams Increase Production," *Personnel Psychology,* 5 (1952), 175–85.

WALKER, CHARLES R. (ed.). *Modern Technology and Civilization.* New York: McGraw-Hill Book Co., 1962.

WHYTE, WILLIAM F. *Human Relations in the Restaurant Industry.* New York: McGraw-Hill Book Co., 1948.

Chapter 11

Human Factors in
Organization Change

THE PREVIOUS CHAPTER dealt with changes in technology, structure, and tasks. Harold Leavitt postulates that planned change involves a four-dimensional structure and that clearly "most efforts to effect change, whether they take off from people, technology, structure, or task, soon must deal with the others,"[1] as is shown in Figure 11–1. In this chapter,

Figure 11–1. Structure of Change

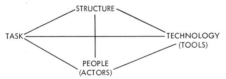

Source: Harold J. Leavitt, "Applied Organizational Change in Industry: Structural, Technical and Human Approaches," in William W. Cooper et al. (eds.), *New Perspectives in Organizational Research* (New York: John Wiley & Sons, Inc., 1964), p. 56.

the focus of attention will be upon the consideration of individuals and groups in the process of planned changes. Initially an examination of resistance to change is undertaken since resistance constitutes the basic reason that human factors enter into considerations for change. Then, factors influencing the ability or inability of managers to effect change are examined. Finally, successful and unsuccessful approaches to change are analyzed in the light of resistance and factors important to generating planned changes.

---

[1] Harold J. Leavitt, "Applied Organizational Change in Industry: Structural, Technical and Human Approaches," in William W. Cooper et al. (eds.), *New Perspectives in Organizational Research* (New York: John Wiley & Sons, Inc., 1964), p. 56.

REASONS FOR RESISTANCE TO CHANGE

There are many reasons why members of the business firm may resist organizational changes. Sometimes an individual may not understand how a proposed modification will affect him, and be reluctant to accept the change essentially because he is "afraid of the unknown." Or, his perceptions of the implications of some organizational rearrangement may be inaccurate, and he may unrealistically and erroneously assume that the new arrangement will somehow threaten the satisfaction of certain of his needs. In still other cases, a particular form of organizational redesign may pose a *real* threat to the individual, of which he is aware and does perceive accurately; and he may attempt to take some actions to prevent such an occurrence. Some of the more specific factors which may give rise to resistance to organizational change are now examined. For purposes of exposition, we will classify these as (1) psychological and sociological, and (2) economic.

Psychological and Sociological Factors

Disruption of Interpersonal Relationships. As was pointed out in Chapter 7, friendship cliques are frequently formed in firms as a means of meeting individuals' belongingness needs, and the formation of such groups is conditioned by the formal task and command structure of the organization to the extent that physical proximity facilitates friendship associations.

Sometimes organizational redesign will mean that individuals who have been in association with each other will be assigned to other tasks and relocated to other departments, thereby effecting a disruption of bonds of friendship and common social activities which have developed over a period of time. Separated from those co-workers toward whom he has developed positive sentiments, the individual may find himself placed in association with new and unknown colleagues, whom he may or may not like, or who may like or not like him. Such uncertainties as to how one will be accepted by, and "fit in" with a new work group can, quite obviously, pose a threat to the belongingness needs of the individual.

Threats to Status. Organizational change may also effect, or, at least, be perceived to be, a threat to the individual's status position, and hence to the satisfaction of his esteem needs. That such may be the case may be illustrated by an organizational change which took place in one large accounting department of a firm. In this department, the rapid turnover of clerical personnel made it necessary for supervisors to spend considerable time training new clerks as replacements. Part of this turnover was planned in that some college graduates were assigned to clerical positions for training purposes and to ascertain their capabilities for advancement within the accounting management hierarchy. Many of the other clerks were women whose turnover often resulted from marriage or pregnancy. Further, the firm was located in an area where an acute labor shortage existed and where worker mobility was often generally high.

Top management in the accounting department believed that some of the clerks were not being trained adequately and that an excessive amount of learning time was often being required before new clerks achieved satisfactory performance levels. As a result of this belief, it was decided to establish a special staff group within the department to train new clerical and other accounting personnel. This organizational modification was strongly resented by a number of the supervisors in the department. Seeing that the scope of their positions was being reduced by transferring their training responsibilities to the staff group, the supervisors perceived this change as reducing their status, and anticipated that they might, in consequence, be less highly esteemed by their subordinates and other managers in the organization. Top management in the accounting department had not anticipated this reaction by the supervisors. When the reasons for the reactions to the change became clear, however, an attempt was made to overcome the resistance. Arrangements were made for the trainers to work under the direction of a supervisor whenever any of his new clerks required training. This modification was perceived favorably by most of the supervisors, who felt that their "lost" status had now been regained.

Fear of Increased Responsibilities. Organizational changes may sometimes be resisted because individuals fear their own inability to handle the increased work responsibilities which such modifications may effect. It is for this reason that some nonmanagerial employees are reluctant to accept the job enlargement redesign approach which we discussed in Chapter 8. Such reluctance may be observed sometimes at the managerial level where an individual may balk at having the scope of his job expanded, or may even refuse to accept a promotion to a higher organizational level. In terms of the ideas which were presented in Chapter 6, individuals resisting such increases in responsibilities will tend to be those whose dependence needs are fairly strong.

Economic Factors

Members of the business organization may view organizational restructuring as a threat to their economic security, and hence to their physiological, safety, and esteem needs. Such fears are not without foundation, for technological changes have on many occasions resulted in (1) jobs calling for relatively high skill levels being replaced by lower skilled (and lower paid) work on more highly mechanized equipment, and/or (2) the total elimination of some jobs, accompanied by layoffs.

As organizations have grown, with the volume of their operations becoming sufficiently large to justify mass-production methods, increased specialization with the replacement of highly skilled jobs by those calling for fewer skills, has been common. Further, at the present time, considerable task restructuring is taking place in many firms due to automation. Although some newly created jobs in automated operations have called for *higher* skill levels than those required for many of the jobs existing theretofore, in many cases, however, the converse has been true.[2] In addition, at times considerable numbers of workers may be displaced by automation. In one electric power firm which expanded its operations by the addition of a new "automated" power plant it was reported that the man-power required in the new plant was about half the number which would be needed in the older plants to generate the same level of output.[3] Although no workers were actually displaced in this operation since the power plant constituted an *addition* to the firm's capacity:

> The effects of these reduced personnel needs are reflected in a greater feeling of job insecurity for the workers in . . . [the firm's] . . . older plant. These men recognize that technological developments will soon force them to acquire new skills or to supplement their present skills. . . .[4]

Viewing the American economy as a whole in the longer run, the assumption that technological change and automation leads to greater unemployment or lower pay levels can be questioned. As Peter Drucker has pointed out, from 1961 through 1964:

> . . . the blue-collar manufacturing jobs that automation supposedly devours have been growing particularly fast—by 1,600,000 altogether since 1961; that is, at twice the rate of the other job classes. There has been no drop in the past 10 or 15 years either in the proportion of the American labor force employed on the factory floor (a third of total employment in the country) or in the number of man-hours per week needed to get the nation's work done. The average weekly take-home pay of the factor worker is at

---

[2] For a discussion of the extent to which automation lowers as opposed to raising skill levels, see James R. Bright, "Does Automation Raise Skill Requirements?" *Harvard Business Review*, 36 (July-August 1958), pp. 85–98. Bright holds that although it seems "logical that automatic machinery does result in higher work-force skills. . . . despite a number of exceptions here and there, the opposite is a truer picture of reality."

[3] F. C. Mann and R. L. Hoffman, "Case History in Two Power Plants," in *Man and Automation: Report of the Proceedings of a Conference Sponsored by the Society for Applied Anthropology at Yale University*, as reprinted in Charles R. Walker, *Modern Technology and Civilization* (New York: McGraw-Hill Book Co., 1962), p. 168.

[4] Ibid., p. 169.

an all-time peak and likely to grow further in 1965 as a result of sharp pay raises in the new union contracts.[5]

However, in the short run, in certain specific companies and industries, numerous individuals have without doubt been adversely affected by technological change. Witness for example the chronic unemployment existing in areas dependent upon steel plants whose technology has become outmoded. Thus when mechanization and automation occur or are being considered, resistance to such changes is not unusual or irrational from the vantage point of the affected individual.

Not only does such resistance come from individuals, but also from work groups and from unions. Since union income is dependent upon the number of dues-paying members, union officers, both at the international[6] and local levels, may view changes which will mean lower levels of employment as a threat to their own (and the union's) economic security. Such threats are of special significance at the international level, of course, when technological changes portend the reduction of employment throughout an industry (e.g., the effects of dieselization of the railroads upon firemen). Further, union leaders may be under serious pressures to resist technological changes from their membership, for if they do not support member desires, they may lose their positions in the union at the next election of officers.

The reader should not infer from the above discussion that unions always resist organizational change; for, in fact, union leadership has sometimes given support to technological changes calling for worker displacement. For example, John L. Lewis, long the president of the United Mine Workers, considered technological change in the coal industry desirable since it would mean the removal of men working in undesirable coal mines and would permit an increase in productivity and pay of the mine workers. Although a considerable number of coal-mining jobs were eliminated, the average rate of pay of the miners who continued to be employed rose considerably as mine technology advanced under encouragement by the union. Thus, the union viewed technological changes in the industry as desirable in an overall, long-run sense, rather than considering each such change as a threat to employment in a particular mine at a particular time.

FACTORS INFLUENCING CHANGE

While some informal organizational adaptation to local problems is a natural and ongoing process in organizations, many of these changes

---

[5] Peter F. Drucker, "Automation Is Not the Villain," *New York Times Magazine*, January 10, 1965, p. 27. © 1965 by the New York Times Company. Reprinted by permission.

[6] National union organizations in this country are usually referred to as "internationals" since they may have members in Canada.

may be likened to patching up an unsatisfactory condition—temporary repairs that will eventually have to be encompassed by formal change. As shown in the preceding paragraphs, these changes are subject to a variety of resistances. To overcome resistance, several conditions must exist; the existence of a single condition is not sufficient to ensure that change will occur. Further, while discussing these factors below, it should be kept in mind that planned change is a *process* that occurs over time. The sequencing of the change process will be discussed after factors bearing upon the process have been discussed. A comparative summary of variables influencing successful and unsuccessful change is given in Figure 11–2.

Figure 11–2. Comparison of Variables Influencing Planned Change

Variable	*Successful Change Efforts*	*Unsuccessful Change Efforts*
Attitudes toward organization's status	Dissatisfaction with status quo, tension	Rigidity, complacency, or lack of awareness of problem
Support for change	Encouragement by high-level management present	Encouragement by higher level management absent
Change agent	Outside, prestigeful	Middle or lower level managers
Objectives of the change	Specific change objectives stated	Generally stated
Exercised power	Shared power from top to lower levels of management; power equalization	1. Unilateral top-management efforts or 2. Delegation of responsibility for change to subordinates
Sequence of change power	Common sequence of change efforts	Disjointed, illogical sequence of efforts

Dissatisfaction with Status Quo

It is extremely difficult to effect a change in an organization if the individual workers and managers do not perceive that a problem exists such that their efforts to achieve change will be worthwhile. They must experience *tension* or *dissatisfaction* to initiate change.[7] If top management is satisfied with a condition that some lower level management members feel could be improved, for example, the latter lower level

---

[7] A discussion of confrontation as a method to examine and bring into the open questions which may be causing dissatisfaction are shown in Robert R. Blake and Jane S. Mouton, *The Managerial Grid* (Houston, Texas: Gulf Publishing Company, 1964).

managers may not want to "rock the boat." They may recognize that their own perceptions are limited such that top management properly views other problems unknown to lower managers as more important. Thus, a perceived lack of total perspective may prevent their dissatisfaction with things as they are. It is, of course, possible for lower level managers to effect changes, but rarely if ever, *major* ones affecting large segments of the organization.

To illustrate how the need for a change may take place, the management of a firm manufacturing consumer products was apparently satisfied with its increasing sales and profit levels over a period of years. Finally, however, one of its board of directors related a conversation he had with his investment counselor who recommended that he switch his investments in the firm for which he was a director to a competitive firm. The counselor's reasoning was based on the faster growth and higher profit levels with a lower investment base that competition was achieving. This information from the director initiated a review of the position of the firm relative to its competitors. The study was prodded no doubt by a possibility that future planned new financing via common stock would suffer if the investment community was recommending sales rather than acquisition of its stock by investors.

The Cyert and March model[8] postulates that managers tend to deal with short-term problems and issues of limited and immediate scope unless serious issues face the firm. This view reinforces the concept that dissatisfaction or tension is a necessary precondition to a search for problems and solutions.

Support for Change

If higher level management does not actively support the change effort, its likelihood of achievement is greatly reduced.[9] There is less inclination for individuals to risk sticking their necks out to achieve change if there appears to be some chance that top management supports some other courses of action. Even if top management only appears neutral toward a proposed change, these attitudes suggest that behaviors other than those associated with the proposed change are more appropriate. Only if members of the organization perceive reward toward changed behavior is the change likely to be achieved. The Pennsylvania and the New York Central Railroads merged in 1968 and a number of unsatisfactory operating conditions existed as a result. Different safety systems prevented locomotives from one line to run on the other. Different billing systems and different computer systems of the two lines as

[8] Richard Cyert and James March, *A Behavioral Theory of the Firm* (Englewood Cliffs, N.J.: Prentice-Hall, Inc., 1963).

[9] Larry E. Greiner, "Patterns of Organization Change," *Harvard Business Review*, 45 (May–June 1967), pp. 119–30.

well as many other duplications of services existed in the premerged companies and remained until the merged Penn Central went bankrupt in June 1970. The conditions generated a great deal of dissatisfaction in the organization but were not changed until top management in the form of a new president[10] started reform in July 1970. Top management had previously focused upon real estate, financial, and governmental guarantees rather than upon operating problems. Lack of higher level managerial attention and support will usually frustrate change efforts even if dissatisfaction with present conditions is otherwise widespread.

It is interesting to note that the information necessary to induce dissatisfaction with the status quo is often available in an organization, but if that information is not congruent with what top management perceives the situation to be, it can lie dormant, ignored, or even refuted. General Dynamics lost over $450 million in its ill-fated entries into the commercial jet market with its 880 and 990 series of aircraft. At one time, an analyst at a relatively low level in General Dynamics accurately foresaw what a debacle the company was getting itself into and recommended the company terminate its contracts, take penalties, and get out at a cost of $50 million in losses. This information was at such a variance with the goals, expectations, and hopes of management that it was ignored. Similar warnings of impending catastrophe were available to the managements of NASA concerning the space capsule fire, to Lockheed about its C5A cost overruns, and to Douglass concerning its DC-8 problems. If this information had been acted upon by top mangement, change could have been effected to minimize many of the resulting dysfunctional operations. Instead of investigating the validity of the information, several of these analysts were fired and others discounted. Top-management recognition and support for change is, obviously, important to effect change.

Shared Power

Top management ordinarily is unable to make a decision to change unilaterally and arbitrarily because the success of the investigation necessary to focus change efforts and the success of implementing change is dependent on a large number of people.[11] Thus for effective change

---

[10] Note that, in this case, the change agent was a member of top management so that dual roles of support for change and the change agent are played by the same individual. This condition is not unusual for a large company or division of a firm.

[11] Leavitt, "Applied Organization Change," proposed "power equilization" rather than shared power. Whether higher and lower levels do or should have equal distribution of influence over change actually cannot be determined from available data on change efforts. Warren C. Bennis in his *Changing Organizations* (New York: McGraw-Hill Book Co., 1966), also points out that planned change entails mutual goal setting, leading to the equalization of power eventually (p. 83).

participative methods such as those discussed in Chapter 7 are important.

The efficacy of this approach under certain conditions has been demonstrated by several research studies. For example, in an experiment conducted by Coch and French at the Harwood Manufacturing Corporation, slight changes were made in the job content of four different groups of employees.[12] Three of these groups were permitted to participate in deciding how the jobs were to be redesigned; in the fourth (control) group, no such participation opportunities were provided. In the control group:

> Resistance developed almost immediately after the change occurred. Marked expressions of aggression against management occurred, such as conflict with the methods engineer, expression of hostility against the supervisor, deliberate restriction of production, and lack of cooperation with the supervisor. There were 17 percent quits in the first forty days. Grievances were filed about the piece rate, but when the rate was checked, it was found to be a little "loose."[13]

In the experimental participative groups, on the other hand, no workers quit their jobs in the first 40 days after the task changes had been introduced, and their average productivity *increased* over what it had been prior to the task restructuring.

As was mentioned in Chapter 7, the participation approach, notwithstanding its usefulness, may not be effective when the individuals concerned do not have the knowledge or skills to help make decisions or when they are apathetic or hostile toward management. Additionally, the efficacy of the participation approach can be seriously questioned in cases in which the necessary organizational changes pose a real, serious threat to the group—e.g., when, say, half of a group knows that they will lose their jobs, and the other half knows that their jobs will be downgraded due to a technological change. In the Harwood experiment, none of the workers was threatened by either loss of job or downgrading of skill levels—as mentioned previously, the changes in job content were only minor ones. Thus, conditions probably more conducive to the participative approach existed at Harwood than would be found in many cases where technological change necessitates job redesign.

Furthermore, management cannot simply delegate all of the authority to institute change and expect that the change effort will be successful. Complete delegation implies to participants in the change process that the innovation is not important enough to warrant top management's attention. It is thus perceived as indicating a lack of complete support for the proposal by top management. In general, the optimal distribution of power in the change process appears to be one in which complete

---

[12] Lester Coch and John R. P. French, Jr., "Overcoming Resistance to Change," *Human Relations*, 1 (1948), pp. 512–32.

[13] Ibid. Quoted by permission of *Human Relations*.

delegation and authoritarian approaches are to be avoided while sharing power is highly desirable, if not necessary.

Presence of a Change Agent

A further factor central to generating change in an organization is the presence of a proponent for the change to act as a catalyst to the process of moving from the present situation to a new one.[14] To spearhead the change and to obtain cooperation, the change agent must be prestigious; his expertise should be recognized and accepted. For this reason, lower and middle-level managers ordinarily do not make good change agents even if they are supported by top management. Many successful change agents are from outside the organization. William Moore, who took over the presidency of Penn Central, had a distinguished record at Southern Railway and in straightening out problems at the St. Louis Terminal Railroad Association. He had prestige and top-management support. Well-known consultants from reputable firms and professors from prestigious universities have been successful as change agents.[15]

When an outsider enters a situation ripe for change, he often is unable to perceive anything different from what is already known by someone in the organization. The comment is often made that the consultant "didn't tell us anything we didn't already know." Yet, he can be effective by providing a new conceptual perspective, and a new way of thinking about the problem to enhance dissatisfaction. He can bring additional expertise and experience, and, with top-management support, can sometimes push more effectively for change. While he cannot ramrod change and expect it to be accepted, part of the attractiveness of an outside change agent is that the people do not have to work with him after the change is completed.

CHANGE PROCESSES

Similar to the process of acquiring a college education, a major planned change in an organization is not something that occurs overnight but rather is a process that is only successful over a period of time. During change, furthermore, distinctly different kinds of processes are

---

[14] Bennis, *Changing Organizations,* for example, states: "The process of planned change involves a *change agent,* who is typically a behavioral scientist brought in to help a *client system,* which refers to the target of the change" (p. 82).

[15] Some of the classic studies providing data most relevant to organizational change has come from professorial sources. See, for example, S. E. Seashore and D. G. Bowers, *Changing the Structure and Functioning of an Organization.* (Ann Arbor, Mich.: University of Michigan Survey Research Center, 1963); and Robert Blake et al., "Breakthrough in Organization Development," *Harvard Business Review,* 32 (November-December 1964), pp. 33–55.

taking place. The purpose of this section is to identify these processes as well as to show their natural sequence.

Gene Dalton, in an excellent summary review article of the research concerning the dynamics of change, postulates an extension of Kurt Lewin's change process model.[16] Lewin held that change consisted of a three-step process:[17]

Dalton extends this by adding "the introduction of a change agent" as a second step. In addition, he identifies four separate components or subprocesses which are effected at each of these four stages of the change process. His model is summarized in Figure 11–3 and provides the basis of much of the following discussion. It should *not be assumed* that if this model is followed, successful change will occur—it is only suggested that the *probabilities* of more effective change will be *higher*.

The Change Process in General

Unfreezing. When a system is in equilibrium with its environment, the internal structure and the external forces impinging upon the organization are in balance. In an equilibrium state, the internal structure is differentiated to accommodate the environmental components with which it must deal and the internal subsystems are harmoniously related to each other. If a change relevant to the firm (e.g., the development of a greatly improved competitive product) comes into existence, the equilibrium is disturbed. Such disturbances when recognized and evaluated destroy the internal harmony, creating dissatisfaction with the status quo in the organization and with its relation to its environment. This dissatisfaction unfreezes previous attitudes and behavior, making it possible for change to occur. As the competitor's new product gains sales volume at the expense of a firm's current product line, for example, the salesmen's attitudes toward customers and the company of which they are a part would tend to change from complacency to concern and dissatisfaction with the current situation. Unfreezing is thus seen to encompass a growing sense of dissatisfaction and lowered self-esteem over a period of time.

---

[16] Gene W. Dalton, "Influence and Organizational Change" first presented (and later published) as a paper at the Conference on Organizational Behavioral Models, Kent State University, May 1969. Also reprinted in C. Dalton, P. Lawrence, and J. L. Greiner, *Organizational Change and Development* (Homewood, Ill.: Richard D. Irwin, Inc., 1970).

[17] Kurt Lewin, "Group Decision and Social Change," in T. M. Newcomb and E. L. Hartley (eds.), *Readings in Social Psychology* (New York: Holt Rinehart & Winston, Inc., 1958).

Figure 11–3. A Model of Induced Change

Tension Experienced within the System	Intervention of a Prestigious Influencing Agent	Individuals Attempt to Implement the Proposed Changes	New Behavior and Attitudes Reinforced by Achievement, Social Ties, and Internalized Values—Accompanied by Decreasing Dependence on Influencing Agent
⟶	Generalized objectives established	Growing specificity of objectives —establishment ⟶ of subgoals	Achievement and resetting of specific objec- ⟶ tives
Tension within existing social ties ⟶	Prior social ties interrupted or attentuated ⟶	Formation of new alliances and relationships centering around⟶ new activities	New social ties reinforce altered behavior and attitudes ⟶
Lowered sense of self-esteem ⟶	Esteem-building begun on basis of agent's atten- ⟶ tion and assurance	Esteem-building based on task accomplishment ⟶	Heightened sense of self-esteem ⟶
⟶	External motive for change ⟶ (New schema provided)	Improvisation and reality-testing ⟶	Internalized motive for change ⟶

Change Agent.   After an interval of time during which tension and lowered self-esteem have been increasing, a change agent can be effective in initiating progress toward planned change. The change agent serves several functions. He may provide the new perspectives within which the problem can be attacked and give the specific overall objectives toward which the change will be directed. He may provide a galvanizing central focus and attention. As a result of his insertion into the situation, past relations with peers and subordinates may be disrupted helping to sever behavior associated with unsatisfactory prior performance. His appearance may provide members with some "hope for the future" and, as a result, an increased level of self-importance which had deteriorated in the unfreezing stage of the change process. For example, when a new plant manager took over one extremely unsuccessful plant in a large corporation, the lack of prior success had led some managers in the plant to believe that they might be made the scapegoat for past failures. Morale was low and apprehension about the future was high. The new manager identified the problem primarily as one of cutting cost and asked for help in solving the plant's problems. Managerial morale immediately improved as a realization that a challenge to improve the situation was being offered. Cutting cost was the overall goal describing in particular terms the previous lack of success.

The Change Process Itself. Following unfreezing and the introduction of a change agent, the actual changing of behavior may take place effectively. The specific plan of attack on the problem outlined by the change agent needs to become detailed goals toward which members of the organization instrumental in carrying out the change will direct their efforts. Successfully explicating goals is undertaken within the framework of shared power described above. That is, participants at lower levels of organization become involved in examining overall objectives, how they can be achieved by specifying subgoals and how their actions will need to be altered in order to accomplish their own subgoals. Participation in these processes is accompanied by *improvising* solutions and *testing* their effectiveness while developing new behavior patterns. Disassociation with past behavior, associates, and attitudes complements the working out of such a change process. This severance helps to assure change by reinforcing the inadequacy of past performance.

In one unsuccessful change effort, a new manager of methods and industrial engineering was brought in to help bring about improved operational efficiency and lowered cost of production. He hired professionals to redesign the operating systems thought necessary to implement these goals, but rather than improving morale in the operating units, morale decayed. Cooperation between the professionals and managers responsible for carrying out the changes was lacking because change was imposed rather than being worked out together. Because of the lack of specific operating knowledge on the part of the professionals, the new system designs often overlooked the realities inherent in the production processes. The overall efforts failed to achieve anticipated goals.

Refreezing. After successfully exploring and testing the means of effecting the changes, refreezing hopefully takes place. This step of the process involves reinforcing those new behaviors and attitudes that are resulting in achieving the goals of the change. The experiences in the changed system may even result in reevaluation of the goals and their levels to elevate or deflate aspiration levels. As noted, there appears to be a tendency of greater success in the change efforts if individuals are able to take the concepts of change suggested by the change agent and to improvise with them in his own way in applying new procedures. As the process unfolds, a reinforcement of the relation between the expected behaviors and the new goals hopefully takes place and as success is achieved, morale tends to improve.

This process is one not limited to organizational change. For example, success or failure of school children to learn at satisfactory rates depends to some extent upon the reinforcing of the school learning behaviors in their home environment. If the attitudes toward learning in the home are apathetic or negative, the probability of low school performance and the creation of "problem children" for the school are increased. Refreezing school behavior is not accomplished. As another example, prisoner rehabilitation efforts toward acceptable societal behavior can be frustrated if, upon release, the prisoner returns to an environment in which his "new self" is not reinforced. The ex-prisoner tends to lapse into preprison acts if his postprison environment encourages it. The need for the individual to try the new behavior in his normal environment and to achieve success with it is critical to continued success of the change effort.

Specific Processes in Change

While the general nature of the change process has been outlined above, achieving success in such efforts involves a complex of movements from the condition existing before change to the different resultant condition. The purpose of the following sections is to deal with these necessary components of the change process:[18] (1) specific changes in objectives, (2) the social system, (3) the attitudes of individuals in the organization towards themselves, and (4) the acceptance of the formal change by members of the organization.

Change in Objectives. The objectives of a planned change process evolve from overall goals of the change agent to more specific subgoals of participants. The major *focus* of the changing goals moves from the change agent to the participants. After changed behaviors are tried out and evaluated, a finalization of these specific goals may take place.

If, in the conceptual framework originally provided by the change agent, the objectives for the change are not provided, altered rational behaviors are not possible. No new goals for change implies that previous goals and behavior are satisfactory. Yet even if the overall goals for the proposed change are set forth, they tend to be too general to guide participant behavior toward new directions. By allowing participants to help specify subgoals, the system achieves the concreteness needed. It also provides a personal investment by the participants in the total process.

Socialization Movements. As was shown in Chapter 7, individuals tend to assume social as well as task relationships so that existing social ties and friendships constitute contributing factors to the resistance to change. As ultimately the tasks and technology of the workplace change,

---

[18] Dalton, "Influence and Organizational Change."

so, too, do the organization structure and the relations among individuals (see Figure 11–1). After structure and task alterations have been achieved, cementing the new social relations is aimed at reducing the resistance stemming from former social relations. Then the new social relations may help reinforce the individual internalization of the new required tasks. Thus the alteration of social arrangements is seen to be an important component of the change process—social evolution during the process can aid and help refreeze desired individual and group behaviors.

Change in Self-Esteem. It was noted above that in the equilibrium of a system with its environment, the internal forces of the system tend toward harmony so that when dissatisfaction and tension (preconditions to change) set in, the members may experience a lower sense of their personal worth. Upon the insertion or emergence of a change agent, however, perceptions of their self-image tend toward improvement because the dissatisfaction has some chance of being alleviated. In successful changes, this enhanced feeling of self-esteem continues to improve as a result of working out their processes of change and implementing them. Upon the completion of a change effort, therefore, perceived self-esteem tends to rise to higher levels as accomplishment and success provide a vehicle for self-expression. It should be noted that if the self-esteem of participants remains low during the change process, these attitudes indicate less than acceptable change performance in that the process of change is progressing in such a way that participant support for an activity directed toward the change is endangered. Successful change appears to be accompanied by movement from low to higher self-esteem.

Internalization. As indicated above, a change can be initiated because of the dissatisfaction brought about by an internal disharmony, or a perceived incongruence of the organization's operations with the environment. To managers and individuals in the affected systems, this need for change may often be perceived as that of top management or the change agent and is not one of their own selection or making. Initially they tend to view it as coming from the outside, but as a successful shared change effort proceeds, it becomes more of their own creation. As they set specific goals, generate solutions, test and implement them, the formerly perceived external impetus hopefully moves toward one in which individuals accept the changed conditions as their own. As the new behavior is accepted and reward for it is received, a reinforcement of this internalization process helps maintain changed behavior.

To ensure success, the internalization process—acceptance of the changed activity as one's own—needs to be reinforced by the environment in which the participant works and acts. Individuals, who in college accept new values, beliefs and life-styles alien to most parts of society, find that to maintain these new orientations successfully over time that they must join subcultures or groups with members possessing similar orientations. More religious converts, too, remain converted if they join churches, thus helping to reinforce their beliefs. The new work situation including peers and superiors need to be supportive to the desired behavior change if that behavior is to be internalized.

Success and Sequence. There is some logical and empirical evidence[19] that in order for a change to be most successful it must (1) exhibit the preconditions to change, (2) follow the sequence in the change processes noted above, and (3) fulfill the suggested directions of objectives, socialization, self-esteem, and internalization within the processes. To illustrate, if a proposed change agent attempts to set general goals prior to the creation of tension and dissatisfaction with the status quo, he will likely be unsuccessful in generating any interest in the change or he may merely be spending his time creating the precondition to change rather than working on the change itself. If he expends his personal efforts and prestige in the organization creating this dissatisfaction, furthermore, he is less likely to be able also to act as the change agent itself. Omission of the unfreezing process prior to introducing the change agent is dysfunctional in achieving alteration in the expected direction. More generally, an illogical sequencing of the processes of change, the failure to provide necessary preconditions, or a failure to achieve the indicated direction of alteration in the subcomponents in the process will jeopardize change. In his study, Greiner states: "In the successful change patterns, we observe some degree of logical consistency between steps, as each seems to make possible the next. But in the less successful changes, there are wide and seemingly illogical gaps in sequence."[20]

CHANGES IN THE STEADY STATE

In Chapter 4, the tendency of open systems (such as organizations) to move toward an equilibrium in which the organizational components are in harmony with each other and their environment was noted. A second tendency toward improvement in the equilibrium position of an open system was also explained. This latter tendency, to improve, reflects the goal-seeking orientations of man—the striving to achieve some end(s). In effect, the *improvement* of steady state means that the ratio of inputs to outputs has decreased and the system is more efficient in using its resources.

In Chapter 5, the process of learning was described. Man is both achieving and versatile. If a general goal for a task is assigned to an individual such that his specific behavior is not set forth, a reasonably

---

[19] Greiner, "Patterns of Organization Change," and Dalton, "Influence and Organizational Change."

[20] Greiner, "Patterns of Organization Change," p. 125.

skillful individual (in relation to the task) will be able to solve problems associated with achieving the generally stated goal. Different approaches are tried, rejected, accepted and altered in the process of adaptation of the general capacities to achieving the goal. As these behaviors become successful, the efficiency with which the individual performs the task increases because relative unsuccessful approaches are rejected in favor of better ones. Learning takes place. Even if versatility is not needed or wanted because of highly restrictive constraints to the task, learning to perform such a highly structured task takes place.

As learning occurs by individual participants at all levels of an organization, change obviously occurs. To some extent, this kind of change is natural and goes on without plans for specific alteration. Managers can, however, enhance the rate that improvement in this steady state of organizational achievement will occur. Guidance and reinforcement of successful behavior are two processes that influence the rate of improvement. Learning can be dysfunctional as well as beneficial. An office supervisor, given little training for managing and only general output goals, could exercise authoritarian leadership indiscriminately and successfully in the short run. This approach may be dysfunctional if the tasks and worker capacities suggest that these conditions are more appropriately managed by participative approaches. If the supervisor has some initial success as an autocrat, however, this behavior will be incorrectly reinforced. Ultimately relearning will be required if he remains on the job. Guidance and training, together with reinforcement of appropriate long-run rather than short-run behavior would increase the rate of improvement in this case. Thus guidance and the reinforcement of behaviors by higher level managers is important in the rates of organizational learning that is experienced.

A careful observer of an organization may note striking changes in its operations from one period to another. There may have been no major changes in the environment, the technology, or the available resources, that would have been cause for formal change in any sense other than the "natural" learning process described above. These evolutionary changes suggest that certain aspects of organizational learning need to be predicted so that proper planning can take place. When new models are introduced to an automobile assembly line, for example, it is important to know the rate of learning for the assembly operations in order to predict the delivery and sales volume that will be possible during different periods of time over the course of its production. In large shipbuilding, aircraft, and space vehicle programs, the work in process inventory can become enormous. The ability to predict learning rates allows a prediction of cash and, therefore borrowing needs to finance the inventory.

Organizational learning is a synergistic combination of processes, not simply the additive effect of individuals' learning. New machinery may be introduced, new procedures for dealing with problems are developed, and new methods of operations introduced. The cumulative impact of these kinds of processes results in improvement of the steady state equilibrium position of a system such that the organization, rather than remaining stationary, appears to be moving always toward higher levels of achievement. The reason that organizations by improving their efficiency do not achieve higher output levels (e.g., higher rates of profits) is that they are in competition with other organizations undergoing similar improvements. Even if an organization improves its efficiency, it may become less successful if competitors are improving at more rapid rates.

SUMMARY

Change is a continuing ongoing process in viable organizations. This natural and sometimes informal process can accurately be described as organization learning, a combination of efforts at individual learning and general improvement efforts. Major changes, in contrast, are conscious efforts to alter important aspects of the functioning of a system or subsystem. Important to success in achieving major change are conditions of dissatisfaction with current operations, support of higher level management for the change effort, and existence of a prestigious proponent of the change. Change may be a lengthy process. Successful attempts appear to be characterized by the sharing of influence to make alterations with the individuals directly affected by the change and a clarification of the problem by a statement from the change agent as to the specific overall objectives of the change.

The change process is complex, consisting of a series of distinctly different kinds of activities being undertaken. If change is successful goals become specified at the lower levels of organization, social ties are altered, individual self-esteem levels increase and internalization of change goals and new behavior takes place. Altering the steps in the change process or failures to achieve change in these subcomponents of change introduce serious doubt that the overall objectives of the change can be accomplished.

DISCUSSION AND STUDY QUESTIONS

1. For what purposes is the concept of organizational learning useful?
2. Explain and describe the changes in the perceived self-esteem of individuals in an organization as influenced by the successful change process.
3. Needed change in an organization is a rational process which considers the factors relevant to the need for change. As a consequence of the rationality involved, highly educated individuals in status positions in an organization tend to recognize the need for change to a greater

extent than do the ordinary worker with a lower educational and status level. Discuss.

4. X Company was approached by an inventor who had developed a process to produce continuously and relatively cheaply a product that had similar properties to the company's major product which was relatively expensive per unit. Management purchased rights to use of the patent on the process and proceeded to design a plant. To gain cooperation, it took its plans for replacing the old with the new product to the union which noted that much of the skill formerly required to produce the old product would no longer be required. Further, many fewer workers would be needed on the new process. In light of the decreased skills in the new jobs, less wages would need be paid if the new plant were to be competitive with those that competitors undoubtedly would be building. Management offered the new jobs at new wage rates to the workers in the new plant at the same location.

The union demanded that the new jobs carry the same job classifications and wages as the old process. In this way, workers with high seniority would not lose income. Further demands were made but not seriously maintained by the union. The company was unable to dissuade the union from its position. Ultimately, the company built the plant in a distant location employing newly hired workers to staff it. Wage rates were competitively established in relation to job skills required. The old plant eventually was closed as the new product replaced the old. The obsolete plant was closed.

Were the management and union socially responsible? Did management create conditions conducive to change?

5. "As president of this company, my job is to develop people to carry the many responsibilities associated with modern progressive management. Each manager worth his salt must be tested under fire. Joe Campbell, while he hasn't had much responsibility as yet and has only been with us a short time needs this testing experience. I am putting him in charge of revamping our sales organization and sales compensation policies. If he can do this job on his own without interference, we'll know that he has high potential in this firm." Evaluate.

6. "As a successful consultant, my function is to go into a situation that management wants changed, push through the change, take the criticisms that might otherwise be directed toward management, get my fee, and get out, fait accompli." Evaluate this statement in the light of your knowledge of change.

7. Which of the following are consistent with successful planned change in our organization? Explain.

   a) Random sequence of change efforts.

   b) Shared power.

   c) Creation of a happy satisfied work force.

   d) Initiation of change before resistance to it can be galvanized.

8. One of the reasons that our products are not competitive on the world market is the difficulty and expense of our industry keeping up technologically with our competitors in other countries. Our union demands

most of the savings from technological change as increased wages or as termination payments to workers laid off as a result of the change. Under these conditions, many changes are uneconomical or maintain our labor cost so high that our prices in the world markets are not competitive. Evalute.

9. One executive states, "I like to make a continual series of changes in tasks and structures going on so that individuals in the organization become accustomed to and receptive to changes. Then when a need for major change arises, we won't have trouble with resistance to change." Evaluate.

10. Some effects of the "student revolution" in U.S. universities and colleges have been successful in creating change in spite of opposition from trustees and top management. Explain this success in light of the preconditions and the change process outlined in the text.

11. Given the conditions for and the processes involved in successful planned change in an organization, how could you, starting after graduation in a new position, initiate successful change in operations that only you and a few compatriots perceive as dysfunctional to the firm as a whole?

12. If change is inevitable, how can an organization that has been operating in a relatively stable and certain environment over a long period of time adapt to change when it happens?

SELECTED REFERENCES

BENNIS, W. D.; BENNE, K. D.; and CHIN, R. (eds.). *The Planning of Change.* New York: Holt, Rinehart & Winston, Inc., 1961.

BLAKE, ROBERT R.; MORTON, J. S.; BARNES, L. B.; and GRIENER, L. "Breakthrough in Organization Development," *Harvard Business Review,* 42 (November-December 1964), 133–55.

BRIGHT, JAMES R. *Research, Development, and Technological Innovation.* Homewood, Ill.: Richard D. Irwin, Inc., 1964.

CARTWRIGHT, DORWIN. "Achieving Change in People: Some Applications of Group Dynamics Theory," *Human Relations,* 4 (1951), 381–92.

CHOWDRY, KAMLA. "Management Development Programs," *Industrial Management Review,* 4 (Spring 1963), 31–40.

DAVEY, NEIL G. "The Consultant's Role in Organizational Change," *MSU Business Topics,* 19 (Spring 1971), 76–79.

GUEST, ROBERT H. *Organizational Change: The Effect of Successful Leadership.* Homewood, Ill.: The Dorsey Press, 1962.

LAWRENCE, PAUL R. *The Changing of Organizational Behavior Patterns.* Boston: Division of Research, Graduate School of Business Administration, Harvard University, 1958.

LEVY, S., and DONAHUE, G. "Exploration of a Biological Model of Industrial Organization," *Journal of Business,* 33 (October 1962).

LIPPIT, RONALD; WATSON, JEANNE; and WESTLEY, BRUCE. *The Dynamics of Planned Change.* New York: Harcourt, Brace, & World, Inc., 1958.

LIVINGSTON, J. STERLING. "Pygmalion in Management," *Harvard Business Review,* 47 (July-August 1969), 81–89.

McMURRY, ROBERT N. "The Problem of Resistance to Change in Industry," *Journal of Applied Psychology,* 31 (December 1947), 589–93.

PHILIPSON, MORRIS (ed.). *Automation Implications for the Future.* New York: Vintage Books, 1962.

ROSS, PAUL R. "How to Deal with Resistance to Change," *Harvard Business Review,* 32 (May-June 1954), 49–57.

SANFORD, RALPH S., and BAILEY, EARL L. *The Product Manager System,* Experiences in Marketing Management, No. 8. New York: National Industrial Conference Board, Inc., 1965.

SHILS, EDWARD B. *Automation and Industrial Relations.* New York: Holt, Rinehart & Winston, Inc., 1963.

TAYLOR, GEORGE W. "Collective Bargaining," *Automation and Technological Change* (ed. JOHN T. DUNLOP). Englewood Cliffs, N.J.: Prentice-Hall, Inc., 1962.

WOODWARD, JOAN. *Industrial Organization Theory and Practice.* London: Oxford University Press, 1965.

Chapter **12**

Planning

THE PURPOSE of this chapter is to focus on one type of decision process—that involving planning. Planning consists of a series of decisions that take into account probable future states and commit resources and activities in an attempt to maximize the operations of the organization at that future period. Management ordinarily cannot make radical changes in current operations or the direction of the firm in the short run. To change work force levels, the size of a plant, the products it will produce, the overall quality of its products, or similar actions that might appear desirable can only take place over time. They cannot occur overnight. Hindsight about what a company should have been doing is only obliquely relevant for planning. While minor adjustments can be effected rapidly, the rate of practical change depends largely upon the effectiveness of planning preceding the time that the change is to take place.

Planning involves estimating the future values of environmental variables, the probable change in these variables, and the decisions the firm should make in light of these changes in order to meet its goals. Because of the uncertainties in these estimates and because the profit returns from decisions made in the planning process are only realized in the (distant) future, the discounted information *value* of planning can be quite low. For this reason, long-range planning is sometimes resisted. In firms with a relatively stable environment, moreover, the estimates and the decisions to accommodate them would possess little surprise content, information, or information value. At the other extreme, a highly volatile environment would be difficult to estimate, the accuracy of estimates being subject to a good deal of questioning by managers in the organization. These limitations to the planning process are slowly being overcome as better planning methods develop.

DEVELOPMENT OF PLANNING

Some descriptive studies of business operations have concluded that managers are more likely to be adaptive to current conditions than be

344

attuned to long-run eventualities.[1] To the extent that competitors behave according to short-run expectations, a manager is provided an opportunity for outflanking them if he seizes the opportunities provided through planning. George Steiner concludes that a number of firms are placing increasing importance on long-run planning, strategy formulation, and goal setting. He sees in modern corporations a professional planning expert emerging with greater organizational power, reporting to or a part of top management, and overseeing an expert planning staff. His conclusions, noting that planning is becoming an "indispensable and indivisible part of the process of managing"[2] contradicts those noted above. Learned and Sproat state, however, that these latter conclusions suggesting that managers pay little attention to long-range planning efforts are more accurately applied to decisions of middle than top management.[3] Viewing these studies in perspective, then, corporations appear to be moving toward more upper level formal corporate planning efforts, keeping planning activities as a line manager's responsibility while supplementing these efforts with staff planning expertise.

RATIONALE FOR PLANNING

The economic, political, technological and social environment within which managers make decisions is a partially ordered one. Social and economic acts of today are predicated, in part, upon what happened in the past in the environment. Events ordinarily do not occur randomly but depend upon past events. To the extent that one may perceive the time dependency of events, he can isolate cause-effect relationships through historical analysis. By applying them to relevant current events and assuming stable relations, predictions about the future can be made. Forecasting the future can often provide a better than random estimate of states and conditions. Forecasts thus provide information, but that information does not have any value unless it increases the utility to the firm.[4]

Forecast information could have utility if it showed a future potential problem for the company *and* if a decision were made to prevent the potential problem from becoming a real one. It should be noted that the plan is (in this case) a decision to overcome a potential problem.

[1] Richard M. Cyert and James G. March, *A Behavioral Theory of the Firm* (Englewood Cliffs, N.J.: Prentice-Hall, Inc., 1963). They characterize the firm as an *"adaptively rational* system" rather than an *omnisciently rational* system" (p. 99). Further, firms tend to seek solutions to current problems or those of the "immediate future" (p. 121).

[2] George Steiner, "Rise of the Corporate Planner," *Harvard Business Review*, 38 (September-October 1970), 139.

[3] Edmund P. Learned and Audrey T. Sproat, *Organization Theory and Policy* (Homewood, Ill.: Richard D. Irwin, Inc., 1966), p. 94.

[4] Supra, chap. 4.

If no decision were made until the problem event occurs, a decision at that time may be incapable of avoiding the problem. The forecast per se, thus, possessed no utility. Hence, a decision taken to overcome an anticipated problem is one form of a plan, but awaiting the event and reacting to it is not planning—that is expediency. Some firms have failed to provide for their president's replacement, for example, until he leaves, even though the event had been well known in advance.

Forecast information can also possess value if it shows formerly unperceived opportunities for profit *and* if the firm plans so as to take advantage of these opportunities.

In the transistor field many firms saw the possible replacement of ordinary semiconductors if MOS technology could be developed. A handful of firms placed a major research effort and several were successful to find acceptable methods for designing and producing these new products. A perception of a potential need does not constitute a plan. Only decisions taken to exploit that opportunity can be considered as a plan.

Both preventing potential problems and exploiting opportunities are examples of plans dictating change. Furthermore, a forecast may possess value if it suggests no change and if there has been some probability (without the new information) that the company would have changed its course. After all, the manager's tendency to continue into the future as he has in the past is not a certainty; it is only probable. Without foresight about the effectiveness of future operations, management cannot be confident that its current strategy and policy are appropriate for the future. For example:

A machine tool manufacturer, Cincinnati Milacron, had always followed the policy of producing the major components for its products rather than subcontracting them. With the development of numerical controls replacing human-mechanical control machine tools, the company reiterated its view by developing a new and different capability for designing and producing electronic equipment—quite a different technology than formerly required. Competitors, meanwhile, adopted a subcontracting strategy, thereby allowing them to deliver numerically controlled machines earlier while Cincinnati was losing $10 million developing its electronic capability. Cincinnati Milacron believed its strategy[5] correct in spite of short-term setbacks, since the electronic portions of machine tools constituted up to 25 percent of the total costs of numerically controlled machines. Not only would it lose the profits on a quarter of the business to subcontractors but also it would be unable to provide rapid repair or troubleshooting experience if it opted to split electronic and mechanical expertise. Ultimately its strategy was successful in producing numerically controlled machine tools. Further, the electronic capability allowed

[5] For a more detailed exposition of Cincinnati Milacron's activities, see Allan T. Demaree, "Kicking the Doldrums at Cincinnati Milacron," *Fortune*, 82 (December 1970), 72 ff.

the firm to diversify to bring out a line of minicomputers for new uses and markets.

The example shows that by forecasting the future nature of the machine tool industry, the company was able to adapt its long-term strategy to best capitalize on the opportunities in that market. While the basic policy of producing "in-house" remained the same, changes in capabilities were required to adapt to the changing market.

In general, then, planning is rational behavior if planning decisions result in an increase in expected utility by means of avoiding problems and unwarranted change and by exploiting opportunities.

COROLLARY PLANNING

The main planning efforts of a firm will be directed toward establishing a set or several sets of plans to take actions anticipating forecasted conditions. Ordinarily, planning would focus on the most important and highest value outcomes. It is uneconomical to plan for every eventuality. At the same time, unanticipated events occur and conditions that, at one time, appeared only remotely possible actually do come to pass. In addition to the major planning, corollary planning efforts can be useful. Corollary plans can take a preventive and a contingency form.[6]

Preventive planning focuses on the potential causes of failure in the main planning effort and takes action to minimize dysfunctional results. In planning for a major space vehicle engine, the design, schedules, specifications, desired performance, and a host of other components related to the vehicle constitute the major planning effort. At the same time, no matter how well-designed the system may be and no matter how carefully purchasing and fabrication may be, the complexity of the engine creates a network of interdependent components such that the failure of one can adversely affect the performance of many other components and the success of the mission. As a result, many preventive measures are undertaken as insurance against failure. Strict quality control and testing programs are examples of preventive plans. Similarly employee training programs can be used to help ensure "doing it right the first time."

Planning redundancy into systems is another common approach in preventive planning. To help ensure that an airplane will not suffer electrical failure due to lack of power, auxillary power systems typically consist of multiple generators independently isolated from each other so that the failure of one generator will not cause undue reductions

---

[6] Charles A. Kepner and Benjamin B. Tregoe, *The Rational Manager* (New York: McGraw-Hill Book Co., June 1965) make the distinction between preventive and contingency plans indicating that both should be used to ensure success of a mission. See their Chapter 11 for a detailed exposition of these views.

in electrical service. Of course, redundancy costs money and the value of a large safety factor is traded off against decreasing the probability of failure.

Contingency plans are established to be used if the original planning effort is no longer appropriate. In some few instances, planning can irrevocably commit the company to a cause of action. If states of nature or competitive conditions different from those estimated to happen do occur, a contingency plan offers a reasoned alternative consistent with the less likely event. Contingency plans also can be made to ensure a degree of success even if preventive plans are not successful. For example, in spite of redundancy in design, failures in parts of the auxillary electrical power in airplanes could occur. In that event, contingency plans dictate that priority is given to flight safety power uses while passenger comfort would be given a somewhat lower priority until those emergency conditions no longer exist.

PROGRAMMING

Programming: The Degree of Detail

Another problem which the decision maker faces is that of determining the degree to which his plans should be programmed—i.e., the degree of precision and detail in which his planning statements should be spelled out.

Under certain conditions it may be advisable for management to develop highly programmed courses of action. Such is almost invariably the case in *close tolerance* situations in which only a small margin of error from some precise specification is permissible if management's objectives are to be met. For example, highly programmed plans are required in the design and manufacture of many electronic components for this reason.

In other cases, however, more generalized planning statements may serve managerial objectives more appropriately. There are at least two reasons why this is so. First, the lesser planning time and costs required for their design may more than offset any advantages which might be gained from developing highly detailed plans. Or, to put it another way, the marginal value of highly detailed programs in terms of objective attainment may be less than the marginal costs of their development. For example, a salesman, in planning a sales presentation to a potential customer:

1. May increase his probability of making the sale considerably if he spends some time in advance outlining his presentation in general terms (as opposed to going in to see the customer "cold"), but

2. May be able to increase the probability only slightly (if at all) by spending many hours in developing a highly programmed word-for-word sales talk.

Since this time could be utilized to call on other customers, the salesman's objectives might be best met by developing generalized planning statements rather than either (1) highly programmed ones, or (2) none at all.

Second, the utilization of generalized, rather than highly programmed, planning statements may be advisable in order to permit *flexible* responses to problem situations when the plans assume the form of *instructions* from the manager to one or more of his subordinates. That is:

1. Under conditions of risk or uncertainty, in which the manager cannot foresee all possible states of nature and/or competitive strategies which may influence the appropriateness of a subordinate's actions (and hence, cannot design adequate sets of statements covering all contingencies),
2. Spelling out in great detail the actions that the subordinate should take rather than allowing him some degree of judgment within the framework of a generally specified plan, may *bind him* to behavior which is inappropriate.

For example, the authors have observed some industrial trainers being bound by their superiors to highly detailed "canned" presentations in management training conferences which "fell flat" because little or no consideration was given to the responses of the training groups involved. Much more effective in such programs is for generally specified training plans to be worked out in advance, permitting the instructor to use his own judgment in responding to any unforeseen reactions of the group.[7]

Programming: The Human Variable

Although highly detailed programs such as that in the above example may be ineffective because they place the subordinate in a "straight-jacket" and do not permit him the flexibility that he needs in order to behave appropriately, there are also dangers involved in developing instructions for subordinates which are too generally programmed. This is because instructions which are too generally specified may not be understood by the subordinate, and/or because he may not have the ability or psychological inclination *to fill in the details* of the plan necessary for its implementation.

Just how highly programmed any instructions should be will, of course,

---

[7] Assuming that the instructor has the ability to respond appropriately in such situations.

vary from situation to situation. As we pointed out in Chapter 6 in discussing leadership directiveness, three classes of variables—the personality of the leader, that of the follower, and the nature of the situation —must be considered in relationship to each other in determining how highly detailed instructions aimed at evoking desired follower responses should be. The complexity of the decision problem, the costs of failure, the ability of the subordinate to "fill in" generally specified programs, his dependence and independence needs, the overall philosophy of the organization toward "general supervision" must be taken into account in the programming of planning statements which are to serve as sets of instructions to subordinates.

TIME HORIZONS IN PLANNING

A number of different values may be obtained by the organization from effective planning efforts.[8] Underlying all of these, however, is one basic function which planning activities serve to perform—to help increase the probability of occurrence of those future activities which must take place if the firm's objectives are to be attained. Suppose, for example, that a firm has just finished developing a new product and wants to be able to sell 10,000 units of it eight months hence. If this objective is to be met, a multitude of appropriately sequenced activities will have to be completed prior to the sale of these units, some of which are illustrated in Figure 12–1. Moreover, these activities will obviously not "just happen," nor is it possible for many of them *to occur immediately* upon management's decision that it wants them

Figure 12–1. Sequence of New Product Activities

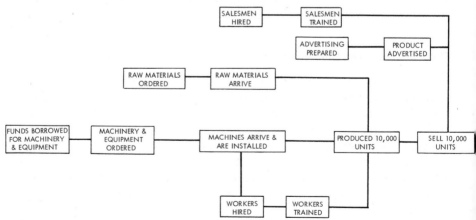

---

[8] See Stewart Thompson, *How Companies Plan* (New York: American Management Association, Inc., 1962), pp. 24–25.

to occur. Rather a considerable amount of advanced planning must be undertaken if the firm's sales objective is to be achieved.

Such planning must recognize several factors: First, *lead times* will be required for the acquisition of the resources necessary for the production and sale of the product. The new machinery needed for the manufacture of the product may not be ready for use until four or five months after it has been ordered; a lead time of two or three weeks may be required for the acquisition of raw materials, and so forth. Certain activities cannot be initiated until others have been completed—e.g., the firm's new product cannot be manufactured until after its employees have been trained; the training cannot begin until after the employees have been hired, and so on.

In effect then, the attainment of the firm's objectives requires planning the design of *means-ends-means chains over time.* As is illustrated in Figure 12–1, attainment of the worker training sub-subobjective, which must be planned prior to its occurrence in April, for example, serves as a means toward accomplishing the manufacturing subobjective which, in turn, serves as a means toward attaining the sales objective.

Second, if a plan involves an investment in capital equipment, planning should extend over the interval of *capital recovery.* If the market for a product line will disappear in five years, investments in equipment that will not be recovered from it before that time need be avoided. We will discuss capital recovery in greater detail in Chapter 15.

Third, if a firm sells durable goods for use by others, a further consideration is the time *span of use* of that equipment by the firm's customers. If customers using a machine tool tend to replace that equipment after eight years, planning to develop products to meet those replacement needs appears rational.

A further factor influencing the time horizon over which a firm's planning might extend is the expected *availability of raw materials,* related somewhat to lead time as discussed above. For a company producing women's dresses, cloth, thread, and notions can ordinarily be delivered in a few days. In contrast, an oil company, in drilling, refining, and distributing, may require 10 years to acquire supplies consistent with its anticipated sales volumes. Planning to ensure the refinery and marketing resources ought to be consistent with its drilling and production plans. The lumber and extractive industries are especially needful of long planning horizons. For example, it takes 25 to 100 years to grow a tree.

Some of these time intervals occur sequentially rather than simultaneously. The period of capital recovery would not necessarily start until the lead time for design and research for a product had been, at least partially, completed. The same sequential relationship does not necessarily apply to a dressmaker since equipment, space, and skilled employees may readily be available in some locations (e.g., the garment district in New York City). Except for anticipating customers' needs for replacement, the dressmaker's planning periods can be quite short and the planning intervals occur simultaneously rather than sequentially. These relations are shown in Figure 12–2.

Figure 12–2. Planning Horizon Determination

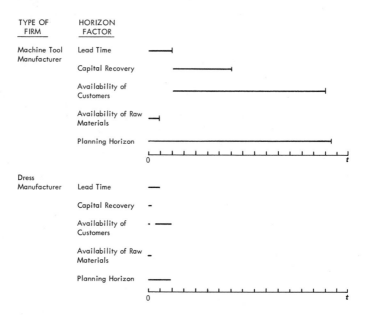

An additional factor influencing the practical length of a planning period is the time value of money. Rationally one should plan if the future expected values as discounted back to the planning period exceed the cost of planning. Assuming that a firm's discount of future earnings is 8 percent per year, a planning effort that saves $1 million at a time 10 years in the future is only worth $149,000 today.[9] As the discount rate is increased, the optimal period over which plans extend would decrease. This factor also influences the type of activities for which planning is done in that it tends to focus long-range attention toward major projects. It is the increase in expected future returns that justify planning. Small-scale and small expected returns as discounted to the present often cannot support their planning costs.

There is managerial resistance to planning for long time periods if there is little confidence in the forecasts upon which the planning depends. As the length of the forecast period increases, the amount of information in the forecast tends to decrease and the error in the estimate increases. If a forecaster is unable to predict any better than a mere

---

[9] A more detailed explanation of present value techniques is given in Chapter 15.

extrapolation of current trends, there is no surprise value and no information in his forecast. Even if extrapolations are avoided, the success of a forecaster may be no better than a random choice. If so, such a forecast contains no information above that already possessed by the organization. Justification for the first time in planning efforts often are made on the faith that it is necessary to start planning, even if poorly done initially, to gain experience in the method and the ultimate benefits. If forecast and planning errors are reduced, confidence to implement plans to extend the planning horizon then increases.

THE REPETITIVENESS VARIABLE

Planning theorists frequently distinguish between *single-use* plans which are designed to deal with unique problems and *standing* plans which are geared toward providing responses to *repetitive* situations. Most of the observations made in the preceding sections have application to both of these two types of plans, although we have not explicitly treated the planning for recurring decision problems. It will be the purpose of this section to discuss some of the special characteristics of standing plans.

Types of Standing Plans

Most business organizations rely on many different kinds of standing plans to aid them in their decision making. Some of these are made up of rather broad, generalized planning imperatives—as is the case with many basic company *policies,* such as the following:

1. We will not discriminate in employing personnel on the basis of race, religion, or color.
2. It is the policy of our (retailing) firm to sell only the highest quality products.

To implement policies such as these as well as to deal with other specific repetitive decision problems, business firms will also design a multitude of more highly programmed statements—in the form of *rules, procedures,* and *methods.* As a means of implementing the employment nondiscrimination policy mentioned above, for instance, the following imperative might be formulated: "When interviewing a prospective employee do not ask him about his religious or ethnic background." A few of the many other kinds of rules, procedures, and methods commonly utilized by business firms are cited below:

1. Employees on production lines frequently are required to follow highly detailed work methods often developed by industrial engineering.

2. Practically all companies have developed a number of rules by which their employees must abide such as reporting to work at specified times, and no smoking in hazardous areas in the plant.
3. Most firms rely on various standard operating procedures. For instance, union employees having grievances should first bring their problems to the attention of their shop stewards; customer refunds in a supermarket must be handled by the store manager; employee claims for medical benefits under the firm's insurance program must be processed by the personnel department, and so on.

Such standing plans, like single-use plans, may be stated as either imperative or conditional planning statements. For example:

1. The above-mentioned statement requiring interviewers to refrain from asking prospective employees about their religious or ethnic backgrounds is of the imperative form.
2. Some firms have developed conditional shop rules specifying that when an employee is absent from work without excuse, he shall be given an oral warning *if* it is his first such offense; a written warning *if* it is his second such offense; and so on.

Thus, standing plans are similar to single-use plans in that they may be programmed to varying degrees of detail and in imperative and/or conditional form.

Values of Standing Plans

There are several advantages which may be gained from the utilization of standing plans. We will now examine three of the more important of these.

First, the design of such plans provides the manager with *relief from decision making*, which provides one type of simplification of the complex as discussed in Chapter 4. That is, the manager does not have to take time out each time a repetitive situation occurs to decide how to handle it—standing plans provide him with pre-programmed *decision rules* which he can apply whenever called for. For instance, the development of vacation policies by a firm—e.g., if an employee has been with the company 1 to 10 years, grant him a two-week vacation; but if he has more than 10 years' service, give him a three-week vacation—serves to relieve its managers of the task of deciding just how many days of vacation each of their subordinates should be granted each year. In short, the design of standing plans simplifies the whole decision-making process by transforming problems of the type: "when x occurs, *decide on* how x is to be handled" to ones of types such as: "When x occurs, do y"; "When x occurs, do y if condition a exists, but if condition b exists, do z"; and so on.

Second, by *routinizing* many decision problems through the utilization of decision rules, standing plans provide an important vehicle for delegating responsibility to lower levels in the organization. For example:

In the absence of any decision rules for deciding upon the quantities of parts and materials needed by a manufacturing plant to be purchased, all ordering decisions may have to be made by the materials manager, or by one of his managerial assistants. With the availability of a quantitative model specifying how many units should be purchased at any given time, however, it may be possible for clerical help in the department to handle the ordering simply by plugging appropriate figures into the model, carrying out the calculations called for, and following the courses of action so generated.[10] Or, as is being increasingly done by business firms with such programmable decision problems, the standing plan may be programmed on a computer, thus obviating the need for human calculations.

Finally, standing plans provide a means of obtaining *uniformity* in the handling of like decision problems. The development of standardized work methods and procedures, for instance, helps ensure that all units of production turned out on the assembly line will meet the same specifications. Or, the design of uniform accounting procedures makes it easier for management to compare operating results from one department to another. Moreover, uniform responses to recurring situations also may serve to provide equitable treatment to either the firm's customers or employees. For example:

1. The vacation policies mentioned above help ensure that favoritism will not be shown to certain employees—e.g., *all* employees with more than 10 years' service are granted three weeks vacation annually.
2. By developing standardized payment schedules, health insurance companies treat all of their customers alike. For instance, whenever the insured or a member of his family undergoes a tonsillectomy, he or his doctor may be paid $100; for all appendectomies, $200; and so on.

Problems Involved in Designing Standing Plans

Notwithstanding their values, there are a number of problems which may be encountered in the design and utilization of standing plans. First, as with single-use plans, such planning statements, if either too generally or too highly programmed may be either ineffective or actually lead to the creation of problems for the organization. Policies which are very generally stated, and not implemented with more specifically detailed rules and procedures may be, in effect, quite meaningless. This is sometimes true with respect to companies which proclaim themselves

---

[10] We will illustrate the application of models of this type in Chapter 18.

as "equal opportunity" employers in their basic policy statements, but which do nothing to see that discrimination is avoided in their employment practices.

At the other extreme, highly programmed standing plans may force organizational employees to be inflexible in their responses to certain decision problems. For example, many instances have been cited of the statutory and administrative requirements that call on civil servants to follow a number of highly detailed rules, regulations and procedures in handling governmental problems.

Additionally, requiring employees to follow highly programmed statements may lead to monotony and boredom on the job and a thwarting of the higher level needs. As we pointed out in Chapter 5 concern has been raised about the number of jobs in today's business organizations which are routine and call for the application of only a few simple skills—jobs which, in terms of our conceptual framework in this chapter, are structured around sets of highly programmed statements, and which leave little room for employee judgment and ingenuity.

Finally, a problem which probably exists in all organizations to some extent is that standing plans may continue to be relied upon even though the conditions which led to their design no longer exist and the plans are no longer needed or appropriate. The authors have frequently observed, for instance, executives continuing to receive reports, accounting data, and other forms of written communications, which were perhaps once useful to them, but which have become unnecessary due to changing conditions within the organization. Such inertial tendencies to continue to follow prescribed methods, rules and regulations (often due largely to individuals' resistance to change) render it important for the firm to review its standing plans periodically.

HIERARCHY AND PLANNING

Plans at any level of the organization are dependent upon the planning undertaken at organization levels both above and below it. In a product division of a corporation, planning may be constrained by top management's plans in several ways. If the corporation as a whole has established a 15 percent return on investment as one of the corporate goals, it is not likely that lower level approval could be gained to build a new cost-reduction facility if its anticipated return is less than the 15 percent goal. Similarly, the development of a new product discovered in the laboratory of one division of a firm may more appropriately be produced in the facilities of another division; and top management would require this to be done.

To illustrate hierarchy further, assume that the product division in a firm is organized so that functional departments (e.g., engineering, production, marketing and finance) report to the divisional manager.

Planning for the division would also be constrained by the lower level plans of the functions. For example:

One goal in a product division of the firm is to grow in sales volume at a 9 percent yearly rate. During one planning session the territorial sales managers were asked to estimate the volume by product they expected to generate during the planning interval. When summed for the division, the estimates were well below the 9 percent goal. Detailed review of the basis for sales estimates showed that in many territories the division's share of the market was so high that continued advances at a 9 percent rate would be extremely costly or incapable of being achieved. To reach the 9 percent sales growth, the division plans were altered to encompass the lower growth estimates and to introduce new product lines so as to approach the overall sales goals. Territorial sales plans had the result of changing higher level plans, hastening the process of introducing new products.

Since the scope of positions at the top of an organization exceeds that of lower levels, the planning at top levels reflects that broader scope and importance. Some planning at lower levels, furthermore, cannot proceed rationally until some guidelines or premises have been previously set forth from above. A production manager needs sales estimates by product by time period and inventory level limits set from above before he can establish rational work force levels and plant schedules. Furthermore, functional plans in order to coordinate with each other require *common* premises from which to plan. If engineering, sales, and production departments are using different product sales forecasts, as an example, the plans of these separate functions will not smoothly interface.

The level of organization at which the planning is taking place ideally is related to the time span being covered by the planning. Top managers

Figure 12–3. Short- v. Long-Range Activities by Management Level

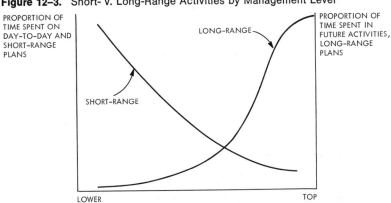

Note: These relations are normatively desirable rather than accurate representations of what managers do. See George Steiner, *Top Management Planning* (Toronto: Collier-Macmillan, Canada, Ltd., 1969), p. 26.

would tend to devote a lesser proportion of their time to short-range plans than would a first-line foreman. Most of the work with which a foreman might deal would encompass a relatively short time span covering days or weeks. Conversely, formal top-management planning would (except in emergencies) rarely encompass time spans of less than a month or a quarter. More typically, top-management planning would encompass multiple-year decisions. (See Figure 12–3.)

OVERALL CORPORATE PLANNING

Since, as indicated previously, the planning at all levels and throughout all functions of an organization is partially determined and constrained by the planning that is done at the top, it will be useful to examine comprehensive planning processes as they might logically be carried out at the corporate level.

Goals

In Chapter 2, the fundamental factors bearing upon establishing goals were identified: the values held and the social responsibilities embraced by top management who are involved in the process of establishing overall corporate objectives, the profit levels necessary for remaining viable, and the externally imposed constraints from the environment.

A firm's objectives rarely can be set arbitrarily at the mere whim of top management, even though there may be considerable latitude both in the nature and the level of goal attainment. A high return on investment objective, while desirable from the view of managers and stockholders, may prove incapable of fullfillment as competitors cut prices or customers refuse to buy. Conversely, setting a lower-than-average profit goal may risk attacks upon management by rival aspirants to top management or by other firms who seek to take over the firm in the belief that high profits can be attained. Similarly, a goal to gain in sales volume at the rate of 50 percent per year would probably be unrealistic within a stable industry. Although some firms have attained such a rate of sales growth, either the base from which the growth was made was small or the increase was unable to be sustained within the industry over time. The range of practical goal levels are, therefore, constrained by competitive acts and other threats (e.g., managerial security).

Further, the level at which a goal can be attained is dependent upon the level of other goals and constraints which the firm attempts to achieve. The president of one firm established a two-year goal deadline for cleaning up all water pollution from its plants. Several division managers reported that this objective could be gained but only at the expense of failure to meet the level of profits expected during the next two years. One vice-president estimated that both the profit and the anti-pollution goal could be achieved if the clean-up period were extended to four years. In spite of these tradeoffs and apparent inconsistencies between goals, the president elected to maintain both original goal levels hoping to spur efforts so that any degradations in performance would be minimized. The combined efforts were mostly realized.

Establishing a set of goals for the firm provides the basis for generating other types of plans. Logically following the setting of goals is strategic planning, to which attention will be turned next.

Strategy

A corporate strategy (as distinguished from a plan) consists of a set of interrelated decisions setting forth the *major* methods the firm will follow to achieve its goals. While a business may establish such multiple objectives as removal of pollution, an 18 percent return on assets and an 11 percent rate of yearly growth, these goals could, conceivably, apply equally well to a number of companies. (Both a grocery retailer and an electronic manufacturer could meet them.) Strategic plans form a pattern to identify the type of business(es) the firm will engage in as well as the general approaches the company will employ in meeting its goals. Thus, a strategic plan will provide the business boundaries within which the firm's resources will be employed. A rational strategy will, as well, exclude opportunities and behavior outside its intended scope.

Product-Market Components of Strategy. A complete set of strategic plans consist of several components. One of these is a determination of the products that the company will sell together with the markets into which the firm will attempt to distribute them. There are four basic product-market strategies available to a firm. The following section describes these and the conditions that suggest employing one strategy over another. Figure 12–4 illustrates these four strategies.

First, if a firm is seeking high rates of growth and profitability, it

Figure 12–4. Strategies of the Product-Market Component

Market \ Product	Present	New
Present	Market penetration	Product development
Future	Market development	Diversification

Source: Adapted from H. Igor Ansoff, *Corporate Strategy* (New York: McGraw-Hill Book Co., 1965), p. 109.

is less likely that it can continue selling its present products to the same customer group. Even if its share of sales to present customers is low, growth through increased *market penetration* (increased share of products sold in the market), is limited over time. Yet a market penetration strategy is relatively inexpensive. No product research or new marketing techniques are needed; only a more intensive selling effort is required. During early stages of corporate life, this strategy may well be the best one. For example, a regional chain of retail novelty stores may decide to extend from its limited geographical coverage toward national coverage. Note that the chain's operations remain basically similar—purchasing, merchandising, promotion, resource acquisition and other activities remain (except for their scope) quite similar to what they have been previously. For this reason, market penetration is considered a "safe" or conservative strategy. Often, considering the firm's capacities, it is the best as well.

Second, if market penetration proves incapable of providing sales volumes or margins anticipated by goals, the firm may consider selling its current line of products to new kinds of customers. An airplane producer may try to expand from the military to the commercial market. A computer manufacturer may attempt to establish a foreign marketing organization. To accomplish new *market development* requires a capability in marketing and promotion. Selling to airlines requires a different marketing expertise than does selling to the military.

A third alternative product-market strategy is to develop new products or services to sell to the firm's current clientele. Sears has been successful in moving into insurance, art, and mutual funds through such a *product development* strategy. The company's type of customers remain basically the same but new products and services are developed to appeal to them. Successful development of new products is a rare art. Less than one fourth of all new products brought to the market are successful. Similarly, research and development projects to develop new products have an even higher casualty rate. A research and developmental capability together with economic and marketing expertise is needed to create and evaluate potential products early enough so that large losses are not incurred by the inevitable failures.

The fourth, and riskiest, product-market strategy of all is *diversification*. While the motive for such a strategy is often to eliminate risk and profit variability by developing products with offsetting cyclical patterns, success in diversification requires both a development of a new marketing expertise as well as a new product research capability. If either fails, the strategy cannot attain expected results. Of course, associated with diversification's riskiness may be high potentials. The lure of exploding sales and profits from new technologies have resulted in fantastic fortunes as well as bankruptcies. (Compare IBM and RCA in the computer business, for example.)

Relative Expertise. A second component of a comprehensive strategy is the determination of the areas in which the firm's relative expertise lies. At one point in its planning, General Mills concluded that its capabilities for creating and promoting consumer products via mass media consisted of one of its basic strengths. Whereas this capacity had been applied to promoting food products in the past, the skill was considered applicable to a wide range of consumer products. At the same time, its technological and production skills were considerably weaker. As part of a diversification program, therefore, the company sought products which required a low technological and production capability but which were susceptible to mass-promotion methods. This determination of strengths and weaknesses led the company into several businesses of which one was the toy business in which it became a major seller.

In the General Mills instance, a determination of the product came *after* a judgment was reached about where the firm's strengths and weaknesses were. Without some relative advantage, the organization can rarely hope to meet goals set at high levels. If competitors possess relative advantages it may well be that the firm with no special expertise will be unable to survive. Thus, rational strategies need to *seek and exploit* the peculiar strengths the firm possesses. Further, if an organization finds that it has no relative superiority over competitors, development of some special expertise would appear warranted. For example:

After World War II, airplane manufacturers found dwindling orders and reconversion from a huge war effort resulting in idle facilities and work forces. Some companies attempted to diversify by designing and producing aluminum boats, pots and pans, or similar products. While airplanes are made of aluminum, these types of attempts were basically failures since the relative expertise for airframe manufacturers consisted of sophisticated engineering, complex production capability, and selling to military markets, strengths hardly applicable to the simpler consumer products under development.

Even though a firm possesses no relative expertise, the potential attractiveness of entering a new domain may be so great that risk taking for the development of that expertise appears warranted. RCA invested huge resources and over 10,000 people in the computer business, for example. Since some complementary advantage might be expected between its electronic business and computer manufacture, the match appeared particularly attractive. Yet the relative marketing and technological expertise possessed by RCA seems to have been lacking because it later abandoned what proved to be an unprofitable operation. In contrast, Xerox bought Scientific Data Systems to acquire an already successful computer expertise. Acquisition of small, scientific engineering-oriented technical firms by established organizations provides a ready technical expertise. If the acquiring firms possess complementary marketing and financial skills, the combined advantages can be substantial.

In new technical areas, many small aspiring firms may emerge. Acquisition of one or more of these can become complex as each may have different advantages and several offers from other acquiring firms. The question of how much to pay to ensure acquisition is critical. Alternatively, technological forecasting is often attempted to identify important future developments so that expertise can be developed and used to exploit the possibilities. This is because active research may precede successful marketing by many years (with color television it was over 10 years).

Synergy. In seeking new products or services through which the firm will meet its goals, a third component of strategy to consider is that of synergy. Ansoff defines synergy as "a measure of joint effects."[11] It results from the use of common resources such that utility is gained at a lesser cost than if the resources were duplicated. Synergy is often spoken of as the "2 + 2 = 5" idea or in systems terms, the "whole is greater than the sum of its parts." One example of this is a cooperative agreement of the airlines whereby spare parts that are infrequently used are stored and replaced from a central pool. Rather than each airline carrying expensive spares rarely needed, a synergistic inventory reduction is effected through the joint pooling effort.

If a company adds products to its line such that they require a different type of plant, different research and development as well as different distribution, little synergy other than financial and, perhaps, management synergy may exist. Financial synergy almost always results from such a combination since the cash reserves and other financial resources required in the larger combined firm is almost always less than the sum of those required for the separate companies.

Synergy can have negative as well as positive effects. In the combination of the New York Central and the Pennsylvania Railroads, the initial management synergy apparently was negative even though overhead reduction was a goal of the merger. Attempts to apply common operating rules, computer routines, and other management systems became so cumbersome and unwieldy that its deliveries and schedules became chaotic, constituting one element that forced eventual bankruptcy. Management teams from both of the original firms attempted to gain power and to force their systems and will upon the other. Negative synergy is a danger if incompatible systems are merged.

The concepts of sales, production, research, financial, and management synergy is somewhat related to determining a firm's relative (dis)advantages. For example, an oversize plant causing excessive depreciation, utility costs, and tax expense can be considered a disadvantage for producing a firm's products. The excess capacity could be an advantage,

---

[11] H. Igor Ansoff, *Corporate Strategy* (New York: McGraw-Hill Book Co., 1965), p. 75. Ansoff's book represents one of the most lucid and logical expositions of strategy formulation.

however, if the products of a newly acquired firm were consolidated with the old.

Analysis of synergy, products-markets, and relative expertise form interrelated components of strategic planning. Obviously, many companies do not make these planning analyses since they result in expensive continuing costs stemming from a staff of strategic planners. Without strategic plans, however, a firm runs the substantial risks of missing opportunities for profit or growth and the risks from unanticipated threats to its performance. Strategic plans provide the focus of where the firm's activities should take place as well as cricumscribing the boundaries of its efforts.

Goal-Strategy Interdependency. The establishment of a high level of profitability above the level that a corporation has achieved in the past will create a gap between corporate aspirations and performance. If this gap is perceived as a problem to its management, a search for new products or new applications of products in other markets may well be a result. The more extensive this search becomes, the closer will the management tend to accomplish comprehensive strategic planning incorporating not only the product-market component implied above but also the relative expertise and synergy analysis. Goal setting is thus seen as suggesting strategic planning.

If a corporation has undertaken a comprehensive strategic analysis and the results incorporated in maximizing expansion to diversification opportunities, it may conclude that it will still be impossible for the firm to meet its preestablished goals. If this happens, a possible conclusion would be that the objectives have been established at too high a level. It is in such an instance that strategy affects a reevaluation and realignment of the objectives of the firm.

Strategy-Structure Relations. Once the strengths, weaknesses, opportunities, and pitfalls have been determined and translated into an acceptable strategy, the decision and organization structures of the business need to be adapted to accommodate the grand strategy. One firm concluded that, in the light of its competencies and the probable growth of potential market that it would be advisable to enter an entirely new product area in which it had little production or research technology. Rather than to spend the time and money to build these capacities internally, the company decided to acquire them through purchase or exchange of stock with some existing corporation possessing the desired abilities. This decision to acquire, in turn, required the formation of an organizational acquisition unit to screen and evaluate possible candidate businesses with which they might combine. The product decision triggered a study resulting in the methods to be used for acquisition and the criteria a candidate firm must meet for acquisition. As we showed in Chapter 8, organizational differentiation is appropriate whenever environmental or task differences are significantly separate from those already existing. It should be emphasized that internal expansion as well as acquisition (as in the above example) may lead to significant task and organizational differentiation.

Periodic Plans to Implement Strategy. After a strategic plan has been developed to show the future nature of businesses the firm will undertake, decisions about how it fits into the present activities, the expertise that will be needed, and assignments to implement the strategy will be required. If, for example, an acquisition program is decided upon, the financial officers will need to determine whether outright purchase of assets, acquisition through exchange of stock, or other methods will be the most effective method of financing. Other assignments to uncover and screen candidate firms for acquisition and to recommend procedures for integrating activities of disparate components of new organization's into current operations might reasonably follow.

These assignments could be incorporated into the regular periodic long-range planning of the firm. The periodic plans most visible to middle- and lower level managers often takes the form of an operating budget for a yearly quarterly or monthly period. At higher levels of organization, however, these current periodic plans are being fashioned to take account of the decisions previously made and incorporated into a plan for a longer period. Five-year planning is not unusual at the corporate level. Carrying out a program to increase the number of college graduates hired in a particular year may merely reflect those needs imposed by a strategic decision made five years ago to enter a new market.

In one survey, 69 percent of the reporting firms indicated periodic plans of five years or less, with longer range planning for particular projects extending further into the future than their regular planning as these projects required.[12] The long-range planning period in American corporations appears to be lengthening as the proportion of firms engaging in planning over longer periods increases.[13]

PLANNING: COMPLEXITY AND UNCERTAINTY

While some might consider planning as a rather straightforward decision process, it is far from easy or simple. Rather, at a corporate level, it tends to be extremely difficult. The difficulty stems from the complexity and uncertainty associated with long-run planning decisions. A comprehensive plan for a corporation is often complex since a great many variables are being considered simultaneously. The information concerning relationships among variables may be severely lacking in spite of the direct influence such variables might have upon a firm's operations.

---

[12] George Steiner, *Top Management Planning* (Toronto: Collier-Macmillan, Canada, Ltd., 1969), pp. 21–25.

[13] Ibid.

The plans of a competitor to build a new plant for the purpose of producing a newly developed product exemplifies the type of information that is important but not readily available to a corporate planning effort.

The risks of error from complexity and uncertainty in planning tend to be higher for those companies whose future acts depend upon advancing the state of technology. Lockheed's C5A transport was developed, but its original costs estimates failed to include unanticipated developmental expenses. Two hundred percent cost overruns, schedule deficiencies, or performance degradations, are evident in other developmental type of projects (e.g., the SST, the operation system for IBM's 360 computers, the SABRE system and Rolls Royce's engines for the air bus). In contrast, large-scale multivariate projects whose technology is known can more easily be brought in at anticipated cost and schedules[14] (e.g., the Ford Mustang).

In large-scale projects whose subsystems must proceed simultaneously and independently, technological uncertainty may increase the difficulty of matching the parts into a whole. In a new rocket, the flow of fuel may cause unforeseen vibration and stability problems. In producing an ocean liner, the technology is much better understood so that design of interfaces between fuel and stability would tend to disrupt plans to a lesser extent than would be the case for a technologically new system.

While complexity and uncertainty tend to dominate planning at the corporate level where comprehensive planning is undertaken, less complexity and more certainty is associated with lower level functional and departmental planning whose premises are decisions already made at higher levels. Planning at lower levels also tends to extend over shorter periods of time so that estimates of the future can be made with greater precision and detail than is reasonable at higher levels. A departmental planning process may be little affected *directly* by external events. The planning for a tooling department depends typically much more upon activity going on in the departments it serves than in the environment external to the firm. The lower level departments tend to view their environment as the other departments in the organization rather than external states of nature or competitive acts.[15] Significantly it is just as important that the subdepartments know the planning going on in the "in company environment" as it is for overall corporate planners to be aware of the external environment. The former suggests a need for an internal information system; the latter presupposes intelligence and forecasting systems.

---

[14] Malcom M. Jones, "Management Problems in Large-Scale Software Developmental Projects," *Industrial Management Review,* 11, (1970), pp. 1–15.

[15] This may be more the case for certain departments in organizations than in others. For example, first-level sales managers may need to know much more about their competitors' actions than first-level production supervisors.

In the light of the differences between planning at the bottom and the top of an organization, it may appear that the nature of the decisions at these two levels require different skills, abilities, and techniques. To some extent, this is probably true, but the purposes served are similar: overcoming anticipated problems and taking advantage of heretofore unseen opportunities.

SUMMARY

This chapter has examined the reasoning behind decisions of a planning nature together with some descriptive materials explaining that both periodic and standing plans have a hierarchial nature. The more widely embracing and all-encompassing plans tend to be made at higher levels in the organization. Further, these comprehensive plans tend to constrain and determine the content of lower level plans. Planning in excessive detail over long periods of time is shown as dysfunctional since the costs of such plans tend to exceed their values.

Plans are decisions setting forth standards of performance and behavior expected in some future time period. The worth of these decisions can only be evaluated as performance can meet or exceed the levels anticipated by the plans. The process of making these evaluations of performance relative to plans is called managerial control, the subject of the following chapter.

DISCUSSION AND STUDY QUESTIONS

1. In Chapter 9, the tendency of an organization to isolate and protect the core technology of an enterprise from environmental variation influencing it was noted. Does planning contribute to this isolation process? Explain.

2. Does establishing goals for a firm determine available strategies for the firm or does a strategy, once selected, determine what goals the firm can attain? Or both? Explain.

3. Other things being equal, the value of planning is less for a firm making high rates of profit than for one experiencing low-profit rates. Comment.

4. In speaking of his long-range planning efforts, a president of his firm noted that most critical to the firm's success was the future acquisition of processing equipment. Considerable time was spent with equipment suppliers, their efforts to refine equipment, and research in processes development. Evaluate this planning effort.

5. Compare the relative expertise required if a firm were to exercise a product development rather than a market development strategy.

6. Highly structured plans and the use of a complex set of standing plans, rules, and regulations is appropriate in an uncertain and complex situation. Comment and evaluate.

7. A worldwide oil firm exploring, producing, refining, and distributing petroleum products had generated a large cash flow and was in a position to expand or diversify by developing new businesses or acquiring already existing firms. The company was evaluating an opportunity to exchange common stock with a firm producing and selling oil field equipment throughout the world. The equipment firm sold drilling equipment and supplies, automatic pumping and distribution systems, and provided consulting services to petroleum firms. What synergistic effects (positive and negative) might be involved in this potential merger?

8. Preventive plans are more applicable to internal operations while contingency plans are relevant corollary planning efforts to meet externally imposed conditions. Comment.

9. Planning may provide new information, but the decisions about what fields or directions the firm will enter may be the same as they were without planning. Comment.

10. While an estimate of the future may possess an extremely high information content, it may have no information value. Comment.

11. "I have just seen some population estimates showing a declining birthrate and a change in the proportion of boys born relative to girls. Since I make diapers, some of this information is important while the other is not." Comment.

12. Firms don't look very far ahead and plan for the future until they get into trouble and are forced to do so. Comment.

13. If a situation facing a firm is relatively stable and certain, planning is mostly a waste of time. Comment.

14. If uncertainty about the future is high, planning will mostly be a waste of time. Comment.

SELECTED REFERENCES

Ackoff, Russell L. *Concept of Corporate Planning*. New York: Interscience Publishers, 1970.

Bright, James R. (ed.). *Technological Planning*. Boston: Harvard University, Graduate School of Business Administration, 1962.

Chandler, A. D., Jr. *Strategy and Structure*. Cambridge, Mass.: The M.I.T. Press, 1962.

Drucker, Peter F. "Long-Range Planning: Challenge to Management Science," *Management Science* 5 (April 1959).

Gilmore, F., and Brandenburg, R. G. "Anatomy of Corporate Planning," *Harvard Business Review*, 40 (November-December 1962).

Harrison, W. B. "Long-Range Planning in a Dynamic Industry," *American Management Association Management Report*, 3. New York: American Management Association, Inc., 1958, 47–53.

Henderson, Bruce D. "Strategy Planning," *Business Horizons*, 7 (Winter 1964).

HOLSTEIN, DAVID. "Comprehensive Systems for Business Planning," *Academy of Management Proceedings,* San Diego, 1970, 396–404.

HOLT, C. C.; MODIGLIANI, F.; MUTH, J. F.; and SIMON, H. A. *Planning Production, Inventories and Work Force.* Englewood Cliffs, N.J.: Prentice-Hall, Inc., 1960.

KATZ, ROBERT L. *Cases and Concepts in Corporate Strategy.* Englewood Cliffs, N.J.: Prentice-Hall, Inc., 1970.

KILMER, DAVID C. "Growth by Acquisition: Some Guidelines for Success," *The McKinsey Quarterly,* 3 (Spring 1969).

MARTING, ELIZABETH (ed.). *Developing a Product Strategy.* New York: American Management Association, Inc., 1959.

NATIONAL INDUSTRIAL CONFERENCE BOARD. *Appraising the Market for New Industrial Products,* Studies in Business Policy, No. 123. New York: N.I.C.B., 1967.

NOVICK, D. "Planning in the Department of Defense," *California Management Review,* 5 (Summer 1963), 35–42.

PRYOR, MILLARD H., JR. "International Corporate Planning: How Is It Different?" *Management Technology,* 4 (December 1964), 139–48.

SCOTT, BRIAN W. *Long-Range Planning in American Industry.* New York: American Management Association, Inc., 1965.

SIEGEL, IRVING H. "Technological Change and Long Run Forecasting," *Journal of Business,* 26 (July 1953).

SMALTER, DONALD J. "The Influence of D-O-D Practices on Corporate Planning," *Management Technology,* 4 (December 1964).

STARR, MARTIN K. "Planning Models," *Management Science,* 13 (December 1966), B115–42.

STEINER, GEORGE A. "The Rise of the Corporate Planner," *Harvard Business Review,* 48 (September-October 1970), 133–39.

THOMPSON, STEWART. *How Companies Plan,* Research Study, 54. New York: American Management Association, Inc., 1962.

TILLES, SEYMOUR. "How to Evaluate Corporate Strategy," *Harvard Business Review,* 41 (July-August 1963).

VANCIL, RICHARD F. "The Accuracy of Long-Range Planning," *Harvard Business Review,* 48 (September-October 1970), 98–101.

WARREN, E. KIRBY. *Long-Range Planning.* Englewood Cliffs, N.J.: Prentice-Hall, Inc., 1966.

Chapter 13

The Control Process

THE PREVIOUS CHAPTER was devoted to a conceptual presentation of understanding the planning process in the organizational system. This chapter focuses attention on another basic facet of organizational decision making—the control process. First, some general observations are made about the nature of control. Then two basic facets of control systems are analyzed: (1) the development and use of performance measures and standards, and (2) the design of information systems to provide data for control decisions.

THE NATURE OF CONTROL

A number of different conceptions of control are reflected in the thinking of management scholars and in the practices of business managers. As a starting point for a discussion of control, examine Douglas S. Sherwin's definition: *"The essence of control is action which adjusts operations to predetermined standards, and its basis is information in the hands of managers."*[1] As may be noted, a central focus of this definition is upon *action* taken to correct performance, with action considered dependent upon information. In addition to acting, however, the manager must *decide* whether the information indicates that action should be taken, and, if so, just what actions are required. Consequently, intervening between information and action in the control process is the control *decision*.

Also central to the control process are the performance standards indicated in Sherwin's definition. Essentially, such standards represent *desired* levels of performance with respect to any one or more variables in the organizational system. For instance, a sales volume of $500,000 or an average worker output of 110 units an hour on a particular opera-

---

[1] Douglas S. Sherwin, "The Meaning of Control," *Dun's Review and Modern Industry* (January 1956), as reprinted in Max D. Richards and William O. Nielander, *Readings in Management* (Cincinnati, Ohio: South-Western Publishing Co., 1958), p. 423.

tion might be established as performance standards. Thus, standards in effect represent *objectives* which the organization hopes to attain. Further, as in our examples of sales volume and average worker output, the utilization of standards involves the development of performance measures—e.g., *dollars* as a measure of sales volume, and *units per hour* as a measure of worker output. After such measures and standards have been developed, management may then *compare* the *actual* performance of its operations with that level *desired,* and depending upon the extent to which the standard is not being met, decide whether corrective action is necessary to bring the system into conformity with the desired standard. These various phases of the control process are illustrated schematically in Figure 13–1.

Figure 13–1. The Control Process

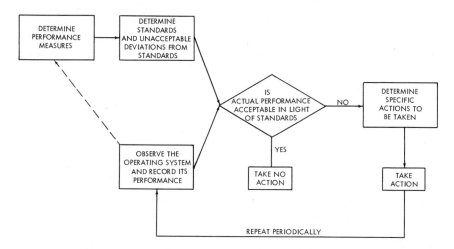

Certain further observations are in order at this point concerning the control process. First, with respect to the relationship between control and the planning process as discussed in the previous chapter, control decisions may be thought of as depending upon and directly related to planning decisions. That is, like planning decisions, control decisions either specify or guide the taking of future action, but such decisions are *specifically geared* toward *correcting* deviations in systems performance from established standards.

Control standards may have been formed directly in the planning process. Further, the control process may be thought of as a corollary plan, one established to help *prevent* a system from deviating excessively from desired levels. A control system is, of course, more than preventive; it is also designed to be corrective when the system's performance has deteriorated from standards.

As indicated previously, the control process involves both determining *when* (or, under what conditions) corrective actions are called for and specifically *what* actions should be undertaken if the performance of the system is inadequate. In some situations, both the when and what of control action may be specified in advance through the utilization of conditional statements. For example, in a quality control system, the following planning (and control) statement might be developed: "If rejects produced on a particular machine exceed 5 percent in any given period, replace the machine's cutting tool." Such preprogramming, of course, requires that management know in advance what should be done should the system get "out of control." In our example, for instance, the effective preprogramming of the retooling decision would be contingent upon management's knowledge that such a course of action would correct the reject problem.

In the previous chapter, it was indicated that in the planning process conditional statements are useful: (1) for dealing with certain repetitive types of decision problems, and/or (2) when insufficient time is available between the occurrence of an event and the point at which managerial actions must be taken to permit such actions to be planned after the event has taken place. The same may be said for the utilization of those conditional statements which specify both when and specifically what corrective actions should be taken in the control process. An example of the use of such conditional statements in dealing with repetitive problems would be provided by our previous retooling example, assuming that, as in many production processes, the periodic wearing down of the cutting tool was creating a recurring problem of the production of an unacceptable number of poor pieces. Or, to provide an example of situations in which the preprogramming of conditional statements would be absolutely essential due to the need for quick action when a process begins to go out of control: when the temperature or pressure in certain chemical processes exceeds a predetermined critical level, the reaction must immediately be halted lest an explosion occur.

The discussion in the preceding paragraphs has assumed that management knows in advance what actions will correct unacceptable deviations in systems performance. In many cases, however, such is not the case. A company may not know, for instance, just why its sales volume has fallen 20 percent below the desired level in a particular week, or why the absenteeism rate among its production workers has suddenly jumped considerably above acceptable levels. In cases such as these, conditional statements may sometimes still be preprogrammed to specify *when* corrective action should be considered (e.g., when absenteeism exceeds 5 percent); but it would not be possible to develop specific plans for correcting systems performance until after subsequent analysis had been undertaken to find out just why the performance was inadequate. An information system designed to provide the data for such analysis could be preplanned, but not the specific cause of action that should be undertaken.

Three final observations are in order concerning the nature of the control process. First, it should *not* be inferred from the previous discussion that control actions are taken *only after* systems performance has *already* become unacceptable. In many cases, management may note: (1) that while performance is still satisfactory, negative trends toward unacceptability are taking place, and (2) corrective action must be taken in an effort to *forestall* the continuance of these trends. For example, a firm may note that while its sales volume is still quite satisfactory, sales have been declining in recent months, and that steps should be taken in an effort to reverse this trend before the decline becomes a really serious one. This exemplifies control's preventive rather than corrective character.

Second, some comments are in order concerning the nature of the control process in terms of the systems view of the organization. In systems terms, the data generated by management concerning the actual performance of the organization represents *feedback* to the control decision system. In the system are stored as *memory* the standards of performance which have been developed and the degrees of deviation from the standards which have been deemed acceptable. By comparing actual with standard performance and deciding whether control actions are necessary, and if so, what actions should be taken, the manager *transforms* the information at his disposal into a decision *output*.

Finally, we should point out that it may often be desirable for business organizations to provide for participation in the control process by their nonmanagerial members. If a manager's subordinates know what performance levels are expected of them, subordinate *self-control* may prove more effective in keeping performance within acceptable limits than if their supervisor specifies what corrective actions should be undertaken. (In fact, as was mentioned in Chapter 4, all open systems must possess some degree of self-control.) Such self-control, of course, assumes not only a technical knowledge of the operation on the part of the subordinate, but also motivation to initiate corrective actions on his own. Further, if self-control is to be possible it is necessary that the control system be designed so that feedback data concerning the subordinate's performance is provided to him. It may be useful to have the subordinates participate initially in establishing performance measures and standards. Such participation may not only help develop an awareness and insight into the control process but also stimulate motivation for exercising self-control.

MEASURES AND STANDARDS FOR CONTROL

As was indicated previously, the design and utilization of both performance measures and standards are essential facets of the control process. This section explores these two aspects of control.

Performance Measures

Many different types of performance measures are utilized by business firms depending upon the systems variables in question. Performance may be measured in terms of dollars and cents, units produced, the number and/or frequency of certain types of human behavior taking place (e.g., number of employee grievances), and so forth. Further, as will be pointed out more fully in the next chapter, it is often most useful to frame performance measures in terms of relationships between two systems variables—e.g., number of grievances *per* 100 employees per month—since relationships provide intelligence as well as information.

Since all organizational systems and subsystems (of any magnitude) have multiple objectives, multiple measures of performance may be required for effective control. Further, constant or periodic monitoring of systems performance is sometimes necessary so that any performance inadequacies or tendencies toward inadequacy may be noted and hopefully corrected before they become serious. (The utilization of computers in recent years has made this more feasible.) For example, in examining the performance of one of his salesmen the sales quota for whose territory is $500,000 per year, a sales manager may want to keep track of sales made on a monthly, weekly, or even on a daily basis. Additionally, in order to pinpoint more precisely any performance inadequacies which may occur, additional information about the salesman's patterns of behavior may be useful such as number of customers seen, frequency of calls on each customer, and percentage of time spent travelling. If the salesman is falling behind in meeting his quota, this information may help enable the salesman and the manager to determine why this is the case. Further, the sales manager may want to develop and apply measures to other variables which are outside his or the salesman's immediate control, but which, nonetheless, may be influencing the latter's performance. For example, such factors as long delays in deliveries of the firm's product to certain key customers, adverse economic conditions, or increased competitive activity in the salesman's territory may be key contributing causes to negative trends in his sales performance.

Two other observations are in order concerning the utilization of multiple performance measures for control purposes. First, it is important for the manager to weigh the advantages of the control measures which he utilizes against their cost. In any organizational system or subsystem of any magnitude, the use of literally thousands of performance measures might be conceivable. To develop, maintain, and evaluate all such measures, however, would be prohibitively time consuming and expensive. In order to overcome the problem of excessive information costs while at the same time providing for adequate control, managers commonly (and perhaps optimally) rely on *selective* control measures—i.e., attention is focused only on certain *key* systems variables. Just which variables are considered key ones, of course, will depend on what particular organizational system and set of decisions are under consideration, and properly designed computerization may be helpful here in examining the key variables desired. Further, additional measures may be developed and/or existing ones excluded from consideration as organizational conditions change. For example, the sales manager may record and examine only the total expense account figures of his salesmen, but should these expenses start getting "out of line" he may call for an itemized analysis of them (e.g., travel, entertainment, and so on) in an effort to find the causes of and ways to correct the problem.

Second, it should be pointed out that the extensive utilization of control measures by management with respect to the performance of particular individuals in the organization may be reacted to negatively by the latter. If a salesman, for example, is required to fill out reports indicating in detail his activities for each hour during every day, he may not only feel that he is not being trusted by his superior, but also resent having to spend considerable time filling out the reports— time which he may consider could more profitably be utilized otherwise. In terms of the conceptual framework which we presented in Chapter 6, the manager's close scrutiny of an extensive number of measures of his subordinates' performance represents one facet of close supervision; and the subordinates' reactions to such close control will be influenced by such aspects of his personality orientation as the relative strength of his dependence and independence needs.

Performance Standards

Once performance measures for a system variable have been selected, it is necessary to determine what standards of performance are to be considered acceptable for the variable. In this section are discussed three different facets of the development and utilization of performance standards. First the need to consider systems variability in designing standards is pointed out. Then some of the approaches commonly utilized by managers in defining standards of acceptable performance for the organizational system are illustrated. Finally, certain psychological aspects of importance to consider in establishing standards are reviewed.

Systems Variability and Standards. In establishing standards, it is important to recognize that the performance of most systems will not remain constant over a period of time, but rather will be subject to some degree of variability. A machine operator, for example, may average 110 units per hour, but his performance might normally be expected to range anywhere from 100 to 120 units in any given hour, depending upon his motivational state, the degree to which he is fatigued, and so on. Or, in manufacturing shafts of a desired diameter of 1.95 inches, the units turned out on any given day might be expected to range in diameter from 1.945 to 1.955 inches. Thus, in developing standards, the manager must define not only desired *levels* of performance, but also the *degree of variation* from these levels which is acceptable to him.

Certain other observations are in order concerning performance variability and control standards. First, for some systems variables, both *positive* and *negative* variations from standards would obviously be considered unacceptable if their magnitude were considerable. For example, for our shafts with a desired diameter of 1.95 inches, pieces turned out which are either too large or too small would be unusable.[2] For many other types of systems variables, however, the manager's primary concern would be in avoiding *negative* variations from standards, with positive variations being welcomed. For instance, if production standards for a particular job have been established at 100 units per hour, and a particular employee with high levels of skill and motivation is able to turn out an average of 170 units per hour, his supervisor might be quite pleased with his performance.

Even where performance levels above standard are generally desirable, however, *extreme* positive variations may be indicative of organizational problems requiring corrective action. Some of the reasons why such may be the case are as follows:

1. If performance is consistently far above standard, it may be that something is wrong with the standards. For example, if all employees working on a particular operation are producing at 200 percent of the performance standard set for their job, it is highly probable that the standards were set unrealistically low.

2. High positive variations from standards on one systems variable may be indicative of the existence of a suboptimization problem within the organization—i.e., the high performance with respect to the one variable may have been attained only at the expense of some other organizational objective. For instance, a division in a large corporation may be showing an unusually good profit picture to a considerable extent because of cutbacks on research and development efforts—a move which may endanger its long-run profitability.

3. In some cases, individuals within organizations may make their performance look good by failing to report performance inadequacies. For example, cases have been reported of supervisors managing to avoid the reporting of minor accidents occurring in their departments in order to make their safety records look better.

One further observation is in order concerning variability in systems performance. For certain variables, performance may normally be expected to fluctuate according to some predictable pattern—e.g., con-

---

[2] It might be possible, of course, to rework those shafts which are too large.

sistently higher sales in a supermarket on Fridays and Saturdays than on Mondays and Tuesdays. When such is the case, definition of standards and acceptable variations for the variable under consideration would have to take into account the particular time period in which performance takes place—e.g., different levels of acceptability would have to be set for sales on different days of the week.

Establishing Performance Standards. There are many different approaches utilized by managers to determine what levels of and variations in systems performance are acceptable. An examination of several of these follow.

In many situations, managers find it useful to utilize data concerning organizational performance in previous time periods as a basis for setting standards of acceptability for the future. For example, if a firm's raw materials costs as a percentage of its total cost of goods sold have stabilized at about 32 percent over the past two or three years, this figure might be considered as an acceptable standard for future performance. Or, a firm might judge a reject rate of 5 percent for a certain part that it manufactures as good based on its prior experience in turning out the part.

The use of historically based standards is valid only under two general types of conditions. The first occurs when the factors influencing the performance of the systems variable under consideration are stable. For instance, if the price of raw materials for the firm mentioned in the preceding paragraph had just decreased by 10 percent, the historical standard of 32 percent would no longer be appropriate (assuming that all other variables influencing materials costs have remained the same). Second, historically based standards may also be valid under nonstable conditions if the key dynamic variables influencing systems performance are *predictable*. For example, a publisher of textbooks for the elementary schools might find that historically changes in the magnitude of its sales volume have closely paralleled increases or decreases in the number of elementary school pupils in the United States each year, and aim for a 5 percent increase in its sales for the forthcoming year based on a like projected percentage increase in elementary pupils.

When such historically based standards are utilized, managers, of course, may hope not simply to maintain previous performance levels (or increase them in proportion to market increases as with the publisher), but rather to improve upon their performance. For example, the book publisher might hope to increase its sales by 8 percent in the forthcoming year through the introduction of a number of new titles.

In addition to simply looking at the previous performance of a particular variable in their own organizational system, managers often find it useful in setting standards to compare their performance with that of other similar business firms. For example, in establishing levels of acceptable performance in the area of safety, management may find it useful to examine accident rate data for other like firms in the industry. Further, in setting standards for a particular subsystem in the organization some consideration may also be given to the performance of *other similar subsystems* within the firm. For instance, in establishing a sales quota for a given salesman, management may give some weight to what other salesmen with similar sales territories have been able to do in the past. Or, cost standards for the newly opened store in a large supermarket chain may be based largely on performance levels achieved in the past by other of the firm's stores of a similar size and type.

When performance levels achieved by either other firms or other organizational subsystems are being considered in setting standards, it is important, first of all, that such performance is considered adequate. That is, the manager would not want to use someone else's poor performance as a standard for his own operations. Additionally, it is important that the system or subsystem for which the standard is being set really is comparable to that from which the performance data is being derived. For example, the cost standards based on the performance of other supermarkets mentioned above may not be valid for the new supermarket in its initial weeks of operations, due to the fact that many "nonnormal" costs would be expected in getting the store started—e.g., unusually large training costs, an extensive advertising program to attract customers, and so on.

Finally, it should be pointed out that in many cases managers will use more sophisticated, analytical, and statistical means for establishing standards and taking control actions than have been discussed thus far. For example, time study analysis is frequently undertaken by industrial engineers to provide (among other things) a basis for establishing incentive standards for workers.[3] Widely used, especially in quality control, are numerous statistical techniques for determining what degree of variation from standards is acceptable, and when control actions should be taken.[4] As with the historically based standards discussed above, those standards developed by analytical and statistical means are valid only for stable systems or when dynamic variables influencing systems performance are predictable. For example, if the work content of a production line job were to be modified, new incentive time standards would have to be developed to take into account this change.

Establishing Standards: Psychological Considerations. As explained in Chapter 5, different individuals vary in several respects as far as personality orientation and need importance is concerned. In performing

---

[3] For a discussion of time study and other work measurement procedures, see J. William Gavett, *Production and Operations Management* (New York: Harcourt, Brace & World, Inc., 1968), chap. 12.
[4] For an introductory discussion of quality control approaches, see ibid., chap. 13; and for a more theoretically based statistical treatment, Edward H. Bowman and Robert B. Fetter, *Analysis for Production and Operations Management* (3d ed.; Homewood, Ill.: Richard D. Irwin, Inc., 1967), chap. 5.

on the job, some individuals have higher *aspiration levels* than others—i.e., the levels of future performance toward which they strive is different. The individual's aspiration level is conditioned to a considerable extent by his past level of actual achievement. Further, his aspiration level over time "tends to adjust to the level of achievement."[5] For example, if a person's achievement is continually below that toward which he has strived in the past, he will tend to reduce his aspiration level downward in order to reduce feelings of failure.

In designing performance standards for individuals within the organization it is important to consider not only what is "fair" or physically possible with "normal" effort, but also what the aspiration levels of the individuals concerned are. If standards are set *below* the individual's own level of aspiration, they will quite obviously not serve to motivate him to improve his performance. Conversely, if standards are set too far above the individual's past achievement level and his related future aspiration level, he may perceive that his performance cannot meet the expectations set for him and become discouraged. In some extreme cases, discouragement may become so pronounced that his performance may actually deteriorate rather than improve.

The importance of considering aspiration levels in developing performance standards may be illustrated by the following example. In one firm, incentive standards were established for a job by the use of time study methods. The job that was studied and for which standards were set was that of accomplishing a major overhaul on a unit of operating equipment. The time standard developed indicated that an overhaul could be completed at a normal pace in 2,400 man-hours. A review of past records, however, showed that 6,000 man-hours had been needed on the average for each overhaul. The incentive plan based on the 2,400-hour standard was placed into operation despite the large discrepancy between it and past performance. The workers' aspiration level was so distant from the 2,400 "normal" level established that they considered the incentive plan ridiculous, and actual performance continued as before at about 6,000 hours per overhaul.

Subsequent management reflection on the problem led to an "adjustment" in the standard. A few minor methods changes were introduced, larger rest and fatigue allowances were added, and the revised standard was set at 3,000 hours per overhaul. At this level, the standard was effective in stimulating improved performance on the part of the maintenance workers. In fact, some subsequent overhauls were completed in as short a period as 1,900 man-hours, indicating that the original standard had not really been an unreasonable one.

This example illustrates that a "fair" standard may not be effective in helping to improve organizational performance. If in the design of

---

[5] James G. March and Herbert A. Simon, *Organizations* (New York: John Wiley & Sons, Inc., 1958), p. 182.

performance standards for a control system, a goal is to improve actual performance, the standards set must not be so far above the aspiration levels of the individuals concerned so as to engender rejection of the standards and/or discouragement.

We should also note that economic considerations are important in determining what levels of performance are deemed acceptable as standards. In most cases, higher levels of systems performance may be realized only through additional expenditures of effort and costs. For example, the percentage of pieces turned out on a machine which will be rejects may be a function of numerous variables such as operator skill and the quality of raw materials utilized. By devoting more effort to operator training, and/or by purchasing higher quality raw materials, management may be able to reduce its average reject rate from, say, 8 to 4 percent. Whether such efforts would be advisable, however, would depend upon the marginal savings realized from reducing the reject percentage as compared with the marginal costs of attaining the improved performance.

Similar considerations would, of course, also apply in determining what variations from standards should be considered acceptable. For instance, the percentage rejects turned out on our machine might also increase as the tooling utilized wears down over time. Although the magnitude of these variations in performance might be reduced by more frequent retooling, the costs of such an action would have to be weighed against the advantages of reducing performance variability.

THE INFORMATION SYSTEM FOR CONTROL

Once satisfactory measures and standards have been established, it is necessary to design a system for reporting feedback data concerning the actual performance of their operations to the managers. From the point of view of the manager, the information feedback system should be designed in such a way that it will increase his chances of identifying and correcting the most important problems which exist in his organization. On the other hand, it is also important to design the system so that the costs of recording and processing the data useful to the manager can be kept at a minimum and do not exceed their value in helping to make better control decisions. In this section we will consider three basic facets of the design and utilization of information feedback systems for control: (1) data relevance, (2) report format, and (3) the timing of feedback data.

Data Relevance

It is important to design information systems in a manner such that the feedback data reported to the manager is *relevant* to possible control actions which he may undertake. For example, information as to how each of a firm's salesmen is progressing in meeting his yearly sales quota would be of no value to a first line production supervisor in improving the performance of his operations. Data relevance, it should be noted, is one type of simplification of the complex techniques which were discussed in Chapter 4.

In speaking of "relevance" it should be emphasized that we do *not* mean that the manager should be given feedback data *only* with respect to variables over which he has control. Often, information provided to the manager relative to states of nature and/or competitive strategies which are beyond his control may be useful to him in making better control decisions. For example, if a production supervisor is aware of the fact that the batch of raw materials which his workers are currently processing is of an inferior quality such that their work pace has to be slowed down, he may avoid taking the inappropriate control action of reprimanding them for poor performance.

Classification.   Although the fact that control reporting should be relevant to possible control decisions is a fairly obvious one, it is sometimes ignored in the design of feedback systems. In one department store, for example, merchandise markdowns (to dispose of slow moving items) were reported periodically by stock number in numerical order. Each departmental manager in utilizing the markdown report would have to seek out and identify the items sold in his department. Much of the information in the report was irrelevant to his own decision making, since it concerned markdown activity in other departments. This particular report was a carryover from the time when the store was small and there were no separate departments. When departmental managers had been appointed to supervise the stores' various merchandise lines, the report was maintained in its old form which had served well prior to the departmentalization.

It should also be noted that the store manager could follow markdown activity on an overall store basis from the report and discern *when* control action was warranted. He could not, however, easily determine *where* action should be initiated. Without further analysis, he could not determine the extent to which, if any, any particular department in the store might be contributing to excessive markdowns.

Eventually, the store's markdown report was revised so as to feed back to each manager information on the items sold by his department. This not only helped to reduce each departmental manager's search activity, but also enabled the store manager (who received the various reports for all departments) to pinpoint those departments which appeared to need assistance in controlling their operations.

This idea of focusing control reports upon data pertinent to the operations for which each manager has responsibility is often referred to as *responsibility reporting*. This concept has in recent years been receiving considerable attention in accounting circles, where, in the past, cost data frequently had been reported solely on a product-by-product basis. For example, in one firm in which cost data had been reported by product but not for each department involved in making its products, management found that its accounting data were extremely useful in determining the profitability of each of its product lines. If the costs of manufacturing a particular product were found to be excessive, however, management was unable to pinpoint the departments responsible for the high costs. A revision of the accounting system to report the costs incurred by each department as well as by product was instituted, and this problem was overcome.

Irrelevant Data. One further observation is in order concerning relevance of control data reported—in some cases irrelevant data may not only increase the manager's search activity, but it may also create other problems.[6] For example, in one plant one item in the report given to each foreman for cost control purposes was the rent charged to his department on a square footage allocation basis. Although rent was a cost to the firm, and each department obviously used space for which rent was charged, the foreman had no control over the rental price or over the amount of space assigned to his department. Foremen soon learned to ignore the item. On their reports it continued as a sort of annoyance. Some people believed that reporting the rent figure actually constituted a disservice since a few foremen had refused to let other supervisors make use of unutilized space in their areas because they "had to pay" for it.

Data Hierarchy. Implied in the discussion of data relevance is a hierarchy of control data corresponding to the hierarchy of organization. Data important to controlling a foreman's department ordinarily is less relevant to his superior, a general foreman, or to a superintendent further up in the organization. Reports designed to meet the needs of managers generally can be of most pertinence, then, if at higher levels of organization, summaries rather than the detail of lower level operations are given. For example, only one foreman in an assembly operation may be having problems associated with the quality level of the products he is producing, while the assembly operations, as a whole, may be experiencing major difficulties as a result of scheduling overloads. It is to the overall scheduling problem that the general assembly manager should devote his major efforts; and data reported to reveal its extent and nature are important. It is desirable, too, that the general assembly manager should know that he cannot have much influence on solving the scheduling problem if he devotes too much time and attention to the area supervised by the one foreman with the quality problem.

---

[6] For an extensive critique of information systems focusing upon misguided criteria, see Russell L. Ackoff, "Management Misinformation Systems," *Management Science,* 4 (December 1967), B147–56.

At the same time, optimal operations for the whole assembly area cannot be achieved without attention being given to both problems. The general assembly manager needs to know which one of the foremen has the problems of quality so that he may follow it up to discover whether the foreman has solved the problem or needs help to solve it. It would be quite disconcerting and dysfunctional, on the other hand, for the general assembly manager to order that *everyone* working under him get busy to solve *both* the quality and the scheduling problems since the former applied to only one foreman.

While higher level managers require only data indicating the locale and nature of problems, those at lower levels who are directly responsible for the troublesome operations need detailed information that aids in revealing the cause of their problems. The further up the organization that a manager is placed, the more general the information may be. Hopefully, data provided to top management reveals the major problems of the corporation. At the same time, however, top management can lose control over parts of its domain if information is not *comprehensive* even though it is summarized. When General Electric and some of its executives were indicted for price fixing, one of the president's defenses was that he did not know about and was not a party to the price fixing. Scholarly observers might claim that the president has the responsibility for seeing that sufficient information be reported to him in such a way that misdeeds would be prevented, or at least revealed so corrective action could be undertaken.

Control Report Format

In addition to determining which performance variables are relevant to the manager for control purposes, consideration must be given in designing control systems to the format of the feedback data being provided. The format of control reports can assume considerable importance, since data relative to the same systems variable presented in one way will often provide greater insight and permit more rapid decision making than if it is presented in other ways.

In its simplest form, a control report may merely provide information as to the *actual performance* of the manager's operations. For example, a report to a first-line production supervisor relative to downtime on the assembly line in his department might be in the following format:

	Actual Level
Line Downtime This Week:	43 minutes

Does this report provide surprise value and, therefore, information? As was shown in Chapter 4, only if the manager perceives that a problem exists is information given by such a report. With such data, the manager must compare in his own mind the actual performance to the standards which have been developed for the variable. This comparison forces him to *recall* what standard performance is supposed to be. In some cases, and especially when he is working in an operation with a complex control system generating many control measures, his personal recall may be incomplete, and, in consequence, a failure to take appropriate control action may result.

To remove the control system's dependence upon human recall of the standard, the downtime report could be expanded so as to include data relative to *both* actual and standard performance—e.g.,

	Actual	*Standard*
Line Downtime This Week:	43 minutes	38 minutes

Reports such as this facilitate comparisons between actual and standard performance, but the manager must still evaluate the extent to which the two levels are in variance from one another, and determine whether it is necessary to redirect the system toward the standard. This evaluation process can be built into the control reporting procedure by providing the manager with *both* the standard level of performance *and* normal variations from it when the actual performance of the system is fed back to him. If, for example, the normal variation of downtime is ± 2 minutes from the standard of 38 minutes, the following form of reporting would allow the manager at a glance to determine that the system's performance is not within acceptable levels:

	Actual	*Standard*	*Normal Variation*
Line Downtime This Week:	43 minutes	38 minutes	36–40 minutes

In terms of the definitions of Chapter 4, the data presented in this form reveal both information and intelligence, the latter from the comparisons afforded. Even with these refinements, however, it is possible to arrive at incorrect conclusions about the status of the system. To give the manager further insight into the performance of his operating system, it is also sometimes useful to provide him with feedback concerning not only the present status of the system, but also its status in the past. In the downtime report, for example, the following data might be provided:

	Average Last Month	*Last Week*	*This Week*	*Normal Variation*
Line Downtime:	57	52	43	36–40

In this example, the historical trend indicates that the performance of the system is improving as time passes. If we assume that this trend will continue (e.g., because forces have already been set in motion in the system to correct its performance), it might *not* be necessary to initiate additional corrective action even though the performance variable is still outside of the acceptable range.

One further method of highlighting areas of performance which are out of control is to restrict feedback data given to the manager only to those conditions which are abnormal. For example, if 25 different performance measures have been developed describing the status of a department's operations, a typical weekly control report might contain data with respect to only the two or three variables, the performance of which is abnormal and to which the manager needs to give immediate attention. This approach is often referred to as *reporting by exception.* It assumes that only exceptionally good or bad performance areas require managerial attention since the manager does not need to take control actions when his system is performing normally. Reporting by exception recognizes that the time and resources of the manager are limited, and that if he directs his efforts toward correcting inadequate performance rather than focusing his attention on all phases of his operation, the probability of improving his operations will be increased. Exception reporting constitutes an important form of filtering information from the environment to simplify the complexity facing the manager.

The Timing of Feedback Data

In addition to determining *what* performance data needs to be fed back to members of the organizational system, management must also give consideration to *when* the feedback information should be provided. Consideration to several facets of the problem of feedback timing will now be given.

One will find considerable variation in different managerial control systems both as to (1) the duration of the time period encompassed in feedback reports, and (2) the immediacy with which the control data is fed back to the system after the performance has occurred. Illustrative of reports covering long durations and fed back slowly would be the annual financial reports of many firms which are sometimes not available to management until two or three months after the fiscal year encompassed has expired. At the other extreme, in certain automated or semiautomated production systems, performance may be measured every second or fraction of a second, and such data fed back to the system almost immediately. For example, at the Newark, Ohio plant of Owens-Corning Fiberglas Corp., a computerized control system was developed to run a glass furnace. The system

. . . has run largely without attendants, monitoring the glass coming out of the furnace, making control decisions, and ordering adjustments to keep the process balanced . . .

The system runs the furnace by detecting changes at a wide range of measuring points in and around the furnace. The computer scans the signals from the thermocouples and other devices at predetermined times. One crucial instrument is read 10 times every second; another instrument, far less critical to the process, is sampled only once every minute and a half.[7]

---

[7] "New Edge in Glass," *Business Week* (April 10, 1965), pp. 60, 62.

If the information-decision control system fails to prevent deterioration in some systems such as these, it fails. If the plant blows up, for example, corrective control measures are immaterial.

In defining the timing of feedback data in control systems, several factors may be of importance. One of the most basic of these for all control systems is, of course, costs. Quite obviously, all other factors remaining the same, the more frequently performance is measured and control data fed back to the manager, the more time and expense will be incurred. From a theoretical point of view, the basic question which should be raised relative to feedback frequency is: "Will the marginal returns of more frequent feedback (in terms of better control decisions) exceed the marginal costs of providing such feedback?"

As far as the *need* for frequent feedback is concerned, one key consideration is the *rapidity* with which it is likely that the system may go out of control. In an automated chemical process, for example, it may be necessary to measure performance and provide feedback data every few seconds, because sudden temperature or pressure changes beyond critical limits are possible which would ruin the processing. On the other hand, in a quality control system in which an excessive number of defective parts turned out is normally due to the wearing down of cutting tools, which takes place relatively slowly, sampling of pieces turned out once a day or every two or three days might be adequate in order to prevent the system from going out of control.

When considering the frequency of feedback to members of the organization (as opposed to that provided within nonhuman automated systems), certain psychological considerations may also be of importance. In learning situations, as we pointed out in Chapter 5, for example, immediate corrective feedback is usually desirable so that the trainee does not develop inappropriate habits, which may be quite difficult to unlearn at a later time. Also, as far as day-to-day supervisor-subordinate relationships are concerned, too frequent monitoring of subordinate performance may not only be disruptive but be resented as representing overly close supervision and control. For example, such was the case with one supervisor known to the authors who would sometimes check every 10 or 15 minutes on the progress of his secretary when she was in the process of typing certain lengthy reports. At the other extreme, of course, supervisory monitoring and feedback which is conducted too infrequently may result in the continuation of and failure to correct inappropriate subordinate performance. Just how frequently supervisory control should be exercised will depend upon the variables as discussed in Chapter 6—the characteristics of the leader, of the follower and of the particular organizational situation under consideration.

One final observation is in order concerning the psychological aspects of feedback frequency. Some research has indicated that the individual's performance may be adversely affected if he is *"overloaded"* with too much *negative* feedback (or criticism) at any given time. In a study of the value of annual performance appraisals of subordinates at the General Electric Company, for example, the following conclusions were drawn:

Employees seem to accept suggestions for improved performance if they are given in a less concentrated form than is the case in comprehensive annual appraisals . . . employees became clearly more prone to reject criticisms as the number of criticisms mount. This indicates that an "overload phenomenon" may be operating. In other words, each individual seems to have a tolerance level for the amount of criticism he can take. And, as this level is approached or passed, it becomes increasingly difficult for him to accept responsibility for the shortcomings pointed out.[8]

From these findings, it was concluded that corrective feedback from supervisors to their subordinates is more effective if it is carried on a day-to-day, rather than on a once-a-year basis.

SUMMARY

The control process centers around ensuring that actual systems performance is in accordance with that desired by the organization. In designing control systems it is first necessary for management to establish measures of performance. Then standards of performance and acceptable deviations from the standards must be defined. In order that members of the organization be made aware of the need to take corrective action, it is also necessary that information be fed back to them concerning the status of their operations. In designing information systems for control purposes, it is important to give consideration to the relevance of feedback data, the format in which the data is reported, and the frequency with which the feedback is provided. In all phases of the design and utilization of control systems, attention must be given both to: (1) the cost of generating and reporting information as compared with its value to improved decision making, and, (2) likely human reactions to the system—e.g., those of individuals to an "overload" of negative feedback. Thus, consideration of both economic and psychological variables is important in the control process.

DISCUSSION AND STUDY QUESTIONS

1. A control decision taking corrective action is predicated on deviance from preconceptions about desirable performance, thus seeking to exploit promising opportunities in the environment. Evaluate this statement.

---

[8] H. H. Meyer, E. Kay, and J. R. P. French, Jr., "Split Roles in Performance Appraisal," *Harvard Business Review*, 43 (January-February 1965), p. 127.

2. If no deviations from standard exist, a report to this effect contains no information or value. In light of this, the system status should go unreported. Comment.

3. "I am the chief engineer supervising a number of projects and functions whose task requirements are unknown, even to me. If a man is sitting with his feet up on the desk staring out the window, he may be dreaming up the most fantastic invention we've ever had. The ordinary concepts of managerial control simply do not apply to evaluating progress in this department." Evaluate this problem in control. How can control be exercised, if at all?

4. The interval between reporting periods for feedback data is directly related to the potential rate of change in the system. Comment.

5. Since organizations tend toward a steady state equilibrium, a control system merely duplicates work to achieve something that is going to happen anyway. Evaluate.

6. "Comprehensive and completely detailed data concerning all facets of the operations are necessary for enlightened management. Let the computer people provide me those data and I'll run the plant." In terms of control and information theory, evaluate this statement.

7. Inaccurately established standards for control may be more dysfunctional than no standards at all. Comment.

8. Fraternity News Corporation operates a chain of newstands selling magazines, dailies, and paperback books throughout a metropolitan area. The manager of each location is responsible for maintaining stocks, generating sales, and overall profitability of his unit. One unit manager and several of his employees were arrested for regularly distributing drugs. The president was considering how this situation developed without the knowledge of anyone else in the organization and how he could take action to prevent its recurrence in other units. Comment.

9. In the light of the concept of steady state improvement in a system, of what value are historically based performance measures?

10. "We are evaluated on such gross measures of performance that quite a bit could be wrong with our operations and it wouldn't show up on these gross measures for a long time. In fact, it can happen that I can make some decisions detrimental to the long-run benefit of the company as a whole and it might even improve my short-run, gross measure—for example, profitably. Using gross measures for control seems to be no control at all." Why would a firm use gross measures for control? How could actual overall performance be opposite of that shown by the measure? Please give examples.

SELECTED REFERENCES

ANTHONY, ROBERT N. *Management Controls in Industrial Research Organizations*. Boston: Graduate School of Business, Harvard University, 1952.

ANTHONY, ROBERT N. *Planning and Control Systems: A Framework for Analysis*. Boston: Harvard University Press, 1965.

BONINI, C. P.; JAEDICKE, R. K.; and WAGNER, H. M. *Management Controls.* New York: McGraw-Hill Book Co., 1964.

CHARNES, A., and STEDRY, A. C. "Search-Theoretic Models of Organization Control by Budgeted Multiple Goals," *Management Science,* 12 (January 1966), 457–82.

DE-LATIL, P. *Thinking by Machine: A Study of Cybernetics.* Boston: Houghton Mifflin Co., 1957.

DUN and BRADSTREET, INC. *Cost Control in Business.* New York: Business Education Division, Dun & Bradstreet, Inc., 1967.

DU PONT COMPANY, *Executive Committee.* Wilmington, Dela.: E. I. Du Pont de Nemours & Company, 1959.

HALL, W. N. "Methods of Evaluating Decentralized Operations," *Management Record,* 25 (January 1963), 26–28.

KAGDIS, JOHN, and LACKNER, MICHAEL R. "A Management Control Systems Simulation Model," *Management Technology,* 3 (December 1963), 145–59.

MCLEAN, JOHN G. "Better Reports for Better Control," *Harvard Business Review,* 35 (May-June 1957), 95–104.

MCLEAN, JOHN G. "How to Evaluate New Capital Investments," *Harvard Business Review,* 36 (November-December 1958).

MILES, RAYMOND E., and VERGIN, ROGER C. "Behavioral Properties and Variance Controls," *California Management Review,* 8 (Spring 1966), 57–65.

PUTNAM, A. O.; BARLOW, E. R.; and STILIAN, G. N. *Unified Operations Management,* Section 3. New York: McGraw-Hill Book Co., 1963.

Quality Control in Action, Management Report No. 9. New York: American Management Association, Inc., 1958.

SHILLINGLAW, GORDON. "Profit Analysis for Abandonment Decisions," *The Journal of Business,* 30 (January 1957), 17–29.

STROLLER, DAVID S., and VAN HORN, RICHARD L. "Design of a Management Information System," *Management Technology,* January 1960, 86–91.

VAZSONYI, ANDREW. "Automated Information Systems in Planning, Control, and Command," *Management Science,* 11 (February 1965), B2–41.

WEINWURM, G. F. "Computer Management Controls Systems through the Looking Glass," *Management Science,* 7 (July 1961), 411–19.

Chapter 14

Analysis of the Firm

IN CHAPTER 3, it was pointed out how models, both quantitative and qualitative, may be utilized by the decision maker to provide understanding and insight, to predict the outcome of proposed strategies, and/or to prescribe future courses of action. Most of the models discussed thus far have been essentially qualitative in nature, with a majority of them having focused attention on the behavior of the firm's human subsystems from a psychological or sociological point of view. In this and succeeding chapters the text will place much greater emphasis upon quantitative models (and tools) designed to aid the manager in analyzing and dealing with the problems of the firm from an economic point of view. A central focus of these quantitative-economic models is upon the question: "What profits and/or costs will be incurred by the firm or by one of its subsystems when different decision strategies are chosen under various conditions?"

The first section of this chapter will be devoted to a discussion of several fundamental economic concepts, knowledge of which is necessary for an analysis of the firm's cost and profit structure. Then, attention will be turned to a simple model for analyzing the profitability performance of the organizational system or one of its subsystems at various levels of output—the break-even model. Next, some of the ways in which percentages and ratios can be utilized by the manager for the comparative analysis of various systems variables, both economic and noneconomic will be pointed out. Finally, consideration will be given to "cost-utility" analysis—situations involving costs but where the output generated by the organization cannot be expressed in dollar terms.

FUNDAMENTAL ECONOMIC CONCEPTS

Many different kinds of costs will be incurred in the operation of the business firm—labor costs, materials costs, the cost of borrowing funds, and so on. For the purpose of analysis, these costs may be classified into five basic types: (1) sunk, (2) opportunity, (3) fixed, (4) variable, and (5) marginal. In this section we will discuss each of these, as well as two other concepts basic to the economic analysis of the firm—marginal revenue and marginal profits.

Sunk Costs

Sunk costs refer to those outlays which have been incurred by the firm in the past, and which are *unrecoverable*. The important fact to recognize concerning such sunk costs is that they should be completely *ignored* as far as the making of *future* decisions is concerned. For example, suppose that:

1. A company bought a machine last month for $40,000, only to find now that a newer one, which performs the same work much more efficiently, has become available, and that

2. Only $5,000 could be realized by selling the old machine if the new one were to be purchased to replace it.

The fact that $35,000 of the $40,000 investment in the old machine would be "lost" if the new machine were purchased should not be considered in deciding whether or not to acquire it. Rather the recent purchase of the old machine, which now appears to have been a mistake, should be ignored in making such a decision.[1] The new machine should be evaluated only on the basis of its own potential value to the firm in the future (although the salvage value of the old machine should be considered). We will consider means for evaluating investment decisions such as this in terms of their future value to the firm in the next chapter.

Opportunity Costs

It is important to recognize that the term "cost" is *not* always used to apply only to expenditures which are *actually made* by the business organization. Such is the case with *opportunity* costs, which refer to those gains which must be *sacrificed* by choosing one course of action rather than another. A prime example of the existence of opportunity costs is seen in the management of the firm's inventories. By tying up funds in inventories, a company must give up the opportunity of investing, and hence realizing earnings on these funds elsewhere. As will be pointed up in greater detail in Chapter 18, it is important for management to consider these foregone opportunities as well as actual cash outlays in deciding on the levels of inventories that it wishes to maintain.

---

[1] Although, from a psychological point of view, some managers who have made the "mistake" may be defensive and reluctant to ignore their sunk costs.

Fixed Costs

In producing and selling goods and/or services, certain of a company's costs may remain fixed regardless of the level of output generated. Such costs are termed *fixed* costs. For example, during any given month, expenses for rent in an insurance office may remain the same whether 4,000 or 5,000 claims are processed; or in a manufacturing plant, salaries paid to supervisors in a particular week may be fixed at $25,000 whether 40,000 or 50,000 units of production are turned out.

It should be recognized, however, that such fixed costs do not remain "fixed" indefinitely—rather, they may be subject to variations from time to time. Supervisory salaries in the manufacturing plant, for example, although fixed at any given time, may be increased annually to reflect cost-of-living changes. Thus, when using the term "fixed costs" we refer to the short run—in the long run, all costs are subject to change.

It should also be pointed out that many of the firm's so-called fixed costs are really *semifixed*—i.e., although remaining fixed for *normal* variations in output, they will vary if output is either exceedingly high or low. For example, if production in a manufacturing plant which normally operates on a three-shift, five-day-a-week basis is cut back to the point where only one or two shifts are required, some production supervisors will probably be laid off. Or, if production is expanded so as to necessitate Saturday and Sunday work as well, additional supervisory personnel

Figure 14–1. Semifixed Costs: Supervisory Salaries/Week (hypothetical example)

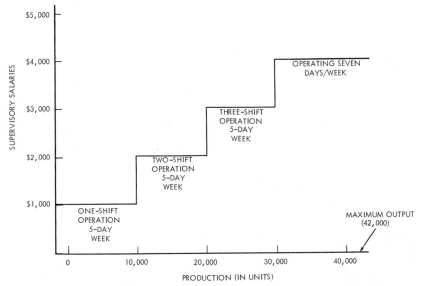

Assumes: Maximum output of 2,000 units per shift per day.

may be needed. For such an operation, the relationship between semi-fixed supervisory salaries and output may be described as a step-function, such as the hypothetical one illustrated in Figure 14–1.

Variable Costs

Other costs incurred by the firm will vary directly with output. These are referred to as *variable* costs. Each unit of production that a manufacturing plant turns out, for instance, might require (1) $4 in materials, and (2) under a piecework incentive system, $1 in wages paid to those employees directly involved in fabricating and assembling the product. As may be observed, the relationship between total variable costs (*TVC*) and output (*X*) may theoretically be expressed by a linear equation—as in the illustration below, where $TVC = \$5X$. (This relationship is shown

Figure 14–2. Relationship between Variable Costs and Output

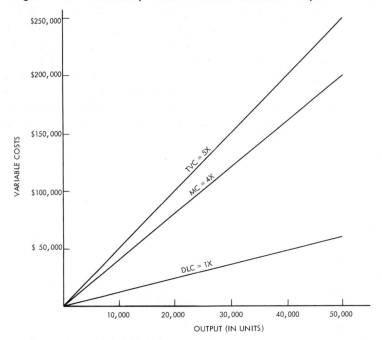

Key: TVC = Total Variable Costs
     DLC = Direct Labor Costs
     MC = Materials Cost
     X = Units of Output

graphically in Figure 14–2.) In actual practice, however, many of the firms costs, although closely linked to output, are not directly and linearly so related. To illustrate this point, let us return to the previous example and add some realistic qualifying conditions.

1. There will probably be some newly hired fabricators and assemblers in the manufacturing plant who have not yet reached full proficiency in their work. As in many piecework systems, however, they may still be paid the "base rate" set for their jobs even though they do not produce up to standards. If so, labor costs for the pieces turned out by these individuals will be greater than $1 per unit.[2]

2. If production were to be increased in the plant sufficiently to require overtime work, time-and-a-half pay would be called for, and the firm's variable labor cost function would look like that illustrated in Figure 14–3.

3. If a number of overtime hours are worked, one would expect

Figure 14–3.   Variable Labor Costs and Output (for both regular and overtime work)

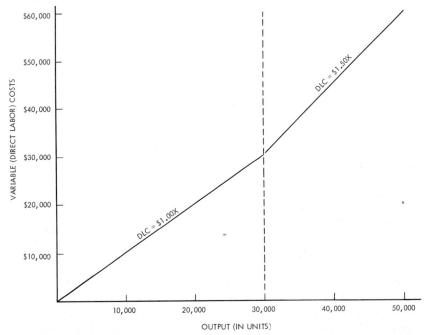

Assumes: Maximum output possible without recourse to overtime is 30,000 units.
Key: DLC = Direct Labor Costs
     X = Units of Output

---

[2] To illustrate more fully how this may be so, let us consider the following example. The hourly base rate for assemblers whose work standard is 20 pieces per hour is $4, and an incentive wage of $0.20 per unit is paid for all units produced above the standard. Thus, direct labor costs for all work performed either at or above the standard is $0.20 per unit. A newly employed worker who is able to produce only 10 pieces per hour, on the other hand, would often be paid the base rate of $4, so that direct labor costs for his work would be $0.40 per piece.

some of the plant's employees to become fatigued to the point where the quality of their work suffers. If their fatigue results in a greater percentage of pieces which have to be scrapped, increasing per unit materials costs such as those illustrated in Figure 14–4 might result.

Figure 14–4. Materials Costs and Output (assuming greater scrap on overtime shifts)

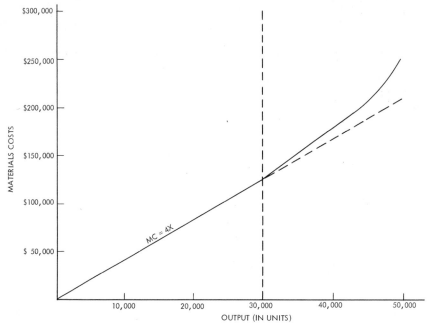

Assumes: (1) Maximum output possible without recourse to overtime is 30,000 units.
(2) Scrap rate does not appreciably increase until overtime hours are worked.

In short, some of the firm's variable costs may not be directly and linearly related to output. In certain such cases, however, they may be considered directly variable for purposes of simplification, without appreciably distorting the analysis—i.e., relatively good approximations of the firm's cost structure may be obtained by treating the relationship between variable costs and output as a linear one. This provides an example of managerial simplification of the complex in open systems.

Marginal Cost-Revenue Concepts

The concept of "marginal" is a basic one for the manager since it underlies all optimizing decision-making models. In the analysis of the firm's operations, the concept may be applied to costs, revenue, and profits (or, theoretically, to any goal). Marginal costs are defined as those *additional* or *extra* costs which are incurred because a particular course of action is undertaken. Frequently, the concept of marginal costs is used to refer to the additional costs which will be incurred when the organizational system produces *one more unit* of output. When such is the case, marginal costs will remain *constant* per unit of output at all levels of output *if all* the firm's cost relationships are *linear*. For example, in the illustration given previously in Figure 14–2, the firm's marginal costs are $5 at all output levels. When certain costs are related nonlinearly to output, on the other hand (such as is the case with materials costs with an output of over 30,000 units as shown in Figure 14–4), the increased costs incurred by producing one more unit will *vary* at different levels of output.[3]

The marginal concept may also be applied in analyzing costs other than those associated with changes in levels of output. For example, in financial analysis, consideration may be given to the marginal cost of capital (the added costs of obtaining additional funds for financing).[4] Or, in dealing with other types of problems, attention may be focused on the additional costs which will be incurred by adopting the strategy of say, hiring one more maintenance man in a production operation or the marginal savings incurred by eliminating one check-out station in a supermarket.[5]

Conceptually paralleling marginal costs is marginal revenue, which is defined as the extra or additional revenue generated by the firm as a result of undertaking a particular course of action. As with marginal costs, marginal revenue: (1) is often used to refer to the extra revenue gained by producing one additional unit of output; but (2) in a more general sense may be utilized to refer to the additional revenue generated from *any* course of action—e.g., the added revenue expected by a supermarket if one more check-out station were added.

The marginal *profit* accruing from any course of managerial action is the difference between marginal revenue and marginal cost. Important to recognize with respect to marginal profit is that in making managerial decisions regarding levels of output, profits will be maximized according to economic theory when *marginal revenue equals marginal costs*, since it is at this output level that marginal profits are zero. At higher output

---

[3] This is also true for the kinked function shown in Figure 14–3, in which marginal labor costs are $1 per unit under a level of output of 30,000; and $1.50 per unit at 30,000 units and above.

[4] See, for example, Joseph F. Bradley, *Administrative Financial Management* (2d ed.; New York: Holt, Rinehart & Winston, Inc., 1969), pp. 124 ff.

[5] Problems such as these in which the number of check-out stations or maintenance men will affect the line *waiting for service* may be dealt with by one branch of operations research—*queueing* theory. It is beyond the scope of this text to present any queueing models. For a discussion of queueing theory, see, for example, Harvey M. Wagner, *Principles of Management Science* (Englewood Cliffs, N.J.: Prentice-Hall, Inc., 1970), chap. 15.

levels, marginal costs increase more than do marginal revenues, so that marginal profits become negative, and total profitability is reduced. This point will be illustrated in greater detail in the section below on nonlinear break-even analysis.

BREAK-EVEN AND PROFITABILITY ANALYSIS

A widely recognized deterministic model for analyzing the firm's cost and profitability position is the *break-even* model. As its name implies, one function served by this model is that of answering the question: "What will be the *break-even point* for either the company as a whole or for any of its individual products (or services)—i.e., the level of output needed for total revenues to meet total costs, and at which profits are zero?"

The usefulness of the break-even model, however, is not limited solely to the determination of the firm's break-even point. Rather, it may be utilized to answer such more general questions as: "What profits (or losses) will be realized at *any* given level of output?" Or, conversely, "What level of output must be generated and sold for the firm to realize any particular desired level of profitability?"

In the following discussion, how the break-even model can be utilized to answer such questions will be illustrated. In doing so, we will first deal with problems in which all relationships between both revenue and output and variable costs and output are linear. We will then demonstrate the applicability of break-even when such relationships are nonlinear. Finally, we will summarize some of the major values and limitations of the break-even model.

Linear Analysis

A firm will just break even (have no profits) on its operations at that level of output for which total costs (TC) equal total revenue (TR). In the simple linear break-even model, it is assumed that the firm incurs no semifixed costs, and that its total costs at any level of output will be equal to the sum of its fixed costs (FC) plus its total variable costs (TVC); or $TC = FC + TVC$. Total variable costs will, of course, depend upon the level of output produced by the firm. Assuming, as we will do in our linear model, the variable costs are directly and linearly related to output:

1. $TVC = VC(X)$; where VC represents variable costs per unit; and X the number of units of output produced, and
2. $TC = FC + VC(X)$.

The total revenue generated by the firm, on the other hand, will equal the price per unit charged (P) times the number of units sold

(X); or $TR = P(X)$. At the break-even point, total costs will equal total revenue: $FC + VC(X) = P(X)$; and $X = \dfrac{FC}{P - VC}$. The solution of this equation for X will provide the level of output at which the firm will break even.[6]

The application of the break-even equation can best be demonstrated by both (1) presenting a specific problem, and (2) depicting graphically the relationships between the variables involved on a *break-even chart*. For illustrative purposes, let us assume that a company wants to determine how much sales volume will be required for it to break even on a new product to be priced at $2, and for which fixed costs are estimated to be $50,000, and variable costs $1.50 per unit. The break-even point may be obtained by substituting these cost and price data in the break-even equation given above, and by solving for X as follows:

1. $X = \dfrac{\$50,000}{\$2.00 - \$1.50}$

2. $X = 100,000$ units

That 100,000 units is the break-even point for the new product may be verified by reference to Figure 14–5, a break-even chart illustrating the cost and revenue relationships involved in the problem. It may be noted that the firm's losses decline at a constant rate of $0.50 per unit as output is increased from zero up to the break-even point of 100,000 units, above and beyond which point each additional unit produced and sold results in a marginal profit of $0.50. This $0.50 figure represents the *difference between price and variable costs per unit*. In effect then, up to the break-even point the company "picks up" from the sale of each unit a $0.50 contribution to the coverage of fixed costs; and the break-even point, fixed costs are fully covered; and above this point,

---

[6] Two observations are in order at this point. First, in speaking of "the level of output at which the firm will break even" here and in the ensuing discussion, it is assumed that the firm will be able to sell all units produced (with the exception of the probabilistic example given below in footnote 12). Second, it should be pointed out that for the firm as a whole which produces several products there will be no single break-even point—i.e., with a different cost and revenue function for each product, many different combinations of output and sales for the various products would result in the company's just breaking even. Because of the enormous complexities of examining all such combinations when the number of products handled is large, formal break-even analysis of the type we are discussing in this chapter may be prohibitive. Thus, it would be single-product firms for which the models discussed on this section would be most *directly* applicable. However, many multiproduct firms are able to utilize the basic cost concepts with which we are dealing to determine approximate break-even points. For example, supermarket chains, by estimating how total sales will be divided among meats, groceries, produce, soft goods, and so on, for any given store, and with a fairly good knowledge of fixed costs, labor costs, markups, and so forth, have been able to approximate the store's weekly break-even point in total sales dollars.

Figure 14–5. Break-Even Chart

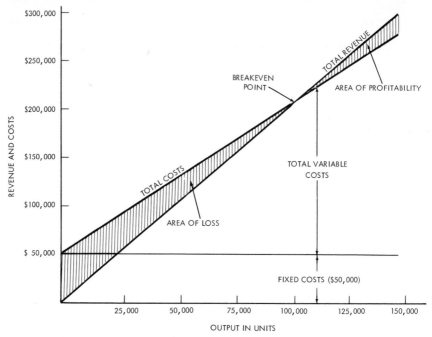

Assumes: Revenue = $2 per unit
         Variable Costs = $1.50 per unit

each $0.50 per unit differential between price and variable costs represents a contribution to profits.

There are certain other important questions which the hypothetical firm manufacturing the new product can answer by utilizing break-even analysis as presented above and/or with certain modifications. For example, it may determine that in order to earn an adequate return on investment[7] on the product, it must realize $75,000 in profit during the forthcoming year; and may want to know how much sales volume must be generated to meet this profit objective. This question may be answered by modifying the break-even equation so as to include the desired profit *as well as* fixed costs as a sum which must be fully covered by the per unit difference between price and variable costs times the number of units of output. Thus, the level of output and sales at which any given profit will be achieved may be obtained by solving the following equation for X:

$$FC + PR + VC(X) = P(X)$$

---

[7] The meaning of return on investment will be discussed later in this chapter.

where *PR* represents the profit desired. Or, with a profit objective of $75,000, and the cost and revenue functions given previously:

1. $50,000 + $75,000 + 1.50X = $2.00X
2. $.50X = $125,000, and
3. X = 250,000 units.

The reasoning behind the modification of the break-even equation may also be visualized graphically by reference to Figure 14–6. It may

Figure 14–6. Modified Break-Even Chart—Point of Desired Profitability

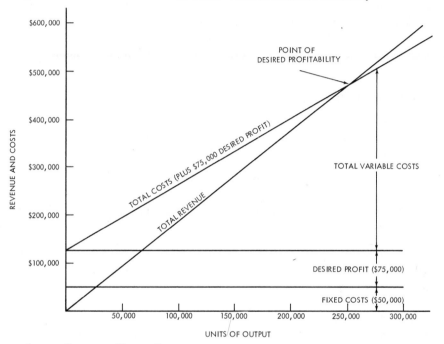

Assumes: Revenue = $2 per unit
        Variable Costs = $1.50 per unit

be noted that the only difference between this "break-even" chart and the one illustrated in Figure 14–5 is that the total costs line has now been "pushed up" by $75,000 (the desired profit), so that its intersection with the total revenue line represents the "break-even plus $75,000 point" rather than the point of zero profitability.[8]

Thus far, it has been demonstrated how the break-even approach may be applied to the analysis of a *single set* of cost data. It should be pointed out that this technique may also be utilized for (1) the

_____

[8] It should be noted that the 250,000 unit level of output needed to obtain the desired $75,000 profit could be read directly by extending the break-even chart in Figure 14–5, without the need to draw up the chart shown in Figure 14–6.

comparative evaluation of alternative decision strategies and/or (2) an analysis of the effect of changes in the firm's existing cost and revenue structure as far as the break-even point and profitability are concerned. For example, a company might use this form of analysis to determine what impact its concession to a 10-cent-an-hour wage increase demanded by the union would have on its break-even point, and/or how much its sales volume would have to be increased with the higher wages in order to maintain its existing level of profitability (assuming that it does not increase the price of its products). Or, a firm considering the purchase of either of two new machines each of which would alter its fixed and variable cost structure differently, might be interested in (1) the projected break-even point for each, and/or (2) the level of sales volume at which the two strategies would be equally profitable.[9]

Nonlinear Analysis

Break-even and profitability analysis are also applicable when either the firm's variable costs and/or revenue is not directly and linearly related to output. Such would be the case when:

1. The firm must lower the price of its product if it is to sell additional units of output.
2. Its per unit variable costs increase or decrease as additional units of output are produced.

The application of nonlinear analysis will now be illustrated by examining a situation in which the variable cost function is linear, but where total revenue increases at a diminishing rate as output is increased.

A firm's fixed costs for a particular product are $2,000, and its variable costs $0.50 per unit. Previous experience has indicated that consumer demand is sensitive to price, and that as the firm's price is lowered, an increasing number of units will be sold as follows:

Price	Units Sold	Total Revenue (Price × Units Sold)
$10.00.........	100	$ 1,000
3.33.........	900	3,000
2.00.........	2,500	5,000
1.00.........	10,000	10,000
0.50.........	40,000	20,000
0.33.........	90,000	30,000

---

[9] Which would be at the level of output at which total costs for each were equal.

These cost and revenue data are illustrated graphically on the break-even chart in Figure 14–7.

It may be noted from Figure 14–7 that two break-even points exist for the firm's product—one at 508 units, and the other at 31,492 units.

Figure 14–7. Nonlinear Break-Even Chart

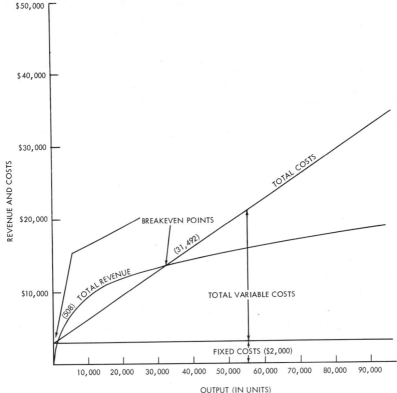

Assumes: Variable Costs/unit = $0.50

Total Revenue = $100 $\sqrt{X}$; where X represents units of output

These points may be obtained by equating total revenue with total costs, as was done previously with the linear analysis. Solution for the break-even points now, however, becomes somewhat more complex since the nonlinear total revenue function in the example is expressed by the equation: $TR = \$100\sqrt{X}$, where X equals units of sales (and output). Equating $\$100\sqrt{X}$ with total costs ($\$2,000 + \$.50X$) and solving for X as follows gives the two break-even points indicated previously (508 and 31,492):

1. $\$100\sqrt{X} = \$2,000 + \$.50X$
2. Squaring both sides of this equation:

$$\$10,000X = \$4,000,000 + \$2,000X + \$.25X^2; \text{ and}$$
$$\$.25X^2 - \$8,000X + \$4,000,000 = 0$$

3.   Next, employing the quadratic formula[10]

$$\frac{-b \pm \sqrt{b^2 - 4ac}}{2a}, \; X = \frac{+\$8,000 \pm \sqrt{\$60,000,000}}{\$.50}, \; \text{or}$$

$$X = 508, \text{ and } 31,492.$$

Now that the two break-even points for the firm's product have been determined, let us answer the question: At what level of output and sales will the greatest profitability be achieved? As mentioned earlier, maximum profits are obtained at that point at which *marginal costs equal marginal revenue*—or, in this example, when the slope of the variable cost line is equal to the slope of the total revenue curve. Up to this point, as may be observed in Figure 14–8 the added revenue

Figure 14–8. Nonlinear Break-Even Chart (point of maximum profitability)*

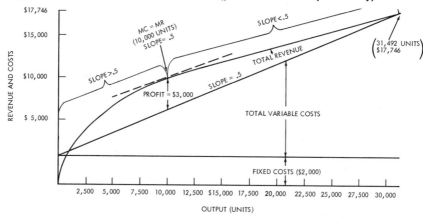

* From Figure 14–7.

obtained from producing and selling one more unit of output is greater than the added cost incurred by doing so. Above this point, however, the costs necessary to produce each additional unit of output are greater than the revenue obtained from its sale.

The point of maximum profitability (which, as shown in Figure 14–8, is 10,000 units) may be determined either (1) by the trial-and-error method of calculating and comparing profitability for various levels of output, or (2) analytically by setting the first derivative of the total revenue curve $\left(\dfrac{dTR}{dX} = \dfrac{50}{X^{\frac{1}{2}}}\right)$ equal to the slope of the variable costs line. This latter approach is detailed in the footnote below for those familiar

[10] As the reader may recall from his algebra, *a* in the quadratic formula represents the coefficient of the x^2 term (.25 in the example); *b*, that of the *x* term (−8,000); and *c* the constant (4,000,000).

with the differential calculus.[11] As may be noted in Figure 14–8, profitability at the optimum point is $3,000.

Break-Even and Profitability Analysis: Values and Limitations

The analytical approaches which have been described in this section
represent simple *deterministic, static* models of the firm's operations.
That is, they provide a "still picture" of certain of the firm's operations
at any given point in time, and include *no probabilistic* variables.[12]
As models, they may serve any or all of the three basic functions of
models which were indicated in Chapter 4:

1. They may provide the manager with *insight and understanding*—
   e.g., What is the break-even point for a particular product?
2. They may permit the manager to *predict* the outcome of proposed
   strategies—e.g., What effect would the acquisition of a new machine
   have on the break-even point of a product?
3. They may help *prescribe* courses of action for the manager—e.g.,
   if projected sales for a proposed new product are below the level re-

---

[11] $a)$ $\dfrac{dtr}{dx} = \dfrac{50}{x^{\frac{1}{2}}}$

   $b)$ $\dfrac{dvc}{dx} = .5$

   $c)$ Equating (a) with (b): $\dfrac{50}{x^{\frac{1}{2}}} = .5$, or $.5x^{\frac{1}{2}} = 50$

   $d)$ Squaring both sides of the equation: $.25x = 2,500$, and $x = 10,000$
It should also be noted that this same method may be used to determine the point
of maximum profitability: (1) when the firm's total revenue is linearly related to
output, but variable costs are related to output curvilinearly, or (2) when both
variable costs and revenue are related curvilinearly to output.

[12] Break-even (and profitability) problems, it should be noted, may be designed
to include probabilistic variables. For example, consider the following simplified
problem. A firm considering introducing a new product anticipates fixed costs of
$100,000 and variable costs of $1 per unit; and plans to price the product at $2
per unit. Its deterministic break-even point will be $X = \dfrac{\$100,000}{\$2 - \$1}$; or 100,000 units.

Suppose, however, that the firm is unsure it will sell enough units over the break-
even point to meet its profitability goals, but does have the following subjective
probabilities from its marketing department as to anticipated sales: 80,000 — 100,000
units, a probability of .3; and 100,001 — 120,000 units, a probability of .7. For
purposes of simplification, assume that management takes the *midpoints* of these
two sales production ranges for analytical purposes—i.e., assume a .3 probability
of 90,000 units in sales for the first, and a .7 probability of 110,000 units for the
second. The results of the 90,000 unit forecast would be $TR - TC$; or $180,000 ($TR$)
— $90,000 ($VC$) — $100,000 ($FC$); or a loss of $10,000. Multiplying this loss by
its probability (.3) would give an expected value of —$3,000. For, the second fore-
cast, the expected value would be .7 ($TR - TC$); or .7 [$220,000 ($TR$) — 110,000
(VC) — 100,000 (FC)]; or $7,000. Summing these two expected values (—$3,000
and $7,000) would give a total expected profitability of $4,000 for the new product.

quired to meet management's desired profitability goals, perhaps the product should not be manufactured.

There are, on the other hand, a number of difficulties encountered in the application of break-even and profitability analysis. The variables in the organizational system are much more complex than have been represented in the models described above—which were made simple for purposes of exposition. In these simplified models, precise knowledge of revenue and cost functions has been assumed, which often is difficult, if not impossible, to obtain in a real business operation. For example, most firms do not know exactly how much sales volume will be generated at various prices, as was assumed in the nonlinear revenue function problem presented earlier. Nor can many firms predict exactly what their materials costs will be during any given period—scrap rates, for instance, may change unexpectedly from time to time. Further, in attempting to utilize break-even for a particular product, it is often far from a simple matter to assess just what percentage of certain overhead expenses (such as the salary of a company's president) should be assigned as fixed costs to that product. Finally, as indicated earlier, precise formalized break-even analysis is prohibitively complex when a firm produces many products with different costs and revenue functions. In short, the break-even model, rather than being a highly precise tool, is simply one which, under conditions of imperfect knowledge, may provide the manager with answers representing relatively good approximations to some of his key questions.

COMPARATIVE ANALYSIS: RATIOS AND PERCENTAGES AS ANALYTICAL TOOLS

In analyzing the organizational system, a great many different variables can be examined such as sales, profits, costs, employee productivity, and number of lost-time accidents on the job. In many cases, examination of any variable takes on significance *only when compared with* certain other variables in the system. For example, one cannot tell whether a monthly sales volume of $100,000 for a firm is good, bad or indifferent until this figure is compared with certain other information about the company. Quite obviously, such a figure would be disastrously low for General Motors; while for a small supermarket, it might be considered excellent.

Most business firms develop and make reference to a wide variety of *percentages* and *ratios* for the purposes of comparative analysis of their operating data. Sales may be examined as a percentage of profits, attention may be focused on the ratio between highly liquid current assets and current liabilities, the number of lost-time accidents may be compared to total man-hours worked, and so on.

The purpose of this section is twofold. First, to add insight into the previous discussion of profitability and to provide a basis for the understanding of some of the ideas which will be presented in the next chapter, a widely used comparative measure of the firm's profit position—return on investment—will be examined. Second, several examples will be presented to show how various operating ratios and percentages may be utilized in the analysis of noneconomic as well as economic variables within the organizational system.

Return on Investment as a Tool of Analysis

As may be inferred from the preceding discussion, the number of dollars per se that a company earns during any given period is a completely inadequate measure of its effectiveness as a profit maker. Rather, in evaluating a firm's profit position, it is important to *compare* its earnings with the funds which have been invested in the company; for the more money that one invests in any enterprise, the greater would be the expected returns, other things being equal. Such a measure of profitability is referred to as the return on investment (ROI).

Several different methods have been devised for measuring the firm's return on investment. Our preference is to define ROI as follows:

$$\text{ROI} = \frac{\text{Net Income Before Taxes}}{\text{Total Tangible Assets}}$$

Income before, rather than after, taxes is chosen in order to provide a more uniform base for comparing a company's profitability with either (1) that which it realized in previous periods (when tax rates may not have been the same) and/or (2) that of other companies, which with varying levels of profit, may be subjected to different rates of taxation. "Total tangible assets" refer to the firm's total capital assets (both fixed and current) minus any intangible assets such as goodwill. Although sometimes calculated on a monthly or quarterly basis, ROI for the firm is most frequently thought of as an annual profitability measure—net income for the fiscal year is compared with total assets as of the end of this period. For example, if a company's income for a particular year were $500,000 and its year ending total tangible assets $2,500,000, its ROI would be: $\frac{\$500,000}{\$2,500,000}$ or 20 percent.

As a measure of profitability, ROI serves as an instrument of both planning and control. For example:

1. A number of business firms define their profit objectives in terms of ROI—e.g., a 20 percent annual return before taxes—and gear their planning activities toward the attainment of such an objective.

2. ROI, although essentially a static deterministic model, may be

highly useful in trend analysis over time. The ROI which a company actually attains during any given year is often compared with its returns in previous years to determine what trends, if any, are taking place. A steadily declining ROI from year to year, for example, might signal to management that an earnings problem exists which it somehow must attempt to resolve.

3. Additional insight may sometimes be gained by comparing a company's ROI figure with that of other firms in the industry. Assume, for instance, that a company's ROI for the past four years has been 15, 16, 17, and 18 percent in that order; and that its objective is to attain a return of 15 percent. Although its profitability objective has consistently been met and the trend is favorable, knowledge that other comparable firms in the industry have been averaging a return of over 25 percent during the four-year period might indicate that the company's ROI objective is inappropriately low.

4. Businesses often find it useful not only to examine their overall ROI but also to compare the rate of return earned on various segments of their operations.[13] A national supermarket chain, for example, comprised of 38 geographically decentralized operating divisions, may note that its ROI position is favorable everywhere but in its Denver and Atlanta operations, on which a return of only 2.5 percent is being attained. On the basis of such information, management might decide to give special attention to the operating problems of these two divisions in an effort to improve their earnings position.

5. The concept of return on investment may also be utilized in making *specific investment decisions*—e.g., a new piece of laborsaving machinery may be evaluated by management in terms of the return on the investment which it will generate. This application of rate of return will be discussed in greater detail in the next chapter.

As may be noted from the above discussion, one major application of ROI is that of helping management to pinpoint existing problems. Knowledge that either its overall return, or that for any of its operating divisions, is inadequate, however, does not by itself indicate to management *why* such problems exist, or what should be done to resolve them. A company's ROI may be poor because it is being undersold by its competitors, the quality of its product is poor, its labor costs are out of line, or for any one of a multitude of other reasons. For this reason, managers will sometimes expand their analysis of ROI so as to make it a more precise analytical tool as follows:

$$\text{ROI} = \frac{\text{Operating Income}}{\text{Sales (\$)}} \times \frac{\text{Sales (\$)}}{\text{Total Tangible Assets}}$$

---

[13] Such an analysis would require an allocation of a portion of the firm's total assets and certain corporate overhead costs (such as its president's salary) to each segment of its operation so examined.

In this expanded form, which is sometimes referred to as the Du Pont formula:

1. The ratio $\dfrac{\text{Operating Income}}{\text{Sales}}$ is referred to as the firm's "margin," and

2. The ratio $\dfrac{\text{Sales}}{\text{Total Tangible Assets}}$ is referred to as "turnover," "asset turnover," or "capital turnover."

The utilization of this formula may enable management to determine whether it has problems with respect to margin, turnover, or both of these variables. If so, as Johnson has pointed out:[14]

1. Margin may be improved either by increasing sales revenue more than operating expenses, or by reducing operating expenses more than sales, while
2. Turnover may be increased by increasing sales revenue more than assets, or reducing assets more than sales.

With respect to improving margin, for example; "Meat markets find that the selling price of boneless meat may be increased by more than enough to offset the added labor cost required to remove the bones."[15] Or in many cases, firms have found it possible to improve turnover by reducing the level of inventories which they carry.

The Du Pont formula, as may be noted, does not answer the question: "Why is the firm's margin and turnover high or low?" To help provide a better answer to this question, the formula may be extended to focus attention on other systems variables and relationships.[16] For example, a partial extension of the formula might include the following:

1. Operating Income = Sales — Cost of Sales
2. Cost of Sales = Factory Cost of Sales + Selling and Administrative Expenses
3. Selling Expenses = Salaries and Commissions to Salesmen + Travel Expenses + Expenses for Maintenance of Sales Offices
4. Total Assets = Fixed Assets + Current Assets
5. Current Assets = Cash + Accounts Receivable + Inventories

Working with series of equations such as these, management may be able to trace changes in its ROI back to changes in the more basic

---

[14] Robert W. Johnson, *Financial Management* (3d ed.; Boston: Allyn and Bacon, Inc., 1966), pp. 49 ff.

[15] Ibid., p. 50.

[16] For a discussion of how profitability analysis has been extended by one firm to include consideration of numerous systems variables, see Kenneth R. Rickey, "How Accountants Can Help Management Manage," *NAA Bulletin*, 44 (July 1963), pp. 25–36.

variables underlying ROI—e.g., costs, sales volume, inventory levels, and so on. For example, this type of analysis may indicate that one reason why a firm's ROI has been declining is that it has been forced to liberalize its credit policy and hence increase its accounts receivable in order to compete effectively with the rest of its industry which has adopted a similar practice. Further, the utilization of series of equations such as those illustrated above may enable management to evaluate the impact of *proposed* policies. For example, a proposed investment in a new automated process might increase the firm's total assets, while at the same time lead to decreased operating costs and a higher margin. Whether the *net effect* of the investment would be to increase or decrease the firm's overall ROI may be determined by the type of analysis we have been suggesting. Also useful in pinpointing organizational problems and evaluating proposed policies are certain ratios other than ROI, to which attention will be turned next.

Ratios and Percentages: Other Applications

Business organizations, as mentioned earlier, rely on many hundreds of different types of ratios and percentages as analytical tools other than ROI. To cover these applications in any detail is beyond the scope of this book. However, the following examples will serve to illustrate some of the many possibilities of comparative analysis.

1. Cost/Cost Relationships. Business firms often find it useful to compare one type of cost with another. For example, in some manufacturing operations, certain employees (indirect labor) will assist those workers actually operating the machines (direct labor) by (1) setting up (adjusting) their machines whenever necessary due to changeovers in production from one size or model of product to another, and/or (2) providing the operators with materials and supplies. In such cases, management may find it useful to examine its indirect labor costs as a percentage of direct labor costs. Experience may show that if this percentage is too high, those employees in the indirect labor category may not be performing up to par; while, on the other hand, a percentage which is too low may mean that not enough indirect labor is being employed to service the direct laborers adequately.

2. Cost/Revenue Relationships. In analyzing a firm's income statement, attention is frequently focused on various costs as a percentage of dollars of sales, and any significant trends noted. For example, it may be observed on the income statements illustrated in Figure 14–9 for a hypothetical firm that profitability is declining as the total cost of goods sold as a percentage of sales income is increasing; and that much of this increase is due to proportionally greater materials costs. Such information may point up the need for management to scrutinize certain phases of its operations more closely—e.g., perhaps materials costs are increas-

Figure 14–9. Income Statement for Hypothetical Firm

	197–	%	197–	%	197–	%
Net Sales...................	$100,000		$105,000		$110,000	
Cost of Goods Sold						
Materials................	31,000	31	42,000	40	47,300	43
Labor	29,000	29	31,500	30	34,100	31
Other Manufacturing						
Expense................	10,000	10	10,000	9.5	12,000	10.9
Total................	70,000	70	83,500	79.5	93,400	84.9
Gross Profit........	30,000	30	21,500	20.5	16,600	15
Operating Expenses						
Administrative Salaries....	8,000	8	10,500	10	8,800	8
Offices and General........	2,000	2	2,100	2	2,200	2
Selling and Advertising....	4,000	4	4,200	4	4,200	3.8
Total................	14,000	14	16,800	16	15,200	13.8
Net Profit..........	16,000	16	4,700	4.5	1,400	1.3

ing due to a larger number of rejected (scrap) pieces being turned out, or because of poor procurement decisions.

3. *Asset/Liability Relationships.* Financial ratios are frequently utilized as a measure of the firm's asset and capital structure position. For example, one commonly used measure of *liquidity*—i.e., a firm's ability to meet its financial obligations to its creditors—is the so-called *acid test*

$ratio: \left(\dfrac{\text{cash and equivalent on hand}}{\text{current liabilities}} \right)$.[17] If this ratio is too low a company

may experience difficulties in paying its bills on time. On the other hand, an acid test ratio which is too high is not desirable either, for some of the excess funds tied up in cash might be more profitably invested elsewhere.

4. *Cost or Revenue/Asset Relationships.* In addition to the income/asset comparison provided by ROI, business firms frequently utilize certain other comparisons between revenue or cost items and assets for analytical purposes. For example, to determine how rapidly their accounts receivable are being converted into cash, managers often examine their receivables turnover, which may be defined as:

$$\frac{\text{Credit Sales During a Year}}{\text{Average Accounts Receivable}}.$$

A low receivables turnover may indicate that numerous of the firm's customers are lax in paying their bills and that its credit policies are not strict enough; while a very high turnover ratio may suggest that its credit policies are too strict, and that, in consequence, it is losing sales by refusing to grant credit to customers who would be fairly good credit

---

[17] "Cash and equivalent" refers to cash, government securities, and other highly liquid assets.

risks. Or, also frequently examined by firms is their *inventory turnover,* which compares cost of goods sold to average inventories. We will discuss the application of this measure in Chapter 18.

5. *Noneconomic Variables.* All of the ratios and percentages which have been discussed thus far have dealt with dollars and cents comparisons. Comparative analysis, however, is frequently utilized with noneconomic data. These noneconomic data may consider both human and physical variables, for example. In the field of safety, as an illustration, companies are usually interested in their accident record—with respect to both the number and severity of employee accidents on the job. Obviously sheer numbers of accidents or man-days of work lost due to accidents is an inadequate measure of performance, since one must also consider how many workers are being employed. For this reason, many firms focus attention on both accident frequency and severity *rates* as a measure of their safety performance. The frequency rate is commonly defined as the number of lost-time accidents *per* million man-hours worked; while the severity rate is defined as: number of working days lost due to accidents per million man-hours worked.[18] Or, with respect to physical variables, certain aircraft manufacturers stock their rivet bins on the basis of number of pounds of rivets per aircraft to be produced.

Several observations are in order concerning the use of ratios and percentages as analytical tools. First, it may be seen that ratios and percentages have wide applicability both for purposes of planning and control. Values defining desired relationships among systems variables are chosen by management as objectives to aim at—e.g., an ROI of 20 percent; or an acid test ratio of 1:1—with unacceptable variations from the standards indicating the existence of problems and the need for corrective actions.

Second, as was indicated with respect to ROI, firms may utilize ratios of actual performance: (1) to compare their operations both with those of other firms; and among subsystems within their own organization, and (2) from a more dynamic trend point of view by examining the comparisons in (1) above on a year-to-year, month-to-month, week-to-week, and so forth basis. For example, the National Safety Council annually publishes statistics on both the accident frequency and severity rates by industry, such as automobile, communications, and shipbuilding, and for all industries as a whole.[19]

---

[18] For figures on accident frequency and severity rates for a number of industries, see, for example, Edwin B. Flippo, *Principles of Personnel Management* (3d ed.; New York: McGraw-Hill Book Co., Inc., 1971), p. 519. It should also be noted that both the accident frequency and accident severity rates (or ratios) have been sharply criticized as being inadequate measures of safety performance. See, for example, Ralph V. Hedian, Jr., "Incidence: A New Tool for Accident Analysis," *Safety Maintenance,* 135 (May 1968), pp. 11–13.

[19] For such 1968 data, see Flippo, *Principles of Personnel Management,* p. 519.

Third, in many cases, actual performance ratios desirable for management are ones which are neither too high nor too low—i.e., if one were plotting ratios of actual performance versus desirability, the more optimal ratios would fall in the middle range, as is illustrated in Figure 14–10.[20]

Figure 14–10. Ratio versus Desirable Performance*

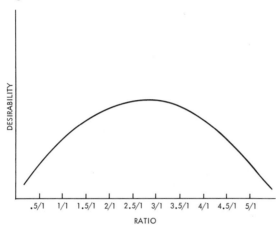

* Hypothetical example.

Fourth, it is important to recognize that ratios and percentages of actual performance represent simply *informational inputs* which management may be able to utilize to pinpoint problems and make decision transformations—i.e., they are *descriptive*, rather than *prescriptive* models. For example, an acid test ratio of 8:1 may well indicate to management that it has a problem of too high a percentage of its assets tied up in highly liquid ones, but the ratio per se does not prescribe what ought to be done about the problem.

Finally, the ratios and percentages which have been discussed above only describe the performance of certain subsystems of the firm. As a consequence, "good" performance on one ratio may not be desirable in light of the fact that it creates dysfunctionalities with respect to the firm as a whole; or, in terms of the discussion in Chapter 3, suboptimization problems may result from the use of ratio analysis. A prime example of this problem occurs in the field of safety. If management

[20] There are obvious exceptions. For example, most firms like to keep their accident frequency and severity rates as low as possible (although as will be indicated later, this may lead to suboptimization problems). There is also evidence to indicate that supervisors may sometimes "hide" accident data from higher level management to make their safety records look "good."

scrupulously enforces all safety regulations (including, for example the use of safety guards on machines), its accident rate may decline. This may occur only at the expense of a lower level of production, however, because the use of all safety equipment may slow down worker productivity. As Strauss and Sayles have put it:

> To the foreman operating under the pressure typical of modern industry, maximum production and maximum safety are *simply incompatible*. One can be achieved *only at the expense of the other* . . . if top management really wants "Safety First," it must clearly indicate that it is willing to pay the possible cost of lower production.[21]

COST-UTILITY ANALYSIS

For all organizational decision alternatives aimed at meeting objectives some resources have to be given up in order to attain certain returns. Often it is possible to attach dollar costs to the *resources* required for each such *alternative* (although, perhaps only approximately). Further, in many cases in business firms the effectiveness or benefits gained from an alternative *can also be framed in dollar terms*. In these cases where *both cost and benefits* can be framed in the same unit (dollar terms) analytical methods, such as break-even and profitability analysis and capital budgeting analysis (which will be discussed in the next chapter) may be utilized to compare decision alternatives. For many programs undertaken in organizations, however, it is not possible to assign a dollar value to the benefits of the decision alternatives or to the *objectives* which they are geared to meet. In such cases, an approach referred to as cost-utility or cost-benefit analysis may be utilized by the decision maker. Brief attention was given to one aspect of cost-utility analysis in Chapter 3—in the discussion of ranking and rating. In this section, a more extensive discussion of the area of cost-utility analysis will be presented.

Cost-utility, or cost-benefit analysis has been given attention to a much greater extent in the evaluation of governmental programs, where services performed are very difficult to measure,[22] than to those in industry, where many measures of output (such as profits) can be framed in dollar terms. There are still many areas, however, in the business firm where it is not possible to assign explicit dollar benefits to the returns generated from a particular program aimed at meeting organizational

---

[21] George Strauss and Leonard Sayles, *Personnel: The Human Problems of Management* (2d ed.; Englewood Cliffs, N.J.: Prentice-Hall, Inc., 1967), pp. 705–6. The italics are ours.

[22] The earlier attempts at applying cost-utility analysis in the government were primarily concentrated on the evaluation of *defense* programs. More recently, however, this form of analysis has been applied to other governmental programs (e.g., health and education) as well.

objectives. A prime example of this would be the evaluation of management training programs.[23]

Cost-Utility Analysis: Some Basic Characteristics

Among the characteristics of cost-utility analysis not indicated in the introductory section above are:

1. Criteria (or standards of measurement) must be set for each program or alternative, and the criteria *must be related* to the organization's ultimate objectives.
2. There are no all-purpose criteria which may be applied to all problems. Each problem must be viewed in light of its own situational context. Further, any overall *single* criterion for evaluating a program's effectiveness is likely to be suspect—most, if not all such problems require the utilization of multiple criteria.
3. "The time context [of the program] is the future (often the distant future)—five, ten or more years."[24] Consequently, the environment is often very uncertain.
4. Usually the environment affecting the analysis is very complex.
5. Because of (3) and (4) above, "purely quantitative work must often be heavily supplemented by qualitative analysis."[25]
6. In building cost-utility models it is important to highlight the important factors and to "suppress (judiciously!) those that are relatively unimportant."[26] Or, in terms of the discussion in Chapter 4, an attempt must be made to simplify the complex in an open system.
7. Attempts must be made to avoid suboptimization problems.
8. The "main role of analysis should be to sharpen . . . [the decision maker's] . . . intuition and judgment." In practically no case should it be assumed that the results of the analysis will *make* the decision.[27]

In short, cost-utility analysis is designed employing both quantitative and qualitative approaches to evaluate problems involving uncertainty and complexity where no dollar cost may be assigned to the effectiveness of alternatives and objectives.

---

[23] One model which attempts (in the authors' opinion inadequately) to measure the returns on training is Jack H. Doty, "Human Capital Budgeting—Maximizing Returns on Training Investment," *Journal of Industrial Engineering*, 16 (March-April 1965), pp. 139–45.

[24] Gene H. Fisher, "The Role of Cost-Utility Analysis in Program Budgeting," in David Novick (ed.), *Program Budgeting: Program Analysis and the Federal Budget* (Cambridge, Mass.: Harvard University Press, 1965), p. 66. Program budgeting will be discussed later in Chapter 16.

[25] Ibid., p. 67.

[26] Ibid., p. 72.

[27] Ibid., p. 67.

Some Inadequate Cost-Utility Approaches

No really optimal approaches have been designed to evaluate the types of cost-utility programs with the characteristics described above. To provide greater insight into *specific* cost-utility problem handling, some inadequate approaches will be presented in this section. Then in the next section, some theoretically sounder approaches will be considered.

First, cost/effectiveness ratios may frequently be misused in cost-utility analysis. For example, suppose that the Department of Defense could develop a bomber system at a cost of $1 billion which would be able to destroy 10 targets; or a new missile system, capable of destroying 200 targets at a cost of $50 billion. Here, the *effectiveness*/cost ratio for the bombers would be 10:1; while the same ratio for the missile system would be only 4:1. Targets may be a poor measure of effectiveness, for any number of reasons. Further, in answering the question, should the bomber system be chosen because its (questionable) effectiveness/cost ratio is higher:

> The answer is surely no, for it might merely be a system which would invite and lose a war inexpensively. To maximize the *ratio* of effectiveness to cost may be a plausible criterion at first glance, but it allows the absolute magnitude of the achievement or the cost to *roam at will*. Surely it would be a mistake to tempt the decision-maker to ignore the absolute amount of damage that the bombing system could do.[28]

In measuring the effectiveness of governmental nondefense programs, numerous other inadequacies have been pointed out by Hatry. Among the most common are work load or output measures and physical standards. An example of a work load measure would be the "number of livestock inspected" by the Department of Agriculture. Although valid as a work load measure per se, it says little about the effectiveness of the program and ignores such vital questions as: "How effective will the livestock inspection . . . be? What would be the effects on citizens if . . . [this program was] . . . reduced? increased? or revised?"[29] As ex-

---

[28] Both this direct quotation and the example given above are drawn from Roland N. McKean, *Efficiency in Government through Systems Analysis* (New York: John Wiley & Sons, Inc., 1958), p. 36. The italics are ours. McKean goes on to point out that if the ratios remained constant for all levels of achievement (or cost), the ratio analysis would be adequate—e.g., if at $50 billion the bombers would destroy 500 targets or at $40 billion, 40 targets, and so on, the bombers would represent a "dominant system" and be preferable. However, "to assume that such ratios are constant is not permissible some of the time and hazardous the rest of the time" (p. 37).

[29] Harry P. Hatry, "Measuring the Effectiveness of Nondefense Public Programs," *Operations Research*, 18 (September-October 1970), p. 773.

amples of physical standards, Hatry indicates the inadequate use of what are essentially ratios—e.g., "x acres of neighborhood parks per 1,000 population, . . . z teachers per so many students."[30] These ratios as Hatry points out, say nothing, for example, about either the *quality* or quantity of recreation or education which will be provided. Further, like the work load measures, they do not really provide any direct answers about the extent to which programs meet *basic* organizational objectives—e.g., providing high-quality food with the livestock inspection, or high-quality education for the nation's children by using teacher/student ratios.

More Adequate Cost-Utility Analysis

Although there have been no optimal approaches to dealing with cost-utility problems yet developed, there are at least two conceptual approaches which may be useful to the decision maker. In examining different alternatives, one is to assume or set "either the costs or gains, seeking the way to get the most for a given cost, or to achieve a specified objective at least cost."[31] A major problem in this type of analysis, however, is how to determine the right level of attainment or cost (budget) to establish for comparing the alternatives. One way of overcoming this problem is to start with several effectiveness levels and several budget sizes. Such an analysis may or may not lead to choosing the most desirable alternative.[32] Regardless, however, the decision maker will still be required to relate the analysis to the *ultimate* objectives of the organization—e.g., with the bomber versus missile illustration provided earlier, is it 50 targets, 100 targets, 300 targets, and so on, for which it is most desirable to have destructive capabilities in light of the *overall objectives* of national defense? This illustrates one of the fundamental characteristics of cost-utility analysis mentioned earlier—the results of the analysis will not make decisions, but rather the analysis should be conceived of as a way of sharpening the decision maker's intuition and judgment.

The second approach which may be useful to the decision maker

---

[30] Ibid., p. 774.

[31] McKean, *Efficiency in Government*, p. 47. As McKean points out, these "two criterion-forms are equivalent, if the size of either gain or cost is the same in the two tests." For his elaboration of this point, see ibid.

[32] According to McKean, if the same alternative is better for all effectiveness or budget (cost) levels, it is "dominant" in the same sense as noted earlier, and should be chosen. However, to continue with the illustration presented earlier, even though the bomber (with a 4:1 effectiveness/cost ratio) were dominant and preferred to the missile, the analysis would still not tell us the number of targets requiring destructive capabilities (and therefore, the number of bombers most desirable). (Ibid., p. 48).

in evaluating and relating alternatives to objectives is that of utilizing "proximate" or "proxy" criteria. That is, since it is not possible to evaluate directly such ultimate objectives as "the best military defense for the nation," or "the best public relations for the firm," *lower level* criteria may be used as substitutes in decision making.[33] For example, "the observed 'going' price of narcotics may be useful as a proxy for the effectiveness of efforts to reduce narcotics flow."[34] Or, in order to meet the subobjective "maternal and infant care" of the overall objective of national health, the program costs of various alternatives may be compared against the number of annual maternal deaths, annual infant deaths, and annual infant defects which would be expected to occur with each alternative.[35] As Hatry has pointed out, however, there is a tendency for analysts to overdo the use of proxy criteria, for example, by "accepting a proxy criterion that is readily quantifiable and that permits 'optimization' [rather] than to attempt the difficult task of finding vital, but less quantifiable, relations."[36] In short, proximate criteria, like the examination of multiple budget and cost levels, only provide *part* of the analysis—it is necessary for the decision maker to relate any such criteria to the ultimate objectives which he seeks to meet, which often must be done on a subjective, intuitive basis.

SUMMARY

In the analysis of the business firm, reliance is placed on a number of fundamental economic concepts: sunk, opportunity, fixed, and variable costs; and marginal revenue, costs, and profit. An important managerial tool for carrying out various forms of profitability analysis is the break-even model. This approach may be utilized to handle situations in which the cost and revenue functions involved are either linear or nonlinear. Additionally, business firms utilize a number of different types of ratios and percentages for comparing the relationship among variables in the organizational system both as yardsticks in the setting of objectives,

---

[33] In a strict sense, the number of targets capable of destruction discussed above could be considered a proxy criterion.

[34] Hatry, "Effectiveness of Nondefense Programs," p. 779.

[35] This example is drawn from a more detailed illustrative one presented in ibid., pp. 781 ff.

[36] Ibid., p. 779. As an example, Hatry indicates how New York City did an analysis of its "emergency ambulance-service system in which the number and location of ambulances were related to response times, e.g., both times until arrival at the scene and round-trip times until the patient was delivered to a hospital for care." One of the charts in this analysis showed a response time reduction of from 14 to 12 minutes. Hatry's criticism of this study was based on the grounds that no one tackled the more important problem in any great depth of exactly *what effect* did the reduction of response time have upon the more *fundamental* objective of better individual health. Ibid., pp. 779–80.

and as a means of pinpointing problem areas. For control purposes, these percentages and ratios may be utilized along the lines suggested in Chapter 13—performance trends may be noted, the firm's performance may be compared with other similar companies, and/or performance comparisons may be made among similar subsystems in the organization. Also, since no explicit costs may be associated with many outputs generated by business firms and other organizations, cost-utility analysis is another useful approach available to the manager. Utilized alone, no single analytical tool discussed in this chapter will provide a complete picture of an organization's operations or problems. However, multiple analyses which focus attention on numerous systems variables and relationships of the types we have been discussing can be useful in helping management to develop more satisfactory solutions to its problems.

DISCUSSION AND STUDY QUESTIONS

1. In cost-utility analysis, one approach in examining different alternatives is to assume either the costs or gains, attempting to get the greatest benefit for a given cost, or to achieve a desired objective at the lowest cost. Comment on the efficacy of this approach.

2. What are some of the limitations of ratio analysis?

3. Evaluate the validity of the following statements concerning cost-utility analysis:

   a) Cost-utility problems rarely create suboptimization problems.

   b) In practically no cases can we assume that the results of the analysis will make a decision for the decision maker.

   c) Cost-utility analysis is geared more to decision making under risk, as opposed to decision making under uncertainty.

   d) In cost-utility analysis, it is often necessary to simplify the complex in an open system as discussed in Chapter 4.

4. A plant manager recently purchased some machines at $100,000. Now, a salesman is attempting to sell him some new machines to replace these. The new machines will require only one-half the labor of the machines the plant manager just purchased. In determining the economic feasibility of the new machines, what data should be taken into account, and which data should be ignored? Explain.

5. When a firm's revenue function is nonlinear, and its variable costs linear, two break-even points will exist. Does this mean that all levels of output *between* the two break-even points or *outside* of them represent levels of profitability for the firm?

6. Since opportunity costs never occur, and therefore, are not real, they should be ignored in analysis. Comment.

7. Since the Du Pont formula will provide a firm with exactly the same ROI figure as simple ROI analysis, why do firms bother to use it?

8. The Sundry Washing Machine Company has set an ROI of 15 percent before taxes as its profitability goal. The firm's income and position statements for the past three years are as follows:

	Three Years Ago	Two Years Ago	Last Year
INCOME			
Sales.....................	$1,000,000	$1,100,000	$1,200,000
Cost of sales..............	800,000	850,000	900,000
Gross Profit.........	200,000	250,000	300,000
Selling and administrative			
expenses................	100,000	160,000	195,000
Profit before taxes....	100,000	90,000	105,000
ASSETS			
Cash.`....................	$ 100,000	$ 80,000	$ 90,000
Receivables...............	100,000	100,000	100,000
Inventory................	75,000	80,000	100,000
Total current.............	275,000	260,000	290,000
Plant and equipment.......	225,000	250,000	260,000
Total assets.........	500,000	510,000	550,000

a) What was the firm's break-even point in each of these years? What assumptions do you have to make to determine the firm's break-even point? Are they valid?

b) Utilizing ratio and percentage analysis, indicate any problems that you believe the firm has faced in these three years.

9. A firm manufactures a product which sells for $1. The firm's variable costs are $0.50 per unit and the firm's fixed cost are $20,000. Its total assets are $200,000, and it wishes to obtain a return on investment of 15 percent per year. Its plant capacity is 80,000 units.

a) What is the firm's break-even point in dollars and units?

b) With these revenue and cost levels will the firm meet its ROI objective?

c) If not, what capacity would be needed to do so?

10. The manager of the Goodman Company has data to determine his firm's break-even point on a new product. His goal is to earn a return of investment on the product of 20 percent on an investment of $100,000. His selling price for the new product is $3 per unit; his variable costs $2 per unit; and fixed costs are $10,000. He is unsure of how many new units he can sell, and his marketing manager has estimated that the probability of selling 40,000 units is .4; and that of selling 20,000 units, .6.

a) What will the firm's break-even point be?

b) Guided by the two marketing estimates will he meet his profitability objective?

11. The Busad Company has a production, the revenue function for which is nonlinear and has been determined to be $100 \sqrt{X}$, where X represents the number of units sold. Its variable cost is $1 per unit, its fixed costs are $1,000 and its maximum production with existing facilities

is 3,000 units. Determine the firm's break-even point(s). At what production level would the company's profits be maximized? Is this level attainable? If not, at what attainable production level will the firm obtain the greatest profits?

SELECTED REFERENCES

Analysis of Cost-Volume-Profit Relationships. National Association of Accountants, Research Reports 16-18 combined, 1949–1950.

ANDERSON, C. W. "Disclosure of Assumptions, Key to Better Break-Even Analysis," *National Association of Accountants Bulletin,* 39 (1957), 25–30.

BARISH, N. N. *Economic Analysis: For Engineering and Managerial Decision Making.* New York: McGraw-Hill Book Co., 1962.

BAUMOL, WILLIAM J. *Economic Theory and Operations Analysis.* 2d ed. Englewood Cliffs, N.J.: Prentice-Hall, Inc., 1965.

DEAN, JOEL. *Managerial Economics.* Englewood Cliffs, N.J.: Prentice-Hall, Inc., 1951.

FISHER, GENE H. "The Role of Cost-Utility Analysis in Program Budgeting," in DAVID NOVICK (ed.). *Program Budgeting: Program Analysis and the Federal Budget.* Cambridge, Mass.: Harvard University Press, 1965.

HARRISON, W. E. "The Contribution of Marginal Costing to Present-Day Problems," *The Cost Accountant,* 33 (1954), 128–31.

HATRY, HARRY P. "Measuring the Effectiveness of Nondefense Public Programs," *Operations Research,* 18 (September-October, 1970), 772–84.

HAYNES, W. WARREN. *Managerial Economics: Analysis and Cases.* rev. ed. Dallas, Texas: Business Publications Inc., 1969.

McKEAN, ROLAND N. *Efficiency in Government through Systems Analysis.* New York: John Wiley & Sons, Inc., 1958.

RAUTENSTRAUCH, W., and VILLERS, R. *Economics of Industrial Management.* rev. ed. New York: Funk & Wagnalls, 1957.

"Report of the Committee on Managerial Accounting," Committee on Managerial Accounting, American Accounting Association. Supplement to *The Counting Review,* 45 (1970), 1–8.

"Report of the Committee on Managerial Decisions Models," Committee on Managerial Decision Models, American Accounting Association, Supplement to *The Accounting Review,* 44 (1969), 43–76.

SHILLINGLAW, GORDON. "Guides to Internal Profit Measurement," *Harvard Business Review,* 35 (1957), 82–94.

STETTLER, HOWARD F. "Break-Even Analysis: Its Uses and Disuses," *The Accounting Review,* 37 (July 1962), 460–63.

TUTTLE, FRED G. "Dynamic Variable Cost Control," *The Controller,* 24 (1956), 62–65, 96. */160, 62*

$FC = 120,000$

$X = S$ at break even point

$.60X = VC + EXP$

$X = 300,000$

$.40X = FC + EXP$

$X - .60X = FC + \bar{X}$

$X = .60X + FC + \bar{X}$

Chapter 15

Acquisition of Resources

CHAPTER 3 proposed that business organizations develop objectives geared toward providing both economic and noneconomic values to society. The attainment of objectives depends to a considerable extent on the manner in which organizations direct the means at their disposal toward these objectives. If the resources of the firm—men, materials, money and time—were unlimited, the fulfillment of most business objectives would pose few major problems. However, since resources are always in scarce supply to one degree or another, a key managerial problem is that of determining their most effective acquisition and allocation to meet the firm's objectives.

The manager faces many different types of problems in planning and controlling the acquisition and allocation of resources. A number of these problems and decision-making approaches designed to deal with them are explained in this and succeeding chapters. To provide a framework for understanding these facets of managerial decision making, a brief overview of resource acquisition and allocation is now presented in systems terms.

RESOURCE ACQUISITION AND ALLOCATION

The business firm may be viewed as a system comprised of a series of transformation cycles, in which both the acquisition and allocation of (1) financial resources, (2) men, materials and machines, or inputs, and (3) goods and services, or outputs, are closely interrelated. As is illustrated in Figure 15–1, each such cycle consists of three phases: the transformation of financial resources into inputs, of inputs into outputs, and of outputs into financial resources. To elaborate more fully:

1. Financial resources (or funds) are either (a) acquired externally by the business firm by borrowing or the issuance of stock, or (b) generated internally through the sale of goods and services.

Figure 15–1. Transformation Cycle

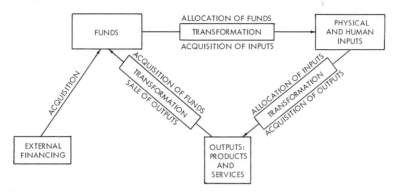

2. These funds are allocated to acquire the various factors of production—labor, materials and machines. Or, in systems terms, the funds are transformed into physical and human inputs.

3. These inputs are then allocated for the production of outputs—i.e., human effort, materials and machine utilization are transformed into goods and services. Here again, both acquisition and allocation are involved—the transformation centers around input allocation to effect output acquisition.

4. The sale of goods and services represents a transformation of outputs into funds. Some of these funds are paid out to the owners of the business firm; the remainder are available for transformation into inputs, thus permitting the above cycle to commence again.

As the preceding discussion indicates, resource acquisition and allocation are closely interrelated aspects of the decision-making process, and many decisions may be considered as being either type depending upon one's point of view. The decision to purchase a new piece of machinery, for example, involves the allocation of financial resources to effect the acquisition of a capital resource. For the purposes of exposition, however, we will treat separately various aspects of the business firm's transformation cycle, considering some of them under the heading "acquisition" in this chapter, and others as "allocation" problems in the following two chapters. This chapter will be devoted to exploring three steps in the acquisition process: (1) determining a need to acquire additional resources, (2) searching for alternative sources of supply for the needed resources, and (3) discussing selection approaches to determine which alternative sources best meet the goals of the system.

DETERMINING THE NEED FOR ACQUISITION

During normal operations of a firm, its resources are used up in the course of transforming them into products and services. Replenishment of expended resources constitutes an ongoing requirement to secure additional resources; employees retire or resign, materials are used up, and equipment wears out. The need to acquire may also arise from growth in the level of transformation activity that the firm is undertaking. To trigger an acquisition decision in either case, the manager needs an information system that will foretell the need to initiate action.

Information systems that trigger acquisition decisions may contain data about the immediate future and/or the long run depending upon how the decision maker needs to use the data. For some resources, it is permissible for the information system to be *reactive* to the exhaustion of resources; other resources will be dependent upon a *predictive* system. For a shipping line loading and off-lifting cargoes, it may be unnecessary to predict when needs will occur or how many longshoremen will be needed if a rapidly deployable cadre of manpower can be made available by the union. If a shortage of men on the job occurs, or if a sudden surge in the need arises, a telephone call to the union hiring hall can be sufficient to provide the needed manpower inputs. If resources are readily available, the information system to show a need for acquisition can be geared simply to denote the time that the resource is exhausted.

Reactive information-decision systems can be appropriate also if the outputs sold to customers are very specialized and/or expensive. The costs of maintaining resources used exclusively for manufacturing a highly specialized machine tool, for example, suggest that these kinds of special resource needs are required each time a (rare) demand is exhibited. Material acquisition reacts to a sale of the specialized tool. Raw materials often are not purchased in other cases if the product is very costly even if it is standardized. Ocean transports provide an example of this. The raw materials typically are ordered upon receipt of a sale since this procedure is cheaper than maintaining an inventory the use of which is dependent upon an uncertain sale.

While reactive information systems may meet the needs for triggering an acquisition system when outputs are specialized and/or expensive or when resources are easily obtainable, these conditions are not always applicable. In some instances, it is always necessary to keep some resources above the exhaustion point because the lead times for acquiring new resources extend over a long period. In managing a blast furnace, the manager cannot wait to reorder until the supply of iron ore is exhausted. In fact, it may be necessary to *predict* the rate of sales orders for the company's steel to ensure that ore will be mined and shipped in sufficient time to be smelted, refined, and formed to meet sales needs. In this case, the company's plans, including estimates of sales activity and the planned rates of production in the operations following those performed by the blast furnace, provide an input into the timing and amount of ore procurement.

The anticipation of the resource needs for a department in the early stages of a long-production process may be a fairly complex task. Manpower planning, for example, can be dependent upon such factors as the future (and as yet unplanned) activity in other departments, the learning rates of workers, the amount of overtime that will be worked, the desired inventory levels and changes in them, and other factors.[1] Thus, departmental planning will often be keyed to some other activity which may be, in turn, dependent upon yet other factors.

The need to acquire is further complicated by an inability or undesirability to change activity levels rapidly. It is usually uneconomical to acquire an expensive machine tool to process a single lot of parts if there is no other anticipated need for that tool. Subcontracting that particular operation may provide a better alternative for the resource needed. Large and temporary changes in manpower requirements are also difficult to accommodate. Rather than to hire and train a new group of employees only to lay them off shortly, it may be more economical to make accommodations elsewhere in the system—e.g., putting present workers on an overtime basis, if technologically feasible.

Keying the need for physical resource acquisition to inventory levels can provide information about when and how much to acquire. Specific analytical models which are capable of providing optimal times and quantities to replenish inventories are explained in Chapter 18. Many such models depend upon constant usage, but other conditions of growth or decline of use will suggest a need to forecast the rates of resource demand. For example, when a design change of an electronic component formerly employing vacuum tubes substitutes semiconductor circuits, past demand experience, even though steady, gives no information about future needs.

Furthermore, it may be that a particular input (such as a specific transistor) will be required in several different products, the amount needed varying from product to product. If past demand rates are believed to be inaccurate estimates of future usage, a parts listing for each product can be combined with the amount of product demand estimated for the desired future time period. The common needs by different products for the same input (e.g., a transistor) can be aggregated to show the future need for that resource. When this result is compared to inventories available, the net need can then be computed.

In summary, determining a need to acquire resources is dependent upon an information system that is either reactive to or predictive of the need to acquire. Predictive systems are the more complex. Their functioning depends upon estimates, forecasts, and plans developed throughout the organization to show anticipated levels of activity and, therefore, resource use.

---

[1] Of course the formal planning efforts discussed in Chapter 12 constitute an important basis for determining the activity and usage rates of resources.

SEARCH SYSTEMS

After a need to procure an input is determined, a search can be initiated to discover acceptable alternate sources of it. When a divisional controller in a large multidivision firm (such as General Electric, Du Pont or General Motors) retires, there exist a number of potential candidates within (and without) the company. This need to replace suggests a search procedure such that reasonably well-qualified individuals could be brought to the attention of the decision maker(s) who will make the replacement selection. Similarly, when a purchasing agent receives a requisition for the purchase of 7,500 of a specific type of transistor he needs a system to seek out qualified suppliers.

Most search systems include files which describe inputs used and their location, together with a procedure of querying the files to identify likely sources. While personal knowledge may be a sufficient source of information for simple search systems, personal capacities are limited and perishable. To search for an important executive such as a controller in a large corporation, for example, requires (1) a formal file of all individuals in managerial positions denoting their qualifications, background, and experience; (2) a specification of the qualifications required in the open position; and (3) a method of matching the job specifications to man qualifications.[2]

The design of files in such a way as to extend the information and intelligence available to the decision maker is, perhaps, obvious. Yet search systems may be erroneously pointed toward ease of file maintenance, operation and cost considerations rather than toward maximizing the net utility they can provide. If a steel buyer in a purchasing department maintains a dossier on each potential supplier, his search capabilities are enhanced if the dossiers are maintained in light of the specific needs for different types of resources that the organization may need to acquire. If an emergency need for stainless steel is requested, for example, the search system should be able to furnish those sources of supply capable of "rapid delivery" of the item even though "price" performance or "long-run viability" of those sources is questionable. Typically not all sources excel in all respects, so the search system, by classifying sources by frequently employed criteria of acquisition choice, can be more responsive to these needs than could a system utilizing a mere alphabetical listing of sources. This does not mean that separate files of sources necessarily be maintained according to all important deci-

---

[2] A number of firms have designed computerized search systems for their executives. These are often referred to as "skills inventories." For example, see W. J. Pedicord, "Advanced Data Systems for Personnel Planning and Placement," *Computers and Automation*, 15 (September 1966), pp. 20–22. This article describes systems designed by the IBM Corporation for its search for both qualified executives already with the firm as well as managers outside the firm.

sion criteria. If efficient search procedures to identify sources possessing *any* relevant criteria are available such as exhibited by some computer systems, a single-source file can be sufficient.[3]

A search system can fail to provide information in another way when the file data are obsolete. Updating data about sources needs to be pursued as diligently as any other aspect of a search system to ensure decision makers information rather than misdirection. When a copper tubing manufacturer installs a new warehouse nearby, the new capabilities the manufacturer may be able to supply will not necessarily be evident. An active query by some individual may be necessary to identify the implications generated by such a change. Further, some systems are designed to be updated *periodically*, such as might be the case of an internal file describing executive talent and experience. If all activities affecting executive status (i.e., performance ratings by superiors, promotions, transfers, changes in compensation, education completed, health examinations, and so on) are updated frequently, the individual files of each executive can provide a good picture of his current capabilities. A system incorporating all such changes runs the risks of maintaining data never used, but, if designed well, the updating system can be made so that excessive costs are minimized.

Once source files have been established to maintain data perceived as useful to the acquisition decisions of the firm, a retrieval procedure is needed to identify relevant sources. Relevance can be and usually is, shown by specifying the criteria that measure the constraints and variables important to the acquisition decision. For filling a position as divisional controller, managerial background and experience in financial or accounting activities may be two criteria stated, and to ensure that neophytes will be eliminated from considerations, this experience criterion may be established at 10 years. To match possible resources to acquisition needs, then, specifying decision criteria is necessary. For many positions in organizations, specifications of the qualifications thought to be necessary are maintained in standard form; a job specification for each position, therefore, is not unusual.[4]

Once specifications by the using organization have been furnished, these can be compared with potential sources in the appropriate files and potential candidates furnished to the decision maker. It should be noted that the more severely constrained the resource specifications are stated, the fewer candidates a finite system will provide for choice while the greater the risk will be that a qualified candidate will be overlooked. If 15 years of managerial experience in accounting and finance is speci-

---

[3] A flexible approach to retrieval using random access file techniques in a computer is shown by James Martin, *Programming Real-Time Computer Systems* (Englewood Cliffs, N.J.: Prentice-Hall, Inc., 1965), chap. 5.

[4] Similarly, the specifications for raw material used to initiate the machining of a part often are stated on the drawings used for processing the part.

fied rather than 10, fewer individuals from a specific file will be able to meet the higher experience requirement. If the best man for the position has only 12 years' experience, he would not even be considered. It should be noted that some position specifications are written in such lofty terms that only an extremely gifted person could match them. These types of specifications are *hopes* rather than *needs* for acquisition.

Systems to determine the need to acquire resources and to search for candidates are designed to provide information concerning the potential resources to the decision maker. Given that list of alternatives from which a selection is to be made leads to a consideration of choice models.

CHOICE MODELS

Once a firm has determined the specifications of the resources it needs, the amount needed, and the time horizon over which these resources are to be used, the firm is ready to apply a choice model to select an alternative that will most closely match its transformation requirements. Certain choice techniques have already been discussed in earlier chapters—e.g., the rating and ranking approach in Chapter 3 and cost-utility analysis in Chapter 14. The following sections devote attention to three basic choice areas facing management. The first two examine acquisition of physical resources:

1. Are expenditures which the firm is considering for capital equipment economically justifiable? For example, should it purchase a new machine costing $80,000 which will effect labor savings of $12,000 a year for 10 years?
2. Should the firm manufacture itself, or purchase from other companies, the materials and parts which it needs? Cost is obviously an important consideration in resolving this question; however, there are other factors which must be taken into account.

The third examines the acquisition process for the obtaining human inputs:

3. How does the need for human resources arise, how are specifications developed, what sorts of search activity are relevant, and how optimal are the choice models that are available?

Investment Decision Making (Capital Budgeting)

Business firms find it necessary to make many major decisions relative to the investment of funds—in new machinery, plant and equipment, and products. In this section is first defined what is meant by investment decision making (or capital budgeting, as it is often called). Then a number of assumptions which must be incorporated into any capital budgeting model if it is to be "theoretically" correct are shown. Finally, three approaches to making investment decisions: (1) payback; (2) present value; and (3) discounted rate of return are examined.

Capital Budgeting: A Definition. Funds spent by the business firm for the acquisition of inputs are often considered as being either (1) *operating expenditures,* the primary returns from which are realized within a year (e.g., for labor and materials) or (2) *capital expenditures,* the major benefits from which are gained over longer periods of time (e.g., for plant and equipment). This distinction is somewhat arbitrary. Moreover, it

. . . is not always applicable in practice. . . . most companies would consider the cost of advertising as a current tax-deductible expense, even though long-run benefits may result. To reduce the number of proposals for capital expenditures, management may decree that those involving less than, say, $100, will be treated as operating expenses. Neither the tax treatment nor the accounting convenience is theoretically correct, because they fail to recognize the durable nature of the benefits produced by expenditures, but both are justifiable on the ground of expediency.[5]

Recognizing that this distinction is somewhat blurred, but that capital budgeting generally refers to acquiring inputs with longer run returns, some of the basic assumptions in making such decisions will be examined.

The Assumptions of Theoretically Correct Investment Models. Of the many investment models used by business firms today, some are considered by most observers as "theoretically" correct; while others, although their application may sometimes be justified on the basis of expediency, are regarded as being based on incorrect assumptions. The underlying rationale behind all "theoretically correct" assumptions is that attention be focused solely on the question: "Will the firm be better off financially if the asset is acquired than if it is not acquired?" Or, in economic terms, considering all opportunity costs, will the marginal revenues (or savings) realized from any investment exceed its marginal costs? Among the considerations which should be taken into account in the theoretically correct investment models are the following:

1. Only changes in future *cash flows* should be taken into account in capital budgeting. For example, suppose that a manufacturing plant

---

[5] Robert W. Johnson, *Financial Management* (3d ed.; Boston: Allyn & Bacon, Inc., 1966), pp. 162–63. With respect to searching for external sources of funds, it should also be noted that a "basic decision guide in financial management is that, in general, the duration for which funds are to be acquired should be *matched* to the duration for which they will be utilized." Paul S. Greenlaw and M. William Frey, *FINANSIM: A Financial Management Simulation* (Scranton, Pa.: The International Textbook Company, 1967), p. 164. Thus, since capital budgeting generally is largely geared to projects realizing longer range returns, management (if it does not generate the funds internally) would normally float, say, 10-year debentures, or issue common stock rather than obtaining three-month bank loans.

is considering the purchase of a new machine which will replace two present ones, and in doing so (1) effect annual labor savings of $5,000 and (2) reduce the floor space utilized by 300 square feet.[6] Suppose also that each department is "charged" $1 per square foot in rent each month for all floor space that it uses. Obviously, the labor savings represent a negative cash outflow (or return) of $5,000 and must be considered in evaluating the profitability of the new machine. However, the $300 less in rent which the department utilizing the machine would be charged would not represent any real cash savings to the firm, and should be ignored.[7]

2. As pointed out in the previous chapter, sunk costs should be ignored in investment decision making since they do not influence future cash flows.

3. The *cost of capital* must be taken into account in evaluating investment proposals. Obviously, the rate of return realized on any proposed investment must exceed the rate of interest which the firm will have to pay to borrow any funds so utilized, lest the decision be an unprofitable one. Moreover, even if the firm is planning to use its *own* funds rather than borrowing, the cost of capital cannot be ignored. This is because, as pointed out in Chapter 14, opportunity costs must be considered in managerial decision making—i.e., the firm must take into account the return that it could realize if it invested its funds elsewhere at its going rates of return.

4. Money has a *time value*. That is, returns earned sometime in the future are not as valuable to the manager as those earnings which are realized today, and hence, must be discounted in evaluating investment proposals. This is again because of opportunity costs—e.g., $1,000 obtained today may generate additional earnings by being reinvested for the next three years; whereas such an opportunity would be foregone with $1,000 obtained three years from now.

5. Depreciation charges should be considered only to the extent that they influence taxes, which represent a future cash outflow. The effect of depreciation on taxes will be illustrated later with an example.

Keeping these assumptions in mind, the first of the investment models—the payback model is discussed.

The Payback Method. One commonly utilized approach to investment decision making is the *payback* method. Application of this approach tells the business firm *how many years* (or periods) will be required for its original investment to be returned from the savings realized on the investment. The savings so generated are usually computed on a *before depreciation but after taxes* basis. Although deprecia-

---

[6] This example parallels one cited in ibid., pp. 169–70.

[7] Unless, of course, releasing the 300 square feet of floor space would either reduce costs (e.g., lower rental payments made by the firm) or increase revenues (by its rental by the firm to someone else).

tion is not considered as savings, its *effect on taxes* must be taken into account, as shall be illustrated below. Mathematically, the payback model may be expressed as follows:

$$PB = \frac{I}{S}$$

where I represents the original investment, and S the net yearly savings after taxes.[8] The application of the payback model is illustrated with an example.

A manufacturing plant is considering the replacement of one of its machines with a newer, more efficient one, which costs $20,000. The new machine would effect annual labor savings of $3,000 and a yearly reduction in the costs of materials of $1,000. The economic life of the new machine is estimated to be 20 years; and, if purchased, it would be depreciated by the firm for tax purposes on a straight-line basis—i.e., $1,000 would be charged for depreciation each year. The firm is taxed 50 percent on its earnings.

Gross annual savings on this investment would obviously be $4,000: $3,000 in labor and $1,000 in materials costs. All of these savings would not be taxable, however, because the yearly depreciation of $1,000 on the machine represents a tax-deductible expense. Thus, the firm's taxes would equal 50 percent of gross savings ($4,000) minus depreciation ($1,000): $0.50($4,000 − $1,000) or $1,500. Subtracting this figure from gross savings gives a yearly net after tax savings of $2,500. Or symbolically, $NS = GS - [(GS - D)(TR)]$; where NS represents net savings; GS, gross savings; D, depreciation; and TR, the tax rate (percentage). Utilizing these net savings in the payback equation:

$$PB = \frac{\$20,000}{\$2,500}$$

the payback period for the new machine would be eight years.

At this point the reader may be wondering: Just what constitutes a "desirable" payback period? Is the eight years for the new machine in the example good, bad, or indifferent? These questions may be answered in two ways. First, if the payback period is longer than the service life of the machine or equipment, the firm will never fully recover its initial investment; and hence, any such investment decision would be a poor one. Second, assuming that this is not the case, many different payback period standards may be chosen, depending upon how rapidly

[8] For the purpose of simplification we assume here and in the following discussion that S remains the same each year. However, the payback approach can still be utilized even if expected savings vary from year to year. For example, if $I = \$10,000$, and savings were $3,000, $2,000, $4,000, $1,000, $3,000 and $5,000 in that order in future years, the payback period would be four years.

the firm believes it must recover its initial investment, the type of investment being considered, the returns on other investment alternatives available to the company, and so forth. For example, in developing many new products, there may be *no returns* expected until several years in the future, whereas normally a new labor saving machine would begin paying off almost immediately. Illustrative of the variations which exist in payback standards are the following figures derived from a survey made by the Machinery and Allied Products Institute:

. . . 60 percent of the surveyed firms use the payback period. On equipment with a service life of 10 years or more, 28 percent of those using the method set a three-year payback, and 34 percent set a five-year payback. Only 16 percent use a payoff period of more than five years, even for such long-lived equipment.[9]

The payback model, as the above survey indicates, is widely used by American business firms. However, it is not a theoretically sound one in light of the assumptions discussed previously. It does not take into account the time value of money by discounting future returns. For example, consider two investment alternatives, each costing $10,000 and having an economic life of four years; but with different savings as follows:

| | Year | | | |
	1	2	3	4
Savings from investment A.......	$8,000	$1,000	$1,000	$1,000
Savings from investment B.......	$ 0	$1,000	$9,000	$1,000

Alternative A would be a superior one in that a greater proportion of its savings are realized *sooner* than is the case with alternative B; yet the payback period for both investments would be the same—three years. Nor does the payback model consider the cost of capital. Finally, the method does not take into account returns over the whole economic life of the investment. In some cases the savings realized from a machine, for example, may be considerable in those years toward the end of its service life *after* the payback period. To ignore these returns, as the payback model does, is to give an inadequate picture of future cash flows generated by the investment decision.

On the other hand, the payback method is simple to understand and relatively easy to utilize. Moreover, the use of the method may be defended when:

. . . a firm which is short of cash must necessarily give great emphasis to a quick return of its funds so that they may be put to use in other places

---

[9] J. Fred Weston and Eugene F. Brigham, *Essentials of Managerial Finance* (2d ed.; New York: Holt, Rinehart & Winston, Inc., 1971), pp. 151–52.

or in meeting other needs. It can only be said that this does not relieve the payback method of its many shortcomings, and that there are better methods for handling the cash shortage situation.[10]

In short, although used by many business firms, the payback model ignores several important considerations. Before discussing those investments models which are more theoretically sound, it will be necessary to examine more fully the concept of the time value of money upon which—unlike the payback model—they are based.

The Time Value of Money. As indicated previously, it is important to consider the time value of money in investment decision making—a dollar earned on an investment sometime in the future does not have as great a present value as a dollar earned today. By utilizing a simple example, we will now illustrate mathematically just how money does have a time value. This analysis will provide the basis for understanding the present value and discounted rate of return models discussed later, both of which call for discounting the value of future returns.

The idea that money has a time value may be grasped most readily if, rather than beginning the discussion with the present value of future earnings on an investment, we first consider the *converse*—i.e., the *future value of presently held funds*. Assume, for example, that a manager has just invested $100 in some securities, and that he will earn 10 percent on his money compounded annually. At the end of one year, his $100 will have grown to $110: (*a*) the original investment (*I*), plus (*b*) the interest rate (*i*) times the $100. Or mathematically, the future value of his investment after one year (FV_1) may be represented as:

(1) $FV_1 = I + i(I)$, or
(2) $FV_1 = I(1 + i)$.

Next, assume that the manager leaves all of his money (now $110) invested in the securities for a *second* year. At the end of this time, its value will be equal to: (*a*) the $110 which he had at the *beginning* of the second year—$I(1 + i)$—plus (*b*) the interest earned on this money *during* the second year, or $i(I[1 - i])$. Thus, the future value of the original investment at the end of *two* years may be expressed as:

(1) $FV_2 = I(1 + i) + i(I[1 + i])$, which simplifies to
(2) $FV_2 = I(1 + i)^2$;

and, for the manager, $FV_2 = 100(1 + .10)^2$, or $121.

The reader will note that the equation which gives the future value of the investment at the end of year two (FV_2) is like that which gives the future value at the end of year one (FV_1), *except that* $(1 + i)$ *is now raised to the second power rather than to the first.* Although it is not done here, it can be shown mathematically that this type of

---

[10] Ibid., p. 152.

relationship holds for *any number* of years or periods—the future value of any present investment at the end of any given number of periods (n) will equal the original investment times $(1 + i)$ to the power n: $FV_n = I(1 + i)^n$.[11] That is, the future value at the end of three periods equals $I(1 + i)^3$; at the end of four periods, $I(1 + i)^4$; and so on, assuming that the interest rate, i, remains the same during all periods.

The Present Value Model. Above it was shown that $100 invested today at an interest rate of 10 percent will have a future value of $121 at the end of two years. Conversely, it follows that $121 earned on an investment two years hence has a *present value* today of $100 if earnings are discounted at a rate of 10 percent per year. Or, in mathematical terms:

(1)   Since $FV_n = I(1 + i)^n$,

(2) $I = \dfrac{FV_n}{(1 + i)^n}$.

This latter equation lies at the heart of the present value investment model. However:

1. Since in investment decision making we are interested not in the future value of presently held funds, but rather in the present value of anticipated future earnings, the following notation is preferable:

$$PV = \frac{R_n}{(1 + i)^n}$$

where R_n represents the returns expected in any given future period and PV, the present value of these returns.

2. Since a firm normally expects to obtain returns on its investments not only in a single future year, but rather *for several years,* we must expand our equation so as to account for any number of a *series* of future returns which management wishes to consider. As the reader might suspect, this may be done simply by *summing each approximately discounted* future return—i.e.,

$$PV = \frac{R_1}{(1 + i)^1} + \frac{R_2}{(1 + i)^2} + \cdot\cdot\cdot + \frac{R_n}{(1 + i)^n},$$

where PV represents the present value of all future returns; R_1, returns in year one; R_2, those in year two, and R_n, those in the last year of the economic life of the investment.

This equation represents the basic present-value model to investment

---

[11] The period (n) can theoretically be of any duration, and does not necessarily have to be a year. For example, if interest on money deposited in a savings bank is compounded quarterly, the future value of any given sum saved after one quarter would equal $(1 + i)^1$; after two quarters, $(1 + i)^2$; and so on, but in this case i would be the quarterly rather than the yearly interest rate.

decision making.[12] Its application may be illustrated by a simple example. Assume that a firm has the opportunity to purchase a new machine for $2,700 which will have a service life of three years, and that the gross savings (returns) realized by its use will be: $1,300 in the first year; $1,520 in the second, and $1,762 in the third. The going interest rate is 10 percent.[13] Taking into account taxes at an assumed rate of 50 percent, and depreciation *only* to the extent that it has a bearing on taxes, the present value of these future returns may be determined as follows. First, assuming straight-line depreciation as with the previous payback example, $\frac{\$2,700}{3}$ or $900 must be subtracted from each year's gross savings to give the taxable savings. Then, these savings must be multiplied by the tax rate (50 percent) to give the taxes which must be paid:

1. Year 1—$1,300 gross savings — $900 depreciation = $400 taxable income; $400 × 50% = $200 taxes.
2. Year 2—$1,520 gross savings — $900 depreciation = $620 taxable income; $620 × 50% = $310 taxes.
3. Year 3—$1,762 gross savings — $900 depreciation = $862 taxable income; $862 × 50% = $431 taxes.

Next, subtracting taxes from gross savings gives net after-tax savings for each year:

1. Year 1—$1,300 — $200 = $1,100 net savings.
2. Year 2—$1,520 — $310 = $1,210 net savings.
3. Year 3—$1,726 — $431 = $1,331 net savings.

Finally, utilizing these net savings figures in the present value equation, we have:

1. $PV = \dfrac{\$1,100}{(1 + .10)^1} + \dfrac{\$1,210}{(1 + .10)^2} + \dfrac{\$1,331}{(1 + .10)^3}$

2. $PV = \dfrac{\$1,100}{1.10} + \dfrac{\$1,210}{1.21} + \dfrac{\$1,331}{1.331}$

3. $PV = \$1,000 + \$1,000 + \$1,000;$ or $3,000.

---

[12] This model assumes that all returns are realized at the *end* of each period, rather than continuously over the whole duration of the period, which would actually be the case with many investment decisions. For example, labor savings on a new machine would be generated continuously, and not all at the end of each year. The error introduced by making this assumption, however, is usually small. We should also note that there are methods involving the use of the calculus which do take into account the continuous inflow of future returns.

[13] For purposes of simplification, we are assuming in this and later examples that the interest rate is known to the decision maker. In actual practice, however, determining of a going "cost of capital" presents many difficulties. For a discussion of the measurement of the cost of capital, see, for example, Johnson, *Financial Management*, chap. 8.

Thus, the present value of all future returns (after taxes) on this investment of $2,700 is $3,000.[14]

Now that we have demonstrated the mechanics of the present value model, let us turn to the critical question involved in this type of analysis: What represents a "good" present value on any given investment? The answer is that an investment is generally desirable if (1) the present value of all future returns is greater than the cost of the investment (if $PV > I$);[15] *provided that* (2) no more favorable investment alternatives are available. Thus, the new machine in the above example would represent a desirable investment since the present value of its future savings ($3,000) is greater than its cost ($I = $2,700) unless the firm could invest the $2,700 elsewhere and generate returns the present value of which would exceed $3,000.[16]

The Discounted Rate of Return Model. The final investment model to be discussed, *discounted rate of return,* is theoretically quite similar to the present value model. As its name implies, it is also conceptually related to ROI, which we treated in the previous chapter. Rather than determining the present value of a series of appropriately discounted future cash inflows, as does the present value model, this approach answers the question: What return on the original investment will such inflows represent? The equation which will give the discounted rate of return resembles that utilized for present value, except that the unknown is now r rather than PV:

$$I = \frac{R_1}{(1 + r)^1} + \frac{R_2}{(1 + r)^2} + \cdots + \frac{R_n}{(1 + r)^n}; \text{ where}$$

I represents the original cost of the investment; $R_1, R_2 \ldots R_n$, the future anticipated savings or returns; and r, the discounted rate of return to be determined.

---

[14] As the reader may have already observed, raising $(1 + i)$ to powers as high as 10, 15 or more which is sometimes necessary in utilizing the present value model would be quite time consuming. Fortunately, tables have been prepared which give the present value of a dollar earned at the end of each future year (up to 50) at various commonly employed interest rates. One such table is provided in Appendix B at the end of the text.

[15] Because whenever $PV > I$ the future discounted returns to the firm obtained from the investment are greater than those returns which could be realized by investing the same sum elsewhere at the going rate of interest, i. We should also note that we have termed such an investment opportunity "generally" desirable, rather than always so, for there may be exceptions. For example, a firm whose financial position is strained and needs to generate returns quickly might deem it inadvisable to make an investment where most of the returns would be generated six or seven years hence, even though $PV > I$.

[16] Analysis of this problem would become more complex if another investment alternative costing other than $2,700 were available—i.e., if a present value of $2,500 could be realized on an investment of $2,200 as compared with the present value of $3,000 on our $2,700 machine. For an approach to ranking numerous alternative proposals when I is different in each case, see Johnson, *Financial Management*, p. 179.

The application of this model will now be illustrated by taking the same example as presented in the previous section. All variables such as savings, depreciation and taxes are treated *exactly the same* with the discounted rate of return model as with the present value model. Thus, the net savings figures which are to be·utilized in the discounted rate of return equation are:

$$I = \$2,700, R_1 = \$1,100, R_2 = \$1,210, \text{ and } R_3 = \$1,331; \text{ and }$$

$$\$2,700 = \frac{\$1,100}{(1 + r)^1} + \frac{\$1,210}{(1 + r)^2} + \frac{\$1,331}{(1 + r)^3}.$$

The discounted rate of return may be obtained from this equation by means of trial and error experimentation with various values of r until one which provides a solution is obtained.[17] Such experimentation, as the reader may wish to verify, provides a value of just over 16 for r in the above example; and hence the discounted rate of return is approximately 16 percent.

Some additional observations are in order at this point to further clarify the meaning of the discounted rate of return model. First, the close relationship between this model and the present value one may again be noted by observing that, for any investment problem:

1. When $PV > I, r > i,$
2. When $PV = I, r = i,$ and
3. When $PV < I, r < i.$

For example, assuming an i of 10 percent again in the last problem, $16\% > 10\%$; as was the present value of $\$3,000 > \$2,700$, utilizing the same data.

This observation leads logically to a second one about the discounted rate of return model. Earlier it was pointed out that an investment may generally be considered "desirable" when $PV > I$, provided that no other more favorable alternatives are available. Thus, since when $PV > I, r > i$, so also may an investment generally be considered desirable when $r > i$, with the same proviso.[18]

Finally, it should be pointed out that the present value and discounted rate of return models will not always yield the same results. A basic reason for this is that the present value approach assumes that all future returns will be reinvested by the firm at the interest rate i; whereas the discounted rate of return model assumes that these returns will be reinvested at the rate r. For example, consider an investment project

---

[17] This substitution may be simplified by the use of tables which give $(1 + r)^n$ for commonly utilized ranges of r and n.

[18] Again, we use the words "generally desirable" for the same reason as indicated above in footnote 15.

which has a discounted rate of return of 187 percent. The discounted rate of return model assumes that the returns obtained from this investment each period are immediately reinvested at 187 percent. While this assumption may be mathematically correct, it is unreasonable in its economic implications. It is beyond the scope of this book to delve deeply into this and other technical differences between the two methods.[19] However, it should be mentioned that:

1. When the firm is examining only a single investment proposal (e.g., replacing an old machine with a new one), generally the same conclusions may be obtained by utilization of either method.
2. When, on the other hand, various alternative proposals are being ranked, with the objective in mind of selecting the best of these, the present value model is theoretically sounder than discounted rate of return.

Present Value and Discounted Rate of Return: Values and Limitations. A major value of both the present value and discounted rate of return models in comparison with other capital budgeting approaches such as the payback method, is that each considers explicitly the time value of money. These two models are, however, not widely utilized in industry today. Rather, quite frequently:

> Rougher techniques are used, sometimes because they are reasonably suitable to the needs of the firm, sometimes because more sophisticated techniques are not understood by management, and sometimes because management is still in process of training and educating its personnel in the use of rate of return or present value.[20]

Moreover, there are several difficult technical problems which have to be faced in the application of present value and discounted rate of return. For one, as indicated previously it is often difficult to determine just what value should be taken to represent the cost of capital. Furthermore, both the present value and discounted rate of return models are based on the assumption that the manager possesses relatively accurate knowledge about the size of the future returns—i.e., both assume *conditions of certainty*. In actual practice, however, it may be very difficult to estimate how much in savings, for example, would be realized on a new machine 10 years hence. Recognizing this limitation, some financial analysts have utilized Monte Carlo simulation techniques and other methods involving statistical analysis to evaluate investment proposals in which future savings as a function of numerous variables

---

[19] For a more thorough discussion of these differences, see Michael P. Hottenstein, "An Analysis of Theoretical and Empirical Models of Capital Investment Decision Processes" (Chap. ii, Ph.D. dissertation, Indiana University, 1964).

[20] Johnson, *Financial Management*, p. 183.

not known for certain.[21] In the next section, a simple present value model under conditions of risk and uncertainty will be illustrated.

Present Value under Risk and Uncertainty. In the literature on finance, risk in capital budgeting is usually ignored, or treated in a "formalistic mathematical manner."[22] As Weston and Brigham have pointed out:

. . . ignoring risk is dangerous at best and downright misleading at worst . . . [while] . . . the mathematical approach is frequently not feasible in business situations because (1) vital statistical information is unavailable and (2) all the theoretical concepts have not yet been completely worked out.[23]

In this section, a simplified example of how risk and uncertainty might be included in present value analysis will be presented. This discussion is designed to provide the reader with some insight into financial risk and uncertainty, utilizing only the approaches discussed previously in Chapter 3.

As an illustration, assume that a business firm is evaluating one capital budgeting alternative: (1) which has an economic life of three years, (2) where $I = \$2,700$, and (3) where the cost of capital (i) is 10 percent—as in the example presented above. Assume further the following conditions. For year 1, the firm believes that its *net* savings are known for certain to be $1,100, which appropriately discounted for one year will equal approximately $1,001.[24]

For year 2, the firm is less certain about the returns from the project. Employing decision making under risk, however, it concludes that if business is "good" (probability of .6), the alternative will generate *net* returns of $1,510, but that if business is "bad" (probability of .4), it will only generate net returns of $759. The expected value of returns for the project discounted for two years will thus be: $1,510 $\times$ .6 $\times$ .83 or $752, plus $759 $\times$ .4 $\times$ .83 or $252; or a total of $1,004.

For year 3, the firm believes that business could be "good," "fair," or "poor" and anticipates *net* returns from the investment alternative of $1,530, $1,330, and $1,130, respectively, for these three possible states of nature. The firm is, however, *completely uncertain* about business prospects for year 3, and decides to use the Laplace criterion to evaluate the alternatives—i.e., to assign an equal probability of .33 to each state

---

[21] See, for example, David B. Hertz, "Risk Analysis in Capital Investment," *Harvard Business Review,* 42 (January-February 1964), pp. 95–106.

[22] Weston and Brigham, *Essentials of Managerial Finance,* p. 167.

[23] Ibid. For a more detailed and sophisticated discussion of capital budgeting under uncertainty, see ibid., chap. 9.

[24] For all calculations in this example, the returns are multiplied by the appropriated discounted value (as given in Appendix B of this text) rounded to *two* decimal places. Thus, the present value figures arrived at are only close approximations to the "real" values.

of nature. Appropriately discounting the three possible returns employing the Laplace criterion gives the following value to be attached to the investment alternative in year 3:

1. $1,530 \times .33 \times .75 = \$379$ if "good business" conditions occur,
2. $1,330 \times .33 \times .75 = \$329$ if "fair" business conditions prevail,
3. $1,130 \times .33 \times .75 = \$280$ if "poor" business conditions happen, and
4. Summing these three values gives a total value for year 3 of $988.

Simply summing the value obtained above for each year will determine the total expected present value of the proposal—i.e., $1,001, for year 1 + $1,004, for year 2 + $988 for year 3 = $2,993. Since this value (PV) is greater than the I of $2,700, the firm should make the investment subject to any of the exceptional conditions discussed previously.

For year 3 in the above example, the decision maker could, of course, have utilized the other uncertainty criteria presented in Chapter 3—e.g., complete pessimism (assuming a net return of $1,130), complete optimism (assuming a net return of $1,550)—except the criterion of regret, since one cannot "discount" regret as can be done with dollars. As pointed out in Chapter 3, none of these uncertainty criteria would be the "best," with the selection of an uncertainty criterion remaining basically a matter of managerial judgment.

Physical Resource Acquisition: Make-or-Buy Decisions

An important question confronting many business firms is whether they should purchase their parts and material from other companies or manufacture (or process) these inputs themselves. For example, should an automotive concern make or buy the tires and batteries used in manufacturing its cars? Or should a retail supermarket chain which sells its own line of private brand canned goods can and label the goods itself, or purchase them from another concern?

There are many factors which have to be taken into account in any make-or-buy decision. One prime question which must be asked in resolving make-or-buy problems is: Can the *quantity* of input desired at the specified *quality* level be obtained through *either* manufacture or purchase? In some cases a negative answer to this question may be obtained, thus dictating the decision alternative which must be chosen. For example:

1. A firm may not believe that it possesses the technical know-how to make a particular part; or it may be possible to make the part only by means of a special process, the patent to which is held by another company.

2. Conversely, there may be no other firms which have the plant capacity or technical knowledge to make the quantity of a particular input required.

In other cases, however, either the manufacture or purchase of the input may be technologically feasible. If so, cost will be a prime consideration—i.e., which of the two alternatives is cheaper? In answering this question, it is necessary not only to compare the purchase price of the input with the costs which would be incurred by its manufacture, but also to consider certain other factors. For instance:

1. The transportation charges which would be required to have the purchased input shipped to the firm's manufacturing facilities would have to be taken into account.

2. If a company would have to purchase additional plant and equipment in order to make its own parts, the return on this investment must be examined. For example, assume that a firm could save $5,000 a year by making a part rather than purchasing it if it invested $30,000 in new machinery and equipment. Would the present value of these future returns justify the investment?

Nor are the above factors the only ones which management may want to consider in making make-or-buy decisions. In some cases firms will prefer to make a certain input themselves so as to be able to keep secret the processes required for its manufacture. Or, in other cases, the "make" alternative may be chosen by a company in order to provide it with a more closely controlled source of supply—e.g., to avoid being put in a position in which a strike against its supplier would force it to curtail or suspend its own production.

The existence of excessive capacity in its own parts manufacturing operation is another factor often suggesting that a firm undertake to make rather than to purchase its parts. Since the capacity is available, the marginal costs of making the parts would only include labor, materials, and variable overhead while excluding the fixed costs which would occur whether or not the parts were to be made. Price quotations from suppliers for the same parts would, on the other hand, ordinarily, include provisions for marginal and fixed costs as well as a profit. Thus, for the firm deciding to make or buy, the comparisons are between internal versus external marginal costs, except that, the external purchase price ordinarily includes both its profit and more items of cost than would the marginal costs of making the parts. With such a "stacked deck," the choice often is to make rather than buy.

Yet, the "make" choice may be fallacious if the excess capacity is a temporary condition. When business is good, the firm's capacity is likely to be strained, forcing it to buy parts from outside suppliers in order to meet its delivery promises to customers. When business declines and excess capacity allows internal production, the former parts suppliers are trying to stay in business with a smaller number of orders. If these suppliers survive until business again is excellent, they are unlikely to provide preferential delivery or price quotations to firms which have stopped purchasing from them and thus, helped accentuate the cyclic nature of their sales. It is because of this potentially negative effect upon reliable suppliers that some firms view the make decision as essentially shortsighted, especially if their own excess capacity is seen to be temporary.

A major make or buy decision is one that involves a strategic choice and should be considered only in light of all other statistics available to the firm. Making its own parts (or backward integration) can be a form of diversification which requires the firm to develop or acquire technological expertise above and beyond that which it already possesses. Since the firm, if making its own resources, will be selling to itself, the diversification *may* not involve new marketing expertise. Unless the firm is a large user of the resource being made, however, the economies of scale may require so large a facility that it must sell a portion of the output of that resource. For example, a large homebuilder acquired a brickyard as a source of bricks. The yard—in order to produce economically—may have such a large capacity that it must sell to other homebuilders. This requirement puts the integrated firm in a position of having to sell to its own competitors. Through the make decision, not only has the firm created needs for new technical and marketing skills, but it may also use these skills against it *own suppliers*—i.e., other firms not only having previously supplied it with bricks but also still supplying it with other building materials. This, of course, may lead to considerable antagonisms.

The range in complexity of make or buy decisions can be from the relatively simple choice involved in evaluating a single criterion (such as technical competence) to highly complex decisions to acquire via integration of a supplier firm into its own corporate structure. In both cases, the guiding factor should be the *net* utility. This criterion should be considered both in the short and the long run and in terms of dollars and whatever other goals that the firm is attempting to achieve.

The Acquisition of Human Resources: Personnel Selection

We will now turn attention to the firm's acquisition of human resources—the selection of personnel. As the reader will recognize from the previous discussion of human behavior, selecting people with certain desired characteristics to fill positions involves dealing with a number of complex and interrelated variables which defy precise definition. For this reason, business organizations have not found it possible to utilize formalized mathematical models in their acquisition of human inputs to anywhere near the same extent they have with the acquisition of physical inputs.[25] Rather, personnel selection is a process in which managerial judgment plays a central role.

[25] Statistical approaches have been frequently utilized for many years to measure the effectiveness of certain selection tools, such as psychological tests. It should

Nevertheless, some of the basic concepts dealt with previously in the discussion of quantitative models are often considered by management at least implicitly in making personnel selection decisions. For example, some observers place emphasis on the fact that the skills and knowledge of the members of the business organization:

> are a form of property or capital, which is part of the deliberate investment. In fact, this capital in western society has grown faster than the rate of accumulation of conventional, physical capital, and has a substantial effect upon the growth and productivity of the firm. This has become a distinctive feature of our economic system.[26]

Moreover, it is often recognized that the acquisition and maintenance of human resources require both (1) an initial investment (hiring and training costs) and (2) subsequent outlays of funds for employee salaries and wages, fringe benefits, additional training and development efforts, and so on. Managers also, of course, hope to obtain an adequate *return* on their investment in human resources, even though it may be exceedingly difficult, if not impossible, to define precisely the benefits derived by the firm from the application of particular human skills. For example, many companies are cautious about hiring individuals who have a history of frequent job changes. This caution is predicated on the following assumptions. First, the probabilities are fairly good that a person who has frequently changed jobs in the past will continue to do so in the future. Second, for many jobs, a period of initial training is required during which the new employee will not perform at high levels of effectiveness (i.e., initially the returns to the company on an investment in human resources will be low). Third, the firm may, in consequence, never obtain a full "payback" on its original investment if the individual's "economic life" with the firm is relatively short.

---

also be noted that some "management science" techniques have been applied to personnel selection in recent years. For example, the simplex technique of linear programming (which will be discussed in Chapter 17) has been applied to minimize recruiting costs in light of filling specified quotas of needed personnel by the IBM Corporation. See Leon Teach and John D. Thompson, "Simulation in Recruitment Planning," *Personnel Journal*, 48 (April 1969), pp. 286–92, 299. Additionally, CPM/PERT analysis (which will be discussed in Chapter 16) has been applied to college recruiting. See Lawrence L. Steinmetz, "PERT Personnel Policies," *Personnel Journal*, 44 (September 1965), pp. 419–24. As a final example, the thought processes of a psychologist in making personnel selection recommendations have been simulated on a computer. The computer prints out for female clerical and clerical-administrative applicants both: (1) a recommendation to "hire," "hire as a fair risk," "obtain a further background check on the applicant," or "reject," and (2) numerous interpretive comments about the applicant. See Robert D. Smith and Paul S. Greenlaw, "Simulation of a Psychological Decision Process in Personnel Selection," *Management Science*, 13 (April 1967), pp. B409–19. (The subject of simulation will be discussed in Chapter 19.)

[26] George S. Odiorne, *Personnel Policy: Issues and Practices* (Columbus, Ohio: Charles G. Merrill Books, Inc., 1963), p. 156.

Finally, as will be discussed more fully below, the concept of marginal analysis may often be useful in determining whether additional information should be obtained in making personnel selection decisions.

Personnel Selection: An Overview.   The purpose in this and the following sections is not to present a detailed description of personnel selection procedures which is more rightly reserved for a text in personnel management. Rather, our aim is to focus attention on certain fundamental aspects of the problems involved in the acquisition of human resources in decision making and systems terms.

There are several basic steps involved in the personnel selection process. First, human input specifications must be determined—i.e., what kinds of people does the firm want to hire? Second, management must engage in one or more forms of *search activity*—it must attempt to find people available for employment with the skills and abilities desired. Third, attention must be given to obtaining specific and detailed information about all human input alternatives available. For instance, if two recent college graduates are applying for the job of personnel assistant with a firm, management might want to know the age, marital and military status, grade point average, and business courses taken in college, and so forth, of each. Finally, these information inputs must be transformed into outputs—the decision must be made as to which individual(s) the firm will offer employment. These facets of personnel selection will now be discussed.

Input Specification and Search Activity.   For our purposes, only a few observations need to be made about the input specification and search activity phases of the selection process. As far as the former is concerned, human input specification like that of the firm's physical inputs will largely be determined by the nature of both the output and the input-output transformations which are desired by management. If an aerospace firm has positions open which call for advanced design work on an intercontinental ballistic missile, it will need to hire engineers; in considering filling the position of head meatcutter in a supermarket, one important human input specification with which the firm may be concerned might be "previous meat cutting experience"; and so on. Further, economic considerations must be taken into account in human input specification—i.e., can the firm afford to pay the salaries or wages demanded by individuals possessing the characteristics desired? A company, for example, may want to hire only Ph.D.s with five years of industrial experience in solid state physics for senior positions in its research laboratory, but have to settle for persons with lesser qualifications because of limitations on the salaries which it can pay.

With respect to search activity, human resources may be sought either (1) within the firm itself by considering individuals for promotion to higher level positions or (2) outside the company. It is beyond the scope of this book to delve into the relative advantages and disadvantages of promotion from within as opposed to external recruitment.[27] However, it should be noted that most companies utilize both of these two approaches to varying extents.

As far as search activity outside the firm is concerned, any one or more of a number of different approaches may be undertaken by a company. Potential job applicants may be located through personal contact by the firm's managers, newspaper and journal advertising, utilization of employment agencies, recruiting trips to colleges and universities, and so on. Further, human inputs may sometimes be obtained without the firm's initiating any formalized search activity—i.e., from time to time it may receive unsolicited applications for employment.[28]

Finally, a point which was made in Chapter 3 concerning the search for human resources should be reiterated: The manager's rationality to obtain the "best" possible candidates for employment is bounded by time and costs. That is, the marginal costs incurred by extending the search activity farther and farther may exceed the marginal returns in terms of obtaining possibly better candidates by doing so.

The Information Generating Process. After one or more potential candidates for a position have been located, it will be necessary to obtain detailed information about each to provide a basis for the final hiring decision(s). As means for obtaining such information, five basic selection "tools" or approaches are frequently utilized by American business firms today:

1. Application forms
2. The personal interview
3. Psychological tests, which attempt to measure the individual's skills, aptitudes, interests, personality characteristics, and so on
4. Reference checks
5. Physical examinations

Each one of these tools may be viewed as a "hurdle" which the applicant must "overcome" if he is to be given a job offer by the firm. That is, a negative showing by him at *any* of these stages in the selection process may result in his being dismissed from further consideration. For example, an individual may make a good impression when interviewed by management, and his test scores may be favorable, but he may be "washed out" when reference checks from one or more of his previous employers indicate poor performance in his past work. Thus,

---

[27] For a discussion of this problem see, for example, George Strauss and Leonard R. Sayles, *Personnel: The Human Problems of Management* (2d ed.; Englewood Cliffs, N.J.: Prentice-Hall, Inc., 1967), pp. 488 ff.

[28] It should be noted that computerized information retrieval systems linking applicants with employers by matching qualifications of applicants with those desired by employers have been developed. See, for example, Walter A. Kleinschrod, "New System Finds Job Applicants Fast," *Administrative Management*, 27 (April 1966), pp. 28, 30; "Instant Job Placement," *Personnel Journal*, 48 (January 1969), p. 60; and "Computers Jobhunt for Undergrads," *Business Week*, February 27, 1971, p. 123.

in terms of planning, the information-gathering (and evaluation) process in personnel selection may be viewed as comprising a series of conditional statements: if the applicant looks desirable on the application form, give him the psychological tests, if not, dismiss him from further consideration; if his test scores are favorable, interview him, if not, dismiss him from further consideration, and so forth.[29]

Two further observations are in order concerning the generation of information inputs in the selection process by means of the above approaches. First, the degree to which the information generating process is programmed will vary considerably from firm to firm. For example, in some companies managers who are called on to interview job applicants are allowed to structure their interviews in any way they may desire. On the other hand, some firms have developed a highly programmed interviewing procedure—the so-called patterned interview—in which each interviewer asks the *same prescribed set* of questions in the *same order* to each applicant. This approach has certain advantages, such as making it easier to compare responses given by the same applicant to each of several managers in the firm who may have interviewed him. On the other hand, the utilization of such a highly programmed approach has been criticized as preventing the interviewer from being flexible in adapting his questions to prior responses of the interviewee.

Second, the marginal costs of obtaining additional (or better) information must again be weighed against the anticipated marginal returns realized by doing so. For example, by spending $50,000 to design and validate a mental alertness test[30] of its own rather than purchasing one of the many such tests which have been developed by firms in the test design business, a company may have a slightly better predictive tool. However, in considering these two decision alternatives, management must ask itself: "Will the results which may be obtained by developing our own test be sufficiently better to justify the $50,000 expenditure?"

The Selection Decision. Transformation of the information inputs obtained about potential employees into the selection decision output involves many different considerations. Some of the more important of these will now be examined.

First, as was mentioned in an earlier chapter, it is essential in personnel selection to look at each individual's personality system *as a whole* rather than at just certain isolated aspects of his behavior and

---

[29] It should be noted that the sequencing of the various selection tools may vary from firm to firm and within firms in different selection situations. For instance, in some cases a job applicant may be given an interview before being tested; while in others he may be given numerous psychological tests prior to any formal interviews.

[30] Validation refers to evaluating the test to see that it measures what it is intended to measure. For example, to what extent are high scores on a mental alertness test correlated with successful managerial performance?

attitudes. This view, often referred to as the "whole man" concept, recognizes that almost all aspects of a person's life may have a bearing on his job performance. Financial difficulties at home, for example, may lead an individual to "moonlight" (take a second job) which may tend to impair his performance on his regular job. It is for reasons such as this that many companies feel justified in probing into many phases of the job applicant's personal life—especially for managerial candidates, who, if hired, may assume major responsibilities for the firm.

Second, another point emphasized in previous chapters should be reiterated—the individual's *basic* personality system is extremely difficult to modify once he has reached adulthood. For this reason, companies usually place considerable weight on patterns of an applicant's previous work behavior. The man who has enjoyed considerable success as a "creative thinker" in past jobs is likely to continue to contribute new ideas in the future; or, on the negative side, the "job drifter" is likely to continue moving about from job to job in the future.

Third, the personality system of the individual should also be viewed in relation to the organizational system in which he will function if hired. That is, in addition to determining whether or not an individual possesses the specific skills required for the job for which he is being considered, questions such as the following may want to be asked:

1. Are his expectations as to future promotional opportunities with the firm in congruence with the upward movement which it can offer?
2. To what extent are he and his family willing to accept the demands placed on him by the organization—e.g., extensive travel away from home, or the need for frequent transfers from one job location to another.

Fourth, due to the complexity of human behavior, it is usually not possible to predict with certainty the degree to which any particular individual will be successful on any given job; except perhaps to predict failure when a person is obviously highly unqualified—e.g., a low-grade moron to do advanced design work on a ballistic missile. Thus, the selection process should be viewed as a probabilistic one, in which improving input generation and decision transformation is designed to *increase* management's *chances* of acquiring better human resources.

Finally, it is possible to develop certain types of programmed decision rules to aid management in evaluating applicants at the various stages of the selection process mentioned previously. For example, in assessing candidates for an engineering position, programmed planning statements such as the following might be appropriate:

1. If the candidate does not have a college degree in engineering, or if he scores below 28 on the firm's mental alertness test, dismiss him from further consideration, but

2. If he meets both of these requirements, consider him further. Both of the above decision rules are of what may be termed the "go, no-go" type. Each prescribes a *specific* imperative (dismiss from further consideration) if the applicant *fails* to meet a given requirement; but only a *generalized* imperative (consider further) if he *does* meet the requirement. Such is generally the case with personnel selection decision rules, again because failure on the part of an applicant to meet a certain criterion may be a fairly good indicator of his being unqualified for a given job, whereas the converse is not necessarily true. For example, many individuals who both have engineering degrees and score above 28 on the firm's mental alertness test may not be qualified because of personality problems or for any one of a host of other reasons.

When two or more applicants for a job meet all of the firm's selection standards, of course, more than simple go, no-go decision rules are required in choosing from among them. What management must attempt to do in such cases is to weight its various criteria, measure each applicant against each criterion considered important, and then select the individual(s) appearing most suitable. For example, if two applicants for an engineering position both meet a company's selection standards, and one has less previous work experience but a higher degree of mental alertness as measured by the firm's tests than the other, management must decide which is more important, and how much so—the additional work experience or the higher mental alertness score. Decisions of this type, which may involve the simultaneous consideration of numerous variables, are generally not amenable to preprogramming, but rather call for the application of managerial judgment to each particular case. In short, personnel selection decision rules are primarily useful in helping the manager to *narrow down his range* of human input alternatives prior to the exercise of subjective judgment in making the final selection decision.

SUMMARY

A fundamental concern of the business organization is the acquisition of inputs, both physical and human. The acquisition process (see Figure 15–2) consists of three phases: (1) determining a need to acquire resources stemming from an analysis of the firm's current status and future needs, (2) developing a search and retrieval process into files containing descriptions of available inputs and their sources, and (3) selecting the particular resource that best meets the goals of the organization. A number of formalized, quantitative, prescriptive models such as payback and present value have been developed to aid the decision maker in his choice of physical inputs. On the other hand, because of the

Figure 15–2. The Acquisition-Decision Process and Information System

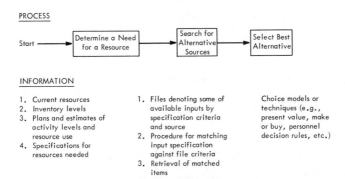

PROCESS

INFORMATION

1. Current resources	1. Files denoting some of	Choice models or
2. Inventory levels	available inputs by	techniques (e.g.,
3. Plans and estimates of	specification criteria	present value, make
activity levels and	and source	or buy, personnel
resource use	2. Procedure for matching	decision rules, etc.)
4. Specifications for	input specification	
resources needed	against file criteria	
	3. Retrieval of matched	
	items	

complexity of the human variables involved, very few models of this type are available for personnel selection. In consequence, managerial judgment assumes a greater role in human than in physical input problems. Nonetheless, programmed decision rules do have some application in dealing with personnel selection, especially in helping the manager to narrow down his range of decision alternatives. Further, the acquisition of both physical and human inputs is similar in that: (1) their specification is conditioned considerably by the types of outputs that the firm wishes to generate, and (2) the economic consideration of obtaining as favorable a return on the firm's investment in the inputs as possible is a paramount one.

DISCUSSION AND STUDY QUESTIONS

1. There are no conditions under which reactive information systems for resource acquisition are really appropriate. Discuss.

2. Which is the more complex—reactive or predictive information systems? Why?

3. Discuss some of the problems involved in developing search systems for the acqustion of resources. How can these problems be overcome?

4. Which of the capital budgeting techniques covered in the text is most useful in personnel selection?

5. A firm purchases a piece of equipment with an economic life of three years for $15,000. In each of the following cases, without making any present value calculations (but assuming that the cost of capital has been considered), can you tell if its present value would exceed the original investment?
   a) Its after-tax returns on the investment are $5,200 per year.
   b) Its after-tax returns on the investment are $5,000 per year.
   c) Its after-tax returns on the investment are $4,800 per year.

6. A firm has purchased a piece of machinery for $10,000, with an economic life of five years, and gross savings per year of $2,500. The firm uses straight-line depreciation, and its tax rate is 50 percent.
   a) What is its payback period?
   b) Do you think this investment would be a desirable one if the present value technique were used instead?
   c) What are the values and limitations of the payback method?

7. The Jones Company is considering buying a piece of equipment costing $1,500, and with an economic life of three years. Utilizing a cost of capital of 10 percent, straight-line depreciation, and with gross savings as follows: year 1, $1,000; year 2, $800, and year 3, $500. Should the firm buy the equipment?
   Note: The firm's annual tax rate is 50 percent.

8. For an investment of $10,000, and given a cost of capital of 10 percent, which of the following statements could you be *sure* are *either* correct *or* incorrect even without undertaking either present value or discounted rate of return calculations? In each case, indicate why.
   a) If the present value of the investment is $8,000, its discounted rate of return is 8 percent.
   b) If the present value of the investment is $16,000, the discounted rate of return is 9 percent.
   c) If the present value is $10,000, the discounted rate of return is 10 percent.
   d) If the present value is $7,000, the discounted rate of return is 10 percent.
   e) If the present value is $16,000, the discounted rate of return is 16 percent.

9. A company is considering making an investment with an economic life of three years of $20,000. Its cost of capital is 10 percent. Its returns are considered to be $8,000 for certain in year 1; and in year 2 management has estimated its returns to be $10,000 if business is good (probability of 60 percent) and $6,000 if business is bad (probability of 40 percent). Business conditions are considered completely uncertain in year 3—if business is good the returns will be $10,000, but if business is bad, the returns are expected to be only $6,000.
   a) If the management of this firm uses the criterion of optimism as an uncertainty approach is used in evaluating this investment, would it be a good investment?
   b) Conversely, if the criterion of pessimism is used, would the investment be worthwhile?

10. Mr. Jones recently purchased a Lifetime muffler for his automobile. The initial cost of the muffler was $27, including installation. Had he purchased a Temp muffler, it would have cost him $15, including installation. The Lifetime muffler is guaranteed for the life of the automobile. The average life of Mr. Jones's automobile is four years. The Temp muffler will last for approximately three years. Mr. Jones has averaged 10 percent per year on his invested money in the past. Has Mr. Jones made a good decision?

SELECTED REFERENCES

AMMER, D. *Materials Management*. rev. ed. Homewood, Ill.: Richard D. Irwin, Inc., 1968.

ANYON, G. J. *Managing an Integrated Purchasing Process*. New York: Holt, Rinehart & Winston, Inc., 1963.

BERANEK, WILLIAM. *Analysis for Financial Decisions*. Homewood, Ill.: Richard D. Irwin, Inc., 1963.

BIERMAN, H. et al. *Quantitative Analysis for Business Decisions*. 3d ed. Homewood, Ill.: Richard D. Irwin, Inc., 1969.

BIERMAN, H., and SMIDT, S. *The Capital Budgeting Decision*. 2d ed. New York: The Macmillan Co., 1966.

CRONBACH, L. J., and GLESER, G. C. *Psychological Tests in Personnel Decisions*. 2d ed. Urbana, Ill.: The University of Illinois Press, 1965.

DEAN, JOEL. *Capital Budgeting*. New York: Columbia University Press, 1951.

ENGLAND, W. G. *Procurement: Principles and Cases*. 5th ed. Homewood, Ill.: Richard D. Irwin, Inc., 1970.

HAYNES, W. WARREN. *Managerial Economics: Analysis and Cases*. rev. ed. Dallas, Texas: Business Publications, Inc., 1969.

HEINRITZ, STEWART F., and FARRELL, PAUL Z. *Purchasing*. 4th ed. Englewood Cliffs, N.J.: Prentice-Hall, Inc., 1965.

HIRSHLEIFER, J. "On the Theory of Optimal Investment Decisions," *Journal of Political Economy*, 66 (1958), 329–52.

JOHNSON, ROBERT W. *Financial Management*. 3d ed. Boston: Allyn and Bacon, Inc., 1966.

LERNER, EUGENE M., and CARLETON, WILLARD T. *A Theory of Financial Analysis*. New York: Harcourt, Brace & World, Inc., 1966.

MAIER, NORMAN. *Psychology in Industry*. 3d ed. Boston: Houghton Mifflin Co., 1965.

PEDICORD, W. J. "Advanced Data Systems for Personnel Planning and Placement," *Computers and Automation*, 15 (September 1966), 20–22.

QUIRIN, G. DAVID. *The Capital Expenditure Decision*. Homewood, Ill.: Richard D. Irwin, Inc., 1967.

TERBORGH, G. *Business Investment Policy*. Washington, D.C.: Machinery and Allied Products Institute, 1958.

WESTING, J. H., and FINE, I. V. *Purchasing Management: Materials in Motion*. 3d ed. New York: John Wiley & Sons, Inc., 1969.

WESTON, J. FRED, and BRIGHAM, EUGENE F. *Essentials of Managerial Finance*. 2d ed. New York: Holt, Rinehart & Winston, Inc., 1971.

Chapter 16

Allocation of Resources

IN THE PREVIOUS CHAPTER, it was pointed out that the operations of the business firm may be viewed as comprising series of resource transformation cycles involving both acquisition and allocation; and the acquisition of both physical and human resources was discussed. Attention will now be turned to two aspects of resource allocation of primary concern to management. First, consideration will be given to some of the problems involved in the periodic planning (and control) of the overall allocation of the firm's financial resources. In this discussion attention will be focused on the utilization of budgets as instruments of planning and control. Second, we will turn to decisions involving planning and controlling the allocation of manpower, materials, and machine ultilization in generating the firm's outputs. It will be indicated how the problems involved in planning and control vary depending upon the type of operations involved, and certain approaches useful in dealing with this phase of managerial decision making (including network models) will be discussed.

THE ALLOCATION OF FINANCIAL RESOURCES: BUDGETING

A key problem for the business firm is that of planning and controlling the overall allocation of its financial resources for future periods of operations. What sales volume is the company to anticipate for the forthcoming week, month, or year? How much revenue will these sales generate? How much money will have to be spent for the manpower, materials and other inputs necessary to produce the projected levels of output? How much profit will be generated by the planned level of operations? What can management do to help assure that its actual costs of operations can be kept in line with projected costs?

This problem can be an extremely complex one, especially for large organizations. Levels of future sales—which taken together with price will determine sales revenue—are dependent on many interrelated variables, and are often difficult to predict with a high degree of accuracy. Considerable difficulty may also be encountered in attempting to project many of the costs required to produce any planned level of output. In short, the overall allocation process is one in which many key decisions must be made under conditions of uncertainty. In light of these complexities, it is not surprising that, as yet, no decision approaches have been developed which will optimize the overall allocation of the firm's resources. The manager does, however, have at his disposal a useful satisficing instrument for planning and control—the operating budget. Further, as we will indicate in the following chapter, algorithms have been developed to achieve cost minimization for certain subphases of the firm's operations.

The Operating Budget

The operating budget is basically a formalized allocation of financial resources for a specified future time period, not uncommonly a year. Projections of several different systems variables may comprise the operating budget: sales, prices, sales revenue, costs, and profits. The inclusion of these projections in a simplified budget for a hypothetical firm is illustrated in Figure 16–1.

Figure 16–1
Operating Budget
Leslie Manufacturing Company

Operating Budget for 19—

Sales Revenue (100,000 units @ $10)..........	$1,000,000
Cost of Goods Sold	
Direct Labor ($4/unit)....................	400,000
Materials ($2/unit)....................	200,000
Factory Expenses........................	80,000
Total.................................	$ 680,000
Selling and Administrative	
Expenses.................................	100,000
Total Expenses........................	$ 780,000
Operating Profit...........................	220,000

A basic step in developing the operating budget is that of projecting the firm's sales and sales revenue for the ensuing budgetary period. Sales will be a function of three basic classes of variables discussed previously in mutual interaction: (1) certain states of nature, such as general economic conditions, (2) competitive strategies, such as competitors' prices, product quality, and advertising, and (3) the company's own quality, marketing, pricing, service, and other strategies. Projected sales revenue will, of course, be a function of both the firm's pricing decisions and its anticipated sales levels.

It is also necessary in developing an operating budget to define both in physical and financial terms the projected input-output relationships for the planning period under consideration—i.e. what levels of manpower, materials, and other inputs will be required to produce the planned level of sales output and how much money will these inputs cost? It should be noted that planned transformation levels may or may not be equivalent to planned levels of sales. For example, a firm with large inventories of finished goods on hand at the beginning of a budgetary period may decide to set its production at a level considerably below that of anticipated sales.

Further, in planning input utilization and costs, it is important to consider not only the expenditures required to produce the projected level of output, but also those financial resources necessary to produce the desired level of *sales*. Advertising, marketing, and sales promotional activities, for example, do not contribute to the production of goods and services per se, but they aid in transforming these goods into dollars.

In some cases, the costs which will be incurred in transforming the firm's inputs into outputs can be predicted with certainty. For instance, the firm may already be committed to certain fixed charges for the forthcoming year, such as interest or rental payments. Other costs, although not as certain to occur, may be projected with a fairly high degree of accuracy. If a company's production workers are being paid on a piecework incentive plan, under which each employee is paid a fixed sum for each unit of work he turns out, the direct labor costs per unit can be estimated quite accurately for any planned level of production. There are still other costs relative to planned levels of output and sales, however, which may be quite difficult to determine. For example, it may be far from a simple matter to determine how much money will need to be spent in advertising a particular product at a given price in order to sell the number of units desired.

Finally, in the budgetary process the subtraction of projected costs from estimated revenues will provide estimates of the firm's profitability for the forthcoming budgetary period. Quite obviously, these profit projections will be only as valid as the other projections upon which they are based; and as pointed out in Chapter 13, it is extremely difficult if not impossible to precisely define many of the benefits derived from any given level of expenditures.

Several additional observations concerning the budgetary process are in order at this point. First, the firm does *not* first forecast sales, then set prices, then project sales revenue, and then its costs. Rather, all budgetary projections must be considered together in light of their mutual impact upon each other. Or, in other words a systems approach must be taken to budgeting. A firm's sales, for example, cannot be predicted without knowing its pricing policies, the attractiveness of the quality characteristics of its product, and so forth; while its costs cannot be accurately projected without good estimates as to what its sales will be. Further, because of the complex interrelationships between the budgetary variables, numerous revisions may be necessary before a company is able to finalize its operating budget. The initial projections may indicate that planned costs are too high in relation to projected sales revenue to achieve the profit goals set by the company. If such were the case, certain programs might be delayed (e.g., research and development); the company's pricing policies might be modified either upward or downward depending upon management's estimates of the elasticity of demand; or additional expenditures might be planned for advertising if management believed that the added efforts would generate sufficiently greater sales revenue to improve profitability. On the other hand, certain programs deemed essential to the long-run success of the firm may be effected regardless of their short-run impact upon the attainment of profit goals. For instance, one firm hired a relatively large engineering force to update and improve its product line even though this course of action considerably increased its costs in the short run.

Second, it is important to recognize the close interrelationship between the operating budget and the capital budgeting process which was discussed in the previous chapter. The decision to purchase additional machinery or to expand a company's existing manufacturing plant will be largely conditioned by its future sales projections. Further, once such a decision has been made, its effects upon costs should be incorporated into the operating budget. If a company plans to borrow $10,000 for a new piece of machinery in the near future, for example, the interest charges incurred, and any labor and/or materials savings realized can be accounted for in the cost projections for the forthcoming operating budgetary period.

Third, allocating funds among several programs, departments, and expense categories involves a series of decisions to determine the *relative values* of these alternative expenditures to the firm. Is a proposed $50,000 equipment overhaul program, for example, more important than a like expenditure for new product research? While from a theoretical point of view, an optimal allocation of resources would exist when the marginal expected present value is equal for all expenditures,[1] determining these values for many expenditures is not feasible. Bounded by the costs involved in accumulating the necessary data and by the time required to prepare such information, firms ordinarily can only hope to approach an optimal allocation. One approach designed to partially overcome this allocation problem is planning-programming budgeting, which will be discussed in the next section.

As a consequence of the difficulty in obtaining data for optimal allocations, less-sophisticated decision rules ordinarily are employed. Often,

---

[1] Assuming that $PV > I$.

intuitive, subjective estimates of the relative worth of competing budget requests reinforced with incomplete objective data are employed. Or, in some firms, across-the-board increases or decreases from the previous year's budget may be utilized, irrespective of marginal values. Further, in some cases, the firm may be operating under certain nonprofit constraints which would render it necessary to keep budgeted expenditures below most profitable levels—e.g., a lack of cash or manpower to carry out certain programs.

Fourth, emphasis should be given to the fact that the operating budget serves as an instrument of financial control as well as planning. As an instrument of control, the budget provides a *standard of performance* with which actual performance may be compared. As in the individual's personal life, significant variations from budgetary plans in organizations represent problems, and signal the need to take corrective action.[2] The operating budget of the type illustrated in Figure 16–1, however, only provides a standard of performance for the firm as a whole. It is not oriented toward providing a basis for controlling the performance of any of the company's operating units, such as divisions or departments, since it focuses attention on activities cutting across departmental lines, and for which no individual manager (except at the very top level in the organization) may be held singly responsible. In consequence, many companies break down their operating budget data by department so as to guide performance and permit a comparison between the planned and actual performance of each manager's entire operational area of responsibility. Such departmental (or divisional) budgets are frequently referred to as *responsibility* budgets. A responsibility budget for one department of a hypothetical firm is presented in Figure 16–2.

Figure 16–2
Responsibility Budget—Fabrication Department
April 19—

Controllable Expenses

Direct labor (400 units @ $2)	$ 800
Indirect Labor	200
Materials (400 units @ $1)	400
Tools	25
Supplies	50
Travel and Transportation	35
Total	$1,510
Expenses Controllable by Others	
Factory Overhead	200
Total Expenses	$1,710

---

[2] That is, to the extent that the budget is realistic. Exceeding one's budget may be impossible to avoid if it is unrealistically low, for example; in such case, the design of the budget, rather than the difference between planned and actual performance, would represent the problem.

It may be noted that this responsibility budget focuses attention only on those costs for which one department manager is to be held responsible. These budgeted costs provide both (1) performance goals to guide the manager in planning and (2) a basis for control. Note that this budget distinguishes between those expenditures which are within the control of the manager and those which are controllable by others. This distinction is made so that the manager will not be held responsible for those expenses charged to his department, such as factory overhead, which are beyond his immediate control.

Brief mention should be made of two approaches often utilized by business firms in recognition of the fact that levels of sales, revenue, and costs may not turn out as forecasted. The first of these is simply to revise the budget at various intervals during the year (assuming a yearly budgetary period), such as each quarter or each month. The second approach is to initially develop a *variable* budget. The variable budget provides for the segregation of the firm's fixed and variable costs, and thus makes possible the projection of costs at various levels of sales and production. For example, if a department's fixed costs are budgeted at $10,000 per month, and its variable costs at $5 per unit of production, its total budgeted costs for a monthly production volume of 5,000 units would be $35,000; for a volume of 6,000 units, $40,000, and so on. Although as was indicated in Chapter 14, difficulties are often encountered in clearly defining some costs as either fixed or variable, the variable budgeting approach is helpful in providing budgetary control of departments when activity levels change.[3]

Planning-Programming Budgeting

To overcome some of the difficulties indicated above, a form of budgeting called planning-programming budgeting (or simply program budgeting) has been developed. This technique dates back to thinking as far as 1910;[4] has been given more attention in the public administration literature than in the writings on business management; and went into effect in May 1966 in all federal departments and most U.S. agencies, following a statement of intent by President Johnson in August 1965. The concept of program budgeting is somewhat ambiguous, however. As Churchman has pointed out: "There are many definitions of program planning and budgeting in the literature on the subject, and most of us have become quite frustrated in our attempts to get a clear-cut and

---

[3] For a more detailed discussion of variable budgeting, see, for example, S. Alden Pendleton, "Variable Budgeting for Planning and Control," *National Association of Cost Accountants Bulletin,* 36 (1954), pp. 323–34. This article is reprinted in B. C. Lemke and James Don Edwards, *Administrative Control and Executive Action* (Columbus, Ohio: Charles E. Merrill Books, Inc., 1961), pp. 644–54.

[4] Roland N. McKean, *Efficiency in Government through Systems Analysis* (New York: John Wiley & Sons, Inc., 1958), p. 249, footnote 3.

unambiguous definition of the method."[5] In this section, some of the basic ideas of program budgeting will be presented.

A basic notion underlying program budgeting is that the organization's budget be directly related to its objectives and major programs *rather* than represent simply a classification of financial obligations and expenditures by object class—i.e., by categories such as personnel, travel expenses, printing and reproduction of company brochures. This does not mean that such object class items be ignored; but in program budgeting, all expenditures should be related to basic goals and subgoals as much as possible. As McKean has pointed out:

> We are anxious, of course, to find cheaper combinations of these objects with which to carry out each program, and to do this we must estimate the effect *on each program's accomplishment* of using various combinations of transportation, printing and personal services. But this is different from attaching a measure of performance to quantities of paper clips or printer's ink that are used up in diverse activities.[6]

In an aircraft manufacturing concern, for example, the organization might have several major programs going, such as the development of a new supersonic commercial airliner and the subcontracting on one phase of the government's missile program; and with program budgeting emphasis *both for planning* and control would be upon the *resources geared* to each of these programs, as well as budgetary sub-breakdowns of resources for subphases and sub-subphases of these programs, and so on. The word planning is emphasized here since, as its name implies, planning-programming budgeting is more planning oriented than many traditional budgetary systems.

A second theme in program budgeting is that departments "apply systematic analyses to the alternative ways in which these objectives are being—or may be—sought."[7] Cost-utility analysis, as discussed in Chapter 14, is considered to be a central tool of analysis in program budgeting, but any operations research, management science, or other technique which will lead to a more efficient allocation of resources in light of the programs desired may be utilized.

Third, program budgeting emphasizes, that in spite of uncertainties, the analysis should go beyond the one-year ahead type, and examine the plan for longer range activities (say up to five years). Thus, program budgeting would take into account the concepts of capital budgeting discussed in the previous chapter.

---

[5] C. West Churchman, *The Systems Approach* (New York: Dell Publishing Co., Inc., 1968), p. 81.

[6] McKean, *Efficiency in Government*, p. 253.

[7] Virginia Held, "PDBS Comes to Washington," *The Public Interest*, No. 4 (Summer 1966), pp. 102–15; as reprinted in *Planning Programming Budgeting*, ed. Fremont J. Lyden and Ernest G. Miller (Chicago: Markham Publishing Co., 1968), p. 11.

One final comment is in order concerning program budgeting. Programs (and program budgeting) cannot be carried out unless they are under the direction of some responsible manager. What is likely to happen in many organizations is that programs, and hence their budgets, cut across departmental boundaries. For example, both an SST and a missile program would use resources from engineering, production, and so on. Anshen has recognized this problem and made some suggestions for dealing with it in the federal government which may have applicability in the business organization. One of these is through interdepartmental committees for each program area, with representation on it by all affected departments. A second is to retain this committee approach, but "place responsibility for chairing and strongly leading each committee in a high-level representative of the administrative unit that presently implements the principal assignment in the committee's area."[8] Anshen wards off the criticism of the use of committees as simply developing compromises at a level of mediocrity, and indicates that both of the approaches he suggests have proven viable. In short, program budgeting has been utilized and given widespread attention, especially in nonbusiness organizations, and has provided a useful approach in managerial decision making.

Cash Budgets

In addition to planning for profitability, it is important for business organizations to be concerned with their liquidity position. For this reason, many business firms also develop a *cash* budget along with the preparation of their operating (or program) budget. The cash budget, like the operating and program budgets is a formalized financial plan for a specified future time period, and is a satisficing rather than an optimizing approach. Unlike the operating or program budget, however, the cash budget focuses attention on projecting the organization's cash needs for future periods, rather than on planned profitability, or other objectives, especially in governmental organizations.

---

[8] Melvin Anshen, "The Program Budget in Operation," in *Program Budgeting: Program Analysis and the Federal Budget,* ed. David Novick (Cambridge, Mass.: Harvard University Press, 1965), p. 361. As an example, Anshen indicates that if the program area were in education, "leadership would be exercised by a top official of the Office of Education in the Department of Health, Education and Welfare." Ibid. Other critics have pointed out that PPBS centralizes authority in organizations. In discussing this criticism with respect to the use of program budgeting in higher education, Dyer has pointed out that: "In actuality, while the result of its use may be an increase in the centralization of authority with respect to the *previously* existing arrangement, PPBS tends to *restore* the authority for decision making to the originally intended units within the organizational structure by reducing the uncertainty inherent in decisions." James S. Dyer, "The Use of PPBS in a Public System of Higher Education: Is it Cost Effective?" *Academy of Management Journal,* 13 (September 1970), p. 297.

A company's cash needs at any particular time will be conditioned considerably by its level of output. As sales and production increase, additional funds will be required for receivables, inventories, materials, wage payments, and so on. Central to the cash budgeting process is an analysis of the flow of funds into and out of the firm in terms of the specific times at which various payments will be due and revenues received. Of special concern is the fact that large cash outlays are often necessary during the design, preproduction, and tooling phases of programs some time in advance of the sale of the product and the receipt of cash. Further, plans must be made to meet periodic cash payroll outlays, and dividend and tax payments. From the point of view of revenues, the firm's credit and collection policies and receivables turnover must be analyzed in order to project patterns of the inflow of funds.

An illustration of a cash budget for a hypothetical firm is presented in Figure 16–3. It may be that this budget includes projected figures

Figure 16–3
Cash Budget
Wilson Company
Cash Budget for April 19—

Receipts
Accounts Receivable Collections.............................. $500,000
Disbursements
Accounts Payable*................................. $150,000
Operating Expenses
Factory Wages.................................... 270,000
Selling and Administrative........................ 50,000
Insurance and Taxes.............................. 8,000
Investment in Equipment......................... 2,000   −480,000
Net Inflow–Outflow
Cash Generated from Operations:
(Accounts Receivable—Total Disbursements)................... $ 20,000
Beginning Cash Balance...................................... 75,000
Projected Ending Cash Balance............................... $ 95,000
Desired Ending Cash Balance................................. 100,000
Projected Cash Needs.. 5,000

* Includes payments for materials, supplies, and so on, purchased prior to the current budgetary period.

for cash on hand at the beginning of the budget period, the inflow and outflow of funds during the period, and both planned and desired cash balances at the end of the period. That the desired ending cash balance of $100,000 is greater than the beginning cash balance of $75,000 for the period might be indicative of large cash needs for an expanded level of production during the following budgetary period. As the budget indicates, it will be necessary for the management of this firm to obtain an additional $5,000 in cash if it is to meet this need. Thus, cash budgetary projections play an important role in guiding managerial decisions to acquire funds from outside the firm.

As is the case with operating budgets, cash budgeting problems, may often arise because actual levels of a firm's activity vary considerably from the budgetary projections. To help overcome this problem, some companies will develop more than one cash budget, each geared to a different possible level of sales. The following is a statement of one company's use of multiple cash budgets:

. . . we . . . establish a budget for a sales volume that is somewhat higher and another for a sales volume that is somewhat lower than the original sales forecast. We also prepare cash budgets based on all three of the operating budgets. The two extra budgets are primarily a safety factor. Our cash budgets may show a drop in profits and a decrease in cash to a dangerously low point and we may need to obtain loans in advance of normal requirements to be on the safe side. On the other hand, the cash budgets may show that an increase in profits will cause an excess amount of cash and we will then be prepared to invest this cash or to pay off any loans that are no longer needed.[9]

In summary, like the operating and program budgets, the cash budget is a tool for both financial planning and control. Courses of future action are charted, actual performance is compared to planned performance, and variances may signal the need for corrective action. The cash budget, however, is oriented primarily toward the firm's liquidity objective. It should be recognized, however, that there is a close interrelationship between operating or program and cash budgeting processes. The operating or program budget provides a basis for cash budgeting in that operating costs and revenues are (at least partially) reflected in cash flows. On the other hand, a projection of cash flows may indicate that a proposed operating or program budget is not feasible since it would require cash resources which are more than a company is able to acquire.

Budgeting: Human Considerations

It has been indicated that the complexity of overall financial resource allocation for large organizations is considerable, and that no optimizing models have yet been developed to deal with this problem in its entirety. Thus, a considerable degree of value judgment is required by managers in making many budgetary decisions. Further, it is important to recognize that the interpersonal relationships among those individuals

---

[9] Quotation from Grover E. Edwards, "Structure and Services of the Cash Budget," *National Association of Accountants Bulletin,* 39 (1957), pp. 67–73, as reprinted in Lemke and Edwards, *Administrative Control and Executive Action,* p. 175.

responsible for the allocation of financial resources may be of considerable importance in budgetary decision making. In fact one may view the budgetary process not only as an economic process but as an influence process as well. Suppose, for example, that both the personnel manager and production control manager of a plant request larger budgets for the forthcoming year, but that the plant manager, who will rule on these requests does not believe that he can justify both increases to his superior. Each of the two managers making the requests has assembled and presented a considerable amount of data to support his position, but there are still a large number of intangibles involved and the reasonability of the requests is largely a matter of judgment. On what basis will the plant manager make his decision? Possibly the decision will be influenced by such noneconomic considerations as his subjective opinion as to the relative importance of the two departments, his personal like or dislike of the two men, or his perceptions of the status, power, or influence of the two. In short, we are indicating that influence patterns, in terms of the bases of social power discussed in Chapter 6, may have an important bearing on allocation decisions such as those involved in the budgetary process. Such patterns of influence probably are of considerably less significance with regard to specific allocation problem decisions, in which the "authority of facts" may clearly indicate a particular decision strategy to be the optimum one from an economic point of view.

In the budgetary process, certain kinds of human relations problems may exist which deserve our attention. Research findings by Chris Argyris, for example, suggest that at least four such problems are fairly common:

1. Budget pressure tends to unite the employees against management, and tends to place the factory supervisor under tension. This tension may lead to inefficiency, aggression, and perhaps a complete breakdown on the part of the supervisor.
2. The finance staff can obtain feelings of success only by finding fault with factory people. These feelings of failure among factory supervisors lead to many human relations problems.
3. The use of budgets as "needlers" by top management tends to make each factory supervisor see only the problem of his own department.
4. Supervisors use budgets as a way of expressing their own patterns of leadership. When this results in people getting hurt, the budget, in itself a neutral thing, often gets blamed.[10]

To overcome such problems, Argyris has suggested permitting a greater degree of participation by supervision in the budgetary decision making, and training in human relations for the financial staff to enable them

---

[10] Quoted from Chris Argyris, "Human Problems with Budgets," *Harvard Business Review*, 31 (January-February 1953), p. 108.

to perceive more accurately the human problems involved in the budgetary process.[11]

More recently, a work entitled *The Game of Budget Control* was based upon a research study of budgetary systems in six manufacturing plants in the Netherlands.[12] A primary focus of this study was upon psychological variables in the budgetary process, and it lends further support to the fact that human variables are critical ones in budgetary systems. In this work, for example, it was pointed out, that "conflict between organizational control and individual autonomy" is present in any management control system. Further, it was emphasized that

> The motivation of a . . . manager working in a budget system . . . is split into two components: the *relevance* of budget standards to the . . . [manager's] tasks, and the *attitude* of the . . . [manager] . . . toward the system. Actual motivation to fulfill budgetary standards depends first of all on the relevance component; the attitude component can either reinforce or counteract the relevance component, but it cannot motivate by itself.[13]

As may be noted, this view of the manager takes an open systems approach as discussed in Chapter 4—open systems cannot be completely controlled entirely from outside; there must be some degree of self-motivation (or control).

INPUT–OUTPUT TRANSFORMATION: OPERATIONS PLANNING AND CONTROL

In the previous section, attention was focused on the overall allocation of financial resources within the business firm. Emphasis will now be on the problems involved in planning and controlling the transformation of the firm's inputs into outputs. The concern here will be with the allocation of men, materials, machine utilization, and time in the production of goods and services; although as will be indicated later, input acquisition decisions must also be made by those responsible for the transformation processes.

Traditionally, many management texts have treated the problems which will be discussed in this section as ones of "production planning and control." We prefer to describe this facet of managerial decision making, however, as that of "operations planning and control," so as to encompass both manufacturing and nonmanufacturing operations—for many of the basic types of decision problems involved both in the production of goods and services are conceptually quite similar.

---

[11] Ibid., pp. 108–110.

[12] G. H. Hofstede, *The Game of Budget Control* (London: Tavistock Publications, Limited, 1968).

[13] Ibid., p. 3.

Operations Planning and Control: Some Basic Considerations

Operations planning and control will vary considerably depending on the characteristics of the work processes involved. Planning and control efforts, however, will usually be comprised of a similar sequence of basic decisions. In manufacturing—working either from sales forecasts or from orders received—plans will first be formulated as to the number of units of each product to be manufactured over a given period of time. Similarly, in nonmanufacturing operations, estimates must be made as to the amount and kinds of work which will be required to service the firm's customers. In the claims department of an insurance company, for example, the manager may project the number of claims likely to need processing for the forthcoming year and the resulting work necessary to carry out this function. In short, regardless of the type of operation in question, the determination of output levels represents an initial step in operations planning.

Once general preliminary plans such as these have been developed, more intensive planning is necessary to ensure that adequate manpower, materials, tools, and machine capacity are available to meet operating needs. That is, certain input acquisition decisions are first made. Then, specific departmental work schedules can be formulated. The essential characteristic of scheduling, as opposed to other forms of planning, is that it centers around the *sequencing* of work in terms of chronological time. At what specific times will a particular piece of work be started and completed on a given machine? What piece of work will be scheduled next on the machine? What priorities will be established for various orders or batches of production?

After the above decisions have been made and the work planned is being performed, control becomes an important consideration. Actual performance must be compared with planned performance, and any important variances noted. Decisions can then be made as to what kinds of action are desirable to correct any excessive variances which may exist. If, in the keypunch section of a computation center, for example, one operator is absent from the job, should the work originally scheduled for that operator be held up or transferred to another worker? If the latter alternative is chosen, to which operator should the work be rescheduled, and how will the work originally scheduled for this employee, but now displaced, be completed? These are among the kinds of questions which must be resolved in planning and controlling the allocation of resources for the production of goods and services.

As may be noted, many aspects of resource acquisition and allocation which have been discussed previously play an important role in the operations planning and control process. Projected input and output levels for a department may be developed in the operating or program budgeting process; the acquisition of additional machine capacity so as to be able to generate the levels of production planned for future periods may call for capital budgeting decisions; and the hiring of additional workers needed to turn out the planned output involves personnel acquisition.

These observations raise the question: To what extent do input acquisition decisions as opposed to those of allocation (input-output transformation) affect the operations planning and control process? In the very short run, the range of alternatives available to the manager is constrained to a considerable extent by resources which have already been acquired by the firm, and his primary problems center around the allocation of the inputs at his immediate disposal. That is, at any given point in time, he must work with the men, materials, and machines available to him; he is relatively restricted in his ability to acquire additional inputs in the short run. For example, in a department comprising four lathes, and 12 lathe operators, of whom 4 are working on each of three eight-hour shifts, the manager on any given day has at his disposal a maximum of 96 man-hours of input. In such a case, the manager's primary problems in planning and controlling production for the day would center around such questions as which jobs should be given priority and which men should be assigned to which jobs. If production were falling behind in the department with the available inputs, additional machine capacity or manpower could be obtained at some future time, but not immediately, because some lead time would be required for their acquisition. Of course, if one was considering a department operating on a single shift per day basis, the manpower input might be immediately augmented to a certain extent by scheduling overtime. In short, it is only in longer range planning that input *acquisition* becomes an important consideration in the operations planning process.

Generalizing from the above observations, it may be stated that in planning in the longer run, the manager's strategy space may be extended as he acquires additional resources as inputs. Even in future periods, however, his choice of alternatives will not be completely free, for his alternatives may be constrained both by lead time required for acquiring more resources and by budgetary limitations. For example, the manager in the previous illustration may wish to acquire two additional lathes for next month's production, but be unable to do so because either (1) funds are not available for their purchase, and/or (2) it will take three months for the lathes to be obtained from the company which manufactures them. These restraints and the role of input acquisition and allocation in the operations planning and control process are illustrated in Figure 16–4.

Finally, it should be pointed out that the objectives sought in opera-

Figure 16–4. Input Acquisition and Allocation in the Operations Planning and Control Process

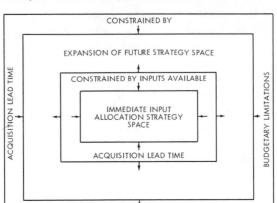

tions planning and control are usually both multiple and interdependent ones. In the allocation of resources for processing work through a system, management is usually interested in: (1) minimizing costs, (2) maximizing the amount of work (e.g., dollar volume) processed in a period of time, and (3) meeting the delivery promises that have been made to its customers.

These three goals are not independent of each other, and the attainment of any one may, and often does, affect the realization of the others. For example, to meet its requests for travel service at a particular time, an airline may schedule a second section of a flight, even though the capacity of the second craft will be only partially utilized. In doing so, costs may be incurred in operating the second plane which exceed the revenue obtained from its passengers. In such an instance, meeting the "delivery" objective would conflict with the firm's cost minimization goal.

As was indicated in Chapter 3, the handling of multiple goals can be simplified considerably if a single measure for all objectives can be developed. For instance, in the airline illustration, if management could estimate the revenue which would be lost due to dissatisfied customers switching to another airline in the future should the second section of the flight not be scheduled, it might be able to frame the scheduling problem in terms of a single profitability measure.

A further complicating factor in understanding the resource allocation process is that the variables which bear upon the three goals which we have mentioned vary considerably in different types of processing systems. In the following sections, some of the more basic of these differences will be illustrated by examining three different types of work processing systems: (1) job lot systems, (2) continuous-type processing operations, and (3) large, complex, limited-volume production.

Job Lot Processing Systems

In this section attention will be given to the fundamental character-istics of job lot processing systems, some of the key variables which must be considered in planning and controlling such operations, and certain approaches utilized by management in job lot planning and control.

The Characteristics of Job Lot Systems. A fundamental characteristic of job lot operations is that many items or lots of items with different specifications are manufactured, each of which is characterized by a small yearly volume *relative to the processing capability* of the system. One optical firm, for example, estimated that it has the capacity to produce 20,000 units of one particular item per year should all its re-sources be concentrated on it. Yet, it has been able to sell only about 250 units of the item each year to its customers, who normally place orders of less than 5 units at a time; and the remainder of its capacity is utilized to produce many other items, each also with a comparatively small yearly demand.

Because the characteristics of the many different orders processed in a job lot system will vary from each other, processing equipment which is *flexible* enough to handle all types of items is employed. In machine shops, for example, most equipment commonly utilized is gen-eral purpose in use (e.g., engine lathes). It is not economical to use special-purpose equipment designed specifically for the most efficient production of any one particular kind of item since the volume for any one item is relatively low. Further, since each piece of processing machinery in the system is employed in the production of many different items, the preparation or *setup* time necessary for producing each differ-ent lot is relatively high compared to manufacturing systems in which a large volume of a single product is turned out.

In some job lot systems, many different lots will be processed through the same sequence of operations, even though the specifications of each lot will vary somewhat. For example, in the manufacture of printing rollers, most lots of rollers are processed through essentially the same production stages, although variations exist from order to order in the length and diameter of the rollers, the type of rubber used in their manufacture, and so on. In many cases, however, the processing se-quences may vary from lot to lot. In a machine shop, for example, the production of an order of pistons, while being turned out on some of the same equipment as an order of axles, would require a different sequence of operations. When the processing sequence frequently varies from order to order, the machines utilized for production cannot be economically arranged to best accommodate the physical handling and flow of any one product, since the processing sequence of other lots will be different. As a consequence, the physical layout for job lot processing systems often does not, except in some very general way, attempt to match the processing sequences. Rather, similar types of processing equipment are often physically grouped together; and the operations may be departmentalized on the basis of process. In a job lot machine shop, for example, it would not be unusual for all of the lathes to be physically grouped together, with all lathe operators reporting to one supervisor, and for the same to be true for the milling machines, the planers, and so forth.

One final characteristic of job lot systems also deserves mention. Since the demand for any one item is small relative to processor capacity (although it may be steady), it is usually uneconomical to produce items on a continuous basis. In determining when the processing of particular lots should be scheduled:

1. The firm may wait until a sales order is received before initiating the processing.
2. It may wait until it has received several orders for an item, and batch these orders together so that they may be processed in the same lot in order to reduce the setup costs per item, or
3. If the firm has experience to show that a particular item is likely to be reordered in the future, it may decide to carry an inventory of the item.

In the latter instance, the processing of lots would be initiated so as to replenish inventories which have been reduced by previous sales. When such is the case, lot sizes are usually determined independently of any particular sales order. Rather they are generally related to the total demand for the item in question over a period of time. Methods for determining optimal lot sizes for the replenishment of inventories will be examined in Chapter 18.

Variables Involved in Job Lot Resource Allocation.   Now that the fundamental characteristics of job lot processing systems have been discussed, an examination will be made of some of the key variables which must be considered in planning and controlling in such operations so as to achieve the allocation goals of cost minimization, maximizing throughput, and the minimizing of delivery delays.

Lot Processing Sequences.   As indicated previously, it is necessary to determine the sequence of operations which need to be performed on each lot in order to complete its production. The determination of the processing sequence for a lot—which is commonly referred to as *routing* since it involves defining the route along which the lot will travel as it is being produced—is conditioned considerably by the product specifications of the lot. In the manufacture of books, for example, the printing operation must precede the binding operation. Routing (and scheduling) decisions, however, may also be conditioned by economic as well as output specification factors. Some processing operations on certain products may be performed equally well (although not equally economically) on either of two alternative machines—e.g., a flat machined surface on a part on either a milling machine or a planer. In such cases, when a lot is being scheduled it may be assigned to that machine which can perform the operation most economically. If no capacity were available on the most efficient machine for the operation, however, the order scheduler might assign the alternative piece of equipment to the lot so as to avoid delivery delays.

Lot Processing Time per Operation.   A second variable which must be considered in operations planning and control is the time it will take to process a lot through each operation in its sequence. For each operation, this time may be calculated by adding: (1) the setup time required for the lot to (2) the number of items in the lot multiplied by the processing time required for each piece. These times are often kept as data on a master route sheet compiled by the individual or individuals responsible for making the routing decisions.

Lot Delivery Date.   In determining when a particular lot is to be scheduled on available facilities, the date when the lot needs to be completed is usually taken as a starting point. This date may represent that on which the items in the lot are to be shipped to the firm's customer; or, if the firm is scheduling the processing of parts which are later to be assembled into a final product, the delivery date for the lot may be set at the day prior to that on which their assembly has been scheduled to begin. If, on the other hand, the lot were processed in order to replenish inventories, the delivery date would be that when existing inventories are expected to be exhausted. In all such cases, provision may be made for scheduling the completion of a lot prior to its desired delivery date in order to help prevent any delay in its delivery should the processing time take longer than planned. The provision for slack time in operations planning to cover such a contingency will be discussed in a later section.

Processing Availability.   Another important variable which must be considered in scheduling a lot to the different operations required for its processing is the amount and nature of other work already assigned to these facilities. If the delivery date for an order awaiting scheduling is 20 days, for example, and a piece of equipment necessary for processing the order has already been reserved for the next month because prior lots have been allocated to it, the scheduler obviously faces a dilemma.

When numerous orders must be scheduled on the same processing equipment, the problems of establishing priorities may become one of considerable importance. By giving processing priority to one lot, the delivery on another may be delayed, especially when the facilities are operating near capacity. In such cases, the scheduling of any given order must be determined in light of the processing requirements of all other lots utilizing the same equipment. To schedule one order requires knowledge not only of the equipment in the shop, but also of the times at which it will be free and available for additional work.

In-Process Inventories.   The manner in which lots are scheduled will influence to a considerable extent inventory levels of the items being processed. For example, if it takes 20 days instead of 10 to complete the processing of a particular lot, the raw materials utilized in turning out the lot must be "tied up" in production (or "carried" as in-process inventories) twice as long. Since there are costs associated with carrying inventories (which will be discussed more thoroughly in Chapter 18) attempts to minimize costs for a job lot operation involve keeping in-process inventory levels under control. It may, however, be more profitable to increase in-process inventories above minimal levels to help meet certain other objectives of the job lot system, as will be indicated in the next section.

Slack.   The allocation of resources is a complex problem especially in large job lot operations; and many of the variables which affect production are not completely predictable. In consequence, allocation decisions frequently may not turn out as well as desired. A scheduler may not have been able to foresee that one large order should have been given priority over a smaller one. Because a worker is absent or a machine breaks down, delays in processing certain lots may occur. As a means of dealing with such contingencies, managers will frequently make provisions for allowing more time for the processing of lots than would be necessary if all work went perfectly according to plan—i.e., *slack* time is provided for. In some cases, extra slack time may be specified both prior to and after each processing step. Or, another method of allowing for slack time on an order is to schedule its processing in such a way that the last operation is to be completed a week (or some other duration) prior to its required delivery date.

It should be noted that providing for slack time increases the firm's inventory requirements and costs (since the lot remains in process longer) in order to increase the probability of meeting scheduled delivery dates. Slack scheduling may also permit supervision to sequence lots so as to reduce setup costs or to be able to utilize more highly skilled operators on complex operations. Thus, slack may help contribute to the reduction of operating costs as well as to the meeting of scheduled deliveries. That it leads to increased inventory costs in doing so, however, again points out that the different objectives sought in resource allocation may be in conflict with each other.

Job Lot Scheduling.   As mentioned previously, the allocation of resources in job lot systems of any magnitude tends to be quite complex. In fact, even in small shops, the amount of data which needs to be considered in routing and scheduling the processing of lots may be quite large. For example, consider a small job lot machine shop in which on the average 25 lots are allocated per week, with an average of 12 operations required for each lot. In such an operation, for each lot, the manager must consider the delivery date, 12 pieces of information about processing sequence, and 12 pieces of information about processing times required; or, *in toto,* 625 informational items must be considered. Further, for effective operations, the impact of scheduling any one lot upon the processing of all other lots being scheduled plus any lots already in process must be taken into account. Consideration of such interdependencies often poses difficult problems since the relationships between all variables in the system are not known precisely and are subject to change as the status of the system changes. For example, placing one lot on a "rush" basis may have little effect on meeting delivery dates for other lots in process when the system is operating at only 75 percent of capacity, but might delay the delivery of several other lots when the plant is operating at 98 percent of capacity.

Scheduling in job lot systems lends itself to the utilization of computers, the large memory systems and rapid computational abilities of which are ideally suited to handling masses of data quickly. Even with computerized scheduling, of course, the complex systems interrelationships must be defined and programmed; and in most cases it is not possible to attain such precise definition as to make possible any truly optimal scheduling-decision approach.[14]

Because of such complexities, many managers in job lot systems rely on one or more relatively simple scheduling rules to allocate processing resources. Furthermore, such rules are often applied sequentially, to one lot at a time, without giving consideration to all variables, lots, and processes in the system simultaneously.

One of the simplest scheduling rules utilized is to process each order on a first-served basis. If each order were assigned an ascending lot number as it was received, foremen in the job shop could be instructed to process the lot with the lowest number first. Consequently, priority would be given to those orders which have been in the shop the longest period of time.

The first-come, first-served rule often may operate satisfactorily when the machines in the job lot system are operating at less than full capacity. A basic weakness of the rule, however, is that it does not give consideration to either the total processing time required for each lot or to delivery dates. For example, an order requiring 15 days of total processing time with a delivery date 16 days in the future, may remain in a department awaiting processing for 5 days while a prior order not due for delivery

---

[14] One method of developing satisfactory scheduling decisions is through computer simulation. This approach would involve developing a model of the operations and testing numerous decision rules which have been developed under typical processing conditions. With such an approach it may be possible to identify the conditions under which any given rule offers the greatest probability of achieving effective allocation. We will discuss simulation as an experimental problem-solving method more fully in Chapter 19.

for three weeks, and requiring only 12 days of processing is being worked on. One way of alleviating this problem is by means of a somewhat different scheduling rule: "Give priority to orders which have the nearest delivery date." Although this rule gives explicit consideration to meeting delivery objectives, it does not give recognition to the processing time required for orders *in relation to* their delivery dates. A lot with a distant delivery date, for example, may await processing for so long that it may be too late to perform all of the operations required for its manufacture before the delivery date. As a consequence, some schedulers have resorted to still another allocation rule which states: "Give priority to lots with the smallest difference between the time remaining before their promised delivery date and the processing time still needed for their completion." Although this rule may be fairly effective in helping to minimize delivery delays, it is by no means an optimizing technique—for example, it does little to further the cost minimization objectives of the job lot system.

In addition to the utilization of scheduling rules, two other approaches are often employed to help facilitate the complex problems of scheduling in job lot systems. First, so as to give greater consideration to costs and to provide greater flexibility, numerous scheduling decision details may be delegated to supervisors of various departments in the plant, rather than attempting to plan centrally the exact start, stop, and handling times for all processing stages for all lots. Assuming sufficient lot slack is introduced, such decentralized scheduling may permit supervisors to employ scheduling rules which would be difficult to employ on a centralized basis due to lack of knowledge about the current status of all operations. Supervisors may gear their scheduling decisions so as to minimize setup costs, to match worker skills with available work, to assign any overtime work required to their employees on an equitable basis, and so forth. Thus, decentralized scheduling may allow more attention to be given to meeting the economic objectives of the system and to the human factors of importance.

Second, it should be pointed out that various visual display and record maintenance aids are frequently utilized to aid schedulers in assigning lots to various machines and in keeping track of the progress of orders being processed in the system. Usually in job lot scheduling, the practice is followed of working backward from the lot delivery date, and scheduling the last operation first, the next to the last operation required, second, and so on. In order to schedule the processing of lots in such a manner, it is necessary for the scheduler to have for planning purposes information showing the time periods at which each type of processing facility is available for assignment to unscheduled lots, and for control purposes, the progress made on lots already in process. One commonly utilized type of visual display device designed to provide such information is the Gantt Chart, to which attention will now be turned.

The Gantt Chart is a form of schematic analysis designed to aid the manager in planning and controlling input allocation for the production of goods and services. Several different types of Gantt Charts have been developed—man and machine record charts, layout charts, load charts, and progress charts.[15] All are similar in form in that they enable the manager to visualize work to be scheduled and/or work actually performed in relation to the dimension of time. Although the Gantt approach has been used most widely for planning and control purposes in job lot manufacturing operations, some of the charts have been employed for other types of work—such as in the merchant marine to keep track of the movement of vessels, and in offices for the scheduling of clerical work. To illustrate the basic characteristics of Gantt analysis and its value to planning and control, one type of Gantt Chart, the project planning chart, will be examined.

The project planning chart is a schematic model which enables the manager to visualize the times required for various stages of an operation and the interrelationship between the stages. It is designed with the time variable indicated horizontally, and the production capacity variable vertically. To illustrate the use of the project planning chart, consider the following example.

The foreman of a job shop is concerned with planning and scheduling the manufacture of a large piece of heavy equipment, the completion date for which has been set at February 16. The piece of equipment is comprised of two subassemblies; each of which, in turn, is made up of three parts which must be fabricated in the shop.[16] Final assembly cannot commence until each subassembly has been completed. Nor can the work on either subassembly begin until the fabrication of each of its three parts has been completed. The time required for each stage of the manufacture of the equipment is as follows:

Operation	Days Required
Fabrication Part No. 1	4
Fabrication Part No. 2	2
Fabrication Part No. 3	5
Subassembly A (of Parts Nos. 1, 2, 3)	3
Fabrication Part No. 4	4
Fabrication Part No. 5	3
Fabrication Part No. 6	2
Subassembly B (of Parts Nos. 4, 5, 6)	5
Final Assembly	3

---

[15] The originator of the Gantt Chart was Henry Gantt, a pioneer in the scientific management movement. For a detailed discussion of each of the different types of Gantt Charts mentioned here, see Wallace Clark, *The Gantt Chart* (3d ed.; New York: Pitman Publishing Corp., 1952).

[16] What would probably be an unrealistically small number of parts and subassemblies have been included in this example for purposes of simplification.

Working backward from the completion date, the manager will first schedule the final assembly, then the two subassemblies, and finally the fabrication of the six parts. That the Gantt project planning chart is valuable in portraying these schedules schematically may be seen by the reference to Figure 16–5. Assuming no delays or slack time be-

Figure 16–5.   Gantt Project Planning Chart

PROCESS	M. FEB. 1	T. FEB. 2	W. FEB. 3	TH. FEB. 4	F. FEB. 5	M. FEB. 8	T. FEB. 9	W. FEB. 10	TH. FEB. 11	F. FEB. 12	M. FEB. 15	T. FEB. 16
PART # 1												
PART # 2												
PART # 3												
SUB-ASSEMBLY A												
PART # 4												
PART # 5												
PART # 6												
SUB-ASSEMBLY B												
FINAL ASSEMBLY												

LEGEND:

⌐ JOB SCHEDULED TO START

⌐ JOB SCHEDULED FOR COMPLETION

└─────┐ TOTAL TIME SCHEDULED FOR JOB

▬ WORK DONE TO DATE

V TIME AT PRESENT

tween operations, the chart indicates the fabrication of Part No. 4 must be initiated on February 1 if the order is to be completed on time, and that minimum time required for producing the piece of equipment is 12 days.

After the production has been scheduled and the work is in progress, the Gantt Chart may be used for control and replanning by enabling the manager to visualize the progress of each stage of the operation. The chart illustrated in Figure 16–5 shows progress in the manufacture of the piece of equipment as of the end of Friday, February 5. It may be noted that work on Parts Nos. 2, 4, 5, and 6 and Subassembly B has proceeded as planned, and that progress on Part No. 3 is one day ahead of schedule. The fabrication of Part No. 1, however, is one day behind schedule, and unless this delay is made up for before the scheduled initiation of work on Subassembly A on February 9, it will not be possible to complete the order on time. Faced with this variance between planned and actual performance, the foreman might decide to take corrective action by scheduling overtime work on Part No. 1.

As the above example illustrates, the project planning chart, by providing a graphic comparison of actual versus planned performance, represents a vehicle for facilitating control as well as a tool for planning and scheduling. Easy to design and read, Gantt Charts have been employed in many industries. On the other hand, keeping the charts up to date may require considerable time, particularly when the operation is a complex one. As a means of partially overcoming this limitation, various mechanical devices have been designed to facilitate Gantt-type analysis. Among these are pegboards which employ different colored pegs to represent the various Gantt symbols. Finally, it should be reemphasized that notwithstanding its usefulness, Gantt analysis is not an optimizing approach and does not consider all key decision variables.

In the above illustration, for example, the Gantt analysis provided no answer as to whether slack time should have been scheduled with the operation to cover possible delays—but at the expense of an increase in in-process inventories. The various units of work may simply be blocked on to the charts on judgmental basis—no formalized search procedures or mathematically based decision rules are prescribed. Although optimum schedules may be developed intuitively by means of Gantt analysis when the operations involved are relatively simple, the manager is not likely to achieve more than a satisfactory work program by this approach when the decision problem is a complex one.

The Focus of Control in Job Lot Systems. Control efforts in the job shop must center around keeping close track of the progress of *each* customer order. Each order must be turned out according to customer specifications by the delivery date promised, or else the manager faces the possibility of its cancellation. If a particular order is behind schedule, it is usually not possible to substitute in lieu thereof another order already completed—as would be the case in highly repetitive manufacturing in which large quantities of identical units are being produced—since different orders are different. Because attention in job shops is so strongly focused upon each customer order, planning and control procedures designed for this type of operation are often referred to as *order control systems.*

Data for control of operations in a job shop include the status of each lot as it progresses through the processing facilities. In some shops, these data are obtained at the completion of each operation and forwarded to scheduling for a comparison with the operation's scheduled completion date. In control terms, the schedule may be considered as a standard against which the actual performance is compared for purposes of deciding if a lot should be rescheduled or expedited. Corrective action may be indicated if it appears that a lot will not be completed in time to meet an important delivery date, or if subsequent processing on the lot will interfere with the processing of other lots. Overtime and Saturday work may be decided upon as a result of identifying performances which are behind schedule. At other times, it may be sufficient to designate a behind schedule lot as "rush" so that it may receive priority in the processing of lots at subsequent operating departments. As indicated above, a Gantt Chart, or its equivalent, is useful for visualizing the probable impact of each kind of corrective action.

Continuous Manufacturing

Characteristics of Continuous Manufacturing Systems. Quite different from job lot manufacturing are those operations which are highly repetitive in nature. Such operations are often referred to as continuous manufacturing. The key characteristic of continuous manufacturing—which is usually associated with mass production industries such as those making automobiles or cigarettes—is that long runs of highly standardized items are produced.

Also characteristic of continuous manufacturing is the production of items for inventories (or stock), as opposed to production to order—i.e., production is planned on the basis of sales forecasts rather than on the basis of specific orders received. Few, if any, manufacturing operations, however, are completely repetitive. In addition, some items are produced to order rather than for stock in many industries characterized as continuous manufacturing. In the automotive industry, for example, a number of different models with different options possible are produced each year, some of which are manufactured to customer or dealer specifications. To the extent that items produced are identical in design, each follows the same manufacturing or servicing operations. Consequently, there is no reiterative requirement to decide upon the *route* that items will take through the operations. Rather the product flow is standardized, going through basically the same operations for all items. Further, special equipment, perhaps designed especially for the manufacture of a single item, may be economical. Such special-purpose equipment is often relatively expensive in initial cost, but is designed to operate at higher speeds and with greater automatic control. The labor savings thus generated can, assuming sufficient product volume, justify the initial cost.

Since both the design of each item and its processing route through production are basically similar, the plant layout of machines can be based upon the processing sequences. In this manner, relatively little handling between operations is needed as work flows directly from one operation to the next. Since adjacent processors perform adjacent sequences, there is no requirement (in terms of minimizing handling costs) to await completion of a lot of parts prior to moving it to the next operation. Rather, each completed item can be moved individually for the relatively small distances involved. In addition, because of the fixed route that items follow through processing and the relatively large volume, automatic handling equipment (such as conveyors) can often be justified, in contrast to job lot operations in which different lots require different routes through production.

Planning, Scheduling, and Control in Continuous Manufacturing. The allocation objectives in continuous processing are the same as those in lot processing, namely: minimizing processing costs, maximizing throughput, and minimizing delivery delays. Because of differences in the nature of continuous processing operations, however, the variables bearing upon the attainment of these goals operate in quite different ways. In continuous manufacturing, processing sequences and operating times are relatively unimportant since they are fixed during the layout of equipment. An electronics firm which plans to produce 1,200 table radios of a particular model each day can establish an assembly line for the model, determine the necessary sequencing of operations, and schedule the whole line as single unit. As long as the firm's production remains approximately at this rate, scheduling decisions are passive—i.e., no basic changes are required in scheduling work on the assembly line. When production requirements do increase or decrease, of course, a greater or smaller number of hours of work would have to be scheduled. Thus, the production scheduling decision in operations producing large numbers of identical outputs basically involves the number of hours that the whole unit will operate in order to meet its production requirements.

All outputs are not identical in most mass-production processes, however. Automobiles, for example, may be purchased with a fairly wide, but limited and standardized, variety of options. Yet, the car with 20 extras goes through the same assembly line in the same length of time as does the stripped down model following it. Quite obviously, however, more man-hours are needed to assemble cars with more options (e.g., installing a radio or air-conditioner).[17] Such variations in work load are accommodated in the original setup of the assembly line by providing line space and manpower to produce the types of options expected.[18] This approach requires that sales forecasters not only estimate the number of cars sold, but also the number of each kind of option which will be required during the year prior to establishing the processing layout. Although some changes from the predicted mix of options may be accommodated on many assembly lines, the ability to deviate widely

---

[17] It should be noted that not all variations in options affect the work load of an assembly line. For example, it may take no longer to mount whitewall tires than blackwall ones.

[18] In addition, part of the extra work required with some options may be handled on subassembly lines. For example, much of the extra work required on a 4-barrel V–8 is done on the engine subassembly line rather than on the final assembly line.

from preplanned option mixes is usually not possible. Further, this basic adherence to preestablished plans is necessary not only over relatively long durations such as a month, but also during each day. For example, if all air-conditioned cars on an assembly line to be produced on a given day were scheduled in the morning, the assembly crew for this operation might not be able to keep up with their work in the morning, and yet have nothing to do in the afternoon.

The focus of control is also different in continuous manufacturing from that in lot processing. Due to the high degree of standardization, it is the *total number* of units produced which is of primary concern rather than each specific order as in job lot operations. For example, a cigarette manufacturer does not have to keep close track of many different orders with various delivery dates to numerous customers; rather his control efforts are geared toward assuring that a specified number of packs be turned out each month. Although always of importance, maintaining close control over the quantity of items produced in continuous manufacturing is especially critical when there are a number of stages involved in the production process, and when production at any one stage is dependent upon a continuous flow of items from a previous stage. Suppose, for example, that the operations of a plant are geared for the final assembly of three subassemblies at a rate of 300 per hour. In such a case, the production rates for the final assembly and each of the subassemblies must be closely coordinated if there is to be a smooth flow of production. If production of one or more of the subassemblies is slowed down to 100 per hour, for example, the final assembly operation cannot proceed as scheduled unless in-process inventories of the subassemblies exist. On the other hand, if the subassembling proceeds at a much faster rate than the final assembling, excessive inprocess inventories will soon build up. In other words, the rate of output being turned out at each operations stage must be *balanced* if an optimum continuous flow of production is to be realized. For a graphic illustration of the production balancing problem, the reader is referred to Figure 16–6, which portrays both a balanced and an unbalanced production line. Because of the large degree of interdependence between each production stage, centralized planning and control is necessary if balancing is to be achieved. The scheduling of each operations process cannot be left to the discretion of each individual department head—coordination by the production control department is necessary. Systems designed to maintain a continuous rate of flow in highly repetitive manufacturing are often referred to as *flow control* systems.

Finally, some observations are in order concerning the difficulties involved in achieving the overall optimization of a continuous manufacturing operation. As was indicated above, the high degree of repetitiveness

Figure 16–6. Production Line Balancing

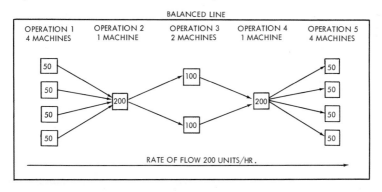

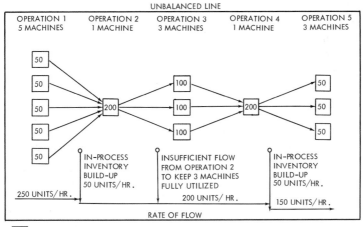

and standardization in continuous processing renders its day-to-day planning and control less difficult than that in the job lot in certain respects—routing is not a major problem nor is it necessary to maintain close control over the progress of each customer order. Nonetheless, the decision variables and their interrelationships in all but extremely small continuous operations entail such a high level of complexity that—as in the job shop—overall optimization is rarely attained. The manager must be concerned with such problems as the minimization of machine breakdowns, the rescheduling of production when breakdowns do occur, and the maintenance of optimum levels of raw materials, as well as in-process and finished goods inventories. Although it is possible to develop optimum solutions for many of these problems, such optimization usually leads to a less than optimum achievement for others, and suboptimization occurs.

Large Complex, Limited Volume Production

Product Characteristics. In contrast to lot processing or continuous production, the manufacture of some large complex products which are turned out in a limited volume does not lend itself to planning and control by the methods previously discussed. Examples of products of this type would be a jet bomber, a weather satellite, an apartment building, or a moon-landing vehicle. Such products are usually typified by the following characteristics:

1. They are produced in relatively small volume, as indicated above.
2. They are comprised of many small individual subassemblies and/or parts.
3. The dollar value per item produced is *relatively* large.
4. Whereas initiating some operations cannot be started until others are completed (e.g., the engine mounting on a plane must wait until the wings have been attached to the wing root), other operations can be processed in parallel. (E.g., wing subassembly may be done at same time as tail assembly.)
5. A separate organization and facilities may be employed exclusively for the item. (E.g., a project manager and a project organization might be given overall responsibility and a separate plant to assemble a large missile.)

In scheduling large complex products, the allocation goals are sometimes not stated in the terms as discussed previously: (1) minimizing cost, (2) maximizing throughput, and (3) minimizing delivery delays. In space projects, for example, on-time delivery may be preeminent and justify large costs and exclusive, although less than full, use of certain facilities. In addition, at the present time, there exists no analytical method for optimal multiproject scheduling in those instances in which more than a few large complex projects are carried out using the same resources. Thus, we may characterize the operations planning and control methods for large complex projects as satisficing rather than optimizing in most respects.

Network Planning and Control Techniques. To deal with large complex projects various *network* planning and control techniques have been developed. One of the earliest types of these is the critical path method (CPM) originated by Morgan Walker and J. E. Kelly for scheduling large construction projects in Du Pont. The early versions of these methods concentrated upon meeting intermediate and final delivery dates. Some subsequent refinements of the methods, however, have also considered costs, cost-time tradeoffs, the leveling of resources, and optimization of expenditure rates.

Independently, the U.S. Navy developed another network technique for planning and controlling the Polaris Fleet Ballistic Missile Program—the Program Evaluation and Review Technique (PERT). Initially, PERT provided for three time estimates and the use of the probabilistic Beta Distribution for each activity in each project; while CPM provided for only one time estimate for each activity.[19] Many problems have been encountered with the three probabilistic time elements; so that most present-day users (including the Department of Defense for most contracts) have abandoned these and gone to simpler deterministic time elements.[20] In fact, although there exist technical differences between CPM and PERT,[21] as Moder and Phillips have pointed out, "the recent versions of the two original methods have become increasingly alike."[22] For purposes of simplification, in the following discussion we will: (1) utilize one deterministic time estimate for each activity rather than the probabilistic approach; (2) rely on the PERT method of diagramming; and, (3) use the word "PERT," rather than PERT/CPM or CPM.

Since its inception, PERT has been found useful as a decision-making technique for handling numerous types of allocation problems in business such as those involving the planning of construction and research and development projects, the introduction of new products, the issuance of new securities, and in wage and salary administration.[23]

In this section, the basic ideas underlying PERT will be discussed and with a highly simplified example we will illustrate some of the ways that PERT may be useful as a decision-making approach. It should be recognized, however, that although the PERT concept is relatively simple to comprehend, actual application of the technique to decision problems of considerable magnitude involves such a large amount of data that computer utilization is almost imperative.[24]

The first step in the application of PERT is to determine (1) all of the significant activities involved in the project under consideration,

---

[19] In the simplified Beta Distribution, the estimate of the mean time for each activity is equal to $\dfrac{a + 4(m) + b}{6}$, where a, m, and b represent the judged optimistic, most likely, and pessimistic times, respectively, for each activity to be carried out in the project.

[20] Elwood S. Buffa, *Modern Production Management* (3d ed.; New York: John Wiley & Sons, Inc., 1969), pp. 196, 217.

[21] These differences are in the ways the networks are diagrammed. See, for example, ibid., pp. 209–10.

[22] Joseph J. Moder and Cecil R. Phillips, *Project Management with CPM and PERT* (2d ed.; New York: Van Nostrand Reinhold Co., 1970), p. 337.

[23] For a discussion of how PERT was utilized in a specific firm in developing a new wage and salary plan, see Glenn H. Varney and Gerard F. Carvalho, "Pert in the Personnel Department," *Personnel*, 38 (January-February 1968), pp. 48–53.

[24] It should be noted that PERT has been utilized successfully without a computer for relatively simple projects. For example, see ibid.

and (2) the interrelationship between each activity. As mentioned previously, characteristic of most complex work programs is that many activities are often carried on simultaneously in parallel but that the initiation of some activities must wait until certain prior activities have been completed. In the construction and equipping of a new office building, for example, the installation of desks, chairs, office machines, and so on, cannot be initiated until after the flooring has been completed, but many of these activities can be carried on simultaneously as soon as their initiation is possible. In the language of PERT, the completion of any such project activity is referred to as an *event;* and in the application of PERT, the relationships between all activities and events are portrayed in a program *network.* An example of such a network is illustrated in Figure 16–7. Each lettered circle in the network represents

Figure 16–7.   PERT Program Network

PATH	PROJECTED TIMES (DAYS)	SLACK (DAYS)
A–C–E–G	17	7
A–B–F–G	19	5
A–C–F–G	22	2
A–C–D–G*	24	0

ACTIVITY	ES	EF	LS	LF	SLACK
A–B	0	7	5	12	5
A–C*	0	7	0	7	0
C–F	7	16	9	18	2
C–D*	7	14	7	14	0
B–F	7	13	12	18	5
F–G	16	22	18	24	2
E–G	12	17	19	24	7
D–G*	14	24	14	24	0
C–E	7	12	14	19	2

LEGEND:

——————► ACTIVITY

◯ EVENT

* Critical path.
† Note: The activity arrows are not to scale as is also true with real PERT networks.
ES = Earliest Start Time
LS = Latest Start Time
EF = Earliest Finish Time
LF = Latest Finish Time

an event, and each arrow connecting two circles represents an activity. With the time variable plotted horizontally on the program network, Figure 16–7 may be interpreted as follows:

Event A must occur before the activities represented by the A–B and A–C arrows can be initiated; event C (the completion of the activity represented by the A–C arrow) must precede the initiation of the activities represented by the C–D, C–E, and C–F arrows and so on until the event G, the completion of the entire project, has been accomplished.

Once the program network has been drawn up, it will be necessary for the decision maker to assess the time required for the completion of each activity. It will also be useful for the decision maker to work out the *ES*, *EF*, *LS*, and *LF* times indicated in Figure 16–7.[25] These times may be calculated as follows. For the start times, if zero is taken as the project starting time, the *ES* for each activity is the earliest time possible that activity can begin, assuming that all of its "predecessors also are started at their *ES*. Then, for that activity, its earliest finish (*EF*) is simply *ES* + activity time."[26] Thus, in Figure 16–7, for example, the *ES* for activity A–C is 0, moving forward in the network, since A–C requires 7 days, the *ES* for both activities C–D, C–E, and C–F would be 7 days after the beginning of the project, their *EF*s would be 14, 12, and 16 days, respectively, and so on. The latest start and finish times for each activity are obtained by working *backward* through the network. For example, in Figure 16–7, the *LS* for activity F–G with a time of 6 days is on day 18, and with the completion date for the project on the 24th day, its *LF* is on that day. Working backwards, the *LF* for activity B–F equals the *LS* for the successor activity F–G; or on day 18, while the *LS* for B–F would be 18 minus its activity time of 6 days; or 12.

The process of development of a program network in the manner described above may be of value to the decision maker in a number of different ways. First, it will provide a basis for pinpointing problems which are most likely to occur in the completion of a proposed project. A key feature of the PERT network is that it enables one to focus attention on the most *critical path* of activities in the project. The critical path is defined as the longest path (in terms of time) leading to any given event. The longest path leading to event F in Figure 16–7, for example, is A–C–F, which involves 16 days of work as compared with only 13 days for the other path leading to F:A–B–F. Similarly, the most critical path leading to the completion of the *entire* project (event G) is A–C–D–G, which takes 24 days. The key role of the critical path is indicated by the fact that any delays which occur on this path will *always* hold up completion of the project. This is not necessarily true for the other paths in the network. To illustrate, in Figure 16–7 a two-day delay anywhere along critical path A–C–D–G will set back the completion date of the project (event G) from 24 to 26 days. A similar delay along path A–B–F–G, on the other hand, will in no way retard the

---

[25] Two notes are in order here. First, some of the ways in which these times are utilized will be brought out below. Second, for a more technical discussion of the development of these times, see Buffa, *Production Management,* pp. 204–9.

[26] Ibid., pp. 204–5.

progress of the project. With such a delay, path A–B–F–G would entail 21 days of work, or 3 days less than that of the critical path—i.e., it contains 3 days of *slack*. This delay will not effect a postponement of event G, since G cannot possibly occur sooner than 24 days after initiation of the project because of the constraint imposed by the critical path.

Analysis of the criticalness of the activity path in a PERT network and slack will not only enable the manager to pinpoint those activities on which delays are most likely to hinder completion of a project—it may also provide a basis for a more efficient allocation of inputs to the project than that initially formulated. By more efficient input allocation, we mean the development of a program which will (1) hasten the completion of a project without requiring the application of additional inputs and/or (2) reduce the costs of input allocation without delaying the completion of a project. Depending upon the particular conditions involved in the problem, the critical path analysis may indicate the advisability of adding or taking away inputs (resources or equipment) from any given path, or of transferring inputs from one path to another.

There are essentially four different ways of, or objectives served by, developing improved PERT networks. These are: (1) load leveling, (2) time-cost tradeoffs, (3) limited resource management, and (4) controlling rates of expenditures. In the following sections, we will illustrate the first two of these specifically with data drawn from Figure 16–7; and then briefly delve into the other two. This is done because limited resource management and controlling rates of expenditures involve certain complexities which do not render them amenable to concretely apply to the simplified example given in Figure 16–7.

Load Leveling. Load leveling, as its name implies, seeks to make even the utilization of various resources in the original PERT program. As Buffa has pointed out, load leveling may reduce labor costs, hiring and separation costs, or "the cost of any resource, such as an equipment rental."[27] He further has indicated that for very complex projects, load leveling simulations have been developed with the possibility of utilizing a beginning leveling solution based on an *ES* schedule. Further, as indicated previously, project completion times may be hastened without the addition of resources by load leveling. Three examples follow which indicate how load leveling may be accomplished with the PERT program network given in Figure 16–7.

1. *Addition of inputs.* Managers sometimes encounter situations in which they desire to provide additional resources to a project so as to hasten its completion. Such a decision may be made during the preliminary planning stages in the development of a new project, for example, because a firm's competition has just announced a new product

---

[27] *Ibid.*, p. 214.

development of its own. Or, delays encountered during the actual work on a project may necessitate the employment of additional resources (such as overtime work) if the project is to be completed by the planned deadline date. When such delays occur, managers are sometimes tempted to place the entire project on a crash basis, as for example, putting employees working on all activities on an overtime schedule. Critical path analysis, however, may indicate that completion dates may be hastened by the application of additional inputs *only to the activities comprising one or a few of the paths in the program network.* Suppose, for example, that any of the activities indicated in the PERT network in Figure 16–7 could be speeded up by as much as 30 percent by scheduling overtime work, and that the manager has decided that he must reduce the overall project time from 24 to 22 days. This objective could be realized simply by scheduling enough overtime work on *any one* of the activities in critical path A–C–D–G to reduce the time needed to complete the activity by two days.[28] No additional inputs need be applied to any of the other activity paths—the whole project does not need to be put on a crash basis. This is because there is slack in all other paths, with the maximum number of days required by any of the other paths in the PERT network being 22 days (path A–C–F–G), which is just equal to the 22-day completion time now desired. If the manager wished to further shorten the total project time, say to 21 days, however, he would find it necessary to shorten both paths A–C–F–G and the critical path to 21 days.

2. *Transfer of inputs.* In a somewhat similar manner, project completion may sometimes be hastened by load leveling by the transfer of inputs from one network path to another. Suppose, for example, that the manager wishes to reduce the total project time as in the above example to 21 days and that the resources which determine the length of time required to complete both activities D–G and E–G are identical, and thus transferable from one to the other. Each activity, for instance, might be one involving the drafting of blueprints, with all draftsmen equally capable of working on either. If such were the case, total project time could be reduced from 24 to 22 days by transferring two man-days of drafting work from activity E–G to D–G without applying any additional inputs to the project.[29] Such a transfer would reduce the length of critical path A–C–D–G to 22 days, while increasing the length of path A–C–E–G to 19 days—which would still be 3 days less than the total project time available.

---

[28] The questions of *which* activities on which it may be most advisable to schedule; and how much additionally such scheduling will cost get into the question of time-cost transfers, will be discussed in the next section.

[29] To determine on which two *specific* days the two men should be transferred from EG to DG is not possible without further cost information and more sophisticated analysis. The outer range of possibilities, however, may be noted by examining the *ES* and *LF* times in Figure 16–7.

3. *Reduction of inputs.* In the above example it was pointed out that it was possible to transfer resources away from a less than critical path without lengthening the time required to complete a project. In some allocation problems, it may be desirable for the manager to simply take away resources from one of the less critical paths in order to lower the costs of the project, rather than to effect a transfer to a more critical path to hasten project completion time. To illustrate this possibility, let us assume that the manager of the project had originally believed that overtime work would be necessary for activity E–G; and that the most likely time of five days planned for this activity was based on the employment of five draftsmen each working a 10-hour day. Assuming a straight-time rate for each draftsman of $3 per hour, and an overtime rate of $4.50 per hour, total labor costs for the overtime schedule would be as follows:

5 draftsmen @ 40 hrs. each straight time = 200 hrs. @ $3.00/hr. or $600
5 draftsmen @ 10 hrs. each overtime   = 50 hrs. @ $4.50/hr. or $225
                                         Total labor costs $825

Critical path analysis indicates that the scheduling of the drafting work on a straight-line basis, which would require $6\frac{1}{4}$ days for completion rather than 5, can be accomplished without delaying the completion of the project. Total labor costs for the straight-time work are:

5 draftsmen @ 50 hrs. each straight time = 250 hrs. @ $3.00/hr. or $750

Thus, a saving of $75 may be effected by leveling the resource load through the elimination of the use of overtime.

Time-Cost Tradeoffs. As indicated above, resources may be added to the critical path to shorten the duration of the project's time. A key question here, however, is specifically what resources should be added to which activities on the critical path so as to minimize the costs of saving time. A number of approaches with different nomenclature and conceptualizations have been developed to deal with this problem of time-cost tradeoffs—i.e., how much cost will management have to "trade-off" to save any particular amount of time?[30]

In the time-cost tradeoff procedure, it is first necessary to develop two different estimates for each activity and path: "(1) a minimum time estimate and its cost; and (2) a minimum cost estimate and its time."[31] It is important to recognize that these two time estimates represent simply the PERT programmers' or management's estimate of what would the minimum time be regardless of costs, and what the minimum

---

[30] For a brief discussion of this problem, see Buffa, *Production Management*, pp. 216–17; or for a more extended discussion, Moder and Phillips, *Production Management with CPM and PERT*, especially chap. 9. In this section, we will draw heavily on the conceptualization of PERT/COST presented by Martin K. Starr, which demonstrates the basics of time-cost tradeoffs in a clearly comprehensible yet not overly technical manner. Martin K. Starr, *Systems Management of Operations* (Englewood Cliffs, N.J.: Prentice-Hall, Inc., 1971), pp. 208–10.

[31] Starr, op. cit., p. 209.

costs would be to complete the activity—they do not represent either the Beta Distribution times or the *ES, LS, EF, LF* times mentioned earlier.

Next, the minimum cost estimate is used for all activities, and the critical path built on *these times*. This will obviously result in a completion date based on minimum cost estimates. To shorten the critical path to meet the requirements, time-cost tradeoffs are made on the critical path. The procedure suggested by Starr for doing so is as follows:

> As a reasonable trade-off rule, we select that *critical path activity* where: ΔCOST/ΔTIME is smallest; then the next biggest ratio is used; and so on; until a satisfactory compromise between time and cost is achieved.[32]

To illustrate, the two time estimates for each activity on the critical path in Figure 16–7 are illustrated together with some hypothetical cost data in Figure 16–8. In this case, for example, if the project, and

Figure 16–8. Time-Cost Tradeoff Example

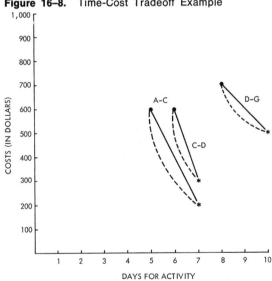

● = MINIMUM TIME LIMIT FOR ACTIVITY

* = MINIMUM COST LIMIT FOR ACTIVITY

Note: The broken lines illustrate that time-cost tradeoffs are usually curvilinear rather than linear.

Activity	Δ Cost	Δ Time	Δ Cost/Δ Time
A–C.......	$400	2	$200
C–D.......	$300	1	$300
D–G.......	$200	2	$100

---

[32] Ibid.

hence, critical path needed to be shortened from 24 to 22 days, the activity to which resources should be added is D–G, where the $\Delta COST/\Delta TIME$ ratio is smallest.

Two final observations may be made concerning this example and time-cost tradeoffs. First, the time-cost tradeoff relationship is usually curvilinear as noted in Figure 16–8 rather than linear as assumed in the example; and techniques for dealing with this phenonemon have been developed.[33] Second, in the above example, it may be noted that as a result of the time-cost tradeoff effected on the critical path, the program now has two 22 day critical paths: A–C–D–G; and A–C–E–F (see Figure 16–7). This poses no special problems except that management should keep closer control over *both* paths, since any delay *in either* will now delay the completion of the project.

Limited Resources Management. In its simpler forms, PERT assumes the availability of unlimited resources. However, in some projects, management may require a critical resource the supply of which is limited. The PERT project plan, for example, may not be feasible if it schedules the same piece of equipment at two different locations at the same time. A model has been developed by Weist called SPAR (Scheduling Program for Allocation of Resources), with one of its features that of dealing with this problem.[34] This is a complex model based on heuristic programming methods and one in which the *ES* times discussed earlier are utilized. As Buffa has summarized the model, it

focuses on available resources which it allocates, period by period, to activities listed in order of their early start times. The most critical jobs have the highest probability of being scheduled first, and as many jobs are initially scheduled as available resources permit. If an available activity fails to be scheduled in one period, an attempt is made to schedule it in the next period. Finally, all jobs that have been postponed become critical and move to the top of the priority list of available activities.[35]

It is beyond the scope of this book to delve into Weist's model in detail except to point out that its application to a space vehicle project resulted in a considerable improvement over a regular PERT schedule in terms of shortening the duration of the project and better manpower planning.

Controlling the Rate of Expenditures. Many PERT projects, such as those involving missiles, call for the investment of considerable outlays

---

[33] For a discussion of ways of dealing with this problem, see Moder and Phillips, *Project Management with CPM and PERT*, chap. 9.

[34] Jerome D. Weist, "A Heuristic Model for Scheduling Large Projects with Limited Resources," *Management Science*, 13 (February 1967), pp. B359–77.

[35] Buffa, *Production Management*, p. 216. For those who are interested in a somewhat more sophisticated summary of SPAR, see Moder and Phillips, *Project Management with CPM and PERT*, pp. 172–75.

of capital over lengthy periods of time for manpower, equipment, and other resources. For this reason, and because money has a time value as indicated in Chapter 15, management may be interested in controlling the *rate* of expenditure invested in the project. One can develop a PERT network with all activities based on their earliest (*ES*) times; or conversely the program could be based on utilization of latest start (*LS*) times. By doing so, a *range* of feasible budgets may be developed. A hypothetical example of a range of cumulative cost curves for a PERT network is shown in Figure 16–9. As Moder and Phillips have pointed

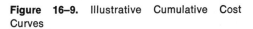

Figure 16–9. Illustrative Cumulative Cost Curves

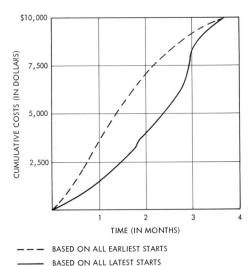

out, "a particular budget curve, lying somewhere between the *ES* and *LS* curves is usually desired."[36] They also point out (1) that in some cases management's funds for a particular period may be constrained, so that the critical path may have to be lengthened; or (2) sometimes it may be desirable to schedule a project so as to "level the requirements for funds within a limitation on the length of the project."[37] At any rate, the key point here is that money is a resource, and that there are certain cases in which controlling the rate of expenditures as a resource may be a constraint to be considered in the use of PERT.

The Limitations of PERT. Although the use of PERT and the types of PERT approaches have expanded considerably since its inception, PERT is not without its limitations. As indicated earlier, the use of

---

[36] Moder and Phillips, *Project Management with CPM and PERT*, p. 242. These authors also point up ways for scheduling start times, a discussion of which is beyond the scope of this book.

[37] Ibid., p. 243.

three probabilistic time elements has been one problem associated with PERT. Others include the following. First, PERT has sometimes been forced on management, with adverse psychological reactions rendering support for and the effective use of the technique extemely difficult, if not impossible. Second, in some cases the time lags in reporting to management the status of activities in a PERT project has caused a loss of faith in the technique. Third, in a few cases (e.g., the Minuteman missile program), projects have been so complex so as to render their use on the computer impossible. Finally, it has been estimated that PERT planning and control costs approximately twice that of conventional techniques. Counterbalancing this fact is that there is a trend toward the development of better PERT programs of a general purpose nature, which should serve to reduce the costs of using PERT in the future.

SUMMARY

A fundamental management problem is the allocation of scarce resources in such a way as to achieve full realization of the firm's objectives. From a prescriptive point of view, the fundamental criterion for the allocation of resources should thus be the maximization of profit or its counterpart, cost minimization, to the extent that the objectives of the firm are economic in nature. In dealing with such broad allocation problems as budgetary decision making for the firm as a whole, and operations planning for complex work processes, the overall optimization of economic objectives (to say nothing of noneconomic ones) is an ideal, rarely, if ever, realized.

The rationality of the decision maker is bounded by the complexity of the key decision variables and their interrelationships in problems of such magnitude. Nor is his rationality in dealing with these problems simply bounded by the complexity of economic variables. Budgetary decisions, for example, often reflect political considerations as well as economic ones, and must be thought of at least in part in terms of the social power and influence of these members of the firm involved in the budgetary process.

Nevertheless, the application of such approaches as operating and cash budgets, as the Gantt Chart, and PERT may enable the manager to satisfice in dealing with his allocation problems. Further, optimization of certain subphases of complex allocation problems is sometimes possible by means of these approaches. Application of time-cost tradeoffs in the analysis of PERT program networks, for example, may permit the minimization of certain expected costs in the planning of work projects. Also of value in optimizing certain kinds of allocation problems is a class of new and powerful decision-making approaches—mathematical programming—to which attention will be turned in the next chapter.

DISCUSSION AND STUDY QUESTIONS

1. If all the outflow of a firm's funds (e.g., taxes, payroll, insurance, and so on) were known for certainty by management, there would be no need to formulate a cash budget. Discuss.

2. One of the few limitations of program budgeting is that it may sometimes be incompatible with the capital budgeting technique of present value discussed in Chapter 15. Discuss.

3. Which budgetary approach—the variable budget, or budgetary revision at various intervals during the year—do you believe to be more valid? Why?

4. Indicate for each of the following type of operations whether PERT, Gantt Charts, or neither of these two approaches would be an appropriate resource allocation method. In each case, give reasons for your answers.
    a) The manufacture of chewing gum.
    b) The construction of a new interstate highway.
    c) Planning a company's college recruiting program.
    d) The manufacture of printing rollers, in which each order must meet customer specifications.
    e) The manufacture of paper clips.

5. Under what conditions would each of the following scheduling rules be satisfactory in a job shop? Explain.
    a) First-come, first-served.
    b) Give priority to orders with the nearest delivery date.
    c) Give priority to orders with the smallest difference between their delivery date and the processing time still needed for their completion.

6. What is meant by line balancing? What basic type of production operation is it applied to?

7. Evaluate the following statement made by a systems analyst: "In the utilization of simple critical path techniques, if you control time, you simultaneously control costs. By reducing the time required to complete a project via PERT methods, you will reduce the total costs of completing the project."

8. PERT is commonly used on short projects involving little complexity. Discuss.

9. The basic focus of control in job lot systems is upon the quality of numerous similar items. Discuss.

10. The foreman of a job shop is utilizing a Gantt Chart to plan the manufacture of a piece of equipment. The piece of equipment is made up of two subassemblies, each of which is made up of two parts which must be fabricated. Final assembly of the equipment cannot begin until each subassembly has been completed, nor can the work on each subassembly begin until both of its parts have been completed. The firm works seven days a week with no overtime and the due date

of the project is April 13. The time required for each stage of the manufacture of the equipment is as follows:

Operation	Days Required
Fabrication Part No. 1	3
Fabrication Part No. 2	2
Subassembly A (of Parts Nos. 1 and 2)	3
Fabrication Part No. 3	5
Fabrication Part No. 4	1
Subassembly B (of Parts Nos. 3 and 4)	4
Final Assembly	3

Draw a Gantt Chart for this operation as in Figure 16–5 in the text, showing operations at the end of April 5, assuming that all operations are proceeding exactly as scheduled. Would the foreman be wise in using a Gantt Chart for this operation?

11. You are given the following network of activities and events. The activity times are stated in days.

NOTE: The activity lines in the schematic below have not been drawn to scale.

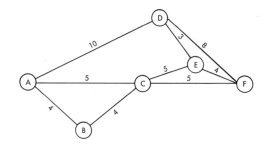

a) Determine the critical path for this network.

b) Determine the times of the other paths. Which has the most slack?

c) Assuming that all resources may be transferred without effecting costs, how much project time could be shortened by just transferring resources from path A–C–F to the critical path?

d) Assume that management must reduce the length of the project by one day, and that no resources are transferable. The present costs, and costs required to meet this objective for four activities are given below. Which activity can be shortened by one day to shorten project time at least cost?

Activity	Present Cost per Day	Cost to Shorten Activity 1 Day
A–D	$400	$800
D–F	$600	$900
A–C	$400	$600
C–F	$400	$500

12. A PERT system assumes no competition for, or multiple use of, resources from other projects. Comment.

13. The more expediting that is done in a job shop in order to speed the flow of lagging items through the shop, the more late orders there will be emerging from the shop. Evaluate.

SELECTED REFERENCES

Arygris, Chris. "Human Problems with Budgets," *Harvard Business Review,* 31 (January-December 1953), 97–110.

Bowman, Edward H., and Fetter, Robert B. *Analysis for Production and Operations Management.* 3d ed. Homewood, Ill.: Richard D. Irwin, Inc., 1967, chaps. 1 and 2.

Buffa, Elwood S. *Modern Production Management.* 3d ed. New York: John Wiley & Sons, Inc., 1969.

Clark, Wallace. *The Gantt Chart.* 3d ed. New York: Pitman Publishing Corp., 1952.

Ford, L. R., and Fulkerson, D. R. *Flows in Networks.* Princeton, N.J.: Princeton University Press, 1962.

Fulkerson, D. R. "A Network Flow Computation for Project Cost Curves," *Management Science,* 7 (January 1961), 167–78.

Hofstede, G. H. *The Game of Budget Control.* London: Tavistock Publications, Limited, 1968.

Holt, C. C.; Modigliani, F.; Muth, J. F.; and Simon, H. A. *Planning Production, Inventories, and Work Force.* Englewood Cliffs, N.J.: Prentice-Hall, Inc., 1960.

Hottenstein, Michael P. (ed.). *Models and Analysis for Production Management.* Scranton, Pa.: International Textbook Co., 1968.

Jewell, William S. "Risk-Taking in Critical Path Analysis," *Management Science,* 11 (January 1965), 438–43.

Lyden, Fremont, and Miller, Ernest G. (eds.). *Planning Programming Budgeting.* Chicago: Markham Publishing Co., 1968.

McCrimmin, K. R., and Ryavec, C. A. "Analytical Study of the PERT Assumptions," The RAND Corporation Memo, Rm-340A-PR (December 1962).

McKean, Roland N. *Efficiency in Government through Systems Analysis.* New York: John Wiley & Sons, Inc., 1958.

Mitchell, William E. "Cash Forecasting: The Four Methods Compared," *The Controller,* 28 (April 1960), 162–66, 194.

Moder, Joseph J., and Phillips, Cecil R. *Project Management with CPM and PERT.* 2d ed. New York: Van Nostrand Reinhold Co., 1970.

Moore, Franklin G., and Jablonski, Ronald. *Production Control.* 3d ed. New York: McGraw-Hill Book Co., 1969.

Muth, J. F., and Thompson, G. E. (eds.). *Industrial Scheduling.* Englewood Cliffs, N.J.: Prentice-Hall, Inc., 1963.

NOVICK, DAVID (Ed.). *Program Budgeting: Program Analysis and the Federal Government.* Cambridge, Mass.: Harvard University Press, 1965.

PENDLETON, S. A. "Variable Budgeting for Planning and Control," *NAA Bulletin,* 36 (1954), 323–34.

STARR, MARTIN K. *Systems Management of Operations.* Englewood Cliffs, N.J.: Prentice-Hall, Inc., 1971.

STEDRY, ANDREW. *Budget Control and Cost Behavior.* Chicago: Markham Publishing Co., 1968.

WEIST, JEROME D. "A Heuristic Model for Scheduling Large Projects with Limited Resources," *Management Science,* 13 (February 1967), B359–77.

WILSON, JAMES D. "Dynamic Budgeting—Getting the Most from Your Program," *Dun's Review and Modern Industry,* 59 (1957), 62, 128–32.

Chapter 17

Allocation of Resources: Mathematical Programming

THE PAST TWO DECADES have witnessed the development and use of a number of mathematical techniques for arriving at optimum solutions for problems involving the allocation of resources. These approaches have made feasible the solution of many types of problems which heretofore could only be dealt with (if at all) by extremely lengthy, cumbersome, and trial-and-error methods. Utilization of the electronic computer has greatly facilitated the application of these techniques, and their use will probably become even more widespread in the future.

In this chapter attention will be focused on several of the better known mathematical programming methods: (1) the algebraic, simplex, and transportation methods of linear programming, (2) nonlinear programming, and (3) dynamic and integer programming. Consideration will also be given to sensitivity analysis in mathematical programming. Specific step-by-step procedures will be presented for the solution to problems by the algebraic and transportation methods, both of which are *linear* programming methods and can easily be handled by those familiar with basic algebra. The other techniques will be treated only in a general way because of the mathematical and/or computational complexities involved in their use. It should also be pointed out that, although the simple problems presented in this chapter can be hand calculated, for all practical purposes, meaningful "real-world" programming problems almost always require the use of a digital computer.

Two conditions must exist for any of the mathematical programming techniques to be applicable. First, the decision maker must state explicitly the objective which he seeks in solution of the problems. This objective must be framed in quantitative terms, such as profit maximization or cost minimization. Thus, mathematical programming cannot be used in problems with multiple goals, unless the goals can be integrated into one sole objective. In programming problems, the objective chosen by the decision maker is referred to as the *objective function*. Second, there must exist one or more restrictions (or constraints) on the resources available to the manager. In other words, we are dealing with problems involving the allocation of *scarce* resources, in which *limited* supplies of men, materials, time, and so forth are available. This is, of course, true of all allocation problems, since with unlimited resources, the decision maker has no allocation problem.

Unlike some quantitative approaches (such as break-even analysis) none of the programming methods provides answers to decision problems through the solution of a *single* equation. Rather, each consists of a *formalized search procedure* or algorithm by means of which the decision maker moves closer and closer to the optimum solution through a series of successive steps or iterations. It is this formalized, logically determined sequencing of problem-solving steps which represents the major advantage of programming over previous trial-and-error approaches.

In addition to providing powerful decision-making tool for the manager, mathematical programming represents an important area for study for at least two other reasons. First, like all quantitative approaches, programming forces the manager to visualize more clearly the key variables and relationships in decision problems by the formulation of the problem in terms of a model, in this case a programming model. Second, a general understanding of these methods is often valuable even for those managers not directly involved in programming work if their organizations are to make most effective use of these tools. As Stockton has pointed out,

Line managers—as differentiated from staff specialists or analysts—play an important role in the initial and final stages of problem-solving projects, that is, in the formulation of the problem and in the evaluation and application of the findings. They must, as a consequence, be capable of effective communication with any staff specialist, including the operations or systems analyst.[1]

In fact, lack of understanding of the potential of mathematical programming by line managers is one important reason why its use is still somewhat limited today.[2]

The reader should not infer from the above that mathematical pro-

---

[1] R. Stansbury Stockton, *Introduction to Linear Programming* (Homewood, Ill.: Richard D. Irwin, Inc., 1971), p. 2.

[2] The applications of linear programming, however, "can be expected to increase in the future as variations and refinements are developed. Tomorrow's business executives will clearly need to be familiar with these methods and capable of applying them to complex problems within their organization." Ibid.

gramming, however powerful, represents a panacea which can be used indiscriminately for the solution of all allocation decision problems. An important consideration in the application of programming techniques, as with all decision approaches, is that of weighing the costs of using the tool against the returns derived from so doing. Employment of programming methods necessitates framing of the decision problem in quantitative terms, the gathering of relevant data and, in many cases, extensive calculations. If the total sum of money involved in making a particular decision or if the difference in results is relatively small, the costs incurred by carrying out these programming steps may well exceed any possible savings or profits that might be realized by the use of programming in lieu of a purely intuitive approach to dealing with the problem.

Nor are the mathematical programming techniques applicable to all types of allocation problems. As will be indicated more fully in the following sections, only problems possessing certain fundamental characteristics may be handled by *some* of the programming methods. For example, as their name implies, the *linear programming* techniques have applicability only to problems framed such that all relationships between variables are *linear* ones. It should be noted that this assumption prevents the use of linear programming in situations where increasing or decreasing returns to scale are important considerations. Further, many important allocation problems involve such a level of complexity that their solution is not feasible by means of mathematical programming because they are too large to be handled on existing computers. For instance, although it is possible under certain conditions to optimize the assignment of men to machines in a job shop through the use of programming, optimization of the entire job shop operation cannot be achieved by the application of programming techniques. (Job shop problems can, however, often be handled by simulation techniques, which will be discussed in Chapter 19.) Thus, it is important for the decision maker to understand not only how mathematical programming may be applied to problems, but also the conditions under which such application is feasible.

It should be noted that developments in mathematical programming methods in recent years have tended to reduce their limitations—i.e., nonlinear programming to overcome the linearity assumption, stochastic programming to deal with problems that could not be handled with programming methods requiring certainty, and so forth. Further, where costs of computation have been excessive, research efforts have tended to focus on better algorithms even at the expense of optimality.

Above, mathematical programming techniques have been referred to as "optimizing" ones. The meaning of the word "optimum," with respect to mathematical programming in the context of management decision making, in general, requires further elaboration. First, although the objective of mathematical programming techniques is to "optimize," if used properly, they usually only provide "very good" solutions. This is because they are only *models* of the real world, and the data fed into them usually only approximate real-world phenomena.[3] Second, in all cases, those models which come close to optimizing, do so typically for only one or more of the firm's subsystems. This results in suboptimization problems elsewhere in the system. For example, a transportation method solution may come close to minimizing total transportation costs, but result in higher inventory costs. Finally, it should be emphasized that no matter how the results of any mathematical programming application turn out, they will be costly unless they are accepted by and actually utilized by line management. Thus, one of the problems of the mathematical programmer is the behavioral one of overcoming any resistance to the use of results by line management.

LINEAR PROGRAMMING: ALGEBRAIC METHOD

The least complex and least useful of the mathematical programming methods designed to arrive at optimum solutions for resource allocation problems is the algebraic method of linear programming. We present the method only to illustrate the optimizing methods and nature of linear programming, rather than to show it as a decision-making technique of value.

The technique calls for the manipulation of a number of simple linear equations and inequalities. It is also sometimes referred to as the graphic-algebraic method, since the algebraic manipulation may be facilitated by the development of a graph to permit visualization of the constraints and the objective function. In fact, optimum solutions to the kinds of problems which may be dealt with by the algebraic method may often be approximated solely by graphic means. In the following sections treatment of the programming mathematics will be supplemented by their graphic presentation so that the reader may visualize the method both algebraically and geometrically.

The algebraic technique is useful in handling *two-variable* product mix problems—i.e., problems in which the decision maker wants to determine the optimum number of each of two products to manufacture when the resources required for their production are limited. A major limitation of the method is its primary applicability to problems involving only two variables. Although three variables can be handled by the technique, their visualization in three-dimensional space is often difficult. (For n variable problems, the simplex technique is employed.) It should be noted, however, that the algebraic method can be employed

---

[3] In spite of this fact, the words "optimum" and "optimizing" will be used in subsequent sections as is conventional in the literature on mathematical programming.

to handle problems involving any number of *restrictions or constraints*. It is only the number of variables which must be so limited.

There are four basic steps involved in the application of the algebraic method: (1) statement of the problem, (2) determination of the restrictions or constraints, (3) the choice of an appropriate objective function, and (4) development of an optimum solution (or solutions). These four steps characterize not only the algebraic method, but all linear program problems. In addition, algebraic problems must possess three fundamental characteristics if the technique is to be employed: (1) both the objective function and all of the restrictions must be expressed in linear terms, (2) all of the profit and cost data relative to the problem must be known for certain, and (3) all parameters in the problem must be continuous rather than discrete variables.[4] These three conditions are often referred to as *linearity, certainty,* and *continuity.*

Statement of the Problem

Application of the algebraic method may be illustrated by the use of an example. As an illustration, the following problem will be considered and each of the steps in its solution treated:

The Atlas Chemical Company produces two chemical compounds, X and Y. The resources available for making the compounds are:

10 hours of labor
600 pounds of chemical element A
900 pounds of element B
1,000 pounds of element C

Each unit of compound X requires: 1/50 hours of labor, 2 pounds of element A and 5 pounds of element C. Element B is not used in its production. Each unit of compound Y requires: 1/50 hours of labor, 1 pound of element A and 2 pounds of element B. Element C is not required. Profits obtained by the Atlas Chemical Company from each unit of compound X are $6; and from each unit of Y, $4.

Management's objective is to determine the number of units of each compound which should be produced if total profits for the firm are to be maximized.

Expression of the Constraints

The first step in dealing with this problem is to develop mathematical expressions for each of the constraints and to illustrate these graphically. First, consider the labor restriction. Each unit of compound X requires

---

[4] For example, in the problem presented in the next paragraph it *must* be possible to utilize any number of hours (including fractional ones) of labor (up to 10)—not just the whole integer number of hours: 0, 1, 2 . . . 10.

1/50 hours of labor. Thus, if only X is produced, the 10 hours of labor available would permit the manufacture of 500 units. Similarly, enough labor is available for the production of 500 units of compound Y if no X is made, since the number of hours of labor required for the manufacture of each unit of compound Y is also 1/50. Further, for every 1/50 man hour taken away from the manufacture of Y and devoted to X, one additional unit of X, and one unit less of Y may be produced, and vice versa. For example, if all 10 hours of labor are allocated to Y, 500 units of Y and zero units of X can be produced; if 9 49/50 hours are allocated to Y, and 1/50 to X, 499 units of Y and 1 unit of X can be manufactured, and so on. This constraint may be expressed in linear terms, since the number of units of either compound which must be given up to permit the production of the other is constant. In this case the *rate of substitution* is one for one.

The reader will recall from his study of algebra that the equation for a straight line may be obtained if two x values and two y values are known by substituting these values in the formula:

$$\frac{y - y_1}{x - x_1} = \frac{y_2 - y_1}{x_2 - x_1}.$$

Substituting in this formula the two sets of x and y values that are given in the chemical problem ($500x$, $0y$; and $0x$, $500y$), we obtain the following linear equation expressing the labor hours restriction: $x + y = 500$.[5] It should be noted, however, that, depending on the other restrictions in the problem, the decision maker may choose to produce a number of units of X and Y, the sum of which is *less than* 500. The labor constraint equation only indicates the *maximum* number of units which may be produced with the labor resources available. Thus, this equation must be transformed to represent an inequality: $x + y \leq 500$.

---

[5] These calculations proceed as follows:

1. $\dfrac{y - 0}{x - 500} = \dfrac{500 - 0}{0 - 500}$
2. $-500(y) = 500(x - 500)$
3. $500x + 500y = 250,000$
4. $x + y = 500$

This same equation can be determined more quickly by solving: $\dfrac{x}{a} + \dfrac{y}{b} = 1$; where

a represents the point at which the line crosses the x-axis; and b, the point at which it crosses the y-axis. Or, for the labor requirements restriction:

(1) $\dfrac{x}{500} + \dfrac{y}{500} = 1$; and

(2) Multiplying both sides of the equation by 500; $x + y = 500$.

For further summary information regarding linear functions which may be useful in dealing with graphic-algebraic problems, the reader is referred to Appendix A at the end of this book.

This inequality is illustrated in Figure 17–1. The shaded area to its lower left indicates the *strategy space* available to the decision maker with respect to the labor constraint. This area represents the range of possible combinations of units of *x* and *y* that can be produced with 10 hours of labor as a restriction. It should be noted that this area

Figure 17–1. Strategy Space Circumscribed by Labor Hours Constraint

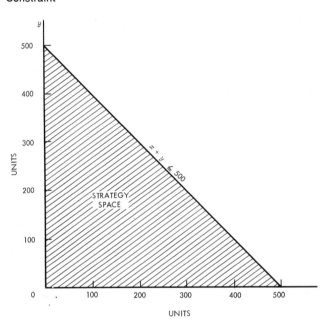

is bounded to the left and at the bottom by the *x*- and *y*-axes, respectively, since negative units of production are an impossibility. Available raw materials constraints will now be examined.

Expressions of linear inequalities may be developed for each of the raw materials constraints in the chemical problem following the procedure outlined above. For element *A*, the expression is $2x + y \leq 600$; for element *B*: $y \leq 450$; and for element *C*: $x \leq 200$. These inequalities have the following meaning:

1. A quantity of element *A* is available for the production of any combination of units of compounds *X* and *Y* as long as the number of units of *Y* plus two times the number of units of *X* does not exceed 600. For example, if 400 units of *Y* are produced, the maximum number of *X* which can be manufactured is 100, since *Y* (400) plus two times *X* (200) equals the limiting value of 600.
2. A quantity of element *B* is available for the production of 450 units of compound *Y*.

3. A quantity of element C is available for the production of 200 units of compound X.

It should be noted that the reason the inequality representing the element B constraint contains no x term, and that for element C, no y term, is that the production of compound X does not require the use of element B; nor does the manufacture of Y call for element C.

Graphing all the constraints in the problem will define the total strategy space available to the decision maker. This space which is represented by the shaded area in Figure 17–2 is often referred to as the

Figure 17–2. Feasibility Polygon

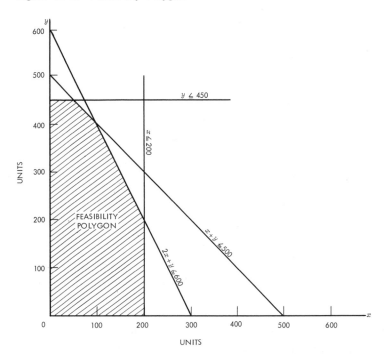

feasibility polygon. The production of any combination of units of X and Y within this polygon is feasible with the resources available, although certain combinations will produce greater profits for the firm than others. It is the determination of that combination of production which will yield the greatest profit for the chemical company to which attention will next be turned.

Expression of the Objective Function

As indicated previously, the chemical manufacturer will realize a profit of $6 from the manufacture (and sale) of each unit of compound X, and a profit of $4 from each unit of Y. To achieve any given level of total profits from the operation, any one of a number of different combinations of X and Y might be produced. For instance, a profit of $300 would be realized by the manufacture of: 50 units of X alone; 75 units of Y alone; 30 units of X and 30 units of Y; and so on. All possible combinations of X and Y which will produce any given amount of profit may be represented by a linear equation, which when superimposed upon the feasibility polygon is referred to as an *iso-profit line*. As will be pointed out below, it is *not* necessary to develop iso-profit equations or graph iso-profit lines to solve problems by the algebraic method. Four isoprofit lines for the chemical problem in Figure 17–3 are illustrated, however, to enable visualization of the possible combinations of production of X and Y which will produce various levels of profit for the manager. As may be noted in Figure 17–3, the slopes

Figure 17–3. Iso-Profit Lines Superimposed on Feasibility Polygon

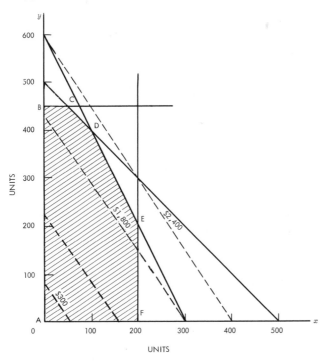

of all of the isoprofit lines are identical $(-\frac{3}{2})$, which will be the case with all problems of the type we are considering. The existence of identical slopes is due to the fact that the per unit contribution to profits of both X and Y is constant regardless of the number of units produced.

In the chemical problem, each unit of Y always contributes $4 to total profits or $\frac{2}{3}$ as much as the per unit contribution of X of $6.

Since profit maximization is the objective function, solution of the programming problem requires finding that iso-profit line representing the greatest profitability within the constraints of the feasibility polygon. A key characteristic of all linear programming problems is that *the optimizing iso-profit line will always intersect one or more of the corner points of the feasibility polygon.* For this reason, to solve the chemical problem one needs only to: (1) examine total profitability at each of points A, B, C, D, E, and F on the feasibility polygon illustrated in Figure 17–3, and (2) select that point which represents the most profitable product mix. Since point A represents zero production, it may be immediately dismissed as an optimum solution, and close examination of only the other five points is required.

Selecting the Optimum Alternative

The total profits which will be realized at corner point B on the y-axis, and at point F on the x-axis may be determined by inspection. At point B, 450 units of Y alone will be manufactured, and total profits at $4 per unit are $1,800. The manufacture of 200 units of X and no units of Y at point F will yield a profit of $6(200)$ or $1,200. The determination of production levels, and hence profits, at points C, D, and E, on the other hand, will require some simple calculations. Each of these points represents the intersection of two of the constraint lines. Therefore, the values of X and Y at each of the points must simultaneously satisfy each of the two equations involved. The determination of these values by means of the solution of the simultaneous equations proceeds as follows:

1. Point C.
$$x + y = 500$$
$$y = 450$$
By subtraction $x = 50$
and $y = 450$

2. Point D.
$$2x + y = 600$$
$$x + y = 500$$
By subtraction $x = 100$
and $y = 400$

3. Point E. By substituting $x = 200$ in the equation $2x + y = 600$, $y = 200$.

The total profit realized from each of the product mix combinations at the corner points may be obtained by multiplying, for both X and Y, the number of units produced by the profit per unit. These calculations, which are illustrated in Figure 17-4, indicate that the optimum

Figure 17–4.   Evaluation of Allocation Strategies

Corner Point	Units of X	@	= Profit from X	Units of Y	@	= Profit from Y	Total Profit
A.....	0	$6	$ 0	0	$4	$ 0	$ 0
B.....	0	6	0	450	4	1,800	1,800
C.....	50	6	300	450	4	1,800	2,100
D.....	100	6	600	400	4	1,600	2,200
E.....	200	6	1,200	200	4	800	2,000
F.....	200	6	1,200	0	4	0	1,200

Source: Corner points, Figure 17–3.

solution to the problem lies at point D, and that 100 units of compound X, and 400 units of compound Y should be manufactured at a total profit of $2,200.

The Existence of Alternative Optimum Solutions

In some linear programming problems, unlike that just examined, a number of equally optimum solutions may exist. Multiple solutions will occur when, and only when, *the slope of the iso-profit lines is equal to the slope of any one of the lines representing binding constraints.* In such a case, all feasible points on the constraint line with its slope identical to that of the iso-profit lines will represent optimum solutions (provided that the points represent whole numbers if the units being dealt with are indivisible).[6]

The existence of multiple solutions may be demonstrated by modifying the chemical manufacturing problem so that the profit per unit for compound Y is $3 instead of $4. The slope of the iso-profit lines now becomes -2 since the per unit profit for compound Y ($3) is one half of that for compound X. This slope is identical to that for the line representing the restriction for element A ($2x + y \leq 600$), and the iso-profit line representing total profits of $1,800 lies on top of the element A constraint line. As may be noted in Figure 17–5, all product mix combinations in whole units falling on these identical lines from point D (100,400)

---

[6] In this example, obviously all such points are not in whole units of X and Y; and hence not possible. This, in a strict sense, violates the continuity assumption of the graphic-algebraic method mentioned earlier. Under certain conditions in which the need arises for the solution of a linear programming problem to be an integer, the method of integer programming which will be discussed later may be used.

Figure 17–5.   Multiple Optimum Solutions

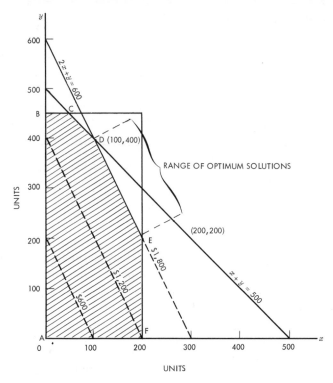

to point E (200,200) are both feasible, and will produce a profit of $1,800. That these points represent optimum mixes may be noted visually, for: (1) moving the iso-profit line to the right brings it outside of the feasibility polygon, while (2) moving it to the left results in a smaller level of production, and hence lower profits, for both compound X and compound Y.

It should be pointed out that the existence of multiple optimum solutions in problems such as the above may be determined without developing and comparing the slopes of the iso-profit and constraint lines to see whether or not they are equal. Rather, the existence of alternative optima may be noted by inspection. All that is required is to determine whether any two corner points yield *identical maximum* profits. If so, all *feasible* points on the constraint line connecting these two corner points also yield optimum solutions. This is due to the fact that all such points fall on the same iso-profit line as do the two corner points.

LINEAR PROGRAMMING: SIMPLEX METHOD

The simplex method, which was developed by George B. Dantzig in 1947, is the most widely applicable of the linear programming techniques. Both the algebraic method and the transportation technique (which will be discussed in the next section) are but special cases of the general simplex procedure. Simplex is by far the most widely used of the mathematical programming techniques—it can handle any number of variables unlike the graphic-algebraic method. It also invariably calls for the use of a computer.[7] Among the wide scope of problems with which it may deal are: product mix, job assignment, production scheduling, transportation routing, the evaluation of complex bids in purchasing, in farm crop assignment to fields, as a substitute for traditional time study methods in work measurement,[8] to help develop wage and salary programs in the field of personnel,[9] and in certain areas of air and water pollution. As indicated earlier, mathematical programming is still not widely used in general. It should be noted, however, that simplex *is* widely utilized especially for product mix problems in two particular types of industries—petroleum, and lumber, paper and allied products. In spite of its usefulness, the simplex method—although not necessarily involving complex mathematics—usually requires a lengthy and involved computational procedure even for problems with as few as four or five variables. Therefore, only some of the key characteristics of the approach will be outlined in general.

Like the algebraic method, conditions of certainty, linearity, and continuity are essential if the simplex method is to be applied. Simplex is further similar to the algebraic method in that the procedure first calls for framing the problem and explicitly stating in quantitative terms both the objective function and the constraints. Once this has been accomplished, an initial (trial) solution to the problem which satisfies

---

[7] Simplex programs may require large computational requirements as is pointed out by Harvey M. Wagner, *Principles of Management Science* (Englewood Cliffs, N.J.: Prentice-Hall, Inc., 1970), p. 101. "For practical applications, several million arithmetic operations are usual. Considerable experience suggests that, as a *rough* approximation, the computational burden increases as the cube of the number of constraints. Thus, a 200-equation problem is likely to require 3 times as many calculations as a comparable 100-equation model." In fact, with some simplex applications the magnitude of the problem is so large that special algorithms are required for them to be run on a computer. One of these is the so-called decomposition algorithm, which "obtains an optimum solution for the given large linear programming problem by decomposing it into a set of smaller linear programming problems and, then, solving these smaller problems." Chaiho Kim, *Introduction to Linear Programming* (New York: Holt, Rinehart & Winston, Inc., 1971), p. 375. For a detailed discussion of the decomposition problem, see ibid, chap. 10, or Frederick S. Hillier and Gerald J. Lieberman, *Introduction to Operations Research* (San Francisco: Holden-Day, Inc., 1967), pp. 520–30.

[8] James A. Chisman, "Using Linear Programming to Determine Time Standards," *The Journal of Industrial Engineering*, 17 (April 1966), pp. 189–91.

[9] See, for example, Frederick P. Rehmus and Harvey M. Wagner, "Applying Linear Programming to Your Pay Structure," *Business Horizons*, 6 (Winter 1963), pp. 89–98, and James E. Bruno, "Using Linear Programming Salary Evaluation Models in Collective Bargaining Negotiations with Teacher Unions," *Socio Econ. Plan. Sci.*, 3 (1969), pp. 103–17.

the constraints is developed. Modifications of the trial solution are then formulated and examined, and the most favorable of these (in terms of the objective function) is incorporated into a second solution. This procedure is repeated until no further modifications improve the solution.[10] Thus, the simplex technique is a step-by-step iterative search procedure in which the optimum solution is progressively approached. The procedure is designed so that the decision maker does not have to fully consider all possible alternative feasible solutions to the problem. This formalized short-cutting represents a major contribution of the method over trial-and-error approaches.

LINEAR PROGRAMMING: TRANSPORTATION METHOD

Another well-known technique for developing optimum solutions for allocation problems is the transportation method of linear programming which is a special case of the simplex technique. Compared to simplex, the transportation method can be understood much more easily with a limited background in mathematics. It does not call for the development and manipulation of linear equations, but rather involves only simple addition, subtraction, and multiplication. On the other hand, application of the method is limited to a much narrower variety of problems than is the simplex.[11] As its name implies, the transportation method is most applicable to problems in which the decision involves selection of optimum transportation routes. As will be indicated later, however, the method may be employed in the solution of other classes of problems as well.

Statement of the Problem

The transportation problem may be stated as follows: Given a number of sources of supply (origins) and destinations, and the costs of shipping a good from each source to each destination, the objective is to select that combination of routes which will minimize total costs. As with the use of both the graphic and simplex methods of linear programming, the transportation technique is applicable only to problems involving: (1) linear relationships between the decision variables, (2) conditions of certainty, and (3) conditions of continuity.[12] That is, the per unit

---

[10] For a discussion of this step-by-step procedure, see, for example, Stockton, *Linear Programming,* chap. 4, or Edward H. Bowman and Robert B. Fetter, *Analysis for Production and Operations Management* (3d ed.; Homewood, Ill.: Richard D. Irwin, Inc., 1967), pp. 82 ff.

[11] It should be noted that all problems amenable to the transportation method could be solved by simplex, but due to the special mathematical structure of the transportation method, they can be solved *faster* than by the use of simplex.

[12] It should be noted, however, that if all the parameters (variables and constraints) in a transportation problem are integers, the method will *always* provide one or more optimum *integer* solutions.

transportation costs from any source to any destination must remain constant regardless of the number of items shipped;[13] and these costs must be known for certain or assumed so by the decision maker in advance. In addition, a third condition must exist if the method is to be applicable—homogeneity or one-for-one substitution. For example, if a manager gives up shipping 50 units from source A to destination X, the condition of homogeneity requires that he be able to substitute in lieu thereof the shipment of exactly 50 units from other sources to this destination. The reader will recall that this condition of homogeneity is not a requisite for the application of the algebraic method (nor is it for simplex). In the problem involving the chemical manufacturer, for example, the production of two units of compound Y had to be given up to release enough element A to produce one unit of compound X.

Developing an Initial Feasible Solution

Like the simplex technique, the transportation method is a formalized search procedure involving a number of successive iterations leading to one or more optimum solutions. The first step called for is that of developing an initial feasible solution. Then, unless this solution happens to be an optimum one, various alternative routes are considered and evaluated one by one until an optimum has been attained. To illustrate the application of the transportation method we will consider an extremely simple problem—one involving only three sources and three destinations. This problem can be solved more quickly by inspection than by use of the transportation technique. However, it will focus attention on the basic aspects of the method without becoming involved with an unduly large number of calculations. Further, exactly the same procedure may be employed regardless of the number of sources and destinations comprising the problem.

As an illustrative example, assume that a manufacturer has three plants with the following monthly production capacities:

Plant 1	200 units
Plant 2	50 units
Plant 3	200 units

and that the company has three warehouses which must be supplied from these factories, with the following monthly demand requirements:

Warehouse A	100 units
Warehouse B	150 units
Warehouse C	200 units

---

[13] Some problems involving step-function costs may be dealt with by the transportation method by treating each step as a separate linear cost source. See, for example, Harvey C. Bunke, *Linear Programming: A Primer* (Iowa City, Iowa: Bureau of Business and Economic Research, College of Business Administration, State University of Iowa, 1960), p. 15.

Given the transportation costs from each factory to each warehouse indicated in Figure 17–6, the problem is to determine the number of units which should be shipped from each source to each destination to minimize these costs.

Figure 17–6. Transportation Costs (in $)

Source	Destination		
	Warehouse A	*Warehouse B*	*Warehouse C*
Plant 1.............	4	1	2
Plant 2.............	6	5	6
Plant 3.............	3	7	4

The first step in developing the initial feasible solution is to design a matrix indicating (1) all plant capacities and warehouse requirements and (2) the transportation costs for each route in the upper diagonal halves of the matrix cells. Such a matrix is shown in Figure 17–7. The

Figure 17–7. Initial Transportation Matrix

Source	Destination			Total Capacity
	Warehouse A	*Warehouse B*	*Warehouse C*	
Plant 1...............	$4	$1	$2	200
Plant 2...............	$6	$5	$6	50
Plant 3...............	$3	$7	$4	200
Total Requirements.....	100	150	200	450

next step is to assign shipments of various numbers of units in the lower diagonal halves of the cells in such a manner that the total number of units shipped from each plant will exactly equal its capacity, and the number of units shipped to each warehouse will exactly meet its requirements.

There are several different ways in which this initial trial assignment may be made.[14] The procedure we recommend is to first assign as many

---

[14] One of the more widely known of these is the so-called northwest corner rule by which the decision maker assigns units first to the cell in the northwest

units as possible to the cell with the lowest transportation cost. Then this step should be repeated for the cell with the next lowest cost, and so on, until all capacity requirements are met. An initial solution to the problem developed by following this procedure is shown in Figure 17–8.

Figure 17–8. Initial Feasible Solution

Source	Destination			Total Capacity
	Warehouse A	Warehouse B	Warehouse C	
Plant 1................	$4	$1 150	$2 50	200
Plant 2................	$6	$5	$6 50	50
Plant 3................	$3 100	$7	$4 100	200
Total Requirements.....	100	150	200	450

It should be noted that in following this procedure, sometimes cells with costs lower than others which are used have to be passed over, since their use would result in either the plant capacities or demand requirements being exceeded. For example, in the matrix in Figure 17–8 as many units as possible were first assigned to the three cells with the lowest costs—1B ($1), 1C ($2), and 3A ($3). The assignment of 150 units to 1B and 50 units to 1C effected the full utilization of Plant 1's capacity of 200 units; and thus cell 1A ($4) had to be passed over. Assignment was next made of 100 units to cell 3C ($4). After this had been accomplished, the only remaining unused cell to which additional units could be assigned without exceeding the capacity or demand requirements was 2C ($6)—cell 2B with lower costs ($5) had to be passed over.

In making the initial assignment, it is also extremely important that the *number of cells used equals the rim requirements of the problem minus one.* "Rim requirements" is defined as the number of sources plus the number of destinations, which in the example is 6. This require-

corner of the matrix, and then proceeds "step by step, away from the northwest corner until, finally, a value is reached in the southeast corner." Churchman, Ackoff & Arnoff, *Introduction to Operations Research* (New York: John Wiley & Sons, Inc., 1957), p. 285. If the manager is analyzing the effectiveness of an existing distribution system, another approach for determining the initial assignment is to select the firm's existing routes, on the assumption that, although not optimum ones, they will probably be closer to an optimum solution than any arbitrary initial assignments.

ment is essential not only in the development of the initial solution, but for all succeeding solutions tried in working out the problem. If the number of used cells is either greater or less than the number of rim requirements minus one, a condition known as *degeneracy* will exist and the problem is not soluble.[15] Methods for dealing with degeneracy, if it is encountered, will be dealt with in a later section after the fundamentals of the transportation procedure have been examined.

Development and Evaluation of Alternative Routes

By following the procedure outlined above, the initial solution shown in Figure 17–8 happens to be an optimum one. This will often be the case with extremely simple transportation problems such as the one under consideration; but will not usually be the case with more complex problems.

In order to illustrate the full transportation procedure we will formulate another trial solution which is considerably less than optimum. This solution is illustrated in Figure 17–9. It may be noted that there are

Figure 17–9.   Initial Trial Transportation Solution

Source	Destination			Total Capacity
	Warehouse A	Warehouse B	Warehouse C	
Plant 1..............	$4 50	$1 150	$2 0	200
Plant 2..............	$6 0	$5 0	$6 50	50
Plant 3..............	$3 50	$7 0	$4 150	200
Total Requirements.....	100	150	200	450

four unused cells in the nonoptimum solution in Figure 17–9—no units have been scheduled for transportation in cells 1C, 2A, 2B, or 3B. The first step involved in developing an alternative, and possibly more optimum, assignment than that in the initial solution is to examine the effect on total costs of the *transfer of one unit* from any of the five used cells to each of the unused cells in turn.

---

[15] Technically it is possible to have degeneracy if the number of used cells equals rim requirements minus 1. Such would be the case with Figure 17–8, if instead of the initial assignment shown here, cells, 1A, 1C, 2B, 3A, and 3C were used.

First consider the transfer of one unit to unused cell $1C$, which is illustrated in Figure 17–10.[16] Note that this transfer necessitates altering the assignment of units in three of the used cells, $1A$, $3A$, and $3C$. These changes are mandatory in order to ensure that the capacities

Figure 17–10. Transfer of One Unit to an Unused Cell

Source	Destination			Total Capacity
	Warehouse A	Warehouse B	Warehouse C	
Plant 1...............	$4 ~~50~~ 49	$1 150	$2 ~~0~~ 1	200
Plant 2...............	$6 0	$5 0	$6 50	50
Plant 3...............	$3 ~~50~~ 51	$7 0	$4 ~~150~~ 149	200
Total Requirements......	100	150	200	450

of each plant continue to be fully utilized and that the demand requirements for each warehouse continue to be fully met. For example, the demand requirements of Warehouse 3 (200 units) are now exactly met by the shipment of 1 unit from Plant 1, 50 units from Plant 2, and 149 units from Plant 3 rather than by 50 units from Plant 2 and 150 units from Plant 3.

Before evaluating the changes in total costs which will result from this transfer of one unit to unused cell $1C$, two observations should be noted. First, the number of cells used at this stage of the transportation procedure does not necessarily have to equal the rim requirements minus one. This is because the transfer of one unit does not represent an alternative solution but rather a tentative exploration. In the above illustration, for example, the number of cells in use is 6 which is *equal* to the number of rim requirements. Second, in deciding which used cells to modify in effecting the transfer of one unit to an unused cell, it is desirable to choose the least cumbersome route—i.e., the one in

---

[16] Other approaches for developing alternative routes have been developed. One of these is the modified transportation method, or *modi.* (See, for example, Stockton, *Linear Programming*, pp. 103–7). Another such approach is that presented in Earl O. Heady and Wilfred Candler, *Linear Programming Methods* (Ames, Iowa: Iowa State College Press, 1958), pp. 350 ff. These methods are somewhat more expedient in the evaluation of unused cells. However, the basic (or "stepping-stone") method is presented in this chapter, based on the authors' experience that this method enables the reader to grasp more easily the *meaning* of the calculations in transportation problems.

which the fewest number of cells require modification. In many cases the simplest transfer procedure may be accomplished as follows:[17]

1. Select one used cell which is in the same row as the unused cell being evaluated, and another used cell which is in the same column as the unused cell; providing that a third used cell exists which is both (1) in the same row as one of the above-mentioned used cells, and (2) in the same column as the other. In Figure 17–10, for example, cell 3C is in the same column as the unused cell being evaluated, 1C; 1A is in the same row as 1C; and 3A is in the same row as 3C and in the same column as 1A.
2. Subtract one unit from each of the first two above-mentioned used cells (3C, 1A), and
3. Add one unit to both the unused cell being evaluated (1C) and the third of the above-mentioned used cells (3A).

Once the single unit has been transferred to one of the unused cells, evaluation of the effect of this modification upon total costs is a relatively simple matter. Reference again to Figure 17–10 indicates that the addition of one unit to cell 1C adds $2 to the transportation costs, and that the costs of adding or subtracting one unit from each of the *used* cells which have been involved in the transfer are as follows: 1A, —$4; 3A, +$3; and 3C, —$4. Summing these four figures indicates that for each unit transferred to cell 1C, total transportation costs are reduced by $3; $2 — $4 + $3 — $4 = —$3. It would therefore be profitable for the decision maker to transfer *as many units as possible* to cell 1C. Before he decides to do so, however, each of the other unused cells should be similarly examined, for the transfer of a unit to any one of them may effect an even greater reduction in total costs than the transfer to 1C. Following the prescribed procedure we find that the cost changes effected by the transfer of one unit to each of the other three unused cells in Figure 17–9 are as shown in Figure 17–11.

Figure 17–11.   Evaluation of Unused Cells

Unused Cell	Cost Change for Individual Cells Involved in Transfer (in $)	Net Change
2A	2A, +6; 2C, —6; 3A, —3; 3C, +4	+1
2B	1A, +4; 1B, —1; 2B, +5; 2C, —6; 3A, —3; 3C, +4	+3
3B	1A, +4; 1B, —1; 3A, —3; 3B, +7	+7

---

[17] In other cases, such simple transfer routes as described here are not possible, and the reader will find it necessary to develop more lengthy routes. This will usually present no major problems as long as it is kept firmly in mind that all source and destination requirements must be exactly met.

The reader will note that each of the above modifications results in *increased* transportation costs.[18] Therefore, only the transfer of as many units as possible to cell 1C should be given further consideration. Sometimes, however, *more than one* of the unused cells to which a unit is transferred may provide the basis for a more satisfactory solution than the initial solution. Or, the transfer of one unit to a particular unused cell may result in *no change* in the transportation costs from the initial solution. If so, the total costs which will be incurred if as many units as possible are transferred to this cell will be the same as they were for the initial assignment.

In deciding to which unused cell, if any, such a transfer should be effected, the following rules are recommended:

1. If the transfer results in a reduction in transportation costs for only one of the unused cells, that cell is to be chosen.

2. If the transfer brings about a reduction in costs for more than one unused cell, choose that cell for which the reduction is the greatest. Or, in other words, select the cell for which the net change has the greatest negative value.[19] If this value is identical for two or more unused cells, evaluate the transfer of as many units as possible to each. Then, select from among these possible transfer routes the one which brings about the greatest reduction in *total costs*. For example, if the transfer of one unit to each of the two unused cells results in a cost reduction of $2, and it is possible to transfer 100 units to one, but only 50 units to the other, in the reassignment, select the former. This will effect a reduction in total costs of $200 as compared with only $100 for the latter. If the greatest reduction in total costs is identical for two or more reassignment routes, either may be chosen.

3. If the transfer does not effect a cost reduction for any of the cells, *the initial solution is an optimum one.* If so, and the transfer results in *increased costs for all* of the unused cells, the initial solution is the *only* optimum solution. If so, but *no change in costs* is effected by transfer to one or more of the unused cells, the transfer of as many units as possible to these cells will provide *alternative optimum* solutions.[20]

The transfer of as many units as possible to the cell so selected may be accomplished quite simply. The transfer of 50 units to cell 1C in

---

[18] It should also be noted that the transfer route involving unused cell 2B is an example of the type mentioned above in footnote 17, in which a larger number of cells must be involved in the transfer.

[19] It is not essential that the cell with the greatest negative value be chosen; any negative cell may be selected. In some cases, in fact, choice of a negative cell which is not the most negative will result in the greatest improvement in the program over the previous solution. For an example of such a case, see Churchman, Ackoff & Arnoff, *Operations Research*, p. 289.

[20] If more than one optimum solution exists, the decision maker may make his choice among these on the basis of their contribution toward other noneconomic objectives. He may prefer, for example, to give as much business as possible to a shipper handling one of the routes on the basis that this firm is a good customer of his company, all economic factors being equal.

the example is illustrated in Figure 17–12. It should be noted that the number of units which it is possible to so transfer is always equal to the number of units in that used cell involved in the transfer containing the *smallest number of units of those used cells from which units are to be subtracted in the reassignment.*

Figure 17–12.   Second Feasible Solution

Source	Destination			Total Capacity
	Warehouse A	Warehouse B	Warehouse C	
Plant 1....................	$4 0	$1 150	$2 50	200
Plant 2....................	$6 0	$5 0	$6 50	50
Plant 3....................	$3 100	$7 0	$4 100	200
Total Requirements........	100	150	200	450

In the problem, cell 1A—which contained 50 units—imposes this restriction. It is also important to reiterate that in the completed reassignment: (1) all of the rim requirements must be exactly satisfied, and (2) the number of cells being used must equal one less than the number of rim requirements. Further, none of the used cells may have a negative number of units assigned to it, since this would represent an impossible condition.

Further Steps in the Transportation Method

The above reassignment represents the second feasible solution to the transportation problem. Once this has been developed, exactly the same procedure as indicated above is *repeated* until the transfer of units to the unused cells effects *no further reduction* in transportation costs. When this stage has been reached, one will have one or more optimum solutions, depending upon the conditions indicated in paragraph (3) in the preceding section. As indicated earlier, any of the alternative solutions, including the initial feasible one (if the manager is fortunate), may represent an optimum.

These further steps may be illustrated by the evaluation of each of the unused cells in the second feasible solution in Figure 17–12. The transfer of one unit to each of the four unused cells effects the changes in the transportation costs (shown in Figure 17–13). These calculations

Figure 17-13.   Evaluation of Unused Cells—Second Feasible Solution

Unused Cell	Cost Changes for Individual Cells Involved in Transfer (in $)	Net Change
1A	1A, +4; 1C, −2; 3A, −3; 3C, +4	+3
2A	2A, +6; 2C, −6; 3A, −3; 3C, +4	+1
2B	1B, −1; 1C, +2; 2B, +5; 2C, −6	0
3B	1B, −1; 1C, +2; 3B, +7; 3C, −4	+4

indicate that the second feasible solution is an optimum one, since in no instance does the transfer of one unit to any of the unused cells effect a reduction in transportation costs. It is only one of *two* optimum solutions, however, since the transfer of units to cell 2B results in no net change in the costs. By effecting the transfer of as many units as possible to this cell, as shown in Figure 17–14, one thus arrives at an

Figure 17-14.   Alternative Optimum Solution

Source	Destination			Total Capacity
	Warehouse A	Warehouse B	Warehouse C	
Plant 1....................	$4 \qquad 0	$1 \qquad 100	$2 \qquad 100	200
Plant 2....................	$6 \qquad 0	$5 \qquad 50	$6 \qquad 0	50
Plant 3....................	$3 \qquad 100	$7 \qquad 0	$4 \qquad 100	200
Total Requirements........	100	150	200	450

alternative optimum solution. That total transportation costs are identical for each of these solutions is indicated in Figures 17–15a and 17–15b.

Introduction of a Slack Variable

Throughout the previous discussion of the transportation method it was assumed that total plant capacity was equal to the total demand of the three warehouses. In many business problems, however, capacity will exceed demand, and it is important to know not only which transportation routes are optimum, but also which production facilities should not be utilized at full capacity. The answers to both of these questions may be determined by introducing a slight modification into the trans-

Figure 17–15a. Transportation Costs—Second Feasible Solution

Cell	Units Shipped	Cost/unit	Transporation Costs
1B.............	150	$1	$ 150
1C.............	50	2	100
2C.............	50	6	300
3A.............	100	3	300
3C.............	100	4	400
Totals..........	450		$1250

Figure 17–15b. Transportation Costs—Alternative Optimum Solution

Cell	Units Shipped	Cost/unit	Transportation Costs
1B.............	100	$1	$ 100
1C.............	100	2	200
2B.............	50	5	250
3A.............	100	3	300
3C.............	100	4	400
Totals..........	450		$1250

portation method as it has been presented thus far. To illustrate this modification, the same data will be employed as in the previous example, except that the capacity of Plant 3 will now assumed to be 300 units instead of 200. This results in a total capacity of 550 units as compared to total demand requirements of 450 units.

To solve this problem, exactly the same procedure as outlined in the previous sections may be employed, except that a *slack variable* is introduced into the transportation matrix. This is slack Warehouse S, shown in Figure 17–16, which represents the hypothetical destination of those 100 units of excess capacity which will neither be produced nor transported. Since no units will actually be shipped to Warehouse S, transportation costs for each cell in its column are set at zero dollars. The cells

Figure 17–16. Transportation Matrix with Slack Variable

Source	Destination Warehouse A	Warehouse B	Warehouse C	Warehouse S	Total Capacity
Plant 1.................	$4	$1 / 150	$2 / 50	$0	200
Plant 2.................	$6	$5	$6	$0 / 50	50
Plant 3.................	$3 / 100	$7	$4 / 150	$0 / 50	300
Total Requirements........	100	150	200	100	550

in this column are treated in exactly the same way as the "real" cells in the matrix, and in each iteration the effect on total costs of the transfer of one unit to each unused slack cell must also be evaluated. Further, in the development of any feasible solution: (1) the demand requirements of the slack warehouse must be exactly fulfilled as must those of the real warehouses; and (2) if degeneracy is to be avoided, six used cells must be employed (since the rim requirements now number seven).

It will be left to the reader to work through each iteration in the solution of this problem, since the procedure is no different than that outlined previously. A few words are in order, however, as to the interpretation of Figure 17–16, which represents the optimum solution. The capacity of Plant 1 will be fully utilized, with 150 units being shipped to Warehouse B, and 50 units to Warehouse C. No units will be produced in Plant 2 since all 50 units from this plant are assigned to the slack warehouse. Similarly, the 50 units from Plant 3 assigned to Warehouse S will not be produced—100 units of its production will be shipped to Warehouse A, and 150 units to Warehouse C.[21]

Degeneracy

Earlier it was indicated that if the number of used cells in any of the transportation solutions is greater or less than the number of rim requirements minus one, degeneracy will occur and the problem is not

---

[21] It has been assumed throughout this discussion that the manager is concerned only with present demand in the period under consideration. It may, of course, be desirable to fully utilize all plants in this example so as to be able to meet future demand. Determination of the desirability of such a course of action would require consideration of many other factors such as inventory carrying costs.

soluble. In this section, both the causes of degeneracy and approaches for dealing with this condition will be discussed.

Degeneracy resulting from an excessive number of used cells can be caused only by an improper initial assignment in formulating the problem. In such cases, it is necessary to return to this assignment and modify it so as to satisfy the rim requirements minus one restriction. Degeneracy due to an inadequate number of used cells, on the other hand, may be brought about either by an improper initial assignment or by the normal mechanics of the transportation method itself. Degeneracy will occur during the normal processes of applying the method when: the number of units contained in two or more of the used cells from which units are to be *subtracted* in the transfer is equal to the number of units which will be subtracted from these cells to give the completed reassignment. When this condition exists, one or more of the used cells will be lost in the reassignment. In the reassignment illustrated in Figure 17–17, for example, all of the 100 units contained in both

Figure 17–17. Occurrence of Degeneracy

Original Assignment

		Destination		Total Capacity
		A	*B*	
S O U R C E	1	~~100~~ 101	~~100~~ 99	200
	2	~~100~~ 99	~~0~~ 1	100
Total Requirements		200	100	300

Reassignment

		Destination		Total Capacity
		A	*B*	
S O U R C E	1	200	0	200
	2	0	100	100
Total Requirements		200	100	300

used cells 1*B* and 2*A* of the original assignment will be subtracted in obtaining the reassignment. In consequence, the number of used cells in the reassignment matrix equals rim requirements minus two, and the matrix is degenerate.

When degeneracy due to an inadequate number of cells is encountered, one should first check the initial assignment to ensure that it is not improper. If not, it will be necessary to add a "dummy" used cell to the transportation matrix. This may be accomplished either: (1) by treating one of the unused cells as a used cell with zero units assigned to it, or (2) by adding an artificial, infinitely small number of units

(ϵ) to one of the unused cells so as to convert it to a used cell.[22] Both of these approaches accomplish the same objective—to increase the number of used cells so as to equal the rim requirements minus one. Further, treatment of either zero or ϵ cells is identical in the transportation procedure. Sometimes the zero or ϵ may drop out of the problem before the final solution is arrived at; in other problems, the zero or ϵ may remain in the optimum solution or solutions. If so, it is simply ignored. For example, if the final assignment to a particular cell is $100 - \epsilon$, the number of units to be shipped would be 100.

Transportation Method: Other Considerations

In this section certain other significant aspects of the transportation method with which the decision maker should be familiar will be considered. First, it is possible for the manager to handle problems with the transportation method in which he wishes to rule out the use of one or more source-destination assignments on the basis of some other criterion than cost minimization. For example, the manager in the previous illustration may want to avoid shipping any units from Plant 1 to Warehouse C because lengthy delays are frequently encountered when this route is employed. In such cases, the undesirable cells may be eliminated from consideration simply by assigning extremely high costs to them, say $50,000 per unit.

It is also important to recognize that the transportation method is equally applicable to problems in which the objective function is profit maximation rather than cost minimization. When such is the case, dollars of profit, rather than costs, are assigned to the cells in the matrix. Nor is the method limited only to problems involving the selection of transportation routes. Many other kinds of problems may be dealt with by the technique providing that they can be similarly framed and possess the characteristics of linearity, homogeneity, and certainty. For example, the method has been used in:

1.   Machine and job assignment problems in which a number of jobs can be done on a number of machines or by a number of people.

2.   Scheduling over several time periods.[23]

Indeed, a key requisite for the successful application of the transportation technique is the ability to visualize ways in which business data may be modified so as to be amenable to treatment by the method. As Bunke has pointed out, a large number of problems "are subject,

[22] Treatment of one of the unused cells as a used cell with zero units assigned to it is suggested by Bunke, *Linear Programming*, p. 12. The use of the artificial ϵ is suggested by Bowman and Fetter, *Production and Operations Management*, pp. 130–33.

[23] Bowman and Fetter, *Production and Operations Management*, p. 134.

to mathematical solution only when the data of the real world are so adapted that they can be fed into the programming model."[24]

NONLINEAR, DYNAMIC, AND INTEGER PROGRAMMING

Three further mathematical programming techniques which have been increasingly utilized in the solution of allocation problems in recent years are *nonlinear, dynamic,* and *integer* programming. Application of these techniques requires a level of mathematical complexity beyond the scope of this book and/or a lengthy computational procedure. In consequence, these three approaches will be treated only in a general manner in this section.

Nonlinear Programming

Nonlinear programming is designed to deal with problems in which the objective function and/or the constraints involve nonlinear expressions. Or, in economic terms it "may be described as the analysis of constrainted maximization problems in which diminishing or increasing returns to scale are present."[25] As an illustration of a nonlinear programming problem, consider the following simple example in which the objective function for one of two products under consideration is nonlinear:

1. A company produces two products, X and Y, the manufacture of which is subject to the linear constraints shown in Figure 17–18.

2. The profit for each unit of product X sold is \$8; consequently total profit from X may be expressed by the following linear expression: $P_x = 8x$.

3. The per unit profit for Y (UP_y) declines as additional units are offered for sale due to consumer resistance in the following manner: $UP_y = 10 - .01y$. That is, if 100 units of Y are offered for sale, the per unit profit will be $10 - (.01)(100)$ or \$9; if 200 units are offered for sale, $10 - (.01)(200)$ or \$8; and so on. The *total* profit obtained from any number of units of Y will equal Y times the unit profit function $(10 - .01y)$ or $y(10 - .01y)$, which simplifies to $10y - .01y^2$. This is a nonlinear expression.

4. The total profit from both products equals the sum of the total profit from each or: $TP = 8x + 10y - .01y^2$.

Any number of nonlinear iso-profit curves may be superimposed upon the restrictions indicated in Figure 17–19 in much the same way as were the linear iso-profit lines in the previous example of the chemical manufacturer faced with the linear allocation problem. Four such curves are illustrated in Figure 17–19. A major difficulty one encounters in

[24] Bunke, *Linear Programming*, p. 13.

[25] William J. Baumol, *Economic Theory and Operations Analysis* (Englewood Cliffs, N.J.: Prentice-Hall, Inc., 1961), p. 98.

Figure 17–18. Linear Constraints for Problem with Nonlinear Objective Function

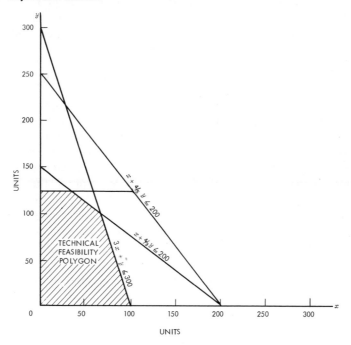

Figure 17–19. Nonlinear Iso-Profit Curves

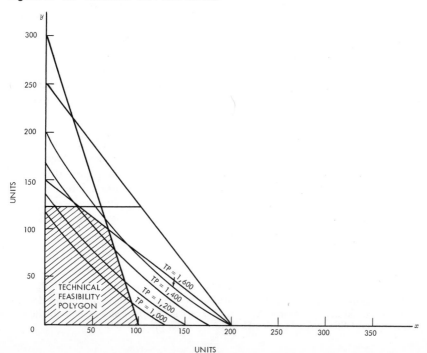

solving nonlinear programming problems arises from the fact that optimum solutions *will not necessarily be found at one of the corners of the technical feasibility polygon,* as is always the case with linear programming problems. In consequence, more sophisticated mathematical approaches are required to arrive at optimum solutions.[26]

Dynamic Programming

Each of the previous programming techniques which have been discussed has been designed to develop an optimum solution for problems calling for a single decision or set of decisions. Many business problems, however, involve *multistage* processes, in which sequences of interdependent decisions are required. For example, suppose that a company has $100,000 at the beginning of a year and wants to decide whether it should: (1) pay out the entire sum in the form of dividends, (2) reinvest the entire sum, or (3) allocate some portion of the $100,000 for reinvestment and pay out the remainder in dividends. If the company's objective is to maximize dividends for the one year, it will obviously pay out the total sum in this form. Suppose, however, that the company is concerned instead with the proportional dividend payout from profits each year over a period of years, with its objective the maximization of dividends over the whole period of time. In such a case, the company will be faced with a series of interdependent decisions. Increasing the amount of money to be reinvested in any given year will result in added funds being available in future years either for dividend payments or further reinvestment, and vice versa.[27] It is for the handling of such multistage problems as this that dynamic programming is designed.

Like the other programming methods which have been discussed, dynamic programming is a formalized iterative search procedure. The fundamentals of this procedure have been summarized by Bowman and Fetter as follows:

The basic feature of dynamic programming is that the optimum decision is reached stepwise, proceeding from one stage to the next. Stages in the problem need not be in terms of time. An optimum solution set is determined, given any conditions in the first stage. Then this optimum solution set (from the first stage) is integrated with the second stage to obtain a new optimum solution set, given any conditions. Then, in a sense ignoring the first and second stages as such, this new optimum solution set is integrated with the third stage to obtain still a further optimum solution set (or decision) under

---

[26] For a discussion of some of these approaches, see ibid., pp. 109 ff.

[27] The dividend problem and its treatment by dynamic programming are described in David W. Miller and Martin K. Starr, *Executive Decisions and Operations Research* (Englewood Cliffs, N.J.: Prentice-Hall, Inc., 1960), pp. 328–34.

any conditions. This new solution is integrated with the fourth stage, and so forth. At each stage an optimum solution from all previous stages, under any conditions, is carried into the next stage. It is this optimum solution which is carried forward rather than all the previous stages.[28]

Unlike the other programming techniques which have been discussed, dynamic programming is designed to handle decision problems under conditions of both certainty and risk. It is also applicable to problems involving both linear and nonlinear relationships. Among the many types of multistage problems which may be dealt with by dynamic programming are those involving production scheduling, equipment investment, and inventory decisions.

Integer Programming

In the multiple optimum solution to the chemical compound mix of products X and Y discussed previously, it was indicated that some points on the feasibility line would not represent feasible solutions since they were not integers. In many linear programming problems, "the decision variables make sense only if they have integer values"[29]—e.g., in a two-product mix problem involving sugar and chocolate cookies, an optimum answer of $150\frac{1}{16}$ chocolate cookies, and $234\frac{6}{7}$ sugar cookies would not be meaningful. As Hillier and Lieberman have pointed out:

In practice, the usual approach to integer linear programming problems has been to use the simplex method (thereby ignoring the integer restriction) and then rounding off the non-integer values to integers in the resulting solution.[30]

Although such an approach may often be satisfactory it has its weakness:

1. The noninteger solution is not necessarily feasible when rounded off,
2. It is often "difficult to see in which way the rounding should be done in order to retain feasibility,"[31] and
3. Even should the rounding be carried out successfully, there is "no guarantee that . . . [it] . . . will be the optimal integer solution. In fact, it may be far from optimal. . . ."[32]

It is for overcoming such difficulties in order to find optimal solutions to linear programming problems when all of the variables have to be integers that represents one basic use of the integer programming algorithm.

---

[28] Bowman and Fetter, *Production and Operations Management,* p. 136.
[29] Hillier and Lieberman, *Operations Research,* p. 553.
[30] Ibid.
[31] Ibid.
[32] Ibid., p. 554.

Additionally, there are certain types of binary (go, no-go) types of problems for which integer programming may be utilized. Integer programming (a special case of what is referred to as "binary" or "zero-one" programming) lends itself to problems in which a sequence of "yes" or "no" decisions must be made. This would be the case, for example,[33] with the following decision problem.

Twenty "good" investment opportunities are available to the management of a pension fund, each with specified differing attributes such as a fixed cost and yield (or interest). Management has a fixed budget, which prevents it from choosing all 20 alternatives. A further constraint that management has placed on the decision problem is that no more than a certain percent of the total amount may be invested in any single class of alternatives (e.g., debentures, preferred stock, common stock, and so on). In this example, the basic decision problem for which management wants an answer is: Which subset of the 20 investment proposals should be chosen in order to maximize its interest or yield while satisfying all other constraints? Assuming a fixed cost for each alternative as indicated above (i.e., an investment of $10,000 may be made in Company A's common stock, but no more or less), the decision problem solution provides management with *binary* choices—it either *invests or does not invest* in any particular alternative.

One final observation is in order concerning integer programming. Next to simplex, integer programming is probably more widely used than any other mathematical programming techniques available today; and its utilization will in all probability increase in future years.

SENSITIVITY ANALYSIS

As indicated at the beginning of this chapter, the data fed into mathematical programs only approximate real-world phenomena. Further, (1) errors in collecting and refining the data may well creep into mathematical programming problems, especially large ones where the data are considerable; and (2) the decision maker would often like to know how "sensitive" is, say a particular simplex solution, to *any* changes (including corrected errors) which might be made to any of the parameters in the model. For example, consider a firm making six products, each requiring eight scarce resources, and each with a profit margin of a certain number of dollars, based upon a currently set price and set of costs. Due to possible market price fluctuations and cost changes for each product, the profit margins for any or all of the six products might be in error. An extremely relevant question is: What magnitude

---

[33] For other binary choice examples which may be dealt with by integer programming, see Alan S. Manne, *Economic Analysis for Business Decisions* (New York: McGraw-Hill Book Co., 1961), chap. 6.

of error will leave the already developed optimum profit solution unchanged? In some cases, changes or errors of a particular parameter will change the optimal solution very little—i.e., it is very *insensitive* to these changes. If the model is not very sensitive to changes in *any* of its parameters, considerable confidence may be placed in the optimum solution developed. However, if the model is very sensitive to any such changes, the operations researcher and management should be aware of this fact. In such cases it may be desirable to ensure more closely data accuracy. Thus, testing the model for sensitivity after it has been developed but *before* it has been used is desirable. This type of analysis is referred to as "sensitivity" or "postoptimality" analysis.

It is beyond the scope of this book to deal with the mathematical aspects of sensitivity analysis.[34] Basically the procedure involves running the model again with some new values assigned to the variables. One cannot usually recalculate for all possible values because of the computation costs; so that the expected value of the information to be gained must be considered in relation to alternative strategies of modifying the variable values. It should be noted, however, that sensitivity analysis is often useful in examining problems of types other than mathematical programming. For example, sensitivity analysis has been applied in the forecasting of manpower requirements in civil aviation in which a model other than a mathematical programming one was utilized.[35]

SUMMARY

In this chapter a number of mathematical programming methods designed to aid the decision maker in effecting the optimum allocation of resources have been examined. Each of these techniques is applicable to constrained maximization or minimization problems in which the strategy space of the decision maker is circumscribed by some restrictions upon resources. Each represents an iterative process by means of which optimum solutions are progressively approached through a series of successive steps. Characteristic of all of the programming methods is the requirement that the objective function and all constraints be explicitly expressed in quantitative terms.

Notwithstanding these similarities, the programming methods vary both in mathematical and computational complexity and in the types of problems to which they may be applied. Figure 17–20 provides a comparison of some of the key characteristics of the programming methods.

Mathematical programming represents a significant contribution to

---

[34] For such a discussion, see Wagner, *Management Science*, pp. 111 ff.

[35] D. Clay Whybark, "Forecasting Manpower Requirements in Civil Aviation," *Personnel Administration*, 33 (March–April 1970), pp. 45–51. Whybark found the forecasts in his model much more sensitive to certain parameters than others.

Figure 17–20. Comparison of Programming Methods

Programming Method	Ease of Application		Characteristics of Problems to which Applicable					
	Mathematical Complexity	Computational Work Required	Number of Variables	Number of Stages	Certainty Required?	Linearity Required?	Homogeneity Required?	Contiguity Required?
Algebraic	simple	little	2–3	single	yes	yes	no	yes
Simplex	moderate-complex	considerable	n	single	yes	yes	no	yes
Transporation	simple	varies with size of matrix	n	single	yes	yes	yes	no
Nonlinear	complex	considerable	n	single	yes	no	no	yes
Dynamic	moderate-complex	considerable	n	multiple	no	no	no	no
Integer	moderate-complex	considerable	n	single	yes	no	no	no

management in that it provides an efficient formalized approach for handling resource allocation problems involving a considerable degree of complexity. By means of the use of electronic computers, even those programming problems requiring extensive computational work for their solution can be handled. With the rapid growth of computer availability in industry, we anticipate increased utilization of mathematical programming in the future. Programming, however, is not a technique which should be indiscriminately applied to all types of allocation problems. In some cases—as, for example, those in which the total costs involved in the decision problem are quite small—the marginal savings which may be realized by the application of programming may be exceeded by the marginal costs of doing so. Further, some allocation problems are so complex that their solution is not possible by the application of programming. Satisfactory solutions to some problems of this level of complexity, however, may be obtained by the use of simulation processes, the treatment of which we will reserve for Chapter 19.

DISCUSSION AND STUDY QUESTIONS

1. What do we mean when we say that mathematical programming techniques are "optimizing" methods and yet that they may not provide optimum answers to managerial problems?

2. What are the problem characteristics with which dynamic programming can deal, but the simplex method cannot?

3. What would the rim requirements be in a transportation problem involving three warehouses with combined total requirements of 750 units and four plants with a combined total capacity of 900 units?

4. The simplex technique may be used in solving problems in which integer solutions are required. Comment on this statement.

5. What is sensitivity analysis? Is its utilization limited to only mathematical programming problems?

6. Which of the following are requisite of all mathematical programming techniques? In each case, give reasons for your answer.
    a)   An objective function.
    b)   Degeneracy.
    c)   Scarce resources.
    d)   An explicitly defined strategy space.
    e)   Utilization of marginal analysis.
    f)   The continuity assumption.
    g)   Single-stage problems.
    h)   A slack variable.
    i)   The homogeneity assumption.

7. Personnel placement tests were given to 100 applicants to measure their aptitude for performing on each of three different jobs: *A*, *B*, and *C*. Each test was scored on a 10-point scale, with a score of 10 representing

the greatest aptitude. Analysis of the test results showed the existence of three distinct applicant groups, as is illustrated in the table below. All 30 individuals in applicant Group 1, for example, had the same scores of 9, 1, and 8 for Jobs A, B, and C, respectively. Also indicated in the table below is the number of job openings for each of the three jobs in question. How should the applicants, if hired, be assigned to the existing job openings so as to maximize the total of all applicants' test scores (for the job to which each is assigned)?

		Applicant Group			
Job Type	1	2	3	Job Openings
A........................	9	6	3	30
B........................	1	4	7	50
C........................	8	5	2	20
Number of applicants.........	40	35	25	

8. Mr. MacDonald, an elderly farmer, is considering the purchase this spring of new stock. Presently he has none. He has decided to buy only steers and pigs. He has steer pens which can accommodate up to 20 steers. His hog pens have a maximum capacity of 40 hogs. Young steers currently are selling for $400 per head, whereas pigs are selling for $200 per head. His available funds total $10,000. He expects that he will net $200 profit per steer and $50 profit per hog, after all expenses, when he sells the animals at the end of two years. In order to maximize profits, how many steers and pigs should he purchase?

9. The Alphagraphic Company produces two products, x and y. It takes 5 minutes to fabricate each unit of x; 10 minutes per unit of y; and the total amount of fabrication time available is 500 minutes. Both products also have to be assembled. 10 minutes of assembly time is required for each product (x and y); and, total available assembly time is 600 minutes. Further, product x alone requires polishing, which takes 5 minutes per unit; and 200 total minutes of polishing time are available.
    a) If the company makes $1 per unit of x and $2 per unit on product y, how many units should be produced to maximize profits?
    b) If, instead, the firm makes $2 per unit on x and $1 on y, how many units should be turned out to maximize profits?

10. The per unit costs of shipping goods from each of a firm's three plants (A, B, C) to each of its three warehouses (1, 2, 3), the plants' monthly capacities, and the warehouses' monthly demand are shown in the matrix below. How many units should be shipped from each plant to each warehouse to minimize costs? What will these minimum costs be? In working this problem (a) use the method of initial trial assignment recommended in the text; (b) use the northwest corner rule as explained in footnote 14 of the text. What differences did you note with these

two initial trial assignments? What are the implications of these differences?

Source	Destination			
	W1	*W2*	*W3*	*Capacity*
PA...............	$6	$2	$4	60
PB...............	$3	$1	$5	100
PC...............	$7	$9	$8	100
Demand...........	70	150	40	260

11. In scheduling work to machines in a job shop, why would linear programming be superior or inferior to simple shop dispatch rules as discussed in Chapter 16?

12. The simplex algorithm is merely a search heuristic. Comment.

SELECTED REFERENCES

BAUMOL, WILLIAM J. *Economic Theory and Operation Analysis.* 2d ed. Englewood Cliffs, N.J.: Prentice-Hall, Inc., 1965.

CHARNES, A., and COOPER, W. W. *Management Models and Industrial Applications of Linear Programming,* Vol. II. New York: John Wiley & Sons, Inc., 1961.

CHISMAN, JAMES A. "Using Linear Programming to Determine Time Standards," *The Journal of Industrial Engineering,* 17 (April 1966), 189–91.

CHURCHMAN, C. W.; ACKOFF, R. L.; and ARNOFF, E. L. *Introduction to Operations Research.* New York: John Wiley & Sons, Inc., 1957.

DORFMAN, R., et al. *Linear Programming and Economic Analysis.* New York: McGraw-Hill Book Co., 1958.

HEADY, EARL O., and CANDLER, WILFRED. *Linear Programming Methods.* Ames, Iowa: Iowa State College Press, 1958.

HENDERSON, A., and SCHLAIFER, R. "Mathematical Programming—Better Information for Decision Making," *Harvard Business Review,* 32 (May-June 1954), 73–100.

HILLIER, FREDERICK S., and LIEBERMAN, GERALD J. *Introduction to Operations Research.* San Francisco: Holden-Day, Inc., 1967.

KIM, CHAIHO. *Introduction to Linear Programming.* New York: Holt, Rinehart & Winston, Inc., 1971.

MCMILLAN, CLAUDE, JR. *Mathematical Programming.* New York: John Wiley & Sons, Inc., 1970.

MANNE, ALAN S. *Economic Analysis for Business Decisions.* New York: McGraw-Hill Book Co., 1961, chap. 6.

MILLER, D. W., and STARR, M. K. *Executive Decisions and Operations Research.* 2d ed. Englewood Cliffs, N.J.: Prentice-Hall, Inc., 1969.

REHMUS, FREDRICK P., and WAGNER, HARVEY M. "Applying Linear Programming to Your Pay Structure," *Business Horizons,* 6 (Winter 1963), 89–98.

STARR, MARTIN. *Systems Management of Operations.* Englewood Cliffs, N.J.: Prentice-Hall, Inc., 1971.

STOCKTON, ROBERT S. *Introduction to Linear Programming.* Homewood, Ill.: Richard D. Irwin, Inc., 1971.

TEACH, LEON, and THOMPSON, JOHN. "Simulation in Recruitment Planning," *Personnel Journal,* 48 (April 1969), 286–92, 299.

THROSBY, C. D. *Elementary Linear Programming.* New York: Random House, 1970.

WAGNER, HARVEY M. *Principles of Management Science.* Englewood Cliffs, N.J.: Prentice-Hall, Inc., 1970.

WAGNER, HARVEY M. *Principles of Operations Research.* Englewood Cliffs, N.J.: Prentice-Hall, Inc., 1969.

Chapter 18

Inventory Decision Making

In the previous two chapters, a number of resource allocation problems and decision-making approaches have been examined. Attention will now be focused on a particular type of allocation problem—that of planning and controlling the inventories of a business firm. Although inventory decision making is being treated in this chapter as separate from other kinds of allocation problems for purposes of exposition, it should be recognized that this distinction is an artificial one. That the maintenance of adequate raw materials inventories, for example, is just as important in the manufacture of goods as ensuring the availability of sufficient manpower or machine capacity, points out that inventory decision making is an integral part of the whole production planning and control process.

Only this century has the problem of controlling inventories come to be recognized as a critical one in managerial decision making. "In past centuries, inventories were considered an indication of wealth; even inventories greatly in excess of the amount needed to carry on the processes of production and distribution were considered beneficial."[1] With the development of modern industrialism and the growth of large-scale enterprises, however, inventories have come to represent very substantial investments for many business firms and their control has been recognized as mandatory. Beginning about 1915, attention was turned to the development of mathematical approaches designed to aid the decision maker in setting optimum inventory levels. Since that time increasingly sophisticated analytical tools have been brought to bear on the problems of inventory management.

The purpose of this chapter is to examine the functions that inventories perform for the business firm, the problems involved in their control,

---

[1] Thomson M. Whitin, *The Theory of Inventory Management* (2d ed.; Princeton, N.J.: Princeton University Press, 1957), p. 3.

and the more commonly employed approaches to inventory decision making. Attention will be given to certain of the simpler mathematical models designed to guide inventory decisions. Treatment of these models is intended to (1) focus attention on the key variables involved in inventory problems, and (2) serve as a point of departure for those interested in ultimately exploring more complex quantitative approaches to inventory decision making.

FUNCTIONS PERFORMED BY INVENTORIES

There are at least three basic functions that inventories can provide to aid in management decision making. The first is to decouple, or make independent, successive stages in the manufacturing and distribution process so as to allow each to operate more economically. For example, inventories "make it possible to make a product at a distance from customers or from raw-material supplies" . . . [and] . . . "make it unnecessary to gear production directly to consumption or, alternatively, to force consumption to adapt to the necessities of production."[2]

The decoupling function may be performed in at least two different ways. First, *process and movement inventories* will be necessary if user demand is to be met when time is required to transport raw materials, goods in the process of being manufactured, or finished products from one location to another. An inventory representing an average week's demand would be needed in movement, for example, if one week were required to ship a finished good from a firm's warehouse to its retail outlet. Second, are *buffer* or *safety stock* inventories. When the demand for a particular item is known to be variable—perhaps seasonally—it may be more economical for a firm to absorb some of the variation by permitting its inventories to fluctuate, rather than its level of production. This is because such fluctuations in production would result in changing levels of employment—with attendant retraining, unemployment compensation, and other costs—and/or the need to schedule overtime work to meet the periods of peak demand. Firms tend to isolate their core technology from environmental variation, and inventory control is one method of doing so. Also, because of *unknown* changes in demand for many items, inventories may be necessary if an adequate supply of items is to be available to the consumer when he wants them, and stockouts are to be minimized. For example, a supermarket may sell 10 cases of a particular canned good per week on the average. Beginning weekly inventory, however—assuming stocks are replenished every Monday morning—would more than likely be kept somewhat above 10 cases so that normal fluctuations above the average demand could be met.

Second, there is the *lot-size* inventory, where more units are purchased

---

[2] John F. Magee, *Production Planning and Inventory Control* (New York: McGraw-Hill Book Co., 1958), p. 17.

or manufactured than are needed for present use because certain economies may be realized from the larger lots. Quantity discounts or smaller
per unit shipping costs due to avoiding less than carload (l.c.l.) shipments often may be gained by making larger purchases at less frequent
intervals. Similarly, in manufacturing, the number of machine setups
and resulting setup costs may be reduced by scheduling longer production runs of an item on a given machine.

Finally, inventories may serve a useful function in *commodity purchasing*. Due to different technologies, there are some companies which purchase large amounts of commodities in doing business, rather than, say,
basic raw materials such as steel or copper, or fabricated parts. Prices
of these commodities (e.g., wheat, coffee beans, cattle) generally tend
to vary to a considerably greater extent during each year than does,
say, the price of steel. To deal with these market fluctuations effectively
companies often resort to the use of specialized techniques of purchasing
their raw materials, thus affecting their inventory levels and costs. These
methods "include hedging and speculative purchases, both of which
involve forward buying."[3]

MINIMIZATION OF COSTS

A fundamental concern of the manager in developing inventory
policies is to minimize the total operating costs of his firm. However,
cost minimization may not be the only decision criterion, for other values
and objectives may be considered important. For example, a company
may maintain a stable level of production during periods of slack demand and thus permit its inventories to increase, in order to provide
steady work for its employees because it considers this policy necessary
to meet a social obligation. It should also be emphasized that the costs
directly incurred by carrying items in inventory are not the only ones
which must be considered in inventory decision making. Rather, it is
important to view the firm as a system and to recognize the mutual
interdependence between inventory policies and many other types of
decisions made by the company. The relationship between fluctuations
in inventory levels and the stabilization of employment indicated above
provides a good example of such interdependence. This example also
illustrates the existence of suboptimization problems with respect to
inventories—the minimization of inventory costs per se, may lead to
higher costs or a lesser realization of objectives elsewhere in the organizational system.

The costs which a firm may incur as a result of the inventory levels
which it establishes may be grouped into three categories. First, there

---

[3] Martin K. Starr, *Systems Management of Operations* (Englewood Cliffs, N.J.:
Prentice-Hall, Inc., 1971), p. 330. In this work Starr provides a detailed example
illustrating the mechanics of hedging (pp. 330–31). He also presents a simple
dynamic programming model in his discussion of commodity purchasing (pp. 331
ff.).

are *inventory carrying* costs. These include the gains sacrificed by tying up funds in inventory which could have been invested elsewhere (opportunity costs). In addition, carrying items in inventory may require the rental of storage space and the payment of taxes and insurance and may result in losses due to the deterioration or obsolescence of the items being carried. Second, there are *procurement* costs which include both *setup* and *ordering* costs. Among the more important setup costs are the retooling and "shakedown" costs[4] which occur when a changeover is required from the manufacture of one item to another on a particular machine; while among ordering costs are those clerical expenses involved in placing an order. Third, losses may be realized by the firm if *stockouts* of items occur. Sales may be lost if inventories are not adequate to meet consumer demand or production may come to a halt if the inventories of critical raw materials or parts are insufficient to meet its needs.

Two mutually interrelated inventory decisions which have a key bearing on the total inventory costs which will be incurred by the firm are: (1) the size of each lot to be purchased or manufactured, and (2) the average inventory levels to be maintained. As the lot size and average inventory increase, certain of the costs indicated above will increase, while others will decrease. In a later section, attention will be turned to one of the better known inventory models designed to minimize total operating costs—the economic lot-size model.

SELECTIVE INVENTORY CONTROL

It is frequently most economical for firms to employ different degrees of control for different classes of inventory items since the administrative cost of the control may exceed its value in some cases. A basic reason for this is that it is not uncommon for a relatively small number of items in the firm's inventories to comprise a major portion of its total inventory value. As Starr has pointed out, it is not unusual for: (*a*) 25 percent of the firm's items to contribute for from between 60 to 75 percent of the total value of the firms' inventories; (*b*) for another 25 percent of items to contribute to from 15 to 20 percent of total inventory value; and (*c*) the remaining 50 percent to contribute to from only 5 to 10 percent of total inventory value.[5] Consequently, a much greater proportion of total inventory investment may be controlled by any given amount of effort for certain types of items—namely, the high-value items.[6] One approach for providing the basis of selective

---

[4] "Shakedown" costs refer to those costs often incurred because of diseconomies encountered initially in a production run—e.g., during the time required to bring quality under control, for workers to reach maximum efficiency levels, and so forth.

[5] Starr, *Systems Management*, p. 336.

[6] By high-value items, we do not necessarily mean a high unit value; but rather those items whose total value contributes significantly to the firm's total inventory investment.

control in management decision making is to deal with the above three classes of items as follows: (1) close control for high-value items, (2) a moderate degree of control for medium-value items, and (3) relatively loose control for the low-value items.[7] It is important to note that when such selective control is employed, item value is not the only criterion upon which the degree of control to be established is determined. Both critical items and items which are subject to rapid deterioration or obsolescence are often placed in the high-value category, regardless of their contribution to total inventory value. Close control over a one-cent critical part, for example, would be justified if an out-of stock condition might result in the complete breakdown of production. Similarly, a complete or near-complete loss in the value of certain items due to rapid spoilage or obsolescence would warrant close control of their inventories.

THE ECONOMIC LOT-SIZE MODEL UNDER CONDITIONS OF CERTAINTY

The focal point of the economic lot-size model is the determination of that lost size for any given item—either purchased or manufactured—which will minimize total inventory costs for the item. If anticipated yearly demand for an item is 3,000 units, should all units for the year be purchased in one lot—or manufactured in a single run? Or, is it more economical to schedule two production runs, or the purchase of two lots during the year—each containing 1,500 units? In addition, application of the lot-size model will also indicate both the optimum *number* of lots to be scheduled over a given period of time and the optimum size of the average inventory of the item under consideration.

Assumptions Underlying the Model

First, the economic lot-size problem will be examined by considering the purchase of a single item of inventory under conditions of certainty. It will be assumed that: (1) demand for the item is at a constant rate and known to the decision maker in advance, and (2) the lead time necessary for acquiring the item (elapsed time between the placement of the order and its receipt into inventory) is also known. Although these assumptions would rarely be completely valid for "real-world" inventory problems, they permit the development of a simplified model which may be incorporated into more realistic complicating factors.

The number of units in inventory at any given time under the above conditions may be portrayed graphically by what is frequently referred

---

[7] Starr refers to these classes as A (high value), B (medium), and C (low value), respectively. Starr, *Systems Management,* p. 336. It should also be noted that closeness of control may be defined as "being synonymous with frequency, accuracy, and completeness of review." Howard L. Timms, *Inventory Management of Purchased Materials* (New York: National Association of Purchasing Agents, 1958), p. 27.

Figure 18–1. The "Saw-Tooth" Model

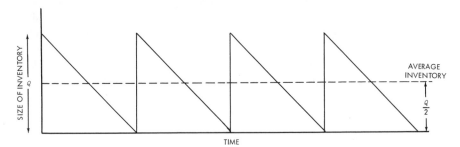

to as the "saw-tooth" model. This is illustrated in Figure 18–1. Here, letting Q represent the order size, it may be noted that the number of units in inventory is equal to Q at the time that each new order enters inventory; and that the inventory is gradually depleted until it reaches zero just at the point at which the next order is received. It may also be observed that: (1) the average inventory of the item is equal to exactly *one half* the number of units in the lot size $\left(\dfrac{Q}{2}\right)$ and (2) because each new order is received into inventory at exactly the time at which the previous order is depleted, no stockouts will occur. This latter condition presupposes that the decision maker has taken full advantage of his knowledge of the constant acquisition lead time and placed each order appropriately in advance.

Opposing Cost Analysis

Since stockouts are assumed not to occur in the basic model, the only two sets of costs which must be considered in determining the lot size which will minimize total inventory costs for an item are the ordering and inventory carrying costs. A key feature of this model is that these represent a set of *opposing costs*—as the lot size increases, the carrying charges will increase, but the ordering costs will decrease. A closer examination of these two costs will indicate why such a relationship exists:

1. *Carrying Costs.* The annual cost of carrying one unit of inventory is frequently calculated by multiplying the value (cost) of the item under consideration (C) by a percentage figure (I)—which represents management's estimate of opportunity costs, taxes and insurance on the items being carried, and so forth, per year as a percentage of the value of the inventory. Total carrying costs are equal to the cost of carrying one unit (CI) multiplied by the average inventory, which as indicated previously is equal to $\dfrac{Q}{2}$. Thus, total annual carrying costs are $\dfrac{Q}{2}\,CI$, and will increase as Q, the lot size, increases.

2. *Ordering Costs.* The number of orders which will be placed during any given period of time is equal to the demand (R) for the period divided by the size of each order (the lot size, Q). Total ordering costs per period are equal to the cost of placing each order (S) times the number of orders per period $\frac{R}{Q}$; or, $\frac{R}{Q} S$. As the lot size increases, fewer orders will be required to meet demand, and thus the ordering costs will decrease.

Figure 18–2 illustrates graphically the nature of the opposing costs

Figure 18–2. Opposing Cost Relationships

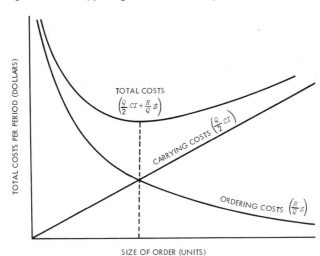

involved in the lot-size problem. It is important to note here that annual total costs—inventory carrying plus ordering costs $\left(\text{or } \frac{Q}{2} CI + \frac{R}{Q} S \right)$—first decrease, and then increase, as the lot size increases;[8] and that the fundamental objective is to find a value for Q which will minimize the total costs. It should also be noted that, with any given demand, total *per unit* costs will be minimized by the same value of Q, since they are equal to $\frac{TC}{R}$.

The *EOQ* Formula

A formula has been developed which will permit one to determine the lot size which will minimize total costs. This is the economic order

---

[8] Assuming that ordering costs remain constant per order, and carrying costs constant per unit of inventory. These relationships also exist when the period under consideration is more or less than a year; although the value of I would have to be adjusted accordingly. For example, if management sets the annual carrying charges for an item at 12 percent of its value, and the period under consideration is three months, a value for I of approximately 3 percent would be used.

quantity formula, which is often referred to as *EOQ*. This formula may be derived by utilizing the differential calculus, as is noted below.[9] Additionally, the logic underlying the *EOQ* formula may be demonstrated algebraically, due to the particular behavior of the variables involved in the model, as follows.

When a curve such as that representing ordering costs in Figure 18–2 and a straight line such as that representing carrying costs in the inventory model exist, it happens that the minimum point on the total cost curve will be at the value for Q at which the *curve and line intersect*.[10] Or, to put it another way, total costs for any period will be minimized with that lot size for which *carrying costs are equal to the ordering costs*. This relationship may be observed graphically by referring to Figure 18–2. Consequently, the economic order quantity may be obtained by equating the ordering costs and carrying costs, and solving for Q as follows:

Equating carrying and procurement costs:

$$(1) \quad \frac{Q}{2} CI = \frac{R}{Q} S$$

Solving for Q:

$$(2) \quad QCI = \frac{2RS}{Q}$$

$$(3) \quad Q^2 CI = 2RS$$

$$(4) \quad Q^2 = \frac{2RS}{CI}$$

$$(5) \quad Q = \sqrt{\frac{2RS}{CI}} = EOQ$$

Equation 5 is the economic order quantity formula and will provide the lot size, Q, which will minimize total costs for the firm.

---

[9] Total costs are minimized when the slope of the total cost curve is zero. Therefore, the *EOQ* formula may be obtained by setting the first derivative of total costs with respect to Q equal to zero, and solving for Q as follows:

$$(1) \quad TC = \frac{Q}{2} CI + \frac{R}{Q} S$$

$$(2) \quad \frac{dTC}{dQ} = \frac{CI}{2} - \frac{RS}{Q^2}$$

(3)　Setting the first derivative equal to zero: $Q^2 CI = 2RS$; and $Q = \sqrt{\dfrac{2RS}{CI}}$

That this represents a minimum point rather than a maximum is indicated by the positive sign of the second derivative:

$$\frac{d^2 TC}{dQ^2} = \frac{2RS}{Q^3}$$

[10] The basic reason for this is that the marginal costs of carrying inventory equal the marginal costs of ordering at this point.

An application of the *EOQ* formula may be illustrated by taking the following data—let $R = 8,000$, $S = \$30$, $C = \$1.00$, and $I = 10\%$:'

$$Q = \sqrt{\frac{(2)(8,000)(30)}{(1)(.10)}}$$

$$= \sqrt{4,800,000}$$

$$= 2,191$$

Substituting this value for Q in the total cost equation, total costs for the year are $\frac{2,191}{2}(1)(.10 + \frac{8,000}{2,191}(30)$; or $\$219.09$. Once the most economic lot size has been so obtained, it is quite simple to determine both: (1) the number of orders placed per period: $\frac{R}{Q}$; and (2) average inventory for the item: $\frac{Q}{2}$; Since the acquisition lead time is assumed constant and known in advance, the date to place each order can also be determined. For example, if the economic order quantity for an item were 500 units, weekly demand 125, and the acquisition lead time one week, each reorder would simply be placed one week prior to the depletion of the existing inventories—or when the inventory level has fallen to 125 units. This number of units represents item usage during the delivery period. The reorder points called for in this example are illustrated diagrammatically in Figure 18–3.

Figure 18–3. Reorder Points

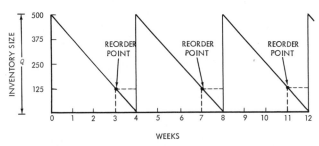

WEEKS

Further Development of the *EOQ* Formula

The *EOQ* model discussed above is a highly simplified one and does not take into account many key variables which often must be considered by the manager. In this section, the effects of two additional variables—quantity discounts and a continuous inflow of items into inventory during production runs—will be considered. These are but two of many variables which analysts have introduced into the simplified lot-size model. They illustrate the ways in which elaboration of the simplified model is possible. In both cases, the assumption that both the acquisition lead time and demand are constant and known in advance to the decision maker will be maintained.

Continuous Inventory Inflow during Production Runs. In the *EOQ* model considered above, all items were treated as being received into the inventory at once. This is not uncommon when items are purchased from an outside supplier. When a firm itself is manufacturing the items, however, a situation may be encountered in which there is a continuous inflow into the inventory as the units are completed during each production run. Assuming a constant rate of inflow, the number of units in inventory at any given time may be represented graphically as in Figure 18–4. This illustration shows that the size of the inventory will increase

Figure 18–4.   Continuous Inflow into Inventories

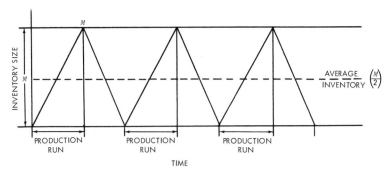

during each production run to the extent that the inflow of items exceeds the number of items being withdrawn for use. Once a run has been completed, the inventory will decrease by the rate of usage until depleted at the time the inflow from the next run commences. For example, if the rate of inflow is 100 units per day during each run, and daily withdrawals to meet demand are 60 units, the inventory will: (1) increase at a rate of 40 units per day during each run; and (2) decrease at a rate of 60 units per day between runs.

A formula for determining the optimum run size may be developed in much the same manner as the economic order quantity equation. Here, there will be procurement costs incurred by "ordering" the production of each run; these are the setup costs referred to previously. These costs are determined in the same way as the ordering costs in the purchase-size model: $\frac{R}{Q} S$. As may be noted by comparing Figures 18–1 and 18–4, however, average inventory, and thus inventory carrying charges, are different when there is a continuous inflow of items into inventory than when the entire lot is received at once. In both cases, however, average inventory is equal to *one half* the maximum number of units in the inventory. In the purchase-size model, the maximum number of units in inventory was Q, the lot size. In the continuous inflow model, on the other hand, inventory is at its maximum size at the time each production run is completed (point M on Figure 18–4). This maximum is equal to the number of days in the run (D)—times daily production (P) minus daily usage (U)—or $D\,(P - U)$. Thus, average inventory is equal to $\dfrac{D(P - U)}{2}$; which, as is noted below, may be simplified to read: $\dfrac{Q}{2}\left(1 - \dfrac{U}{P}\right)$.[11] Following the same reasoning as in the purchase-size model, annual inventory carrying charges are: $\dfrac{Q}{2}\left(1 - \dfrac{U}{P}\right)CI$; and the total costs per year: $\dfrac{Q}{2}\left(1 - \dfrac{U}{P}\right)CI + \dfrac{R}{Q}S$. This total cost equation may be manipulated in much the same way as the economic purchase-size equation to give the following formula for determing the optimum size of a lot with a constant inflow production run: $Q = \sqrt{\dfrac{2RS}{CI\left(1 - \dfrac{U}{P}\right)}}$[12]

It is interesting to note that—given the same procurement costs, carrying costs, and demand—a continuous inflow of items into inventories

---

[11] The number of days in a run (D) will equal the run size (Q) divided by the rate of daily production (P); or $D = \dfrac{Q}{P}$. Substituting this term for D in the equation

$$\dfrac{D(P - U)}{2} \text{ gives us } \dfrac{\dfrac{Q}{P}(P - U)}{2}, \text{ which simplifies to } \dfrac{Q}{2}\left(1 - \dfrac{U}{P}\right).$$

[12] The mathematical proof utilizing the calculus is as follows:

(1) $TC = \dfrac{Q}{2}\left(1 - \dfrac{U}{P}\right)CI + \dfrac{RS}{Q}$

(2) $\dfrac{dTC}{dQ} = \dfrac{CI}{2}\left(1 - \dfrac{U}{P}\right) - \dfrac{RS}{Q^2}$

(3)   Setting the first derivative equal to zero:

$$Q^2\left[CI\left(1 - \dfrac{U}{P}\right)\right] = 2RS; \text{ and } Q = \sqrt{\dfrac{2RS}{CI\left(1 - \dfrac{U}{P}\right)}}$$

Or, since total costs are minimized at the value for Q at which the ordering costs curve and carrying costs line intersect:

(1) $\dfrac{Q}{2}\left(1 - \dfrac{U}{P}\right)CI = \dfrac{R}{Q}S$ (3) $Q^2 = \dfrac{2RS}{\left(1 - \dfrac{U}{P}\right)CI}$

(2) $\left(1 - \dfrac{U}{P}\right)CI = \dfrac{2RS}{Q^2}$ (4) $Q = \sqrt{\dfrac{2RS}{\left(1 - \dfrac{U}{P}\right)CI}}$

results in lower total costs for the firm than when the entire lot is received into inventory at once. This is true because the introduction of the continuous inflow brings about:

1. An increase in the optimum lot size, and thus, fewer orders (runs) and smaller procurement costs.
2. A decrease in the size of the average inventory, and consequently, smaller carrying costs.

A comparison between costs in the two models may be illustrated by taking the same demand and cost data as in the lot-size example, but modifying for: (1) an inflow of 44 units per day while each lot is being produced and (2) a daily outflow (usage) rate of 22 units throughout the year (which for a 365-day year approximates a yearly demand of 8,000). Employing the continuous inflow formula:

$$Q = \sqrt{\frac{(2)(8,000)(30)}{(1)(.10)(1 - 22\!/\!44)}}$$

$$EOQ = 3,098$$

Dividing the demand of 8,000 units per year by this optimum run size, the (average) number of runs which should be scheduled during the year is 2.58; and total costs per year are minimized at approximately $154.92. This may be compared with the minimum total costs of $219.09 per year which were obtained with the simplified formula when each purchased lot entered the inventory all at once.

Quantity Discounts. Another common inventory problem is that of determining the economic lot size if one or more price discounts on all items in the lot may be obtained from the supplier when large quantities are purchased. For example, the per unit cost of an item might be reduced 5 percent if the purchase quantity is more than 1,000 units and 10 percent if the order size is 2,000 units or more. Although it is possible to determine the economic lot size with any number of such successive discounts taking effect as the purchase quantity increases, the following analysis will be limited to the case in which only one discount price is offered.[13]

The basic costs relationships which exist in the quantity discount problem are illustrated graphically in Figure 18–5. It will be noted that procurement (ordering) costs are the same whether or not the lot size purchased is large enough to realize the discount; but that per unit inventory carrying costs are lower when the discount is obtained since the cost (and value) of each item in inventory is less. Minimization

---

[13] The approach presented here is one suggested by C. West Churchman, Russell L. Ackoff, and E. Leonard Arnoff, *Introduction to Operations Research* (New York: John Wiley & Sons, Inc., 1957), pp. 235 ff. For an approach to the quantity discount problem involving more than one discount price, see this same work, pp. 245 ff.

Figure 18–5. Quantity Discount Model (*EOQ* at discount price greater than price break)

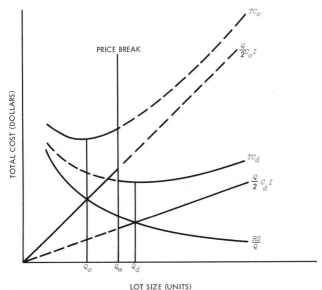

LOT SIZE (UNITS)

of total costs under such conditions may be determined by use of the *EOQ* formula developed previously, although in some cases certain additional calculations are needed. The steps required for the solution to this type of problem first will be indicated, and then the application of this approach by treatment of a specific example will be illustrated.

1.   Using the *EOQ* formula, and taking the cost of the item at the discount price (C_d), determine the economic lot size (Q_d). As Figure 18–5 shows, this economic lot size minimizes total costs. Lot size Q_d, however, will be feasible *only when it is equal to or greater than* the minimum number of units which must be purchased for the discount to take effect (Q_m). Such is the case illustrated in Figure 18–5. (Q_o is eliminated from consideration here since it is always greater than Q_m and Q_d, as may be seen on Figure 18–6.)

2.   If Q_d is less than Q_m and does not represent a feasible solution (as illustrated in Figure 18–6) the following additional steps are required:

   a)   Using the original (nondiscounted) price (C_o), determine the economic order quantity (Q_o) and the total costs which will be incurred when this quantity is purchased (TC_o).

   b)   Determine total costs when the minimum number of items required to obtain the discount is purchased (TC_m). As Figure 18–6 illustrates, total costs *continuously increase* as the lot size increases beyond Q_m. Thus, it will never pay to choose a lot size greater than Q_m. Q_m may represent either a more or less economic lot size than Q_o, and the

Figure 18–6.   Quantity Discount Model (*EOQ* at discount price less than price break)

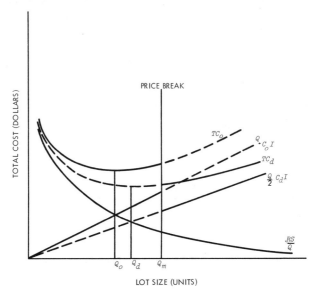

LOT SIZE (UNITS)

two must next be compared to see which provides better solution. In making the comparison, it is necessary not only to compare the total costs computed above (TC_o and TC_m) but also to consider the savings which will be realized from the discount price if Q_m is chosen.

c)   Determine the savings which will be obtained if the discount is obtained. These will be equal to demand times the savings on each unit—which is the difference between the original price and the discount price. Or, mathematically, the savings may be represented by: $R(C_o - C_d)$.

d)   If total variable costs per year at the minimum quantity needed to obtain the discount (TC_m) minus savings are less than total variable costs per year when the economic lot size using the original price is chosen (TC_o), it will pay to take advantage of the discount; and Q_m is the optimal solution. If not, Q_o is the optimal solution.

To illustrate the application of this method, consider the following example. Demand for an item is 8,000 per year, procurement costs are $25, the price of the item is $1 if less than 3,000 units are purchased, and $0.99 if the lot size is equal to or greater than 3,000; and the percentage figure assigned to represent annual carrying charges is 10 percent. Proceeding step by step as indicated above:

1.   The economic order quantity using the discount price is

$$\sqrt{\frac{(2)(8,000)(25)}{(.99)(.10)}} \text{ or } 2,009$$

This solution is not feasible since it is less than the 3,000 units which must be purchased for the discount price to apply, and the following steps must be taken.

2. Using the nondiscounted price, the economic lot size is

$$\sqrt{\frac{(2)(8,000)(25)}{(1.00)(.10)}}$$ or 2,000. Total yearly costs $\left(\frac{Q_o}{2} C_oI + \frac{RS}{Q_o}\right)$ are

$$\frac{2,000}{2} (1.00)(.10) + \frac{(8,000)(25)}{2,000}; \text{ or } \$200$$

3. Total variable costs per year when the minimum number of units required to obtain the discount (3,000) are purchased

$$\left(\frac{Q_m}{2} C_dI + \frac{RS}{Q_m}\right) \text{ are } \frac{3,000}{2} (.99)(.10) + \frac{(8,000)(25)}{3,000}; \text{ or } \$215.17$$

4. Savings of \$0.01 will be realized on each unit if the discount is obtained (\$1.00 — \$0.99), and for 8,000 units, total savings are \$80. Thus, although total yearly costs at Q_m are \$15.17 greater than at Q_o, the \$80 in yearly savings obtained by the discount more than offsets this figure and Q_m represents the optimal solution.

Values and Limitations of the *EOQ* Models under Certainty

The most obvious limitation of the inventory models discussed above is that certainty does not exist in most business situations. For example, both acquisition lead time and the demand for items usually fluctuate in a manner not completely known to the decision maker in advance. In those cases in which these two factors are relatively constant and predictable in advance, however, these models will provide us with a close approximation of reality. Another problem which may often be encountered in the application of the models is that accurate cost information may be difficult to obtain. The clerical costs incurred by placing an order may defy precise measurement. Nor may it be a simple matter to assess accurately any losses due to obsolescence in determining the inventory carrying costs. However, relatively good approximations of minimal total costs may be arrived at even with quite crude cost data, for *"the total cost in the neighborhood of the optimum-order quantity is relatively insensitive to moderately small changes in the amount ordered."*[14]

This important characteristic of the *EOQ* model may be demonstrated by the use of an example. Assume that a firm's yearly demand for an item is 8,000 units, its procurement costs, \$25 per order, and its inventory

---

[14] Magee, *Production Planning*, p. 66.

carrying costs 10 cents per unit (10 percent of the value of the item costing $1). Employing the *EOQ* formula, the economic lot size is

$$\sqrt{\frac{(2)(8,000)(25)}{.10}};$$

or 2,000; and total yearly costs with this lot size are $200. Next, suppose that management has erroneously estimated the procurement cost to be $12.50 instead of $25. If this erroneous figure were used instead of the correct one of $25 in applying the *EOQ* formula, the optimum lot size arrived at would be 1,414 instead of 2,000. Using what we know to be the correct procurement cost ($25), total variable costs per year for a lot size of 1,414 would be $212. Thus, even with procurement costs in error by a factor of two, total costs in the example are only $12 or 6 percent more than they would have been had the correct cost figure been employed. This relative insensitiveness due to the flatness of the total cost curve on either side of the optimum lot size of 2,000 units in the example is illustrated in Figure 18–7.

Figure 18–7.   Total Cost Curve Insensitiveness

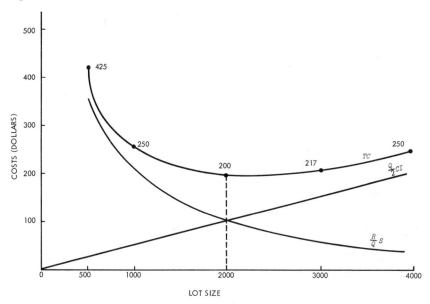

The inventory models, as is the case with most mathematical models, are also of considerable value to the manager in that they focus attention on and reveal the key relationships which exist between the variables in the decision-making problem. For example, the *EOQ* models indicate that under conditions of certainty, optimally both the order (or run) size and average inventory should vary in proportion to changes in the *square root* of the demand of the item. As demand doubles, for example, the new economic order quantity will equal the previous *EOQ* times $\sqrt{2}$; as demand triples, times $\sqrt{3}$; and so forth. Average inventory follows the same pattern since it is always equal to $\dfrac{Q}{2}$. These relationships are illustrated in Figure 18–8 which is based on the same cost data in the previous example ($S = \$25$; $C = \$1$; and $I = 10\%$):

Figure 18–8

Demand	EOQ	Average Inventory
2,000	1,000	500
4,000	1,414	707
8,000	2,000	1,000
16,000	2,828	1,414

Another important relationship between the key variables in the inventory problem follows from the above analysis. Since the average inventory should optimally increase only in proportion to the square root of any increases in demand, a *smaller average inventory per unit of sales* is required as demand for an item becomes greater.

INVENTORY DECISION MAKING UNDER RISK AND UNCERTAINTY

As indicated previously, neither demand nor acquisition lead time for the items under control are constant or completely known to the decision maker in advance in most business situations. In some cases, the decision maker may have no idea whatsoever of what variations to expect in these two variables. In such cases we have the problem of decision making under uncertainty. More frequently, however, he will be in a position to estimate the probability of occurrence of various demand levels and acquisition lead times on the basis of past experience. This involves decision making under risk. With either risk or uncertainty the inventory decisions are considerably more complex than in the certainty models previously discussed. It is important to note, however, that it is *not* the lack of certainty about demand for the items under control alone which causes this added complexity. Rather it is the lack of certainty about demand *coupled with* the existence of an acquisition lead time. The maintenance of adequate inventory levels would pose few major problems, regardless of the degree of uncertainty and variation in demand, if *instantaneous replenishment were possible.* Such is usually not the case, however, and the manager—if he is to avoid stockouts—must protect himself against those occasions when inventories are being reduced more rapidly than anticipated, and a lead time renders replenishment impossible until after stocks are depleted.

In the lot-size models considered previously—in which a constant known demand and acquisition lead time existed—both the size of orders (or manufacturing runs) and length of time between the placement of orders (or initiation of runs) were constant (see Figures 18–1 and 18–4). When variations in demand exist, however, both of these factors cannot remain constant if stockouts are to be avoided. The two most commonly employed approaches to inventory control under conditions of risk or uncertainty in which demand varies are: (1) to hold the lot size constant and vary the time between the placement of orders or scheduling of production runs, or (2) conversely, to hold the time between the placement of orders or initiation of production runs constant but to vary the lot size. A discussion of these two approaches as well as a newer method which combines features of both will be found in the following sections.

Continuous Review Method

First, consider the acquisition or scheduling of fixed lot sizes at variable intervals. This approach for purchased lots is illustrated graphically in Figure 18–9, and is frequently referred to as the *continuous review*

Figure 18–9.   Continuous Review Method

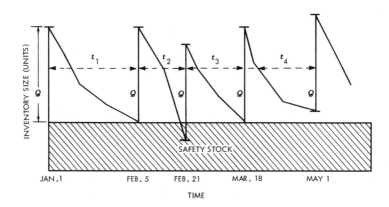

method. The fixed lot size may be determined either by use of the *EOQ* formula, or on the basis of the decision maker's judgment. In either case, it is necessary to provide for a *safety stock*—as shown by the cross-hatched area in Figure 18–9—to protect against unpredictable fluctuations in demand and possibly also in the acquisition lead time. Discussion of setting safety stocks will be reserved until a later section.

One form of the continuous review method—the two-bin system—has been used for certain types of items by many companies for a number of years. The items are placed in two bins. One contains the number of items needed to cover both: (1) average expected demand during the acquisition lead time, and (2) the safety stock. Initially, items needed for use are drawn from the second bin. The depletion of this bin signals that just enough items to cover expected demand during the lead time (plus the safety allowance) remain in the inventory (i.e., in the first bin)—and that it is time to place the replenishment order.[15] This system is often utilized in parts warehouses, for manufacturing floor stocks and under similar conditions where primarily high (Class A) but sometimes medium (Class B) items are controlled. It is "simple to operate and requires a minimum of record keeping."[16] The lot sizes chosen in utilizing this approach, however, should be reviewed periodically in order to make adjustments as changes take place in demand patterns, inventory carrying costs, and so forth.

Periodic Review Method

The second major approach employed in controlling inventories under risk and uncertainty is to vary the lot and size as demand changes, while keeping the interval between the placement of orders or production runs constant. This approach—frequently called the *periodic review* method—is illustrated diagrammatically for purchased lots in Figure 18–10.

Figure 18–10.   Periodic Review Method

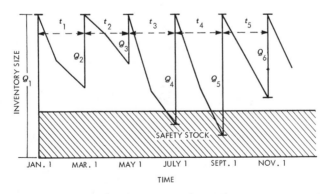

[15] "Sometimes, however, average expected demand during the acquisition period may exceed the purchase quantity, and inventories then would never be as high as the reorder point; in terms of bins, . . . [one] . . . is always empty and the . . . [other] . . . never contains the required quantity." (Whitin, *Inventory Management*, p. 52.) For an approach to the treatment of the problem under such circumstances, see ibid., pp. 52 ff.

[16] Magee, *Production Planning*, p. 70.

The fixed intervals when inventories are reviewed and orders placed or production runs scheduled may sometimes be quite lengthy—perhaps once every several months. Frequently, however, it is necessary to maintain close constant control over the inventories, and in such cases the review may take place more frequently.

The mechanics of the periodic review method may be illustrated by the use of an example. Consider a case in which: (1) the plant manager of a firm and his staff review inventories of a particular item on the last day of each month as a basis for scheduling the following month's production in light of anticipated demand, and (2) management has decided to set safety stocks for the end of each month equal to one half of the forecasted demand for the following month.

Under these conditions, the number of items scheduled for production in any given month will be equal to expected demand for the month plus the desired ending inventory for the month minus the beginning inventory on hand. For example, assume that:

1. The firm's expected monthly demand for a six-month period is that indicated in Figure 18–11.
2. Actual demand will always equal expected demand.
3. No lead time is required for scheduling the production.
4. The beginning inventory for January is 2,000 units.
5. The desired ending inventory for June is 2,000 units.

In such a case, monthly production would be scheduled as follows using the periodic review method:

Figure 18–11. Periodic Review Method

Month	Expected Demand	+ Desired Ending Inventory	= Total Requirements	− Beginning Inventory	= Production
January...........	4,000	2,100	6,100	2,000	4,100
February.........	4,200	1,800	6,000	2,100	3,900
March...........	3,600	2,400	6,000	1,800	4,200
April............	4,800	2,300	6,100	2,400	3,700
May.............	4,600	2,000	6,600	2,300	4,300
June............	4,000	2,000	6,000	2,000	4,000

When actual demand does not equal forecasted demand—which is often likely—the variance may be adjusted by a review at the end of each month. For example, if actual demand during January in the example were 4,200 units instead of the anticipated 4,000, ending inventory would be 1,900, or 200 short of the desired 2,100. Since the desired ending inventory for February is 1,800 and anticipated demand 4,200 units, production for this month would be set at 4,100 units rather than 3,900 as in Figure 18–11.

Four other observations concerning the periodic review method should be noted. First, the method is not basically an optimizing approach, although mathematical and statistical techniques may be employed to determine both the frequency of the acquisition intervals and the size of the safety allowances. Second, as in the continuous review approach, changing conditions may necessitate altering the frequency of review, and of the acquisition intervals.[17] Third, essentially the same method used in Figure 18–11 for scheduling production may be applied to inventory problems when purchasing lots from an outside supplier. Acquisition lead time—assumed away in the production example—is normally an additional important consideration, however, and must enter into the calculations. Finally, the periodic review method is used primarily for medium value items (Class B), but sometimes for high value (Class A) items, when the periodic review period is comparatively short.

The s, S or Optional Replenishment System

A newer approach to inventory decision making under risk and uncertainty, is one which is frequently called the s, S, or optional replenishment system. This system combines features of both the continuous and periodic review systems. What this system provides for is a *maximum* level of inventories on hand (and on order), S, and a reorder point, s. These two "levels" are illustrated in Figure 18–12. The way that the s, S system operates is as follows. Each time that any inventory is *taken from stock,* management *reviews* its inventory levels. If the level is above the reorder point (s), *no new inventories* are ordered.[18] If, however, the inventories have fallen to a level ≤ s, management will place an order equal to S, the maximum inventory minus the existing inventory (points x on Figure 18–12).

It is beyond the scope of this text to describe how the parameters of this approach (s, S) may be mathematically determined.[19] However, certain observations may be made concerning this system. First, it is

---

[17] It should not be inferred from this discussion that an order must necessarily be placed each time inventories are reviewed, for sometimes the review may indicate that existing inventories are high enough to protect against stockouts until the following review is to take place.

[18] The s, S system can be utilized both when inventories are ordered from outside the firm, and when inventories are obtained from production runs inside the firm. In both cases, the lead times for the inventories to arrive are assumed to be short, as is shown in Figure 18–12. As of this writing, analytical methods for dealing with s, S systems with long lead times, and overlapping orders have not yet been developed.

[19] Mathematical algorithms for determining the values of s, and S, may be found in J. William Gavett, *Production and Operations Management* (New York: Harcourt, Brace & World, Inc., 1968), pp. 504 ff.

Figure 18–12.   s, S Replenishment System

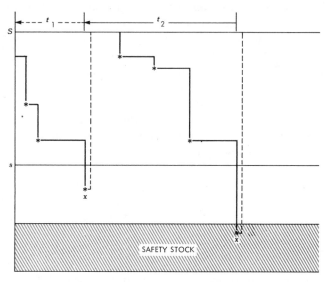

* = STOCK TAKEN FROM INVENTORY AND REVIEW TAKES PLACE

x = EXISTING INVENTORIES ≤ s, AND AN ORDER PLACED

¦ = SIZE OF ORDER PLACED (S - x)

-- = LEAD TIME FOR ORDER TO ARRIVE (ASSUMED TO BE SHORT)

a discrete policy system—i.e., each time *any* inventory is removed from stock a review takes place (compare Figure 18–11 with Figures 18–9 and 18–11). Second, the time intervals between the placement of orders will vary as in the continuous review system. Third, as Buffa has pointed out, the s, S system "places a lower limit on the size of an order which can be placed . . . [S − s] . . . yet maintains the close surveillance over inventory levels and demand rates associated with . . . [shorter periodic reviews]. . ."[20] Finally, at the time of this writing, this approach has been utilized primarily by large corporations, with the aid of computerization, and for the Class A and B (but not C) types of inventory items discussed previously. Its utilization is also increasing primarily because it does combine the desirable features of both the periodic and continuous review systems.

Determination of Safety Stocks

Under conditions of risk or uncertainty the periodic, continuous, and s, S systems all require the maintenance of safety stocks if stockouts

---

[20] Elwood S. Buffa, *Production-Inventory Systems: Planning and Control* (Homewood, Ill.: Richard D. Irwin, Inc., 1968), p. 98.

are to be minimized. The fundamental question upon which the decision maker must focus attention in determining the size of safety stocks is that of whether the costs of carrying the items will be justified by the probable reduction in losses due to stockouts. Or, in other words, are the marginal costs of extra inventory exceeded by the marginal savings realized by avoiding lost sales as the size of the safety stock is increased? It is important here to emphasize *reduction* in losses due to stockouts, rather than complete avoidance of such losses. For many demand situations, the probability of extreme fluctuations above average demand will exist, but be very small, and the costs incurred by carrying inventories large enough to cover *all possible* demand levels would greatly exceed the losses from stockouts which would be avoided by doing so.

It is beyond the scope of this book to delve into the mathematics and statistics required to determine optimal safety stocks. However, the ideas presented above may be illustrated graphically in a statistical demand distribution manner in Figure 18–13.[21] As may be noted from

Figure 18–13. Safety Stock-Demand Illustration

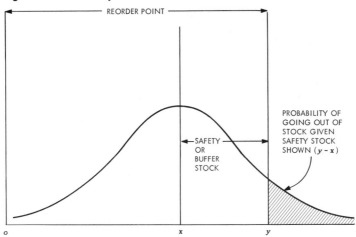

Source: Adapted from Martin K. Starr, *Systems Management Operations* (Englewood Cliffs, N.J.: Prentice-Hall, Inc., 1971), p. 358.

Figure 18–13, inventory must be provided to cover expected demand in the lead time, x; then a safety or buffer stock must be provided which "gives some specified level of protection . . . against going out of stock during the lead time interval."[22] Finally, the area of the demand

---

[21] Adapted from Starr, *Systems Management*, p. 358. It should be noted that Starr's diagram would be valid for all three of the risk and uncertainty approaches discussed previously.

[22] Ibid.

distribution to the right of point y on Figure 18–13 represents the probability of going out of stock given the safety stock level portrayed in this illustration.[23]

Certain other generalizations may be made concerning the establishment of safety stock levels. All other factors being equal, the size of the stock should increase as: (1) stockout costs increase, (2) the inventory carrying charges decrease, (3) the fluctuations in demand increase, and (4) the acquisition lead time increases.[24] In addition, proportionate to lot size, a little larger safety stocks will be required as the lot size decreases, since the possibility of depletion will occur more frequently.

OTHER INVENTORY CONSIDERATIONS

Total Dollar Limitations

Management may sometimes believe that some of the firm's funds tied up in inventories could more profitably be invested elsewhere and that a total dollar limitation should be placed upon the value of its inventories. Under conditions of risk or uncertainty in which a safety stock is maintained, the average inventory value for an item may be reduced to satisfy the limitation imposed in either or both of two ways: (1) more frequent and smaller lot sizes may be purchased (or shorter and more frequent production runs scheduled); or (2) the size of the safety stock may be reduced. For example, assume that yearly demand for an item is 8,000 units; that the item value is $1; that four orders of 2,000 units are presently being placed each year; and that the safety stock is 500 units. In this case, average inventory value is $\frac{Q}{2}$ C ($1,000) plus $500 for the safety stock; or $1,500. If the manager decided to limit the value of the average inventory to $1,000, he could: (1) reduce the safety stock to zero, (2) maintain the safety stock at 500 units, but place eight orders of 1,000 units during the year, which would reduce the average inventory value of the "live" stock to $500; or (3) reduce the safety stock partially and place somewhere between four and eight orders per year.

When a total dollar limitation has been placed on an inventory containing a large number of different kinds of items, the manager must decide by how much the average inventory value of each item should be reduced. A number of factors must be considered in making such a decision. As Starr has shown, optimal inventory reductions given a total dollar constraint limitation can be calculated analytically for all

---

[23] For information concerning an algorithm for determining the reorder point, see ibid.

[24] Whitin, *Inventory Management*, pp. 55–56.

classes of items.[25] Whether it is more desirable to order more frequently or reduce the level of the safety stock for the items depends on the relative importance that management gives to incurring additional procurement costs as opposed to increasing the probability that stockouts will occur. Elimination of the 500 unit safety stock in the previous illustration, for example, would increase the probability of stockouts without affecting the procurement costs. Increasing the number of orders from four to eight per year, on the other hand, would double the procurement costs, but would not increase the probability of incurring stockouts nearly as much as would elimination of the safety stock.[26] Finally, if the increased profitability attainable by releasing funds from the inventories is thought of in terms of a percentage return on investment, inventory reductions can be effected by manipuation of the *EOQ* formula in those cases in which it is employed. For example, if that portion of inventory carrying costs which has in the past been assigned to cover opportunity costs is 6 percent of the value of an item, and management decides that its funds can now earn 10 percent if invested elsewhere, a new economic order quantity reflecting this change can be determined by increasing *I* in the *EOQ* formula by 4 percent.

Inventory Turnover

An analytical tool which is often employed to determine inventory problems is the inventory turnover ratio. This ratio is computed by dividing the firm's annual cost of goods sold by its average inventory value. The average inventory value for the overall firm is usually determined by averaging the total value of the beginning and ending inventories for the financial year as given in the company's position statements. It is also possible to determine the turnover ratio for any single item in the inventory. Under conditions of certainty, in which no safety stock is maintained, the turnover is approximately equal to: $\dfrac{RC}{\dfrac{Q}{2}C}$, or $\dfrac{2R}{Q}$.[27]

---

[25] Starr, *Systems Management*, pp. 353–54. Starr has also presented an algorithm which, when there are managerial constraints on the *number* of orders which may be placed (but no total dollar constraint) will provide for an optimal inventory policy. (See ibid., pp. 353–55.) It should be noted that both of these algorithms are deterministic rather than probabilistic ones.

[26] As indicated previously, the probability of incurring stockouts will increase to an extent as smaller orders are placed more frequently, since the frequency of exposure to depletion is thereby increased.

[27] Where *R* represents the yearly demand, *Q*, the lot size, and *C*, the value of the item. The inventory turnover approximates $\dfrac{2R}{Q}$ to the extent that demand and the acquisition lead time are constant as assumed in the previous discussion of the lot-size problem under conditions of certainty.

With the addition of a safety stock (SS), the turnover becomes approximately: $\dfrac{RC}{\dfrac{Q}{2}C + (SS)C}$, or $\dfrac{2R}{Q + 2SS}$.

It may be noted that when only one item is being considered, its value (C) in both the numerator and the denominator cancels out, and the turnover ratio may be computed without reference to the item value. Computation of the turnover for the entire inventory of the firm, however, requires consideration of dollar values—since differently valued items invariably make up the inventory.

Turnover ratios vary considerably not only from industry to industry but also for different items carried by a firm. In the retail food industry, for example, produce items invariably turn over much more rapidly than any of the soft goods lines which a supermarket may carry. Consequently, there is no single turnover ratio which may be considered universally optimal. Comparisons of turnover figures with either (1) past ratios for the firm, or (2) current figures for other firms in the industry, however, may be useful in pointing up possible problem areas in the company's operations. A comparatively low turnover, for example, may indicate that too many slow-moving items are being carried. This may be due to the company making too many different sizes of models of a particular good. On the other hand, a comparatively high ratio may be an indication that insufficient inventories are being carried and that excessive stockouts are occurring. On the other hand, rational inventory policies on the part of management may lead to a normally high turnover ratio. For example, in cases where management's control over items is close, or in which expediting has been carried out, one would normally expect to find high turnover ratios. It should also be noted that turnover ratios—even for the same item—do not, and often should not, remain constant for long periods of time. As shown by the *EOQ* formula, for example, the average inventory for an item should optimally change only in proportion to the square root of changes in demand. Consequently, when the demand for a particular item increases, the turnover ratio should also increase.

Information-Feedback and Inventory Control

The previous sections dealing with *EOQ* and inventory decision making under conditions of risk and uncertainty have focused prime attention on examining inventory policies for *one item,* as opposed to the case where there are a number of items, say on a production line, where there is a *sequential flow* of these items through the system. This latter case, which is quite common, might include fabrication of subassemblies, assembling the latter into a finished product, inspecting it, warehousing it, and finally shipping it to the firm's customers. What one has in such a situation is a number of independent but interrelated inventory stock points—finished goods inventories in the warehouse, in-process inventory points such as final assembled but yet uninspected items, and raw materials inventories. Each of these sequential stock points *can* be operated independently. For example, when finished goods inventories are down to their reorder point, an *EOQ* can be placed with the final assembly department; when its inventories reach this reorder point, it can place an *EOQ* with each of the firm's subassembly departments, and so forth. However, when this is done "the demand for the item becomes progressively more erratic the further the stock point is removed from the point of original consumer demand."[28] For example, under relatively constant demand conditions, when the reorder point for finished goods is reached, a replenishment order would be placed with the assembly department. Then:

this demand on the assembly department will be passed on to the next stock points for subassemblies and components. In this sense, the demand on the intermediate stock points is *bunched*. The effect of this is to force a large safety stock to take care of this *more erratic demand.*[29]

The primary way of overcoming these unstable reponse problems in sequential inventory systems is to "pass customer demand *information* directly back to each point in the sequence."[30] This information feedback is illustrated in Figure 18–14. This results in each stock point responding directly to customer orders rather than to replenishment orders from the next sequential stock point. For example, in Figure 18–14 materials

Figure 18–14. Information-Feedback System

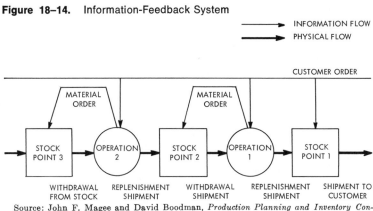

Source: John F. Magee and David Boodman, *Production Planning and Inventory Control*, 2d ed., pp. 142–43. © 1967 by McGraw-Hill, Inc. Used by permission of McGraw-Hill Book Company.

---

[28] Gavett, *Production and Operations Management*, p. 528.

[29] Ibid. The italics are ours. It should also be noted that Gavett points out that this problem would be magnified if original customer demand is variable. Ibid., pp. 528–29.

[30] Ibid., p. 528. The italics are ours.

would be ordered at Stock point 3 from Operation 2 based directly on customer demand information at Operation 2 rather than upon a replenishment order from Stock point 2 to Operation 2 which would be based on a material order from Operation 1. What this approach does is to *minimize information lags* which often *generate delays* in the system, thus preventing the problems of erratic demand and the consequent requirement for larger safety stocks is mentioned earlier.[31]

SUMMARY

As the importance of adequate inventory control methods has gained more recognition, increasing analytical approaches have been developed to aid the decision maker in dealing with inventory problems. Although inventory decisions may serve to meet a number of objectives, the fundamental decision criterion on which all of these approaches center is the minimization of the total variable inventory costs. Some of the techniques for handling inventory problems—such as the *EOQ* formula—are structured around mathematical models and are designed to develop optimum solutions. Because of the complexities encountered in dealing with inventories when demand and acquisition lead time are not certain, other approaches—such as the periodic review approach—are designed simply to satisfice rather than to optimize. In the presentation of all of these approaches, the primary focus has been upon decision making and analysis of the key decision variables and their interrelationships.

DISCUSSION AND STUDY QUESTIONS

1. An *EOQ* system of inventory control presumes that the organization is operating as a closed system. Comment.

2. An executive of a small company whose demand is fairly constant said, "I don't need inventory models to solve my problems. I just use intuition and follow a 'middle-of-the-road' inventory policy." Comment on these statements. If his demand fluctuates, would his statement be relevant?

3. How many items will be reordered each time an order is placed with the continuous, the periodic, and the *s, S* inventory systems?

4. The minimum number of items that can be ordered at any one time under the *s, S* system is what?

5. A firm manufacturing phonographs, turntables, and loudspeakers recently installed a new inventory control system. The firm manufactures items

---

[31] There are also several other characteristics of the information-feedback system type of control. (See ibid., p. 528); or, for a fuller description of this type of system (sometimes referred to as base stock), see John F. Magee and David Boodman, *Production Planning and Inventory Control* (2d ed.; New York: McGraw-Hill Book Co., 1967), pp. 141–48. It should also be noted that this type of control can be utilized with all of the risk and uncertainty approaches discussed previously: continuous review, periodic review, and the *s, S* system.

both for stock and to meet specific customer orders. Its controller stated that a major advantage of the new system was that it provided accurate and timely information for controlling inventory levels. The system provides for daily reports on all items showing the number of parts, in-process and finished goods inventories on hand, the number of parts on purchase order, the number of items in process reserved for customer orders, and so on. These reports are furnished to the inventory control manager, the controller, the purchasing agent, the production planning staff, the marketing vice-president, and the manufacturing vice-president.

a) Comment on this system from the viewpoint of:
   (1) Information cost versus value.
   (2) Report format.
   (3) Exception reporting.
   (4) Differing data needs for different executives.

b) Does this system as described assure optimal inventory decisions? Explain.

6. Under conditions of certainty, as sales double, the *EOQ* should double; as sales triple, the *EOQ* should triple, and so forth. Comment on this statement.

7. a) What is meant by selective inventory control? Is this type of system optimal? Doesn't selective control imply that part of the inventory in the system is not controlled at all?

   b) Discuss selective control under conditions of risk with *s*, *S* continuous, and periodic review systems. Which is used most with Class C items?

8. The Smithson Company, manufacturers of home appliances, estimates that demand for one of its component parts which it orders from an outside supplier will be 100,000 next year. The firm estimates that its ordering costs are $20 per order. Each components costs $10, and it is estimated that the inventory carrying costs for each component is 10 percent per year of the value of average inventory on hand. Utilizing the *EOQ* formula, determine:

a) The economic order quantity.
b) What total costs for the year will be.
c) What the number of orders placed per year will be.
d) What the average inventory level for the components will be.

9. A firm with the following demand, output rate, and cost data wants to determine its optimum production run size.

Yearly demand.....................	72,000 units
Daily output......................	400 units
Carrying cost per unit.............	$1
Cost per setup....................	$10

Assuming a 360-day year:
a) What will be the optimum size of each production run?
b) What is the optimum length (in days) for each run?
c) What are its yearly costs?
d) What is its average inventory?

e) How many runs are placed per year?

f) If its daily output rate were 200 units rather than 400, what would the optimum run size and length be?

10. Yearly demand for an item is 5,000 units. Ordering costs are $40 per order, and the item costs $1 if purchased in quantities up to 2,500 units, but only 90 cents per unit if the volume of a purchased lot is equal to or greater than 2,500 units. Annual carrying costs are 10 percent of the purchase price. What is the most economical order quantity?

11. A firm manufactures gear units for farm equipment. The nature of the demand for its product requires that the firm utilize intermittent manufacturing. The sales forecast for gear units for the forthcoming year is as follows:

Quarter of Year	Estimated Number of Units
First................	6,000
Second..............	5,800
Third................	6,200
Fourth..............	5,600

The firm establishes production schedules on a quarterly basis. Its inventory policy specifies that the desired ending inventory of finished gear units for each quarter should be equal to one-half of its expected sales for the *subsequent quarter*. The firm's management estimates that the forth-coming year will commence with 2,000 units of completely assembled gear units in its finished goods inventories. Management has decided that it would like to end the forthcoming year with 3,000 units of finished goods in its inventories.

Using the periodic review method of inventory management, determine how many gear units should be produced in each quarter of the forthcoming year. Assume that actual sales equal forecasted sales.

12. Chapter 8 noted the tendency of organizations to isolate their core technologies from environmental variation to minimize coordination costs. Do inventories do this for a job shop producing to customer order? Explain.

SELECTED REFERENCES

Ammer, Dean. *Materials Management.* rev. ed. Homewood, Ill.: Richard D. Irwin, Inc., 1968.

Brown, R. G. *Decision Rules for Inventory Management.* New York: Holt, Rinehart & Winston, Inc., 1967.

Buffa, Elwood S. *Production-Inventory Systems: Planning and Control.* Homewood, Ill.: Richard D. Irwin, Inc., 1968.

Churchman, C. W.; Ackoff, R.; and Arnoff, E. L. *Introduction to Operations Research.* New York: John Wiley & Sons, Inc., 1957.

Gavett, J. William. *Production and Operations Management.* New York: Harcourt, Brace & World, Inc., 1968.

HADLEY, G., and WHITIN, T. M. *Analysis of Inventory Systems.* Englewood Cliffs, N.J.: Prentice-Hall, Inc., 1963.

HOLT, CHARLES C. et al. *Planning Production, Inventories, and Work Force* Englewood Cliffs, N.J.: Prentice-Hall, Inc., 1960.

MAGEE, JOHN F., and BOODMAN, DAVID. *Production Planning and Inventory Control.* 2d ed. New York: The McGraw-Hill Book Co., 1967.

MILLER, D., and STARR, M. *Executive Decisions and Operations Research.* 2d ed. Englewood Cliffs, N.J.: Prentice-Hall, Inc., 1969.

STARR, MARTIN K. *Systems Management of Operations.* Englewood Cliffs, N.J.: Prentice-Hall, Inc., 1971.

STARR, M. K., and MILLER, D. W. *Inventory Control: Theory and Practice.* Englewood Cliffs, N.J.: Prentice-Hall, Inc. 1962.

TIMMS, HOWARD L. *Inventory Management of Purchased Materials.* New York: National Association of Purchasing Agents, 1958.

VIENOTT, A. F. "The Status of Mathematical Inventory Theory," *Management Science,* 12 (July 1966), 745–77.

WAGNER, HARVEY M. *Principles of Operations Research.* Englewood Cliffs, N.J.: Prentice-Hall, Inc., 1969.

Chapter 19

Simulation Models

IN THE PREVIOUS TWO CHAPTERS, attention was focused on the application of several different optimizing models to managerial problems. Certain of these, such as the simple *EOQ* and continuous inflow inventory models, provide optimal solutions to problems *directly* by the substitution of values in an equation. Others, such as the transportation model, do not provide for such direct solutions, but rather require the use of iterative methods. All of these models represent what will be referred to as *analytical* models. That is, they consist of known mathematical procedures or algorithms, which when manipulated, either directly or iteratively, provide an optimum solution.[1]

Many types of managerial problems are so complex that neither direct nor iterative analytical procedures exist for their solution, or, if such methods do exist, they present such great difficulties in application that their utilization is impractical. In such cases (or as Harvey Wagner has put it in his comprehensive work on operations research, "when all else fails"),[2] the manager may turn to the use of a technique called *simulation*. In this chapter, several facets of simulation for managerial decision making will be explored.

THE NATURE OF SIMULATION

Simulation involves designing and utilizing a model which replicates some aspect of the firm's operations. Simulation models, like those discussed in previous chapters, may be utilized to provide understanding about a system, to predict behavior, and/or to help prescribe courses

---

[1] It should be noted that some writers prefer to define "analytical" procedures in a narrower sense—e.g., as ones generally involving "the use of calculus to obtain the maximum point of a profit function or the minimum point of a cost function." Donald Clough, *Concepts in Management Science* (Englewood Cliffs, N.J.: Prentice-Hall, Inc., 1963), p. 372.

[2] Harvey M. Wagner, *Principles of Operations Research* (Englewood Cliffs, N.J.: Prentice-Hall, Inc., 1969), p. 887. He uses this phrase as a title of one of his sections since most "operations researchers look upon . . . computer simulation as a 'method of last resort' . . ." (ibid., p. 890).

of action. In general, simulation models may be distinguished from other operations research models in that they are generally *nonanalytical* in nature, calling for an *experimental* approach, in which *numerous* trials or *iterations* are carried out by means of which workable, satisficing solutions rather than optimal ones are usually provided. These characteristics of simulation will now be examined in greater detail.

Nonanalytical Nature of Simulation

Simulation models, in their entirety, usually cannot be manipulated directly by mathematical means so as to arrive at an optimum solution.[3] As mentioned previously, simulation models are utilized rather than those by means of which optimal solutions may be determined by one or more mathematical algorithms because the latter either do not exist or are not practically applicable. Illustrative of a problem of such complexity as to render simulation appropriate was that of one consumer goods manufacturer which attempted to determine whether or not it should initiate its own sales finance company. A simulation model of the proposed finance company was designed and run to estimate how profitable the operation might be under various possible conditions. Even though the model was "simplified" to the extent that no probabilistic functions were included in it, and certain elements which might have rendered it more useful were excluded:

The model used . . . twenty-three input variables. . . . In total, forty-seven equations were developed to represent the operation of a finance company branch on a monthly basis . . . [and with an IBM 7090 utilizing FORTRAN] the entire simulation consists of approximately 8,000 program steps.[4]

Even in some cases in which a more straightforward mathematical statement of a problem can be made than in the finance model (with its 47 equations), there may be no known algorithm for determining an optimal solution, and simulation techniques may be called for. For example, in discussing one equation which describes the materials handling costs associated with the location of facilities in a plant, Armour and Buffa state:

While this equation does furnish a mechanism for conceptualizing the problems, it unfortunately does not carry the analyst to a solution. The authors do not know of any algorithm which can *feasibly* be used to resolve this . . . problem.[5]

[3] Mathematical routines such as *EOQ* or linear programming may be incorporated into, and comprise one or more parts of, a total simulation model.

[4] Gordon B. Davis, Howard Ambill, and Herbert Whitecraft, "Simulation of Finance Company Operations for Decision Making," *Management Technology*, 2 (December 1961), pp. 86, 87, 89.

[5] G. C. Armour and E. S. Buffa, "A Heuristic Algorithm and Simulation Approach to Relative Location of Facilities," *Management Science*, 9 (January 1963), p. 297.

Illustrative of the usefulness of simulation techniques when analytical procedures do exist but pose such difficult computational problems that their application is not feasible, is with dealing with the so-called assembly line-balancing problem.[6] An optimum solution to this problem is computationally possible but the expense of analytical computational means is considered excessive. Through the use of heuristic line-balancing procedures which simulate the human thought processes of an industrial engineer when he balances a line, however, a "satisfactory" solution to this problem may be arrived at. Analytical balancing procedures probably could provide a better line balance, but the heuristic simulation techniques are almost as good and are considerably cheaper to operate.[7]

There are, of course, many managerial problems (including human ones) which, as indicated previously, cannot be solved by any known analytical technique. Further, within the "operations research area" *itself*, Wagner has specified three particular types of problems, for which operations research techniques "for now and in the foreseeable future . . . cannot be relied on to provide a complete analysis . . . [for] . . . management decision-making. . . ."[8] These are:

1.   The choice of investment *policies* for strategic planning—i.e. comprehensive policies that consider such factors as new product development, entry into new markets, determining types of financing, and so on,
2.   The choice of facilities in operations planning—e.g., determining how many check-out stands should be in a supermarket, and
3.   The design of information-feedback scheduling and operations rules—e.g., scheduling in a job shop manufacturing operation.[9]

Simulation as an Experimental Process

A second basic characteristic of the simulation approach is that it is generally an experimental one. By experimenting with a number of variables incorporated into a simulation model, its user can compare the results from each experimental trial with those from other trials; and then select that set of decisions which the simulation results indicate would be most preferable. Although different simulation models vary

---

[6] Balance "refers to the equality of output of each of the successive operations in the sequence of a line. If they are all equal, we say that we have perfect balance, and we expect smooth flow. If they are unequal, we know that the maximum possible output for the line as a whole will be dictated by the slowest operation in the sequence." Elwood S. Buffa, *Modern Production Management* (New York: John Wiley & Sons, Inc., 1961), p. 415.

[7] For a discussion of a heuristic approach to the line-balancing problem, see Fred M. Tonge, *A Heuristic Program for Assembly Line Balancing* (Englewood Cliffs, N.J.: Prentice-Hall, Inc., 1961).

[8] Wagner, *Operations Research*, p. 888.

[9] Drawn from ibid., pp. 888–89.

considerably as far as the *specific* variables which are incorporated in them is concerned, they generally are structured around consideration of the *types* of variables which were discussed in Chapter 3—strategies which the firm may employ to meet its objectives; and states of nature in which the firm anticipates it may operate and/or competitive strategies which may be employed by other firms. Through such experimentation, several alternative strategies may first be tested under one set of possible competitor actions and states of nature. Then, the same alternatives may be tested under a second, third, and fourth set of external conditions, and so on. This process of systematically varying the firm's own alternatives, states of nature, and competitive strategies can be continued for as long as considered necessary to determine which courses of action would be preferable.

An example of how various conditions of interest to management may be experimentally examined via simulation is provided by a simulation of the activities involved in operating a large airport developed by United Air Lines. In this simulation such factors have been included as weather conditions, need for maintenance, type and length of repair jobs, availability of spare aircraft, number of maintenance personnel, and so on.[10] With this model:

> Management can change the number of spare aircraft, or the manpower schedule, and simulate operations under any new conditions which it would like to test. The computer is programmed to provide such data as expected idle manpower, expected idle equipment, utilization of maintenance docks, and delays in take-off. By comparing the expected performance in terms of these data with the cost of obtaining that performance, decisions can be arrived at that will produce the best over-all operation of the complex airport system.[11]

One final observation is in order concerning the experimental nature of simulation. While simulation is an experimental process, the experiments may be performed on a model of the firm's operations rather than with the real operations themselves. In consequence, proposed courses of action can be tested *without disrupting* the actual operations of the firm. As the designers of the finance company simulation discussed previously have pointed out:

> Simulating a system allows those conducting the study to expand or compress real time . . . management . . . can simulate years of operations in a few minutes on a computer. Conversely they can slow it down to study special problem areas in detail. In short, they have a laboratory to analyze the proposed operation . . . simulation allows management to look before they leap and to test ideas in advance. The results can be evaluated and

---

[10] Franc M. Ricciardi et al., *Top Management Decision Simulation: The AMA Approach* (New York: American Management Association, Inc., 1957), p. 51.

[11] Ibid.

new ideas tried *without disrupting* current operations or incurring unnecessary costs for an uneconomical operation.[12]

Repeated Trials in Simulation

A third characteristic of simulations is that their utilization usually involves the carrying out of numerous trials or iterations. Repeated trials in simulation models may be necessitated for several reasons. First, as indicated previously, management often desires to examine the impact of numerous possible strategies under a number of varied states of nature and/or competitive conditions. Additionally, it is necessary to simulate certain types of systems for numerous *time periods* if the impact of any given management decision, or of changes in external conditions are to be fully understood. Such would be the case in those dynamic systems: (1) the state of which in any time period is conditioned by their states in previous time periods and; (2) which take several time periods before reaching a new equilibrium state after having been "disturbed" from a previous equilibrium state. For example, in a simulation model of a production system described by Clough, the responses of certain system variables to a sudden 50 percent increase in customer order rates are long-term ones. With such an increase:

> The work-in-process level starts to oscillate and eventually settles at a level 50% higher than its original level. The warehouse inventory level begins to oscillate and then settles back to its original level. The interesting point is that the system does not reach equilibrium again until about 50 weeks after the step change in order rate.[13]

Systems such as that illustrated in the previous example requiring simulation over a number of periods of time because of their dynamic nature may be either stochastic or deterministic—i.e., they may or may not include any probabilistic relationships among variables. When a system being simulated includes probabilistic relationships, on the other hand, the necessity arises for repeated trials *regardless* of whether it is dynamic or not. This is because it is necessary to obtain an adequate *sample* of observations if statistical confidence is to be ascribed to the simulation results. Just how many experimental trials are necessary in utilizing simulations is a problem falling within the domain of statistical techniques, the discussion of which is beyond the scope of this book. It should be noted, however, that the number of iterations considered adequate may vary considerably from simulation to simulation depending upon their characteristics. In some relatively simple models, a sample size of less than 100 may be sufficient to produce useful estimates with

---

[12] Davis, Ambill and Whitecraft, "Simulation of Finance Company Operations," p. 84. The emphasis is ours.

[13] Clough, *Management Science,* p. 378. Copyright © 1963 by Prentice-Hall, Inc.

a 95 percent level of confidence.[14] On the other hand, in one simulation with which the authors are familiar, about 50,000 iterations were considered necessary by its designer.[15]

THE GROWTH OF SIMULATION

Both the number of simulations developed and the types of problems to which they have addressed themselves have increased greatly in recent years. With respect to number, one survey with a sample response of 323 indicated that among these firms 63 were already using simulations or currently developed them in 1969, and that an additional 39 of the respondents indicated that they planned to begin developing a model within the next year; with the major efforts having started in 1966 "when 13 companies began developing their first model."[16] Interestingly enough, this researcher made an attempt to see if any particular industry predominated in simulation development but found that: "An extensive amount of correlation analysis was undertaken . . . but nothing conclusive could be determined."[17] In this same study, however, it was found that 65 percent of companies developed models which began by examining the total corporation in very little detail, while only 35 percent "chose to start by looking at a part of the company in detail with the idea of proceeding to develop a total corporate model function by function."[18]

With respect to the scope of models developed, many different types have been developed within the business firm such as production scheduling, financial planning, a crude oil supply model,[19] and a computerized simulation of psychological thought processes in personnel selection.[20]

Simulations have been designed in many types of organizations and

---

[14] Murray A. Geisler, "The Size of Simulation Samples . . .", *Management Science,* 10 (January 1964), pp. 261–86.

[15] Richard L. Reich, "A Simulation Approach to the Solution of a Machine Interference Problem," Unpublished thesis (University Park, Pa.: The Pennsylvania State University, 1964), pp. 59–60.

[16] George Gershefski, "Corporate Models—The State of the Art," in Albert N. Schreiber (ed.), *Corporate Simulation Models* (Providence, R.I.: College on Simulation and Gaming of the Institute of Management Science; and Seattle, Wash.: Graduate School of Business Administration of the University of Washington, 1970), p. 29. It should be noted that this survey included responses on other types of models than simulation; but 95 percent of the models in the study were simulations.

[17] Ibid., p. 31. Why some companies have models while others do not, it was speculated, "appeared to be a matter of individual initiative. Models appear to exist in these companies where someone has heard about them and proceeded to 'sell' management." Ibid., p. 30.

[18] Ibid., p. 41.

[19] See, for example, Vahe Nalbandian and David Bailin, "A Crude Oil Simulation Model," in Schreiber, *Corporate Simulation Models,* pp. 431–48.

[20] See, for example, Robert D. Smith and Paul S. Greenlaw, "Simulation of a Psychological Thought Process in Personnel Selection," *Management Science,* 13 (April 1967), pp. B409–19.

for many different purposes than solving managerial problems. Transportation systems, ecological models (such as the simulation of pesticide application), bio-medicine/clinical models, models dealing with federal policies for requiring residential housing, resource allocation to school districts in Illinois—these are but a few of the many differing problems dealt with by simulation.[21] At the macro level, a simulation of certain facets of the world as a system has even been developed by Jay Forrester. In this model, which is generalized to a high' degree, five basic levels were chosen as "cornerstones" on which to build the simulation structure: population, capital investment, natural resources, fraction of capital allocated to agriculture, and pollution.[22] Whether such a highly macro effort will prove fruitful is open to question, but it does illustrate the modeling of the largest social system known to man—the world itself.

The above illustrations raise an important question: Why has simulation expanded as a problem-solving tool? There are at least three answers to this question: (1) many simulations have worked providing highly satisfactory answers;[23] (2) computers themselves have improved greatly in their ability to deal with complex simulation models over the last decade; and (3) considerable research has been devoted and led to the development of computer languages designed especially for simulating, and which have made simulation easier to carry out. Comment will be made briefly on these simulation languages in a later section.

TYPES OF SIMULATION

Now that the fundamental characteristics of simulation models have been discussed, some of the different types of simulation utilized by management will be indicated. There are several different ways in which managerial simulations may be classified. One preference is to classify such models as (1) hand, (2) machine, and (3) man-machine.

With hand simulations, all calculations required in utilizing the model are performed by individuals either by hand or by the manual operation of calculating equipment, such as adding machines or comptometers. Machine simulations, on the other hand, are those in which calculations are carried out by an electronic computer. Man-machine simulation models are those in which humans perform as *active participants* in the model, as will be illustrated more fully later.

Hand simulation may be used when relatively simple problems are

---

[21] All of these models appear in the *Proceedings of the 1971 Summer Computer Simulation Conference* (Denver, Colo.: Board of Simulation Conference, 1971).

[22] Jay W. Forrester, *World Dynamics* (Cambridge, Mass.: Wright-Allen Press, Inc., 1971), p. 19.

[23] In the survey cited earlier (Gershefski, "Corporate Models") when asked what weight their management placed on results of simulation models as opposed to other analytical studies: 42 percent said the same; 50 percent said more; and only 8 percent said less. Further, 91 percent of the respondents believed the benefits gained from models were worth the efforts expended to design them (p. 38).

being considered in which only a few variables or time periods are being examined. In such cases, it may not pay the decision maker to incur the expense of computer programming and operation.[24] Further, hand computations are also frequently employed to test and "debug" a simulation model before it is programmed for a computer. For example, in the simulation of the finance company operations which was discussed earlier:

Since the simulation . . . involved the use of the computer to solve a relatively large number of rather simple equations, it was feasible to compute one solution by hand. This hand-calculated solution was compared against the same solution as calculated by the computer and any corrections or differences were rectified. Once the preliminary solution was completed, it was possible to proceed with additional problems using a wide range of input values.[25]

For large-scale simulated experimentation, utilization of computers is mandatory. Many such experiments are pure machine simulations—resort is simply made to computerization without introducing people into the model as active participants. Man-machine simulations, on the other hand, may be employed when: (1) it is necessary to simulate certain facets of human behavior if the simulation results are to be adequate; and (2) either the expense of or probable error resulting from developing a program to simulate such behavior on the computer is likely to be excessive. If the particular behavior which the simulation designer is interested in is overly complex, defining and programming it may exceed the cost of using people themselves in the simulation. Additionally, a pure machine simulation into which certain aspects of human behavior have been programmed may be in error due to an inadequate knowledge of how this behavior is exhibited in the real system.[26]

Man-machine simulations may also be employed for the specific purpose of determining how individuals will react in a *proposed* system. For example, one may want to know how much stress certain individuals will experience under a new organizational structure. Since the proposed organization does not yet exist, it might be very difficult to predict just which kinds of situations would occur in it. If, however, one was able to simulate the information flows, the interpersonal relationships

---

[24] In Gershefski, "Corporate Models," it was indicated that among the models indicated by respondents in his study, 94 percent were computerized (p. 42).

[25] Davis, Ambill and Whitecraft, "Simulation of Finance Company Operations," p. 89.

[26] This may be the case with the controversial "MANPLAN: A Micro-Simulator for Manpower Planning," by James R. Miller, III, and Mason Haire, *Behavioral Science,* 15 (November 1970), pp. 524–31. It was noted at the beginning of this work that "Reviewers disagreed on the merits of this paper. It exemplifies the problems encountered when an effort is made to provide explicit operational definitions for procedures that usually are handled according to complex but not fully formalized rules." (Ibid., p. 524.)

and other factors which would exist in the proposed system, he might be able to determine how individuals would behave in it and whether its operation would be adversely affected because of the stress they experience. This type of man-machine simulation is sometimes referred to as *operational gaming*. The application of operational gaming may be illustrated by reference to a study of the supply systems for aircraft logistic support made by the RAND Corporation.[27] In this study, RAND developed new rules for making decisions about inventory levels, reorders to manufacturing plants, and other activities in a proposed defense supply system. Before recommending the new system to the Air Force, RAND designed a man-machine simulation of the proposed system to test its effectiveness. Air Force personnel were used as integral elements in the simulation, acting in the same capacities as they might in the real supply system if it were to become operational in the Air Force. Computer-generated reports necessary for logistics decisions were given to these people. Their decisions were fed into the computerized portion of the simulation and the impact of these decisions was determined. Usage rates under conditions of both war and peace were simulated to discover whether the supply system proposed and the individuals in it would be effective in both cases. Since Air Force personnel would eventually operate the system, their participation in the simulation was also helpful in determining how the selection and training of persons at different hierarchical and functional positions of the proposed supply system might best be effected.

Extending this RAND experience in designing new systems for the Air Force, Geisler and Steger have suggested that proposed business organizations can be tested by means of man-machine simulation.[28] When a firm reorganizes, modifications in existing power relationships, information patterns, and content of jobs often take place. If individuals could be placed in a system which simulates such changes, it might be possible to determine the adequacy of proposed information networks, work loads, influence patterns, and so forth. Appropriate improvements might then be made *before* the new organization is placed into operation. Such simulation may also serve the auxiliary function of providing *training* to potential incumbents slated for revised positions. Although such operational experiments have been proposed, their practical feasibility for business firms has not yet really been shown. Perhaps someday operational gaming could be used in business, but thus far its application has been almost exclusively limited to military systems. Probably the prime reason for this is cost, since, for example, some of the RAND

---

[27] The RAND simulation experiments have been widely published. For a general evaluation of them, see Murray A. Geisler, "Appraisal of Laboratory Simulation Experiences," *Management Science*, 8 (April 1962), pp. 239–45.

[28] Murray A. Geisler and Wilbur A. Steger, "How to Plan for Management of New Systems," *Harvard Business Review*, 40 (September-October 1962), pp. 103–10.

air defense experiments have been very costly to develop,[29] justified only on the basis of the importance of national security.[30]

THE STRUCTURE OF SIMULATION MODELS

The design of simulation models involves many of the same considerations as does the development of other types of mathematical models utilized in managerial decision making. Simulation models, however, are often structured somewhat differently from the models which have been discussed in previous chapters, due to their nonanalytical, iterative-experimental replication of often fairly complex systems.[31] In this section, several aspects of the structuring of simulation models will be examined. The purpose of this examination is not to enable one to become proficient in simulation design. Rather, it is intended to provide him with greater insight into and understanding of the simulation approach.

Simulation Languages

As indicated above, the development of special simulation-oriented computer languages has helped facilitate the design and growth of simulations. There are two basic classes of simulation languages:

1. Continuous, which includes the computer simulation languages DYNAMO and GPSS (General-Purpose System Simulator), and

---

[29] For example, the air defense simulation described in Robert L. Chapman et al., "The System Research Laboratory's Air Defense Experiments," *Management Science*, 5 (April 1959), pp. 250–68.

[30] Two other notes are in order here. First a "man-hand" (rather than man-machine) noncomputerized simulation has been suggested for systems training purposes in a mail-order house by Elias D. Porter, in his *Manpower Development* (New York: Harper & Row, Publishers, Inc., 1964), pp. 116–22. Second, business games or simulations are a type of simulation that have been used widely in recent years for training in industry and in colleges and universities. A business simulation is a sequential decision-making problem structured around a model of a business (or other organizational) operation in which the participants assume the role of managing a simulated organization. To go into business simulation is beyond the scope of this book. For further information on this subject, the reader is referred to Paul S. Greenlaw et al., *Business Simulation in Industrial and University Education* (Englewood Cliffs, N.J.: Prentice-Hall, Inc., 1962), and Robert C. Graham and Clifford C. Grey, *Business Games Handbook* (New York: American Management Association, 1969). Several business simulations have been published and are readily available for use. Among these are three computerized simulations co-authored by one of the authors of this text: Paul S. Greenlaw and Fred W. Kniffin, *MARKSIM: A Marketing Decision Simulation* (Scranton, Pa.: International Textbook Co., 1964); Paul S. Greenlaw and M. William Frey, *FINANSIM: A Financial Management Simulation* (Scranton, Pa.: International Textbook Co., 1967); and Paul S. Greenlaw and Michael P. Hottenstein, *PROSIM: A Production Management Simulation* (Scranton, Pa.: International Textbook Co., 1969).

[31] As Wagner has pointed out: "Unlike the situation with mathematical programming, there are as yet no underlying principles guiding the formulation of simulation models. Each application is ad hoc to a large extent." Wagner, *Principles of Operations Research*, p. 891.

2.   Discrete, which includes the computer languages CSMP (Continuous System Modeling Program) and SIMSCRIPT.[32]

It is beyond the scope of this book to delve further into simulation languages except to point out that the continous-discrete classification is not a dichotomous one. As Gordon has pointed out comparing aircraft and factory systems with respect to simulation languages

. . . aircraft and factory systems . . . respond to environmental changes in different ways. The movement of . . . aircraft occurs smoothly, whereas the changes in the factory occur discontinuously. The ordering of raw materials or the completion of a product, for example, occurs at specific points in time.

Systems such as the aircraft, in which the changes are predominantly smooth, are called *continuous systems*. Systems like the factory, in which changes are predominantly discontinuous, will be called *discrete systems*. Few systems are wholly continuous or discrete. The aircraft, for example, may make discrete adjustments to its trim as altitude changes, while, in the factory example, machining proceeds continuously, even though the start and finish of a job are discrete changes. However, in most systems one type of change predominates, so that systems can usually be classified as being continuous or discrete.[33]

Iteration Specification

As indicated previously the simulation approach is characterized by iterative experimentation. The operations of a system may be simulated for numerous time periods and/or a repeated number of trials for any one or more periods may be carried out to ensure obtaining an adequate sample of data. When the simulation being utilized is a manual one, the experimenter can simply go ahead and run the model for as many iterations as considered desirable, keeping track of each trial as it is carried out. When the simulation is to be computer-run, on the other hand, specification of the iterative procedures to be utilized must be programmed in advance. For example, suppose that a firm is simulating certain phases of its production system in order to determine the effect of various proposed raw materials ordering rules on its inventory levels, and that it has been decided to simulate the operations on a weekly period basis for four years. If only one proposed ordering rule is to be tested at a time, the computer would have to be instructed to carry out 208 iterations (4 years times 52 weeks). Each such iteration is sometimes referred to as a model *cycle*. Further, it would be necessary in the programming to define the *end point* for each cycle—i.e., to specify

---

[32] All of these languages except CSMP are discussed in Geoffrey Gordon, *System Simulation* (Englewood Cliffs, N.J.: Prentice-Hall, Inc., 1969). For greater depth into the widely used SIMSCRIPT, see Forrest Paul Wyman, *Simulation Modeling: A Guide to Using SIMSCRIPT* (New York: John Wiley & Sons, Inc., 1970).

[33] Gordon, *System Simulation*, p. 4.

that when the last necessary calculation for any given cycle has been completed, the computer should initiate computations for the next cycle (week). It would also be necessary to program the simulation so that the number of cycles already completed in the run are kept track of—this would be accomplished by building an *index* into the program which is incremented by one each time that a cycle of the model is iterated. After the index has reached the desired number of cycles (208 in the example) the computer would be instructed to terminate the run.

If the firm wanted to test numerous ordering rules as indicated previously, it might well not want to test them one at a time as we have been describing. Rather the computer program might be structured so as to permit several (or all) of the proposed rules to be tested in one run. This would obviate the necessity of setting up the experiment and reading the simulation program into the computer several different times. If such multiple testing were undertaken, of course, additional end point and indexing specifications would be necessary—i.e., the computer would have to be instructed to initiate testing of the second ordering rule for the first week of operation after the last calculation for the 208th week with the first rule tested had been completed, and so on; and the computer would have to keep track of the number of 208-cycle tests already completed as well as the number of cycles completed in each test.

Input-Output Specification

In addition to specifying the iterative procedures to be utilized, it is necessary for the simulation designer to give attention both to the data which he plans to "feed in" to his model (input) and to the results which he wants the model to generate (output). In this section some of the characteristics of simulation inputs and outputs will be discussed.

Simulation Inputs. Some simulation inputs represent values which define the state of the system being simulated at a given point in time. In a simulation of a production operation, for example, an input value of 500 might be fed into the model to specify that 500 units of raw materials inventory are to exist for a particular item at the beginning of week one of the simulation. Other input values may be ones which help describe the relationships between certain variables in the simulation—e.g., in a production simulation the value $2.50 might be inputted to specify that labor costs are to be $2.50 for each nonovertime hour of work performed on certain operations in the system.[34]

---

[34] It should be noted that values such as the one given in this example may or may not be structured as inputs to a computer program in a strict technical sense. In some cases, the $2.50 labor cost definition may be written into the computer program itself—e.g., as in the following equation $NLC = \$2.50\ NHW$; where NLC represents nonovertime labor costs, and NHW, nonovertime hours worked. It is often more convenient, however, to structure a program so that the $2.50 would

In some simulations, all inputs are defined prior to the beginning of the first cycle of the run. In certain such cases, the outputs from the first cycle of the run may then serve as inputs to the second cycle, and so on. To use the production system as an example again, after week one of operations has been simulated, the raw materials inventories may have increased from an initial value of 500 to a level of 700 units, and this ending inventory level for week one (an output from cycle 1) would serve as an input into the second cycle. In certain types of simulations, on the other hand, it may be necessary to "plug in" new input values as the simulation progresses. For example, in a man-machine simulation of an air-defense direction center, numerous input data such as blips on a radarscope simulating the locating of aircraft were continually "fed in" to the system to be responded to by personnel participating in the experimentation.[35]

Simulation Outputs. The kinds of results generated from a simulation, or its outputs, will vary considerably depending upon the objectives of the experimentation. In some cases, management may be interested only in certain overall measures of system performance. For example, in a simple computerized simulation designed by one of the authors, probability distributions for two variables effecting cost savings with a new machine investment over a period of years are fed into the model, and a frequency distribution of present values for the investment are outputted.[36] In this model, the program was not written to print out cost savings data for each year, since the objective of the simulation was simply to provide present value data for the whole economic life of the investment. In other cases, however, management may find it desirable to print out data for each cycle of the simulation run. This would be the case when a dynamic oscillating system was being simulated, and management was interested in the patterns of change in the system over time. For instance, in testing new ordering rules in a production system as was discussed previously, it might be important to know how, and by how much inventory levels fluctuated each week. Finally, with respect to outputs, it should be pointed out that sometimes it is essential to know something not only about overall system performance, but also about

---

represent an input—e.g., to write in the program the equation $NLC = C_n NHW$; where C_n represents the hourly nonovertime labor rate. In this way C_n the hourly nonovertime labor cost parameter can be *varied* any time the simulation user so desires, by simply punching a new input card (assuming the computer utilizes this type of input). If the $2.50 were specified in the program *itself*, on the other hand, it would be necessary to *recompile* the program every time this figure needed to be changed. (Compilation is a process in which programs written in such computer languages as FORTRAN are translated by the computer into machine language).

[35] See, Robert L. Chapman et al., "Air Defense Experiments."

[36] This unpublished model is patterned after the approach suggested in David B. Hertz, "Risk Analysis in Capital Investment," *Harvard Business Review*, 42 (January-February 1964), pp. 95–106.

the performance of one or more of the system's *subsystems*—either with respect to their state at each cycle of the run or to their performance for the run *in toto*. It is to this facet of simulation structuring—the design of subsystems—that attention will next be turned.

Subsystems

Systems being simulated, especially more complex ones, may often be made up of fairly well-defined subsystems, which are linked together in one manner or another. For example, physical production in a furniture factory moves sequentially through four operational subsystems—rough mill to finish mill to assembly to final finishing. It is useful in designing simulations of such systems to segment the model into parts corresponding to these subsystems. Such subsystem segmentation may permit greater flexibility both in the design and operation of a simulation. For example, suppose that the management of a furniture factory wished to test among other things via simulation the advisability of purchasing kilns to dry green lumber as opposed to its present practice of buying already dried lumber. If the total simulation were segmented into subsystems paralleling those in the real operation, a subsystem representing the drying operation might easily be inserted into the model prior to the rough mill subsystem in place of the existing "purchasing of dried lumber" subsystem. Without this segmentation in the model, the simulation might require considerable redesign each time that management wanted to test the effect of such changes in the operations. In addition, subsystem segmentation may make it possible to test the effects of proposed policies on only one (or more) subsystems without the need to run the *total* simulation. The management of the furniture firm, for instance, may seek to test the impact of substituting improved machines for existing equipment in the finishing mill. This modification might have no impact outside of the finish mill subsystem. In such a case considerable savings could be realized by restricting the experimentation to just this one subsystem.

As was indicated in the previous section, it is often desirable to design simulations so that subsystem as well as overall system outputs are generated. The uefulness of such an approach may be illustrated by reference again to the furniture factory example. Suppose that management were simulating the impact upon its cost structure of increasing the variety of its furniture suites to be produced. Such a proposed course of action might increase labor costs considerably in the finish mill, moderately in rough milling and assembly, and only slightly in the finishing subsystem. Without the generation of subsystem cost outputs, the firm's only knowledge of its proposed policy would be with respect to total costs. Such overall data might, of course, be sufficient for evaluating the proposed course of action. Subsystems analysis, however, would permit a greater insight into the specific factors contributing to total costs. Management could determine, for example, the number and type of extra workers that it would need to acquire in each department. If no such information were generated from the simulation as to what would happen *within* the individual departments (subsystems), additional detailed studies might be required before the new policy could be effected.

Variables and Relationships

Of prime importance in designing simulations is specifying the variables which are to be incorporated into the model and defining the relationships which are to exist among the variables. Attention will now be focused on these facets of simulation structuring.

Variables. As mentioned previously, variables may be classed as independent, dependent, or intervening. In simulations, independent variables—which represent experimentally controlled factors, the value of which affects the values of other variables—are invariably structured as model inputs. For example, if management were testing the impact of a number of ordering rules upon total costs in a production-inventory simulation, the quantity of parts or materials purchased as specified by the rules would represent an independent variable. Conversely, in such a simulation, total costs, which are determined by the quantities purchased (among other factors), would represent a dependent variable, and a simulation output. Intervening between total costs and quantities purchased would be a number of other variables—e.g., average inventory levels, which when multiplied by carrying costs/unit would give total carrying costs; and ordering costs, which when added to total carrying costs, would give total inventory costs.

Three other observations are in order concerning simulation variables. First, the dependent variables are invariably outputted from the model, since it is how they behave when any one or more independent variables are manipulated that the simulation designer is primarily interested in. Second, intervening variables, on the other hand, may or may not be so outputted, depending upon the objectives of the simulation. As indicated earlier, for example, in simulating some dynamic production systems, management may be interested in examining the intervening variable "inventory levels" at the end of each simulation cycle. In other cases, however, it may be considered necessary only to output values for a dependent variable such as "total costs." Finally, it should be mentioned that the distinction between independent, intervening, and dependent variables is somewhat arbitrary. In some man-machine simulations, for example, certain human variables under such may be interdependent—e.g., positive sentiments among two or more group members may help contribute to "successful" performance, while successful performance may also serve to increase positive sentiments. Further, the *same* variable may be structured as one of a different type from one simulation to another. To illustrate with reference to a production-inventory system again, in one simulation an ordering policy may be the experimentally controlled independent variable as described earlier; while in another, management may frame the simulation problem as follows: "*given* an ordering rule that we have already decided to use, how would our total costs be influenced by different worker assignment decision rules?" In this latter case, the "given" set of ordering decisions would intervene (somewhere in the model) between the independent variable being experimentally tested (worker assignment) and the dependent variable, total costs.

Relationships among Variables. In addition to specifying simulation variables, the model designer must define the relationships which are to exist among these variables. For purposes of convenience, simulation relationships may be classified as being either of the two types mentioned briefly earlier—deterministic, and probabilistic (or stochastic). In deterministic relationships, the value of the dependent variable is absolutely determined by the values of the other variables in the relation. Such relationships may be linear or curvilinear, or step- or kinked-functions may be utilized depending upon just what relations management is attempting to simulate.

A relation among two or more variables is classed as stochastic if at least one of the variables assumes multiple values, the frequency of occurrence of which may be described by a probability distribution. For example, management might find that the service life of one of the parts of a machine which it utilizes conforms to the probability distribution illustrated in Figure 19–1. Probability distributions utilized

Figure 19–1.   Probability Distribution (hypothetical example)

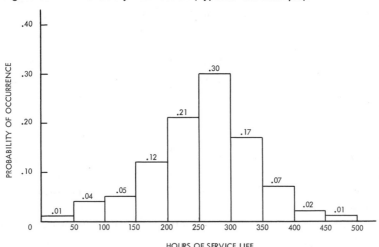

HOURS OF SERVICE LIFE

in simulation models are sometimes standard statistical ones, such as the normal or Poisson. In many cases, however, they are not. In fact, it is frequently for those situations in which actual distributions observed in the real system *cannot* be approximated by any standard distributions that simulation processes may be most useful.

One other observation is in order concerning the relationships among simulation variables. As was pointed out previously, simulation is utilized primarily when algorithms do not exist for the solution of managerial problems, or when the application of such analytical techniques is not feasible. Further, variables which are related stochastically involve more computational and manipulative problems than those related deterministically, *ceteris paribus*. For these reasons, it has been for systems (or problems) involving stochastic relationships that a great many simulation models have been designed. If the relationships among variables in a system can all be stated deterministically, the problem can often be dealt with analytically *unless* the system is a fairly complex one. Thus, simulation is primarily utilized with stochastic or *complex* deterministic systems; its use is rarely justified with simple deterministic problems.

Handling Stochastic Variables: The Monte Carlo Technique

In designing stochastic simulation models, it is necessary to have a means for dealing with those probabilistic variables, the values of which assume a frequency distribution. One commonly utilized method for working with stochastic variables in simulation models is the so-called Monte Carlo technique. This technique is one which both has application to an almost endless variety of simulation problems and at the same time, is relatively simple to comprehend and easy to utilize (although for many problems it requires the use of a computer). In this section the application of the Monte Carlo technique will be illustrated by utilizing an inventory problem under conditions of risk as an example.

Assume that a retailing firm wants to develop an inventory ordering rule for a product for which both demand on any given day and the lead time required between its order and receipt are variable. Assume further that, on the basis of previous experience, the firm's management has derived probability distributions for both demand and lead time, as illustrated in Figure 19–2.

By simulating numerous days of experience given these probabilities, management could determine the impact of various possible ordering rules upon such variables as inventory levels, number of orders placed, and lost sales. Then, if costs could be assigned to these variables, a basis would be provided for evaluating the proposed ordering rules and choosing from among them a preferred course of action.

To illustrate the utilization of Monte Carlo with this problem, assume

Figure 19–2. Demand and Lead Time Probabilities

Daily Demand (Units)	Probability of Occurrence*	Lead Time (Days)	Probability of Occurrence
30	.10	1	.10
35	.20	2	.50
40	.40	3	.40
45	.25	Σ	1.00
50	.05		
Σ	1.00		

* These probabilities are assumed to be the same regardless of day of week for purpose of simplification.

that management wants to test over a 15-day period the following two ordering rules:

1. Whenever inventories at the beginning of a day have fallen to a level of 80 or below, reorder 80 units.
2. Whenever inventories at the beginning of a day have fallen to 120 or below, reorder 120 units.

In actual practice, of course, management would probably try out more possible rules than these two (the choice of which was somewhat arbitrary) and a simulated experience of more than 15 days would be required to obtain an adequate sample. However, this limited examination of two rules will serve to illustrate the application of the Monte Carlo technique.

A basic problem in running this simulation is to select values for lead times and demand such that they will represent or mirror the probabilities assumed to exist in the real system. This would mean that, as the model is iterated, lead times with a length of from one to three days, and demand levels of from 30 to 50 units per day be utilized *in proportion to* the frequency that each of these conditions is expected to occur in the real system. One method of achieving this objective would be as follows:

1. To simulate the demand distribution, place 100 balls in an urn: with 10 of them marked "30 units" (since this demand level occurs *10 percent of the time*); 20 marked "35 units" (which occurs 20 percent of the time); and so on. Next, "select" a ball at random,

and use the number of units indicated thereon as demand for the first day of the simulation. Replacing this ball, then draw another to provide a demand value for the second day of the simulation, and so on, for each of the 15 days to be simulated.

2. To simulate the lead times, place 100 balls in an urn, with 10 of them marked "1 day"; 50, "2 days"; and 40, "3 days." Then, each time that it is necessary to place an order (following the proposed ordering rule), draw a ball at random to obtain a value for the lead time required for that order.

As yet, computers have not been designed to accommodate either urns or balls, nor is it convenient for managers, professors, or students to carry such equipment around with them. Fortunately, however, an equivalent process for random sampling with replacement has been developed. This involves first taking 100 *numbers* (say 0–99) rather than balls, and assigning the occurrence of an event to a *proportion* of these numbers *equal to* the probability of the event's occurrence. Thus, in the problem, we would assign to the numbers 0–99, lead times and daily demand levels as is shown in Figure 19–3. Then, a number from

Figure 19–3. Assignment of Lead Times and Daily Demand Levels

Lead Time (Days)	Probability of Occurrence	Occurrence Assigned to Numbers:	Daily Demand (Units)	Probability of Occurrence	Occurrence Assigned to Numbers:
1	.10	0–09	30	.10	0–9
2	.50	10–59	35	.20	10–29
3	.40	60–99	40	.40	30–69
			45	.25	70–94
			50	.05	95–99

0 to 99 is generated randomly for each demand and lead time iteration (as one would draw a ball randomly if an urn were to be used); and the event assigned to the number generated is considered as having occurred in the simulation. This random selection of numbers may be accomplished:

1. In manual simulations by using a *table of random numbers,* numerous of which have been published and are readily available.[37]

---

[37] Frequently utilized is the RAND Corporation's *A Million Random Digits,* (Glencoe, Ill.: The Free Press, 1955). See, for example, Ricciardi et al., *Top Management Decision Simulation,* pp. 36–37; or Clough, *Management Science,* p. 394. A table

2. In computerized simulations, by building a random number generator into the simulation program.[38]

These various stages of the Monte Carlo process are schematically diagrammed in Figure 19–4.

Figure 19–4. The Monte Carlo Process

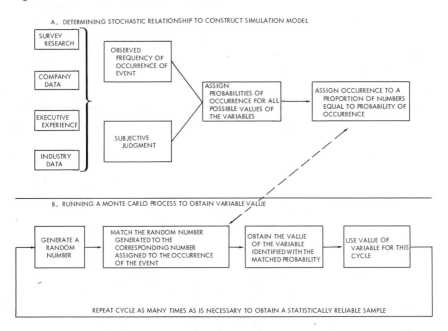

Returning to the inventory problem, the random numbers shown in Figure 19–5 were selected randomly from Appendix C, following the procedures outlined above, were assigned to the demand levels and lead times as also illustrated in Figure 19–5.

Given these data the inventory problem may be simulated with both of the proposed ordering rules specified previously. Taking the "reorder 80 units when inventory falls to 80 or below" rule and assuming that the system starts with an inventory of just 80 units (with the first order thus being placed at the beginning of the first day), the simulated system

of pseudo-random numbers is also provided for the reader's use in Appendix C at the end of this text. The word pseudo is used here for the following reason. From the "purist theoretical" point of view, no random number generator developed is *completely* random. For practical purposes, however, generators have been developed which are random enough for the solution of problems. The pseudo-random number generator used in this example and in Appendix C of the text was developed by utilization of a computer routine.

[38] Or, with some computers it is possible to program the simulation so as to make use of a random number generating subroutine incorporated in the computer system itself.

Figure 19–5. Monte Carlo Generation of Demand Levels and Lead Times

	For the 80-Unit Rule			For the 120-Unit Rule	
	Demand Levels			Demand Levels	
Day	Random Number Chosen	Represents Demand Level of:*	Day	Random Number Chosen	Represents Demand Level of:*
1	46	40	1	86	45
2	31	40	2	13	35
3	19	35	3	40	40
4	48	40	4	83	45
5	57	40	5	54	40
6	92	45	6	60	40
7	00	30	7	04	30
8	34	40	8	86	45
9	51	40	9	03	30
10	11	35	10	44	40
11	79	45	11	97	50
12	23	35	12	47	40
13	16	35	13	73	45
14	33	40	14	49	40
15	56	40	15	49	40
	Lead Times			Lead Times	
Order Number	Random Number Chosen	Represents Lead Time of:*	Order Number	Random Number Chosen	Represents Lead Time of:*
1	69	3	1	38	2
2	61	3	2	82	3
3	24	2	3	38	2
4	53	2	4	64	3
5	51	2	5	09	1
6	22	2			

*From Figure 19–3.

Note: Random numbers were chosen as follows. One number in Appendix C was randomly chosen for the 80-unit rule and the remainder of the random numbers down to all 15 days and including those for all orders were those numbers succeeding it consecutively columnwise. The same procedure was followed for the 120-unit rule. The starting random numbers randomly chosen happened to be the 10th number in column 1 of Appendix C (46) for the 80-unit rule; and the 9th number in column 6 of Appendix C (86) for the 120-unit rule.

Figure 19–6.   Inventory Simulation with 80-Unit Reorder Rule

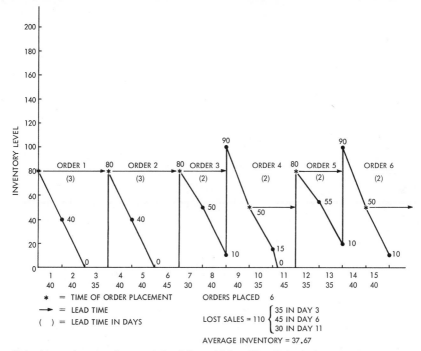

Note: Average inventory is computed as follows: (1) by adding the beginning and ending inventory figures for each day; (2) summing these 15 sums, (3) dividing this figure by 2 to get an average inventory figure, and (4) finally dividing this result by 15, the number of days in the simulation. (In days 3, 6, and 11, ending inventory will be zero, not the 80 figure shown, since this represents the new order arriving at the *beginning* of the following day.)

for the 15 days behaves as is illustrated in Figure 19–6. With the 120-unit reorder rule (and assuming an inventory of 120 units at the beginning of the first day), the system will behave as is shown in Figure 19–7.[39] As may be noted from these figures (and as would be expected from the discussion of inventories in the previous chapter), with the 120-unit reorder rule:

1. Average inventories are higher (68.33 as opposed to 37.67 units with the 80-unit rule),
2. Fewer lost sales occur as compared with the 80-unit rule (45 as opposed to 110), and
3. One less order is placed (5 as opposed to 6).

One important point should be stressed with respect to these data. The two ordering rules were simulated only *once*, with one set of random

---

[39] With both of these ordering rules, we are assuming that no orders will be placed while any previous order is still outstanding—e.g., no order is placed in days 2 and 3 in Figure 19–6 since the order placed in day 1 has not yet been received.

Figure 19–7. Inventory Simulation with 120-Unit Reorder Rule

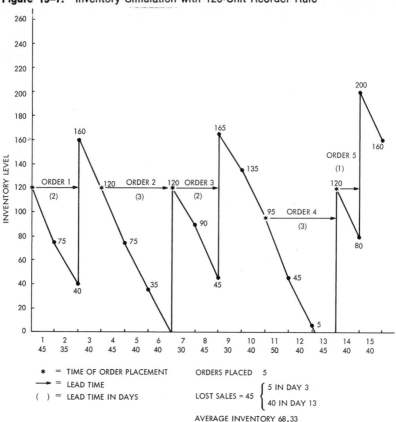

Note: Average inventory is computed as noted in Figure 19–6.

numbers. If a second simulation were run with different random numbers, the data might well be different—e.g., average inventories might be higher *or* lower, say 73 or 63, and 42 or 32, for the 120- and 80-unit rules, respectively. If enough samples were run, however, the variables such as average inventory or lost sales would tend to *converge*, however, so that the data would provide a fairly accurate representation of the real system.

To evaluate these two ordering rules, management would have to next define the costs which would be expected with each. For illustrative purposes, assume that it costs $5 to place each order; that the cost of each "lost sale" is estimated to be $1; and that, for a 15-day period, as simulated, inventory carrying costs are believed to be about $2 for each unit of average inventory carried. In such a case, the total costs expected for each ordering rule would be computed as is illustrated in Figure 19–8. As may be noted from Figure 19–8, with the *specific*

Figure 19–8.   Comparison of Costs for Two Ordering Rules

80-Unit Ordering Rule	*120-Unit Ordering Rule*
Lost Sales 110 $\times$ \$1 = \$110	45 $\times$ \$1 = \$45
Ordering Costs 6 $\times$ \$5 = \$30	5 $\times$ \$5 = \$25
Inventory Costs 37.67 $\times$ \$2 = \$75.34	68.33 $\times$ \$2 = \$136.66
Total Costs = \$215.34	Total Costs = \$206.66

parameters given and with *only one iteration* with each ordering rule, the 120-unit rule would be least costly for management.

THE FUTURE OF SIMULATION

As was indicated previously, simulation has increased in utilization considerably in recent years, not only in many different areas within the business organization, but by other organizations and for other purposes as well. Current evidence indicates that this trend will continue in the future.

Among the types of simulation that appear to hold special promise for the manager are on-line simulations, sometimes referred to as Interactive Decision Simulation. The essential characteristic of on-line simulations which distinguishes them from other simulations, is that they permit the manager to "communicate" directly with the computerized simulation and receive immediate answers to his questions. As Boulden has pointed out, with Interactive Decision Simulation, the manager must "continue to be an active partner in the decision-making process. The computer is invaluable for its memory capacity and computational ability, but the manager must be on line for his judgment, experience and intuition."[40] Boulden goes on to point out that on line simulation is *conversational*. That is: "Interaction between the computer and the manager is essential. . . . The response [from the computer] must be immediate to facilitate the manager's creative process and maintain his continuity of thought. The manager asks the computer 'what if' questions, and the computer quickly responds."[41]

Although at least 300 on-line decision models for 40 major corporations had been developed as of 1970,[42] some questions may be raised concerning this apparently promising approach. First, not only must the manager

[40] James B. Boulden, "Interactive Decision Simulation: A Revolution in Management," *Academy of Management Proceedings,* Thirtieth Annual Meeting, San Diego, California, August 23–26, 1970, p. 349.

[41] Ibid.

[42] Ibid., p. 346.

favor and support the use of the system, but he must also understand how he can operate it most effectively. Second, often considerable time is needed after the completion of an experimental test of proposed courses of action before the meaning of its results is known because lengthy analysis of the simulation outputs is required. The simulation may take but a short period whereas the analysis of it may take weeks. Therefore to employ a simulation for on-line operating decisions would require construction of methods of data reduction and analysis such that rapid conclusions could be reached when the manager "converses" with the computer. If this is accomplished, and as long as the operating characteristics of the real system undergo no fundamental changes, rapidity of analysis can be built into an integrated data processing and simulation decision system.

SUMMARY

Simulation provides an approach for dealing with managerial decision problems for which analytical methods either do not exist, or cannot be feasibly applied. Iterative and experimental in nature, simulation permits the testing of various proposed managerial strategies under different conditions without disrupting the real system. Further, simulation is a more flexible tool than are many currently used operations research techniques (e.g., linear programming)—the technique has been applied to many diverse types of managerial and other types of problems. In spite of this diversity, there are many general characteristics of model structuring common to most simulations—e.g., the specification of the iterative procedures to be utilized, and of the inputs, outputs, variables, and relationships among variables.

Simulations have been designed to replicate both deterministic and stochastic systems. When stochastic variables are being simulated, the Monte Carlo technique is often highly useful. Through random number generation, Monte Carlo provides a means of selecting values for the stochastic variables in the model so that they will approximate those probabilities assumed to exist in the real system. Simulation is being increasingly used to deal with managerial problems. In the future, this utilization should continue to grow, with on-line simulations holding considerable promise for management decision making.

DISCUSSION AND STUDY QUESTIONS

1. Why is simulation utilized as an optimizing technique "when all else fails"?
2. Why has simulation expanded so rapidly as a useful problem-solving technique?
3. What are the two basic types of computer simulation languages which have been developed?

4. In designing simulation models, what do we mean by "iteration specification"?

5. What are the differences between ordinary and on-line simulations? What are the values and limitations of each?

6. Comment on the following: "Since simulations are basically nonanalytical in nature, one will not find simulations using such analytical techniques discussed earlier in this text, as the transportation method."

7. Why do simulations usually call for repeated trials?

8. What advantages may be obtained from providing for the subsystem analysis approach when designing simulation models?

9. How may simulations be utilized in training individuals in an organization?

10. *a)* Given the probability distribution as in Figure 19–3, randomly select a number from Appendix C and following the procedure given in Figure 19–5 use the random numbers you have chosen to get lead times and demand for 15 days of inventory simulation as in the text.

    b) Draw diagrams of the simulation behavior you obtained as in Figures 19–6 and 19–7 of the text.

    c) Compute the total costs associated with each ordering rule using the same ordering, inventory and cost of lost sales given in the Monte Carlo example in the text. How does your cost data compare with that given for two examples in the text. Why?

    d) Following the same procedure as above, test over a 15-day period, the ordering rules: (1) whenever inventories at the beginning of the day have fallen to 40 units, reorder 40; and whenever inventories have fallen to 200 units at the beginning of the day, reorder 200.

    e) How can you relate your findings in this problem to inventory theory?

11. Sensitivity analysis as discussed in relation to linear programming in Chapter 17 is essentially a simulation approach. Comment.

12. A job shop producing to order is considering testing alternate dispatch rules to be used by departmental foremen in selecting which orders in the shop to process first. A series of orders received during the last six months is to be used to test the alternate policies. How would you go about designing a simulation to do this? Explain what information you would need, and how you would use it.

SELECTED REFERENCES

BAUER, R. A., and BUZZELL, R. D. "Mating Behavioral Science and Simulation," *Harvard Business Review*, 42 (September-October 1964), 116–24.

BORKO, HAROLD (ed.). *Computer Applications in the Behavioral Sciences.* Englewood Cliffs, N.J.: Prentice-Hall, Inc., 1962, chaps. 14, 15, 21, 23, 24.

BOULDEN, JAMES B. "Interactive Decision Simulation: A Revolution in Management," in the *Academy of Management Proceedings,* Thirtieth Annual Meeting, San Diego, California, August 23–26, 1970, 345–54.

BOWMAN, EDWARD H., and FETTER, ROBERT. *Analysis for Production and Operations Management.* 3d ed. Richard D. Irwin, Inc., 1967, chap. 11.

CHAPMAN, ROBERT, et al. "The System Research Laboratory's Air Defense Experiments," *Management Science,* 5 (April 1959), 250–68.

CHU, KONG. *Quantitative Methods for Business and Economic Analysis.* Scranton, Pa.: International Textbook Company, 1969, chap. 9.

CHU, KONG, and NAYLOR, THOMAS H. "A Dynamic Model of the Firm," *Management Science,* 11 (May 1965), 736–50.

CONWAY, R. W.; JOHNSON, B. M.; and MAXWELL, W. L. "Some Problems of Digital Systems Simulation," *Management Science,* 6 (October 1959).

FORRESTER, JAY W. *Industrial Dynamics.* Cambridge, Mass.: The MIT Press, 1961.

FORRESTER, JAY W. *World Dynamics.* Cambridge, Mass.: Wright-Allen Press, Inc., 1971.

GEISLER, M. A. "The Simulation of a Large-Scale Military Activity," *Management Science,* 5 (July 1959).

GORDON, GEOFFREY. *System Simulation.* Englewood Cliffs, N.J.: Prentice-Hall, Inc., 1969.

GUETZKOW, HAROLD (ed.). *Simulation in Social Science.* Englewood Cliffs, N.J.: Prentice-Hall, Inc., 1962.

HOGGATT, A. C., and BALDERSTON, F. E. (eds.). *Symposium on Simulation Models: Methodology and Applications to the Behavioral Science.* Cincinnati, Ohio: South-Western Publishing Co., 1963.

HOVLAND, C. I. "Computer Simulation of Learning," *American Psychologist,* 15 (1960).

JACKSON, J. R. "Simulation Research on Job Shop Production," *Naval Research Logistics Quarterly,* December 1957.

KAUFMAN, GORDON M., and PENCHANSKY, ROY. "Simulation Study of Union Health and Benefit Funds," *Industrial Management Review,* 10 (Fall 1968), 41–60.

MALCOLM, D. G. (ed.). *Report of System Simulation Symposium.* Baltimore, Md.: Waverly Press, Inc., 1957.

NAYLOR, THOMAS H. et al. *Computer Simulation Techniques.* New York: John Wiley & Sons, Inc., 1966.

Proceedings of the 1971 Summer Computer Simulation Conference. Denver, Colo.: Board of Simulation Conferences, 1971.

SCHREIBER, ALBERT N. (ed.) *Corporate Simulation Models.* Providence, R.I.: College on Simulation and Gaming of the Institute of Management Science; and Seattle, Wash.: Graduate School of Business Administration of the University of Washington, 1970.

SHUBIK, M. "Bibliography on Simulation, Gaming, Artificial Intelligence, and Allied Topics," *American Statistical Association Journal,* 55 (December 1960), 736–38.

SMITH, ROBERT D., and GREENLAW, PAUL S. "Simulation of a Psychological Thought Process in Personnel Selection," *Management Science*, 13 (April 1967), B409–19.

TOCHER, K. D. *The Art of Simulation*. Princeton, N.J.: D. Van Nostrand Co., 1963.

WAGNER, HARVEY. *Principles of Operations Research*. Englewood Cliffs, N.J.: Prentice-Hall, Inc., 1969, chap. 21.

Patterns in Management: A Tentative Theory

THE PREVIOUS CHAPTERS have been devoted to an examination of the many aspects of organizational and managerial behavior presented around a decision-making framework. The primary purpose of this chapter is to integrate these parts into an overall insightful conceptual view of the management process. It should be pointed out that the discussion of aspects of management systems in this conceptual framework is simply *suggestive* rather than *exhaustive*. Further, it is important to note that the word "tentative" has been used in entitling this chapter for the following reasons. Some of the specific propositions put forth have been based directly on research results previously reported in the text. Others have been based on the inferences drawn from both sound research and management thought in general. Still others are of a more hypothetical nature based on logical extensions from research and theory.

TYPES OF PROBLEMS

Since management is centrally concerned with making decisions to solve problems, it is useful to classify the types of problems in such a way that different decision-making techniques, organization structures, leadership styles, planning methods and control processes can be related to these distinct types of problems.

For this purpose, it is possible to distinguish among problems by classifying them along two dimensions: (1) *complexity*, with few variables bearing upon a problem indicating relative simplicity and a large number of factors indicating complexity, and (2) *uncertainty*, with deterministic problem variables indicating certainty, probabalistic variables suggesting some uncertainty and ignorance indicating high uncertainty.

Figure 20–1. Problem Types

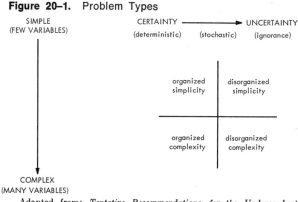

Adapted from: *Tentative Recommendations for the Undergraduate Mathematics Program of Students in the Biological, Management and Social Sciences* (Berkeley, Calif.: Committee on the Undergraduate Program in Mathematics, 1964), p. 12.

This classificatory framework is shown in Figure 20–1. Lawrence and Lorsch describe uncertainty (in discussing environmental factors influencing decision making) as information which (1) lacks clarity, (2) has a long time span for definitive feedback, and (3) possesses uncertainty about causal relationships.[1] Their definition is appropriate to the discussion that follows. Highly certain problems possess the opposing information characteristics of clarity, short-term feedback, and relative certainty concerning causal relations.

The classification in Figure 20–1 is somewhat arbitrary since both uncertainty and complexity actually range over a continuum rather than being dichotomized into the two classes shown. Obviously, the number of certain variables can range from one to thousands, and similarly for the number of stochastic variables or those about which there is little prior information. Thus, both uncertainty and complexity are relative matters.

Organizations versus Problem Types

For an organization whose problems are relatively simple and certain, a relatively nondifferentiated plain line type of organization structure tends to be sufficient and appropriate (see Figure 20–2).

A company owning its own timber and selling furniture it manufactures in long-term contracts would exemplify a company in a situation of organized simplicity. The processes it has to deal with are few and relatively certain. If such a company were very large, however, holding

---

[1] Paul Lawrence and Jay Lorsch, *Organization and Environment* (Homewood, Ill.: Richard D. Irwin, Inc., 1969), chap. 4.

Figure 20–2. Organization Features versus Problem Types

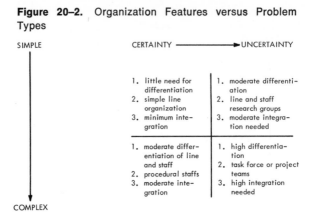

a number of different timber sources (or hedging its lumber buying) with multiple manufacturing plants, the uncertainty of their decision variables is not greatly different. There are just more variables than in the simple case. As a consequence, the increased complexity resulting from more factors would suggest a need for a staff of people to set forth these relations in the forms of policies and procedures that each of the line departments will follow. Differentiation of staff structure tends to occur because of the greater complexity.

If the number of factors inherent in the problems facing the firm is small but some of them are uncertain, a different tendency toward differentiation is observed. Standard procedures cannot be applied because of the difficulty in predicting what will happen. Rather, studies to determine the nature of uncertainty in the influencing variables is needed. A research task group, possibly in the form of staff differentiation, appears appropriate. Thus, either complexity or uncertainty creates the need for differentiation, but the former tends to introducing procedural development while the latter suggests a research staff.

A firm with a relatively simple product line might experience unexplained variation in the demands for its products over time. Such variation, if predicted, could be taken into account by production planning, manpower planning, inventory control, and the purchasing functions in the firm. The basic causes of product demand variation might arise from differing seasonal demands by several customer groups, customer orders being dependent upon the types of variation in their customer's uses or ordering policies, and so forth. To identify and predict such fluctuations, an expert statistical and marketing specialist rather than a line supervisor appears appropriate. Such need for expertise suggests differentiation of tasks in the firm to provide the staff research function in marketing. Such a solution deals effectively with disorganized simplicity.

When a task facing the firm is both complex and highly uncertain (a case of disorganized complexity) it is dysfunctional to attempt to utilize a fixed structure of organization to deal with it. Existing procedures and components of the organization are established to deal with familiar problems. The complex uncertain situation is unusual and a manager is unable to predetermine the appropriate approaches, techniques, or variables. Under these conditions, a flexible rather than fixed group or organization appears most useful. A project group or task force approach, usually temporary in nature, is appropriate for a solution of these types of problems. If the problem is transitory, the project team may be able to identify and define the nature of the complexity and uncertainty, establish decision approaches to be utilized in dealing with the problem and turn the results over to regular line and staff groups for operating on a day-to-day basis.

Most complex organizations have some components whose decision problems differ from those facing its other components. Thus, the type of structure most appropriate in a research and development lab might approach a project-matrix organizational form, while in the same firm the administration of the selling functions might more appropriately be a simple line organization form. All kinds of organizational variation appropriate to the varying degrees of complexity and uncertainty in task variables could conceivably exist within a single firm.

Furthermore, even within any one organizational unit, different types of problems occur although one type may predominate and exert the major influence on the type of organizational structure. In line and procedural staff organization for a manufacturing plant, for example, the decision to expand the plant and to rearrange the departmental locations is sufficiently different from the day-to-day activities that a committee or task force composed of members from the affected units might reasonably be formed to deal with the temporary increase in complexity and uncertainty facing the organization. Especially in view of the change process described in Chapter 11, in such an organization differentiation would appear to be appropriate. As the nature of problems facing a system varies, structural changes geared to dealing with these problems appear desirable even if the basic tasks remain unaltered.

Planning versus Problem Types

As organization structure varies with uncertainty and complexity of problems, so does planning tend to be affected in a similar manner. In the unit faced with organized simplicity, the need for long-range planning is at a minimum because the future is relatively predictable. Behavior and operating rules can be highly explicated. Standing plans can deal with the relatively few contingencies that occur. Habit oftentimes represents acceptable behavior. Many complex organizations would not fall into this planning category, but some subunits of complex forms when isolated from environmental variations could in effect, operate effectively with this mechanized planning approach.

As the number of relatively certain variables facing a decision group increase, the number of standing plans tend to increase to match the increased in variety. Therefore, the planning system is more complex to include variety and more interrelationships needing to be dealt with in the planning process. Plans are essentially short run although the planning lead time itself creates a reason for lengthening the planning horizon over that which obtains in the simplest case of a few variables characterized by certainty (see Figure 20–3).

Figure 20–3. Planning and Problem Types

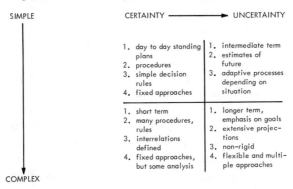

In considering the planning required by a system facing disorganized simplicity, the need for longer term planning becomes important. Variations in the variables affecting planning occur over time and, therefore, need to be estimated if planning is to accommodate these conditions. It is not possible to use fixed procedures since the proper course of action to take will depend upon the condition that exists in the future. Thus the use of standing plans will be contingent upon the condition appearing. The operational behavior is similarly adaptive to estimates and environmental cues about the nature of the condition the organization is experiencing.

For highly complex and uncertain problems, fixed rules, procedures, or standing plans also tend to be inappropriate. A greater tendency toward tailor-made, single-use planning is evident compared to the less uncertain and complex situations. The need for intermediate and long-term planning horizons to identify the probable movements in the variables is greater. Flexible, contingent, and innovative planning decisions are appropriate to the uncertain and complex situations.

The above discussion is in somewhat black and white terms with little consideration of the grays. A large complex organization may be faced with all types of problems simultaneously and be forced to engage in a corresponding variety of planning efforts. A market research unit dealing with a variety of customer, consumer, and environmental effects deals with uncertainty and complexity and if successful, tends to plan accordingly. Yet, at the same time, it may develop highly structured inviolate rules concerning the expense accounts for its members.

As pointed out in Chapter 12, the relative lack of planning for firms in a simple certain environment can be understood in those contexts. Little extra knowledge is gained by estimating future events. The information content of these estimates are low; there is little or no surprise in them. To plan ahead involves some staff costs, however, so that the tradeoffs between the costs and values of planning tend to indicate minimizing the planning function in the organized simplicity case.

Control versus Problem Types

Since plans form the basis for many variables to be controlled and their measures, the variations observed in the planning process have their counterparts in controlling operations. In an organization facing few problem variables possessing a relatively certain character, it is possible to maintain a close, if not continuous, watch over operations. Controls can be fairly comprehensive to encompass observation and adjustments as any operations deviate from norms. There is no need for a massive information system, however, because the number of variables influencing operations is relatively small. Furthermore, personal experience of managers and operators in the system leads to their learning the expected status of the system as part of their personal knowledge. Thus while extremely formalized controls are possible, there is less need for them (see Figure 20–4).

Figure 20–4. Control versus Problem Type

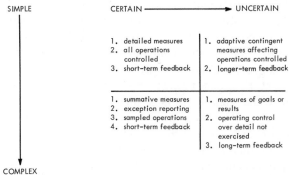

Consider the more complex but certain, case of controls in an organization facing problems with a great many variables. Here, relying upon only personal knowledge of the operating system would lack completeness and a formal control system is more of a necessity. In fact, there may be so many factors bearing upon a situation that the control system needs to be simplified from the masses of data that would be required if every variable were monitored. Data may consist of samples of organizational performance rather than reports involving a constant review. Exception reporting can reduce human processing time. Summative performance measures incorporating the combined effect of a number of variables can be reported instead of data concerning the detail. In such a case, deviations from normal may require a study to reveal which of the detailed variables are out of control. As a consequence, the corrective process includes an analytical phase, increasing the effective span of correction.

For organizations dealing with uncertain problems, the control process is, again, different. The span of corrective action tends to be longer because the control limits within which performance is acceptable tend to be wider than in the certain cases. Observations of a variance outside the control limits may represent a random deviation or an unacceptable performance. Corrective control taken in the former instance is wasted since the system really is not out of limits. Following this reasoning, the feedback interval for definitive information in uncertain problems tends to be longer than for the more certain instances.

Uncertainty of the causal factors bearing upon operations makes it difficult or impossible to establish a fixed corrective response rule for deviant observations. If the operating system has been studied over time, it may be possible to develop a repertoire of responses, each of which is appropriate to a particular out-of-control situation. If the control system is not so mature, however, innovative decisions for correction will be needed until the system learns which responses are appropriate to the sort of variance observed. In both the mature and less mature situations, adaptive responsiveness appropriate to the problem observed is relevant while fixed responses tend to be less useful.

In groups facing both high complexity and great uncertainty, the ability to exercise preconceived controls over detailed behaviors is severely restricted. In this instance, the work involves exploring possible relationships and testing alternatives for problems about which very little is known. The fact that one project expended $10.20 of computer cost per man-hour while another project only expended $3.67 is irrelevant for purposes of control over complex disorganized problems. More appropriate is control over achieving the objective of the work group involved. Of course, the original decision to enter into the work anticipated some costs and some benefits to the firm. Recognizing that these estimates must necessarily be imprecise, management initiates some uncertain, complex activities such as those partially on faith. Yet these activities cannot continue indefinitely without producing some results. As a consequence, these kinds of work normally are reviewed on some periodic basis to determine whether the original objectives can be achieved at all and, if so, what progress has been made toward that achievement. These status measures can be compared to the original cost estimates to see whether or not the cost/benefit ratios or other measures originally anticipated are still reasonable.

In authorizing high-risk work that involves high uncertainty and complexity, management is aware that failures and partial successes will occur; it gambles that the successes will outweigh the losses. At some point in the review process, management must have the fortitude to eliminate originally promising work on which excessive sums have been spent only to achieve a modicum of success. The agonizing aspect of such a cutoff is the realization that a breakthough may occur at any moment to allow original expectation to be achieved. Since the people working on the activity have invested heavily of their time and reputations, they often present an optimistic evaluation of eventual achievement. It is for these reasons that many projects drag on past their usefulness and constitute a drain on the resources of the firm. In contrast, too quick a cutoff results in the firm abandoning much work that could have been successful. Control judgment is obviously called for.

It should be noted that work of an uncertain and complex nature does not remain that way if it is repeated. The first time an organization undertakes its own advertising campaign, a great deal of uncertainty about effectiveness, costs, schedules, and relevance would be encountered even if the firm employed experienced advertising people. As experience is gained, less uncertainty about each of these factors exists, because a generalized experience allows closer predictions even though each advertising campaign is different. Departments working at the edges of the state of a rapidly advancing or changing knowledge are susceptible to uncertainty and, typically, complexity. Research groups for consumer analysis, transformation changes, and product development attempt to reduce the uncertainty and ignorance associated with the phenomena they are studying. The knowledge developed is relayed to other groups to use while the research groups revert to new problems. Thus the compatriot subsystems tend to deal with the more certain and less complex problems than do those groups dealing with problems at the edge of the state of the art.

Leadership versus Problem Types

In the previous sections, the nature of decision-making approaches, organization, planning, and controlling has been shown to differ with the degree of complexity and uncertainty of the problems facing the firm. As might be expected, variances in leader and follower behavior stem from these fundamentally different operating systems. In both the simple and complex but certain systems, operational methods and procedures, being predetermined on the basis of known variables, allow relatively little variability or innovative action. Only a small portion of the capabilities of individuals may be utilized and monotony of repetitive work may characterize the work force. Individuals with creative flair or an innovative bent will find less opportunity to employ these abilities than in the more uncertain environments. Some analytical skills are called for by the staffs in developing the planning and control systems, especially for the complex case, but a bureaucratic atmosphere is typical (see Figure 20–5).

Figure 20–5. Leadership versus Problem Types

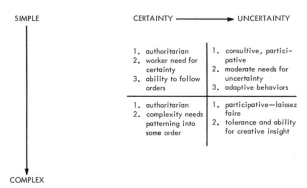

Leadership, in the certain case, tends to be autocratic in form because there are relatively few choices with which consultation or participation could be effective. While the system facing problems of a certain nature tend to call for authoritarian leadership, this need may be in conflict with the needs of individual workers for variety, variability, and exercise of discretion. One approach to this dilemma is to recruit and place in those jobs only individuals with high needs of dependency, for order, and for certainty. Then task requirements, leadership, and follower needs are congruent. Another approach is to seek worker participation in non-task activities such as the recreational or civic activities of the firm. Further, job enlargement and job rotation approaches change the task to introduce variety in a worker's job. By allowing participation in designing and scheduling these task rearrangements, a greater proportion of individuals may be able to be motivated than through an authoritarian approach alone. Enlargement and rotation tend to move the task from a case of organized simplicity to one of organized complexity, in effect. Furthermore, use of participation in the certainty cases is based on the needs of workers rather than those of the task system. If these two needs conflict, how is the problem to be resolved? Care needs to be taken by the leader to ensure that participative approaches not be used where the task requirements will lead to overruling his subordinates' decisions. As a compromise, the leader may consult with subordinates (reserving decisions to himself or his superiors) and utilize open communications rather than a clear shared power approach to leadership. Clearly, the nature of the relatively certain problems suggests less need for participative styles. Planning change, as was shown in Chapter 11, is most successful as shared powers, a participative approaches to the change are used. Switching leadership styles to accommodate participation may be especially difficult for an authoritarian manager if his previous success has been based on nonparticipative methods. Thus change efforts may be jeopardized if the system is geared to certain rather than changing conditions.

The incongruence between the task requirements in a simple-certain problem and individual needs raises the question of whether a human being is the appropriate "worker" to employ in dealing with work at that level. Indeed, it is precisely in this segment that automation is most effective.

Unlike the certain instances, uncertain problems are the ones calling for abilities of a more diverse and adaptable nature. In the highly complex and uncertain tasks, in fact, there may be few guidelines of acceptable behavior or performance. It may be possible to establish only a general goal of achievement. The individual may need to work through the means-ends-means chain to the solution himself. He is required to exhibit innovative and creative behavior for success. An individual who has a high aversion to risky choices and who wants to be told what to do and where he stands will tend to be unhappy with the responsibility for complex uncertain tasks.

Task requirements in the uncertain kinds of problems are suggestive of participative leadership styles and a considerable delegation of authority. If the proper approach to a problem can only be dimly perceived by management, the workers are going to need to test, adapt, and create. The degree of worker initiative required by the task appears to be directly related to the extent of uncertainty and complexity. In the highly uncertain and complex environment, the task may suggest a completely free laissez-faire leadership (even though workers might prefer more order and direction), and, as was shown above, the simple-certain task suggests an authoritarian style (even though workers might prefer less order and direction). Between these extremes, consultative and participative leadership appear appropriate.

Repetitiveness of Complexity and Uncertainty

It may be that a firm faces a degree of uncertainty about which external event it will face in a future period, but it may know that one of three events will occur. Furthermore, it may know the probability of occurrence of such event. Based on previous actions, a firm may know that if it introduces a new model of a product its main competitor will react with price cutting and increased advertising outlays, and hence plans can be made to offset these responses. However, there is always the possibility of a completely unanticipated unique competitive response. There is a degree of uncertainty in all external activities but the greater the repetitiveness of events in the uncertain environment, the greater is the possibility that appropriate programmed responses can be devised. Further, for completely different external events, it may be possible to use or adapt an already existing response. In general, the greater the repetitiveness of uncertainty and complexity factors, the more structured can the internal management system become.

Consistency in the Management System

If a management system is defined as the combined effect of structure, planning, control, leadership, individual behavior and decision making, one can observe patterns in the preceding discussions of these components as they are influenced by complexity and uncertainty. As less variety of variables and less uncertainty exist, a more structured system in terms of task needs, at least, is appropriate. Conversely, as more variables and greater uncertainty exist in the problems faced, the less structure and greater need for adaptability in the management system. While both uncertainty and complexity influence the system, it may be that uncertainty has the greatest influence. In his examination of decision systems (including hierarchy of authority, participation in decision making, impersonality in decisions, rule and procedures, and division of labor), Duncan found that groups were better able to deal with complexity than uncertainty.[2] If this finding holds across the total system, it implies that groups are better able to identify and deal effectively with a large number of variables than they are able to estimate uncertain factors and interrelations.

A management system is inconsistent if one or more of its components responds inappropriately to the degree of uncertainty and complexity of the problems it faces. If a highly articulate, talented, and innovative individual is placed in a simple organized system, he will tend to be a "duck out of water," unable to utilize his skills in the predetermined and highly structured system. College graduates, for example, may fail to get excited about routine military service which has a reputation (probably mostly undeserved) for placing the right man in the wrong job.

One firm selling consumer products exclusively to mail-order firms decided to market and distribute a similar product line itself. It patterned its new sales organization upon its former relatively simple

---

[2] Robert B. Duncan, "Characteristics of Organizational Environments and Perceived Environmental Uncertainty," Graduate School of Management, Northwestern University, working paper no. 62-71. Duncan examines uncertainty in what he calls a static-dynamic dimension, somewhat akin to the uncertainty concept described here.

organization structure. It floundered a long time before it realized that the greater uncertainty in its new selling functions required a differentiated staff for market research, product development, and advertising formerly performed by their customers. These new functions introduced new highly paid experts to the firm. The work of these groups needed to be coordinated with each other and with already existing departments such as production planning and customer service. The new "prima donnas," as they were viewed by the long-tenure employees, received little voluntary cooperation from them. No new coordinative positions were established so that the old information system became overburdened. The whole system faced greater variety of product demand and greater uncertainty, but management had not developed changes in structure, planning, controls, or expected behavior to deal with the changes. The firm floundered as it slowly "learned the ropes" in this new environment. The old system was partially inconsistent with the new needs.

Conditional Management

Throughout this book, we have noted that the most appropriate leadership style, decision technique, organization structure, and other elements in management decision making are "conditional," "dependent on a number of factors," or "situational." There is no one best way to manage. There are, instead, a variety of ways to manage appropriately, but there is much less variety in appropriate management systems *given the conditions* in which the decisions need to be made. That is, if the conditions *indigenous* upon the tasks that a particular unit has the responsibility for are complex and uncertain, then flexible innovative approaches are appropriate while fixed structured approaches are not. Since there are huge numbers of conditions that conceivably could influence a firm's operations and since the conditions facing each firm are unique to some extent, it would be possible that the management system for each firm could be appropriate and unique. This does not mean that there is no management theory. The discussions in this and other chapters has suggested that both complexity and uncertainty affect both normatively and descriptively the type of management system. Thus, one can both predict and prescribe the management system if he knows enough about the conditions affecting decision making in the organization. A conditional theory of management also suggests that copying the systems, the techniques, and the strategies of another firm, can be dysfunctional unless conditions facing them are similar.

Factors Underlying Complexity and Uncertainty

It has been shown that management systems are influenced by complexity and uncertainty. This section reviews and summarizes their sources. Partly the technology and its rate of change cause complexity and uncertainty. A firm building engine lathes faces a great deal less uncertainty in its research, product development, component manufacturing and assembly than does a computer manufacturer whose technology is in a state of flux. Other environmental elements such as the firm's customers, its competitors, governmental agencies, environmental societies, and civic groups can, from time to time, have either a transitory or a continuing influence upon the uncertainty or complexity facing the firm. The consumer and environmental movements in the United States are introducing a number of new factors to consider and evaluate in a firm's decision making and projections. The directions these movements may take are not certain so that it is not possible to program wholly appropriate responses in advance.

In Chapters 8 and 12, the concept of a strategic domain for the business was introduced as a factor influencing organizational differentiation and integration. When a firm chooses a strategy, of course, it carves out a portion of the environment with which it is going to deal and thus determines the degrees of complexity and uncertainty with which it will face. In evaluating strategies to diversify, expand or acquire, failure to give consideration to whether changes in the existing management system will be needed to accommodate different types of strategic uncertainty or complexity, can lead to inconsistencies in the management systems of the firm.

VARIATIONS FROM CONDITIONAL THEORY

While the preceding discussion in this chapter has suggested that the appropriate management system should or would be one that conforms to the degree of complexity and certainty of the decision variables facing it, some successful organizations have deviated from this expected congruence. It has already been shown that to accommodate needs for wider expression and variety on the part of workers some firms have introduced job rotation and enlargement despite the fact that the nature of task problems does not require it.

Another deviation in the expected structure of management system was reported in continuous process industries. (The reader may wish to refer to Figure 8–2, p. 243, in Chapter 8 where these observations by Woodward are summarized.) A continuous process plant is one that produces a limited range of products in large volumes. The production system is highly preprogrammed, interrelations are predetermined, and control systems established. The uncertainty and complexity of the system was taken into account when the process was designed. Such a structured situation might, according to the arguments already presented, reasonably be expected to be consistent with a relatively highly structured management system. Yet the research describing management systems in continuous process industries reveals small spans of control and task force types of operating groups typical of those found in highly uncertain, complex climates. The answer extends beyond the day-to-day complexity-uncertainty components of the work situation.

Consider in more detail the nature of the continuous process plant. Products are produced in high volumes of throughput per hour. Often, achieving higher volume in a chemical process, for example, will require higher operating temperatures and pressures, more expensive catalysts, and, particularly, higher levels of capital equipment than systems with lower throughput levels. Such systems may also require automatic rather than human process controllers to ascertain and adjust to any changes in the rapidity of throughput. Consider further what happens when a malfunction in the process equipment occurs. At that time, quick action may be needed to prevent the system from possible disaster. While the system has been predesigned to eliminate as much as possible, perhaps, to account for complexity, and to eliminate complexity, the automaticity of equipment *adds* uncertainty as to its failure. More control components (which we in effect substitute for human equipment operators) need monitoring and repair as inevitable breakdowns do occur.

The frequency of failures may be quite low, especially if redundant components are included in the design, but the importance is noted of any failure having the potential of blowing up the plant. Thus the conditional value of failures justifies keeping a task force structure on hand, idle some of the time, but available to deal with and prevent emergencies. During harmonious operating conditions, the management system may be underemployed. Its value comes when the exceptional conditions occur. Even if these occurrences are infrequent, their possible high expected disutility justifies an "overmanaged" system.

MANAGEMENT SCHOOLS OF THOUGHT

In light of the variations shown in decisions resulting from differences in complexity and uncertainty, it may be useful to reexamine the schools of management thought in light of these conceptions (see Figure 20–6). The purpose of this section is not to discredit any school of thought but to show how each may contribute to a conditional theory of management. As stated in Chapter 1, concepts from the different schools still apply under specified conditions.

Scientific management focused upon removing complexity and uncertainty from the job of managing. Major attention was given to specifying and improving methods, standardizing tasks, controlling variations caused by different materials or improper planning, selecting workers with the *same* high skill level, and training all workers to do programmed tasks. In retrospect, it appears that scientific management thought pre-

Figure 20–6. Schools of Management Thought versus Problem Types

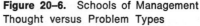
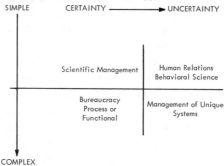

Note: This categorizing of management schools by the types of problems they presumed is somewhat general and is used to clarify their major characteristics and limitations rather than to be definitive and comprehensive in their explanation.

sumed that the system with which they were dealing was one of relative simplicity and certainty. As one could identify and correct deficiencies, the system would become highly predictable and easy to manage. A belief in *laws* of interaction existed and were only awaiting discovery.

Some scientific management thinkers did deal with aspects of organizational complexity. A primitive line and staff organization (Taylor's functional foremanship) was developed; but it was the bureaucratic and the process or functional schools of management thought that really focused on the complexity of large organizations. Bureaucratic thought, particularly, developed differentiated tasks and structures. It established fixed positions, rules, procedures, and protocol to deal with the complex of administrative tasks. It is inaccurate to characterize the work of these schools as ignoring uncertainty, but the thrust of thought in the process and bureaucratic schools implies a presumption that the system they were dealing with was certain but complex.

The human relations and behavioral science schools of management thought revealed the impact of human variables upon the functioning of organizational systems. In so doing, they addressed an implied (if not direct) criticism upon the mechanized fixity they perceived as characteristic of the scientific management, bureaucratic, and functional schools. Not only did the human relations movement insert greater complexity into the formulae for managing, but also uncertainty. Individual and group behaviors are not completely predictable. Their consideration in managing obviously involves uncertainty not explicitly posited in the structured tasks and systems of scientific management, bureaucracy, and the process school. On the other hand, the human relations group tended to examine individual and group variables, sometimes without much consideration of the complexity of variables influencing an organization's functioning. With some exceptions, it is fair to consider their parameters as encompassing a case of disorganized simplicity.

With the advent of large systems to produce areospace hardware, project management, research and development management and similar management systems received considerable attention. The question was asked whether there was anything different about managing a group of highly educated, creative, and versatile engineers from that of managing assembly-line workers whose task needs for education, skill, creativeness and versatility was at a minimum. While the answer was obviously "yes" in light of the analysis already presented in this chapter, the tasks of research economists, marketeers, consultants, and analysts of various types also required creativity, education, and versatility. Thus engineering or research management is not unique in these respects. Perhaps part of the criticism of project management as a separate kind of management system evolved because the experts in organization and management behavior could not conceive of engineers developing a new kind of management system. It appears clear that many research and development organizations are operating in an environment of high uncertainty and complexity. It is these factors, not the fact that engineers are involved, which call for a relatively unstructured, innovative, and adaptive management system. Perhaps, however, research and development management should be considered as a separate school of management thought, although we did not do so in Chapter 1.

The systems school of management thought deals directly with problems of whatever level of uncertainty or complexity faces an organization. Since a firm is considered as a subsystem with input-output to others or as a system interacting with its environment, the systems school is capable of dealing with any kind or amount of variables, internally or externally imposed.

The quantitative approaches of operations research and management science have been discussed as decision techniques above. It is clear that some of the techniques of the quantitative school are applicable in all of the complexity-uncertainty quadrants. Since the mathematics and the computation is easier if certainty is assumed, however, lesser attention was given to uncertainty in early quantitative developments. Since then, however, a recognition that many of the application limitations to quantitative techniques rest with their certainty assumptions. More research has been undertaken to apply models utilizing stochastic variables (e.g., with Monte Carlo simulation).

While the development of management thought can be categorized into the complexity-uncertainty quadrants as has been shown above, it should be recognized that these dimensions were not specifically recognized during the evolution of these approaches to management. It may be, therefore, somewhat presumptuous and arbitrary to so classify them in this way at this time. Yet, we believe this discussion provides an additional perspective to these differing schools of management thought and to the concept of a conditional theory of management.

SOCIETAL TRENDS VERSUS ORGANIZATIONAL TENDENCIES

It is instructive to compare some social tendencies to those of institutions in society with which individuals deal. There has been a general movement toward mass education in the United States with more children finishing high schools and a larger proportion of individuals entering college and post-high school education. Further, there has been an increased sympathy for everyone "doing his own thing," self-actualizing in the sense that an individual is given the opportunity to exercise his highest level of talents in whatever he undertakes. Increased aversion to authoritarianism, repression, and inequality of opportunity is coupled with desires for openness and freedom.

While organizations are open systems adapting to and anticipating their environments, they, at the same time attempt to reduce the uncertainty and complexity facing them because these factors make decision making more difficult as was shown in Chapter 4 and make organizational structures simpler to avoid greater coordinative costs as shown in Chapter 8. Thus by eliminating or organizationally isolating uncertainty and complexity facing it, an organization can increase the efficiency with which it meets its goals. In doing this, however, it should be noted that the management system moves from less to more structure, from the need for creativeness and adaptability to a need for conformity and compliance, from a system congruent with the social trends noted above to one less so. These tendencies in management systems are not restricted to business firms; they are general tendencies observable in univerities, government agencies, and elsewhere. In light of this, where is the "action"? Where can one self-actualize?

Figure 20–7. Societal Trends and Organizational Tendencies

SIMPLE   —SOCIETAL TRENDS————▶   COMPLEX

CERTAIN   ◀—ORGANIZATIONAL TENDENCIES———   UNCERTAIN

This dilemma (see Figure 20–7) between the growing social movement towards individuality and freedom versus the organizational tendency toward closedness and structure has led to experiments for altering the effect of the organization tendencies. For example, job enlargement, rotation, and participation in these activities have, as shown above, altered the authoritarian systems appropriate to organized simplicity. Some firms, for example, have given the responsibility for the complete assembly of a product to each of its workers rather than to assemble it on an assembly line in the sometimes realized hope that variety and product responsibility will develop less man-hours per product, less absenteeism and turnover, and less need for quality control.

These systems changes do not, however, directly address the notion of changing values in society. Filley examines this question by suggesting utopian organizations in which status, social, and economic differentials among individuals would be eliminated, leaders would be elected, decisions would be made by consensus or vote, and conflict would be resolved by consensus rather than fiat or vote. He believes such organizations would and that some organizations do now "minimize what I regard as obscenities: fears, guilt, loneliness, jealousy, failure, possessiveness, and war."[3]

It should be recognized, however, that the design of a management system is a compromise or a tradeoff in values. In Chapter 8, it was noted that the psychological benefits of job enlargement are gained at the expense of economic replacement and training costs. All organizations provide multiple values as outputs. Business organizations have traditionally been charged with the responsibility of focusing upon economic values. As shown in Chapter 2, the singular attention to one goal may be dysfunctional in terms of creating other values. The unintended consequences of business behavior provide both positive and negative values. To some degree, all organiziations face the same question of which societal values it should create.

The fact that society's values are changing does not necessarily alter the impact that values have upon an organization. The real question is whether an organization should attempt to maximize all social values in its functioning or whether, within the levels of constraints of values impinging upon it, it should focus on those values it is best fitted to create. Relatedly, can an organization simultaneously create effectively a wide spectrum of values? Or will it, by so doing, fritter away resources and be dysfunctional to society as a whole? Can creative leaders working with an enlightened work force build systems capable of increasing the material well-being while providing the changing values sought by society?

DISCUSSION AND STUDY QUESTIONS

1. What is the difference between complex and uncertain problems?
2. "If invention is 99 percent perspiration and 1 percent innovation, what the research and development organization needs is a plodder rather than a creator." Comment.

---

[3] Allen C. Filley, "Some Major Issues in the Future of Management: Practice and Teaching," *Academy of Management Proceedings* of 1970, p. 26.

3. Why might the chief executive, upon deciding to introduce a new functional specialty into the organization, decide to establish the new function as a separate unit rather than to integrate it logically into the existing operations with which it is most closely allied?

4. Two grocery chains are both aggressive in locating promising new locations, evaluation of current stores, and dropping stores in unprofitable locations. Both chains select store managers by promoting the more successful departmental managers in existing stores. New store managers are, ordinarily, assigned to smaller stores and then are moved to larger ones if they are successful.

   In opening new stores, Chain A selects the manager they ultimately want to manage the store. He is given power to stock the stores to meet local needs within the constraints of the merchandise available from regional headquarters, he selects departmental managers as his subordinates, he expedites the problems associated with final construction of the store and deals with the building contractor, establishes the advertising needed, and hires and trains personnel.

   Chain B has an expert in opening stores. As the building is being completed, he is assigned as store manager. He performs the same functions as the store manager in Chain A. Then after the new store is shaken down, a new and permanent store manager is brought in and the "store opener" moves on to another store being opened. Evaluate these two approaches to opening stores.

5. In light of considerations in this chapter, can you explain why the research and developmental functions often are established to report to the top management of a company separated from the operating divisions? This organizational separation is, in addition, often accompanied by physically separating these functions from those of day-to-day operations.

6. Why is it that project groups or task forces as organizational forms tend to be temporary?

7. Distinguish between the tasks of staff groups concerned with research and staff groups dealing with procedural matters.

8. A successful and well-known college football coach holds that authoritarianism on the part of the coaching fraternity must be abandoned because autocratic leadership is inconsistent with the values and intelligence of modern-day college athletes. Is his view consistent with the task requirements of football? Explain.

SELECTED REFERENCES

BURNS, TOM, and STALKER, G. M. *The Management of Innovation.* London: Tavistock Publications, Ltd., 1961.

CHANDLER, A. D., JR. *Strategy and Structure.* Cambridge, Mass.: The M.I.T. Press, 1962.

GRIMES, A. J., and KLEIN, S. M. "The Technological Imperative: The Relative Impact of Task Unit, Modal Technology, and Hierarchy on Structure," *Academy of Management Proceedings,* San Diego, Calif., 1970.

HALL, R. H. "Intraorganizational Structure Variables," *Administrative Science Quarterly,* 7 (December 1962).

KOONTZ, HAROLD. *Toward a Unified Theory of Management.* New York: McGraw-Hill Book Co., 1964.

LAWRENCE, PAUL, and LORSCH, JAY W. *Organization and Environment.* Homewood, Ill.: Richard D. Irwin, Inc., 1969.

MARCH, JAMES G., and SIMON, HERBERT A. *Organizations.* New York: John Wiley & Sons, Inc., 1958.

MILLER, ERIC J. "Technology, Territory, and Time," *Human Relations,* 12 (1959), 243–72.

MINGO, KENT, and SMITH, RUSSELL. "A Factor Analysis of the Dimensions of an International Business Environment," *Academy of Management Proceedings,* San Diego, Calif., 1970.

RICE, A. K. *The Enterprise and Its Environment.* London: Tavistock Publications, Ltd., 1963.

SHULL, FREMONT A. *Matrix Structure and Project Authority.* Carbondale Ill.: Business Research Bureau, Southern Illinois University, 1965.

WOODWARD, JOAN. *Industrial Organization and Practice.* London: Oxford University Press, 1965.

Appendix A

A SUMMARY OF LINEAR FUNCTIONS*

The following will be an aid in review of linear equations.

1. A Standard Form of the Equation of a Straight Line is: $y = a + bx$
   Where: y = the dependent variable
   x = the independent variable
   a = a constant, called the "y intercept"; i.e., it is the value of y when x is equal to 0, or it is the value of y where the line in question crosses the vertical, or y axis.
   b = a constant, called the slope of the line; i.e., it is the amount of change in y with a given change in x, or $\Delta y / \Delta x$. This quotient is the slope or rate of change of y with respect to a given change in x.

   Example A
   Suppose that we have the following equation: $y = 1x$
   Here $a = 0$; i.e., when $x = 0$, $y = 0$
   $b = 1$
   A plot of this line looks like the following:

POINT	WHEN x IS:	y IS:
o	0	0
p	1	1
q	2	2
r	3	3
s	4	4
t	5	5

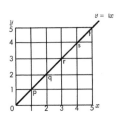

Notice that $a = 0$. Notice also that from any point on the line to any other point on the line, the change in y divided by the change in x is a constant, one; i.e., from point p to point q, the relationship is $1/1$; from q to s, it is $2/2 = 1$; from t to q it is $-3/-3 = 1$. This is of course the slope of the line (i.e., $b = 1$).

Example B

Let us look at another equation: $y = 2$. When plotted it looks as follows:

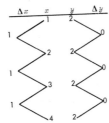
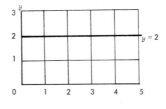

Notice that when x changes by 1, y changes by zero, hence $b = 0$.

Example C

Suppose that we now add these two equations together, calling the first, y_a, the second y_b, and the sum of $y_a + y_b$, y_c, so that $y_a + y_b = y_c$.

$$y_a = 0 + 1x$$
$$y_b = 2 + 0x$$
$$\overline{y_c = 2 + 1x}$$

Plotting this we have:

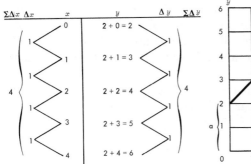
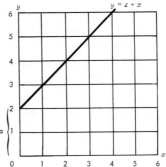

$a = 2; b = 1/1 = 4/4 = 1$.

Notice here that the line looks essentially the same as that in Example A above (i.e., it has the same slope) except that it has been moved up an amount equal to a.

Example D
The equation $y = \frac{1}{2}x$ looks like the following:

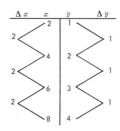
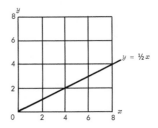

2. Nonlinear Functions

What distinguishes a straight line from a nonstraight line? Let us take another example, $y = x^2$, and plot it.

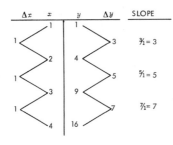
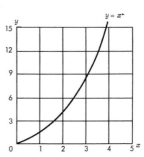

Notice that the change in y divided by the change in x ($\Delta y / \Delta x$) is *not* a constant between values of x and y. The main distinguishing feature of a straight line is thus illustrated; the change of one variable with respect to the other; i.e., the slope, is a constant.

Example
Let us look at another function. Given the following, do we have a linear or nonlinear function?

We have a linear function. The slope $\Delta y/\Delta x$ is equal to 2 and is constant for each pair of values. The value of a by inspection is zero, thus the equation of the line is $y = 2x$.

3. Negatively Sloped Lines

The equations $y_a = -x$ and $y_b = 3$ look like the following:

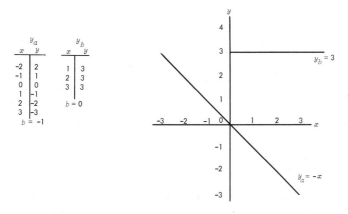

When the two equations are summed, letting $y_a + y_b = y_c$, we have the following equation:

$$y_c = 3 - 1x$$

Notice that this line slopes in a direction opposite to those previously considered, and that it therefore has a negative slope; i.e., $b = -1$.

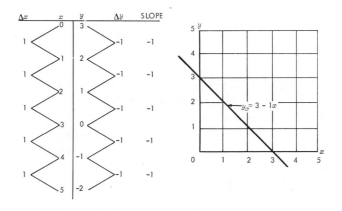

We can show that the slope of a line can have any real number for its value, that is, it can range from plus infinity through zero to minus infinity. The following diagram illustrates the point:

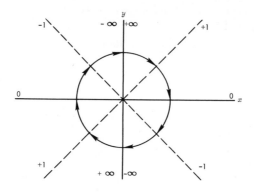

4. Point Determination

Another skill required is that of finding x and y when two lines cross or intersect. The key characteristic of the point of intersection which helps us locate these values is that at that point, $x_1 = x_2$, and $y_1 = y_2$. As an example, let us consider the following two lines:

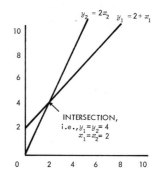

By knowing that $y_1 = y_2$, and $x_1 = x_2$ at the point of intersection, we can find the coordinates of the point by:

a. Setting the equations equal to each other, i.e., $y_1 = y_2$, which gives us $2 + x = 2x$, hence $x = 2$. Substituting in either y_1 or y_2 we have $y_1 = 2 + 2 = y_2 = 2 \times 2 = 4$. The values of x and y for the point of intersection are then $x = 2$, $y = 4$.

b. Subtracting one equation from the other:

$$\begin{array}{ll} y = 2 + x & \\ \underline{-(y = \quad\quad 2x)} & \text{OR} \\ 0 = 2 - x & \\ x = 2 & \end{array} \qquad \begin{array}{l} y = \quad\quad 2x \\ \underline{-(y = \ 2 + x)} \\ 0 = -2 + x \\ x = 2 \end{array}$$

5. Equation Determination Given Any Two Points
   Suppose that we wish to write an equation, given the coordinates (i.e., value of x and value of y) for two points:

   e.g., $y_1 = 4$; $x_1 = 6$
   $\quad\ y_2 = 5$; $x_2 = 9$

   A. One method of determining the equation would be by inspection.

   We can quickly notice that the slope, or change in y divided by change in x, is a positive $\frac{1}{3}$.

   $$\text{Slope} = \frac{\Delta y}{\Delta x} = \frac{y_2 - y_1}{x_2 - x_1} = +\frac{1}{3}$$

   By back tracking we can find a; i.e., value of y when $x = 0$, which here is 2. Hence, we can write the equation which satisfies these points as $y = 2 + \frac{1}{3}x$. This is a laborious and inexact process. Other methods are preferred.

   B. Another method is to learn and apply the following equation:

   $$\frac{y - y_1}{x - x_1} = \frac{y_2 - y_1}{x_2 - x_1} \quad \text{Substituting:} \quad \frac{y - 4}{x - 6} = \frac{5 - 4}{9 - 6}$$

   Hence our equation for the line is again $y = 2 + \frac{1}{3}x$.

   C. The subtraction method is a third alternative.

   $$\begin{array}{lll} y_1 = a + bx_1 & \text{substituting} & 4 = a + b6 \\ -(y_2 = a + bx_2) & & -(5 = a + b9) \\ \hline & & -1 = -3b, \text{ or } b = +\frac{1}{3} \end{array}$$

   Substituting in either of the original equations we have:

   $$4 = a + \frac{1}{3} \cdot 6 \quad \text{OR} \quad 5 = a + \frac{1}{3} \cdot 9$$

   Hence, $a = 2$, and our equation is $y = 2 + \frac{1}{3}x$.

6. Equation Determination Given Axis Intercepts
   One final problem remains. Suppose that we know the values of x and y where one particular line crosses the axes, e.g.,

   Where $x = 0$; $y = 2$ this is the y intercept, or a.
   $\quad\quad\quad y = 0$; $x = 4$ this is the x intercept, or c.

There is a simple way to write the equation of the line which passes through these two points, the intercept form of an equation for a straight line:

$$\frac{y}{a} + \frac{x}{c} = 1 \qquad \text{Note: } b = \text{slope} = -a/c$$

We can quickly write:

$$\frac{y}{2} + \frac{x}{4} = 1 \qquad \text{OR} \qquad y = a + bx, \text{ where } b = -a/c, a = 2, \text{ and}$$
$$y = 2 - \tfrac{1}{2}x \qquad\qquad c = 4, \text{ hence } b = -\tfrac{1}{2}$$
$$\qquad\qquad\qquad\qquad\qquad y = 2 - \tfrac{1}{2}x$$

This method is especially useful for dealing with algebraic linear programming problems as covered in Chapter 16.

SUMMARY

The above summarizes the requisite knowledge of linear functions. The student should develop and solve examples for each type of problem, so that recognition and manipulation of such problems become "second nature" with him. Some problems and answers follow.

LINEAR FUNCTION PROBLEMS AND ANSWERS

1. Plot the equation $y = 3 + 2x$.
    What is the value of the y intercept?
    (Answer: 3)
    What is the slope of the line?
    (Answer: $+2$)
    What is the value of the x intercept, i.e., when $y = 0$?
    (Answer: $-\tfrac{3}{2}$)
2. Determine the slope and y intercept of the following:

Equations	Put in standard form	Y intercept	Slope
$3y + 2x = 7$	$y = \tfrac{7}{3} - \tfrac{2}{3}x$	$\tfrac{7}{3}$	$-\tfrac{2}{3}$
$2y + 3x = 6$	$y = 3 - \tfrac{3}{2}x$	3	$-\tfrac{3}{2}$
$y - x = 2$	$y = 2 + x$	2	1
$4y - 3x = 12$	$y = 3 + \tfrac{3}{4}x$	3	$\tfrac{3}{4}$

3. Which of the following equations is (are) not linear?

	Linear	Nonlinear
A. $y = \tfrac{1}{2}x + 6$	✓	
B. $y^2 = \tfrac{1}{2}x + 6$		✓
C. $y = x^{1/2} + 6$		✓
D. $y = \tfrac{1}{2}x + 6^2$	✓	
E. $3y + 2x = \sqrt{10}$	✓	

4. In words, what is the difference between a positive and a negative slope of a linear function?

Answer

For a line with a positive slope, as the value of the independent variable (x) increases, the value of the dependent variable (y) also increases.

For a line with a negative slope, as the value of the independent variable (x) increases, the value of the dependent variable (y) decreases.

5. Given the following sets of two linear equations, find the points of intersection first by setting the equations equal to each other and second by subtracting one equation from the other.

    A. $3y + 4x = 7$
         $4y + 3x = 12$

Method 1. Set the equations in standard form.

$$y = \tfrac{7}{3} - \tfrac{4}{3}x$$
$$y = 3 - \tfrac{3}{4}x$$

Set equations equal to each other.

$$\tfrac{7}{3} - \tfrac{4}{3}x = 3 - \tfrac{3}{4}x$$
$$\tfrac{7}{12}x = -\tfrac{2}{3} \qquad x = -\tfrac{2}{3} \times \tfrac{12}{7} = -\tfrac{8}{7}$$

Substituting in the value for x in either equation, we have

$$3y + 4x = 7$$
$$3y + 4(-\tfrac{8}{7}) = 7$$
$$3y - \tfrac{32}{7} = 7$$
$$3y = 7 + \tfrac{32}{7} = \tfrac{49}{7} + \tfrac{32}{7} = \tfrac{81}{7}$$
$$y = \tfrac{36}{7}$$

Method 2. Multiply the first equation by 4 and the second equation by 3, yielding

$$
\begin{array}{r}
12y + 16x = 28 \\
-(12y + 9x = 36) \\
\hline
7x = -8 \\
x = -\tfrac{8}{7},\, y = \tfrac{27}{7}
\end{array}
$$

OR

Multiply the first equation by 3 and the second equation by 4 yielding

$$
\begin{array}{r}
9y + 12x = 21 \\
-(16y + 12x = 48) \\
\hline
-7y \qquad = -27 \\
7y = 27 \\
y = \tfrac{27}{7} = \tfrac{36}{7};\, x = -\tfrac{8}{7}
\end{array}
$$

    B. $y + \tfrac{1}{2}x = 6$
         $3y + x = 2$

Method 1. Set the equations in standard form.

$$y = 6 - \tfrac{1}{2}x$$
$$y = \tfrac{2}{3} - \tfrac{1}{3}x$$

Set the equations equal to each other.

$$6 - \tfrac{1}{2}x = \tfrac{2}{3} - \tfrac{1}{3}x$$
$$5\tfrac{1}{3} = \tfrac{1}{6}x$$

or

$$\tfrac{1}{6}x = 5\tfrac{1}{3} = {}^{16}\!\!/_{3}$$
$$x = ({}^{16}\!\!/_{3})(6)$$
$$x = 32$$

Substitute in either equation the value obtained for x.

$$3y + x = 2$$
$$3y + 32 = 2$$
$$3y = -30$$
$$y = -10$$

Method 2. Multiply the first equation by 3, holding the second constant.

$$3y + \tfrac{3}{2}x = 18$$
$$-(3y + x = 2)$$
$$\overline{\tfrac{1}{2}x = 16}$$
$$x = 32$$

by substitution $y = -10$

OR

Multiply the first equation by 2 holding the second constant.

$$2y + x = 12$$
$$-(3y + x = 2)$$
$$\overline{{-y} = 10}$$
$$y = -10$$

by substitution $x = 32$

C. $2y + x = 9$
$\phantom{\textbf{C.}\ }3y + 2x = 7$

Method 1. Set the equations in standard form.

$$y = \tfrac{9}{2} - \tfrac{1}{2}x$$
$$y = \tfrac{7}{3} - \tfrac{2}{3}x$$

Set the equations equal to each other.

$$\tfrac{9}{2} - \tfrac{1}{2}x = \tfrac{7}{3} - \tfrac{2}{3}x$$
$$\tfrac{1}{6}x = -1\tfrac{3}{6}$$
$$x = (-1\tfrac{3}{6})(6) = -13$$

By substituting in the value obtained for x, the value for y will be obtained.

$$2y + x = 9$$
$$2y - 13 = 9$$
$$2y = 22$$
$$y = 11$$

Method 2. Multiply the first equation by 3 and the second equation by 2.

$$6y + 3x = 27$$
$$-(6y + 4x = 14)$$
$$\overline{\qquad -x = 13}$$
$$x = -13$$

by substitution $y = 11$

OR

Multiply the first equation by 2, holding the second equation constant.

$$4y + 2x = 18$$
$$-(3y + 2x = 7)$$
$$\overline{\qquad\qquad y = 11}$$

by substitution $x = -13$

6. Using the equation for determining a line given the coordinates of two points on the line, determine the equation of the lines designated by the following pairs of points.

A. $y_1 = 3 \qquad x_1 = 5$
$\ y_2 = 4 \qquad x_2 = 6$

$$\frac{y - y_1}{x - x_1} = \frac{y_2 - y_1}{x_2 - x_1}$$

$$\frac{y - 3}{x - 5} = \frac{4 - 3}{6 - 5}$$

$$\frac{y - 3}{x - 5} = \frac{1}{1} = 1$$

$$y - 3 = 1(x - 5)$$
$$y - 3 = x - 5$$
$$y = x - 2$$

C. $y_1 = 0 \qquad x_1 = -5$
$\ y_2 = 5 \qquad x_2 = 4$

$$\frac{y - y_1}{x - x_1} = \frac{y_2 - y_1}{x_2 - x_1}$$

$$\frac{y - 0}{x - (-5)} = \frac{5 - 0}{4 - (-5)}$$

$$\frac{y}{x + 5} = \frac{5}{9}$$

$$y = \tfrac{5}{9}(x + 5)$$
$$y = \tfrac{5}{9}x + 2\tfrac{5}{9}$$

B. $y_1 = 2 \qquad x_1 = 3$
$\ y_2 = 4 \qquad x_2 = 7$

$$\frac{y - y_1}{x - x_1} = \frac{y_2 - y_1}{x_2 - x_1}$$

$$\frac{y - 2}{x - 3} = \frac{4 - 2}{7 - 3}$$

$$\frac{y - 2}{x - 3} = \frac{2}{4} = \frac{1}{2}$$

$$y - 2 = \tfrac{1}{2}(x - 3)$$
$$y - 2 = \tfrac{1}{2}x - \tfrac{3}{2}$$
$$y = \tfrac{1}{2}x + \tfrac{1}{2}$$

D. Using the same values for x and y, determine the equations of the lines using the subtraction method.

1)　$y_1 = 3$　　　　$x_1 = 5$　　　　Substituting in
　　$y_2 = 4$　　　　$x_2 = 6$　　　　either equation we
　　　　　　　　　　　　　　　　　　　can get the value
　　　　　　　　　　　　　　　　　　　for a.

$$y_1 = a + bx_1$$
$$\underline{-(y_2 = a + bx_2)}$$

$3 = a + b5$
$\underline{-(4 = a + b6)}$
$-1 = -b$
$b = 1$

$3 = a + b5$
$3 = a + (1)(5)$
$3 = a + 5$
$a = -2$
Hence, with
$a = -2$ and $b = 1$,
we have the equation
$$y = -2 + x$$

2)　$y_1 = 2$　　　　$x_1 = 3$　　　　Substituting in
　　$y_2 = 4$　　　　$x_2 = 7$　　　　either equation we
　　　　　　　　　　　　　　　　　　　can get the value
　　　　　　　　　　　　　　　　　　　for a.

$$y_1 = a + bx_1$$
$$\underline{-(y_2 = a + bx_2)}$$

$2 = a + b3$
$\underline{-(4 = a + b7)}$
$-2 = -4b$
$b = 1\frac{1}{2}$

$4 = a + b7$
$4 = a + (\frac{1}{2})7$
$4 = a + 3\frac{1}{2}$
$a = \frac{1}{2}$
Hence, with
$a = \frac{1}{2}$ and $b = \frac{1}{2}$,
we have the equation
$$y = \frac{1}{2} + \frac{1}{2}x$$

3)　$y_1 = 0$　　　　$x_1 = -5$　　　Substituting in
　　$y_2 = 5$　　　　$x_2 = 4$　　　　either equation we
　　　　　　　　　　　　　　　　　　　can get the value
　　　　　　　　　　　　　　　　　　　for a.

$$y_1 = a + bx_1$$
$$\underline{-(y_2 = a + bx_2)}$$

$0 = a + b(-5)$
$\underline{-(5 = a + b4)}$
$-5 = -9b$
$b = \frac{5}{9}$

$0 = a + b(-5)$
$0 = a + \frac{5}{9}(-5)$
$0 = a - \frac{25}{9}$
$a = \frac{25}{9}$
Hence, with
$a = \frac{25}{9}$ and
$b = \frac{5}{9}$, the equation becomes
$$y = \frac{25}{9} + \frac{5}{9}x$$

7. Using the formula for line determination given the values of the variables at the points where the line crosses the axes, determine the lines for the following points.

A. $x = 0; \quad y = 3$
$y = 0; \quad x = 4$

$$\frac{y}{a} + \frac{x}{c} = 1$$

$$\frac{y}{3} + \frac{x}{4} = 1$$

$$\frac{y}{3} = 1 - \frac{x}{4}$$

$$y = 3 - \tfrac{3}{4}x$$

OR

$$y = a + bx, \text{ where } b = -\frac{a}{c}$$

$$y = 3 + (-\tfrac{3}{4})x$$
$$y = 3 - \tfrac{3}{4}x$$

B. $x = 0 \quad y = 5$
$y = 0 \quad x = 2$

$$\frac{y}{a} + \frac{x}{c} = 1$$

$$\frac{y}{5} + \frac{x}{2} = 1$$

$$\frac{y}{5} = 1 - \frac{x}{2}$$

$$y = 5 - \tfrac{5}{2}x$$

OR

$$y = a + bx$$

$$y = 5 + (-\tfrac{5}{2})x$$
$$y = 5 - \tfrac{5}{2}x$$

C. $x = 0 \quad y = -3$
$y = 0 \quad x = 2$

$$\frac{y}{a} + \frac{x}{c} = 1$$

$$\frac{y}{-3} + \frac{x}{2} = 1$$

$$\frac{-y}{3} = 1 - \frac{x}{2}$$

$$-y = 3 - \tfrac{3}{2}x$$
$$y = -3 + \tfrac{3}{2}x$$

OR

$$y = a + bx$$

$$y = -3 + \frac{-(-3)}{2}x$$

$$y = -3 + \tfrac{3}{2}x$$

D. $x = 0 \quad y = -1$
$y = 0 \quad x = 1$

$$\frac{y}{-1} + \frac{x}{1} = 1$$

$$\frac{y}{-1} = 1 - x$$

$$-y = 1 - x$$

$$y = -1 + x$$

OR

$$y = a + bx$$

$$y = -1 + \frac{-(-1)}{1}x$$

$$y = -1 + x$$

Appendix B

PRESENT VALUE OF $1

$(1 + r)^{-n}$

n	1%	2%	3%	4%	5%	6%	7%	8%	9%	10%
1	0.9901	0.9804	0.9709	0.9615	0.9524	0.9434	0.9346	0.9259	0.9174	0.9091
2	0.9803	0.9612	0.9426	0.9246	0.9070	0.8900	0.8734	0.8573	0.8417	0.8264
3	0.9706	0.9423	0.9151	0.8890	0.8638	0.8396	0.8163	0.7938	0.7722	0.7513
4	0.9610	0.9238	0.8885	0.8548	0.8227	0.7921	0.7629	0.7350	0.7084	0.6830
5	0.9515	0.9057	0.8626	0.8219	0.7835	0.7473	0.7130	0.6806	0.6499	0.6209
6	0.9420	0.8880	0.8375	0.7903	0.7462	0.7050	0.6663	0.6302	0.5963	0.5645
7	0.9327	0.8706	0.8131	0.7599	0.7107	0.6651	0.6227	0.5835	0.5470	0.5132
8	0.9235	0.8535	0.7894	0.7307	0.6768	0.6274	0.5820	0.5403	0.5019	0.4665
9	0.9143	0.8368	0.7664	0.7026	0.6446	0.5919	0.5439	0.5002	0.4604	0.4241
10	0.9053	0.8203	0.7441	0.6756	0.6139	0.5584	0.5083	0.4632	0.4224	0.3855
11	0.8963	0.8043	0.7224	0.6496	0.5847	0.5268	0.4751	0.4289	0.3875	0.3505
12	0.8874	0.7885	0.7014	0.6246	0.5568	0.4970	0.4440	0.3971	0.3555	0.3186
13	0.8787	0.7730	0.6810	0.6006	0.5303	0.4688	0.4150	0.3677	0.3262	0.2897
14	0.8700	0.7579	0.6611	0.5775	0.5051	0.4423	0.3878	0.3405	0.2992	0.2633
15	0.8613	0.7430	0.6419	0.5553	0.4810	0.4173	0.3624	0.3152	0.2745	0.2394
16	0.8528	0.7284	0.6232	0.5339	0.4581	0.3936	0.3387	0.2919	0.2519	0.2176
17	0.8444	0.7142	0.6050	0.5134	0.4363	0.3714	0.3166	0.2703	0.2311	0.1978
18	0.8360	0.7002	0.5874	0.4936	0.4155	0.3503	0.2959	0.2502	0.2120	0.1799
19	0.8277	0.6864	0.5703	0.4746	0.3957	0.3305	0.2765	0.2317	0.1945	0.1635
20	0.8195	0.6730	0.5537	0.4564	0.3769	0.3118	0.2584	0.2145	0.1784	0.1486
21	0.8114	0.6598	0.5375	0.4388	0.3589	0.2942	0.2415	0.1987	0.1637	0.1351
22	0.8034	0.6468	0.5219	0.4220	0.3418	0.2775	0.2257	0.1839	0.1502	0.1228
23	0.7954	0.6342	0.5067	0.4057	0.3256	0.2618	0.2109	0.1703	0.1378	0.1117
24	0.7876	0.6217	0.4919	0.3901	0.3101	0.2470	0.1971	0.1577	0.1264	0.1015
25	0.7798	0.6095	0.4776	0.3751	0.2953	0.2330	0.1842	0.1460	0.1160	0.0923
26	0.7720	0.5976	0.4637	0.3607	0.2812	0.2198	0.1722	0.1352	0.1064	0.0839
27	0.7644	0.5859	0.4502	0.3468	0.2678	0.2074	0.1609	0.1252	0.0976	0.0763
28	0.7568	0.5744	0.4371	0.3335	0.2551	0.1956	0.1504	0.1159	0.0895	0.0693
29	0.7493	0.5631	0.4243	0.3207	0.2429	0.1846	0.1406	0.1073	0.0822	0.0630
30	0.7419	0.5521	0.4120	0.3083	0.2314	0.1741	0.1314	0.0994	0.0754	0.0573
35	0.7059	0.5000	0.3554	0.2534	0.1813	0.1301	0.0937	0.0676	0.0490	0.0356
40	0.6717	0.4529	0.3066	0.2083	0.1420	0.0972	0.0668	0.0460	0.0318	0.0221
45	0.6391	0.4102	0.2644	0.1712	0.1113	0.0727	0.0476	0.0313	0.0207	0.0137
50	0.6080	0.3715	0.2281	0.1407	0.0872	0.0543	0.0339	0.0213	0.0134	0.0085

Source: Bierman, H.; Bonini, C. P.; Fouraker, L. E.; and Jaedicke, R. K., *Quantitative Analysis for Business Decisions* (rev. ed.; Homewood, Ill.: Richard D. Irwin, Inc., 1965), p. 427. Reprinted by permission.

Appendix C

TABLE OF PSEUDO-RANDOM NUMBERS

17	57	89	67	26	06	55	79	96	77
49	49	19	98	24	68	53	32	39	95
36	58	57	33	07	62	30	22	47	09
80	37	50	16	11	36	45	31	09	87
84	15	86	27	60	33	79	98	76	16
56	97	98	83	59	93	41	18	65	98
11	65	65	37	98	52	61	41	54	50
63	75	07	76	52	40	93	74	87	08
33	61	89	25	78	86	17	80	72	19
46	32	21	44	18	13	36	78	81	51
31	73	56	29	99	40	77	41	49	86
19	45	92	13	31	83	89	02	76	20
48	85	69	65	08	54	50	47	27	69
57	06	73	88	07	60	56	18	27	62
92	98	34	22	91	04	31	14	69	45
00	25	23	45	07	86	22	90	10	80
34	29	60	68	83	03	00	57	67	45
51	27	04	40	35	44	60	81	26	34
11	12	62	45	60	97	20	85	34	56
79	52	83	03	40	47	23	48	02	38
23	94	59	71	41	73	37	05	06	22
16	58	28	41	15	49	52	45	87	65
33	42	72	41	93	49	83	17	46	41
56	18	16	36	96	38	69	22	53	41
69	35	29	25	24	82	73	20	39	70
61	19	24	46	63	38	82	24	99	50
24	71	58	71	85	64	06	07	94	19
53	69	33	08	43	09	80	93	46	31
51	64	95	01	75	23	64	68	44	56
22	86	31	30	03	48	41	68	40	80
73	41	77	12	33	23	16	89	48	05
18	09	08	00	55	85	21	81	49	48
72	48	47	81	44	65	11	51	86	44
57	90	58	79	57	91	65	63	67	42
97	46	51	56	37	85	86	33	64	09
20	99	79	08	09	68	00	38	13	26
58	11	40	66	84	55	58	09	12	92
49	19	74	99	56	57	36	30	26	19
33	37	66	12	03	83	32	47	82	39
54	53	48	45	86	35	69	56	73	97
61	33	90	73	53	12	93	13	53	55
06	17	12	11	33	12	77	29	43	90
45	23	73	04	39	25	14	70	26	98
40	44	80	39	72	38	24	60	50	87
54	49	81	35	11	35	49	76	26	83
56	84	70	49	24	96	57	53	30	30
19	68	84	73	60	96	37	83	02	84
19	00	05	35	54	08	06	12	46	19
37	52	58	00	24	97	02	42	29	25

Name Index

Subject Index